Australia's Economy in its International Context

Cover photos published with kind permission of Peter Morris/Courtesy of Fairfaxphotos.com, Nicholas Gruen, ANU ePress, Butlin Archives ANU, The University of Melbourne Archives, World Bank, wikicommons.

L-R: Robert Menzies, Peter Petri, Peter Phillips, Fred Gruen, Anne Krueger, Paul Krugman.

Australia's Economy in its International Context

The *Joseph Fisher* Lectures

VOLUME 2: 1956 - 2012

Edited by Kym Anderson

UNIVERSITY OF ADELAIDE PRESS

THE UNIVERSITY OF ADELAIDE
AUSTRALIA

UNIVERSITY OF
ADELAIDE PRESS

THE UNIVERSITY
OF ADELAIDE
AUSTRALIA

Published in Adelaide by
University of Adelaide Press
Barr Smith Library
The University of Adelaide
South Australia
5005
press@adelaide.edu.au
www.adelaide.edu.au/press

The University of Adelaide Press publishes externally refereed scholarly books by staff of the University of Adelaide. It aims to maximise the accessibility to its best research by publishing works through the internet as free downloads and as high quality printed volumes on demand.

Electronic Index: this book is available from the website as a down-loadable PDF with fully searchable text. Please use the electronic version to complement the index.

Originally published April 2001 by the Centre for International Economic Studies, University of Adelaide, and re-published by the University of Adelaide Press in 2009 with 5 additional lectures. This revised edition includes a further 3 new lectures.

Subject Keywords
International economic relations - Australia Economic conditions 20th century - Australia Economic conditions 21st century - Australia Economic policy 20th century - Australia Economic policy 21st century - Australia Foreign Economic relations - Australia Commercial policy

For the full Cataloguing-in-Publication data please contact National Library of Australia: cip@nla.gov.au

ISBN 978-1-922064-42-4 (paperback)
ISBN 978-1-922064-43-1 (ebook)

Cover design: Fiona Cameron and Emma Spoehr
Text: Céline Lawrence and Zoë Stokes
Paperback copy printed and bound by Griffin Press, South Australia

Contents
Volume 2 (1956 - 2012)

Preface

This two-volume collection brings together the first 56 Joseph Fisher Lectures in economics and commerce, presented at the Adelaide University every other year since 1904. Funds for the Lectures, together with a medal for the top accounting student each year, were kindly provided by a £1,000 endowment to the University by the prominent Adelaide businessman Joseph Fisher in 1903 - before his death, to avoid 10 per cent going to the government! (Since the average adult male wage is now well over 200 times greater than it was in 1903 in nominal dollar terms, that endowment represents more than $0.5 million in terms of today's spending power.) An additional sum of $10,500 was donated to the Adelaide University Centenary Appeal in 1974 by Trustees of Settlements made by Joseph Fisher. The Lectures, which are free and open to the public, have been published by the University as stand-alone booklets, and copies distributed at the fund's expense.

The Lectures are mostly on economic issues and reflect Fisher's interests in liberal markets and non-interventionist government. They have stood the test of time extremely well, while also providing a reminder of the events and concerns that were prominent at different times during the past century. That, plus the fact that many of the earlier Lectures are now out of print and only a small subset of them were reprinted in scholarly journals, justifies putting them together in this collection for posterity.

The timing of this collection's first publication, in 2001, celebrated the centenary of economics teaching at Adelaide, which began with the Federation of Australia in 1901. It also celebrated the fact that it was 50 years since the 2001 Joseph Fisher Lecturer, Peter Karmel, took the Chair of Economics at the University of Adelaide and built the department to an outstanding level (before Peter moved on in the mid-1960s to establish the Flinders University of South Australia). Since 2001, five more Lectures have been added to this second edition of the collection. (See List of lectures in volume 1, 1904-1954 following this Preface.)

The Centre for International Economic Studies (CIES) at the University of Adelaide is proud to be the publisher of the collection, particularly since so many of the Lectures deal with international economic issues or Australian issues that were influenced by major international events.

The lectures have been reproduced fully, preserving the spelling, punctuation and citation forms of the day, with reproduction of figures wherever possible.

This collection would not have been published had it not been for the thorough bibliographical research and editorial assistance including copy-editing and typesetting provided by Jane Russell. Our thanks go to her, and to Bob Fisher and Keith Hancock in providing material for the opening chapters. Finally, to the descendents of Joseph Fisher, we thank them for their on-going support to the University of Adelaide.

Kym Anderson
October 2012

List of lectures in volume 1 (1904 - 1954)

18 1938 – Australian economic progress against a world background by **Colin Clark**

19 1940 – Economic coordination by **Roland Wilson**

20 1942 – The Australian economy during War by **Robert G. Menzies**

21 1944 – Problems of a high employment economy by **H. C. Coombs**

22 1946 – Necessary principles for satisfactory agricultural development in Australia by **S. M. Wadham**

23 1948 – The importance of the iron and steel industry by **Essington Lewis**

24 1950 – The economic consequences of scientific research by **John B. Condliffe**

25 1952 – Australian agricultural policy by **John G. Crawford**

26 1954 – The economics of Federal-State finance by **Wilfred Prest**

Contributors to opening chapters

Kym Anderson (FASSA) is George Gollin Professor of Economics and was the foundation Executive Director of the Centre for International Economic Studies at the University of Adelaide, where he has been associated since 1984. Prior to that he spent 7 years at the Institute of Advanced Studies at the Australian National University in Canberra, following doctoral studies at the University of Chicago and Stanford University. During 1990-92 he was on leave at the GATT (now WTO) Secretariat in Geneva, as deputy to the director of economic research, and he spent 2004-07 as Lead Economist (Trade Policy) at the World Bank's Development Research Group in Washington DC.

F. R. (Bob) Fisher (AO 1990) is a great grandson of Joseph Fisher. A graduate in law from Adelaide University, he became a QC in 1970 and was a Judge of the Federal Court, 1978-89, when he was also Deputy President of the Administrative Appeals Tribunal. He served on the Council of Flinders University of South Australia from 1969 to 1988, and in the latter part of that period he was Pro Chancellor and then Chancellor.

Keith J. Hancock (AO 1987, FASSA) is a graduate of the University of Melbourne and the London School of Economics. His first academic appointment was as a Lecturer at the University of Adelaide, before he transferred to the new Flinders University of South Australia in 1964 as first Professor of Economics and then Pro Vice-Chancellor (1974-79), Vice-Chancellor (1980-87), and thereafter Emeritus Professor. He spent 1987-89 in the Australian Conciliation and Arbitration Commission and was then appointed Deputy President of the Australian Industrial Relations Commission where he served until 1997. Since then he has been an Honorary Fellow in Economics at the University of Adelaide.

The benefactor Joseph Fisher

Extract from *Joseph Fisher – A Pioneer Colonist* by F. R. Fisher (Printed by Open Book Publishers, Adelaide, in 1998)

Joseph Fisher was born in Yorkshire on 14 September 1834, to Joshua and Hannah Fisher. Joseph and his parents and sisters sailed for South Australia in the *Pestonjee Bomanjee*, leaving from London on 11 June and arriving in Glenelg on 12 October 1838, when Joseph was 3 years old.

A family friend, Anthony Forster, probably influenced their decision to choose South Australia. Forster himself travelled to South Australia in early 1841, to take possession for George Fife Angas of the latter's Barossa Estates. This was a fortunate event for Joseph, with whom Forster had a particularly close association both as a friend and mentor consequent upon Joshua's untimely death on 3 September 1841.

Joseph appears to have had the bulk of his schooling at the Oddfellows School and subsequently in Anthony's Forster's old home. He left school at age 12, five years after his father's death, to work in the mercantile business established by Anthony Forster. Two years later Forster took up an offer of a share in the *Register* and *Observer* newspapers, and Joseph joined the *Register's* commercial department. In an interview in 1903 Joseph described his duties as follows:

> "I had to assist the bookkeeper, deliver papers, take a turn at the old hand press, occasionally read proofs and also numerous other odd jobs at the office. I frequently remained on duty for 12-14 hours a day and I soon gained a practical knowledge of the work in almost every department of the newspaper office."

In his article entitled 'A Man of Honor', which appeared on 17 February 1958 in the Adelaide *News*, Douglas Pike (a distinguished historian at Adelaide University) wrote the following about Joseph's early activities:

> "With its new copper wealth and heavy immigration, Adelaide in 1846 was full of opportunities. At 14 Joseph needed no prompting. For two years he quietly imported potatoes from Tasmania and had £2,000 in the bank before his little monopoly was invaded. He was still employed in the *Register* when it came up for sale in 1853. With his potato money he joined the syndicate that bought the newspaper."

Shortly after that time Joseph took over the management of the commercial department of the paper, in which position it was his function, in the words of Dr Pike, to know 'the ins and outs of every business deal in town'. It appears that he also acted as shipping reporter for the paper.

By 1857 Joseph had acquired a quarter share as a proprietor of the *Register*. During that year he both married and purchased the 8-acre property *Woodfield*, his home until his death, in what is now the State Heritage-listed building at 78 Fisher Street, Fullarton. His wife for the next 50 years was Anne Wood Farrar, the eldest daughter of Henry Wilkinson Farrar, a 'highly respected Melbourne Merchant' and also originally from Yorkshire. Joseph appears to have been intensely interested in and proud of his home and gardens. His obituary states that in the later years of his life he spent several hours daily in his garden and was never happier than when tending his roses and fruit trees. Tragedy hit the family at the end of 1865, however, with the death of three of their children of diphtheria. Subsequently three further children were born.

Joseph sold his interest in the *Register* and left his employment there in October 1865, at age 31. In recording his retirement, the newspaper made reference to his 'recent domestic afflictions and the fact that his retirement would give him leisure for which he and his family would be grateful.'

At the time of his retirement he had already acquired what appears to have been his first outside interest, having accepted appointment as one of the trustees for shareholders of the Deed of Settlement of the Bank of Adelaide. This institution was established in August 1865 and Joseph's association extended over the next 23 years, he having been appointed a director in 1868. He is quoted as having been a shrewd and industrious director, and acting for a time as Chairman.

Another South Australian Bank in whose foundation Joseph was involved was the Commercial Bank of South Australia. Trevor Sykes, in his book *Two Centuries of Panic: A History of Corporate Collapses in Australia,* says that the Bank was 'the brainchild of Joseph Fisher, a shrewd, restless entrepreneur'. It was as a Member of the Legislative Council that Joseph in 1878 sponsored a Bill of Parliament and presented a petition to the House of Assembly. Hansard quoted Joseph as saying on the second reading that the Bill was almost a verbatim copy of the Acts under which the National Bank and the Bank of Adelaide had been incorporated. The shares had been subscribed three times over, he said, and five gentlemen who stood high in the colony for honour and probity had been named as directors. However, the accounts of the Commercial Bank were signed by a Manager appropriately bearing the surname 'Crooks'. The Bank collapsed in 1886 and Crooks was convicted of embezzlement and sentenced to eight years in gaol. It is unlikely that Joseph was ever a director of this bank because, throughout the years in question, he was a director of a competing bank, the Bank of Adelaide. Neither he, nor any members of his family, at any time owned shares in the Commercial Bank of South Australia.

Joseph's advice was, as Douglas Pike says in his newspaper article in 1958, greatly sought after and he became director of a number of companies in addition to the Bank of Adelaide. He served on the Boards of the South Australian Gas Company, the Port Adelaide Dock Company (as chairman), the Adelaide Steamship Company, the Adelaide Marine and Fire Insurance Company (as Chairman) and the Momba Pastoral Company. He was also on the local Board of Advice in South Australia of the South Australian Company, established in England in 1835.

The centenary history of the Stock Exchange of Adelaide, entitled *Bulls, Bears and Wildcats,* has this to say of Joseph and his assiduous interest in the performance of Adelaide companies:

> "Several city capitalists, with holdings in a number of companies, customarily attended company meetings to hear of current progress. One of the best known was Joseph Fisher. A doughty supporter of private enterprise, by his own practice of it he had become an early proprietor of the *Register* and a director of several companies. Fisher also served in Parliament, though he was better known for his business investments and astuteness. His remarks at the Gas

> Company's annual meeting in 1895 were typical of his attention to company affairs. He claimed that on a visit to England and to Europe he had taken as much interest in the Gas Company as if he had been in South Australia. He had walked the foreign streets to see how gas was competing with electricity, and was delighted that Adelaide's citizens had turned down the Corporation's proposal to light the streets with electricity."

In addition to his interest in urban business, Joseph was involved in pastoral investments, frequently in association with a number of other South Australians such as Barr Smith, Elder and James Francis Cudmore. It would appear that his interests were financial in nature, however, rather than those of an active pastoralist. His first venture into this field was probably the property north of Adelaide known as Hummocks Run, comprising 97,000 acres of freehold land as well as some leasehold.

In 1870 Joseph and Anthony Forster each acquired a one-eighth interest in the partnership that owned the Mount Murchison Run in New South Wales. In 1872 the partnership acquired a one-third interest in the Momba Run and the ownerships were amalgamated. The other partners at this time were Robert Barr Smith, McCullock Sellar & Co. of Melbourne (the then proprietors of Mt Gipps Pastoral Company of Broken Hill which was the employer of Charles Rasp, the discoverer of the Broken Hill lodes), Peter Waite, W.C. Swann, and Thomas Elder. In 1888 the interests of the partners were acquired by a limited company in which Joseph became a partner. In 1881 Thomas Elder and Joseph each acquired a one-eight interest in the Ned's Corner Run, which held 1300 square miles in Victoria just over the South Australian Border. On 1 August 1899 Joseph transferred half of his interest to the Fisher Trust.

Joseph made five visits in all to England. The first of these was in late 1866 or early 1867. Upon his return, at the age of 33, Joseph entered the Legislative Assembly representing the District of Sturt. He served there until February 1870, and then in the Legislative Council from July 1873 to March 1881. In the obituary published on his death, the *Register* commented that 'he was at all times plain spoken and was not the man to make compromises of principle for the sake of securing any private advantage'. His speeches in the House were usually shorter than those of many of his colleagues, but he made his points clearly and forcefully. In his opening speech he expressed two strong views, which he was often to repeat in later years: a distaste for waste and profligacy, and insistence on his own imperviousness to pressure from any quarter.

During his next seven years at the Legislative Council, Joseph gave his views on a wide variety of matters in a typically uninhibited manner. In his first speech in the Council on July 30 he touched on an issue that was eventually to lead to his political downfall: immigration.

In November 1873 Joseph opposed a Bill that would increase the Ministry from five to six members. He said he would be glad to see a Government that did not seek to be judged by the large number of Bills it introduced. In his view many of the Bills involved an expenditure of time and money for which there was not the slightest necessity.

Then in December that year, in an unusually lengthy speech, Joseph vigorously opposed a Bill providing for compulsory education and State schools. He said the voluntary system of education had not failed, whereas a Government system introduced in 1851 had been an utter failure. He was not opposed to education, but to the compulsory clauses in the Bill. He objected to the unwarrantable interference with the rights and duties of parents, and believed some parents who could afford private schools would no longer be able to if they had to contribute also to the cost of State education.

In the following year, 1874, he berated the Government for its lack of enterprise. He urged, not for the first or last time, that telegraphic communication be extended to Cape Borda to avoid uncertainty about shipping movements. He regretted that 'no action had been taken in the matter of inter-colonial free trade' and wanted 'this colony to step forward and invite the more important colonies to come in'.

He also stressed what he believed was an urgent need for a new railway to tap the Murray River trade. He said a Murray rail connection would enable the Riverina wool then being shipped through Melbourne to be diverted to Port Adelaide. This, he felt, would give employment to thousands: there would be 30 extra ships at the Port within twelve months of the line opening, and the squatters of Riverina would make their headquarters in Adelaide.

As well, he wanted better shipping arrangements than those provided by P&O steamers for landing mail to Glenelg; he opposed a Customs Bill imposing new tariffs to foster manufacturing; and he opposed a Bill to close hotels on Sundays to all but travellers (on the grounds that it simply would make people sneaks).

In 1877 Joseph strongly supported a no-confidence motion carried against the Chief Secretary, Sir Henry Ayers, the only Minister in the Legislative Council. The dissatisfaction with Ayers arose from a Government contract to build a new Parliament House, with an estimated cost of £200,000 and without the proposal being put before the Council. Joseph took exception not only to the Council being ignored but also to the proposed site of the new Parliament House, at the corner of North Terrace and King William Street. The site, he contended, should be reserved for the future railway station. He looked forward to the time when the colony would be regarded as the great centre of Australia. He thought mail steamers would possibly make Adelaide their terminus, with the mails being conveyed to the other colonies by railway. He believed the new Parliament House, with the University and the Institute, should be designed together on North Terrace and become 'three of the grandest buildings in any of the colonies'.

In December 1877 Joseph successfully moved for an award of up to £4,000 to John Ridley, the inventor of the reaping machine, for whom he had acted as an agent before entering Parliament. He said it was a standing disgrace to the colony that no substantial public recognition had been made of Mr Ridley's services: had he taken the precaution to patent his invention, he would have been one of the richest men in South Australia.

Joseph's parliamentary career, which he had never seen as the most important phase of his life, ended in 1881. His failure to win re-election was widely attributed to his opposition to legislation intended to restrict Chinese immigration, legislation that he regarded as unchristian, uneconomic and meddling in imperial matters. Joseph spoke about his election defeat in an interview published in the *Register* on 15 April 1903 as follows:

"Some of my friends thought that I was unnecessarily outspoken at times, and I was frequently told that it would be better for me to give more diplomatic answers when questions were put to me on the hustings respecting popular measures which I could not support; but I refused to make compromises in connection with matters of principle merely for the purpose of gaining a seat in the House."

It was during the decade of the 1890s that Joseph established what thereafter became known to his descendants, somewhat incorrectly, as The Fisher Trust.

On 14 April 1903, Joseph wrote a letter to the Editor of the *Register* newspaper in which he made charitable donations totalling £3,315, which he requested the *Register* to distribute on his behalf. In his letter he sets out his reasons for making the donations during his lifetime rather than by will on his death. The letter reads as follows:

"Sir – I have much pleasure in sending you herewith a list of donations, which I have decided to give to the various institutions enumerated therein. Will you kindly communicate with the representatives of those institutions so that they may collect the amounts in which they are respectively concerned. Subject to your consent, the sums are payable at The *Register* Offices, in Grenfell Street, Adelaide.

"In explanation I may say that for many years past I have made provision in my will for charitable and other public purposes, but I am now led by several considerations to anticipate the date on which effect can be given to that document. The only one of these which I need mention here is the law now in force that all moneys given in his will by a testator for charitable purposes are subject to a deduction of 10 per cent payable to the Government. I regard this exaction as equally unjust and unwise, and as one tending to check the flow of public-spirited benevolence. In these circumstances I have resolved to make during my lifetime the distribution, which I have intended to reserve until after my decease."

The first item reads:

"Adelaide University – To encourage commercial education – (1) a perpetual gold medal to the student of exceptional merit on completion of the course for the advanced commercial certificate; (2) a special lectureship on the commercial side – a lecture to be delivered in alternate years, and published; and (3) the remuneration of lecturers, examiners, and professors engaged in the general work of the commercial course – £1,000."

For the last 20 years of his life, Joseph had been suffering from gout and diabetes. In mid-September 1907 he suffered an attack of influenza which, on 26 September, assumed a serious form and he died the same day at *Woodfield*.

He left a will in which he appointed his two sons his executors. It was signed on 21 May 1903 in the presence of G.J.R. Murray, subsequently Sir George Murray, Chief Justice, Lieutenant Governor and Chancellor of Adelaide University, and W.A. Magarey, Queen's Counsel and donor of the Magarey Medal.

On 5 October 1907 the *Register* published an obituary, which concluded as follows:

"The late Mr Fisher was a man highly respected in business and private life, and though in recent years he had taken little active part in public affairs, in his earlier political career he expressed himself as sternly opposed to many of the political ideals which have since found favour in certain quarters, and refused to shirk what he deemed to be his duties and responsibilities merely to retain his seat. He was at all times plain spoken, and was not the man to make compromises of principle for the sake of securing any private advantage. He always manifested a deep interest in the district in which he dwelt, and progressive municipal movements found in him a warm supporter."

Half a century later, Dr Douglas Pike wrote in his article 'A Man of Honor' (the *News*, 17 February 1958):

"What makes a pioneer and brings him honour? Publicity, land ownership, and pastoral wealth? Does a townsman qualify? Some early arrivals did not care. Sincerity meant more to them than fame.

Joseph Fisher was content to boast that he had spent his life in sight of Adelaide. Parliament claimed him for 10 prosperous years when honest men were scarce. Reporters sharpened their pencils whenever Fisher rose to speak, but landjobbers and speculators quailed before his revelations. He knew the ins and outs of every business deal in town. His advice was sought by high and low. Proposals below his moral standards he denounced in plain unvarnished terms; what he approved was supported with equal vigour. He had too much candour to be accepted by the genteel, yet a dozen boards sought him as a director. Even the Cricket Association made him its president for 25 years. As agent for colonists retired to England he had further inside knowledge, but he rarely used it for personal gain. His own investments were varied, safe, and seldom changed. His family and home meant more to him than power. Solid and unpretentious *Woodfield* at Fullarton gave Fisher Street his name. Its roses and trees were his pride. The full extent of his charity was revealed only after influenza laid him low in 1907."

The Lectures

Kym Anderson

There is of course no sense in trying to summarize as eclectic a set of Lectures as this one. The purpose of this note is simply to whet the reader's appetite by describing the range of economic issues discussed over the almost one hundred years the Lectures cover.

Given the interest of Joseph Fisher in fostering higher education in matters commercial, it is not surprising that the first Lecture was on precisely that topic. The Lecturer, who headed a major bank at the time, was evidently very widely traveled and well informed of the embryonic attempts in other affluent countries to introduce economics and commerce courses into universities. The Inaugural Lecture provides fascinating reading for today's graduate economists and accountants unaware that their courses had hardly begun to be established a century ago. Adelaide University can take pride in being at the global forefront in developing a course as early as 1901. Its initial requirements were not as tough as the University of Birmingham's though, where commerce students had to master at least two modern foreign languages in addition to English!

The next few Lectures cover practical commerce/business issues before the topics turn to mainstream economics and finance issues that were important at the time and, in numerous cases, have remained so.

The issue of price stability concerned Copland in 1919 in the aftermath of the Great War, for which he saw a return to the gold standard as an inadequate solution. That issue also concerned Gregory, Davidson and Melville at the time of the Depression in the early 1930s, where it was addressed more in an international context.

Another big economic issue discussed just prior to the Depression was public finance, particularly in relation to Australia's rapidly growing public debt. Prime Minister Bruce provided a political perspective while Professor Mills gave an academic economist's view. It is also a crucial issue in times of war, as Irvine's

Lecture in 1917 and Wilson's in 1940 make clear. Within the public finance field, Federal-State financial issues are never far from the top of the agenda in a federation. It is surprising, therefore, that only one Lecture has been devoted to the topic, namely by Prest and not until 1954.

Shortly after the Depression, Giblin provided a detailed analysis of the effects of import tariffs. This had been a hot political topic before federation in 1901, and it continued to be so well into the twentieth century. At a superficial level the issue seems to have not changed, with Giblin referring in 1936, just as we do today, to the highly protected sectors of textiles and motor vehicles. But analytically the economics profession has come a long way since then. A comparison with Corden's Lectures three and then again six decades later (1967 and 1995) reveals a progressive development of understanding, not only by economists but also by the public at large, of the economic cost and distributional consequences of tariffs. Also noteworthy is a warning by Menzies at the end of his Lecture in 1942: despite his predisposition to favour import tariffs, he acknowledged that Australia would have to do its part in reducing barriers to international trade once the war was over. As Corden's 1995 Lecture makes clear, Australia took a long time to get to that stage, but in the final quarter of the 20th century it did eventually liberalize its markets.

Just before World War II broke out, Colin Clark treated his Adelaide audience to an application to Australia of ideas that appeared shortly thereafter in his classic treatise on *The Conditions of Economic Progress* (1st edition 1940). His estimates suggest Australia in 1938 was the 4th most affluent country in the world after New Zealand, the United States and Great Britain, and perhaps equal to Argentina – down from first or second at the time of federation and a sharp contrast to today's ranking of around 20th (using similar purchasing power parity measures). As if to link with the previous Lecture, by Giblin on tariffs, Clark points to the comparatively poor labour productivity performance in Australian manufacturing. He also stated that the future for Australian farm exports lies in the politics of trade agreements rather than in the economics of comparative costs of production – precisely what the post-war history of the GATT/WTO has revealed.

Following World War II, attention turned to ensuring full employment. Among the chosen approaches were efforts to boost agricultural and industrial development, including through infrastructural and research investments. These are the themes of the next five Lectures, by Coombs, Wadham, Lewis, Condliffe and Crawford. Coombs focused on the macroeconomic challenge of ensuring full employment once wartime activities ceased, suggesting the need for non-trivial government intervention. However Wadham, a Professor of Agriculture, warned that trying to boost employment by allocating land in small parcels for one-person farms could lead – as it did -- to them being uneconomic, and at the same time adding to environmental and resource management problems associated with soil, water and forests. On the positive side, he stressed the crucial importance of education for rural people if they were to share in the fruits of economic growth.

Condliffe in 1950, like Williams in 1962, drew attention to the growth-enhancing role of investments in research and development and the probable underinvestment in such activities by Australia. This topic has risen again in 2001 as an election issue, along with the perennial concern with brain drain problems. Less emphasis is being given by today's government to the other great contributor to economic growth, namely investments in formal education — despite the strong empirical evidence linking educational attainment and income, as demonstrated for example in Ashenfelter's 1993 Lecture.

Another lecture topic in the 1950s that has a contemporary resonance is superannuation. Downing in 1958 argued that the Australian system of age pensions subject to a means test was not necessarily inferior to the compulsory national superannuation systems operating in numerous other countries at that time.

The 1970s was a period when serious concerns with inflation and associated wages policy and unemployment arose. Some if their effects on economists' activities are surveyed in Gruen's 1978 Lecture, including the increased use of macroeconometric modeling designed to assist policy makers. Related lectures are the ones by Henderson in 1971 on inflation, by Laidler in 1986 on monetary policy, and in between by Gregory in 1981 on unemployment.

Not surprisingly, as globalization has proceeded, international issues of relevance to Australia are more prominent in the second volume of these lectures. Important among those in the 1950s was the issue on which Nobel Laureate James

Meade focused in his 1956 Lecture, namely, why post-war Japan's membership of the GATT should be expedited. The arguments presented are remarkably similar to those currently being used in connection with China's application to re-join the GATT/WTO system. Japan is also the subject of Bronfenbrenner's Lecture three decades later, when that country had become far more affluent. At that time (1985), Bronfenbrenner argued that Japan was not yet suffering from the sclerosis problems of other advanced economies, a claim that would be less easy to make today.

Trade issues were the subject of several other Lectures since the 1950s. The two by Corden have already been mentioned. His analysis of Australian tariff policy in 1967 is still regarded as a classic reference. It provides great detail and insight into the tariff policy formation process and a critique of, and suggested alternatives to, the method of setting tariff rates at that time. His retrospecive analysis in 1995 reviews the extent and causes of the massive trade liberalization in Australia since his first Lecture, and compares it with the forces at work in many developing countries. One of the key forces aiding reform in Australia was greater policy transparency, thanks to the transformation of the Tariff Board in 1973 to the Industries Assistance Commission (subsequently changed to the Industry Comission and most recently to the Productivity Commission). Its first Chairman, Alf Rattigan, contrasts in his 1976 Lecture the IAC's approach with that of the more interventionist Jackson Committee's proposal for boosting industrial development.

Regionalism and American trade policy were the focus of the Lecture in 1994 by Krueger (the only female Fisher Lecturer to date). She expresses concern that regional arrangements such as the North American Free Trade Agreement are being designed in ways that make them more stumbling blocks than stepping stones to freer global trade, for example through diverting the attention of trade negotiators away from the GATT (and now WTO). Since then regional agreements have sprung up like mushrooms, making this Lecture even more pertinent now than in 1994.

Food trade problems wax and wane, but the perceived long run problem of population outstripping supply growth, commonly associated with the name of Malthus, is erroneous according to Johnson in his 1996 Lecture. With population growth slowing and new farm technologies expanding supplies, food-exporting countries will be under continual pressure to adjust to a long-run decline in international food prices – notwithstanding potential food import growth by China in the 21st century. This view contrasts sharply with that of the Australian government in the early 1950s when, according to Crawford's Lecture of 1952, the prime aim of agricultural policy was to produce more.

External payments problems also received attention. In 1969, Phelps-Brown focused on it from a UK perspective, prior to the freeing of currency exchange rates. The issue was revisited by Krugman in 1988, in his case focusing on the persistent US deficit which he saw as the other side of the coin to persistent trade surpluses in Japan, South Korea and Taiwan. He claimed he would not be surprised if the high value of the US dollar was sustained for a long time, as indeed it has been.

Problems of developing countries had been barely touched on in this Lecture series until recently. The three exceptions in addition to Johnson's Lecture on population and food are Arndt's treatment of foreign aid policy (1964), an assessment of the impact of strengthening intellectual property rights in developing Asia (Maskus, 1997), and an economist's perspective on the transmission of infectious diseases (Gersovitz, 1999).

Only a few of the Lectures since at least the mid-1920s are not part of mainstream economic thinking of the time. One in particular is worthy of mention, namely that by the British social historian Asa Briggs, in 1960, on the mass entertainment industry. It provides a fascinating history of that industry's development since the 1800s. According to Lord Briggs, it has been quoted more than any other lecture he has given.

Joseph Fisher would have been pleased that this series not only started with a Lecture on higher education, but also includes the 2001 Lecture by Peter Karmel who has had a distinguished career in higher education administration since leaving the George Gollin Chair in Economics at Adelaide in the mid-1960s. Unlike the first Fisher Lecture by Turner, Karmel's is focused not on the education of economists but on the need for better economic analysis to inform the higher education policy reform process.

Several of the lectures since 2001 focus on issues associated with globalization, including its impact on trade, natural resources and the environment.

In a collection that covers a period longer than a century, the Lecturers' word usage reveals changing social norms. Readers should be warned that the use of gender-neutral language does not become common until well into the second half of these Lectures!

The Lecturers

Kym Anderson and Keith Hancock

The Joseph Fisher Lecturers to date have been a mixture of prominent economists in academia and government, senior politicians including two Prime Ministers, and influential Australian bankers and businessmen. Most shared Joseph Fisher's interests in liberal markets and small, non-interventionist government. Only one female has given a Fisher Lecture so far, a reflection of the male dominance until recently of the world of economics and business. Fifteen of the past Lecturers appear in *Who's Who in Economics* (3rd edition, edited by M. Blaug, London: Edward Elgar, 1999), eighteen appear in *A Biographical Dictionary of Australian and New Zealand Economists* (edited by J. E. King, London: Edward Elgar, 2007) fourteen were knighted, two became lords, and one was awarded the Nobel Prize in Economics. Brief biographies of each of them follow. They are listed in alphabetical order, with the Fisher Lecture number and date given after their name.

Arndt, Heinz W., 1915-2002 (No. 31, 1964): Economist. After moving from Germany to Oxford with his parents in 1933, Arndt studied politics and sociology there and took up economics only after taking an appointment at Chatham House and then the University of Manchester under John Hicks. The University of Sydney attracted him to Australia in 1946, and by 1950 he moved to the new Chair of Economics at Canberra University College (later ANU), where he remained affiliated as an Emeritus Professor and continued to write and edit journals profusely until his untimely death on his way to Sir Leslie Melville's funeral. Arndt did more than anyone to link Australian and Southeast Asian (especially Indonesian) economists.

Ashenfelter, Orley, 1942- (No. 42, 1993): Economist and wine enthusiast. Ashenfelter specializes in labour economics, law and economics, and econometrics, with some of the latter skill being dedicated to understanding the viticultural determinants of the ultimate quality of premium wines, including Penfold's Grange. A professor of economics at Princeton since 1971, he has directed the industrial relations group there most of that time. From 1985 to 2001 he was

Editor of the *American Economic Review*, and was President of the American Economic Association in 2011-12, but that did not stop his own research program from flourishing.

Barbier, Professor Edward Barbier 1957- (No. 49, 2002): Economist. Professor Barbier is currently with the University of Wyoming but he has previously served at the University of York, UK and as Director of the London Environmental Economics Centre at University College London. As an environmental and resource economist, he has worked mainly on the economics of environment and development issues, including land degradation, wildlife management, trade and natural resources, coastal and wetland use, tropical deforestation, biological invasions and biodiversity loss. His latest book, *Natural Resources and Economic Development*, was published by Cambridge University Press in 2005.

Bhagwati, Jagdish N., 1934- (No. 56, 2012): International economist. Based in New York as University Professor in economics and law at Columbia University and senior fellow for international economics at the Council on Foreign Relations, Bhagwati has combined seminal scientific contributions to the theory of commercial policy with several bestselling books and myriad essays in leading newspapers and magazines. He has been a senior advisor to the heads of the UN and WTO, and remains one of the world's strongest advocates for liberal trade and a rules-based multilateral trading system.

Braddon, Sir Henry Yule, 1863-1955 (No. 5, 1912 and No. 11, 1925): Businessman. Braddon worked for 44 years with Dalgety's, the livestock and station agency, and was director of numerous companies. He was President of the Employers' Federation of New South Wales in 1905-07, of the Sydney Chamber of Commerce in 1912-14, and of the Associated Chambers of Commerce of Australia in 1913-14. He also lectured on business principles and practice at the University of Sydney, and he served terms in the New South Wales Legislative Council as both an appointed and an elected member.

Briggs, Asa (later Lord Briggs), 1921- (No. 29, 1960): Social and cultural historian of the 19th and 20th century. Born in Yorkshire, Briggs became Professor of Modern History at Leeds University (1955-61) before moving to the (then) new University of Sussex where he rose to Vice-Chancellor by 1967. He spent

1976-91 as Provost of Worcester College, Oxford and 1978-94 as Chancellor of the Open University. He is President of the British Social History Society and of the Victorian Society. His trilogy, *Victorian Things, Victorian Cities*, and *Victorian People* is published by Penguin.

Bronfenbrenner, Martin, 1914-1994 (No. 39, 1985): Macro-economist. Shortly after finishing his PhD at Chicago in 1939, Bronfenbrenner was engaged in the US Navy in Japan, which gave him an abiding interest in that country. In addition to economics professorships at such universities as Wisconsin, Michigan State, Minnesota and Carnegie-Mellon, he was Professor of Japanese History and Kenan Professor of Economics in Duke University (1971-84) and then of International Economics in Aoyama Gakuin University, Tokyo (1984-90).

Bruce, Rt. Hon. Stanley Melbourne (later Viscount Bruce of Melbourne), 1883-1967 (No. 12, 1927): Prime Minister 1923-29. Bruce entered the conservative side of politics in 1918 with strong business connections. He was a strong believer in Empire economic development, a supporter of tariff protection for selected industries, and a successful protagonist of reform in Commonwealth-state financial relations. His government was defeated in 1929 after Bruce failed to persuade the Parliament to pass legislation for abolition of the federal conciliation and arbitration system. Offices he later held included that of Australian High Commissioner in London.

Butchart, James R. (No. 10, 1923): Banker and dealer. At the time of the Lecture he was a foreign exchange dealer with Edward Dyason and Company. Previously he had been an Inspector in Victoria with the London Bank of Australia. In 1918 he wrote a text on *Money and its Purchasing Power*.

Clark, Colin Grant, 1905-1989, (No. 18, 1938): Economist, public servant. Clark originated many of the concepts of national accounting and was a major contributor to the economics of economic development. He arrived from England in Australia in 1938 to take up an appointment at the University of Western Australia, but soon moved to Queensland as Director of the Bureau of Industry. He remained in Queensland until 1952. After a further period in England, at Oxford University, he returned to Australia, where he spent his later years.

Condliffe, John B., 1891-1981 (No. 24, 1950): Economist. At the time of his Lecture Condliffe was a Professor of Economics at the University of California, but his first appointment to a Chair was at Canterbury University College in New Zealand in 1920. In 1931 he joined to the Economic Intelligence Unit of the League of Nations in Geneva for a time.

Coombs, Herbert Cole ('Nugget') (AC 1975, resigned 1976), 1906-1997 (No. 21, 1944): Central banker, public servant, university leader, advocate of aboriginal rights, supporter of the arts. Formerly an assistant economist in the Commonwealth Bank, Coombs transferred to the federal Treasury in 1939, was appointed to the Commonwealth Bank Board in 1942 and in the same year became Director of Rationing. In 1943, he was appointed Director-General of Post-war Reconstruction. He became Governor of the Commonwealth Bank in 1949 and of the Reserve Bank in 1960. He also served as Chancellor of the Australian National University (1968-76), which he helped found in 1946. He retired in 1968 to take up a Visiting Fellowship at the ANU in Canberra (1976-95). In 1972 he was named Australian of the Year.

Copeland, Brian, 1956- (No. 53, 2009): Economist. At the time of his Lecture, Professor Copeland was Head of the Department of Economics at the University of British Columbia, where he was an undergraduate before completing his PhD at Stanford. His research has focused on developing analytical techniques to study the interaction between international trade and the natural environment. He (with Scott Taylor) wrote the seminal book on *Trade and the Environment: Theory and Evidence*, published by Princeton University Press in 2003. He has been co-editor of the *Journal of Environmental Economics and Management* and an Associate Editor of the *Journal of International Economics.*

Copland, (later Sir) Douglas Berry, 1894-1971 (No. 9, 1921): Economist, administrator and diplomat. Copland, a New Zealander, was appointed a Lecturer in the University of Tasmania in 1917 and Professor in 1920. He was a Professor in the University of Melbourne from 1924 until 1945. During World War II, he was Prices Commissioner. Copland was the first Vice-Chancellor of the Australian National University, the first Principal of the Australian Administrative Staff College and founder of the Committee for the Economic Development of Australia. He held diplomatic appointments in China and Canada.

Corden, Warner Max (AC 2001, FASSA), 1927- (No. 32, 1967 and No. 44, 1995): International economist. One of the world's best-known analysts of tariff policy, Corden in more recent years has focused on the international monetary system, following a period as senior advisor to the IMF (1986-88). He has had long periods on the faculty of such universities as Oxford, Melbourne, ANU and, since 1989, Johns Hopkins University. He was instrumental in having the first official estimates of effective rates of protection included in the *Vernon Committee of Economic Enquiry* report of 1965. His writings on Australian economic policy are published in *The Road to Reform* (1997), but his globally influential works are *Trade policy and Economic Welfare* (1974) and *Inflation, Exchange Rates and the World Economy* (1977).

Crawford, (later Sir) John Grenfell, 1910-1984 (No. 25, 1952): Economist and administrator. After humble beginnings, Crawford became Economic Advisor to the Rural Bank of NSW before moving to Canberra as the head of a new Bureau of Agricultural Economics (1945-50) and then the Department of Commerce and Agriculture which became the Department of Trade. In 1960 he returned to academia as Professor of Economics and head of the Research School of Pacific Studies, became Vice-Chancellor (1967-73) and then Chancellor (1976-84). His impacts on agricultural economics, trade policy (especially towards Japan) and international development assistance were profound. In 1982 he was declared 'Australian of the Year'.

Davidson, (later Sir) Alfred Charles, 1882-1952 (No. 15, 1932): Banker. Davidson, at the time of the lecture, was General Manager of the Bank of New South Wales. He had played a leading role in the financial adjustments of the early phase of the depression. His actions included initiation of the breach of parity of the Australian pound with sterling. He was an advocate of an independent central bank. Davidson, in 1936, was a major witness before the Royal Commission on Monetary and Banking Systems.

Downing, Richard Ivan, 1915-1975 (No. 28, 1958): Economist. In 1954, after service as a lecturer at Melbourne, wartime public servant and economist at the International Labour Office, Downing was appointed to the Ritchie Chair of Economic Research at the University of Melbourne. He had wide interests and occupied various public positions. At the time of his death, he was Chairman of the Australian Broadcasting Commission. Throughout his career, Downing displayed a strong conviction of the obligation of economists to improve the lot of people. His interest in national superannuation reflected this conviction.

Elles, J. Currie, 1852-1934 (No. 3, 1908): A self-described commercial man who dealt in investment stocks and mining shares, Elles also refers to himself as a Member of the University of Glasgow, Honorary Member of the Institute of Bankers of New South Wales and Correspondent in New South Wales of the Board of Trade of Great Britain (Intelligence Department). He also joined the NSW Stock Exchange and then, after its demise, the Sydney Stock Exchange. He spent some time in China, and was fluent in several languages.

French, Sir John Russell, 1847-1921 (No. 4, 1910): Banker. French was for the last 27 years of his life the General Manager of the Bank of New South Wales. He was a founder of the Institute of Bankers of New South Wales, President of the Sydney Camber of Commerce and President of the Associated Chambers of Commerce of Australia. As the leader of Australia's largest bank, he played an important role in relations between government and the banks, especially during World War I.

Gersovitz, Mark, 1949- (No. 47, 1999): Economist. Following his PhD at Yale in 1995, Gersovitz has had faculty appointments at Princeton University, the University of Michigan and currently Johns Hopkins University. He has also taken time out to be Editor of the *World Bank Economic Review* and *World Bank Research Observer*, 1992-94. As an applied microeconomist, he has focused his research on the problems of poor countries, traveling widely to many African and Asian countries.

Giblin, Lyndhurst Falkiner, 1872-1951 (No. 17, 1936): Economist. Formerly government statistician in Tasmania and advisor to the Premier, Giblin was appointed in 1929 to the Ritchie Chair of Economic Research in the University of Melbourne. He was actively involved in the policy debates of the 1920s and 1930s and served on various advisory bodies, including the inaugural Commonwealth Grants Commission and the Bridgen Committee of enquiry into the Australian tariff. As Acting Commonwealth Statistician, he prepared the 1933 census. A friend of J. M. Keynes, Giblin did much to introduce Keynesian ideas into the Australian debate.

Gordon, (later Sir) David John, 1865-1946 (No. 6, 1914): South Australian journalist and politician. Gordon had been employed by the *South Australian Register* in various capacities. He became active in the non-Labor side of politics and in 1911 was elected as member for the federal seat of Boothby, which he lost in 1913. In the same year, he was elected to the Legislative Council, of which he was President from 1932 until 1934. He served a brief term, in 1917, as Minister of Education. Gordon was an enthusiast for rural economic development.

Gregory, Robert George (AO 1996, FASSA), 1939- (No. 38, 1981): Economist. Following doctoral studies at LSE and a short teaching period at Northwestern University, Gregory has been based at ANU's Research School of Social Sciences where he has been Professor of Economics since 1987. He shot to fame in the mid-1970s with the 'Gregory thesis', on the structural changes that a mining boom inflicts on an economy, but since the 1980s has focused mainly on labour market and associated welfare issues where his research has been very influential through being widely disseminated. He has served on many government committees and was on the Board of the Reserve Bank from 1985 to 1995.

Gregory, (later Sir) Theodore Emanuel Gugenheim, 1893-1970 (No. 14, 1930): Economist. Gregory was, at the time of the Lecture, a Professor of Economics at the London School of Economics. He accompanied Sir Otto Niemeyer, who visited Australia in 1930 as a representative of the Bank of England to advise the federal government and the Commonwealth Bank on Australian economic problems.

Gruen, Fred H. (AO 1986, FASSA), 1921-1997 (No. 37, 1978): Economist. Gruen was born in Austria, lost his father when he was 15, was sent to boarding school in England in 1937 knowing no English, heard his mother died in the Auschwitz camp, was deported on the ship *Dunera* to Sydney in 1940, and then was interned in Hay, NSW until war's end. Few would have risen from that beginning to become one of the country's most widely appreciated economists. Starting as an agricultural economist for the NSW government and then as Professor at Monash University, he moved to general economics at ANU's Research School of Social Sciences in 1972. From there he made a formidable contribution to a wide range of economic policy debates, and mentored generations of economists including his two sons.

Henderson, Ronald Frank (CMG 1976, AO 1988, FASSA), 1917-1994 (No. 34, 1971): Applied social economist. Henderson took economics at Cambridge and, after World War II, was appointed a Lecturer in Economics there and a Fellow of Corpus Christi College. He visited relatives in Australia from time to time and took part in policy debates here. In 1962 he accepted an appointment to the University of Melbourne where he built up a team that became the Institute for Applied Economic and Social Research. When Henderson retired in 1979 the Institute had 50 staff and a reputation as the country's most influential unit analyzing economic and social policy issues, particularly poverty.

Irvine, Robert Francis, 1861-1941 (No. 7, 1917): Economist. In 1912 Irvine was appointed as the first Professor of Economics in the University of Sydney. He resigned, in controversial circumstances, in 1922. His views about economics, both during his tenure as a Professor and thereafter, were unorthodox.

Jessop, Lewis Angelo, 1842-1922 (No.2, 1906): General Agent. Little is known of this Lecturer beyond the facts that he lived in North Adelaide, was married in 1879, addressed the Free Trade Association of South Australia on 26 November 1898, and at the time of the Lecture he was employed at the Alliance Assurance Office in Adelaide.

Johnson, David Gale, 1916-2003 (No. 45, 1996): Agricultural economist. Johnson was a member of the Economics Department in the University of Chicago from 1944, a full Professor from 1954, and then Eliakim Hastings Distinguished Service Professor from 1970. During that long tenure he served in a wide number of University positions including Provost. Outside the University he was equally influential in a vast array of offices, including as President of the American Economic Association in 1999. Notwithstanding, he was a prolific researcher and for decades was the world's most influential agricultural trade economist. He is best known for his book *World Agriculture in Disarray.*

Karmel, Peter Henry (CBE 1967, AC 1976, FASSA), 1922-2008 (No. 48, 2001): Economist, educationalist and administrator. Appointed Professor of Economics at Adelaide University at the age of 28 (in May 1950), Karmel built up a vigorous and highly regarded Department. In 1961 he became Principal-Designate of Adelaide University's Bedford Park campus. This became Flinders University in 1966, with Karmel as its first Vice-Chancellor. He was later Chairman of the Australian Universities Commission and the Commonwealth Tertiary Education Commission, and Vice-Chancellor of the Australian National University. He served as chairman or member of many governmental, university-related and public-interest entities, and was the first Chancellor of the University of Papua New Guinea. In 1965 he was appointed an Emeritus Professor with the University of Adelaide.

Krueger, Anne O., 1934- (No. 43, 1994): International economist. Krueger, the only female Joseph Fisher Lecturer to date, has been on the faculty of the universities of Wisconsin (1955-59) and Minnesota (1959-82) before spending a period as Vice President of the World Bank (1982-86). She then moved to Duke University until 1991 when she transferred to her present position at Stanford University. A prolific researcher in the areas of economic development and international trade, she is author or many influential books on the scope for policy reform, and an advisor to numerous developing countries. In 1996 she was President of the American Economic Association.

Krugman, Paul, 1953- (No. 41, 1988): Economist. A PhD from MIT in 1977 launched this brilliant analyst and advocate onto the world stage. He has since taught at Stanford and Yale universities as well as MIT, before moving in 2000 to Princeton. In addition to profound academic writings in international economics he is one of the most prolific and successful popularizers of complex economic ideas via the mass media. All of those popular writings get posted on his website which must be the most visited of any economist. In 1991 he was awarded the John Bates Clark Medal, given by the American Economic Association every two years to the top economist under 40.

Laidler, David, 1938- (No. 40, 1986): Monetary economist. English born and raised, PhD from Chicago in 1964, a professor back in England (Manchester) until 1975, and then Laidler migrated to Canada to take up a Chair at the

University of Western Ontario whre he still is employed. In addition to research for his books and articles on monetary theory, Laidler has been heavily involved in monetary policy debates, particularly in Canada. In 1987/88 he was President of the Canadian Economic Association.

Lewis, Essington, CH, 1881-1961 (No. 23, 1948): Industrialist. A diplomate of the South Australian School of Mines and Industries (now the University of South Australia) and with major involvements in the Port Pirie smelters, Lewis remained with the BHP Company after its disposal of the smelters. He became general manager of BHP in 1921 and Managing Director in 1926. During World War II, Lewis occupied the major office of Director of Munitions, returning to the iron and steel industry in 1945. He was Chairman of BHP during the Korean War years (1950-52).

Maskus, Keith E. 1954- (No. 46, 1997): Economist. Maskus has been on the faculty of the University of Colorado ever since he completed his PhD at the University of Michigan in 1981, and a full Professor since 1995. He has been a Research Fellow with the Institute for International Economics in Washington, D.C. since 1998, and was also appointed as an Adjunct Professor at the CIES in Adelaide University in 2001. As a specialist in international trade policy and in intellectual property rights, he has been widely sought as a consultant/visiting scholar by international agencies, government and business.

Meade, James Edward, 1907-1995, (No. 27, 1956): Economist. From 1947 until 1957, Meade was Professor of Commerce at the London School of Economics. During this period he wrote several seminal books about international trade. He was Professor of Political Economy at Cambridge University from 1957 until 1968. Meade served a term as President of the Royal Economic Society. In 1977, he was awarded the Nobel Prize in Economics. During a visit to Australia in 1956, Meade collaborated with Adelaide's Professor Eric Russell in producing an important paper on wages, prices and the balance of payments.

Melville, (later Sir) Leslie Galfreid (FASSA), 1902-2002 (No. 16, 1934): Economist, public servant, Vice-Chancellor. Trained as an actuary and employed in the South Australian Treasury, Melville in 1929 was appointed at age 27 as the first Professor of Economics in the Adelaide University. He left his Chair in 1931 to become the first economist in the Commonwealth Bank. His later distinguished career included leadership of the Australian delegation at the Bretton Woods conference in 1944, Vice-Chancellor of the Australian National University (1953-60), Chairman of the Australian Tariff Board (1960-63), and Board member of the Reserve Bank of Australia (1965-74).

Menzies, Right Hon. (later Sir) Robert Gordon, 1894-1978, (No. 20, 1942): Australia's longest-serving Prime Minister, holding office between 1939 and 1941 and between 1949 and 1966. Prime Minister at the outbreak of World War II, he resigned in 1941 as Leader of the United Australia Party and Prime Minister. When the Labor Government led by John Curtin came to power later in 1941, Menzies moved to the Opposition benches. He became Leader of the Opposition in 1943 and in 1944 founded the Liberal Party.

Mills, Richard Charles (OBE), 1886-1952, (No. 13, 1927): Economist. As Professor of Economics in the University of Sydney (1922-45), Mills was one of the founders of the Economic Society of Australia and New Zealand in 1924. He had previously undertaken a searching analysis of the Wakefieldian experiments in South Australia and elsewhere. He was later to serve on the Royal Commission on the monetary and banking systems, chaired by Mr Justice (later Sir Mellis) Napier. Near the end of his life, Mills served with distinction as a public servant and was much involved in the early federal funding of universities.

Moore, Right Hon. Mike, 1949-, (No. 50, 2003): After serving as New Zealand's Prime Minister in 1990 and as minister in charge of numerous other portfolios including Foreign Affairs, Trade, Tourism and Sports and Recreation, Mike Moore became the second Director General of the World Trade Organisation (1999-2002). He has been honoured and recognised for his contributions by various governments and universities and has been awarded New Zealand's highest honour, the Order of New Zealand. He is a member of the Privy Council. He has published at least nine books, including *A World Without Walls*, published in 2003.

Mussen, (later Sir) Gerald, 1872-1960 (No. 8, 1919): Industrial relations consultant, newspaper proprietor and promoter. In 1915-19, Mussen assisted Broken Hill Associated Smelters in its efforts to improve conditions of working and living at Port Pirie. He then undertook a similar task at Broken Hill. Mussen was an initial proprietor of the Adelaide tabloid *The News*. He played a major role in the establishment of the paper industry in northern Tasmania and also (from 1937) developed the fish-canning industry at Port Lincoln.

Petri, Peter A., 1946- (No. 55, 2011): International economist. Petri's research addresses international trade, finance, investment and economic integration, with emphasis on East Asia. He has been a member of the Brandeis Economics Department since 1974 and served as the founding dean of the Brandeis International Business School (1994-2006). He is also a Senior Fellow of the East-West Center in Honolulu and has held a variety of consulting assignments with various international organizations including the Asian Development Bank, the OECD, the United Nations, and the World Bank.

Phelps Brown, (later Sir) Ernest Henry, 1906-1994 (No. 33, 1969): Economist. Between 1947 and 1968, Phelps Brown was Professor of the Economics of Labour at the London School of Economics. In 1969, he held concurrent visiting appointments at Adelaide and Flinders universities and gave the Lecture during the term of this visit to Adelaide. He was later President of the Royal Economic Society.

Phillips, Peter C. B., 1948- (No. 54, 2010): Econometrician. Having grown up in New Zealand and completed his PhD at LSE, Phillips has been based since the late 1970s as a distinguished Professor of Economics and Professor of Statistics at Yale University. He has been highly awarded for his research, and elected a Fellow to numerous professional bodies including the Econometric Society (1981), the American Statistical Association (1993) and the American Academy of Arts and Sciences (1996).

Prest, Wilfred (CBE 1966), 1907-1994 (No. 26, 1954): Economist. Prest was a staff member at the University of Melbourne from his arrival in Australia in 1938 until his retirement in 1972, and succeeded D. B. Copland as Truby Williams

Professor. He was a member of the Commonwealth Grants Commission from 1953 until 1965. Originally a specialist in industry economics, Prest became an expert in federal-state financial relations.

Rattigan, Godfrey Alf, 1911-2000 (No. 36, 1976): Public servant. From his position as Comptroller-General of Customs, Rattigan was suddenly appointed as Chair of the Tariff Board in 1963 when Leslie Melville resigned in protest at John McEwan's attempts to circumvent due process in tariff policy formation. The move from law enforcement to policy advising suited him, and with his chief of staff, Bill Carmichael, he brought order, transparency and an economy-wide approach to the Board and its successor, the Industries Assistance (now Productivity) Commission. That facilitated greatly the opening up and deregulation of the Australian economy from the 1970s.

Throsby, C. David, 1939- (FASSA) (No. 51, 2006): Economist. Internationally known for his work in the economics of the arts and culture, Professor Throsby has analysed the economic role of artists, the economics of public intervention in arts markets, cultural development, cultural policy, heritage issues, and sustainability of cultural processes. He has also written extensively on the theory of public goods and the economics of higher education. His most recent book is *Economics and Culture*, published in 2001 by Cambridge University Press. His PhD is from the London School of Economics, but he has been Professor of Economics at Macquarie University in Sydney since 1974.

Turner, Henry Gyles, 1831-1920 (No. 1, 1904): Banker. Turner was the General Manager of the Commercial Bank of Australia and a Fellow of the Institute of Bankers, London. He had occupied that position in 1893, when the Bank suspended, reconstructed and reopened.

Vaizey, John (later Lord), 1929-1984 (No. 35, 1974): Economist. For more than a decade from his mid-teens Vaizey suffered with osteomyelitis, and even thereafter he was often in considerable pain. That did not stop him excelling at Cambridge and being appointed a Lecturer in Economics and Economic History at Oxford (1955-66), before accepting the Chair of Economics at Brunel University. His writing helped to pioneer the economics of education. He was offered the Vice-Chancellorship of Monash University in 1975 but decided to stay in the UK, where he received a life peerage.

Wadham, (later Sir) Samuel Macmahon, 1891-1972 (No. 22, 1946): Agriculural scientist. Wadham was the professor of Agriculture in the University of Melbourne at the time of his Lecture, having previously been a teacher of botany at the University of Cambridge. He came to Melbourne with the firm view that the economics of agricultural practice needed to be emphasized far more than it was at Cambridge. His keen interest in the history of agricultural development was reflected in the four editions (1939-64) of his textbook on *Land Utilization in Australia*, and it led him to write, in his retirement, a book on *Australian Farming, 1788-1965*.

Williams, (later Sir) Bruce Rodda (FASSA), 1919-2010 (No. 30, 1962): Economist and administrator. Williams began his teaching as an Economics Lecturer at Adelaide University (1940-45) before moving to the UK for appointments at Queens College Belfast, Keele University and then Manchester, prior to his return to Australia to become Vice-Chancellor of the University of Sydney (1967-81). He held many prominent board positions including on the Reserve Bank (1969-81). His music interests included chairing the Sydney International Piano Competition.

Williamson, Jeffrey, 1935- (No. 52, 2008): Economic historian. Williamson has written extensively on globalization issues over the long term. His books (no less than 25) and myriad journal articles have focused on its effects not only on economic growth but also on income inequality, industrialization, urbanization and farmers. He was Chairman of the Harvard University's Economics Department from 1997 to 2000, and before that was President of the Economic History Association (1994-95). He has been highly awarded as a teacher too. A prolific traveller, he has had several spells at the Australian National University including as the F.H. Gruen Distinguished Professor in 2003. He is also a research fellow with the London-based Centre for Economic Policy Research, and on the editorial board of a wide range of economic history and development economics journals.

Wilson, (later Sir) Roland, 1904-1996 (No. 19, 1940): Economist, public servant and director. After lecturing at the University of Tasmania, Wilson joined the Commonwealth public service in 1932. In 1936, he became Commonwealth Statistician. He was Director of the Department of Labour and National Service from its inception in 1940 until 1946 and was Secretary of the Commonwealth Treasury from 1951 until 1966. From 1966 until 1975 he was Chairman of the Commonwealth Banking Corporation.

27

Japan and the General Agreement on Tariffs and Trade

James E. Meade[1]

I am much honoured by the invitation which the University of Adelaide has extended to me to give this Joseph Fisher Lecture in Commerce. The subject which I have chosen to discuss is a current issue in commercial policy of great interest to Australians and Englishmen alike. But being an English man, it is my intention to discuss the problem today primarily from the point of view of the United Kingdom. I propose, therefore, in this lecture to examine the Japanese case for an easier access for her exports to world markets, to discuss what would be the effects of the treatment of Japan by the United Kingdom as a full member of the General Agreement on Tariffs and Trade, and to consider the difficulties which this course presents for the United Kingdom.

Let me start, then, by considering the basic facts of the present Japanese economy. Japan is a country with a large population relatively to her resources. If the following figures can be trusted, the density of population per square mile of cultivated land is more than twice as high as in such densely populated countries as China and the United Kingdom, fifteen times as high as in the United States, and more than twenty times as high as in Australia.

1 Twenty-seventh Joseph Fisher Lecture, 8 August 1956.

Table 27.1: Density of population per square mile (1948-50)

	Total area	Cultivated area
Australia	3	164
United States	42	213
China	203	1639
United Kingdom	537	1,764
Japan	563	3,596

Source: "Outlook of the Japanese Economy Today" Ministry of Finance, Japanese Government, Tokyo, 1951. Quoted by Jerome B. Cohen, "Economic Problems of Free Japan", Centre of International Studies, Princeton University, 1952.

Moreover, the Japanese population is growing rapidly. As the following figures show, the Japanese death-rate since pre-war years has been drastically reduced as a result of improvements in medical practice and hygiene, and it is now as low as the death-rate in such rich and advanced communities as the United States, the United Kingdom, and Australia.

Table 27.2: Crude birth-rates (BR) and death-rates (DR) per thousand of total population

		1937	1938	1953	1954
Australia	BR	17.4	17.5	22.9	22.5
	DR	9.4	9.6	9.1	9.1
United States	BR	17.1	17.6	24.6	24.9
	DR	11.3	10.6	9.6	9.2
United Kingdom	BR	15.3	15.5	15.9	15.6
	DR	12.6	11.8	11.4	11.4
Japan	BR	30.8	27.1	21.5	20.1
	DR	17.0	17.7	8.9	8.2

The Japanese birth rate has also fallen, but it has fallen rather less than the death rate, with the consequence that the natural rate of increase in the Japanese population is now as high as before the war. In 1938 it was just under and is now just over 1 per cent per annum. It is true that, as a result of a marked rise in fertility since the pre-war years, the natural rate of increase of population in a number of rich countries like the United States and Australia is of the same order of magnitude. But it is a different problem in Japan with its 3,600 persons per square mile of cultivated land than in Australia with its 160 or the United States with its 210 persons per square mile of cultivated land. I do not myself believe that an overpopulated country should countenance a rapid and unrestrained further increase in its population and expect the other countries of the world to take the steps which are necessary to relieve the effects of its growing population pressure. It is up to the Japanese Government and people themselves to avoid ultimate economic catastrophe by restricting births in Japan. But such demographic changes are bound to be slow in their effects. We are inevitably faced by an overpopulated Japan with a rapidly growing population for many years to come.

Relatively to her population Japan is poorly endowed not only with land, but also with other natural resources. She must import some 20 per cent of her requirements of food; although she is again the world's leading exporter of textiles, she must import all her raw cotton; she must import 100 per cent of her requirements of raw wool, phosphates, rubber, nickel and bauxite, some 90 per cent of her oil, 80 per cent of her iron ore, tin, and salt, and 70 per cent of her cooking coal.

This dependence of Japan upon imported raw materials combined with the dense and rapidly growing population of Japan raises another important problem – that of maintaining full employment in Japan. If Japan cannot import her essential raw materials, she cannot maintain her factories at a level of operations which will avoid heavy unemployment among her workers. Japan is already experiencing difficulties of this kind. Some reflationary expansion of total domestic money expenditure (through lower taxes and more ample supplies of money by the banks) would be needed to stimulate economic activity in order to give employment at home. But Japan has had to do exactly the opposite. In recent years she has adopted a fairly restrictive domestic financial policy in order to restrain the growth of demand and the rise of prices at home so as to damp down the Japanese demand for imported raw materials and foodstuffs, to make the price of her exports more competitive in world markets, and so to keep the deficit on her balance of trade within manage able limits. This policy has been fairly successful in affording some immediate relief to the balance of payments; for there has recently been a considerable increase in Japanese exports and reduction in her imports. But it has naturally had an adverse effect upon the employment situation. The number of workers recorded as wholly unemployed has grown from 450,000 in 1953 and 580,000 in 1954 to 680,000 in 1955. Moreover, these figures greatly underestimate the unemployment problem in Japan, where, as a result of the country's social and economic institutions, unemployment is likely to take the form of short time or of unrecorded unemployed persons supported without real opportunity for work on the land or in other similar positions. According to a recent official Japanese survey, the number of persons without jobs but seeking employment was in fact more than 3,000,000 in October 1954. It must also be remembered that some 700,000 new persons (a number equal to somewhat more than 3 per cent of the non-agricultural working population) seek employment each year.[2] The maintenance of full employment has become a testing point for the efficiency of the economic systems of the free countries of the world. If Japan is to be attracted to the free and democratic way of life, she must be able to sell her manufactures on world markets in sufficient quantities to pay for the imports of foodstuffs and raw materials needed to make possible a domestic full-employment policy.

Now what would one expect to be the economic situation in a country which, like Japan, is endowed with much labour but little land and other natural resources? Labour which is plentiful will be cheap; and land and natural resources which are scarce will be expensive. For this reason it will be easy and cheap to produce labour-intensive products (like cotton textiles) which require little land but much labour to produce; and it will be excessively difficult and expensive to produce land intensive products (like wheat and wool) which require much land but little labour to produce. Indeed, it may well be impossible for such a country to produce adequate supplies of food and raw materials for itself. In such a case, either its excess population must emigrate or it must be able to export large quantities of its cheap manufactures in order to acquire the foreign exchange needed for the purchase of a large part of its own foodstuffs, for the purchase of raw materials for the production of the manufactures needed for its own use, and for the purchase of the raw materials to be embodied in the manufactures which it is exporting.

2 *Economic Survey of Japan, 1954-55*, p. 19. Published by the Japanese Economic Planning Board.

We can, I think, rule out as totally impracticable any solution of this problem through the mass emigration of-the Japanese into less densely populated areas. The Japanese in pre-war years, when there were overseas territories into which they could have moved, showed little willingness to migrate. Human beings are in any ease expensive things to move in a civilised manner, particularly when regard is paid to the need to provide new houses and other social services which cannot be transported with the migrants from their old to their new land. Any emigration from Japan on a scale which would appreciably affect the economic position of that country would be a fantastically expensive operation. Finally, I need not remind an Australian audience of the very real difficulties of linguistic, cultural, social, and political assimilation involved, and – since this is a lecture on economic problems – I will not pause to consider them now. There remains only the solution through foreign trade. A country like Japan which is very densely populated, which lacks most natural resources, and for which there is no possibility of large-scale emigration, must rely on selling its labour-intensive manufactured exports and upon importing land-intensive food stuffs and raw materials. Let us accordingly consider what is in fact the present position of Japan in international trade. As the following figures show, Japanese domestic production has shown a very remark able recovery since the end of the Second World War.

Table 27.3: Japanese population, industrial production and foreign trade

	1934-36	1954	1955
Population	100	128	130
Industrial Production	100	167	181
Volume of Exports	100	55	72
Volume of Imports	100	86	90

In 1955 the Japanese population was some 129.5 per cent of the pre-war level, but her industrial production was 181 per cent of the pre-war figure, or in-other words, her output of industrial products per head of the population was 140 per cent of its level before the war. But her position in world export markets had lagged alarmingly behind this domestic recovery and expansion. The volume of her total exports in 1955 was only 72 per cent of the pre-war level, which means that the volume of her exports per head of her population was as low as 56 per cent of the pre-war figure. Before the Second World War, in 1937, Japanese exports accounted for about 5.1 per cent of total world exports; in 1954 the corresponding percentage was only 2.1 per cent.[3] Japan has indeed a long way to go to achieve an adequate volume of exports to support her domestic economy; and she could expand her exports greatly before she regained the share of world markets which she enjoyed immediately before the second World War.

In view of the figures which I have just quoted, one may well ask how the Japanese economy has been able to sustain itself upon so exiguous a volume of exports. A part of the answer to this question is to be found in the fact that, because of direct and indirect United States aid and support, Japan has been able to acquire a larger volume of essential imports than she could purchase with the very low level of exports revealed in the figures which I have just quoted. Indeed, whereas the volume of Japanese exports in 1955 was only 72 per cent of its pre-war level, the volume of her imports was as much as 90 per cent of pre-war. During the occupation of Japan, the United States, as is the way with those wealthy and generous victors, instead of extracting reparations gave no less than $2,000m in direct economic aid to Japan. It is true that since the end of the occupation direct United States economic aid to Japan has amounted to the much smaller figure of $150m. But since the outbreak of the Korean War in June 1950 the United States has spent about $3,000m in Japan on special procurements for its armed forces in that part of the world; and the receipt of these dollars has, of course, enabled Japan to spend so much more on imports from the outside world than its receipts from its exports to the outside world.

But even so, Japanese imports in 1955 were 10 per cent lower than pre-war although her population (which affects her need for imported foods) was 29.5 per cent higher than pre war and her industrial production (which affects her need for imported raw materials) was 81 per cent above pre-war. Japan has been able to manage on so low a volume of imports only by means of the most severe quantitative restriction and licensing of imports so as to limit them to the most essential items.

3 United Nations. Yearbook of International Trade Statistics, 1954.

If my argument is correct there are four important reasons why Japan needs to increase her exports substantially. First, as an unrepentant, if somewhat old-fashioned, believer in the gains to be won all round by freer trade and the international division of labour, I personally would stress the undesirability of a system which makes it necessary for a country to restrict its imports as rigidly as Japan is restricting hers at present. If Japan could export more of the products (like cheap textiles) in the production of which she has a clear comparative advantage and could thereby earn the foreign exchange which would enable her to import more freely the products (like United Kingdom machinery or Australian raw wool) in the production of which other countries have a marked comparative advantage, then it should be possible for standards of living to be raised all round. Second, it cannot be assumed that American aid to Japan or the expenditure by the United States on special procurements for her forces in that part of the world will continue indefinitely at the high level of recent years. At present the Japanese balance of payments is kept in good shape by these exceptional receipts, but their disappearance or substantial reduction would mean that Japan would have to increase her exports substantially in order to maintain even her present low level of imports. Third, if Japan, like other countries in the free world, is to have an effective full-employment policy, then she must be able to finance through larger exports the increased imports of raw materials which will be required to raise the level of output and production in her factories. Fourth, the increase in population in Japan over the next years will also necessitate substantial increases in imports of foodstuffs and raw materials. I cannot now enter into a discussion of the various estimates which have been made of the increase in Japanese exports which would be necessary to meet these different needs. Suffice it to say that the needed increase is very great. But may I remind you that the volume of Japanese exports in 1955 would have had to have been more than 1¾ times as great as it was to have regained the pre-war level of exports per head of population, over 2½ times as great as it was to have regained the pre-war relationship with domestic industrial production, and about 2.33 times as great as it was to have regained its pre-war share of world trade? It is necessary to think in terms of a doubling of Japanese exports over the next few years. But granted that Japan needs to find additional openings for her foreign trade, would it not be possible for her to find a solution by the restoration of her trade with China to its important pre-war level? The following figures[4] show how much the reduction in Japan's foreign trade is to be ascribed to the loss of her trade with this part of the world, in large measure as a result of the embargo on trade with communist China.

Table 27.4: Volume of Japanese trade (Measured in millions of US dollars with trade valued at 1934-36 prices)

	Japanese exports to:		Japanese imports from:	
	Mainland China and Korea	**Rest of the world**	**Mainland China and Korea**	**Rest of the world**
1934-36 (annual ave.)	307	599	197	744
1954	23	404	15	731

A little simple arithmetic from these figures leads to the conclusion that if in 1954 Japan had been able to send the same volume of exports to Mainland China and Korea as before the war without diverting any of her exports from other foreign markets, this would have involved an increase of roughly 66 per cent in her total exports. From this we can, I think, conclude that a re-opening of trade with the Chinese Mainland might make a substantial contribution to the solution of Japan's trading problem. I have no desire in this lecture to enter into the important political issue whether the restrictions on trade with communist China should be relaxed or not. But it is clear that even if all such restrictions were removed, Japan's export problem would be alleviated but not wholly solved. For in the first place as I have already argued, we must think in terms of a doubling of the volume of Japanese exports rather than in terms of a 66 per cent increase in it. And, secondly, it is certainly very over optimistic to think of Japan restoring her pre-war position in these markets. Before the war she was herself in control of much of the Chinese mainland. She imported from these markets large quantities of ore, coking coal, salt, and similar raw materials for her heavy and chemical industries; and in exchange she exported to them her textiles and other manufactured products. But the probability now is that China will need much of her own ore, coal, and other materials for her own industrial development, which will reduce the supplies of these things available for export to Japan, while

4 Based on a report of the US Department of State, 29th March, 1955.

her own industrialisation will lessen her own need for Japanese textiles and other manufactured goods.

There are perhaps other hopeful possibilities for the expansion of Japanese trade. Japan has reasonably low costs in the production of some forms of capital equipment. Such goods might be produced for the countries of South-East Asia to help them in their programmes of economic development, and Japan might import from these countries increased quantities of some of the primary products which she needs. This concept of Japan playing a leading role in the industrialisation of South East Asia is perhaps a promising one, and there have in recent years been some developments of this kind.

But all these developments are somewhat problematic and the Japanese need for expanded export markets is great. The full solution of the problem therefore involves also an expansion of Japanese trade with the main trading countries of the Western world – with the countries of Europe, the United States, and the members of the British Commonwealth. The admission of Japan as a full and equal member into the General Agreement on Tariffs and Trade – or the GATT as I shall call it in the rest of this lecture – has naturally come to stand as a symbol for this development. I intend, therefore, now to describe briefly the steps which have been taken towards the treatment of Japan as a full member of GATT, the attitude of the United Kingdom to this development, and the difficulties which this development raises for the United Kingdom.

The GATT is a multilateral trade agreement. Each contracting party – or, as I shall inaccurately call it in what follows, each member of the GATT – must in general be prepared to undertake a bilateral tariff negotiation with each of the other members. Each of these negotiations results in the binding or reduction of certain rates of duty which the two members concerned levy on their imports from each other. But the benefits of these tariff concessions are then passed on to all the other members of the GATT through the operation of the Most-Favoured-Nation clause which provides that, when any member undertakes to reduce any duty which it levies on imports from any particular country, it must reduce the duty also on the same imports coming from any other member of the GATT.

In addition to the obligation to enter into tariff negotiations of this kind and to grant to all other GATT members treatment which is as favourable as that which it grants to any other country, the GATT contains a number of additional articles, some of which (as for example, the article which in general prohibits the use of quantitative import restrictions) are designed to set limits to trade barriers other than tariffs, and others of which (such as the article which allows countries with serious balance-of-payments difficulties to restrict their imports) are designed to allow certain escapes and exceptions to the general rules for the freeing of trade.

The members of the GATT are able to admit new members to the agreement by a two-thirds majority vote. The admission of a new member to the GATT would automatically entitle that new member to receive Most-Favoured-Nation treatment from all the existing members; or in other words, the new member would automatically receive the advantages of all the reductions or bindings of duties which the existing members had previously negotiated among themselves. In order to prevent a new member from obtaining such benefits without itself giving similar concessions in the form of reductions and bindings in the rates of its own import duties, the practice has grown up of admitting new members to GATT only after there has been a series of bilateral tariff negotiations between the new member and a sufficient number of the existing members. By this means it is hoped to achieve a sufficiently extensive reduction in the tariff of the new member to make its admission a fair bargain for the existing members of the GATT. Finally, I must mention the important Article 35 of the GATT, which may be invoked by any existing member who has not entered into tariff negotiations with the new member. Any existing member who invokes Article 35 can refuse to extend to the new member the concessions and benefits which it would other wise be obliged to extend to it; and in this case, of course, the new member is similarly relieved of the obligations which it would otherwise have incurred towards the member which had invoked Article 35. In other words, a new member may be admitted into the club by a two-thirds majority vote of existing members; it is normally not admitted unless it has paid, as it were, its entrance fee in the form of negotiating a suitable reduction in the duties which it imposes on imports from other members; but any old member can decide to treat the new member as if he were not a member of the club, in which case the new member in turn can treat the old member as if he were not a member of the club.

Japan made formal application for membership in July 1952. There then followed a long period of enquiry, negotiation, and discussion, into the details of which I will not enter. Certain countries of which the United Kingdom may be taken as the leading example expressed their inability to commit themselves to extend the full privileges of membership of GATT to Japan. The United Kingdom was influenced by memories of the nineteen thirties when many existing lines of trade and production were disrupted by a sudden incursion of. cheap Japanese products, sold in many cases by means of questionable commercial devices which misled customers about the original content, or quality of the goods, which relied upon the copying of other traders' designs, and which involved export subsidies of one kind or another.

In the course of these negotiations the question arose whether there were not sufficient escape clauses already in the GATT for it to be possible for a country like the United Kingdom to take the necessary remedial measures against any repeated experience of this kind even if she had accepted Japan as a full member of the GATT. There are two provisions in the GATT which are relevant in this connection. The first is Article XIX which allows a country to take emergency action to restrict the import of particular products if as the result of concessions given under the GATT imports are coming into its territories in such quantities as to cause serious injury to its domestic producers. The argument against relying on this provision was that it did not exempt a member of GATT from its obligation not to discriminate against imports from any other member. In other words, if cheap Japanese textiles flooded into the United Kingdom, the United Kingdom would have had to restrict imports of textiles from all members of the GATT, which it might not wish to do, in order to protect her own textile industry from an expansion of cheap Japanese textiles. The other escape clause on which, in the opinion of some, reliance might have been placed was Article XXIII, under which, if action was taken by any member which had the effect of nullifying or impairing the purposes of the GATT, other members might, with the agreement of GATT as a whole, take action to offset the effects of the offending member. A proposal was made for an official GATT interpretation of this Article which would remove some of its procedural delays; but in spite of this the United Kingdom was not ready to rely upon it since, in its opinion, action under it was too uncertain.

In October 1953 a temporary compromise was reached. Japan was invited by the members of GATT as a whole to take part in all the meetings, discussions, and work of GATT. At the same time a declaration was drawn up under which any particular member of GATT which wished to do so could state that commercial relations between it and Japan would be governed by the provisions of GATT for the period which must elapse before Japan could finally accede to the GATT after suitable tariff negotiations between it and the other members of GATT. A number of GATT countries accepted this declaration and so in effect extended the full privileges of GATT membership forthwith to Japan. A number of other countries, including Australia and the United Kingdom, did not do so.

In February 1955 tariff negotiations were opened in Geneva between Japan and a number of the GATT countries, including the United States, as a result of which Japan gave concessions in her duties and received further concessions in the duties of the other negotiating countries. In September 1955 Japan was admitted as a full member of the GATT. But that was by no means the end of the story; for no less than fourteen countries, including Australia and the United Kingdom, and accounting for more than 40 per cent of Japan's trade with GATT countries, did not undertake tariff negotiations with Japan and invoked Article 35 of the GATT, so that in effect commercial relations between these countries and Japan remain as if Japan had not been admitted to the GATT.

So far I have considered only the negative side of the United Kingdom's position. But the United Kingdom has stressed the fact that there was at no time any desire on her part to prevent Japan from regaining her status as a great trading nation. Membership of the GATT had become a symbol of this status, and Japanese membership of the GATT as such was not opposed by the United Kingdom. Indeed, it its official statement of policy on this subject, issued in April 1955, the United Kingdom Government expressed the "hope that the United Kingdom's trading relations with Japan and Japan's trading relations with the rest of the world will so develop as to enable the United Kingdom and the Colonial territories in due course to accept the full application of the provisions of the General Agreement to their trade with Japan". But until there was more assurance of the course which Japanese trading practices would take, the United Kingdom required more adequate safeguards against excessive competition from Japan than were written into the existing GATT. Nor had the Untied Kingdom any desire to prevent the expansion of Japanese export trade. Indeed, in a series of bilateral trade and payments arrangements outside the GATT, which concerned the total trade of Japan with the sterling area, and to which I shall return shortly, the United Kingdom, had taken steps to make possible an expansion off trade between Japan and the sterling area. But the United Kingdom was unwilling to undertake to impose no more controls over her trade with Japan than over trade with the other members of GATT. She would have preferred that the issue of principle should not have been raised, so that she could have continued gradually to relax her controls over Japanese reader by the *ad hoc* development of her special trade and payments agreements with Japan. Experience could then have shown whether the dangers which were feared in some quarters in the United Kingdom would or would not prove well grounded.

But Japan did raise the issue of principle by applying for membership of GATT. In the first place, she needed an expansion of her export markets; and the commercial benefits which she would obtain not only in the markets of the United kingdom, but in those of the other members of GATT through the application of GATT principles to her trade were of importance to her. Secondly, exclusion from GATT carried with it some stigma; and it was politically important to Japan to re-establish herself as a full member of the commercial club of the main trading countries of the free world.

Let me turn now to a brief description of the development of trade and payments between Japan and the United Kingdom since the end of the Second World War. At first during the Occupation of Japan trade between Japan and the countries of the sterling area was very low. It would in any case have been low because of the initial disruption of Japan's economy after the war. But it was specially restricted by the fact that the payments arrangements were such as to make Japan for currency purposes a member of the dollar area. Any excess of payments by the sterling area would have had to be settled in gold or dollars and thus imports from Japan had to be restricted as severely as imports from the United States. This was altered by the Anglo-Japanese payments agreement of September 1951, whereby payments between Japan and the sterling area sere to be settled in sterling. If Japan ran up a balance of sterling because of heavy imports of Japanese products into sterling area countries, these sums could not be converted by Japan into gold or dollars. The intention was that a broad bilateral balance should be maintained between Japanese payments to the sterling area and the sterling-area payments in Japan. If an unbalance developed, then this would be corrected by a change in import controls on the one side or the other so as to encourage Japanese purchases from the sterling area and to discourage sterling-area purchases from Japan when Japan had large balances of sterling, and vice versa.

This original Anglo-Japanese agreement was to run for twelve months. It has been followed by a number of new agreements which are basically of the same pattern. There have been times when Japan has accumulated large balances of sterling. Such situations have been met to some extent bay a tightening of restrictions on imports of Japanese products into sterling-area countries, but also by a relaxation of Japanese restrictions in imports from the sterling-area. At other times Japan has been running down her sterling balances; and in this case the situation has been met partly by a tightening of Japanese restrictions on imports from the sterling area, but also by a relaxation of sterling-area restrictions on imports from Japan. The general development of these Anglo-Japanese payments agreements has been to plan each time for an expanded, but still a bilaterally balanced, volume of transactions between Japan and the sterling area.

At first these Anglo-Japanese agreements were reach multilaterally between Japan on the one side and many countries of the sterling area on the other side. That is to say, delegation form the Untied Kingdom) would attempt to work out simultaneously with the Japanese a programme of Japanese imports from the various sterling-area countries concerned and a set of programmes of imports of Japanese products into the sterling-area countries concerned which would result in a balance between Japanese payments to, and receipts from, the sterling area as a whole. But the more recent agreements have been strictly bilateral agreements between Japan and the United Kingdom. In these negotiations statistical estimates have been made of the total amount which, under their separate trade arrangements, independent sterling-area countries are likely to spend on Japanese products. Moreover, since 1954 there have been virtually no quota restrictions on the import of Japanese products into the dependent colonies of the United Kingdom, so that the imports of these territories can also merely be taken as a statistical estimate of what will be the result of such free importation into the colonies. Balance between the sterling payments and receipts of Japan as a whole can then be maintained in the Anglo-Japanese agreement only by changing the restrictions on imports of Japanese products into the United Kingdom itself or, on the other side, by a change in Japanese restrictions on imports from the sterling area. It is in terms of these two variables that a balance has been sought in the most recent Anglo-Japanese agreements.

As the following figures show, these Anglo-Japanese payments agreements have made possible an expansion of Japan's export markets in the United Kingdom and in the rest of the sterling area. But this expansion has been at an uneven rate. In particular in 1953 there was a severe cut-back in the United Kingdom and other sterling-area imports from Japan to meet the situation which had arisen from the greatly increased – purchases of the sterling area from Japan in 1951 and 1952 with the resulting heavy accumulation of sterling balances by Japan.

Table 27.5: Value of Japan's exports, monthly averages (million yen)

	Exports to United Kingdom	Exports to rest of Sterling area	Total exports
1949	1,264	6,195	15,293
1950	781	8,140	24,606
1951	1,620	16,758	40,637
1952	2,194	14,009	38,187
1953	994	8,526	38,245
1954	1,534	13,242	48,880
1955	1,823	17,649	60,320

The sterling area provides an important market for Japan. The proportion of Japanese exports going to the sterling area has ranged from nearly one half in 1949 to one quarter in 1953, and in 1955 was about one third.

Let us now consider against the background of these arrangements the particular difficulties which the United Kingdom would encounter if she were to accept full GATT obligations towards Japan.

As far as tariffs are concerned, there would be no difficulties. Both the United Kingdom and her Colonies (unlike Australia) already extend Most-Favoured-Nation treatment to Japanese imports in so far as import duties are concerned. That is to say they do not levy higher duties on Japanese products than those which they levy on the products of any other country which does not enjoy Imperial Preference in the United Kingdom and Colonial markets. Of course, the United Kingdom and the Colonies do give preferential tariff treatment to other Commonwealth countries; but these existing Imperial Preferences are permitted under the GATT rules and they would not be counted as a discrimination against Japanese products.

The difficulties which the United Kingdom would experience relate to the quantitative restriction of imports by import licensing. In this connection we must consider, first, the question of the restriction of imports of Japanese products into the British Colonies and, secondly, the restriction of imports of Japanese products into the United Kingdom itself.

In the nineteen thirties quantitative restrictions were placed on imports of Japanese products into many of the British Colonies as part of the general development of commercial policy to counteract the disruptive effects of the great flood of cheap Japanese manufactures. After the second World War imports of Japanese products into the Colonial territories, just as imports of Japanese products into other sterling-area countries, were at first controlled on balance-of-payments grounds in order to prevent the accumulation in Japanese hands of excessive balances of sterling which directly or indirectly would lead to a pressure on the gold and dollar reserves of the sterling area. But since 1954, as I have already explained, restrictions on Japanese imports into the Colonies have not been used in this way. Colonial governments have been free to licence the import of Japanese products in any quantities which they desire. The old criticism that the United Kingdom has employed quota restrictions in order to protect expensive Lancashire products against cheap Japanese products at the cost of the inhabitants of Colonial areas can no longer be sustained.

It is true that the apparatus of import licensing is maintained in the Colonies against Japanese products, but not against the products of the sterling area or of the European countries which are members of the European Payments Union. But the quotas set for Japanese products are now so large that they are in many cases ineffective and not fully used; and where the quotas are fully used, additional licences are fairly freely obtainable upon application. The reason for the maintenance of this system is in order that the United Kingdom may hold ready in reserve a weapon which it might need to use once more on balance-of-payments grounds, if there were another sudden surge of cheap Japanese products into sterling markets. This system is, of course, formally discriminatory under the GATT rules and would have to be abolished if the United Kingdom applied the GATT rules to Japanese trade. This might have some slight beneficial effect upon Japanese exports, since the maintenance of the apparatus of licensing may itself somewhat discourage Japanese trade. A Colonial importer must go through the tiresome drill of using an import licence if he buys from Japan, but not if he buys from Europe or the British Commonwealth; and there may be a tendency for the issue of the licences to concentrate the trade in the hands of existing traders who, be cause of their existing commercial connections, are somewhat less likely to buy from Japanese than from other sources. But the discriminatory effect is no longer substantial and the abolition of this system would not have any very direct favourable effect upon Japanese, or adverse effects upon British, trade.

Quantitative restrictions on the import of Japanese products into the United Kingdom itself are quite a different matter. In this case there are quotas on the import of Japanese products which effectively restrain the imports of Japanese textiles, toys, and other products. To give GATT non-discriminatory treatment to Japan would mean the removal of these restrictions; for the import of these products is not similarly restricted when they come from other countries of the Commonwealth or of Western Europe. It is this requirement which presents the most direct and obvious difficulty which stands in the way of the United Kingdom giving GATT treatment to Japan. To let these Japanese products enter the United Kingdom without licence restrictions would not be catastrophic for the United Kingdom. These products are not basic essentials; and neither on military nor on economic grounds would a contraction of these industries in the United Kingdom be disastrous. Moreover, the problem of industrial readjustment would be easier now than it was in the nineteen thirties. In the first place, we now live in an inflationary instead of a deflationary atmosphere. Alternative opportunities for employment would now exist in the rest of the country for workers dismissed from factories hit by Japanese competition. Secondly, largely as a result of readjustments made in the second World War industry is now more diversified in Lancashire where there are now many light engineering and other industries available to give more local employment if the cotton industry were contracted.

But the transitional problems would nevertheless be very real ones. The difficulty of the problem for the United Kingdom is particularly great because the increased competition from Japanese products would be highly concentrated on a few industries in the United Kingdom. The removal of import restriction on Japanese products would not cause a little extra competition for a large number of industries; it would cause a great deal of extra competition for a small number of industries. Certain branches of the textile industry would be very seriously cut back. Certain small industries, like the cheap toy industry or the net-making industry, might be faced virtually with complete ruin. It is politically and economically a serious matter to take steps which may substantially effect the fortunes of a traditionally basic industry like the Lancashire cotton industry and which may bring concentrated loss on a few small producers.

There is another possible danger for the United Kingdom which might turn out to be more important economically, although it presents less obvious political difficulty. Japan since the war has continuously spent a great deal more on dollar products than she has earned by her sales to the dollar area. There have been some structural changes in Japan's trade which have emphasised this lack of dollar balance. For example, the development of competing synthetic fabrics in the United States has greatly restricted the United States demand for natural silks, one of Japan's most important exports to the United States; and the collapse of the Chinese mainland as a main source of supply of important Japanese imports like cooking coal has meant that Japan must make heavy purchases of these products in the United States. This natural and perhaps inevitable structural change has been artificially reinforced by certain types of United States aid to Japan. For example, disposals of United States surplus wheat on special payments terms in Japan may have restricted the Japanese demand for Australian and so for sterling wheat. In 1954 the volume of Japanese exports to North America was only 57 per cent of its pre war level, whereas the volume of Japanese imports from North America was 135 per cent of its pre-war level. In 1954 Japan's exports to North America were worth $349m, but her imports from North America were $1,102m. On the other hand, in many post-war years there has been a tendency for the purchases of the sterling area from Japan to exceed Japan's imports from the sterling area. In these circumstances there might well be an underlying tendency for Japan to earn sterling for her exports and to convert this into dollars for the purchase of her imports, thus putting a strain upon the sterling areas gold and dollar reserves in London.

This tendency has up to now been avoided by the Anglo Japanese trade and payments agreements to which I have already referred. United Kingdom restrictions on purchases from Japan have been deliberately maintained and Japanese restrictions on sterling-area products have been deliberately relaxed so as to keep a rough balance between Japan's sales and purchases in sterling. It is not at all certain that this would be permissible if Japan and the United Kingdom applied GATT rules to their mutual commercial relations. Under the GATT rules a country can restrict imports so long as its balance of payments is in serious disequilibrium. But the general GATT rule is that such restrictions should be non-discriminatory; and if Japan were not free to discriminate in favour of sterling products and the United Kingdom were not free to discriminate against Japanese products, it would not be possible to offset any underlying tendency for Japan to sell to the sterling area but to buy from the dollar area. It is true that the GATT rules do in certain circumstances also permit discriminations in import restrictions on balance-of-payments grounds. I cannot on this occasion go into these complicated rules in detail. Suffice it to say that the freedom of Japan and the United Kingdom to seek a bilateral yen-sterling balance would be more circumscribed than at present.

Thus there are some very real difficulties in the way of the extension by the United Kingdom of full GATT treatment to Japanese products. There would, of course, probably be some compensating advantages to the United Kingdom in achieving a removal of barriers to Anglo-Japanese trade. While the transitional difficulties might be considerable, the change in the structure of United Kingdom industries would probably in the long-run bring some gains. Consumers in the United Kingdom would obtain cheaper supplies of certain products (like textiles and toys) which would be obtained from the export of products (like machinery) in the production of which United Kingdom industry was more economical. The main danger would be the instability of industrial production which would occur if there were ever once more a sudden surge of cheap Japanese products into the relatively unprotected markets of the United Kingdom, as happened in the nineteen thirties. But that development was a product of the Great Depression. In the early nineteen thirties the American market for Japanese silk and other pro ducts collapsed as a result of the collapse of buying power inside the United States combined with the erection of the excessive Hawley-Smoot tariff by that country. This was the main reason why the Japanese suddenly sought alternative outlets for their exports at excessively low prices and by questionable commercial devices in markets such as the British which enjoyed little protection from them. In my view, we can rule out the possibility that the United States will once again permit a major domestic economic depression to develop, or will reverse their commercial policy and build once more an excessively high tariff. And if these things should occur, it is certain that the GATT, as we know it now, would not long survive. In present conditions Japanese products are not so excessively cheap as to cause an overwhelming flood of cheap goods into British markets.

Of course, the United Kingdom is not the only country which has difficulty in giving full GATT treatment to Japanese trade. There are the thirteen other members of the GATT – Australia, Austria, Belgium, Brazil, Cuba, France, Haiti, India, Luxembourg, the Netherlands, New Zealand, Rhodesia and Nyasaland, and the Union of South Africa – which have followed the same course as the United Kingdom in invoking Article 35 so as not to be obliged to give GATT treatment to Japanese trade. But the United Kingdom is the leading trading country which has invoked Article 35 of the GATT in order to refrain from giving GATT treatment to Japan. It is probable that the United Kingdom's example has been important. If she ceased to invoke Article 35, a number of the other thirteen countries which at present also invoke Article 35 might be persuaded not to do so. The indirect effects of this might be important for the United Kingdom. Suppose that some third countries remove some barriers on imports of Japanese products. In so far as similar products were previously being imported from the United Kingdom the result may be that Japanese products are purchased instead of United Kingdom products by the countries concerned; and this would mean contraction in the market for United Kingdom products. Such unfavourable developments are in fact likely to occur in some cases as Japan finds an easier access into third countries. But in so far as the easier access into third markets enables Japanese products to compete successfully in those markets against the domestic production of the third countries themselves, the effect may be to ease the pressure on the United Kingdom. For the more readily Japanese products are absorbed into such third markets, the less plentiful and cheap will be the remaining supplies of Japanese products available for sale in United Kingdom markets or in markets in which they compete directly with United Kingdom products. The extension of full GATT treatment to Japan by all the other members of GATT might thus have some adverse effects upon United Kingdom exports, but at the same time it might relieve the pressure of Japanese competition in other United Kingdom markets.

Even those members of the GATT who did not invoke Article 35 have experienced difficulties in extending full GATT treatment to Japan. There was, for example, a very considerable expansion of cheap Japanese textiles into the United States after the mutual tariff reductions which took place before Japan's entry into GATT relationships with the United States. This caused some considerable concern among the New England textile producers. It became clear that the United States Administration might be forced to take steps (either through the escape clause in GATT which can be invoked if a domestic industry suffers serious injury from imports or by other means) to prevent this natural expansion of Japan's cheap labour intensive products. In fact, an uneasy *modus vivendi* has been found only through the agreement of the Japanese to restrict their exports to the United States. The formal GATT relationship between Japan and the United States has been accepted; but nevertheless some special restrictions on the trade with Japan have thus been continued. In other cases, of which Germany may be cited as an example, countries which have accepted Japan as a full member of the GATT have not yet found it possible so to liberalise their quota restrictions over imports of Japanese goods as fully to carry out the obligations which they have thus incurred. The United Kingdom should not per haps be too severely criticised for having been willing to incur the odium of stating in advance that she could not extend full GATT treatment to Japan.

Is the assumption by Japan of the obligation to give GATT treatment to those members of GATT who do not invoke Article 35 likely to give rise to serious difficulties for Japan? Japan at the present is operating a system of very strict controls over her imports. As long as her balance of payments remains in its present difficult position it will be legitimate for her under the GATT rules to continue to control her imports. But her import controls will now be subject to review and challenge by the other members of the GATT on two counts: the Japanese restrictions must not be more severe than is necessary to cope with the Japanese balance-of-payments problem and they must be non-discriminatory as between the products of the other members of GATT which have accepted Japan as a full member of the GATT. It is possible that on both these counts Japan may need to revise her restrictions. In particular, there have been serious complaints that the Japanese import restrictions have on occasions been administered in an arbitrary manner which has discriminated against the exports of particular countries.

Another feature of the Japanese trading system to which serious exception can be taken is the well-known "link system" in Japanese foreign exchange control. Under this system the right to acquire foreign exchange for the purchase of certain imports has been linked to the export of certain other products. Often the right to purchase imports of a certain raw material has been linked with the export of products made out of that material. But occasionally there has been no such obvious connection between the exported product and the imported product which is linked with it. Thus in the past the export of machinery, ships, and silk has carried with it a right to receive foreign exchange for the import of textile raw materials, sugar, petroleum, and bananas. This system is equivalent to a system of export subsidies. For the exporter will be willing to export, if necessary, at a price which does not fully cover his costs of production because his loss will be linked with the acquisition of a valuable right to acquire certain scarce imports. Until recently, the GATT rules did not include any direct prohibition of export subsidies on manufactured goods. They required only that such subsidies should be notified to the GATT and should be the subject of consultation with other aggrieved members. But the new GATT rules on this subject, proposed at the revision of the GATT in 1955, would provide for a standstill on export subsidies on industrial products until the end of 1957 and for their abolition at the earliest possible date after that. Japan has, in fact, recognised that the "link system" would be subject to criticism as not being in the spirit, even if it were within the letter, of the existing GATT rules. She is in the process of dismantling the whole system.

Japanese traders have been the subject of severe criticism in many countries and, above all, in the United Kingdom, for adopting unfair methods of competition, such as the copying of designs which are in reality the property of their competitors. There is no doubt that these complaints have in the past been justified. Recently after discussions with the British traders concerned steps have been taken to attempt to stop the pirating of designs in the case of textiles. A Japanese Textile Colour Design Centre has been set up and all members of the Japanese Cotton Textile Exporters' Association are required to obtain the approval of the Design Centre for their designs before concluding a foreign sale. This method of control might have two forms of weakness. First, there is the problem how the Design Centre is to make sure that the foreign buyer of Japanese textiles who says that he is the owner of a foreign design is really the owner of that design. Secondly, there is the need to control the exports of the small Japanese producers and exporters who are not members of the Japanese Cotton Textile Exporters' Association. Recent legislation in Japan has enabled regulations controlling the designs used in Japanese exports to be applied to the producers and exporters who are not members of the Exporters' Association. It remains to be seen whether these measures will effectively put an end to objectionable trading practices in the case of textiles, and whether similar safeguards can be applied to other trades.

It is, in my opinion, greatly to be hoped that trading conditions will so develop, and that such safeguards will be found, that the United Kingdom will be able soon to apply GATT treatment to Japanese products. As I have tried to show, Japan is a country whose economic survival depends above all things upon being able to sell her manufactured produce in overseas markets; and for this reason there must be a reasonably ready access for Japanese products to world markets, if a healthy and contented Japan is to be attracted to the democratic and free way of life. In the nineteen thirties the countries of the free world made a double mistake in their attitude towards Japan. In the first place, they should have opposed Japanese military aggression more firmly. But, in the second place, they should have taken a more liberal line towards the expansion of Japanese export markets. They should have said to Japan: "You may not acquire the raw materials and foodstuffs which are necessary for your existence by force of arms; but it is possible for you to acquire them through a commercial expansion of your exports into our markets". Alas, they said something which was almost the exact reverse to this. Today we must avoid finding ourselves in the position of saying to Japan: "You may not, of course, sell your exports on equal terms with the products of other free countries in our markets; nor should you trade with communist China. But, pray, join with us in the prosperity which is offered by the free, democratic, western way of life". The old-fashioned, Cobdenite view that a reduction of trade barriers is a bulwark of this free, democratic, western way of life has often been overstated; but it is not always totally wrong.

28

National superannuation: Means test or contributions?

Richard I. Downing[1]

The income of retired people gives them a claim on the flow of goods and services currently being produced by the active population. Whatever form their income takes, it must be paid at the expense of this active population. Retired people may be living on capital and the income from their investments (an annuity or an income from a superannuation scheme is a combination of the two) or on private gifts or national age-pensions. In all these cases, their spending is directly or indirectly, a charge on those currently producing any earning who save, pay taxes and pay rent, interest and dividends on the capital they use in production. This paper discusses how the amount of income accruing to retired people in these ways is to be determined.

Private insurance

It is a common assumption that people should, both for their own good and for the community's, provide for their own retirement. This is believed to promote the virtue of self-reliance and to reduce dependence on the welfare State.

We may take as our exemplar the man who, either alone or jointly with his employer, pays premiums on an endowment policy or contributions to a superannuation scheme. (I shall not be discussing here the question of relative contributions to superannuation schemes by employees, employers and

1 Twenty-eighth Joseph Fisher Lecture, 24 September 1958. The late Mr. F. H. Rowe, former Director-General of the Commonwealth Department of Social Services, and Mr. Max Wryell and his officers in the Research Section of that Department, gave me invaluable and friendly help in assembling a mass of detailed information about superannuation schemes in various countries. None of these people is in any way associated with either the analysis or the suggestions contained in this Lecture.

governments; in effect, I treat all contributions as being, directly or in directly, a charge on earners' incomes.) These payments accumulate in a fund, earn substantial compound interest and can be used, on retirement, to purchase an annuity.

There is an increasing acceptance of the idea that the income so provided for retirement should be a substantial proportion of the individual's income received while working. This relation of retirement income to earned income is a natural extension of the acceptance of income as a socio-economic criterion. The income a man earns during his working life determines not only the real income of goods and services he can enjoy, but also his material status in relation to other people in his community.

With income playing this important socio-economic role, it is natural that a man should be anxious to ensure that, after his retirement, he will have an income adequate not only to meet his reduced need for goods and services, but also to maintain his material status relative to other retired people. The British Labour Party, for instance, bases its proposals for a national superannuation scheme on the desire to extend to workers, as well as to "the privileged minority" (that is, those who are in private superannuation schemes) the benefit of "between half pay and two-thirds of pay on retirement" rather than relying on a low flat-rate National Insurance benefit.[2] It claims that "wage related pensions satisfy the social requirements of the second half of the twentieth century just as flat-rate pensions suited the first half". (One commentator, Professor A. T. Peacock, points out that, since the scheme proposed by the British Labour Party will not operate fully at least until the year 2030, it would really be necessary to ask one's great-grandchildren whether a system designed for the second half of the twentieth century would suit the first half of the twenty-first century.)

For a man wanting an annuity equal to one-half his average earnings over his life-time, and with no widow to provide for, the cost through an Australian insurance office would be about 5 per cent of his income if he began his provision at age 15, 7 per cent at age 25, and 12 per cent at age 35. The cost would be greater if he wished to provide, as some schemes do, for a benefit related to his

2 *National Superannuation: Labour's Policy for Security in Old Age* (published by the British Labour Party, Transport House, Smith Square London, 1957).

income in his last 5 or 10 years of earning, or his best 15 years; and if he wished to provide for a surviving widow. The United Nations' pension fund, for instance, is based on thirty years' contributions. It provides a pension equal to half the salary earned in the last ten years of the contributors' career, with a half-pension for a surviving widow. It is financed by contributions totalling about 22 per cent of the salary, two thirds being paid by the employer who also carries any deficit in the fund.

The case for Government intervention

It would appear within our reach to provide decently through private insurance schemes for our own retirement. What case is there for any intervention by the Government? Why not leave people to look after themselves? The case for the Government intervention rests on three bases:

Improvidence

The first is the natural improvidence of man – his inability to look ahead and see that his future needs, when he comes to them, are going to be as urgent as his present needs. Pigou, in his *Economics of Welfare*, describes this irrationality as "a far-reaching economic disharmony . . . People distribute their resources between the present, the near future and the remote future on the basis of a wholly irrational preference . . . they will often devote themselves to . . . obtaining a small (satisfaction) now in preference to a much larger one some years hence" (p. 25, 4th edition).

Because people do not realise, during their working years, the full importance of an income during their retirement, there is a case for the Government to introduce a compulsory system of superannuation. There is also an implication that anyone who prefers to provide his own endowment, or join a private superannuation scheme, provided the private arrangement gives at least as good cover as the nationally-prescribed minimum.

Redistribution of income

Second, there is the age-old question of income-distribution. If community opinion was satisfied with the existing pattern on income distribution among income-earners, it might be reasonable to suppose it would also be satisfied with the similar pattern of income-distribution among retired people that would be achieved by, say, half-pensions for all, financed by uniform, percentage contributions from all. If the community is not satisfied with the existing pattern, it might be reasonable to suppose that it should seek to change relative incomes both directly, and indirectly through progressive taxation and social services, so as to bring out a pattern of income-distribution more nearly conforming to its ideals. Individuals could still be left to provide incomes for their own retirement related to the incomes the received while working.

There are, nevertheless, two reasons why considerations of income-distribution might support government intervention in superannuation. Firstly, while the community may be satisfied with an income range for earners of, say £500 to £5000, it may, for the reduced incomes of retired people, prefer an income range of, say £300 to £2000 rather than the £250 to £2500, that would be achieved on a uniform insurance basis.

Furthermore, the community may feel that the task of changing income-distribution, either directly or through the Government budget, is so difficult that the process could be made more effective if reinforced through the medium of a national superannuation scheme.

For both these reasons then, the community may consider it desirable that the provision made by lower-income groups for their retirement should be supplemented, either out of the insurance contributions collected from higher incomes or out of consolidate revenue.

Inflation

Out third basis for believing that there is a case for Government intervention arises from the fact that, in this question of provision for retirement, we are dealing essentially with a problem with a long time-scale. It will normally be a 40 to 60-year period between the time when a man begins providing for his retirement and the time when he dies and needs no further provision. During such a period we can be sure that there will be substantial increase in productivity, bringing corresponding increases in average real income to the whole community.

If the average level of incomes remained stable in money terms throughout the period, there would be continuing price reductions and/or improvements in the quality of products, so that the real value of these stable money incomes would be correspondingly increased. Thus, if a man received £1000 a year during his working life, he would enjoy, along with his fellow-earners, a steady increase in his real income as he and his fellows became more productive. The provision of an annuity of £500 a year would preserve his (reduced) relative income status during his retirement, enabling him to go on sharing in any increase of productivity accruing to the community as a whole in the form of price reductions or quality improvements.

In fact, average money incomes do not remain stable over time. Indeed, it does not any longer seem even to be accepted as a socio-economic objective that they should. It is often stated as an alternative that prices should remain stable, the implication being that money incomes should rise with productivity. If this objective were achieved, an average earner would then share in any gains of productivity during his working life. After retirement, however, his income, fixed in money terms, should also be fixed in real terms. He would no longer share in the community's increasing productivity and his relative income status would sink as productivity rose.

Moreover, in view of our last 20 years' experience, we must go further and acknowledge that, even if stable prices are our objective, it is one we have failed to achieve. In this period, prices in Australia have increased threefold. Many people have come to fear that prices are likely to go on increasing, if not at the rapid rate of the last 20 years, then anyhow by an average of, say, 2 per cent or 3 per cent a year. Over the 40-60 years in which we are interested, this implies prices tripling or quadrupling. Our average earner, who keeps up with the average incomes, is, of course, protected against inflation during his working life. But on retirement, his life savings, designed to give him an annuity equal to half of his average earnings, might buy him an annuity of only one-quarter or one-fifth of his average earnings at retirement; and he would have no protection against inflation after his retirement. Not only his relative income status, but also his ability to provide a stable real income of goods and services, would be destroyed.

It is often suggested that money accumulating in personal or group retirement-funds should be invested in securities that could be expected to rise in value with the general price-level rather than in the usual trustee-type security with a redemption value fixed in money terms. But inflation-hedged securities are not easy to identify and inevitably entail other risks from which trustee-type securities are free. Moreover, the supply of "growth-stocks" is limited. A substantial and sustained switch of funds into them would raise their prices immediately, partly defeating their usefulness as a hedge against inflation.

There is a real resentment that people are thus precluded, through no apparent fault of their own, from providing decently for their retirement. Moreover, the basic cause of inflation is the failure of the community as a whole to provide enough savings to finance the investment required for our development. There is a bitter irony in the fact that the very who, by saving, have done their bit to prevent failure of others to match their efforts.

It is especially the fact of inflation to date, and the widening fear of inflation in the future, which has brought the present ferment of anxiety and thinking about the problem of provision for retirement, and about the responsibility of Governments to protect people against an inflation which is the result of the community's act rather than the individual's.

We have found, then, three reasons for Government intervention in the provision of income for retired people. First, many people are so short-sighted that they will provide adequately for themselves only under a statutory obligation. Second, the provision which lower-income groups can afford to make for themselves may need to be supplemented by the Government at the expense of higher-income groups. Third, to an increasing extent people are coming to expect that the Government should protect their savings against loss by an inflation which is not of their causing, and should even make it possible for them to share in increases of productivity accruing to the community as a whole.

Two basic types of national superannuation schemes have been designed, particularly in Western European countries, to meet the objections raised against pure insurance schemes which tie retirement-benefits to actual contributions. An examination of these will help us to assess the present Australian system and to suggest ways in which it might be modified.

The British Labour Party's insurance-type proposals

The first type of scheme I shall describe is one which retains some of the features of insurance schemes. In particular, it accumulates contributions in a fund and the benefits are related to the contribution-history of the retired earner. I shall take as a basis for analysis the system recently proposed for adoption in the United Kingdom by the British Labour Party. The scheme is not, of course in operation there, but schemes incorporating similar principles are already in operation in a number of Western European and other countries – notably Germany, France, Italy, Belgium, Austria, Greece, Israel, Japan and Brazil.

There are several essential features of the British Labour Party's proposals. Firstly, it is to be compulsory for all who are not members of approved private schemes. A condition of approval for opting out the national scheme is that the private scheme is that the private scheme should grant full transferability of accrued pension rights to anyone who wishes to change his job. It is a regrettable feature of most private superannuation schemes that, if a member changes his job, he gets back, at most his own contributions and loses his employer's.

Secondly, the retirement-benefit paid is to be related to the individual's average earnings during his working life. A typical wage-earner would get a benefit of about 60 percent of his income. But the scheme is so arranged as to give a higher ration of benefit to income for lower-income groups than for higher-income groups. There are also both a floor and a ceiling to the rate of benefit, and a ceiling on contributions. The pension entitlement accrues to retired earners, whether single or married. A reduced pension will be paid to surviving widows.

Thirdly, in calculating the individual's average earnings, his actual earnings in each year of his working life are to be revalued by means of an earnings index, to bring them to equivalence with the average rate of earning in his year of retirement.

(Thus, if the earnings index in the year of retirement say 1990, was four times the earnings index in 1960, the contributions paid and the actual earnings in 1960 would be multiplied by four in order to calculate the pension right he would be credited with, in 1990 on account of his earnings and contributions in 1960). This adjustment will correct fully for any inflation of money incomes that occurs during the individual's working life up to the time of his retirement.

Fourthly, during the individual's retirement, his benefit is to be varied, each year, with an index of old people's cost of living. This adjustment will correct fully for any inflation of prices that occurs after the individual's retirement. The French and German schemes, already in operation, go still further and vary the benefit after retirement with the average earnings index. This not only protects the individual against any price inflation, but also enables him to share fully in any increases of productivity accruing to the community as a whole after his retirement.

Fifthly, a higher rate of benefits is paid to those who postpone their entitlement. Thus, in France, a man retiring at 60 receives 20 per cent of his average income as benefit; at 65, 40 per cent; at 70, 60 per cent and so on. In Germany, after 40 years of contributions he receives 60 per cent benefit, after 50 years, 75 per cent.

Sixthly, receipt of the full benefit is conditional on a full working-life of contribution. (The estimated rate of contribution under the British Labour Party proposals is 10 per cent of earnings, 3 per cent paid by the earner, 5 per cent by the employer and 2 per cent by the Government; self-employed persons will contribute 8 per cent). The scheme will not, in fact, become fully operative until some 50 years or so after its introduction, that is, till some time in the next century, depending on when the British Labour Party goes into office. In the transition period, some minimum benefit will be paid regardless of contributions.

Finally, the British Labour Party believes that, during this transition period, contributions will exceed benefits, so that a fund will accumulate and be available to supplement resources available for investment. It is important to note, however, that the net addition to savings of such schemes will be less than might be expected. In the first place, people may make part of their superannuation contribution at the expense of other savings they would have undertaken anyhow; and secondly, the fund will also be depleted to the extent that the desire to achieve some redistribution of incomes and to offset inflation forces the payment of benefits in excess of recipients' contributions. Thus, for instance, the present National Insurance Fund in the United Kingdom, which is more strictly based on the insurance principle than the British Labour Party proposals will be, is expected to be in deficit by £126m in 1960-1, by £322m in 1969-70 and by £475m in 1979-80.

The insurance element in these schemes turns out, in fact, to be largely a masquerade. This is inevitable. You can have a true insurance scheme, based on contributions determined by an actuarial calculation of what an individual has to contribute during his working life in order to receive an agree proportion of average earnings after retirement, only if you can make your calculations in terms of a money which retains indefinitely its value in relation to average earnings. You could even build into such a scheme a moderate degree of redistribution. But once you have to vary benefits to take account of changes in the general level of money-earnings, the insurance principle and actuarial calculations become a mere front, behind which you carry on the essential operation – namely the transfer from today's earners of whatever part of their income is needed to support today's retired people. Lewis Meriam comments, in *The Cost of Financing Social Security*: "Adoption of the term 'insurance' by the proponents of social security was a stroke of promotional genius. Thus social security has capitalised on the goodwill of private insurance and, through the establishment of a reserve fund, has clothed itself with an aura of financial soundness".[3]

The Netherlands distributive scheme

The second type of scheme I shall describe retains the principle of contributions but abandons entirely the pretence of an accumulating insurance fund. It is known as a "distributive" or "assessment" scheme. I shall take as a basis for discussion the scheme which has been operating in the Netherlands since 1955.[4]

3 Quoted in A.T. Peacock, *The Economics of National Insurance* (William Hodges, London 1952), p. 41.

4 A summary of the relevant legislation is published in *Industry and Labour* (International Labour Office, Geneva), Vol. XVI, No. 8, 15 October, 1956, p. 346.

This scheme pays a benefit equal to about 27 per cent of average hourly wage rates for all single people, and about 45 per cent for married couples. The rate is varied automatically with the index of hourly wages. Retired people have thus full protection against inflation and enjoy full participation in any increases of productivity that accrues to the community as a whole.

The essential feature of the scheme is that contributions are levied on today's income-earners aged 15 and under 65, at whatever rate is necessary to finance the benefits being paid to today's population aged 65 and over. No fund is accumulated – today's contributors support today's retired people. The size of contribution needed will vary according to the ratio of these two populations. For Australia, at present, I estimate that provision of benefits similar to those paid in the Netherlands would require contributions of about 6 or 7 per cent of our national income. If our population growth slackened so that the proportion of older people rose, the cost would be higher.

It would appear at first sight that a distributive scheme of this sort must cost more than insurance scheme of this sort much cost more than an insurance scheme, in which contributions are multiplied by the powerful force of compound interest. This would certainly be so if, thanks to the funds made available while an insurance fund was building up, investment was higher than it would otherwise have been and if this led to increases of productivity greater than would otherwise have occurred. If, however, the community ensures through its general economic policy, as we are now trying to do, that it has always full employment and an optimum allocation of resources between consumption and investment, the rate of growth of productivity will in any case also be optimum. If this optimum growth is achieved, the real burden on the community, in any year, of supporting its retired population at, say, half-pay will be the same, whether it is financed by contributions levied on the distributive principle, or by a lower rate of contributions levied on the insurance principle plus interest payments on earlier contributions. The contributions paid by an individual may well be different according to whether he is contributing to an insurance or to a distributive scheme. But these contributions cannot be considered alone – they must be considered as part of his total payment of contributions, taxes and interest. Fiscal policy could be used to achieve any desired distribution of this total burden.

A second and corollary feature of a distributive scheme is that, while the receipt of full benefit will ultimately be conditional on contributions having been paid throughout the beneficiary's working life, all people over the age of 15 when the Dutch scheme came into operation in 1955 are deemed to have been contributing since the age of 15. The entire population thus qualifies, as soon as retiring age is reached, for the full rate of benefit, instead of waiting until some time in the next century. This follows naturally from the principle that today's retired people are supported by today's earners, leaving to the earners of the future the responsibility of supporting today's earners when they retire. For this reason, the national scheme is compulsory for all, with no provision for opting out into private schemes.

An incidental feature of the Dutch scheme, and one that makes it more re-distributive of income than the British Labour Party proposals, is that while it too is financed by a proportional levy on incomes (subject to an upper limit), supplemented by a government contribution which is presumably progressive in its incidence on income, the benefits paid are a flat rate for all. The benefits under the British Labour Party scheme, it will be recalled, are largely proportional to the individual's own earnings.

A distributive scheme could easily be designed to pay benefits related to individual earnings, particularly once it has been operating long enough for a complete contributions-history of all beneficiaries to have been built up.[5] In fact, in France, private schemes have been established for particular professional or occupational groups – notably civil servants, teachers, bankers, doctors and lawyers – on this same distributive basis.[6] Under these schemes, retired members receive benefits varying according to the status they enjoyed while earning. Thus the pension of a retired Assistant Secretary to the Treasury or of a Professor would be determined in each year as a percentage of the salary currently being paid to the present occupants of these particular posts. The pensions would be financed by current contributions collected from currently employed members of the groups. The administration of a scheme of this type would be much simpler than the British Labour Party's proposals.

5 A distributive scheme granting differential benefits could operate immediately, on the basis of information as to the beneficiary's occupational history and his past income-tax returns. This would give a fitting reward to those who have not understated their incomes in the past.

6 See V. S. Garibian and P. J. D. Wiles "Pensions and Rising Prices" *Oxford Economic Papers* (N.S.), Vol. IV, No. 2, July, 1952, p. 131.

Any identifiable occupational group of private individuals, which is large enough "to carry its own insurance" and stable enough not to be threatened with a contraction in the future, could establish such distributive schemes. I commend them, in particular, to the Universities of Australia. Individuals in such private distributive schemes could be permitted to opt out of a national distributive scheme.

Any superannuation scheme financed out of current revenue rather than a capitalized fund is essentially of the distributive type. Thus in Australia, Eire and South Africa, pensions are paid, subject to a means test, out of consolidated revenue. In New Zealand and in Canada, flat-rate benefits are paid to all, free of means test, out of current tax revenues. Moreover, the adjustments that have to be made to schemes which pretend to be based on the insurance principle, in order to incorporate in them some measure of redistribution and some protection against inflation, have made more obvious the extent to which any system of provision for retired persons has to be based on the distributive principle. It has been said of the present British National Insurance system: "It is difficult to regard (it) as genuine 'insurance' in any strict sense of the word, for . . . as it is compulsory and there is no adjustment of premium to risk, it is, in fact, a social service financed by a poll tax (on workers) by an indirect tax on employers and by general taxation levied by the Government."[7]

This being so, I believe that there are enormous advantages of ease of administration and clear understanding of the nature of the scheme, in adopting a simple distributive scheme like the Dutch one, rather than a complicated insurance scheme like the British Labour Party's.

The present Australian system

The two schemes we have been discussing provide benefits for the whole retired population and compel the whole working population to contribute. The present Australian system offers benefits to any person over the prescribed ages, 65 for a man and 60 for a woman, who can prove need under the means test. No specific pension-contribution is collected, the pensions being financed out of consolidated revenue to which everyone contributes in the various taxes they pay.

7 Peacock, *op. cit.*, p. 42.

People are left to decide for themselves what private provision they will make for their retirement. According to the amount they so provide, they may receive in addition a full or a reduced national pension, or they may be disqualified under the means test from receiving any at all.

The rate of benefit paid is fixed from time to time by legislation. Experience shows that, while there is a time lag, the rate of pension is adjusted upwards to match increases in prices and wages, thus providing a protection against inflation and enabling pensioners to share in increases of productivity accruing to the community as a whole. Indeed, compared with 1939 when the pension was 25 per cent of the basic wage, the rate has, in recent years, been between 30 and 35 per cent of the basic wage. Before, however, we can conclude that we are making better provision for old people now than we were before the war, we should allow for the facts, first, that the excess of actual average earnings over the Federal basic wage is now relatively greater than it was before the war; and secondly, that some important items in many old people's living costs – particularly the rent of furnished rooms – may have increased more than has the average level of prices and wages.

These age benefits, financed out of general revenue, cost only about 2 per cent of our national income. It seems reasonable to suppose that the incidence of public revenues in Australia, which include no substantial levy of contributions proportionate to income, is significantly more progressive in relation to income than is the incidence of public revenues in a country which, in addition to normal taxes, levies a substantial superannuation contribution proportionate to income.

So, with benefits confined to those, presumably primarily from the lower income groups, who can pass the means test, and with finance raised by relatively progressive taxes, it seems likely that our system of age benefits is substantially more re-distributive of income than are national superannuation systems of the contributory type.

Improving the present Australian system

Of all the countries about which I have been able to obtain information, only Eire and South Africa have non-contributory means-tested schemes similar to Australia's. All other countries have contributory systems paying benefits to all free of means test.[8] It is often assumed that our scheme, so different from most other countries', must be wrong and that we also should change to a contributory system of national superannuation free of means test. Before accepting this conclusion, however, we should look at the arguments specifically raised against our present system and, where they seem valid, at the extent to which they might be met by improvements of that system.

The basic rate

What the basic rate of pension should be is essentially a matter for political argument as to how income should be distributed between those who are earning and those who have retired. The rate of benefit payable under Australia's national scheme is reasonable by international standards – the present rate of £4/7/6 a week, established in the 1957-8 Budget, represents 23 per cent of average earnings for employed single males, 34 per cent of the male basic wage rate and 46 per cent of the female basic wage rate. For a married couple both eligible for the pension, the rates are double these percentages. This is only slightly less generous than the Dutch scheme. For married people and for surviving widows and for spinsters, though not for retired males, it is not much less generous than the most advanced of the Western European insurance-type schemes – and it is available immediately and has been since 1909. We do not have to wait until some time next century for the scheme to come into operation.

Whatever may be done about the basic rate, I should like to see the rate varied automatically with an index of average earnings. And I should like to see the principle of differential pensions according to need, established in the last Federal Budget for some of those who have to pay rent, and extended to other special cases. Pensioners who live alone and cannot share overhead expenses of rent, heating and light are especially in need of extra income. Many overseas countries pay to single people 60 to 65 per cent of the rate for married couples, rather than the 50 per cent paid in Australia. On this basis, if married couples receive £8/15/- as they do now in Australia, a single pensioner would receive about £5/10/-. Others deserving differential pensions are those with no supplementary income

8 It is, however, significant that both New Zealand and Canada find it necessary to supplement their national pension system, which is free of means test, with a means-tested pension for those who need it earlier than the age at which they become eligible for the national pension.

or with other special needs. I should also like to see more substantial government subsidies given to municipal or private organisations who provide communal or domiciliary services for old people.[9]

These improvements are important and have to be fought for. If we could get them, we would not need to feel our basic pro vision for the aged was mean.

The means test

Several objections to the present Australian system of providing for retired people centre around the effects of the means test. First, it is said that the means test destroys any incentive to provide for one's own old age. This is simply not true. Today more than half the population eligible by age – 52 per cent- does not draw the pension and has presumably therefore made enough provision to put them above the limit of the means test. More important, the means test is framed in such a way as to leave ample incentive for people to make supplementary pro vision for their old age without affecting at all their right to draw the full pension. Thus a married couple can own a house and all its contents, the land on which it stands and a car; they can have £400 in cash or other property; and they can have income from earnings, superannuation or annuities up to £7 a week. The capital value of all this might be £10,000 to £12,000, yet they can still draw the full pension totalling £8/15/- a week.

Poverty and improvidence may inhibit our savings, but I do not believe that they are inhibited by the means test which leaves such great scope for saving.

Certainly the means test could be improved. In particular the property test, which is grossly discriminatory against property, should be abolished. Even with the liberalisation introduced in the last Budget, no pension is paid to an applicant with property, other than a house, in excess of £2,250. On this property, he might be receiving an income of £2 a week or less, according to how it was invested. Yet if he used his capital to buy an annuity of £4/10/- a week, he could in addition

9 See *Raising Age Pensions* (Melbourne University Press, l9S7) for a discussion of the case for differential pensions, by the author and a group of his colleagues. This case has recently been argued strongly also by the Brotherhood of St. Laurence in their pamphlet, 100,000 Depressed Pensioners (Melbourne, 1958).

receive a pension of £3/7/6 (the full rate of £4/7/6 a week being reduced by the £1 a week excess of his annuity-over the prescribed maximum of £3/10/- a week). So, if he chooses to remain a small property owner – supposed to be the ideal citizen of our liberal democracy – he may be condemned to an income of £2 a week or less. If he gives up his capital and becomes an annuitant, he can receive an income of £7/17/6 a week.

There is no reason to force people to give up the capital they want to keep, partly as a reserve for emergencies, partly as some thing to leave their families. These advantages accruing to the small property owner could be allowed for fully by valuing property, not on the basis of the income actually received from it, but on the basis of the annuity that could be purchased by the capital value of the property. I suggest that the property means test should be abolished, and that we should have only an in come means test. Full Pension would be paid to any person whose income from earnings, superannuation or annuities, plus the annuity that could be purchased by the value of his property in excess of £200, did not exceed the prescribed amount, at pre sent £3/10/- a week.

This would leave people with complete freedom to dispose of their asset holdings as they wished.

Another aspect of the means test needs modification. At pre sent, the pension is reduced by any amount of income from earnings, superannuation or annuities in excess of £3/10/- a week, the pension cutting out altogether when income from these sources reaches £7/17/6 a week. This, in effect, imposes a 100 per cent tax on such income over this range. It would be better to have a partial reduction, the pension being reduced by l/- for every, say, 2/- or 3/- of excess income. If considered desirable to accommodate this modification, the amount of in come permitted without any reduction of pension might be reduced below £3/10/- per week.

It is also objected that the means test subtracts from human dignity – that people should not have officials prying into their private affairs. This sense of indignity probably looms larger in the imagination of those who do not have to undergo it than it does in the experience of those who do. In the last 20 years there has evidently been a great change in the attitude to social services. Any sense of social stigma attaching to them has practically disappeared, encouraged by more sensible thinking and public discussion, by the universal acceptance of social services like child endowment and blind pensions which happen not to be subject to the means test, and by the fact that you can now get your pension by means of a cheque posted to you in a plain envelope, instead of having to stand in a queue in the post office on pension day.

From the economist's point of view, the main effect of the means test is, by excluding higher income-groups, to make the Australian scheme more substantially re-distributive of income. If, then, you want a substantially re distributive scheme, you will favour a means test. If not, then you won't.

Age qualification

It would be desirable to reconsider the age-qualification for our pension. Of the 945,000 people qualified by age to receive the pension at the time of the 1954 Census, 200,000 were women aged 60-64. Few overseas countries now have a lower age qualification for women than for men, and in still fewer is the differential as great as our present five years.

Another 300,000 were men and women aged 65-69. Most overseas superannuation schemes incorporate some inducement to people to go on working after the age of 65. We might, under our present system, at least offer an easing of the means test for such people. Whatever system of providing for retired people we adopt, it is desirable to include some inducement for people to go on working while they are capable. This is tremendously important for the welfare of the old people themselves. With the prospect of a continuing growth in the proportion of old people in the community, it is also tremendously important to minimise the burden of supporting them.

Taxes versus contributions

It is argued against our present system that there are several advantages in financing retirement benefits by contributions rather than by taxes. The British Labour Party, in putting forward its proposals, argues that a contributory scheme is the only way to secure adequate benefit rates, since there are limits to what can be raised by taxes (as distinct, apparently from insurance contributions);

and that it is the only way of ensuring that the benefits are never slashed "to weather an economic storm" and that they are received "as of right" and not as a social service. Australian experience shows, however, that it is perfectly possible, especially if benefits are confined to those who prove need under a means test, to pay adequate rates out of consolidated revenue. Those eligible do regard age pensions as a right, the receipt of which incurs no social stigma. It would be politically impossible to cut the rates significantly to weather an economic storm. And it is not unreasonable to argue that those who want, as of right, a retirement benefit greater than the basic rate should provide it themselves, through private savings or superannuation schemes.

It is also often argued in favour of contributory schemes that contributions are popularly regarded less as taxes than as an instalment-purchase of a retirement benefit. They will therefore arouse less political opposition than taxes, and should be less disincentive to effort and risk-taking. In reply to this, I would argue, firstly, that, whatever may be the reactions of people in other countries, I cannot see Australians regarding a national superannuation contribution as any thing other than a tax. Certainly Mr. Chifley's well-meaning attempt to disguise part of his income tax as a Social Service Contribution never fooled anyone, the separate levy was quickly abandoned by the present Federal Treasurer, in his 1950-51 Budget. Secondly, insofar as contributions do have smaller disincentive effects than income taxes, it is because they are proportional to income, not progressive. It is this very lack of progressiveness in the incidence of contributions that makes some people prefer taxes for their distributional effect.

Accumulation of funds

Finally, the present Australian system provides no interim accumulation of funds. It is argued that a national superannuation scheme, collecting contributions now and paying out considerably less in benefits for the next 40 or 50 years, would provide forced savings which would be quite invaluable at this vital stage of Australia's development. We desperately want to maintain and even to increase our investment, but are chronically threatened by inflation because we cannot match that investment by voluntary personal savings, budget surpluses, business savings and overseas borrowing.

We certainly need a high level of savings to permit a high rate of economic development without an intolerable degree of inflation. But I do not accept that a national insurance scheme is necessarily the best way to achieve this.

I have already pointed out that, by the time we allow for the replacement of other savings by contributions, for payments to beneficiaries during the transition period in excess of the actuarial value of their contributions, and for the raising of benefits in step with prices and earnings, the extra funds available for investment will be much smaller than we might expect from a first consideration of the scheme. We know that the present British National Insurance Fund is actually about to go into a rapidly increasing deficit.

An insurance-type superannuation scheme, insofar as it does succeed in securing a net increase in savings, is essentially a device for financing investment by postponing an intended improvement in the living standards of a particular section of the population, namely, retired people. It is a device for making taxation more palatable to taxpayers, particularly in the lower income-groups.

Its introduction for these reasons would degrade the contributory principle as a measure of self-reliance and community virtue. If we are to have a tax designed to yield forced savings, I should prefer us to take the plunge into educating ourselves to a higher standard of community responsibility. I should, in fact, call such a tax a "tax for investment" and not disguise it as a "social security contribution". The institution of such a tax for investment would have two clear advantages over a social security contribution. In the first place, it could be varied from time to time according to whether economic pressures at the time were making for inflation or deflation. If the happy day comes when we can devote a smaller proportion of our resources to investment and more to consumption, then we could reduce or abolish our "tax for investment". It would be difficult, on the other hand, to vary a social security contribution purporting to be determined on an actuarial basis. Secondly, social service contributions are traditionally levied proportionate to income. It could, however, be separately argued whether a tax for investment should be levied progressively, proportionately or even regressively (e.g., a tax on consumption) to income.

Protection against inflation for people providing for their own retirement

I want finally to spend a few minutes discussing the problem of the many people in Australia who want to make provision for their own retirement without becoming dependent on the age pension. It is this group which has become so keenly aware of how difficult it is to make such provision because of the erosion of the real value of their savings by inflation. They fear they will eventually be forced anyhow to take the pension despite the sacrifices they have made. There is a real resentment in this group that they should suffer so from inflation, when the age pensioner and the retired civil servant are protected against this threat by the Federal Government, which is ultimately responsible – "or perhaps more accurately irresponsible" – for having allowed inflation to occur.

If we want to retain our present system under which the majority of people make independent provision for their own retirement and all people are encouraged to make at least supplementary provision – and such a system has, I think, significant advantages, economic, social and moral, over a compulsory system of national superannuation – then we must be prepared to explore ways in which people who save can be protected at least in part against inflation.[10]

Private individuals who are employed in suitable occupational groups could protect themselves by organising distributive superannuation schemes of the type now operating in some French professions. Governments could acknowledge their liability for the inflationary threat which has given rise to the need for schemes of this sort, by introducing legislation to enable occupational groups to compel members to join the system and to keep it going indefinitely in the future.

10 Professor Ludwig Erhard, Minister for Economic Affairs in the German Federal Republic, says, in his *Prosperity Through Competition* (Thames and Hudson, London, 1958): "The trend towards a Welfare State begins when State compulsion extends beyond the circle of the needy, to include people who as a result of their position in economic life consider such compulsion and dependence as unwarranted". It is significant, however, that Professor Erhard simultaneously emphasizes the implication that inflation must be avoided – as he has avoided it during his ministry: "Any social policy," he writes, "which does not regard the stabilization of the currency as of first importance must create the greatest dangers for the market economy". (Quoted in the London *Sunday Times*, 19 January, 1958.)

Many individuals, however, will not be able to organise themselves in schemes of this sort. They could hope to protect themselves by investing, directly or indirectly, in inflation-hedged securities. As I have said earlier, however, this is not as easy as it sounds. For many investors, government securities are the desirable investment. It has been suggested, for instance, that governments should protect their bondholders by tying the redemption value of securities to a price index. This would not only give greater justice to bondholders, but would also provide an extra incentive to governments to avoid inflation.

Many people, however, want to make their provision for retirement directly or indirectly through insurance companies. This not only frees them from the burden and risks of under taking their own investments, but also gives them protection for their dependents in the event of their own premature death. For these people, I see great advantages in a system recently adopted in Denmark. In that country, a rather low basic pension, varied automatically with the cost of living, is paid to all, free of means test. But in addition, any individual can take out through an insurance office, so-called "index-contracts" up to a maximum which is about double the basic national pension.

These index-contracts are, in effect, endowment policies, pur chased during working life and used on retirement to buy an annuity. The premium to be paid on such a policy is determined in the first instance in the usual way, according to the amount of the policy and the age of the insured person. But thereafter the premiums are varied each year with the cost of living index. On retirement, the original annuity provided in the contract is also increased in accordance with the rise in this index since the contract was made. Thereafter the annuity is varied automatically with the index. Any deficit in this scheme is financed by the Government. In this way, individuals can secure an inflation-protected pension equal in all to nearly three times the basic national pension.

These are three suggestions of methods for protecting savers against inflation. There are others. From them we should try to find some method that suits us. Unless we do give some measure of protection, we must expect a decline of self-provision for retirement. If some protection could be given, we could honestly encourage people to provide for their own retirement, or at least to provide privately for a substantial supplement to the age pension. There is, for instance, a great opportunity here for insurance companies to develop schemes to make it easier for lower-income groups to take fuller advantage of the provisions of the means test, particularly with regard to home-ownership and annuity income. Employers could usefully extend the coverage of their private superannuation schemes, now mostly restricted to the salaried class, to wage-employees, by introducing schemes designed to provide benefits at least up to the limits set by the means test. I would suggest, however, that we do need legislation to force employers to give full transferability of all accrued pension rights to employees who wish to change their jobs.

Conclusion

To sum up, I should like, first, to emphasize that I have, in this paper, been discussing, not visionary or Utopian schemes of providing for retired people, but schemes all of which are actually in operation in one country or another.

It is also, I think, worth saying that, when I first began thinking about this subject, I had a strong prejudice in favour of national superannuation systems based on the insurance-fund principle. I was attracted to them because they eliminate the means test, they make people realize that they must provide for their own retirement, and they provide an interim accumulation of funds vital to our economic development.

However, looking into and thinking about the implications of various schemes being operated throughout the world has persuaded me that our present national system of age pensions subject to a means test has substantial advantages which should not be overlooked. It needs improvements, particularly to meet special needs, and anomalies in the means test should be removed. With such modifications, however, the system would give adequate help to retired people who need it, it would confine public help to those who have not made adequate pro vision for themselves and it would effect a substantial measure of redistribution of income to the poor.

Our present system leaves people with ample incentive to make supplementary or independent provision for their own retirement. For the many people who will always want to make such private provision, it is urgent that they should be given some protection against the erosion of their savings by inflation. Some occupational groups would be able to protect themselves by establishing distributive systems similar to those now operating in the French professions. For the rest, if the Government is not willing to tie the redemption value of its securities to an index which measures inflation, it should at least make avail able some protection along the lines of Denmark's "index contracts".

If finally we wish, however, to abandon our present mixed system and adopt a national contributory system, paying benefits to all free of means test, we should do it on the distributive principle, not on the outmoded, discredited and dying insurance fund principle. Distributive schemes automatically protect participants against inflation of income and prices. They can be administered so as to achieve any desired pattern of income distribution. They can give full scope to appropriate private superannuation schemes, provided they also are based on the distributive principle.

If forced savings are needed to finance economic development, we should obtain them by means of a tax designed for that purpose, and not by a tax masquerading as a social security contribution.

29

Mass entertainment: The origins of a modern industry

Asa Briggs[1]

The provision of entertainment has never been a subject of great interest either to economists or to economic historians – at least in their working hours. Yet in twentieth-century conditions it is proper to talk of a highly organised entertainment industry, to distinguish within it between production and distribution, to examine forces making for competition, integration, concentration and control, and to relate such study to the statistics of national income and output, the development of advertising, international economic relations and – not least – to the central economic concept of the market which in the twentieth century is as much concerned with leisure as it is with work.

In this Fisher Lecture I shall be directly concerned not so much with the present as with the recent past. I want to try to show how and why a so-called mass entertainment industry emerged. An understanding of this history, I believe, is necessary to an understanding of contemporary economy and society, above all to an understanding of the fascinating but formidable frontier areas of modern society where commerce touches questions of taste, discrimination and, deeper still, of human values. I am honoured to be asked as a historian to deliver the Fisher Memorial Lecture on this still neglected theme. Joseph Fisher himself as commercial director of the *South Australian Register* would have appreciated its importance. An additional pleasure is that Fisher was born only a few miles away from my own birth place in Yorkshire. Surely it is not fanciful to suggest that one of the biggest social differences between his world and ours has been the

1 Twenty-ninth Joseph Fisher Lecture, 19 October 1960. Reprinted, with slight revisions, in Briggs, A. (1991), *Collected Essays, Vol. III,* Hemel Hempstead: Harvester Press and Chicago: University of Illinois Press.

revolutionary change in the amount and use of leisure and within that leisure a transformation in the provision of entertainment. Neither Yorkshire nor South Australia – each with its own strong cultural foundations – has been immune from assault, although neither area has been a centre of innovation.

How far back is it necessary to go to understand the story? Some people would say the fall of the Roman Empire. "In the sixth century the barbarians closed the Roman theatres, amphitheatres and circuses. The dispossessed entertainers became wanderers on the face of the earth. "[2] Entertainment was decentralised, the status of the full-time entertainer was under mined, the travelling fair became the main institution. Although the entertainment of the few might on occasion be sophisticated and expensive, the entertainment of the many – with the exception of self-entertainment or home entertainment – was local, intermittent, boisterous, and cheap. In 1834, the year when Fisher was born, the biggest of the London pleasure fairs, Bartholomew Fair in Smithfield, was still going strong, as it had done in Ben Jonson's day. For one penny you could see the Black Wild Indian Woman and Child, the White Indian Youth and the Welsh Dwarf; you could join a thousand other spectators in visiting Richardson's Theatre with a twenty-five minute show of melodrama, pantomime, comic songs and incidental music (Dickens described it); you could take your pick of two menageries – one of them, Wombwell's Menagerie, collected £1,700 in sixpences from satisfied clients in the three days of the Fair in 1828; or, if you wished, you could restrict your spending to one halfpenny and see real Chinese jugglers. The sponsor of these jugglers collected £50 in halfpennies in 1828.[3]

Such figures give a fleeting but vivid glimpse of the limited economic dimensions of show business at what was then one of the biggest fairs in the world. The businessmen behind the scenes were obviously far from being tycoons. They were still wanderers: some of them, as in Jonson's times, were hucksters and tricksters, adept in judging the levels of popular credulity. But there was plenty of subsidiary and lucrative commerce at the Fair – in transport, accommodation, ballad selling (one of the biggest scale sectors of nineteenth-century entertainment), and, probably the most important of all, in the supply of

2 S. McKechnie, *Popular Entertainment Through the Ages* (1931), p. 1.
3 *Ibid,* p. 52.

food and drink. The retailing of commodities and the provision of entertainment were already associated.

Bartholomew Fair disappeared before the rise of modern mass entertainment. It was too rowdy for the respectable mid Victorians and was held for the last time in 1855. In other parts of the country also, as a very shrewd observer noted just over twenty years later, fairs were becoming institutions which in their old form were "almost out of date." "The showman's van which, a quarter of a century since, collected the whole countryside to view its contents, has almost ceased to exist."[4] Big changes had also taken place during the middle nineteenth century in the provision of other kinds of entertainment. Vauxhall Gardens, the great seventeenth and eighteenth-century centre of outdoor entertainment in London, closed its gates for the last time in 1850 after a lavish fireworks display. A year later the Great Exhibition of 1851, housed in the Crystal Palace, was a triumphant landmark in the history both of "improvement" and entertainment, attended by over six million people drawn by cheap transport not only from London but from all parts of the country and overseas. The road to the Crystal Palace was full of stalls and sideshows, and the incidental business carried on in connection with the Exhibition was prodigious. The earnestness of the so-called lessons of 1851 should not eclipse the incidental fun surrounding the event.

There was no doubt about the fun in a long-term development, the biggest single development in entertainment during the next thirty years – the rise of the music halls. The first buildings specifically erected for this purpose were the Canterbury in Lambeth and the Oxford in Oxford Street. Charles Morton, their proprietor, had acquired his initial capital from receipts from so-called "free-and-easies" in a London tavern. During the next thirty years the growth of music halls destroyed the hold of the old elaborate pantomime on the London audience.

In sport there were big changes, too, as the rough, crude and often dangerous sports of earlier centuries gave way to more highly organised, more precisely regulated games. Football was one of these: eight years after the death of Bartholomew Fair the Football Association was founded – a small enough

4 T. H. Escott, *England, Its People, Polity and Pursuits*, Vol. II (1879), p. 419.

association in all conscience, with an income in its first year of only £5,[5] but a portent of the shape of things to come. The first admission charges to football games were made in Britain in 1870: the Aston Villa Club in Birmingham, founded as a Sunday School team, took 5s. 3d. at its first game when spectators were called upon to pay in 1874. Gates remained small throughout the 1870's and professionalism was not legalised until 188S, but journalists were beginning to see the possibilities of sport appealing to spectators – or even mere readers – as much as to players. The participants would be few: the spectators and readers would be many. In 1867 Routledge's *Handbook of Football* was the first important publisher's response to the new developments.

Publishers were usually in the vanguard of the mass entertainment business. I have already mentioned the sale of ballads. An early nineteenth-century publisher, James Catnach, specialised in sensational cheap books, ballads and broadsides to bewitch and tintillate the "masses" of his age. In 1828, the same year for which the statistics of Bartholomew Fair are available, he is said to have sold over 1,100,000 copies of the "Last Dying Speech and Confession" of William Corder, the murderer of Maria Marten in the Red Barn. In 1837 he sold 1,650,000 copies (with illustrations) of the last thoughts before execution of another murderer, James Greenacre. That was the pinnacle of his success, for another spectacular murder took place just too soon afterwards for another publishing success. There is a modern ring in a Victorian comment on his inability to make good use of the second of the two murders. "That took the beauty off him. Two murders together is no good to anybody."[6] Catnach operated from the heart of London. He employed a team of helpers known as "The Seven Bards of Seven Dials" who knew their public and composed fluently to order. During the middle years of Victorian England – a very different age from that described in most nineteenth-century history books or even in the pages of Lytton Strachey – there was a regular sale of "penny dreadfuls," and at least one publisher "pre-tested" his manuscripts by having them read first by a servant or a machine-boy.[7]

5 M. Marples, *History of Football* (1954), p. 176.
6 See C. Hindley, *The Life and Times of James Catnach* (1878).
7 T. Frost, *Forty Years' Recollections, Literary and Political* (1880).

At the same time the Sunday newspapers first came into their own. They still lack a serious historian. A. P. Wadsworth, the economic historian and late editor of the *Manchester Guardian*, briefly described them in a most interesting lecture he gave to the Manchester Statistical Society in 1955. He pointed out that as early as 1812, when eighteen Sunday newspapers were being published in London, they were as renowned for their ribaldry as for their radicalism. "They were far from being mainly political, and their attention to crime and sport anticipated later publications, and in sheer frankness excelled them."[8] *The Observer*, for instance, specialised in wood-cuts of murders, Edward Lloyd's newspaper named after him (1842) and G. W. M. Reynolds's *Reynolds Weekly News* (1850) were pioneers of sensationalism, and the *News of the World* (1843) was selling 109,000 copies a week by 1854. These Sunday papers were the real precursors of the mass circulation papers of today.

In the United States of America as early as 1833 Benjamin Day, with a few associates, started a paper specifically intended – in his own words – for "mechanics and the masses generally."[9] The price of this paper – the *Sun* – was only one cent at a time when the other New York papers were selling for six cents. The publishers in what is now a familiar fashion expected to make up by larger circulation and by advertising the loss sustained by the lower price. This was the same successful formula later applied by Joseph Pulitzer and James Gordon Bennett, the publisher of the *New York Herald*, in New York and by Edward Harmsworth, later Lord Northcliffe, in London. The founding of the Daily Mail in 1896 should be seen against this background and not simply, as it far too often is, against the cultural back ground of the so-called new reading public created by the British Education Act of 1870. *Titbits* and *Answers*, the weekly papers which provided a cultural and a business prelude to the *Daily Mail* were part of an earlier tradition which linked reading and entertainment. *The Daily Mail* and Northcliffe's later venture the *Daily Mirror* were attacked as earlier publications had been attacked – the first as the paper for people who could not think, the second (the pioneer of the tabloids) as the paper for people who could not read – but they survived. During

8 P. Wadsworth, "Newspaper Circulations, 1800-1954," a Paper read to the Manchester Statistical Society, March, 1955.

9 See R. E. Park, "The Natural History of the Newspaper" in R. E. Park and E. W. Burgess (eds.), *The City* (Chicago, 1925).

the first twelve months of its existence the average daily sale of the *Daily Mail* was over 200 thousand: three years later it was well over half-a million. The *Mirror*, designed at first as a women's paper, had a more shaky start and passed through a number of business hands. In time, however, it became the daily paper with the biggest circulation in the world, appealing as much through the picture as through the word.

The year 1896 is an important date in the history of mass entertainment, a vantage point from which to look backwards and forwards. In the same year that Harmsworth created the *Daily Mail* a young Italian inventor, Guglielmo Marconi, arrived in London to demonstrate for the British Post Office how he could send signals by wireless for a hundred yards. Later in the year he filed his first wireless patent. Also in the same year the first moving picture show was presented in London. A February showing at the Regent Street Polytechnic was so successful that the cinema show was transferred to the Empire Music Hall, Leicester Square, where it subsequently ran for eighteen months.[10]

The economic conditions for the development of a mass entertainment industry were all there in 1896. Five conditions stood out. First, a large and concentrated urban population had come into existence in the course of the nineteenth century: the citizens of the towns and cities, provided for half a century with only limited means of entertainment, made up the first segment of what has since been called "the great audience." Second, the incomes in real terms of large sections of this urban population had risen sufficiently during the previous fifty years to enable people to afford to buy regular, cheap entertainment. Third, an increase in the amount of available leisure time had prepared the way for its commercial exploitation. Fourth, urban public transport systems had improved sufficiently in the 1880's and early 1890's to permit late night travel from city centres to residential suburbs; trams (and in London underground railways) were the latest instruments of this transport revolution. Fifth, technology was being applied to entertainment, sometimes falteringly and uncertainly, but, in retrospect at least, decisively.

10 See P.E.P., *The British Film Industry* (1952), p. 23.

Each of these five economic conditions – and particularly the first four – were also essential to the development of the retail trade in the 1880's and 1890's, and it is not an accident that the merchandising of entertainment and the large-scale mass merchandising of branded retail products lead back to the same initial historical situation.[11]

The term "mass market" precedes the terms "mass communications" and "mass culture": the department store preceded the cinema. Advertising provides an additional link between retailing and entertainment. Advertising and showmanship were closely associated in the 1880's, and the successful proprietor of a departmental store had to have some of the qualities of a successful showman. Like his predecessors in the fairs and his contemporaries in the development of patent medicines, he had to understand and, if need be, tap human credulity.

P. T. Barnum (1810-1891) was the classic figure in this context: a second was W. F. Cody, "Buffalo Bill," whose *Wild West Show*, "the show of shows," netted one million dollars in receipts in a year and profits of $100,00.[12] In 1841, Barnum took over Scudder's American Museum, which had been started in the year of his birth and had become New York's greatest storehouse of "curiosities." It was at Barnum's American Museum that Tom Thumb first made his public appearance: it was this Museum which toured parts of Europe in 1844, Barnum having boldly announced that he intended to take over Buckingham Palace as his headquarters. Barnum's later ventures were sometimes more sophisticated. For instance, he sponsored the American tour of Jenny Lind, "the Swedish Nightingale," in 1849, paying her 1,000 dollars a time for her one-hundred-and-fifty appearances, along with one-fifth of the net profits. This, incidentally, was an early example of the "star system," but Barnum did not invent it: in London in 1847 the crowds were so thick in the Haymarket where Jenny Lind was appearing at Her Majesty's Theatre that the crush was later called "the Jenny Lind crush"[13] Barnum went on later in 1871 to develop the circus, which in the new familiar language of superlatives was proudly called "the greatest show on earth." He remained in close

11 See my book *Friends of the People* (1956) for an account of the British "retail revolution."

12 See V. Weybright and H. B. Sell, *Buffalo Bill and the Wild West* (1956), p. 140. Queen Victoria described the show as a "very extraordinary and interesting sight."

13 M. R. Werner, *Barnum* (New York, 1923), p. 133.

touch with retailers and advertisers: he had met the great Boucicaut in Paris in the 1840's and in the 1880's at least one pioneer English retailer deliberately set out to imitate Barnum's methods in his departmental store.[14] Although Barnum's career had its ups-and-downs (bankruptcy, for example, in 1856), he achieved a hitherto unparalleled success in mass entertainment. He tried to tell his public the secret in a book published in the last year of his life with a touch of Samuel Smiles as well as of the showman in its title – *Dollars and Sense or How to get on: The Whole Secret in a Nutshell.* The sub-title was even more Smilesian – "Sketches of the Lives of Successful Men who 'rose from the Ranks' and from the most Humble Starting Point achieved Honourable Fame."[15]

The didactic side even of entertainment was never overlooked by the Victorians. Advertising, too, a superb mirror of social history, reflects the same features. And advertising was more than an historical link between developments in the expansion of the retail market and in entertainment. From the start it entered into calculations about the financing of mass entertainment, providing a hidden or overt subsidy from various forms of business to one particular business, the entertainment business. Newspaper history brings out this point very clearly, as does the later history of commercial radio. That it was not lost sight of even in the early days of the mass entertainment industry is shown by an incident in the history of the gramophone. In 1894 the United States Gramophone Company offered as a "novel form of advertising" to record any musical selection along with a sponsor's advertisement. "Nobody would refuse," the Company claimed, "to listen free to a fine song or concert piece or an oration – even if it is interrupted by a modest remark, 'Tartar's Baking Powder is Best'."[16]

Of the five economic conditions, the fifth – the application of technology to entertainment – is in some ways most interesting. A characteristic cluster of inventions was developed in the last quarter of the nineteenth century. They were as basic to new ways of life in the twentieth century as were the inventions of the last quarter of the eighteenth century in textiles, iron and power to the new

14 David Lewis of Liverpool. See Briggs, *op. cit.*

15 See also *The Life of P. T. Barnum* written by Himself (New York 19SS). This book was subsequently reprinted in many different editions.

16 W. Abbot and R. L. Rider, *Handbook of Broadcasting* (4th edn., New York, 1957), p. 387.

industrial pattern of the nineteenth century. The difference between them is that the eighteenth-century inventions transformed the material standard of living and the nineteenth-century inventions the forms of culture. Critics of the first talked of "exploitation," critics of the second have already talked of "manipulation." Yet both clusters of inventions are related to each other. Without the existence of the first cluster there could not have been the second. One point of special interest, which must be elaborated later, is that the social consequences of the second cluster were not clearly foreseen: there was a great gulf between prediction and prophecy on the one hand and what has actually happened on the other.

It is amazing how many of the inventions came out of the American laboratory of Thomas A. Edison, born one year after "Buffalo Bill", in 1847. Edison's formal education was limited to three months in a public school. At the age of twelve he had his first taste of communications – as a railroad newsboy – and at the age of fifteen he became a telegraph operator. He took out his first patent in 1868 for an electrical vote recorder. Later, among the thousand patents he took out, he devised telephones, gramophones, electric lamps and kinetoscope cameras. He lived until 1931 when all these key objects of the twentieth century were already taken for granted. He still lacks a good up-to-date biographer,[17] but it is clear that he is the James Watt and Richard Arkwright (rolled into one) of the modern mass entertainment revolution. He had little direct to do with the early development of wireless before and after Marconi's patent of 1896, but the invention of the thermionic valve, without which subsequent wireless history in the pre-transistor phase would have been very different, owed much to his work with electric lamps, the one invention of the four I mentioned above which, at first sight, seems out of place in the list.

Paradoxically the telephone, which also may seem a little out of place, was associated by contemporaries with entertainment as well as with work, while wireless was at first thought of entirely as a means of point-to-point communication – a substitute for line telegraphy – rather than a possible medium of entertainment. It was certainly in relation to the telephone not in relation

17 The "official" biography was written as long ago as 1910 when he was still in his prime. See F. L. Dyer and T. C. Martin, *Edison, His Life and Inventions* (1910).

to wireless that the idea of scattering "sound-at-a-distance" was first mooted. A short story of 1878 published in a Sydney magazine, The Australian, includes this passage:

> "The telephone wire was laid on between Abney Hall and the village church of Mortham, so that the Hall people could have the benefit of Mr. Earle's pulpit oratory without going outside their own doors."[18]

Frank Gill, in later years a leading figure in the 1922 talks leading up to the inauguration of broadcasting in Britain, wrote that "telephony has some of the properties both of the letter and of the newspaper: it can be clothed with privacy, given to one individual only, or it can be broadcast to millions simultaneously."

In some towns and cities of Britain the practicability of the telephone as a technical instrument was first demonstrated by the transmission of music, from a "distant source," and in 1892 performances at the Lyric Theatre in London and the theatres and concerts in Birmingham, Liverpool, Manchester and other places were successfully transmitted "with entire success" to an Electrical Exhibition at the Crystal Palace. Ten years before this experiment, a Hungarian, Theodore Puskas, had demonstrated a "telephoned newspaper" at an Electrical Exhibition in Paris, and his son went on to introduce a regular news-paper of this type in Budapest. In 1894 an Electrophone Company was formed in London to provide "listening facilities," including four pairs of headphones and an answering-back "hand microphone" for every subscriber. Musical performances, public lectures and addresses, and church services were "electrophoned." The service was neither a technical nor a business success: after twelve years of activity sounds were distorted and there were only six hundred subscribers. In its restricted way, however, it pointed to the existence not only of a potential demand for diffused entertainment but of a wide range of available "programmes."[19]

It took longer for Edison to realise the possibilities for organised entertainment of either the gramophone or the motion picture camera, the first of which he invented (in simple form as a phonograph or speaking machine) in 1877, the latter in 1889. Both of them were thought of as ingenious "novelties"

---

18 "The Days of the Telephone, A Tale of the Future," *The Australian,* October 1878.
19 This brief account of the electrophone is taken from my fothcoming *History of the BBC,* Vol 1.

rather than as instruments of mass entertainment, while Edison himself, the prototype of what David Riesman would call an "inner directed man," attached chief importance to the "serious" rather than to the frivolous use of both, the first as an "aid to the businessman," the second as an aid to the educators.

The showmen of the day were more percipient in relation to their immediate interests if not to an extended vision of the future. The early phonograph would "speak" in Dutch, German, French, Spanish and Hebrew and "imitate the barking of dogs and the crowing of cocks." Showmen could collect as much as $1,800 a week by playing it at exhibitions.[20] Edison was very annoyed in 1891 when some of his salesmen went further and offered to lease phonographs to cafes and stores for coin-in-slot playing. "The coin-in-slot" he wrote, with a sublime ignorance of the future of the juke box, "is calculated to injure the phonograph in the opinion of those seeing it only in that form, as it has the appearance of being nothing more than a mere toy."[21] It was not until three years later – after competitors, notably Emile Berliner and the Pathe brothers in Paris had entered the field – that Edison began to see the future of the gramophone in terms of entertainment.

He was more dilatory still with the kinetoscope, so much so that Gilbert Seldes, one of the first serious writers on mass entertainment, has suggested that the history of the motion picture industry should be called "The Mistakes of Edison." Edison himself thought of the kinetoscope as a toy, developed it slowly, and, even after he had seen a moving picture, stated that he thought the basic inventions (the camera and the so called peep-show machine) would be useful only because they made possible photographic reproduction of scenes from natural life, operas or plays. He saw no future in the projector. His reasoning was as follows: if hundreds of people could see a picture at one time, the public would be very quickly exhausted. In other words he failed to see the existence of either a potential mass or a market. As Seldes goes on, "The moving picture had to be taken away from its inventors by aggressive and ignorant men without taste or tradition, but with a highly developed sense of business, before it could be transformed from a mechanical toy into the medium of the first popular art."[22]

20 R. Gelatt, *The Fabulous Phonograph* (1956), p.9.
21 *The Phonogram,* January, 1891.
22 G. Seldes, The Movies Come from America (New York, 1931), p. 18.

It was certainly humble men who first took up the new invention, men already in the entertainment business. The first films were made in single rolls, fifty feet long, and were shown in "peep-show machines." Peep shows had always been popular at Bartholomew Fair – one of the most popular of the last of them was the Murder in the Red Barn – and as early as the 1820's sequences of pictures could be manipulated through the peep hole. Edison applied the invention of the motion picture camera to the peep show, offering pictures of a performing dog, a trained bear and a strong man.[23] The first cinema peep show was opened in Broadway, New York, in 1894. The business was thought to be so disreputable that even after the peep-show had been replaced by the more respectable-sounding nickel Odeon, David Warfield, a well-known actor, kept secret his investment in one of these enterprises for fear that publication would ruin his stage reputation.[24] The title of one of the first peep-show films of 1894 – "Doloritain the Passion Dance" – suggests that he may have been right.[25]

The first full screening of a motion picture took place in New York in 1896, the same year that the first motion picture was screened in London. In both cases the *rendezvous* was a music hall – Koster and Bial's in New York and, as we have seen, the Empire Music Hall in London. The men responsible for developing the new medium – although it could not be so described at that stage – were men associated with old forms of entertainment The first American films were offered to the public for ten years in the composite package "Vaudeville and Pictures": it was only after ten years that the label was changed to "Pictures and Vaudeville."[26] The first show at the Empire consisted of an overture, a ten minutes programme of Tyrolean singers and dancers, a ballet, a trio, a group of Russian dancers ("first performance in England"), a display by Cinquevalli, the great juggler, then – and only then – the films, very modestly placed, to be followed by acrobats, a singer, an hour's performance of Faust and, to close the four-hour show, a pair of "eccentrics."[27] There were four films – the *Arrival of the Paris Express, A Practical Joke on the Governess, The Fall of a Wall* and *Boating in the Mediterranean.*

23 MCKechnie, *op. cit.*, p. 177.

24 M. D. Huettig, *Economic Control of the Motion Picture Industry* (Philadelphia, 1944), p. 10.

25 T. Ramsaye, "The Rise and Place of the Motion Picture" in *Annals of the American Academy of Political and Social Science,* Vol. 254 (1947).

26 Huettig, *op. cit.*, p. 10.

27 P.E.P., *op. cit.*, p. 24.

The most numerous of the first British distributors of films were music hall proprietors and showmen who put up their booths at fair grounds. From 1904 onwards they were able to hire films as well as buy them. A third type of distributor, however, the real innovators, held the key to the future. A number of more specialised dealers travelled round the country with films, booking a local hall and giving shows at 2d. or 8d. a time for as long as they could hold an audience. The dealers were sometimes known as "town hall" showmen because town halls were frequently the most convenient places to show the films. Other places chosen were shops, theatres, music halls or even skating rinks. It was not until 1908 that the first building specially built for film shows was opened at Colne in Lancashire.[28] By then there were three exhibiting companies in Britain with a total capital of £110,000: one of them was controlled by Albany Ward, a "town hall" showman, who by 1914 owned 29 cinemas, a second in Scotland was controlled by George Green, whose first activities had been in the fair grounds. It was not until 1909 that bigger business entered the field of film distribution, and Provincial Cinematograph Theatres Ltd. was set up with a nominal capital of £100,000, and a leading British financier, Sir William Bass, as its chairman. Progress was rapid – to use a film phrase "spectacular" – in the years immediately before the First World War. In 1914 there were at least 3,500 cinemas in Britain, and 1,833 companies were in existence with a combined capital of £11,304,500.[29]

At this stage the United States did not completely dominate either distribution or production. Demand for films was greatly in excess of supply, and A. C. Bromhead, who was later to become the chairman of the Gaumont-British Picture Corporation, has reported how in the early days of the cinema "American showmen, unable to find enough films on their own side, visited England and the Continent seeking films."[30] France was a main source of supply, as it was also in the gramophone business. Yet by 1914 the United States came second in the world export market and during the first two years of the First World War American Exports almost doubled. In the already large American overseas

28 R. Low and R. Manvell, *The History of the British Film*, Vol. 11 (1949), p. 18. Another very early cinema was the Alpha Theatre at St. Albans. See *The Bioscope*, 18 September 1908.

29 P.E.P., *op. cit.*, pp. 33-4, 26.

30 A. C. Bromhead, "Reminiscences of the British Film Trade," An Address given to the British Kinematograph Society, 11 December 1933.

market in 1918 Britain was the most important customer, Canada the second and Australia the third. American pictures by then had acquired something like 80 per cent of the world's screen time. As in so many other sectors of twentieth-century economic life war has favoured the position of the United States in the world economy.

Having started the story of technical invention in the laboratory of Edison, it is important to qualify the claim that technical change was primarily dependent on his personal contribution. He was no more the only inventor of the new entertainment devices than most of the eighteenth-century inventors were sole inventors of new industrial devices. Like them he was engaged in fierce patent battles which dominated the early years of business exploitation. It is possible to understand the early development of the mass entertainment industry only if two kinds of conflict associated with the business side of the story are unravelled. The first kind of conflict was that between one form of entertainment and another. This conflict did not always end in the supplanting of one kind of entertainment by another but more frequently by their commercial integration. The second kind of conflict was between different contestants seeking to provide the same kind of entertainment. This conflict centred on patent rights and invoked frequent litigation. Again, it was more likely to end in integration – mergers, trusts and the erection of a network of holding companies – than in complete victory or defeat. The details are frequently intricate and difficult: the pattern, however, is plain and straightforward.

The early history of the cinema illustrates both kinds of conflict. E. V. Lucas visited Barnet Fair in 1906, nearly two years before the first cinema was opened. He noted that "many of the old shows had given place to animated pictures, and at the Fêtes of the Invalides in Paris a few weeks later I observed the same development. Instead of taking the place of the illustrated paper, as the cinematograph did at first almost exclusively, it was taking the place of the theatre." A year later a writer in Encore, the music hall journal, claimed that as early as 1900 he had "pointed out to the profession that the greatest enemies the artistes had were the film merchants. The kinematograph picture shows have come here to stay, was my argument, and each time an operator is employed two or three single items are ousted. How thoroughly my predictions were borne out by events is patent to everyone today although at the time I was being accused of being alarmist and pessimistic."

There was some truth in these verdicts, particularly as far as music halls and vaudeville were concerned, but there was a real element of pessimism, too. The truth was twofold. First there was inevitable technological unemployment of a number of people in the old entertainment business, and second there were unprecedented and dazzling prospects for the artist who could adapt himself or be adapted to the new medium. The "star" system in the cinema dates back to Adolph Zukor's activities before 1912. Charlie Chaplin is by far the best early example of the financial effects of the development of mass entertainment on the financial prospects of the mass entertainer. In the summer of 1913 he was appearing in vaudeville and refused an offer to appear in films for $75 a week. The offer was doubled and Chaplin accepted. His first feature-length comedy *Tillie's Punctured Romance* was so successful that other companies began to bid for his services, and he soon signed for another company at $1,250 a week. It is said that in the course of the negotiations he was offered $1,000 a week and in reply asked for $1,075. When asked why he wanted so much, he said he had to have $75 a week to live on.[31] A year after receiving $1,250 a week, he signed a contract in 1915 for $10,000 a week with a bonus of $150,000. The immediate consequences were first that Mary Pickford, working for a rival concern, had to have her salary put up, too, and second that the company producing Chaplin recouped its heavy costs at once by selling the British Empire rights of Chaplin's comedies for $670,000. The size of these transactions emphasises the element of caution and pessimism in the critical verdicts of 1906 and 1907. Just as important as the "stars" to the success of the cinema were the "fans": indeed it goes without saying that without "fans" there could have been no "stars."

Over a long period the cinema did not so much divert an older audience from other kinds of entertainment as create an enormous new one. From its first beginnings until the end of the First World War the cinema attracted a steadily increasing international audience, including a large number of people who were regular habitues, neither of theatres nor music halls, and a very high proportion of young people (up to 30 per cent of the total cinema audiences below the age of 17) for whom the local cinema was the first institution of entertainment they had ever encountered. From 1918 to 1926-7 the attendance rate appears to have

31 Seldes, *op. cit.*, p.29.

fluctuated within narrow limits until in 1926-7 there was a definite "slump" and the cinema appeared to be losing its hold. This slump was overcome first by the development of a new invention, the "talkie" – the first talking picture being shown in 1926 and second by a re-styling of cinemas and their amenities until they became "luxury palaces" for the masses of the population, the Granadas, Rialtos, Eldorados and Ritzes of modern urban life. From 1929 onwards attendances increased until in Britain they had reached 19 millions a week in 1939. They reached a peak of over 31 millions in 1946, when the American peak of 98 millions was also reached, and since then – in a period which lies outside the scope of today's lecture – they have fallen very sharply indeed. In Britain, for example, they fell by 16 per cent during the twelve months ending in March this year, and since 1945 more than a quarter of Britain's cinemas have closed. In the United States average weekly attendances dropped from 98 millions in 1946 to 41 millions in 1953. They are still falling.[32]

These statistics measure the rise and fall of the greatest public audience ever collected. The facts of the fall, however, should not eclipse the facts of the rise. Superlatives are strictly appropriate in this context. The British public in the five years after the Second World War was spending twice as much (£105 million a year) on attendance at cinemas as on going to theatres concert halls, music halls, dance halls, skating rinks, sporting events (including football and racing) and all other places of public entertainment. Comparative American figures – they run into much bigger aggregates – are not easy to come by, but before the Second World War, in 1937, motion picture corporations in America, constituting 44 per cent of all so-called amusement corporations, accounted for 78 per cent of the gross income and 92 per cent of the total net income of the group.[33] The people who were afraid of the competition of films in 1906 and 1907 had no conception of the dimensions of the future demand for entertainment. They saw only the

32 Available British statistics are set out in P.E.P., *op. cit.,* Ch. XIII. For America, see P. P. Lazarsfeld "Audience Research in the Movie Field," in *Annals of the American Academy of Political and Social Science*, vol. 254 (1947); U.S. Dept. of Commerce, Bureau of the Census, *Report on Motion Picture Theatres* (1953). The 1926-7 slump is an interesting phenomenon. The threat to the cinema was due partly to the poor quality of films, partly to the competition of radio. One response to it was the provision of additional attractions (eg., double features, cinema organs orchestras). Another was "give-aways" (dishes, refrigerators, etc.). Higher admission prices, the consequences of such policies, aggravated the problem.

33 Huettig, *op. cit.,* pp. 57-8.

shadows of conflict between different entertainment interests and were afraid just as today established film interests, saddled by high capital costs, are themselves afraid of the future.

The established film interests are the product of bitter and prolonged internal conflicts within the rapidly growing industry. Edison's patents were challenged. Other inventors in several different countries were responsible either for parallel inventions or basic improvements, and it is historically accurate to say of most cinema inventions as of radio and gramophone inventions that they were products not of one particular man but of an epoch. Since in any case Edison's patents were not international there was always foreign competition in the early days as well as domestic American development of thinly disguised Edison discoveries. An attempt in 1908 by the ten leading American producing and supplying companies of equipment and films – all using Edison patents on the basis of an agreement with Edison – to monopolise the industry through a Motion Picture Patents Company failed. The so-called "Independents," who opposed the Patents Company, moved far away from New York the Company's headquarters, to what Billie Burke has described as "a pepper-tree-lined village which had begun a few years before as a suburb (of Los Angeles) for retired Iowans."[34] The suburb was Hollywood, and some of the "Independents" were men who subsequently became the moguls of the growing inter national industry. The Motion Picture Patents Company was finally broken up in 1915 as a monopoly by order of the Federal Court.

Zukor, the chief of the Independents, changed from rebel into mogul between 1911 and 1921. With the destruction of his enemy he turned to integration himself, passing from production to distribution and then into exhibition. In 1919 he raised funds through a $10 million issue of preferred stock, the first major attempt to finance cinema development from capital raised on the market. By 1921 he controlled over 300 cinemas. It was his turn now to be accused of the same monopolistic tendencies which he had condemned in the Motion Picture Patents Company. "It is made difficult," ran a complaint made to the Federal Trade Commission in 1921, "for small and independent producers

34 B. Burke, *With a Feather on My Nose* (19-0), p. 141.

or distributors of films to enter into or remain in the moving picture industry or market, or to lease individual pictures on merit . . . By the said methods Famous Players-Lasky Corporation (Zukor's group) has unduly hindered, and is unduly hindering competitors, lessening competition, and restraining trade in the motion picture industry."[35] Zukor's group was not the only menace to the new Independents, and by 1923 it was clear that they were fighting an inevitable losing battle. The American industry had taken on the shape which it was to retain until 1950 – throughout the whole golden age of the cinema. There were several large completely integrated units, including Paramount, Loew's and Fox, (with unequal strength, however, in production, distribution and exhibition), a number of powerful unaffiliated chains of cinemas dominated by the so-called "first run" cinemas; and more numerous but less powerful individual cinema proprietors competing with the chains for "product and patronage."

The most important shift in power after 1923 was the rise of Warner Brothers, who had grown from nickelodeon operators to a medium-scale enterprise, and who became one of the giants, the so-called "Big-Five," because they were the first concern to exploit the commercial development of sound. Other companies were conservative in technical matters, concentrating, as is so often the case in economic history, on commercial rather than technical development. They were really impressed only when Warner Brothers' first all-sound feature The Jazz Singer, which cost £500,000 to make, netted $2,500,000 in box-office receipts. Warner Brothers converted earlier business losses into a profit of $17 million in 1929. In 1928 they were a corporation with capital assets of only $16 million: in 1930 – with the financial crash of 1929 intervening – their assets totalled $230 million.[36] Their stupendous progress was a measure not only of their own initiative and drive but of business acceptance of the film industry as a profitable field of activity.

The most revealing expression of overseas alarm at the dominance of Hollywood in economic – and indirectly of cultural life – was the British Cinematograph Films Act of December, 1927. When the British film industry

35 Quoted Huettig, *op. cit.*, pp. 36-37.
36 *Ibid*, p. 45.

(producers and exhibitors) failed to agree voluntarily on measures to preserve itself from threatened extinction, the government intervened directly in the industry. It controlled advance and block booking of films, established a quota system and created a Cinematograph Films Advisory Committee to advise the Board of Trade on the administration of the Act. Hitherto the government's only measure of control over the industry was an Act of 1909 which regulated the licensing of cinemas and the censorship of films: it now maintained that while it saw no reason to give financial assistance to the British film industry, as one section of the trade wished, it had the right to intervene in the industry because of the magnitude of what were described as "the industrial, commercial, educational, and Imperial interests involved."[37] "Should we be content," the President of the Board of Trade asked, "if we depended upon foreign literature or upon a foreign Press in this country?" At this point questions of mass entertainment were bound up with questions of propaganda and prestige. From a strictly business point of view, however, the Act had important consequences. With the prospect of quotas and a guaranteed market a new company, British International Pictures, founded a few months before the Films Act, quickly raised £1 million on the open market. Production increased, large scale vertical integration took place in the industry, and a decade of investment in the British film industry began.[38]

I have spent a large part of this lecture discussing the history of the film industry because during the twentieth century it became by far the biggest element in the provision of mass entertainment. The story of the gramophone industry, however, has many features in common with the story of the cinema, while the story of radio touches the history of the cinema at several points and at the same time provides illuminating contrasts as well as comparisons.

In the early years of the gramophone industry there were fierce struggles between the Bell and the Edison interests – a continuation of the telephone struggle – the rapid bankruptcy in 1890 of a businessman outsider J. H. Lippincott, who

37 The phrase was Lord Newton's. As early as May 1925, he had called attention in the House of Lords to the state of the British film industry and asked for the setting up of a Committee of Enquiry. This request was not accepted, but in 1926 the trade itself was asked to work out agreed arrangements which the government might then support. The first official enquiry into films in Britain was the Moyne Report of 1936, *Cinematograph Films Act,* 1927. *Report of a Committee appointed by the Board of Trade.*

38 P.E.P. *op. cit.*, p. 50.

for a brief spell of two years secured control of both Edison and Bell inventions, the successful challenge of gramophone records to the discs which Edison employed on his early phonographs, and an agreement about the pooling of patents in 1902 – the same year as the famous American steel merger- of two of the biggest gramophone interests in America – the Victor and Gramophone Companies. Together they achieved a dominance in the American gramophone industry which endured for more than half a century.[39] At the end of the First World War the Victor Company's capital assets amounted to nearly $38 million. By 1921 a hundred million records were sold in the United States, four times as many as in 1914.

Like the cinema industry, the gramophone record industry faced troubles in the mid-twenties, a little earlier than the cinema industry, particularly during the period from 1921 to 1925, but unlike the cinema industry it also faced a major crisis from 1929 to 1932. Only six million records were sold in the United States in 1932, six per cent of the total sales in 1927.[40] Immediate recovery was not spectacular, but during the difficult 1930's it was a highly integrated industry on both sides of the Atlantic which faced the continued depression. Technical progress was not rapid, and it was not until much later in 1947-48 that magnetic tape recording and long-playing records introduced a new technical phase associated also with very substantial commercial expansion. The "battle of the speeds" was reserved for the post-Second World War generation. In the meantime, however, the "hit parade" established itself and by 1939 there were 225,000 juke boxes in the United States.

Integration on the business side led to many mergers and the formation in 1931 of one new company which was later to be of international importance – the Electrical and Musical Industries Ltd. EMI was a merger of the Columbia Gramophone Company and the Gramophone Company: it was to be the first company to produce cathode-ray tubes for television sets.[41] This to point to the future. A fascinating side glance at the past is that in 1929, the year of another huge American merger, that between the Victor Company and the Radio Corporation

39 Gelatt, *op. cit.,* P 97.
40 *Ibid,* p. 195.
41 G. Sturmey, *The Economic Development of Radio* (1958), p. 42.

of America – a merger facilitated by the development of the radio gramophone – the Edison Company completely suspended the building of gramophones. Edison himself was then aged 82. It might be very revealing to have a record from that date of his impressions of fifty years of the mass entertainment industry.

Mention of the Radio Corporation of America and earlier of the British Cinematograph Act directs attention to the place of wireless in this story. RCA, founded in 1919, was the biggest of the American radio interests, while on January 1st, 1927, the same year as the Cinematograph Act, the British Broadcasting Corporation came into existence, an experiment in public control which went much further than public control over the film industry. The British Cinematograph Act reflected British fear of American economic dominance in the film industry: the foundation of RCA eight years earlier reflected American fear of British dominance – through the Marconi Company network – of the international wireless business. From its foundation in 1898 to the end of the First World War the Marconi Company with its subsidiaries had controlled a number of key wireless patents. The big American electrical companies, such as Westinghouse and American Telephone and Telegraph, could not exploit radio fully unless they used Marconi-controlled patents in addition to the patents in their own possession. In 1919, therefore, the three biggest American electric firms, with substantial United States government backing, agreed to pool their resources, buy out American Marconi and, following a suggestion of Owen D. Young, Chairman of the Board of General Electric, form a new company, the Radio Corporation of America. The corporation or consortium, as it is more properly regarded, was less concerned with the manufacture of radio sets than with their distribution, and far less concerned with broadcasting matter than with business expansion. The Corporation was drawn during the course of the 1920's both into the gramophone business and after the advent of "talkies" into films: the RKO Film Corporation, founded in 1929 was an offshoot of RCA and soon became "an active, aggressive force in production, distribution and exhibition."[42] The chairman of its Board was a Vice President of RCA Films and radio were thus drawn directly into relation with each other.

42 Huettig, *op.cit.*, p. 47.

Broadcasting developed as a by-product of business pressure, not as an end in itself. Of all the new inventions of the late nineteenth century which were to transform twentieth-century social life, radio inventions were least clearly appreciated as potential agents of social transformation. Wireless was thought of, as we have seen, as a substitute for telegraphic communication by wire, and it was not until the First World War that the possibility of broadcasting regular programmes was recognised. Paradoxically it was believed in the early days that broadcasting was a disadvantage of wireless not an advantage: confidential messages designed for one person or place could be picked up indiscriminately by other people. Moreover, because free transmission of radio messages from individual to individual was known to involve a great deal of "mutual interference," it was wrongly assumed that radio could not be fully exploited in populous areas. "Wireless telegraphy," a witness told a British Select Committee in 1906, "can only be used in lines removed from each other's disturbing influences, as in sparsely populated countries and underdeveloped regions."[43] To have restricted the use of radio to underdeveloped regions, lighthouses and ships at sea would have been like using the telephone only as an internal instrument within the house. Yet the use of radio in the Titanic disaster and the arrest of Dr. Crippen was what interested people most before 1914, not its possible use as an instrument of instruction or entertainment. The idea of a radio audience was stumbled upon not deliberately planned.

Two young prophets saw more clearly than their contemporaries during the First World War that wireless could transform society. The first was David Sarnoff, later the first Vice President of RCA: the second was Arthur Burrows, later the first Programmes Director of the BBC In 1906, the same year that an American, R. A. Fessenden, made a pioneer broadcast of music and the human voice from Brant Rock, Massachusetts – the technical break-through from wireless telegraphy to wireless telephony – Sarnoff, then fifteen years old, became an office boy on the staff of the Marconi Wireless Telegraph Company of America at a salary of five and a half dollars a week. He grew up with radio till he became the commanding figure in the American radio business. It was in 1916 that he made his first striking prophecy about the future of radio. "A

43 *Select Committee of the House of Commons on the International Radio Telegraphic Convention* (1906).

radio telephone transmitter," he wrote, "having a range of say twenty-five to fifty miles can be installed at a fixed point where instrumental or vocal music or both are produced. The problem of transmitting music has already been solved in principle and therefore all the receivers attuned to the transmitting wave length shall be capable of receiving such music. The receiver can be disguised in the form of a simple 'Radio Music Box' and arranged for several different wave lengths, which should be changeable with the throwing of a single switch or pressing of a single button." Sarnoff did not stop at what we now call the "wireless set." He went on to describe the potential radio audience, a large number of people all receiving simultaneously from a single transmitter. He even forecast the kind of programmes which would attract this new audience – broadcasting of events of national importance, concerts, lectures and baseball scores. Modestly he added that "there are numerous other fields to which the principle can be extended."

On this side of the Atlantic Arthur Burrows, employed by the government in collecting, editing and distributing to government departments the wireless propaganda of the Central Powers, was also successful in peering even further into the future. "There appears to be no serious reason why," he wrote, "before we are many years older, politicians speaking, say, in Parliament, should not be heard simultaneously by wireless in the reporting room of every newspaper office in the United Kingdom. The same idea might be extended to make possible the concert re production in all private residences of Albert Hall or Queen's Hall concerts, or the important recitals at the lesser rendezvous of the music world . . . Such departures would expose us, of course, to all sorts of logical but unwelcome developments. There would be no technical difficulty in the way of an enterprising advertisement agency arranging for intervals in the musical programme to be filled with audible advertisements, pathetic or forcible appeals – in appropriate tones -on behalf of somebody's soap or tomato ketchup."

Burrows in Britain looked further into the future than Sarnoff in the United States, for Sarnoff did not reconcile himself to the arguments for commercial broadcasting until the late 1920's. In looking forward, however, Burrows was also looking back. Given the likely transition from radio to broadcasting, he realised that a prophet had to take into account not only technical but social forces. Broadcasting would never be left to the scientists and engineers alone. He turned back to the previous thirty or forty years of history and selected a number of elements in British history which would help to shape the use of the new invention. Today we can see them more clearly still, and they are in the background of all that I have said in this lecture – the attitude of government; the power of the press; the strength of business – particularly business in so-called "consumer goods," those which were bought over the counter and, as the market was extended, were advertised for all the world to buy; the organisation of entertainment, both local and national, and, not least in importance, the level of education of the potential radio audience. Given the transition from radio to broadcasting, all these became factors to take into the reckoning.

On both sides of the Atlantic the radio audience grew rapidly during the early 1920's, America leading the way in the boom of 1922 and 1923. There were only three American radio stations in 1920: by the spring of 1923 there were nearly 600, and the number of radio retail dealers had risen to 15,000; 60,000 radios were in use in the United States at the beginning of 1922: 2,850,000 by the end of 1925.[44] In Britain, where a licensing system was in operation, 35,744 licences had been issued by the end of 1922, 1,645,207 by the end of 1925, and 2,178,259 by the end of 1926.

American broadcasting was provided by a welter of stations, relying increasingly – against Sarnoff's own personal predilections – own commercial advertising for their revenue. There was no Federal direction either of financial control or the allocation of wavelengths until the Federal Radio Commission was set up in 1927.

The "chaos of the ether" in the United States served as a warning in the United Kingdom, where, with the approval of the Post Office, broadcasting was established as a monopoly by a consortium of business interests in December, 1922. Six manufacturing companies subscribed the bulk of the original £100,000 capital of the British Broadcasting Company. Revenue was to be raised from royalties on the sale of receiving sets and from a share (50 per cent) of the licence fee which was to be exacted from everyone who bought a receiving set in Britain. Profits on the working of the Company were to be restricted to 7 per cent Per annum and there was to be no opportunity for windfall capital gains.

44 The above account of the history of radio is from my forthcoming book on the BBC. For statistics see W. Schramm (ed.), *Mass Communications* (Urbana, 1949), pp. 547-52.

There were thus two completely different kinds of broadcasting systems in operation in Britain and the United States by the mid-1920's – the American system resting on advertising subsidies and suggesting to the listener that radio broadcasting was like "manna from heaven" coming to them without money and without price, entertainment that was as free as air,"[45] the British system directed as a public service but compelling the listener (sometimes against his will) to pay for benefits which he did not always appreciate. The gap between the two systems was further widened – formally at least – when on January 1st 1927, the British Broadcasting Company was converted into the British radio and electrical trade were broken, and under the continued regime of John Reith, who had been General Manager and Managing Director of the old Company and became Director General of the new Corporation, emphasis on the public service aspect of broadcasting continued to dominate all discussion of policy.

In the meantime, the volume and cost of American radio advertising sharply increased. It is impossible to give exact figures for the early years or to trace in detail the history of the great advertising agencies, one of the most important of which – the A. C. Nielson Company – was founded in 1923. Again, however, the big American networks, the products of difficult and often complicated business mergers, of which the National Broadcasting System of 1927 the second,[46] looked for attractive broadcast programmes and then sought advertisers "who would take a fling at broadcasting."[47] After 1930 the agencies came in direct. By 1935 the net incomes of NBC and CBS had soared to $3,656,907 and $3,228,194 respectively. The financing of radio by advertisement followed the same kind of formula which had been followed successfully in relation to the press by Lord

45 G. Archer, *Big Business and Radio* (New York, 1939), p. 64.

46 NBC was a subsidiary of RCA, General Electric and Westinghouse holding 50 per cent, 30 per cent and 20 per cent of the stock respectively: it also had an agreement with American Tel. And Tel. CBS incorporated the United Independent Broadcasters and was briefly affiliated with the Columbia Phonograph Broadcasting System. Its success was due largely to the financial backing of W.S. Paley, a businessman with no previous interest in radio. In 1929 a short-lived deal was made with a motion picture company, Paramount Public Corporation. The linking of entertainment interests was further brought out in 1938 when CBS purchased from Consolidated Film Industries Inc. the capital stock of the American Record Company and its subsidiaries, changing the name to the Columbia Recording Corporation.

47 N.W. Ayer of the N.W Ayer Advertising Company, quoted by L. White, *The American Radio* (Chicago 1947).

Northcliffe in the 1890's. When television developed as a natural growth within the radio and broadcasting business, the income (and profits) from advertising moved up sharply, and Britain itself succumbed to commercial television time in 1954 – along with $137 million for radio advertising. One advertiser alone, the Proctor and Gamble Company, spent over $36 million.[48]

These figures are far removed from the figures of receipt of Bartholomew Fair in 1828. Mass entertainment had become big business and the bigger and more organised it grew, the higher the costs of entry became. When J. G. Bennett started the *New York Herald* as a mass paper he had a capital of 500 dollars: today to launch a metropolitan paper would take at least ten million dollars.[49] Press power has become increasingly concentrated in the hands of a small number of interests: it has also become increasingly concerned with entertainment, even in its own particular domain. The comic strip, for example, is the substitute for or perhaps complement to the image on the screen. But the mutual influence is not limited to cultural forms. After feuding with new agencies, particularly radio, the press has in some cases, as in Australia, penetrated them. There has also been marked economic interpenetration of sport by the different entertainment agencies – press, television, cinema and so on. Sport is a subject I have not touched on since an early part of my lecture, but it is common knowledge that there are many signs in the middle of the twentieth century that the small business of sport (leaving on one side amateur sport) is giving way to big business. Contemporary trends already have their history: by the late 1940's there were 14 million people in Britain betting regularly on football pools and spending more than £60 million a year on them.[50] Taxation introduced in 1948 meant that a share of this sum passed into the hands of the State. By the outbreak of the Second World War the annual turnover of the football pools in Britain was at least ten times as great as the annual turnover of all the football clubs put together: by a recent court action in Britain (1959) it was laid down that a share of football pool revenue should also pass directly to the Football League. Television, as the newest and most aggressive of the new entertainment interests, has already made an impact

48 G. Chester and G.R Garrison, *Television and Radio* (2nd edn., New York, 1956), p. 100.
49 M. Lerner, *America as a Civilization* (1958), p. 763.
50 These figures are taken from the *Royal Commission on Betting Lotteries and Gaming* (1949-51). There were only 4 million people betting regularly off-course on horse racing.

(still a controversial impact) on the organization of sport. British television companies, for example, have recently acquired a controlling interest in the Wembley Stadium, Britain's greatest sports arena, while the televising of football matches has begun to revolutionise football finance. All this again is far removed from what at the time was a prophetic cartoon in the *Strand Magazine* of 1898 showing a silk-hatted pedestrian at a rugby match equipped with a kind of walky-talky set listening to the half-time scores, which he was about to pass on to a distant friend.[51]

To an economic historian pausing briefly after surveying the vast field described in this lecture, the main conclusion must be that the chief theme of the story is the way in which massive market interests have come to dominate an area of life which until recently was dominated by individuals themselves with the intermittent help of showmen and the more regular help of two groups I have scarcely talked about at all – innkeepers and bookmakers. The massiveness of the control is certainly more revealing than the often dubious statements made by the controllers about the character of the "masses" whose wants they claim they are satisfying. For the sake of simplification in this lecture and in its title – I have talked throughout of "mass entertainment," a now common term like a score of other terms beginning with mass like "mass media," "mass communication" and "mass culture." I must end, however, by querying the use of the term "masses" in this context since it begs more questions than almost any term which is used in business or society today. To see people as "masses" is not to know them or to think of them in terms of a market formula. To talk of "mass communications" is to mislead: the agencies of so-called "mass communication" are really agencies of mass or multiple transmission. These points have been well made by Raymond Williams in Britain and by Max Lerner in the United States. Let me quote Max Lerner's comment on the idea of the "masses" applied to mass entertainment. "The editors of the big papers and magazines, the producers of movie, radio and TV shows, the publishers of paperbacks and comic books, and of popular records fall into the habit of abstracting some common denominator from all these audiences. I suppose they have to in order to keep themselves from going crazy. Yet the hardheaded, sharp-featured men must know that those whom they have

51 M. Marples, *op. cit.,* p. 232.

thus abstracted continue to be individuals with a variety of tastes. If they forget this they forget it at their peril, for an audience whose varied and changing taste is neglected will dissolve into thin air. Hence the continuing search for 'fresh ideas,' new 'formulas' and 'formats.' If the 'mass' of the 'mass media' were uniform, passive and plastic, there would be no need to woo it by novelties or to watch the fever chart of the changes and chances."[52] In judgements of this kind we cross what I described at the beginning of this lecture as the fascinating but formidable frontier between problems of commerce and problems of taste, and we must remember that minority audiences as well as mass audiences have grown in the twentieth century. Even briefly to discuss the issues raised by this would take not one lecture but a dozen.

Yet this is not the only theme in the story I have been telling. On the technical side scattered developments have led to the creation of an international electronics industry with a top tier interested in a large number of fields, producing a wide range of products and maintaining (sometimes with limited business results) large and impressive research laboratories. On the industrial relations side not only has a group of trade unions and employers associations been created – of which ASCAP and the Musicians' Union in the United States have been the most notorious – but a huge network of agency organizations is now interspersed between the artist and his employer. On the social side, institutions of entertainment have come and gone in peaks and troughs of acceptance and rejection. The music hall, for example, has almost completely gone, while other new institutions the bowling alley in the United States, for example, are on the way in. Paradoxically some of the changes have reinforced the position of the home. Before the rise of radio and television, the revolution in mass entertainment was a revolution outside the home: now it is a revolution from within. Given the sequence and the pattern, there is need for greater public knowledge and discussion of what is going on and what has already gone on. The want of entertainment is basically a simple want which we all share: "show business" and "sporting business" are news. They are also history.

52 M. Lerner, *op. cit.,* p. 766. See also R. Williams, "Culture is Ordinary" in *Conviction* (ed. N. Mackenzie, 1958). For a different view see Dwight Macdonald, "A Theory of Mass Culture," first published in *Diogenes* (1953) and reprinted in B. Rosenberg and D. M. White (eds.), *Mass Culture, The Popular Arts in America* (Chicago, 1957).

30

Industrial research and economic growth in Australia

Bruce R. Williams[1]

Alfred North Whitehead once wrote that the greatest invention of the nineteenth century was the invention of the art of invention. He anticipated many later writers who have claimed this invention for our time. But whenever, if ever, the art of invention was invented, there is no doubt the use of science in agriculture and industry has made a profound difference to our lives. It has brought a truly remarkable increase in food and population, exciting new processes such at atomic power stations and computer-controlled machines and plants, and an extra ordinary array of new drugs, man-made fibres, TV, radar, jet aircraft, moon rockets, and bombs that could end it all.

In the short time that I have been back in Australia, I have read and heard much of the need for more research. Australian expenditure on research is often compared very unfavourably with that in Britain and America. Whereas Britain and America spend more than 2 per cent of their gross national products on research and development, Australia is said to spend little more than one-half of 1 per cent; and whereas Britain spends over 3 per cent of net industrial output on purely industrial research and development, Australian industry, it is said, spends a mere quarter of 1 per cent and most of that on "development rather than research."[2]

It is usually taken for granted that not keeping up with Britain and America is a sign of "backwardness". To say, in this context, that Australia is backward

1 Thirtieth Joseph Fisher Lecture, 24 July 1962. Reprinted in Williams, B.R. (1967), *Technology, Investment and Growth*, Chapman and Hall.

2 See S. Encel, *Science*, July 28,1961, pp. 260-266.

implies that spending a higher proportion of national product on research and development would ensure a higher rate of economic growth; and Dr. Encel's comment, which reflects the views of many scientists in universities and research organizations, that Australian industry spends very little on research and development and that "almost all of this is development rather than research" implies that to increase the rate of economic growth special attention should be given to research.

In this lecture I will not take all this for granted. Instead I will examine whether these judgments are based on the avail able evidence. Is it true that Australian economic growth could be increased by spending a higher proportion of national product on research and development? Is there a special deficiency in research expenditure? In an attempt to answer these questions, I will first define the terms involved, and then examine the expenditure on various types of research and development.

How much research?

Research is the activity of extending the bounds of scientific knowledge. *Basic research* is concerned with fundamental scientific problems, which may be quite unrelated to the current problems of industry, agriculture, medicine and defence; by contrast, *applied research* is concerned with application to such current problems. Such applied research may be short-term and direct. It may, however, be *background* applied and difficult to distinguish from basic research, as suggested by a research worker in a large industrial laboratory who remarked that "if you want me to do it, it's applied, if I want to do it myself, it's basic." *Development*, the process of appraising the results of research, of selecting the most promising, and of making them ready for actual application in industry, includes the process of building and testing pilot plants or prototypes. *Application* or *innovation* is the process of adopting a development and of getting it to perform as it was designed to perform, or better. It is only this final step that gives us the new or improved products or processes. It is therefore this final process of innovation that counts in growth.

In Australia, Government research agencies dominate the field. The Department of Supply conducts Defence Standards Laboratories, Weapons Research Establishments and Aeronautical Research Laboratories for military research and development, costing more than £12 million a year. The Commonwealth Scientific and Industrial Research Organization is concerned with civil research and development over a very wide field, ranging from basic research in such things as genetics and radio astronomy, to development work in textile technology and rain-making. It now spends more than £10 million a year. Other Commonwealth Government agencies – the Atomic Energy Commission, the Commonwealth Health Department, the Bureau of Mineral Resources, the Bureau of Meteorology, the Forestry and Timber Bureau and the Ionospheric Prediction Service – spend another £7-8 million on research.

Universities play a small but important part in research. Their research is mostly basic, and the conduct of this research is usually associated with the training of high-grade research workers. Because of this, and of the other teaching duties of professors and lecturers, estimates of spending on research in Universities depend in some measure on assumptions made about the proportion of time that members of staff devote to research. Recent estimates of University research have ranged from £3 million to £5 million.

There is a notable lack of information about research and development in industry. In 1955 the Research Survey Committee of the Institution of Engineers inquired into the amount of *industrial* research but as the response was poor it could only conclude that "104 firms with production in excess of ~500 million spent £1.7m."[3] Two investigators from the Stanford Research Institute recently blew up this estimate to allow for incomplete response, for later salary increases, and for the sub sequent growth of secondary industry, and they concluded that in 1960 industrial research was £15 million.[4] By contrast Dr. Encel used the same original estimate, but after inquiries in BHP and the Colonial Sugar Refining Company decided that it could be "said with some assurance that the total amount spent in 1958-9 did not exceed £5 million."[5]

3 *Australian Industrial Research*, 1955.

4 *Applied Research on the Development of Australia.*

5 "Financing Scientific Research in Australia", *Science*, July 28, 1961.

Two estimates of research and development

	Encel 1958-59	Stanford 1959-60
	£m	£m
CSIRO	8.5	9.2
Supply Department	11.7	(12.5)[a]
AAEC	2.7	3.8
Other Commonwealth Government	4.5	2.5
State Governments	2.5	2.0
Universities	4.0	3.0
Industry	3.0-5.0	15.0
	37-39	48
Percentage of GNP	0.6	0.7

(a. The Stanford estimate excluded defence. I have added the figure in brackets to make the two estimates comparable.)

We have no reason to trust either guesstimate of industrial research. To get a check I have tried an alternative approach by way of the manpower statistics of the Department of Labour.[6] These statistics are not very satisfactory – they were built up from a purely voluntary register, the definitions of qualified scientists and engineers were loose, and the interpretation of research and development activity was far from strict – but more satisfactory information from CSIRO and the Department of Supply makes possible some necessary adjustments.

The unadjusted Department of Labour statistics imply that 8,000 scientists and engineers were engaged in non-university research and development in 1959 – one-third of this number in "industry". Now we know the expenditure on research and development in CSIRO and the number of qualified scientists and engineers (as usually defined). From these we can deduce the cost of research and development per qualified CSIRO scientist or engineer. This was £6,800 in 1959. In the Department of Supply the comparable cost was about £10,000. If we use an average figure of £8,000 for Government research and

6 *Reports on The Employment of Scientists, The Employment of Engineers, The Employment of Chemists, The Employment of Physicists.*

development, the implication is that approximately 3,750 qualified scientists and engineers were employed on research and development. Using the Department of Labour ratio of industrial to Government employment, we arrive at a figure of approximately 1,900 qualified scientists and engineers employed in industrial research and development. In Britain the cost per qualified industrial research and development man was at this time just under £8,000. We do not know the figure for Australia, though from the few inquiries that I have been able to make it appears to have been in the region of £4,500-£5,000. If so, the cost of industrial research and development done by the 1,900 qualified scientists and engineers was between £8½ and £9½ million. This estimate is almost the average of the Encel and Stanford estimates. This is an accident from which I derive no comfort or assurance. My estimate is based on "informed guessing", which is a beguiling but often misleading activity. However, the knowledge that in the seven large firms that are frequently named when industrial research is discussed the expenditure is near £5 million, makes me hope that my guess will prove to be "informed."

Recently Mr. L. Weickhardt[7] argued that if we make proper allowance for the small number of large companies in Australia it is unrealistic to expect Australian industry to spend more than £7 million on research and development. However, this estimate is based on the assumption that the minimum cost of an effective research and development department is £100,000 per annum. This may be true of the chemical industry, but it is not true generally; and in any case there will be many firms engaged only in development work.

The nature of Australian research and development

The overall position in research and development is that the Government effort costs £30 million, the University effort, say, £5 million, the industrial effort, say, £9 million. It is clear that Government agencies dominate the field. Defence accounts for more than 40 per cent of Government research and development. Commonwealth Government expenditure on the peaceful development of atomic

7 "The Future of Manufacturing Industry": a paper read at the Autumn Forum of the Victorian branch of the Economic Society, to be published as a monograph by the Committee for Economic Development of Australia.

energy, medical research, re search into forestry, timber and mineral resources, and State Government research in agriculture account for another one quarter of the Government effort, and the remaining 30 per cent is provided by CSIRO.

In the civil field, both Government and private, CSIRO is the dominant organization. Fortunately it publishes a good deal of information about the nature of its activities. Until 1938, when defence problems pushed it into a range of industrial research, CSIRO's research was centred on primary industry. After the war when defence research was transferred to other Government agencies, the reconstituted CSIRO did not take the occasion to "go bush" again. In 1960-61 CSIRO's research budget was £10 million. £5½ million of this went on research and development related to primary industries. The other £4½ million was spread over chemical research (almost £1 million), the National Standards Laboratory (£848,000), Radio Physics (£500,000), Meteorological Physics (£128,000), Wool-Textile Technology (£450,000) Coal Technology (£280,0.00), Building (£207,000), and a range of smaller items. The expenditure that was consciously directed to the needs of Australian industry was in the region of £2½ million.

To the CSIRO expenditure of £2½ million on secondary industry research and development, we can add industry's own expenditure of £8½-£9½ million. This total of £11-12 million was approximately 0.6 per cent of the net value of secondary production in 1959.

Primary industry research and development in CSIRO, in other-Commonwealth, and in State research organizations, was approximately £9 million. This was 0.7 per cent of the net value of primary production in 1959.

To go further and to break down these civil figures into basic research, applied research and development involves a deal of guessing. However, CSIRO publications such as *Research Review* and *Annual Report* make possible informed guessing about the main civil spender. Let us start by allocating to basic research all the University expenditure of £5 million. Basic research in CSIRO appears to cost about £4½ million; in AAEC it may be £1 million. Total expenditure on basic research, then, is £10-11 million.

In applied research CSIRO spends £3½ million and State Government and other-Commonwealth agencies £3½ million. AAEC spends £2½-3 million and industry £2-3 million. Total expenditure on applied research, then, appears to be in the region of £11-12 million.

On development, industry spends £6-7 million, CSIRO £1 million, and other Government agencies £2 million – a total of £9-10 million.

These estimates are necessarily rough and are meant only to indicate the order of the problem. The Australian civil research and development effort appears to be fairly evenly distributed between basic research, applied research and development. The cost of each of these activities is a little less than the cost of military research and development.

After this outline of the facts of the situation, so far as I have been able to establish them, I came on to the teasing problems of evaluation. Is the overall expenditure too low? Is there a sensible distribution of effort between primary and secondary industry? Is there an appropriate balance between research and development? These are the critical questions to which we would all like the answers. I wish that it were possible to give them, but in the present state of knowledge of Australian conditions it is easier to expose the wrong answers than to provide the correct ones. Still, this is something; and I hope to go further and indicate the appropriate lines of further inquiry.

Statistical relations between research and growth

It is important to emphasize that there is no established statistical link between research and growth. Britain and the United States devote a relatively high proportion of their national products to research and development but they have not achieved notably high rates of growth. The Australian rate of growth in real product per man hour has been higher than the British despite its much lower ratio of research and development to output. Nor in Britain and the U.S. has there been any apparent acceleration in the rate of economic growth with the post-war acceleration of growth in research and development. It is not possible to provide simple statistical evidence that it would pay Australia to raise its ratio of research to output. The bald assertion that Australian industry is backward because it spends a small portion of net output on research, reminds me of Belloc's jibe:

The scientists who ought to know
Assure us that it must be so;
Oh, let us never, never doubt,
What nobody is sure about.

In fact the lack of a close statistical relationship between research and growth should not be a matter of surprise. The use of science in industry depends on research, on development and on application, as previously defined. But these are not measured and successive steps required for each innovation.

In some innovations, basic research, applied research, development and application, do appear as measured and successive steps. Thus Rutherford's atom-splitting experiments were followed a short time later by applied research on atomic fission, by development work on making bombs, and by the industrial application of the results of this research and development. But this is by no means a typical case. J. J. Thomson's basic research on electrons also provided, in the end, for a new industry, but the time lag was 50 years and there was not an orderly sequence of events from research to application.

Just as a contemporary innovation may draw on the basic or applied research of an earlier generation, so it may draw on the research work of another country. Sir Alexander Fleming's original observation on penicillin mould in 1928 was the starting point for Florey's work between 1938 and 1942, Although Florey was able to produce enough penicillin for clinical trials, the high-yield methods of growth suitable for commercial exploitation were developed in America. The original work on silicones was done by 1908 by Kipping of Nottingham; the development and application between 1932 and 1942 was the work of the Corning Glass Works of America and The Dow Chemical Company. Most of the applied research and development leading to the atom bomb took place in North America; after the war, Britain built on this and developed the first atomic power stations.

It is quite possible for a country to provide more than its share of the world's scientific output but less than its share of development and innovation. This, it is often said, is the position in Britain: "Britain invents, foreigners apply." Although this is a conceit that Britain shares with other nations, it is true that if there were not a “development gap” British science would have a much bigger impact on British industry.[8] Research may be relatively inefficient in generating growth because it is not followed through to the point of application. This follow through is by no means simple, as we shall see. Another country might produce less than its share of science but more than its share of development. Until fairly recently this was true of America. Other countries could decide to do little about either research or development and to concentrate on the effective application of foreign developed processes and products. This is a development gap in reverse. Switzerland followed this policy until the 1930’s, and in some measure Japan follows it still. Australia in its reliance on branches or subsidiaries of foreign companies, has acquired growth from Britain and America’s research and development. We can call this Australia’s vicarious research. If in our foreign dominated industries such as chemicals and vehicles, research and development was the relevant British percentage of net output (less present Australian percentage in these industries) industrial research and development would be £15-20 million more than the actual £9 million. This gives a rough idea of the importance of vicarious research and development in the Australian economy.

The links between a country’s growth and its research and development expenditure are also complicated by military affairs. In 1958 Britain spent 2.3 per cent of net output on research and development. However, more than one-half of this total expenditure was for defence research and development.[9] The position in the United States was very similar. Some defence research and development yields civil benefit, but by no means.

The uses of scientific manpower

I have already mentioned that the follow through from research to application provides complex problems. It is obvious that scientists and engineers are needed for industrial research and development. They are also needed for the actual application of science to industrial processes. In the chemical industry in Britain,

8 For an appraisal of this and related issues see C. F. Carter and B. R. Williams, *Industry and Technical Progress*, Chapter 3.

9 *Industrial Research and Development Expenditure*, 1958 (Department of Scientific and Industrial Research).

qualified scientists and engineers make up 3.7 per cent of the total labour force, though only one-third of them are engaged in research and development. In aircraft, electrical engineering and precision instruments, only one-half of the scientists and engineers are employed on research and development work. For the whole economy, 40 per cent of the qualified scientists and engineers were engaged on research and development. The final application of science to industry often cannot take place unless scientific manpower is employed for the control of production processes. When even the day-to day operation of sophisticated industrial processes requires highly qualified technologists, the successful introduction of new processes in factories is likely to be still more dependent on them. The use of science in industry has very much reduced the usefulness of production men "qualified only by experience."

The need not to concentrate scientific manpower in research and development is increased by the problem of identifying the relevant lines of research. Efficiency in industrial research is largely a matter of choosing the right problems. There are thousands upon thousands of possible research projects – the crucial task is to choose those few projects which are made relevant by the market position, the financial resources, the production problems, and the management skills of the firm. Unless the research workers are guided by experts in production, costing, finance and marketing, they are unlikely to identify the promising lines of research; they are more likely to tangle their feet in the clouds. Perhaps Mark Spade had this in mind when in Business for Pleasure he sardonically advised Directors to "Give the Research Department only Big, Long Term Problems and leave the results in trust for your heirs."

It follows that there is an important problem of finding an efficient distribution of scientific manpower between teaching, basic research, applied research, development, application, control of production processes, and technical selling. It is quite possible to impede the application of science to industry by drawing scientists into research and so impoverishing activities in development and production departments. Since the purpose of applied research and development is presumably to generate innovations in industry and agriculture, it is usually better to think in terms of the overall use of scientific manpower and not simply in terms of money spent on research. In some circumstances more research means less growth.

The special problems of research in Australia

The number of qualified scientists and engineers in Australia is small, both in number and as a percentage of the population.[10] It follows that it would be foolish to spread our research and development efforts as widely as, say, the British do. It follows too, that in some fields it may pay us to rely on the research and/or the development work of other countries. This sets a problem in identification. In which fields should we rely on others; in which should we concentrate our efforts?

Let us start with defence. In both Britain and America defence research and development absorbs a large part of the scientific manpower. This is a field in which size really matters; a field on which we could not hope to make much of an impression. At most it could be sensible to take on a few marginal problems to complement the work of allied countries. The Weapons Research Establishment, operating at Salisbury and Woomera, which co-operates with the Britain's Ministry of Defence, is an example of such a complementary effort. The Australian defence research effort at 30 per cent of the total spending on research and development uses a significantly smaller percentage of scientific manpower than do the British and American efforts. Given the low level of scientific manpower in Australia this seems wise.

In primary industry, there are special problems set by climate and soil. We cannot rely on the research of others, and primary industry, with a net value of production of over £1,200 million, is big enough to justify a substantial effort in both research and development. There is in fact a substantial effort. In 1959 the expenditure was £9 million, 0.7 per cent of the net value of primary production. I know of no way of deducing from these figures whether we ought to be spending more, and I do not know enough about either the detail of the research effort or the problems of application to judge whether the research and development resources have been deployed in the best way. My general impression is that the resources have been deployed well, but a definite answer to this question requires a more careful joint scientific and economic appraisal of research programmes and their results than CSIRO, and State Departments of Agriculture or independent researchers have given them.

10 As a percentage of population the Australian supply of scientists and engineers appears to be 60 per cent of the British figure.

In secondary industries the problems of applying science are both more complex and less special than in agriculture. They are more complex in the sense that the isolated socialization of research is likely to be less efficient than in primary industry. The range of output is much less in wheat or wool or dairy farms than in engineering or chemical or electrical factories. And, because so much less of the actual production can be left to nature, the dependence on scientific manpower is generally greater within factories than on farms. Research and development isolated from production is therefore generally less successful in secondary than in primary industry. The problems are less special in the sense that our raw materials and climate do not render irrelevant much of the research work of other countries. This is fortunate, because any attempt to cover the whole field would lead to the growth of many inefficiently small and ineffective research departments and to a drain of scientific manpower out of other important work. (I assume, I think realistically, that the increased demand for scientific manpower would not be met by increased imports from abroad.) In development, too, the work of other countries is generally relevant, though there are some special problems of adapting foreign techniques to Australian climate, raw materials and cost structure.

It does not follow from the fact that our problems are not for the most part special, that it must pay us to ignore industrial research. In some fields it will pay us, in others not. In some fields the cost of buying know-how may be so high that it would be more economical to develop our own technologies. The cost of buying know-how tends to be high in the "patent sensitive fields" in which, it so happens, small countries can sometimes compete with the big: witness the success of Switzerland in pharmaceuticals and dyes, and Holland in electronics. Where our Universities and Research Institutes make significant contributions to basic research in the relevant "patent sensitive" fields, we can expect to find opportunities for profitable industrial research and development.

It is, however, misleading to think of research and development as the general alternative to buying know-how. Often the relevant alternative will be between spending money on development or on buying know-how. Given that the objective is the fruitful *application* of science to industry it is reason able to assume that it would be wise for a country with a special shortage of scientific manpower (in the sense already explained) to concentrate more of its manpower near the point of application than in countries with a less acute shortage. In other words, we should expect Australian industrial research and development to be more concentrated on development than in say Britain or America, unless a range of Australian industry is made so dependent on foreign technology that there ceases to be a shortage of scientific manpower to deal with the problems of the other industries. As I have indicated in my calculation of vicarious research, certain Australian industries, notably chemicals and vehicles, do draw consider ably on foreign research and development. But this does not keep them out of the market for scientific manpower. The vehicles industry uses engineers for local development and for production; the chemical industry is a large employer of scientists and engineers for research, development and production.

Looked at in this way the roughly equal distribution of expenditure between basic research, applied research and development does not look ideal. Even by comparison with the US – a large economy with a relatively good supply of scientific manpower – the ratios of applied to basic research and of development to applied research are low. For industry alone, development expenditure is approximately equal to the total of relevant basic and applied research, which again by comparison with the industrial sector even in large countries suggests that development is very low in relation to research.

There is another problem that calls for further investigation. A high percentage of expenditure on research relevant to industry is conducted by institutions with no direct interests in production and selling. There is evidence from other countries that does not encourage a rapid application of science to industry.[11] Research detached from production problems and facilities is quite likely to increase the sum of unused applied science, to add to the development gap. In primary industry, CSIRO for example has experimental farms and is able to develop the results of its research under field conditions. In part of its coal research it is able to find solutions to particular problems referred to it by industry. In textile technology it has created production facilities to carry through its development work on processing and finishing to the point of application. But elsewhere CSIRO has not given such attention to the problem of the development

11 See C. F. Carter and B. R. Williams, *Science in Industry* (O.U.P.).

gap. Part of this problem must remain unsolved until manufacturers employ a sufficient number of scientists and technologists to make possible a fruitful collaboration, but even so I suspect that CSIRO is not giving sufficient attention to the choice of fields in which it could make its biggest contribution to Australian industry. I do not pretend to know what these fields are. The knowledge cannot be acquired without a considerable joint research effort by economists and scientists.

The role of overseas companies

I referred earlier to the importance of vicarious research and development. I have argued that these foreign companies do not relieve Australia of its special shortage of scientific manpower. But do they overcome the apparent under-emphasis on development? This is an important question. Australian subsidiaries or branches of overseas companies can draw on the results of research and development that costs very much more than £15-20 million, and, more importantly, they draw on the successful results. It is therefore reasonable to treat most of this vicarious expenditure as equivalent to development. It is this operation of overseas companies that begins to make sense of the Australian use of scientific manpower. I put the matter in this way quite deliberately. Much of the argument about the need for more research in Australia arises from the belief that we spend too much on buying foreign know-how.

It is interesting to note that the role of Research Associations in Australia has been small. There are Research Associations for bread, wine coal and tobacco, but the total expenditure is very small – it is about one-twentieth of what it would be if we used Research Associations as they are used in Britain for co-operative research in industries where there are many small firms.

Significantly, and shamefully, we do not know-how much is spent, but even if we did, the fact would remain that we lack the scientific manpower to be self-sufficient in our technology, and that the more we tried to be, the more it would be necessary in the interests of economic growth (though not necessarily of scientific fun) to put more money into development rather than research.

At the beginning of this lecture I quoted Dr. Encel's estimate that Australian industry spends a mere quarter of 1 per cent of net industrial output on research and development. If Australian industry spent the same percentage as British industry, industrial research and development would cost £70 million. Such a comparison, though it is often used, is rendered meaning less by the different industrial structures of the two countries. The British weights are wrong for Australian conditions. If instead of using the British average net industrial output on research and development, we use the appropriate percentage for each industry – 36 per cent for aircraft, 12 per cent for electronics, 6 per cent for chemicals, one-quarter of 1 per cent for wood paper and pulp, and so on – then the comparable figure for Australia is not £70 million but something like £40 million. (The eccentric way in which Australian production statistics are compiled makes an accurate estimate impossible.) If to the direct Australian industrial expenditure of (the calculated) £9 million we add the vicarious expenditure of £15-20 million (and, in the interests of realism, some such addition should be made to the direct expenditure) the Australian effort does not look quite so puny. In saying this I do not want to give the impression that there is good reason for complacency. The special shortage of scientific manpower is in part due to a low ratio of scientific to total manpower. If this ratio is raised the opportunities to make and to use science will be increased. And though I have stressed the very important role of overseas companies I have not implied that we do get the benefits of these companies on the most favourable terms. Indeed I do not think that we do, and I think it high time that more attention was given both to the capital structure and to the limited trading opportunities of the Australian parts of overseas companies. These, however, are distinct issues.

Summary and conclusions

a) The relation between research and growth is complex. Growth in output per head depends on new or improved products and processes of production. The life history of such innovations is made up of the *basic research* from which *applied research* grows, the *development* of the results of applied research to prepare them for use in production, the *decision* to use the new development or design and where necessary to *invest* in the planned innovation, the *application* of the new method to the farm or the factory processes, and the *marketing* of any new products which in some cases involves sophisticated technical selling and service.

b) These events in the life history of innovations do not usually follow each other in a consistent time sequence. Nor need all these events take place in the same industry, or in the same country. In any country, the life history may start with research or with development or with application.

c) All these events in the life history of innovation depend in some measure on the use of scientific manpower. Research and development depend on the employment of scientists and engineers. So, too, does the actual introduction of the new method to the farm or the factory – whether in the form of field officers or production engineers. Sometimes operating the new processes is fairly simple and only calls for occasional servicing by experts; frequently, as in a chemical plant, day to-day operation depends on highly qualified technologists. The use of science in industry has very much reduced the usefulness of those "qualified only by experience."

d) It is misleading to think of the possible contributions of science to industry just in terms of research, or even in terms of research and development. It is possible to have too much research. It is possible to produce many more useful scientific ideas than can be developed and applied by the scientists and engineers employed in development and production. It :is also possible to have too much research in another sense namely, that a higher rate of innovation could be achieved by using a higher proportion of a country's scientific manpower to develop and/or apply the research results of other countries. In other words, it is possible to aim for an inefficiently high level of self-sufficiency in research as well as in production. The key problem is not how much applied research, but how best to distribute the scientific manpower between research, development and other activities. Much of the talk about the need for more and more research implies either that there is an unlimited supply of scientists and engineers, or that they are only good for research and development work.

e) It is not possible to speak with confidence (at any rate not possible for me to speak with confidence) about the precise balance of the Australian effort. The information on which such a judgment should be based is often conspicuous by its absence. However, such calculations as I have been able to make lead me to suspect that Australian industry is backward in its use, or lack of use, of qualified scientists and engineers for both production and development. I suspect also that too high a proportion of the applied research effort is too detached from production interests and development facilities. Such remoteness usually leads to a mixture of irrelevance in applied science and of failure to bridge the gaps between invention and innovation. Such remoteness is therefore likely to impede growth.

f) To get to the answers to these questions we need accurate information on research and development expenditure in industry and on the size and distribution of scientific manpower. We need research into possible lines of innovation that look promising on both scientific and economic grounds, into the problems of distributing scientific manpower efficiently, into the cost of making innovations at home compared to the cost of buying them from abroad. These are important and interesting lines of research, and I take this occasion to express surprise that so very few resident Australian scientists, both natural and social, have not found them so. If this lecture should help in any way to stimulate such research, I should have some reason to think that I had done my duty to Joseph Fisher.

31

Australian foreign aid policy

Heinz W. Arndt[1]

I do not in this lecture propose to state the case for economic aid or for more economic aid by Australia to developing countries. This has recently been done well by a group of Melbourne colleagues.[2] What I want to do is to discuss some of the difficult choices that confront a willing donor country in foreign aid policy. What kinds of aid are most effective? More especially, what is the most sensible foreign aid policy for Australia?

Foreign aid has been the subject of much earnest and anxious re-thinking overseas in the last year or two. In the United States which for a decade and more had carried the burden almost alone, there was a good deal of disillusionment. The ordinary American often found it hard to see what there was to show for many billions of dollars other than the resentment so often and unfairly earned by charity. The new approach to foreign aid which formed part of President Kennedy's New Frontier did not still all doubts whether American aid was being used as effectively as it might, doubts which were voiced again last year in the Clay Report. A similar re-appraisal has been going on in Britain and other donor countries, and in the United Nations and its specialised agencies. As *The Times* pointed out a while ago, "at a time when most economists are agreed that more aid than ever will be required in the next decade both the effectiveness of aid and the question of whether other countries can share the burden with the United States are coming under close scrutiny".[3]

1 Thirty-first Joseph Fisher Lecture, 9 September 1964. Reprinted in Arndt, H.W. (1968), *A Small Rich Industrial Country: Studies in Australian Development, Aid and Trade*, Melbourne: Cheshire.

2 A Clunies Ross, and others, *One Per Cent*, Melbourne University Press., 1963.

3 *The Times*, London, 3 October 1963.

Australians have so far left the job of thinking about foreign aid policy very largely to a few officials of the Department of External Affairs. If, as I hope, Australia will substantially increase its aid effort in the next few years to the point when it begins to hurt just a little, the issues of foreign aid policy will provoke public interest also in this country.

The ends of aid

The first difficulty in formulating an effective foreign aid policy has everywhere been found to be uncertainty about the ends which foreign aid is to serve. "Effective" for what? There is no simple answer to this question. The wide range of motives behind national foreign aid policies has recently been neatly summarised by the United Nations economist, Dr. H. W. Singer:

> "There is a strictly humanitarian feeling that social welfare measures should not stop at home. There is the shock of world poverty in the midst of plenty. There is a feeling that such a world is not stable and the affluent nations will not be safe unless they help the others to higher standards (the 'insurance policy argument' for foreign aid). There is the desire to win friends and influence people. There is the desire to maintain open and democratic societies in the underdeveloped countries. There is the competition of the Cold War. There is the desire, or feeling of commitment as now in Western Europe, to repay help received in their hour of need, i.e. under the Marshall Plan. There is the desire to support one's actual or potential customers. There is the desire to reduce one's unemployment or get rid of surplus food or surplus industrial capacities.
>
> "As may be seen even from this short list, the motives range all the way from the sublime to the, well, less sublime."[4]

The fact that in the democratic countries Governments lean over backwards to stress the selfish arguments for aid unfortunately hides the novel and exciting fact that very many of their ordinary citizens today accept, and indeed passionately

4 H. W. Singer, "International Aid for Economic Development: Problems and Tendencies", *International Development Review*, March, 1964, p. 17.

believe in, the humanitarian case for aid to the developing countries. In the words of the authors of *One Per Cent*, they believe that "the simple fact that we, as a rich nation, can afford to help those whose needs are desperate is reason enough." [5] But even to assume, over-optimistically, that the object of aid is simply to help the poorer countries is to pose questions, rather than to answer them.

Mere relief of poverty or distress, it is now generally agreed, is not enough. Of course, relief is often imperative. It is hard to refuse food to starving people or medicines and doctors to fight epidemics. But such help does good only while it lasts. At best, it temporarily raises current standards of living in the poorer countries – or postpones a fall. It does little or nothing to further their economic development. This applies also to all technical assistance that merely helps out temporarily with scarce expertise of one kind or another. If – *pace* Shaw – foreign experts do not teach as well as do, technical assistance ensures at best that, for a time, the job is done better. It may even do harm by weakening the incentive to develop these skills locally.

Aid must seek to accelerate economic development in the poorer countries, not merely to raise current living standards. In the broadest sense, it must be aid to investment rather than to consumption. Hence the increasing emphasis in all aid policies on capital assistance to supplement inadequate local saving for capital formation and scarce foreign exchange, and on technical assistance in education, training and research.

But even this definition leaves two major questions unresolved. Should aid policy concentrate on those countries which need aid most or on those which are likely to make the best use of it? Is the target a rate of economic development sufficient to enable the underdeveloped countries to catch up, to close the gap between the rich and the poor, or at least a rate equal to that of the advanced countries?

To take the latter question first, recent overseas thinking about foreign aid has moved away from either answer. For most parts of the underdeveloped world, a closing of the gap between rich and poor countries is for the foreseeable future

5 *Op. cit.*, p. 26.

an impossibly ambitious target. Since World War II the gap has been widening because the rich countries have, on average, enjoyed much faster growth than the poor. Merely to aim at equalling the rate of growth of the advanced countries, which would still leave the absolute gap in living standards growing larger and larger, will seem too modest a target to most of the developing countries themselves, but is in any case of little relevance to aid policy.

The target for foreign aid must be, not any particular level of income or rate of growth, but to make the developing countries independent of the need for further aid; in other words, in the current phrase, to aim at self-sustaining growth. On this basis, the haul may be a long one but there is an end to the road – in the sense in which the US Administration was able to announce last June that aid to Taiwan and Greece will shortly end because these countries have outgrown the need for it.[6]

Discussion of the other question, the best distribution of aid among recipient countries, has yielded a similar conclusion. Since capacity to make effective use of aid, like almost every thing else, improves with economic development, the two criteria are liable to point to opposite policies: the countries most likely to make good use of aid will generally be countries, like Malaya or Taiwan, already well on the road towards economic development, while the capacity to absorb aid of very poor countries may be very limited. A better criterion than either is that pro posed by President Kennedy's chief adviser on foreign aid, Dr. Rodan: "Ideally, aid should be allocated where it will have the maximum catalytic effect of mobilising additional national effort or preventing a fall in national effort. The primary criterion is thus to maximise additional effort, not to maximise income created per dollar of aid."[7]

In practice, this will not be an easy test to apply. Additional national effort is hard to measure or predict. But as a broad guide to aid policy, it offers the best chance of channelling aid where it will do most good, in terms not merely of growth but of self-sustaining growth.

6 *Sydney Morning Herald*, June 10, 1964.

7 P. N. Rosenstein-Rodan, "International Aid for Underdeveloped Countries," *Review of Economics and Statistics*, May, 1961, p. 107.

The means of aid

While the economic objectives of aid policy have now been reasonably clarified, there is still much argument about the relative merits of different forms and kinds of aid: capital aid versus technical assistance; multilateral versus bilateral aid; loans versus grants; tied versus untied aid; project versus programme aid; the role o£ surplus disposal, trade credit, and private investment; supply of experts versus training programmes; and last but not least, aid versus trade. Even to summarise the pros and cons of each one of them would take all my time and more. I will confine myself to some that may have particular relevance to Australia.

The choice between capital aid and technical assistance is obviously not mutually exclusive. All the developing countries need both. They need external capital because their poverty does not allow them to finance an adequate rate of capital formation from domestic saving. It is estimated that total aid – international financial assistance from public funds for economic development – at the present rate of $5-6 billion a year constitutes about 30 per cent of total net investment in the under developed countries.[8] While there is no simple mechanical relation between the rate of capital formation and growth of living standards, it is doubtful whether even the current rate of growth in per capita incomes in the developing countries, on average perhaps 1-1.5 per cent per year, could be sustained without this aid.

Technical assistance has the advantage to the donor country that it costs less than capital aid – for the simple reason that the quantity of it that can be organised in any year, or for that matter absorbed, is limited. But there is little sense in the currently fashionable notion that education and technical progress are more important for growth than capital formation. Both must go hand in hand, and this holds for foreign aid policies as much as for planning for economic growth in one country.

Much the same applies to the prolonged debate over the relative merits of multilateral aid, through the United Nations, the World Bank and other international agencies, and bilateral aid from country to country. There are still

8 H.W. Singer, *op cit.,* p.16.

very great advantages in channelling at least some part of aid through multilateral channels. Such aid is less liable to be suspected of having political or other strings attached to it, particularly where, as in the case of the United Nations, the agency straddles both sides of the Iron Curtain; the usefulness of funds is less likely to be limited by their being tied to the exports of individual donor countries; in the case of some international agencies, like the World Bank aid will be administered with unrivalled expertise; finally, the United Nations and other organs of international co-operation deserve support for their own sake, and using them as channels of aid is support of the most telling kind.

But there is also much to be said for bilateral aid, even from an international or from the recipients' point of view. As the number of donor countries has increased, the opportunity to play off one against the other has made bilateral aid quite attractive to receiving countries and has diminished fear of interference or political strings. Arrangements like the Colombo Plan and the Aid-India consortium have, by exercising a measure of co ordination, alleviated one of the more obvious disadvantages of bilateral aid. When it comes to efficiency, some of the inter national agencies, hamstrung by country quotas in staffing and other respects, have a checkered record. The bulk of aid will in any case continue to be bilateral simply because bilateral aid is overwhelmingly more attractive to the donors. Each donor country cherishes its "freedom to be more generous to a decent, friendly government than to an indecent, unfriendly one";[9] all donors "have political objectives, regional loyalties, security interests, and special relationships which move them to provide assistance over and above what is available from elsewhere".[10] What may look like interference to the recipient may to the donor seem no more than a minimum assurance that aid will not be wasted. Even the developing countries would suffer on balance "if exclusive reliance on multilateral agencies resulted in substantial economies but even greater reductions in the total availability of aid for developmental purposes".[11]

9 R. E. Asher, "Multilateral versus Bilateral Aid. An Old Controversy Re-visited", *International Organization*, Autumn, 1962, p. 705.

10 Ibid., p. 719.

11 Ibid., p. 709.

Ten years ago, it was common to urge donor countries to give aid by way of outright grants, rather than by loans with their burdens of interest and ultimate repayment. On this point there has been a change of emphasis. The problem of debt service has not disappeared; indeed, the International Bank has stressed that many poor countries are nearing the limit of their ability to borrow on present terms.[12] But the answer is now seen, not so much in grants, as in "soft" loans, loans for fifty or more years, at low interest, with debt service waived for an initial period which, rather in line with Soviet thinking and practice, are felt to be more businesslike.[13]

On another major issue, tied lending, there has been some clarification of thinking. It is obviously in the interests of the developing countries that loan money should be freely available to be spent where their needs can be met most effectively and cheaply. It is no less obviously tempting to donor governments to buy domestic support for aid by tying loans and – thus making aid a vehicle of export promotion. What has come to be more clearly recognised is that tied lending is legitimate where the donor country is in balance of payments difficulties and that explicit provision should he made for this. Ideally, countries in balance of payments surplus would agree "to untie their aid while permitting the countries in deficit to tie theirs".[14]

Technical assistance as a form of international aid is little more than ten years old. It is the subject of second thoughts both in relation to the supply of experts to developing countries and to the training of their nationals in the advanced countries. To quote just one observation made some years ago by one of the experts of the Ford Foundation: "A large part of this [technical] assistance has been wasted, in the long view, because it was not related to the process of achieving relative institutional self sufficiency in the countries receiving it… For the most part technical assistance has dealt with immediate problems. Only now, I believe, is it being applied to the long-range job of institution building."[15] On this principle, the Ford Foundation is, for example, helping to establish more than

12 *The Times*, London, 3 October 1963.

13 H. J. P. Arnold, *Aid for Developing Countries*, Bodley Head, 1962, p. 36.

14 H. W. Singer, *op. cit.*, p. 19, *cf.* also Rosenstein-Rodan, op. cit., p. 111.

15 George F. Gant, "Technical Assistance in the Sub-Continent", paper delivered at the London School of Oriental and African Studies, London, January 8, 1960, Ford Foundation (roneoed), pp. 6, 7.

50 polytechnics in Pakistan. This approach is also receiving increasing emphasis in the work of the Special Fund and other United Nations agencies.

There is, finally, the large subject of Aid and Trade. It has frequently been pointed out that the developing countries lost as much through the deterioration in their terms of trade during the nineteen-fifties as they received in aid. The recent United Nations Conference on Trade and development was called to seek some agreed answers to the desperate trade needs of the developing countries. If UNCTAD achieved little agreement except on the establishment of another international organisation, it did secure all-round recognition that "the play of market forces is an inadequate basis for the economic relations between rich and poor countries".[16] It is a paradoxical fact that the rich countries seem willing to pour out aid, but are niggardly to a degree with trade concessions. The reason is no doubt that "the burden of trade concessions and trade adjustments may be concentrated upon influential, if narrow, vested interest; whereas the burden of aid is more widely spread among the general body of taxpayers and less clearly defined".[17] There would seem to be scope here for breaking down some of the opposition through tax-financed assistance to the vested interests in undertaking the required adjustments of production and trade. As Dr. Prebisch said in his preparatory report to UNCTAD, "it is no good to preach the need for them [the developing countries] to develop by their own efforts and at the same time to limit their possibilities of giving practical expression to that effort in the inter national field through the expansion of their exports".[18]

These then are some of the ideas on foreign aid policy that have emerged in recent overseas discussion. What is a sound approach to foreign aid for the major donor countries like the United States or the United Kingdom, however, does not necessarily make a sensible foreign aid policy for a country in Australia's in many ways very different circumstances. Before we can test Australia's present performance in the light of these principles, we should look more closely at her special circumstances.

16 Lynceus (*The Economist*, London), "After the Geneva Trade Talks", *Canberra Times*, June 25, 1964.
17 H. W. Singer, *op. cit.*, p. 19.
18 *Towards a New Trade Policy for Development*, Report by the Secretary General, UNCTAD, United Nations, New York, 1964, p. 124.

Australia's circumstances

The first of these, which places Australia much more nearly in the position of Britain or France than the United States, is her responsibility for a large underdeveloped dependent territory in Papua and New Guinea. While the United States has some dependent territories, their claims are negligible in relation to the total of American aid. More than 90 per cent of aid given by Britain and France, on the other hand, goes to their present or former Colonies.[19]

The case for giving first priority in aid to "the territory politically dependent on ourselves"[20] is obvious: being politically de pendent, it can get aid only from us or through us. At the same time, while we control its government and administration we will feel confident, perhaps unduly confident, that aid will be effectively used. It is not perhaps so obvious why Australia should not, like Britain and France, channel almost the whole of her aid effort in this direction. The answer is partly that, at least in the short run, the absorptive capacity of Papua and New Guinea is limited, but mainly that the former British and French Colonies represent a large part of the underdeveloped world. In Australia's case, a policy of giving all aid to New Guinea and none for multilateral aid or bilaterally to other underdeveloped countries would, from a purely self-interest point of view, have a double disadvantage: it would mean giving up all the diplomatic, commercial or other purposes that aid can serve while making Australia look selfish in the eyes of the world.

The second feature which obviously distinguishes Australia from the major donors is that she is small. On a generous reckoning, Australia is this year contributing no more than 1.5 per cent to the world total of aid to developing countries and only one fortieth of the American contribution. If we, in common with all other rich countries, raised our aid to 1 per cent of national income, our share would be much the same as now.[21]

---

19 Sir John Maud, *Aid for Developing Countries*, Stamp Memorial Lecture,1963, University of London, 1964, p. 11; H. J. P. Arnold, *op. cit.*, p. 87.

20 Sir John Maud, *op. cit.,* p. 9.

21 Estimates given by Rosenstein-Rodan (*op cit.,* p.118) suggest that Australia accounts for about 1.3 per cent of the aggregate national income of all the developed countries.

It at once follows from this that, unlike the United States, Australia can never through her aid alone make a significant difference to the capital resources and therefore the rate of economic growth of the developing countries. What is happening to the overall rate of economic development of the recipient countries – New Guinea excepted – can never be a test of the efficacy of Australian aid. And this would remain true even if it were practicable, as it is not, to concentrate all our aid on one country, say Malaysia or Thailand. We can, of course, con tribute our mite to joint efforts large enough to make a difference – whether through the United Nations or through consortia – but only at the price of relative anonymity. The modest dimensions of what we can give also imply that we cannot, generally speaking, attach major conditions to our aid, while not weighty enough to insist on conditions which might reassure us as to the effective use of our aid, we have the correlative advantage that we are much less likely than a major donor to be suspected of interference in the recipient countries' internal affairs. And, of course, we can, if we choose, help by setting the pace for other donor countries.

A third closely related fact is that Australia is not a Great Power. We are free from the burden of leadership of the Western Alliance which inevitably colours most aspects of American foreign aid policy. It should therefore be easier for us than for the United States to concentrate on economic criteria in aid policy. But Australia is neither so small as to be effectively in capable of aspiring to a foreign policy of her own nor in the position – a by no means inexpensive position – of neutrals like Switzerland, Austria and (in some respects) Sweden. Even the smallest country is liable to pay regard at least to goodwill in its allocation of aid, because even the smallest country -like Ike – likes to be liked. To a greater extent than New Zealand, Australia has foreign policy interests which to her are vitally important and which she cannot ignore in her foreign aid policy. Unlike Canada, Australia lies close to one of the world's trouble spots and has all kinds among her neighbours. Aid is to her in part a means of undoing some of the damage done in Asia by her restrictive immigration policy. Last but not least, Australia is a member of the Western Alliance and carries the obligations of this membership in her part of the world with respect to both military aid and the allocation of economic aid.

Finally, there is the notion that, in the words of her official spokesman at UNCTAD, Australia is "in something of a midway position between the developed and the developing countries".[22] This is true in a sense but much less relevant to foreign aid (or trade) policy than is sometimes suggested. It is true that, as a country exporting primary products, we share the interest of most developing countries in more stable and expanding world markets for such products. On the other hand, we share the reluctance of the advanced industrial countries in giving the manufactures of the Asian countries freer access to our home markets. And to suggest that we resemble the poorer countries in being a "developing" and "capital importing" country and that this, in some way, excuses us from helping them through aid and trade in the same measure as other rich countries is sheer humbug. No doubt Australia is developing, but so are the United States, France Japan, Germany, and some of these a good deal faster. No doubt our immigration policy makes heavy demands on our capital resources, but it is a policy which is not in anyone's national interest but ours. No doubt Australia is importing capital, but her capacity to "attract from overseas investors a large inflow of funds which those investors . . . would not invest in poorer countries"[23] might well be thought to enhance rather than diminish her obligation to make what aid she can available to her less fortunate neighbours. I was shocked to hear that the resolution adopted at UNCTAD, asking each economically advanced country to give not less than 1 per cent of its national income in aid to developing countries, was qualified, apparently at the insistence of and for the special benefit of Australia, by the phrase "having regard, however, to the special position of certain countries which are net importers of capital".[24] I hope we will not use this miserable loophole to crawl out of an obligation which less wealthy countries are shouldering willingly. Here I must leave the discussion of principles in order to leave myself time to say something about what Australia is now doing, and what she might be doing, in the field of foreign aid.

Australia's performance

Table 31.1 gives an overall statistical picture of Australia's past record and present performance. In 1963/64 Australian Government expenditure on foreign aid in all forms amounted to £45 million. Expressed as a percentage of national income this was two-thirds of 1 per cent. No equally up-to-date figures are as yet at my disposal for other countries. Since foreign aid effort has increased almost

22 Statement to UNCTAD by Mr. John McEwen, March 26, 1964.
23 A. Clunies Ross, *op. cit.*, p. 43.
24 UNCTAD, Final Act, Annex A, p. 86. E/CONF. 46/L.28, 16 June, 1964.

everywhere in the last few years, any comparison with figures for earlier years in other countries may put Australia in an unduly favourable light. For what it is worth such an international league table placed Australia well behind the leader, France (1.9 per cent), and also behind the United States (0.8 per cent) and two smaller countries with whom she might well compare herself, Belgium (0.9 per cent) and the Netherlands (0.8 per cent), but on a par with the United Kingdom and Germany in fifth place.[25]

In addition to aid from public funds, Australians contribute a not insignificant amount, estimated at something over £3 million in 1963/64, through private channels such as the Churches, the Volunteer Graduates Scheme, the Freedom from Hunger Campaign and Community Aid Abroad.[26] But if this is mentioned, one might feel constrained to mention also the perhaps not dissimilar amount of "technical assistance" which Australia still receives, mainly from American public agencies and foundations for research in Australia and training of Australians abroad.[27]

Almost two-thirds of the £45 million of official aid last year was accounted for by net government expenditure in Papua and New Guinea. While one might blush at some of the items included in this definition of "aid" to the Papuans, it seems to me entirely reasonable, as I have said before, not only to treat such expenditure as aid but indeed for Australia to accord this form of aid high priority.

Of the rest of Australia's official foreign aid last year, some £6.5 million constituted bilateral aid, the bulk of it under the Colombo Plan and SEATO Economic Assistance. Some £9.5 million was multilateral aid, of which £6 million went to the International Bank, its subsidiary the International Development Association and the Bank-sponsored Indus Waters Project, and most of the rest to the Special Fund and other agencies of the United Nations. Even if the contribution to the Indus Waters Scheme is treated as bilateral, Australia was doing rather better than most countries in the share of aid given in multilateral form.[28]

25 The percentages for other countries are those calculated by A. Clunies Ross for OECD data for 1962 (*op. cit.*, p. 12).

26 Nancy Anderson, "Australia's Voluntary Foreign Aid Activities", *Australian Outlook*, August, 1964.

27 *Cf.* statement by Dr. P. A. Siple, Scientific Attaché, US Embassy Canberra, quoted *Daily Telegraph*, May 1, 1964.

28 "Only some 10 per cent of total world aid is in multilateral form, 90 per cent being bilateral, and the proportions o£ our British aid are much the same" (Sir John Maud, *op. cit.*, p. 9)

Table 31.1: Australia's foreign aid (£A '000)
(Australian grants and grant-like contributions to international development and relief, and assistance to Papua New Guinea)

	1945-46 to 1962-63	Annual average 1958-69 to 1962-63	1962-63	1963-64 estimate
Multilateral				
International financial institutions:				
IBRD gold and dollar payments	2,379	119	-	-
IBRD release of 18 per cent subscription	18,583	2,817	2,672	2,672
IFC	998	-	-	-
IDA	1,909	382	1,346	2,724
Others:				
UN Special Fund	-	-	-	375
UNRRA	22,522	-	-	-
Post UNRRA	1,830	-	-	-
UNKRA	1,799	-	-	-
UNICEF	6,068	230	240	240
UNHCR	479	51	50	75
UNRWA	1,300	88	90	90
UNEPTA	2,926	299	279	335
UN Fund for Congo	335	67	-	-
ICEM Far East Refugees	265	48	50	50
Indus Waters Scheme	2,594	519	968	2,770
World Food Programme	202	40	202	240
WHO Malaria Eradication	48	9	-	-
FAO Freedom from Hunger	8	2	-	-
WRY	50	10	-	-
Total	**67,657**	**4,687**	**5,906**	**9,529**

Table 31.1: Australia's foreign aid (£A '000)
(Australian grants and grant-like contributions to international development and relief, and assistance to Papua New Guinea) cont.

	1945-46 to 1962-63	Annual average 1958-69 to 1962-63	1962-63	1963-64 estimate
Bilateral				
Laos Stabilisation Fund	-	-	-	179
Colombo Plan:				
Economic development	35,783	2,638	2,764	2,700
Technical assistance	12,716	1,588	2,082	2,300
Gifts to United Kingdom	45,000	-	-	-
SEATO: Economic Assistance	3,774	717	1,248	1,000
SCAAP	96	30	76	150
Scholarships	685	110	273	322
Flood and disaster relief	429	42	89	35
Refugees	291	4	22	-
Congo Medical Team	19	27	-	-
Total	**98,793**	**5,156**	**6,554**	**6,686**
Papua/New Guinea				
Grants to administration	143,619	15,275	20,000	25,250
Identifiable departmental expenditures	12,434	1,448	3,000	3,000
Agricultural loans to ex-servicemen (Net)	2,327	463	634	354
Total	**158,380**	**17,186**	**23,634**	**28,604**
Grand total	**324,830**	**27,029**	**36,094**	**44,819**

Source: Department of External Affairs, Canberra.

It is the £5 million of Australian Colombo Plan aid that Australians hear most about because, though given in response to specific requests by the receiving countries, it consists of Australian products, experts and training facilities and thus comes into the lives of numerous Australians. Since the beginning of the scheme in 1950, Australia has given more than £35 million in economic aid, a good part in the form of commodities such as wheat, flour and skimmed milk, but also buses, tractors, road building and agricultural machinery, radio sets for schools, books scientific instruments – a great range of things selected largely from specialties incorporating Australian know-how. Under Colombo Plan technical assistance, Australia has supplied some 600 experts to give assistance and advice,[29] and has provided training facilities at universities, secondary schools, technical and other colleges for some 5,200 students from Asia.[30] In addition, some 400 Australians have undertaken technical assistance missions under United Nations and other auspices,[31] and some 3,000 Asian students a year study privately at Australian universities, like Australian university students very largely at the expense of the Australian taxpayer.[32]

Table 31.2 shows the country distribution of Australian Colombo Plan Aid – in the nature of the case no similar breakdown is possible for multilateral aid. More than one-half of the total has gone to India, Pakistan and Ceylon; but most of this has been economic development aid, a not inconsiderable portion in wheat and flour. The largest recipient of Australian technical assistance (in all three forms, training, experts and equipment) has been Malaysia; followed for training facilities by Indonesia, India, Burma, Thailand, Pakistan and the Philippines; by Indonesia, Pakistan, Ceylon, Vietnam and Thailand for experts; and by Vietnam, Thailand, Pakistan, India and Indonesia for equipment.

So far so good. But is this record good enough for a country as wealthy as Australia and, through her geographic position, so intimately associated with many poor neighbours? Certainly our performance so far does not justify excessive self-congratulation.

29 J J. Pratt, Deputy Director, Commonwealth OffIce of Education, "The Services of Australians Overseas", paper delivered at Fifth Annual Conference, Australian College of Education, Canberra, May 15-18, 1964 (roneoed), Table 1.

30 Senator Gorton, Acting Minister for External Affairs, *Canberra Times*, July 1, 1964.

31 J. J. Pratt, *op. cit.*

32 G. Caiger, "What are we doing for Foreign Students in Universities?" paper delivered at Fifth Annual Conference, Australian College of Education, Canberra, May lS-18, 1964 (roneoed), p. 7.

It was only last year that Australia's total official aid expenditure, including expenditure on New Guinea, reached two-thirds of the one per cent target. In 1962-63 Australia's multilateral aid contribution was under £6 million, less than one-tenth of 1 per cent of her national income. Until that year, Australia was one of the few developed countries which did not contribute to the United Nations Special Fund. By June, 1964, Australia had contributed in all some £24 million to the International Bank (and its subsidiaries) from which it had, in return, obtained loans totalling almost £170 million.[33] Most of the rest of Australia's multilateral aid (apart from steady support for the United Nations Children's Fund) had been for refugee relief, a laudable cause, but not perhaps entirely unconnected with the immigration programme towards the cost of which a not inconsiderable contribution has been made by international agencies and over seas governments.[34] Even in 1963-64, Australia's total aid effort of £45 million was less than one-fifth of the amount she borrowed from overseas and not much more than the amount she lent – very sensibly, in my view – as 12 months' trade credit to Communist China.[35]

Australia will, I hope, without quibbling, aim to fulfil the obligation assumed by the developed countries at UNCTAD to raise their contribution to foreign aid to at least 1 per cent of national income. If expenditure is to be thus increased, it becomes correspondingly more important that the money is well spent.

Comparing Australia's present foreign aid policy with the principles I discussed earlier in this lecture, I do not feel that there is much seriously wrong with the forms or directions of Australian aid. In particular, none of the suggestions for radical reform one hears from time to time – such as that all or none of Australia's aid should go to particular countries or assume particular forms – does justice to the complexity of the problem. But there are a number of suggestions I would make.

33 *Commonwealth Year Book*, 1963, p. 973; Commonwealth Statistician, Balance of Payments 1963/64.
34 Attempts to estimate this contribution have so far failed.
35 Total sales of wheat to Mainland China in 1963/64 were worth £64 million; one-half of this was on 12 months' credit, 40 per cent on shorter-term credit, 10 per cent in cash.

Suggestions for the future

Australia is committed to an all-out effort to prepare New Guinea for independence, economically as well as politically. This will require raising Australian government expenditure to the limit of the Territory's absorptive capacity, and attracting private capital by any means which will not store up trouble for the future. Nor should we be too proud, at the Papuans' expense, to ask for United Nations and other multilateral aid in this task.

Table 31.2: Australia's expenditure on the Colombo Plan
(cumulative total 1947 to 31/12/63)

	Head of expenditure				Total		
Country	**Economic development**	**Training**	**Experts**	**Equipment**	**£A'000**	**Per head (of recipient country – 1961)**	
	£A'000	**£A'000**	**£A'000**	**£A'000**		**s.**	**d.**
Brunei	-	32	1	-	32	7	5
Burma	682	569	58	187	1,496	1	5
Cambodia	780	45	82	69	976	4	0
Ceylon	3,450	357	186	158	4,152	8	2
India	13,112	725	87	258	14,183	0	7
Indonesia	3,347	1,710	451	235	5,743	1	2
Korea	-	16	-	-	16	0	0
Laos	308	33	25	61	427	4	10
Malaysia	832	2,348	827	524	4,531	9	0
Nepal	132	51	25	13	222	0	6
Pakistan	10,950	548	217	293	12,008	2	7
Philippines	43	405	57	204	709	0	7
Thailand	1,351	550	119	306	2,326	2	0
Vietnam	1,504	327	160	340	2,330	3	5
Mekong Survey	-	-	170	65			
Miscellaneous	250						
Total	**36,740**	**7,717**	**2,464**	**2,713**			

Source: Department of External Affairs, Australia in the Colombo Plan, Progress Report to December 31, 1963, Canberra, 1964.

In return, Australia might well increase her contribution to multilateral aid, especially to the United Nations Special Fund and by joining the India and Pakistan consortia.

Australia is almost unique among the rich donor countries in that all her aid has hitherto consisted of grants, virtually none of it of loans. Such a policy, as we saw before, no longer earns the high marks it would have done ten years ago. In Australia refusal to lend to developing countries tends to be justified by her own large-scale borrowing from overseas. This is a specious argument. Why should not Australia make her contribution in part by passing on to the developing countries some of the benefits of her high international credit standing and other attractions to overseas investors? Through such institutions as the Inter national Development Association, or a regional Development Bank in the ECAFE area or in other ways, Australia might per form a modest role as an international financial intermediary – not for profit but as a contribution to the common purpose of aid. If our balance of payments situation demands it -as it surely does not at present – let us by all means offer tied loans which are better than no loans.

Without suggesting that Australia's aid programme under the Colombo Plan is not in general soundly conceived, there is a case for re-appraisal of some of its features. How effective is the technical assistance Australia gives through the supply of experts? Could it be made more effective by better selection or briefing here or by more careful preparation at the other end? Would money be better spent by taking up the Ford Foundation's principle of "institution-building"? Is the student training programme as useful to the students and their countries, and as productive of goodwill for Australia, as is commonly assumed? What happens to the Asian students when they return? Are they dissatisfied, nostalgic for western fleshpots? Do they find jobs for which they were trained, or for that matter, any jobs at all? Without departing from the Colombo Plan principle of acting only in response to specific requests for aid by the receiving countries, could aid be made more effective by Australian advice on the selection of aid projects, for instance by the appointment of some capable and sympathetic Australian of standing as Aid Adviser? To some of these questions we are now, at the Australian National University, seeking answers through a research programme financed by the Ford Foundation.

There may be scope for greater participation in Australia's aid effort, and particularly in technical assistance, by Australian private enterprise. The US Government has recently set up an Executive Service Corps which "will provide American business men with an opportunity to furnish, on request, technical and managerial advice to businessmen in developing countries".[36] Australia's capacity to help in this area is obviously much more limited, but it is not negligible. CEDA – the Committee for Economic Development of Australia – is the obvious body to examine the possibilities for a larger aid contribution by Australian business.

One has the impression that in Australia the politicians are reluctant to adopt a more ambitious foreign aid policy for fear of hostile public reaction while large sections of the public, particularly among the younger people, are increasingly impatient for the Government to give a stronger lead. Could this gulf be bridged by following the example of the Netherlands where the Ministry of Foreign Affairs has recently set up a Foreign Aid Advisory Council to ensure continuous contact between Government, voluntary agencies, universities, business, trade unions and other groups actually or potentially concerned with foreign aid issues.

Finally, a few words on trade and aid. Australia has every right to fight side by side with the developing countries for a better deal for primary products in the markets of the industrial countries. But she also shares the duty of the rich industrial countries to stop discriminating against the exports of manufactures of the so-called "low-wage" countries and, indeed, to examine some of the ways suggested in the Prebisch Report by which the principle of non-discrimination might be waived in their favour, so as to compensate them for their initial infant industry handicap. In her trade agreements with Japan, Australia has gone some way in this direction. But much more is needed. Yet it will not be done if every increase in imports from Asia threatens some Australian vested interest, some existing local industry. It can be done only in the context of a long-range programme for Australia's own industrial development which links the pattern of expansion of Australian manufacturing production with the pattern of mutual trade in manufactures most likely to be beneficial both to Australia and to her Asian trading partners.

36 President Johnson, Message to Congress on "The US Foreign Aid Program", March 19, 1964.

In turn, Australia should not be backward or mealy-mouthed about linking aid in some measure to her own trading interests. Aid in kind, soft loans, technical assistance – all these can be of genuine help to the developing countries and at the same time assist Australian manufacturers in overcoming the difficulties of breaking into new export markets in competition with the major overseas industrial countries. As has been pointed out, even "Soviet aid, just like the market operations of Western commerce, ought to be regarded as a method of securing foreign markets".[37]

In 1919 Alfred Marshall wrote: "It is becoming clear that this [Britain] and every other western country can now afford to make increased sacrifices of material wealth for the purpose of raising the quality of life throughout their whole populations. A time may come when such matters will be treated as of cosmopolitan rather than national obligation: but that time is not in sight."[38]

Today, much sooner perhaps than Marshall expected, we can say that the time has come. Foreign aid is the extension to the international sphere of the principles of the Welfare State. To rich countries like Australia foreign aid is as much a matter both of moral obligation and of self-interest as were progressive income tax and social services for the well-to-do in Marshall's England.

37 K. Billerbeck, *Soviet Bloc Foreign Aid to the Underdeveloped Countries,* Hamburg Archives of World Economy, 1960, p. 100, quoted H. J. P. Arnold, *op. cit.,* p. 117

38 Alfred Marshall, *Industry and Trade*, Macmillan, 1919, p. 5.

32

Australian tariff policy

W. Max Corden[1]

Tariff policy has recently been a matter of controversy. Criticisms of government policy have been along two lines. First, it is said that there have been important increases in tariffs and extensions of the field of protection so that in many cases protection is now excessive. Secondly, it is said that the Government is not leaving it to the Tariff Board to decide which industries should be protected and how much protection there should be, but that it is limiting the Board or by-passing it in various ways. While the two issues are in principle distinct, in practice they tend to get mixed up because the Tariff Board has come to be regarded to some extent as a guardian of tariff moderation against the supposed protectionist inclinations of the Government.[2]

Here my purposes are as follows. First, I shall present briefly some of the main facts about recent tariff policy bearing on the two criticisms above. This is not an easy task since our tariffs, and the machinery for changing them, are very complicated and are in fact in a continuous state of change. It is therefore not surprising that most people find it very difficult to get a clear perspective on what has been happening. Secondly, I shall discuss a central issue of long-term tariff policy, namely the question of the "bench mark."

1 Thirty-second Joseph Fisher Lecture, 27 July 1967. Since published as chapter 6 in Corden, W. M. (1997) *The Road to Reform: Essays on Australian Political Economy*, Sydney: Addison-Wesley

2 The debate and the general development of tariff policy have been fully reported by Mr. Alan Wood in the columns of *The Australian Financial Review*. A review of the issues and the political background by Mr. Peter Samuel appeared in *The Bulletin*, May 13, 1967.

I. Recent tariff changes

Between January 1965 and April 1967, 57 Tariff Board reports were tabled in Parliament. These covered a wide range of products and industries, from the trivially unimportant, such as pins, cycle saddles and bubble levels, to such major reports as those on motor cars and components and on industrial chemicals. To obtain proper perspective it is necessary to be selective. My basis of selection is the size of the industry or activity affected by a report, judging primarily by employment. There were 15 reports affecting manufacturing industries which employed at least 800 persons. In addition there is the report on crude petroleum which must be included in a list of important reports. The 16 reports are listed in the Appendix. Most of the other reports affected quite minor products or industries. Of the 16 reports on which my discussion will be based, the two most important ones by far are those on motor cars and components and on industrial chemicals. Much of the political controversy has been provoked by tariff changes resulting from this last report. It must be stressed that the tariffs reviewed in all these reports are only the top of the iceberg which happened to emerge in the period considered; many important tariffs were not looked at and indeed have not been looked at for many years.

First I shall outline the level of protection provided as well as the devices that are being used. For each tariff item there are usually two rates, the General and British Preferential rates; I shall always cite the former. Every thing I shall say will be oversimplified and thus somewhat inaccurate. I am looking for a broad picture. Details can be found in the relevant Tariff Board reports and Ministerial statements. At this stage I shall describe not Tariff Board recommendations but actual tariff changes imposed by the Government. As will be indicated later, in important cases these have not been in line with Tariff Board recommendations. I begin with the two major cases.

Motor cars and chemicals

In the motor car field we may broadly distinguish the vehicle manufacturers from the manufacturers of components. The former were until recently protected by a 35 per cent tariff. The tariff rate for most components was also 35 per cent, but the crucial complication was that manufacturers were allowed to import a high proportion of the components they used under by-law, that is free of duty or at a rate of 7.5 per cent. This was not important for those cars, notably the Holden and the Falcon, which in fact have an Australian content of 95 per cent or more. But for manufacturers such as Volkswagen it meant that their effective protection[3] was well above 35 per cent; in view of the limited volume production of all producers other than GMH and Ford they clearly needed very high effective rates to survive. In 1964 the Government decided to enforce a higher Australian content on the smaller motor car manufacturers. Continuation of the privilege of importing their components under by-law was made subject to an undertaking to increase steadily the Australian content of their vehicles, a time-limit having been set to reach 95 per cent Australian content for all but the very lowest volume producers. The details of these arrangements have been varied several times; a complete assessment is difficult because information about the content percentages of the different firms and the Government's requirements for them is insufficient. Essentially it means that protection for the components manufacturers is being increased sharply at the expense of protection for the smaller vehicle manufacturers. At first sight it seems that the tariff on components is really no more than 35 per cent since the vehicle manufacturers appear to have the option of moving to 95 per cent Australian content or simply paying a 35 per cent duty on all parts. But this is not really so. It is clear that the Government is determined to increase the Australian content of locally assembled vehicles and in fact to induce a movement towards 95 per cent. If many manufacturers chose the option of not following such a "plan", the Government would no doubt raise the duty on components until the manufacturers made the desired decision. Thus the new arrangements are really the equivalent of the gradual imposition on components of a near-prohibitive duty. In addition there has been a rise in the tariff on completed vehicles from 35 per cent to 45 per cent. This was designed to discourage increased imports but might also be regarded as part compensation for the "forced march" to Australian content. On balance there appears to have been a large increase in protection for components producers paid for partly by the lower-volume vehicle manufacturers and partly, through the rise in the tariff on fully assembled cars, by the consumer.

3 I use the term "effective protection" as meaning the rate of protection in relation to value added. The concept is explained in the Vernon Report and in my review of this report in *The Economic Record*, XLII, 1966. Figures cited in this paper are apparent, not effective rates, unless indicated otherwise.

The great chemicals case covered numerous industrial chemicals and plastic materials. This was a comprehensive case covering many items which had been investigated several times separately before. In fact in the last few years chemicals have kept the Tariff Board busier than textiles. The normal tariff rates were simplified and consolidated. Most chemicals were given either a 25 per cent or a 40 per cent tariff. Certain products, namely synthetic rubber, PVC, polyethylene and vinyl acetate monomer, were given a 60 per cent tariff. The tariff was extended to cover substitutes which had previously not been protected and provision was made for future substitution resulting from technical developments. There were some unimportant tariff reductions; on important items there were increases or extensions of the tariff.

The innovation coming out of the chemical industry review was the system of "support prices". A price is fixed which is regarded as a "normal" duty-paid import value. If duty-paid import prices fall below this, 90 per cent of the difference is charged in tariff. Currently support prices apply to about forty chemical items. Let me take an example of how the system works. Say the support price is $134, that the normal tariff rate is 40 per cent and that normally transport accounts for 15 per cent of the landed duty-free cost of goods. This implies that the normal f.o.b. price is $85 and the normal c.i.f. price $100. Now if the actual f.o.b. price is $70 and the actual c.i.f. price $82, the normal tariff will be $28 and the special duty $21.60, the consumer thus paying $131.60. The impact of the system depends of course completely on the level at which support prices are fixed and on actual import prices, and is very difficult to assess. Its object seems to be to provide almost complete protection against "disruptive pricing" from abroad. It is a form of "ultra-protection" which the European Economic Community uses for its agriculture.

There are interesting contrasts between the motor car and the chemical cases. The motor car and components industry must be regarded as broadly an economic industry for Australia. If there were little or no tariff on cars and components there would still be a substantial Australian industry, even though protection was no doubt required in its early stages and some components would, very rightly, not be produced in Australia. With a uniform tariff of 30 per cent (and no by-law imports) there would probably be a readjustment involving expansion of components manufacture and some contraction of marginal vehicle manufacture. By contrast there must be serious doubt whether a substantial section of the chemical industry is economic, in the sense of having reasonable prospects of being able to manage in time with moderate protection. With a uniform tariff of 30 per cent and nothing else, important parts of this industry would, on their own evidence, be in serious and probably long-term difficulty. There is another contrast. The motor car components manufacturers have not been in difficulties. They have been expanding and profits have been good. The Government's move to increase Australian content has thus not been a rescue operation. Rather, there seems to have been a deliberate decision to expand this section of Australian industry. The reason for this has not emerged from Government statements; perhaps it reflects an ideology of forced manufacturing development, the motor car having the same mystic role in Australia as the steel mill has in some underdeveloped countries, or per haps it was in response to specific pressures. On the other hand, the increase in protection to the chemical industry has more the appearance of a rescue operation for the companies concerned (mainly six foreign controlled companies), though it is not clear from the evidence just how great the need really has been.

These are the two major cases which dominate the tariff history of 1965 and 1966. The chemical case may go down in history as a high-water mark of Australian postwar protectionism. Let me now quickly run through some of the other cases listed in the Appendix.

Other industries

Protection for *crude petroleum* production has been provided for the first time; the object is to stimulate exploration, but of course it will also stimulate production. A domestic price above the price of imported crude has been fixed; together with arrangements designed to ensure that refiners absorb all the crude produced domestically, it has an effect equivalent to a tariff (c.i.f. basis) of about 45 per cent. In the short run the cost is borne by the refiners, who are themselves not protected – so that it gives them a negative effective rate – but in the long run they are likely to be allowed to raise prices to take account of the higher cost of domestic crude so that the cost will be borne by consumers.

For *small engines* a tariff of 65 per cent has been provided, with a specific alternative duty which may yield even higher protection. This tariff rate is to be reviewed within three to five years. The three foreign-owned companies producing *electrical capacitors* were until 1966 receiving a 100 per cent tariff, except for those capacitors used by electricity supply authorities on which the tariff was 50 per cent. These were all reduced in 1966 to 45 per cent. The effective rate would now be about 100 per cent. The industry *producing air conditioning and refrigerating equipment* was reviewed this year and the tariff was left undisturbed. For its main item the tariff is at least 57.5 per cent, and more for lower-priced imports. For the average price of sealed compressors from Japan the duty would be about 75 per cent.

The changes in the *glassware* tariff reflected a fairly typical pattern. Consider heat-resisting glassware. The normal tariff had been 40 per cent. In addition there had been a temporary duty imposed by the Special Advisory Authority in specific form. In *ad valorem* terms, the total duty had ranged from 55 per cent to 130 per cent. Now the normal tariff was raised to 60 per cent. Thus the tariff change to some extent consolidated the temporary duty by making it permanent, but not wholly so, since for lower-priced items there was a tariff reduction. The duty on table glassware was in creased to 45 per cent or 30 cents per dozen, whichever is the higher.

An important case is the *footwear* industry's. It is important because this highly labour-intensive industry employs about 23,000 persons. For leather footwear there is now a single rate of 45 per cent; previously the rate had been 4S per cent for men's shoes and 40 per cent for ladies' and children's shoes. Leather is obtained at or near world prices and the effective rate is probably over 100 per cent. The rubber footwear industry obtains much higher duties.

The tariff on *man-made fibre yarns* is fantastically complicated with many types of products and complex rates of duty. So far as I can tell, the main items seem to be nylon and terylene yarn, produced by a subsidiary of ICIANZ, for which the tariff is now about 40-50 per cent, with the effective rate much higher.

Finally, I come to those habitues of Tariff Board hearings, the manufacturers of textile fabrics. There have been two important cases in the period. For *cotton fabrics* the tariff has been greatly simplified, a great mass of complex tariffs having been replaced by a single rate of 55 per cent. This applies only to those items (accounting for about one-quarter of the Australian market by value) which are produced domestically, tariffs on other cotton items being at non-protective levels. The 55 per cent rate for the protective items seems to be roughly an average of pre-existing duties but represents a substantial decrease in the tariff for certain sections that were previously protected at very high rates, notably that producing canvas and duck. The effective rate for cotton fabrics would be well above 55 per cent. Similarly a uniform duty of 55 per cent was provided for *man-made fibre fabrics*, though in this case an alternative specific duty would yield higher protection for very low-priced fabrics. Previously the *ad valorem* equivalent of duties had been much higher than 55 per cent for the lower-priced fabrics, this being the type of fabric competitive with most Australian production. I would estimate the tariff on relevant items to have averaged 75 per cent, so that there has been a significant decrease in protection for what has been one of Australia's most highly protected larger industries. On the other hand, protection for higher-priced fabrics has been increased.

So as not to present an unbalanced picture, let me end with another case. *Tubes of iron and steel* paid a tariff of 35 per cent up to 1965, when the tariff was reduced to 20 per cent. There has been virtually no import competition. The principal producer is the British-owned firm of Tubemakers and it was found to be making high profits.

What emerges from this? The difficulties in tariff averages are well-known and I have not attempted to summarize the story in a few figures. One is struck above all by the high rates of protection provided in almost all cases. This is so even though I have not been able to calculate the implications in *ad valorem* terms of support prices for chemicals. These high tariffs must be regarded in many cases as the long-term consequences of the period of import licensing. In major cases there have been increases in protection or consolidations of temporary duties into normal duties. But this has not been an invariable trend. Some tariffs have been reduced, the major examples being electrical capacitors (to 45 per cent) and lower-priced man-made fibre fabrics (to 45 per cent), and others have remained constant, though often at very high levels. The assessment of these tariff levels depends on many considerations, some of which I shall explore later in my discussion of the "benchmark".

The Government and the Tariff Board

Some people think that all tariff decisions, other than purely administrative ones, should be made upon the advice of the Tariff Board and that the Board should be completely independent in its approach. Let us see what this might imply in any particular case. First, the Department of Trade and Industry would send a tariff reference to the Board that would simply ask the Board to recommend "whether assistance should be accorded the production in Australia" of the products concerned, and what rates of duty should be provided. There would be no "writing of policy into the reference". Secondly the Board would make its recommendations without taking into account what sort of recommendations it thinks the Department would welcome; it might perhaps provide a choice of policies, indicating its own preference. In other words, it would be independent. Thirdly, the Government would accept the recommendations and propose the relevant legislation. It would not vary them nor send the reference back to the Board. Fourthly, the Government would not within a short period send any of the tariff items concerned to the Special Advisory Authority. Fifthly, the Government would not send the case back to the Board for reconsideration within the following few years, unless indeed the Board itself requested that it do so.

I am unable to say anything definite on the second point. But on the other points I have assembled some information from my sixteen cases.

Motor cars and chemicals

Let me begin again with motor cars and chemicals. In both cases the policy was written into the reference in considerable detail. The motor car reference began:

> "Having regard to the Government's policy of ensuring the sustained development of an economic and efficient automotive industry in Australia, in relation to the production of complete motor vehicles with max mum Australian content. . . .

> "The chemical industry reference was very specific, and made it clear that the Government wanted "a reasonably profitable development of a soundly based chemical industry" and that it was looking for something like support prices to deal with "disruptive low prices".

In the case of motor cars, the main features of the Board's recommendations were not accepted. It proposed a scheme for relating by-law admission of components to scale of output of motor car producers without in general any time-limit element. The details are too complicated to pursue here, but the essential point is that the Board's scheme would have involved less protection for the components manufacturers and less difficulties for the marginal motor car manufacturers and assemblers than the Government's scheme. In fact the Government was already half committed to its scheme which had been under way before it sent the reference to the Board. It modified its original scheme a little, but the main features of the Board's recommendations were not accepted. The Board gave detailed and convincing reasons for its recommendations; by contrast the Government's policy statement was quite curt.

In the case of chemicals, the Board proposed a scheme of bounties and tariffs combined or, as a second preference, a scheme of protection by tariffs alone. The Government rejected the bounty proposal and chose the second preference. But apart from this it accepted all the Board's proposals, including those for extending the field of protection and for support prices.

Other industries

As for the remaining fourteen cases there were nine where the policy was *not* written into the reference, where the Tariff Board recommendations were fully accepted, where significant parts of the industry have not so far gone before the Special Advisory Authority since these reports were produced, and where the cases have not been sent back to the Board before it wanted them sent back. Now let us look briefly at the remaining cases.

The policy was written into the reference in two other cases, crude petroleum and man-made fibre yarns. The petroleum reference was extremely detailed, stating that Government policy was "that crude oil shall be utilized when found in Australia in quantities which, having regard to the location, may be regarded as commercial" and affirmed "the Government's desire to encourage oil exploration . . . ". It set out at length five guiding considerations for the benefit of the Board. The man-made fibre yarn reference clearly hinted at support prices.

The Board's recommendations were not wholly accepted in these two cases, nor in the cases relating to small engines, man-made fibre fabrics and agricultural tractors. The Government's variations in the last two cases were rather minor,[4] so let me just refer to crude petroleum, man-made fibre yarns and small engines. In the case of crude petroleum the Board was asked to provide a price valuation for domestic crude. It arrived at a price which can be calculated as equivalent to a 24 per cent tariff (this is c.i.f. basis; the equivalent would be higher on an f.o.b. basis). This incorporated an incentive margin for exploration.

But the Government decided to raise this margin, in effect increasing the protection to about 45 per cent, saying no more than that "it is very important that exploration in Australia should be at a high level and the level of the stimulus adopted by the Government should provide a significant incentive". In the man-made fibre yarns case the three Board members who conducted the inquiry examined the case for support prices at length, but rejected it, while the Chairman of the Board came in with a minority recommendation recommending support prices. The Government rejected the report and sent it back to the Board asking it to look more closely at the reference – which is understood to be a direction to propose support prices. Meanwhile the Government sent some of the main items to the Special Advisory Authority who continued or even increased the pre existing temporary duties and recommended some support prices. In the small engines case two Board members recommended 55 per cent and two 75 per cent. The Government rejected both recommendations, criticized the Board for producing a divided report and decided upon 65 per cent. But this is not really the significant feature of this case. The Tariff Board had looked at this industry in early 1961 and in late 1962; on both occasions it recommended and the Government apparently accepted a duty of 42 per cent or £6.10.0, whichever is the higher. In fact the specific rate was normally equivalent to 50 per cent or even

4 There was also a very minor variation in the case of cotton fabrics which I have ignored.

more, so it was the operative normal duty. Thus for seven years a normal duty of £6.10.0 had operated. But on three occasions temporary duties were added by the Special Advisory Authority or his predecessor, with the net result that for half of the seven years the operative duty was far above £6.10.0, at least for one of the two major types of engines. This type of situation has not been unusual in recent tariff history.

The role of the Tariff Board

An inevitable question is: does it really matter whether tariff policy is made upon the advice of the Tariff Board or not? In fact, why do we need a Tariff Board at all? The issue is an old one. The last Joseph Fisher Lecture to be devoted to the Australian tariff was delivered 31 years ago by Professor Giblin. He was quite eloquent about the virtues and role of the Tariff Board and expressed his concern that the Board had been ignored by the Government on two important occasions.[5]

Three reasons in favour of the Tariff Board system can be suggested. First, tariff investigations are a specialized and detailed matter; for this work to be done adequately there must be a specialized agency. If there were no Tariff Board one would need a separate government department. This would not be so if we had just a few tariff rates which were infrequently changed, but it is essential given the present approach to tariff making in Australia. Secondly, it seems essential that this type of work be done by a body removed one stage at least from politics. Tariff decisions have vast effects on the profits of individual companies, so that the temptations for questionable connections or pressures must be immense. If the detailed application of tariff policy, as distinct from the broad principles, is made in a political way – as it has been made lately – it becomes at least possible

5 I cannot refrain from quoting Professor Giblin: "There have been at times hesitations and postponements but in the end the Tariff Board's recommendations have been substantially carried out. It appeared likely that this policy if pursued would give the Board a status in public confidence that would be increasingly difficult to upset; so that even a die-hard freetrader or protectionist in the Ministerial Chair, though he might impede, would find it impracticable entirely to frustrate the Board's guidance to a sane and balanced protective economy. . . This pious hope has been rudely dashed by the new trade policy promulgated from Canberra. [He then details three cases] . . . By this action the Government appears to have undone the good work in the past, to have destroyed the promising building it has been patiently erecting, and to have exposed the whole structure of our tariff policy to the vagaries of future political expediency, and the log-rolling of interested parties."

that contributions to party funds would have some effect on actual policies. The Tariff Board system of public enquiries is particularly important in bringing issues and facts out into the open and so reducing the scope for tariff decisions being made in an underhand way. Incidentally, it might be wisest if the Tariff Board were attached to the Prime Minister's Department rather than to the Office of Secondary Industry of the Department of Trade (even though the Office might continue to be the source of tariff references). The latter sees itself, perhaps rightly, as primarily concerned with the interests of secondary industry.[6] But tariff policy is more a matter of adjudicating between tariff applicants on the one hand and consumers and other industries on the other. Thirdly, the Tariff Board's custom of providing in its reports a great deal of information as background and in support of its recommendations is valuable. By contrast, the Minister for Trade and Industry has provided the minimum of information and reasons for his decisions on tariff matters.

The Tariff Board can obviously be no better than its members and staff. If one day all its members were incompetent or lacking in detachment we should all want to reduce the role of the Tariff Board. And it is always within the power of the Government to make this so by its appointments. To judge by the limited evidence available, excessive enthusiasm about a number of recent Tariff Board members would be unwarranted. Nevertheless detachment should be somewhat easier for Tariff Board members than for the Minister for Trade and Industry.

The problem is both to have a genuinely independent and influential Board and to ensure that its members and staff are of adequate quality. Some of the 16 reports which form the basis of my discussion here have been very good, containing most of the relevant information, drawing attention to relevant characteristics of the industry, clear in their analysis and making the essential calculations about the impact of the duties proposed. Some others have been inadequate. Thus the chemical industry report tells us a lot about the industry and its point of view. But it is quite devoid of information enabling the reader to assess the impact of the recommendations, nor does it contain a critical examination of the issues

6 See the speech by Mr. W. Callaghan, the Head of the Office of Secondary Industry, to the Australian Industries Development Association, 24 October 1966.

involved in protecting by support prices. I have the impression that the quality of a report and of the recommendations seem to depend a good deal on which Board members sat on the case concerned.

The benchmark

Is there a simple guiding principle for tariff policy, one which can be used as a "benchmark" even though it may be modified by various other considerations? The Minister for Trade and Industry has a ready answer in his only recent statement of government tariff policy:

> "The Tariff Board is bound to recommend protection only to those industries which it judges are reasonably assured of sound opportunities of success – industries which are efficient and economic – and at levels which it considers will not prevent reasonable competition from imports on the basis of economic and efficient production in the Australian economic environment. This is a policy of this Government. It is a policy of previous governments."[7]

The magic, oft repeated words are "economic and efficient". But what is "economic"? Certainly no clear answer emerges from the Minister's statement or from the discussion of "the principles and procedures in tariff making" which were contained in the Tariff Board's Annual Report for 1958-59 and which he quotes with approval. The Vernon Committee attempted to give some meaning to the concept. It made an impact on the Tariff Board, which commented on the Committee's suggestions for a "benchmark" at length in the form of a majority and a minority view in their Annual Report for 1965-66. An important talk given recently by the Chairman of the Tariff Board also reflects keen concern with the fundamental issues.[8]

7 *Commonwealth Parliamentary Debates*, H. of R. 1967, p. 804.

8 G. A. Rattigan, "The Tariff Board and Today", delivered in Perth, May 24, 1967; see also the talk by Mr. E. J. L. Tucker, a member of the Board, "The Tariff Board and Tariff Policy", delivered in Melbourne, 11 July 1967.

The subject of course is complex and no single, simple approach is likely to be ideal. But the more questing attitude of members of the Tariff Board, the widespread desire for some coherence in tariff policy and for making the logic of policies explicit, and the unease with which recent policies have been received all suggest that it may be useful to put forward an analysis of various alternative approaches as well as some concrete suggestions.

I shall assume a fixed exchange rate and rule out radical "overnight" changes.[9] I shall ignore a variety of special arguments for or against protection which concern particular industries, and which deal with such matters as whether industries are foreign or Australian-owned and whether economies of scale, dumping or fluctuating import prices (what the Government and the chemical industry call "disruptive low pricing") justify special protection. In order to cover a good deal of ground the approach will have to be somewhat less rigorous than might be appropriate. A more rigorous discussion covering some of the same ground can be found in my review of the tariff chapters of the Vernon Report.[10] Inevitably, the policy suggestions advanced depend on implicit assumptions, first about the working of the economic system, secondly about orders of magnitude of various elements in the system, thirdly about the relative valuations to be placed on the real incomes of relevant sections of the community, and fourthly about political possibilities.

Free trade approach

Given full employment and balance of payments equilibrium, it is at least arguable that free trade would yield the optimum allocation of resources, or at least a better allocation than any likely protective system. So one could take the view that the only proper direction in which to move is towards free trade, the only desirable movements in tariffs therefore being down ward movements. This view would lead to the following practical recommendations: (a) Tariffs which protect existing industries should be brought down as far as possible, the downward movement being faster wherever political resistance is less; and (b) No new tariffs should be

9 To assume a fixed exchange rate is not of course to advocate that it should be fixed. But for various reasons it seems a realistic assumption.

10 W. M. Corden, "Protection", *Economic Record*, XLII, 1966.

imposed, and no import-competing industries or activities should be encouraged to come into existence if they would require tariffs for their survival.

Those critics who regarded the Vernon Committee's tariff chapters as too protectionist probably subscribe to a view of this kind. The Vernon Committee suggested that tariffs at a "benchmark" rate of, say, 30 per cent should be provided

readily. But in this view such a policy would represent an undesirable movement in the wrong direction, further away from free trade.

There are at least four objections to this free trade position. The first is that there may be some general arguments for protection of manufacturing in Australia – generalized external economies associated with industrialization, "infant economy" arguments, arguments for diversification, for improving the terms of trade and the distribution of income, and so on. I shall not elaborate them here as they are well known. It is doubtful whether one should give these much weight in present Australian conditions, though no doubt some protection in the past was justified, above all by "infant economy" arguments. A second objection is probably more important. If existing tariffs were indeed dismantled completely while the exchange rate remained unaltered, either unemployment or a balance-of-payments deficit would result. Non-frictional unemployment could be avoided by expansion of demand through fiscal and monetary policy, but only at the cost of a balance-of-payments deficit, while external deficit could be avoided by contraction of demand but only at the cost of unemployment. Thus some significant downward movement in existing tariffs would be practicable only when (with a given tariff level and full employment) balance-of-payments trends were favourable. Such an opportunity would result from an improvement in the export situation (such as might result from present mineral developments) or if the Australian wage and price levels could be made to increase more slowly than wages and prices abroad.

The third objection is of a different kind and applies only to tariffs protecting existing industry. It may be politically impossible to bring about by deliberate policy a substantial reduction in the size of any major protected industry even though full employment and balance-of-payments equilibrium can in general be ensured. A change might have to be so gradual that the reality of some continued protection has to be accepted. The fourth objection follows from the third one and applies to tariffs for new activities. If existing tariffs are not substantially dismantled the argument for providing some protection for new import-competing industries becomes much stronger. If existing industries were protected but no protection were provided for new potential developments there would be a misallocation of resources as between existing and new activities. This would be so even if existing resources in existing industries were completely immobile. For existing industries would tend to be extended, in preference to the development of new industries or activities, even when the latter would require much less protection.

Existence principle

At the opposite extreme to the free trade approach is a view which may be crudely summarized as follows. Any industry or economic activity which is actively in operation and which has involved the investment of substantial capital or the employment of a significant labour force shall be protected sufficiently to enable it to continue in existence. In this view it is the role of the Tariff Board and the Special Advisory Authority to recommend the use of whatever devices are possible, whether straight-out tariffs, temporary duties, anti-dumping duties or support prices, to achieve the object of a tariff made-to-measure for existence. It is usually conceded that this tariff should not "over-protect" but should normally allow "reasonable competition from imports" and should not be so high as to yield the industry abnormal profits. But even quantitative restrictions or devices with equivalent effects could be used.

But who decides which industries shall exist? To some extent history – wars, a period of import licensing, and a variety of past circumstances – bequeaths industries whose survival the tariff must then ratify. To this extent the principle is simply one of economic conservatism – hardly a prescription for economic progress. To some extent the initiative comes from private enterprise. But in recent years the Commonwealth and State governments have in fact played a crucial role in giving encouragement to new developments and, in the case of the Commonwealth, in giving explicit or implicit assurances about adequate protection. Clearly the

Altona petro-chemical complex, which appears to be rather a costly venture for Australian users of synthetic rubber and other chemical products, cannot have been started without Commonwealth encouragement. Thus the argument with regard to extensions of the field of protection is really that the Government should decide who shall be protected and the Tariff Board and the Special Advisory Authority recommend the form or degree of protection required.

How then should the Government decide who shall be protected? One answer might be that it can be left to chance, to the relative pressures and initiatives from the interests concerned, to "political considerations". An other approach might be to promise protection to any activity at all which is likely to yield substantial import replacement, irrespective of the excess cost of the new production over the value of the imports replaced. This view, which completely disregards cost considerations, might be justified if there were a desperate balance-of-payments or employment problem. But otherwise it can only reflect ignorance of the elementary economic concept of opportunity cost. If economics is to come back into the picture, then for any new venture involving extension of protection the question must be asked: "In the light of estimates of expected costs, markets and overseas supply prices, what long-term level of tariff protection may be required to sustain the new activity?" And if the degree of tariff protection expected to be required turns out to be too high, the new venture should not be given any assurances about protection but should rather be discouraged. The question remains of what is "too high" a degree of protection? This in fact brings us back to the unavoidable problem of a tariff benchmark.

Cost approach: simple uniform tariff version

One way of discriminating between activities and industries on the basis of cost is the application of a simple uniform tariff. The logic behind this idea is well-known. In addition to its merits as an allocator of resources it has the appeal of simplicity and of some degree of certainty. There are really two aspects of a decision to apply a uniform tariff:

i. It involves an acceptance of protection, perhaps because of generalized external economies believed to attach to import-replacing industrialization or other of the general arguments for protection listed earlier, perhaps for balance-of-payments reasons or perhaps as a second-best policy of political realism.

ii. It ensures an optimum allocation of resources within the import-competing sector, at least in so far as relative private costs of various import-competing activities reflect also the relative social costs, and provided that private enterprise is efficient from its own point of view; it uses the cost criterion for this aspect of resource allocation, even though, because of the fixed exchange rate, the allocation of resources as between the import-competing and the export sectors may remain distorted.

An appropriate rate of uniform protection must be selected. In any period this must be determined primarily (though not wholly) with a view to the balance of payments. If we go some way towards accepting the free trade approach this uniform tariff might be reduced over time, at least whenever balance-of-payments prospects permit, with free trade as the long-term objective.

The general idea is thus quite simple. There are certain complications arising from the input-output relations between products – that is, the need to consider effective rather than apparent rates – which I shall consider in Part 7 below. Until then, my discussion will refer only to apparent rates and I shall assume that effective rates are equal to apparent rates.

Two problems would be created by a uniform tariff, the problem of "under-protection" and the problem of "over-protection". The uniform tariff will inevitably be too low for some industries and too high for others. Modifications to the simple uniform tariff approach can take some account of these problems. But as we shall see, the modifications would create new problems.

Cost approach: Two uniform tariffs

If the uniform tariff rate were fixed at so high a level that it would maintain the output from every existing activity and would protect adequately every conceivable new activity then it would have no discriminating effects on resource allocation within the import-competing sector. To have any effects on resource allocation it must under-protect some existing industries, causing a contraction of output or even the closing down of industries. Similarly it must "discriminate out" some potential new activities. The under-protection of potential import replacement creates no problems, provided it is clearly made known in advance what uniform tariff rate will apply. But the under-protection of existing activities is a different matter. The political and social reality which motivates the existence approach to tariff-making cannot be ignored. One approach might be to apply the uniform tariff or benchmark only to new activities. This is what a minority of the Tariff Board appear to have in mind in their comment in the Annual Report for 1965-66. They might argue that one cannot do much about the resource allocation mistakes already made, but at least one can avoid new mistakes. Another, less conservative, approach would be to have two uniform tariffs to start with – a relatively low one for new activities, say 30 per cent, and a higher one for existing activities, say 45 per cent or even 55 per cent. Notice would be given that the higher tariff would over a long period be reduced until it reached the lower one. Between the two extremes of not applying the uniform tariff at all to existing activities and of having two uniform tariffs, with the one for existing activities relatively high, there are a variety of compromises all of which would involve concessions for those existing industries which depend on high protection.

The difficulty is that one cannot distinguish clearly between tariffs which protect existing production and tariffs which induce new production. The economy is not static and even a tariff which has given an existing industry the whole domestic market, and which applies to a product with no close substitutes, will induce new production as the size of the market expands. But the problem is greatest where there is significant substitution. The chemical industry may be correct that a 60 per cent tariff on high density polyethylene is needed to protect the existing production of low density polyethylene. But the fact is that this extension of the tariff has induced for the first time domestic production of the high density product. In such a case the distinction between a tariff which protects existing production and a tariff which protects new production completely breaks down.

If high tariffs applied to some or all existing activities, in so far as these could be narrowly defined, while a lower uniform tariff rate applied generally to new industries or extensions of existing industries, we should have the odd result that new industries obtain less protection than old ones. This is odd because it conflicts with the widely accepted view that infant industries should obtain an extra margin of protection. The validity of the various versions of the infant industry argument I cannot discuss here; but in so far as some argument of this type is valid, the following further modification might be made to the policy outlined above. New activities obtain a high rate (say 50 per cent) in their first year, dropping in steps for three years down to the benchmark rate for newly protected products. If the benchmark is to mean anything at all there would have to be complete certainty that the tariff will indeed drop to the benchmark within a short specified period.

Cost approach: Made-to-measure version

Inevitably, a uniform tariff would provide more protection for some industries than they need; that is, it would over-protect them. This may simply mean that some part of the tariff is redundant, the Australian market price being below the duty-paid import price. But it may also provide opportunities for monopolies or oligopolies to raise their prices above the minimum required to make normal profits. The excess profits may eventually induce new entrants and so lead to inefficient fragmentation of production. All this may lead to the conclusion that tariffs should be made-to-measure to the needs or costs of different industries, the calculations being based on the assumption that each industry consists of an optimum number of firms and that individual firms are managerially and technically efficient. This sort of made-to-measure approach under lies much current thinking about tariff-making. It is supplemented by the view that there should never be a tariff when it would have little or no protective effect, that the worst tariff is one that does not protect, especially when it is a tariff on an input.[11]

The case for made-to-measure tariffs is in fact similar to the case for price control; and it is subject to the same objections. To begin with, there is simply the difficulty of measuring the right tariff rate. Any suggestion of accuracy implied in fine variations of rates must be spurious. A tariff rate that yields minimum profits to one firm producing a product will give excess profits to another producing the same product. Secondly, the whole concept of a single made-to-measure tariff rate for each product valid for a reasonable period of time is doubtful. A rate which is just right for existing production may keep out new production as the market expands. Thus a tariff on a particular product may have been squeezed down to ten per cent to deprive existing producers of excess profits; yet as demand expands

11 *Ibid.*, p. 139.

there might be scope for extra production provided a 20 per cent tariff were provided. Thirdly, one can argue that industries which require tariff rates below the benchmark should be allowed to make excess profits. These are the industries that have the greatest potentialities for exporting, and the high profits may help to finance their expansion for export production and make possible exporting at marginal cost. Furthermore, the low tariff requirement may be an indication of managerial efficiency, which it is certainly desirable to reward.

In spite of these qualifications, one should probably take some account of the made-to-measure principle. The benchmark rate would be an upper limit. Those industries, for example steel, which clearly need less than the benchmark rate, could continue to receive a somewhat lower rate. There may also be cases where a tariff below the benchmark rate would clearly prevent monopolistic exploitation or undue fragmentation of production. The benchmark rate need not be imposed where it would bring forth little or no domestic production, especially if the product concerned is an input into export or into other protected industries. But new developments which would be economical at the benchmark rate must not be discouraged by this policy; thus anticipatory protection at or below the benchmark rate could be provided, with free-of-duty (by-law) entry for imports until the possibility of domestic production arises.

Industry rates approach

It is clear from recent Tariff Board reports, from the Annual Report for 19-66 and from the Chairman's recent speech that there is a movement towards simplifying the tariff and aiming in general at a limited number of "industry rates". Thus we now have an industry rate of 55 per cent for woven cotton and man-made fibre piecegoods and two industry rates, 25 per cent and 40 per cent, for the chemical industry. There has been an industry rate for motor car components since 1957. (These are not the only rates applying in these industries; furthermore, in the case of chemicals and motor car components they are partly overlaid by the other arrangements I mentioned earlier). The virtues of industry rates are considerable and are the same in nature as those of a single uniform tariff, though less in degree. Resource allocation as between different products produced by the "industry" is left to market forces, tariff administration is simplified, and a clearer under standing of the height and pattern of tariffs results. Furthermore, the establishment of a limited number of such rates might be regarded as a step towards a modified benchmark approach. The industry rates approach is a compromise between the more radical uniform tariff approach and two of the other approaches discussed above, namely the approach which takes into account the impracticability of greatly under-protecting existing industries, and the made-to-measure approach.

But it is clearly inadequate as a guiding principle for tariff-making. It does not deal at all with the problem of resource allocation as between industries. Perhaps one must accept, at least in the short-term, the choice of high industry rates which are designed to avoid major areas of under protection for long-established industries. The main objection is rather that industry rates may provide the wrong signals for resource allocation as between new developments. Even though an existing industry may require for its survival a 55 per cent tariff, it does not follow at all that new developments in the industry must also be protected at 55 per cent.

Thus, while the general tendency towards industry rates is probably to be welcomed, where industry rates are especially high or low they should clearly not be applied rigidly to extensions of the field of protection. In any case, industry rates can only be a step, if an important one, on the way to a coherent tariff policy based on economic considerations.

Effective protective rates

So far the complications presented by the input-output relations between products have been ignored. These are allowed for in the concept of the effective protective rate. It is these effective rates, and not apparent rates, which are relevant for assessing the impact of a tariff system on resource allocation. The whole of the preceding discussion should have referred to effective, not apparent rates. Thus, if the degree of protection for a group of products is to be uniform, it is their effective rates, and not necessarily their apparent rates, which must be uniform. The difficulty is that effective rates are not easy to calculate. There are many problems in the concept itself. The calculation depends on information about the shares of certain types of inputs in costs; there are difficulties about deciding which inputs are relevant for the calculation; furthermore, the input shares differ for different firms and vary year by year as a result of changes in techniques and relative prices.

Is this then a reason for giving up the whole idea of a benchmark? Is a benchmark in terms of apparent rates wrong and in terms of effective rates impossible? Should one let the benchmark wait until reliable calculations of effective rates on a large-scale have been made? These are reasonable questions, but the answers are really a matter of commonsense. If we wait until all the calculations have been made we shall have to wait a long time – and meanwhile decisions about tariff rates must still be made. We must be careful not to allow the important complication of effective rates to prevent the evolution of more coherent tariff policies. Effective rates often cannot be calculated precisely or require an inordinate amount of work. But rough calculations indicating the broad order of magnitude by which in any particular case the effective rate is likely to be above or below the apparent rate are certainly possible and in fact have been made frequently by the present author and probably also by the Tariff Board. And this will usually be enough.

Undoubtedly effective rates differ frequently from apparent rates. This would be true even if there were a completely uniform tariff with raw materials and intermediate goods all paying the same apparent rate as finished goods. For products which use exportable inputs purchased in Australia at world prices such as wool, steel and leather, would obtain effective protection higher than the uniform tariff rate. But when most imported inputs come in duty-free or at low non-protective rates of duty, perhaps under by-law, the possibility of divergence between effective and apparent rates is much increased.

The solution to the problem seems to me to be along the following lines. The uniform tariff or benchmark rate (or the two rates, one for existing industry and one for new developments) should be expressed in *ad valorem* apparent terms. Where there is clear evidence that the effective rate would be significantly above the apparent rate, the tariff-makers should diverge below the apparent rate benchmark. Thus the apparent-rate benchmark would have some of the characteristics of an upper limit even when the made-to-measure complication is not introduced.

There is of course the possibility that the effective rate is less than the apparent rate, in which case the divergence should be above the apparent rate benchmark. But such cases would be rare. It must be remembered that for the effective rate to be less than the apparent rate it is not sufficient that there are tariffs on the relevant inputs; the input tariff rates must actually be higher than the apparent tariff rate on the final good.

The divergence between apparent and effective rates might be similar for the various products of an industry; if this were so there would be an industry apparent rate which reflected the general divergence from the benchmark appropriate for these products; this would yield a partial re habilitation of the idea of industry rates. But I do not think one could explain or justify much of the present pattern of industry rates in this way.

Effects on exports

In so far as protection of import-replacing industries draws resources out of export industries which are unsubsidized, or at least subsidized at lower rates than the effective protection of the import-competing industries, and in so far as there are no special arguments for protection, there is a misallocation of resources. The balance-of-payments-cum-employment argument for protection to which I referred earlier and upon which a case for a uniform tariff could be based assumes that, in the absence of exchange devaluation, the resources absorbed by protected import-competing industry could not be employed in export industry. In general, the more easily the resources could be absorbed at the constant exchange rate in the export industries and the extra output sold without undue price falls, the weaker the argument for protection and hence the lower the optimum uniform tariff or benchmark. Thus the scope for increasing export production and selling the extra output must be taken into account when determining the long-term level of the benchmark.

Effects on exports may also justify divergences from the benchmark. In general, those import-replacing industries which use resources that are close substitutes for resources in unsubsidized actual or potential export industries should be protected at rates less than the benchmark. Furthermore, tariffs on products which are significant inputs into export industries will raise the costs of export industries. If, like wool and meat, the export industries them selves are not protected, they obtain in fact negative effective rates. This is obviously undesirable from a resource allocation point of view and suggests that tariffs on products which are important inputs into export industries should in general be somewhat lower than they would be otherwise.

Conclusion: The benchmark

To conclude, what should the benchmark rate be? This is clearly a matter of judgment rather than precise calculation. It should be the higher, the higher existing tariffs; to this extent calculations of tariff averages are relevant in determining the benchmark rate. It should also be the higher, the higher are the tariff rates that seem to be required to get any new import-replacing development. On the other hand, the better the balance of payments prospects and the more scope there is for expansion of export industries, the lower it should be. Perhaps a benchmark (in apparent rate terms) of 30 per cent for new activities and 45 per cent for existing activities would be reasonable at present. The benchmark for existing activities would involve lopping off the substantial high protection areas, an operation which would have to be gradual, perhaps in steps announced precisely in advance. The lower benchmark rate would be readily available to new activities.

The two benchmarks would be upper limits exceeded only rarely, except during the transitional period for existing high protection industries and during a short "infant" period for some new industries. Apparent rates would be reduced below the relevant benchmark for any of three reasons: (a) made-to-measure reasons (avoidance of excess profits, of fragmentation of production, and of tariffs on inputs which have no protective effect at all); (b) effective rates clearly exceeding apparent rates; and (c) adverse effects of protection on exports. There are also some special reasons, which I do not have time to discuss here, that may justify departure from the benchmark upward or downward in limited cases.

These are suggestions which take into account the constraints of what is possible. They are close to, though somewhat more radical than, the approach towards which some members of the Tariff Board seem to be moving, especially the three members who wrote the minority comment in the Annual Report for 1965-66, but to a lesser extent also the Chairman. Practical "benchmark policy" involves a balancing of various opposing considerations: on the one hand the arguments for tariff simplicity, for firm guides to tariff-making and for a little ruthlessness in the interests of economic efficiency, and on the other, the arguments for providing for numerous complications and repercussions and avoiding sudden or unexpected discomfort to any section of the community or foreign investors.

Appendix

Between January 1965 and April 1967, 57 Tariff Board reports were tabled in Parliament. Of these 15 dealt with industries or sections of industries employing at least 800 persons. These 15 reports, along with the report on crude oil, are listed below. The date of the report follows in each case. In those seven cases where the Tariff Board recommendations were not wholly adopted the date of the relevant Ministerial statement is also given.

Satisfactory employment figures for many of the industries or products concerned are not available. But using information in the reports, combined with some guessing, one can give the following indication of orders of magnitude involved. The motor vehicle and components industry is by far the biggest employer in the group, with over 64,000 employees. Next comes the footwear industry with about 23,000. The production of industrial chemicals and synthetic resins employs about 9,000, and all the other industries listed, other than crude oil, together about 25,000. Most of these others, except small engines (860) and man-made fibre yarns, employ between 1,500 and 2,500 persons. While the figures are likely to be too low rather than too high, one must be impressed by the small proportion of the Australian manufacturing workforce which appears to be concerned in these cases.

The largest capital investment is in motor vehicles and components and in chemicals followed no doubt by crude oil exploration and production.

The list, which does not include the important report on aluminium which was made public in July 1967 is as follows:
Copper and Brass Strip, etc. (25 February 1967 and 19 November 1965).

Hollow Bars, Tubes and Pipes of Iron or Steel (22 June 1965).

Sulphuric Acid and Pyrites Bounty Acts (30 June 1965).

Crude Oil (23 July 1965). See also statement by Minister for Trade and Industry September 8, 1965; A. Hunter, "Investment in Petroleum Exploration in Australia", *Economic Record*, XLII, 1966; and S. McL. Cochrane, "The Pricing of Australian Crude Oil", *Australian Quarterly*, XXXIX, 1967.

Agricultural Tractors (2 September 1966). See also Commonwealth Parliamentary Debates, H. of R. LIII, 1966, pp. 2102-2103.

Motor Vehicles and Concessional Admission of Components (24 September 1965). See also statements by Minister for Trade and Industry, 8 February 1966, and July 29, 1966.

Tinned Iron and Steel Hoop, Strip, Plates and Sheets (24 September 1965). (These items were not protected; deferred duty provisions were cancelled.)

Woven Cotton Fabrics, Bed Linen, etc. (6 August 1966).

Woven Man-made Fabrics (6 August 1965). See also Commonwealth Parliamentary Debates, H. of R. XLVIII, 1965, pp. 2346-2353.

Glassware (22 December 1965).

Industrial Chemicals and Synthetic Resins (13 April 1966). See also Commonwealth Parliamentary Debates, H. of R. LIII, 1966, pp. 2103-2105 and H. of R. 1967, p. 1863.

Electrical Capacitors (30 November 1966).

Air-cooled Engines not Exceeding 10 B.H.P. and Parts (December 15, 1966). See also Commonwealth Parliamentary Debates, H. of R. 1967, pp. 613-614.

Man-made Fibres and Yarn, Tyre Cord and Tyre Cord Fabric (15 December 1966). See also Commonwealth Parliamentary Debates, H. of R. 1961, p. 548; and Report of Special Advisory Authority on *High Tenacity Man-made Fibre Yarns, etc.* (23 June 1967).

Air Conditioning and Refrigerating Equipment (17 February 1967).

33

Balancing external payments by adjusting domestic income

E. H. Phelps Brown[1]

I owe my hearers an apology at the outset for taking a subject that has so much immediate application to the United Kingdom, and so little to the happier land of Australia. The external balance has been a recurrent source of embarrassment to the United Kingdom for many years past: no such difficulties afflict or threaten the Australia of today. The regulation of money income by means of a national incomes policy has been attempted in recent years by a number of countries, the United Kingdom among them, in which wages and salaries are generally changed by collective bargaining without the intervention of third parties: but Australia has inherited a different procedure, whose availability has largely spared her the need to devise new institutions in order to check cost inflation under full employment. Yet if nonetheless I invite you to consider these issues, it is not only because it is they alone that I can speak of from my own experience in the United Kingdom, but also because I believe they have their relevance to Australian thinking. For in the weather map of international trade, high and low pressure systems are apt to succeed one another unexpectedly; especially where the external balance is supported by an inflow of capital, change may set in rapidly; he would be a rash man in any country who would say that its balance of payments could not become adverse in the foreseeable future. And not only if such a change should ever come about again in Australia, but already for many years past, the Conciliation and Arbitration Commission in its major awards has had to have regard, among other things, to the prospective impact of those awards on the level of costs in Australian industry, and on Australian foreign trade. Although,

1 Thirty-third Joseph Fisher Lecture, 26 June 1969. The author is very much indebted to Professors Keith Hancock and E. A. Russell for comment.

therefore, the thoughts I shall lay before you have been formed mostly in the light of United Kingdom experience, and will be couched in corresponding terms, I hope you will find the question of how far the adjustment of domestic incomes can help to balance external payments not without its relevance to economic policy in Australia.

I

Any government that commits itself to a National Incomes Policy soon finds out how to lose friends and fail to influence people. What has pushed many governments into that commitment nonetheless has been a pressing need to right the balance of payments. At least three countries, the Netherlands, Sweden and the United Kingdom, maintained a wage stop for some time in the later 1940s, when their first necessity was to restore their export trade – and, in the United Kingdom, to raise it far above its pre-war level. Through all the subsequent vicissitudes of Dutch incomes policy there has run a concern with the prospective "room", as the Dutch say, for rises in pay, and in a country whose exports yield more than half its national income that "room" has meant the greatest rise in domestic incomes compatible with balancing external payments. Similarly in Sweden: there, it is true, the government itself eschews all overt commitment to incomes policy: but exports yield a quarter of the national income; and when the national organisations of employers and labour meet to negotiate a central framework agreement that will regulate the course of wages throughout the economy for the next two or three years, the question of how much rise in wages will be consistent with maintaining exports is crucial. It was remarkable that President Kennedy commended to the Congress an elaborate set of guideposts for pay and prices, at a time – early in 1962 – when prices in the United States had been comparatively stable for some years. The purpose in great part was to ensure that the spending to be released by tax remissions would not simply be mopped up by rises in pay and prices in the sector of existing employment; but so controversial a step might not have been taken had there not also been a mounting concern about the balance of payments. Most evidently of all, in the United Kingdom, it was the crisis of sterling in 1957 that induced a Conservative government, dedicated to restoring the working of the free market, to set up the Council on Prices, Productivity and Incomes and so take the first step along a road that the continuing troubles of the British balance of payments have driven governments farther and farther down since then, until a Labour government has taken statutory power to defer for up to twelve months rises in pay that its trade union supporters might obtain in negotiation.

The restraints that these essays in incomes policy have imposed have often been resented by those on whom they bore, without solving the problems of the economy as a whole. There have been uneasy compromises, chops and changes of the policy, outright defeats for it. If nonetheless the policy has been adopted by governments, and accepted in principle by national organisations of management and labour, that is because no other way has offered itself of checking inflation while maintaining full employment. The immediate compulsion to apply that policy has often been exerted by the effects of inflation on the balance of payments. In particular, incomes policy has been invoked as a means of stemming a deficit in the balance of payments in the short run, and of preventing one from being set up in the long. Let us consider those two purposes in turn.

II

In the short run the contribution that incomes policy can make to righting the balance of payments is small. Certainly the determination of a government to bring in or stiffen an incomes policy will have its effect on confidence: if government can be credited both with willingness to undergo the opprobrium it must incur by attempting to check the rise of wages and salaries, and with the power to make that attempt good, the prospects of the economy escaping from the inflationary spiral will be visibly enhanced, and that will take its effect on world opinion. But the embarrassments and rebuffs that have attended on incomes policy hitherto tend to deny credibility to the announced intention of governments to apply it anew. Even, moreover, if they do make it take hold, its immediate effect on the balance of payments can hardly be pronounced. For the function of incomes policy is to check the parallel rise of unit labour costs and prices, not to hold back money incomes relatively to prices so that real demand is restrained. Certainly, insofar as incomes policy does check the rise in costs and prices, it will help to keep imports down and exports up, but this price effect will not be great in the short run. In any case, what is needed to restore the balance of payments quickly will almost always be a reduction in aggregate real demand. In the experience of the United Kingdom, for instance, a rapidly mounting deficit in the balance of payments has been set up not by any rapid turn for the worse in relative costs and prices but by a rapid rise in aggregate real demand – a rise that cannot be satisfied by domestic output and spills over into imports. This surge of aggregate real demand will not have been brought about by increases in pay, for it has been of the essence of the process that, insofar as rises in pay exceed those in productivity and so raise unit labour costs, they carry prices up with them. The surge must have been due to a rise in a form of outlay largely independent of money incomes, and not like them currently linked through costs and margins to prices. That form of outlay is investment. There is no reason why firms' decisions to increase their outlay on investment should be matched by an increase in voluntary saving. Nor, so far as it impinges on the home market, will much of the increased investment outlay be quickly absorbed by higher prices, because unlike a rise in spending due to higher pay it does not tend to raise costs at its point of origin, and it is to rises in cost, not to extensions of demand, that administered prices respond. Insofar, then, as the increase in investment outlay impinges on domestic output it can only set up queuing, as delivery dates recede; the frustrated customer turns to the foreign supplier; the excess of real demand is met by higher imports. Since the upset does not begin with spending out of income, we cannot look to incomes policy to put it right. True, if incomes policy did actually check the rise of money incomes while the rise in prices went on, it would reduce aggregate real demand, but this is not how it is meant to work, or likely to be allowed to work for long in practice.

In the short run, then, though incomes policy has in practice been included among the measures adopted by governments that need immediate relief from balance of payment troubles, its virtue at the time lies largely in its announcement effect. This in turn depends on its capability of preventing inflation from worsening the balance of payments in the long run.

We look to it to do this by guiding the course of costs and prices. The assumption is that the higher the domestic level of costs and prices, with a fixed exchange rate, the bigger imports will be, and the smaller exports. How, then, do we want costs and prices to behave? A country with persistent balance of payments difficulties might well want to aim at what has sometimes come about in the past – constancy of money incomes, with costs and prices falling as productivity rises, and real incomes rising with productivity through the rise in the purchasing power of money. But we are all so accustomed nowadays to taking out the rise in productivity in the form of higher money incomes, that this aim seems visionary, and most governments would be gratified if their incomes policy could achieve the aim set by President Kennedy's economic advisers in 1962, of holding the general level of costs and prices constant. In practice, many governments would be content if they could even ensure only that costs and prices rose more slowly in the future than in the past. Looking around them in the world market for manufactures, they would have reason to expect that if they could achieve only so much as this, they would still not be undercut by their competitors.

The effectiveness of such a policy must be assessed differently according as it is required only to prevent fresh trouble being created by a rise in domestic costs and prices relatively to those of other countries, or is expected to remedy an external deficit arising from other causes.

III

If incomes policy is looked to only in the first of these ways, as a way of avoiding a relatively high rate of inflation, no question arises of its usefulness if only it can succeed in its own immediate aim. We should all agree that the more slowly a country inflates, the less likely it is to run into fresh balance of payments difficulties through its costs becoming uncompetitive. But many of us will ask, granted that you want to check inflation, why resort to such a clumsy: laborious and unproven type of interventionism as incomes policy? Why not rely on the familiar fiscal and monetary restraints, working impersonally through market forces?

The answer is not merely that if those restraints are familiar, so also is the unemployment which they inflict when they are imposed, and which if created deliberately by any western government would be likely to bring it down. If that were all, then the aim of incomes policy would be to keep the economy in a state of suppressed demand inflation – to keep demand high enough to ensure full employment, while preventing the pull of demand from raising costs. But its aim is not that. It has the same aim as the fiscal and financial restraints, namely to avoid inflation altogether. If it imposes itself in their place, that is because, unlike them, it goes to the source of inflation in the contemporary economy.

For this source proves to be on the side not of demand but of costs. The world has known for centuries the inflation that is caused by excess demand – be it when Spanish gold and silver spread across Europe, or when governments created fiat money, especially to pay their way in time of war: then excess demand set up shortages, and the pay of labour and the prices of products were pulled up by the competition of buyers. But a study of what has actually been happening in recent years soon reveals a process quite other than that. Excess demand has not been an invariable condition of rises in pay and prices. In the industries that are shedding labour, or carry a substantial margin of unemployment, pay has risen at much the same rate as in the others. In Denmark down to 1959 the prevailing level of unemployment was around 6 per cent, and in some districts and occupations it was more like 10 per cent; but pay went up at much the same rate in Denmark as in its Scandinavian neighbours where employment was full. The sequence, so far as that can be distinguished in a spiral, has been not that pay follows prices up, or even that pay and prices move together, but that prices follow pay. They have done so because the rises in pay have generally been greater than those in productivity, so that unit costs have been raised. Pay has been able to rise so fast, because the habit has grown up of raising it annually at a rate that has emerged from a spontaneous alignment of decisions. The rate has varied somewhat from year to year, but not in a way that can be systematically related to the state of the labour market. What has happened is rather that a consensus has grown up about the rate of change that will prevail from time to time. Management in any one firm or industry will find it hard to settle for less than this; nor has it any incentive to involve itself in a painful struggle to do so, when it knows from experience that so long as it does not raisc its own costs faster than others are doing all around it, it will be able later to maintain its profit margins by raising its selling prices, without losing business. What the rate is about which the consensus grows up is within wide limits arbitrary. Those who take part in negotiations and settlements feel individually that little discretion is left them; but collectively they are largely autonomous. So far at least as they sell in the home market, they can afford any rise, provided enough of them are tacitly agreed on it.

At the root of cost inflation, then, there is an alignment of expectations about a norm. It is the specific merit of incomes policy that it does go to this, the root of the matter. In a word, its purpose is to align expectations about a norm that is non-inflationary.

It may well be objected, however, that expectations never could have become aligned about an inflationary norm unless experience had shown that the government would provide the money needed to support a growing real turnover at a rising level of prices. Even if cost inflation does arise independently of an extension of the flow of spending, it still depends on such extension for its continuance. So, it will be said, even if inflation under full employment is cost inflation *ex ante*, it is demand inflation *ex post*: let the government only make it clear that demand is not going to be raised so as to float firms off whatever level of costs they allow to accrue, and the accrual will cease. One proposal is that the government should announce its intention of increasing the monetary base by no less but also no more than the expected increase in tumover at constant prices – say three per cent per annum. It would thereby serve-notice on the pay-fixers that if their determinations raised the general level of costs and prices, sales would fall and unemployment would rise. But in this proposal the difficulty is twofold. How far will individual decisions be influenced by a sanction that is activated only by the aggregate of decisions? And how far will the threat of that sanction be credible, when it is itself so painful, so invidious in its incidence, and so easily lifted? – for should the community collectively overshoot the mark, the pressure on the government of the day to provide the once-for-all addition to the stock of money, which was all that was needed to cure unemployment and restore prosperity, would surely be irresistible.

An alternative proposal is that governments should guide the decisions of pay-fixers not by direct intervention but by using fiscal and monetary controls to adjust the balance of aggregate supply and demand. In one form, this proposal would keep industry running with a rather wider margin of unused capacity than of late, so as to avoid bottlenecks in which competitive bidding for scarce resources raises costs, and to give firms a continuing incentive to keep prices down in order to get additional orders which they will now have the capacity to fill if only they can get them. We can agree that aggregate demand cannot be raised beyond a certain level without excess demand being set up at particular points, and without firms generally becoming much less concerned with keeping costs down than with getting production up. We must accordingly accept the necessity of using fiscal and monetary restraints to prevent aggregate demand from passing through the level at which costs begin to rise in bottlenecks and cost control is loosened widely. But this is not to say that so long as we achieve this there need be no fear of cost inflation: for in recent years the movement of costs has come to depend on something other than the balance of supply and demand.

That this is so appears when we examine another proposed way of adjusting that balance – the proposal, namely, to maintain a rather higher level of unemployment than has prevailed of late. Higher unemployment is seen as marking a changed balance of supply and demand in the labour market, and it is believed that the rates of pay arrived at in that market would then rise more slowly. This belief rests upon an association observed in the past between the change of the general level of wages on the one side, and the current unemployment rate, together with the direction in which that rate was changing, on the other. But the labour market is not a produce market. It is arbitrary to interpret the observed association as the outcome simply of the changing balance between job vacancies and job applicants. All that the observed association shows is that the movements of wages varied with the phases of the eight-year trade cycle; the rate of unemployment, and the direction in which the rate is changing, serve only as an indicator of the phases. If we take an alternative indicator, namely the deviations of pig-iron output from trend, we get an equally close association, but no one would suggest that by regulating pig-iron output the government could control the movement of wages. It seems likely that what determined wage movements was not so much the rate of unemployment itself as the state of expectations prevailing in each phase of the cycle. Today, however, estimates of firms' current and prospective ability to pay no longer rise and fall with the course of a trade cycle that seemed to be no less exogenous than cycles in the weather. We all know now that we can spend our way out of depression, and that governments can reduce unemployment if only they choose to. This knowledge, fortified by a quarter century of full employment, has given our current expectations a new base and a force of self-propulsion. It is these expectations that govern the rises in pay that the community has come to expect and that employers have come to believe they can concede without harm to their businesses; and it is these expectations that must be changed by any policy that is to influence the rise in pay. A plunge into depression would shatter them, but this is precluded. The alternative is to try to mould and guide them through incomes policy.

These are the reasons, I believe, for which governments concerned to avoid the worsening of their external balance by a rise in their costs have turned to incomes policy. They have done so because incomes policy goes directly to the point at which cost inflation under full employment arises, and because fiscal and monetary restraints of themselves offer no politically practicable or ultimately effective alternative. They have persisted in it, for all its embarrassments, because their external balance forbids them to let cost inflation go unchecked, and they know no better way of checking it in the state of mind induced by years of full employment.

IV

The case we have just been considering is that for using incomes policy to prevent inflation from bringing a country into balance-of-payments difficulties. What has been at issue is the appropriateness of the instrument, namely incomes policy, and not of the operation, namely, regulating domestic money income. But as we now come to consider the regulation of income as a remedy for a deficit in the external balance arising from causes other than domestic inflation, what is in doubt is the effectiveness of the operation. Balances of payments can go wrong for many reasons other than the domestic level of costs and prices. An inflow of capital may dry up; an outflow of capital may set in; or the government may undertake additional expenditure overseas for aid or defence. Especially in countries at an early stage of development, but not in them alone, an increase in the rate of growth may systematically raise imports more than exports. As between different sectors of one economy, so between different economies, there may be structural changes, arising from the advance of techniques and shifts in consumers' demand. Some of these factors can be dealt with directly by government, but by no means all: in particular, governments are inhibited by the rules of GATT, or the apprehension of counter-measures, from restricting imports or subsidising exports. How much can regulation of incomes do to restore the external balance, when it is not with incomes that the trouble begins? Much can be done, we know from sad experience, by restraining not monetary income merely but real income. Let us consider for a moment why we hear so much of the balance of payments between one country and the rest of the world, and so little of that between one region and the rest of the same country. Forty years ago I heard Edwin Cannan in a lecture at Oxford ask why there was no public concern about the balance of payments of the Isle of Wight, and I would like to follow him now, though not, as I remember, to the conclusions he then drew. If the balance of payments between one region and the rest of the same currency area becomes passive, it will be corrected by a ruthless deflation within the region. The multiplier effect of a passive balance will not be offset in the interests of sustained activity by fiscal and monetary easements at the centre; the quantity of money within the region will be reduced by the amount of the deficit; and this will go on until the region's bill for imports from the rest of the country ceases to exceed what it earns by selling to it. The major part in that adjustment will be played by the reduction of spending on the region's imports. But this will be only part of the total reduction in spending within the region that will have to be brought about. If a quarter of the spending that is cut would have been spent on the region's imports, then the whole cut in spending will be four times the required reduction in the region's imports, and output within the region will have been cut back to the tune of three times the required reduction in imports. This loss of employment, output and consumption, moreover, itself contributes nothing to the restoration of the balance, except insofar as the resources now made idle can be diverted into sales outside the region, and there is no assurance that they will lend themselves to that. The cut in external purchases is thus achieved only through a waste of resources, and an invidious infliction of unemployment on particular men and women. For a monetary problem there has been substituted a structural. No regional imbalance of payments troubles the authorities; but the region may become a depressed area. And this may be no less the plight of any entire economy that holds down domestic income in order to counter a persistent tendency of imports to exceed exports. There come to mind the examples of the United Kingdom in the inter-war years, and of Denmark with its high unemployment between the Second World War and the righting of its balance of payments in 1959. Yet when governments obligated to maintain full employment refuse to allow an external deficit to reduce real income, the deficit will persist. Is there any way out?

One way of diagnosing this dilemma is to see it as arising from a gap in the system of incentives in the market economy. Generally, when the economy needs an increase in a given line of output, the market gives producers an incentive to supply it. But when a persistent tendency to import more calls for an increase in exports, the market gives producers no incentives whatever to bring this about if domestic income is maintained; while even if domestic income is cut they are given only the doubtful incentive of needing to find fresh markets, at a time of depression and dubiety, for what they cannot now sell at home. What the market should be doing, we feel, is to make exports immediately more profitable. But this is just what it would do if the external value of the currency were not pegged regardless of supply and demand, but allowed to float. For then as imports rose the rate of exchange would fall, and the yield in domestic currency of exports selling at unchanged prices abroad would be raised. There is no gap after all in the market system of incentives if the external value of the currency is in the market too.

Another line of diagnosis leads to the same conclusion. By this we view both the persistence of an excess of imports in the absence of a cut in domestic incomes and the wastefulness of the cut in incomes that will restore the balance as alike derived from our inability to separate the money that will buy abroad from the money that will buy at home. The two are not separate so long as the central bank will at need provide foreign currency at a fixed price in terms of domestic: for then anyone who holds the domestic currency is a potential buyer abroad; and the availability of foreign currency cannot be reduced save by a reduction in the domestic currency for all purposes. What is wanted is a way of separating the domestic currency from the money that will buy abroad, and limiting the amount of that money to so much as is being currently offered in exchange for the domestic currency. This can be done, with a fixed rate of exchange, only if there is rationing of imports. One form of rationing is by administrative allocation of licences to import. It has been suggested that the allocation would be more efficient as well as simpler if it were left to the market – if import licences were put up to auction. The procedure would be simpler still if there were no licences, but those who wanted foreign currency had to bid for the available supply. But this is only a way of describing a floating exchange rate.

Two lines of diagnosis of the malady of the persistently passive balance of payments have thus brought us to the same prescription: let the exchange rate float. Needless to say, there is more to the argument than this. Governments would not have held on to fixed exchange rates so long and been at such pains to re-establish them when they broke down, if the only case for them were that they are traditional and suited the convenience of bankers. Nonetheless, it is the usefulness of a floating exchange rate that we come upon when we ask how a persistent deficit in the external balance can be removed without a wasteful contraction of domestic income, and follow the argument where it leads.

Yet this is by no means to say that a floating exchange rate would make incomes policy needless: on the contrary, incomes policy would be an essential complement of a floating exchange. And this for two reasons. First, it is the great political danger of the floating exchange that it might be taken to remove all checks on cost inflation: no longer could an inflationary rise in the general level of pay be resisted because of the threat to the balance of payments through higher costs, for these, it would be said, would be offset automatically by a depreciation of the exchange rate. With this, secondly, goes the danger of a vicious spiral, in which a high rate of rise of pay leads to a fall in the exchange rate, which raises the price of imports and the cost of living, and this in turn prompts claims for a further rise in pay. The removal of a deficit in the balance of payments can never be painless, for – save insofar as it can be provided for out of the annual increase in production – it means a reduction of the resources available in the home market. When the deficit is removed by a fall in the exchange rate, the reduction of resources imposes itself in great part by way of a rise in the price of imports. In modern economies that rise may have to go a long way – for price is only one of the factors on which the volume of imports and exports depends. As the articles traded have become more elaborate and more dependent for their appeal on their design, and as the promotion of trade has come to require more investment in sales effort, stocks and service, changes in the volume of imports and exports have shown persistent trends. The changes in prices required to remove an external deficit, whether by promoting exports or checking imports, may therefore have to be big; and where imports enter substantially into consumption, the cost of living may have to be pushed up sharply. If the improvement is to be maintained, money incomes must not rise correspondingly. There as elsewhere, the movement of those incomes requires to be guided by a policy that has regard to the many-sided needs and prospects of the economy.

V

There remains one observation of particular relevance to Australia. At several points I have urged the usefulness, even the indispensability, of a national incomes policy in meeting problems arising on the side of the external balance. The prime function of that policy is to avoid cost inflation in economies that maintain full employment and mean to go on maintaining it, so that firms in the aggregate have no reason to resist inflationary rises in pay on the ground that higher costs will reduce their profit margins or their sales. The requirements of the policy are mainly two: the participation, in the reaching of particular decisions, of a spokesman of the common interest; and an understanding of the grounds on which decisions are reached. I wish at the last to state my belief that both those requirements are met, more fully than through the institutions of most other countries, by the conciliation and arbitration system of Australia. For this provides for the participation in major decisions about pay of a third party, concerned both to do justice to the cases put forward by the two sides and to see the particular award in the context of the needs and prospects of the whole economy; while the public hearings, and the deliverance of reasoned judgements, serve to inform opinion, and gain acceptance for the awards. It may be an accident of history that long before the need for a national incomes policy was apprehended, Australia came to adopt procedures so propitious to one; but that they should now be available to meet the needs of the hour seems to me a precious legacy of their history to the Australian people.

34

Income inflation in Australia

Ronald F. Henderson[1]

1971 will go on record as the year in which the general public in Australia began to worry about cost inflation or income inflation as I prefer to describe it. This concern was expressed clearly in the Commonwealth Treasurer's budget speech; unfortunately the action taken in the budget did not correspond, for it was aimed at further restraint of demand which was already sagging below the level of full employment. In public discussion it is now understood that the 1971 variety of inflation is significantly different from previous bouts, in that this time the general level of demand, profits, and activity are not very high as they have been on previous occasions pulling prices up. Indeed the use of the term "stagflation" to describe the 1971 situation is becoming common to indicate the combination of a stagnant level of activity combined with a rapid rise of prices.

The problem of cost inflation is not really economic; it's more difficult than that; it is social and political. It is another variant of a very old political problem how to prevent a pressure group, whose interests are immediately and obviously affected, from prevailing over the greater interest of the whole of the community. In the United States recently it has been how to prevent the well organised militant coal miners' union from wrecking the whole of President Nixon's prices and incomes policy to restrain inflation and reduce unemployment.

But while recognition of the disease is fairly general there is still a long way to go in the difficult process of analysis and discussion of causes and remedies. It is to that discussion that I hope to make a small contribution this evening.

1 Thirty-fourth Joseph Fisher Lecture, 2 December 1971.

My first point is that this income inflation was only recognised in Australia a year after it had been prevalent and carefully documented throughout the rich countries which constituted the membership of OECD in 1970 – USA , Canada, Japan and Western European countries (Australia joined belatedly in 1971). A special report on the subject was published by OECD in December 1970 showing that for the group as a whole the rise in prices in 1970 was 5.5 per cent as compared with an average of 2.6 per cent for the years 1960-65. It was only towards the end of 1969 and in early 1970 that a general acceleration took place throughout the OECD countries. This happened in the absence of strong pressure of demand. Demand was particularly low and unemployment high in both Britain and the United States. In 1969-70 in all these countries except France the share of wages and salaries in national income was rising to well above its long term trend value and profits were being squeezed. As a proportion of national income profits in the United States fell from 12.5 per cent in the period 1955-64 to 9.7 per cent in the first half of 1970. This, of course, is clean contrary to what one expects to happen when a boom is caused by demand inflation.

The first condition I want to draw from international experience is that as this disease is so widespread it is most unlikely that its main cause in Australia is a purely local phenomenon such as the rate of immigration. Yet this is being forcibly suggested by the Institute of Public Affairs. Further consideration suggests that the upsurge of inflation in 1971 cannot really be attributed to long term immigration policy; the inflationary influence of high migration, which is real, is exerted on the demand side through demand for new housing and new factories, not on the cost side. The influence of an inflow of migrants of working age is to moderate rather than aggravate the rate of increase of wages and salaries. Thus a reduction in the rate of migration is not a remedy for income inflation.

Another local phenomenon that has been suggested as a substantial cause of the 1971 inflation is the high level of government expenditure, with the corresponding remedy cut "government expenditure". The main part of the answer to this has been given by Dr. P. J. Sheehan in *The Australian Economic Review*, Issue 3, 1971[2] in which he points out the remarkable stability of government

2 P. J. Sheehan, "In Defence of Public Expenditure", *The Australian Economic Review*, Vol. 3. 1971, pp. 37-44.

expenditure as a proportion of gross national product. For the decade 1959-60 to 1970-71 it averaged 20.4 per cent; for the 1970-71 it was 20.3 per cent. One need only add that there was no upsurge in government expenditure throughout the OECD areas either to account for the upsurge of income inflation on an international scale.

There is not yet a consensus of opinion among economists as to the precise causes of this burst of income inflation. Many I think would agree with professor Meade in his Wincott Memorial Lecture[3] that one reason is that "wage earners have become more conscious of rises in the cost of living and more insistent that it is real wages rather than money wages in which they are interested". Moreover, he continues, "a marked increase in the rate of rise of money wages rates may have given individual trade unions an unexpected glimpse into the very large monopolistic powers which they posses for pushing money wage rates up and which they have not fully exploited in the past. The consequence may have been a basic change in their attitudes. The order of magnitude of what is regarded as a reasonable annual claim may have been more or less permanently changed; and trade union leaders may have become much more acutely aware of their power to obtain concessions through the threat to disrupt basic economic activities."

I would wish to add that this increased awareness of inflation is not confined to wage earners. In Australia it is clearly evident among salary earners such as engineers, teachers and public servants who have also changed their expectations as to a reasonable rate of increase of their money incomes, have made much bigger claims and have succeeded in getting much bigger rise sin money incomes. These rises in incomes, of course, raise costs of production and lead to rises in prices just as rises in wages do. So to control this type of inflation the rate of increase of all incomes – not just of wages – must be reduced. This is the economic justification for an incomes policy as distinct from a wages policy. There is also a social or political justification for an incomes policy; trade unions will certainly not acquiesce in a policy that restrains wages while increases of a thousand dollars a year or more are obtained by judges, doctors and professors.

3 *Inflation the Present Problem.* Reports of the Secretary General OECD. December 1970.

Why has there been this apparently sudden acceleration in the rate of increase of incomes in the rich countries in the past three years? Is this a sudden gust of wind that has blown us of course and can we expect to return to a comfortable situation in which the pursuit of sensible monetary and fiscal policies to prevent over-full employment will be sufficient to prevent prices from rising at more than three per cent per year? If so, all we need, presumably, is some temporary corrective such as a six month income freeze before returning to business as usual. President Nixon in his speech of October 7 introducing phase 2 of his New Economic Policy, with a pay board, a price commission and a cost of living council, said specifically "we will not make controls a permanent feature of American life".

I think this analysis is mistaken, for I believe that the experience of inflation has caused such a change in expectations and modes of action that we cannot hope to get back to the conditions of the early 1960s when inflation could be controlled by monetary and fiscal policy alone. In technical terms I think the Phillips curve has shifted right out and cannot be pushed back by a short term incomes policy. There is no longer a moderate, politically acceptable level of unemployment which will prevent an unacceptable price inflation. On the contrary we have seen in Britain, the United States and are threatened with I Australia the combination of unacceptably large unemployment at the same time as unacceptably rapid inflation.

One important underlying reason for this change is that one generation is succeeding another in the seats where important decisions are taken. Men and women over 50 years of age grew up in a world of stable prices. For many of them, subconsciously perhaps, that is still the normal world from which aberrations occur but to which, with a bit of luck, things will return. So they act accordingly, they put up their prices when they have to, they stick to price stability as long as they can. But that generation is being replaced by a younger one that never knew price stability; for them rising prices are the normal state of things and so they act differently, young professional men adjust their fees to allow for rising prices, young trade union leaders claim larger wage increases, business men expect their costs to rise further and so raise their prices. As this replacement of the generation is completed it will become even more difficult to check inflation.

So I submit that what is needed is not just a temporary set of controls over prices and incomes but something built to last. In the future there must be three main elements in control over the economy, fiscal policy, monetary policy and controls over prices and incomes.

Evidence in support of this view can be culled from European experience. In Britain and in Holland it can be seen in retrospect that "wage freezes" failed because they were temporary. OECD studies of inflation stress that these short run efforts have been disappointing and a broader, longer term approach is needed. The report[4] by the Secretary General of OECD, for instance, states in its conclusions, "The question remains of how in practical terms to make price incomes policy more effective over the longer run".

This conclusion that a structural change has occurred that requires a change in long term policies is reinforced, I think, by careful study of the sequence of events in the 1960s in Britain and in USA In both countries there was growing awareness of the cost inflation problem throughout the period and under the Wilson and Johnson governments. In USA the Council of Economic Advisers set up guideposts for wages and prices and engaged in continuous efforts to prevent wage and price increases greater than these. It is probable that in the years 1962-65 when demand was not excessive these efforts did moderate price increases. They were swept away by the strong demand pressure that developed with the escalation of the Vietnam War. Then with a change of government in 1969 President Nixon abandoned attempts to influence prices and incomes by "jawboning" and resorted to an old fashioned policy of demand restraint. This failed. It created heavy unemployment but prices continued to rise. So in August 1971 the New Economic Policies of price and income control were introduced.

In Britain there was a rather similar pattern with a National Board for Prices and Incomes exerting some pressure on prices and wages under the Wilson government. This was swept away by the Heath government devoted at first, like that of President Nixon, to orthodox restraints of demand as a counter to inflation; but it too failed to cure stagflation by these orthodox measures. After considering

4 *Inflation the Present Problem*. Reports of the Secretary General OECD, December 1970.

a policy of heavy differential taxation on all companies giving wage and salary rises of more than the established norm it shelved this when the Confederation of British Industry introduced a policy of pledges by leading companies not to raise prices by more than 5 per cent over the next 12 months.

Thus in both countries governments initially hostile to any form of prices or incomes policy introduced or welcomed such policies after two years with out them – years of heavy unemployment and rapid rises in prices.

The other protagonists in this drama are the central bankers who have to carry out monetary policy with the aim of restraining inflation without causing too much unemployment. Dr. Arthur Burns, President of the Federal Reserve Board of the United States, has been one of the most persistent and persuasive advocates of some form of prices and incomes policy to supplement fiscal and monetary policy. Others of this persuasion include the Governor of the Bank of Norway who said recently,[5] "An incomes policy is obviously no panacea in itself but is a vitally important supplement to demand management policies. In Norway the expert reports on the effects of alternative wage awards on price developments have proved very helpful. These estimates have been worked out by an expert committee chaired by a prominent economist and with members representing both the trade unions and the employers organisations. A remarkable degree of agreement has been reached and this has probably had some influence in moderating wage and price increases. This, of course, is facilitated by the centralized character of the wage and price negotiations in Norway."

Overseas observers often suggest that Australia has had something like an incomes policy for many years, as the Commonwealth Arbitration Commission gives judgements on wage and salary increases. But the objective of the Commission, as its President has stated clearly, is to preserve industrial peace not to prevent inflation; and it has not prevented inflation. That is and must be the direct responsibility of the government, a responsibility that cannot be discharged simply by giving evidence before the Commission but must be discharged by action.

5 *The Banker*, London, August 1971.

This action must be a long term programme in which monetary, fiscal and incomes policy are co-ordinated.

Thus I disagree with a recent statement by Mr. Snedden who said, "With Australia's system of independent arbitral tribunals a complete incomes policy would be possible only if the Government in its public interest interventions is able to persuade tribunals to make decisions which accord with the established criteria". I do not think this will achieve success. I believe that the government must introduce legislation laying down norms, a permissible range of income increases within which in future the arbitral tribunals must operate. This would be a major change, but I am convinced that major changes in our apparatus of control over the economy are required. Insufficient attention has been paid, I suggest, to the question "In what circumstances has an incomes policy a chance of success?" Clearly it has little or no chance at a time of strong demand inflation as in USA in 1967. What is perhaps not so obvious is that it may well break down if the government is responsible for a severe recession as in Britain in 1971. For in those circumstances wage earners and trade union bodies may flatly refuse to co-operate in any way, and without some such co-operation no incomes policy, statutory or voluntary, can hope to succeed.

So a reasonably high level of demand, activity and employment must be maintained by monetary and fiscal policy without bursting into over-full employment. Australia has had a good record in this respect since 1962.

In such conditions prices will not escalate unless incomes do, but there is no longer any reason to be confident that trade unions and professional bodies will refrain from using their monopoly power to drive up their incomes and cause an income inflation. This must be controlled and is the nub of the problem. In order to achieve acceptance of that control by those affected it may be necessary to erect a control mechanism over prices and dividends, but that mechanism is of secondary importance. It may be sufficient, as has been done in the United States to exercise direct price controls only over a small number of the largest companies. If incomes escalate out of control no control over prices and dividends will be sufficient to check inflation.

Control over incomes must be exercised in both the public and the private sectors of the economy. A norm must be set and should be below the average aimed at in order to leave room for a little upgrading for special reasons. If we estimate productivity per employee to be increasing at two per cent a year and are willing to allow prices to rise at three per cent our target average income rise will be five per cent and our long term norm four per cent. When introducing the policy to reduce unfairness between those who have recently had a rise and those who have not, a three-year base period might be used. Ideally using four per cent this would mean that par would be 12 per cent in the past three years. But such large increases in incomes have been gained in this period that some higher norm will have to be accepted as par and a gradual transition made to the four per cent. Within the public sector it is particularly important that restraint is seen to start at the top with the salaries of the Prime Minister, the cabinet, the judiciary, and senior public servants, and extend downwards as far as the influence of the government extends. This would include the fees of doctors for instance.

To regulate incomes in the private sector it may be useful to have a series of committees with representatives of labour, employers and the government as has been done by President Nixon in stage 2 of his operation. These may help to secure an informed consensus of opinion and to secure voluntary compliance with the norm. But behind this there must be a stiffening of compulsion and sanctions against those who refuse to comply. There are a number of possible methods and the choice in Australia will depend on constitutional and political considerations as well as economic ones. We can, however, distinguish certain characteristics that are common to schemes under discussion. The penalty for non-compliance – arranging for too big an increase in income – may be imposed on either the employer or the employee (theoretically it could be imposed on both but I have not yet heard of such a proposal). The penalty may be prosecution or loss of certain privileges or it may be liability to substantially increased taxation.

Australian experience suggests that attempts to impose legal penalties on large trade unions are unlikely to be effective. Professor Meade has proposed for Britain a modified scheme of penalties which will only apply to strikes in support of a claim judged to be in excess of the norm by an independent tribunal. These include loss of accumulated rights to redundancy payments and charging the cost of supplementary benefits to wives and children of strikers to the trade union or individual concerned. I doubt whether any modification of such measures for Australian conditions would be acceptable. Moreover, such reliance on penalties on employees on strike will only be effective in preventing inflationary wage and salary settlements if the employers resist large claims. A few years ago such resistance could be taken for granted. But this is no longer the case. The most flagrant example in the private sector is the Metal Industries Trades Association acceptance of an increase of $6 a week for tradesmen and $4.50 a week for others awarded on 16 July 1971. This did not even occur at the peak of a boom but at a period of some slack in the economy when unemployment was 30 per cent higher than in the previous year and when we were suggesting in The Australian Economic Review that a stimulus should be given to the economy in the budget.

Thus we must accept the fact that employers can no longer be relied on unaided to resist inflationary claims even when the level of activity in the economy is not excessive. Although this is regrettable it is hardly surprising when no effective steps are taken to restrain even greater increases in the public sector such as a 15 per cent increase in salaries for second division public servants, a big increase for judges and a large increase in doctors' fees.

In these circumstances neither legal penalties nor a tax on employees seem likely to be sufficient to restrain income inflation even if they were politically acceptable.

Professor Weintraub[6] has set out a proposal for using company tax policy to restrain employers from granting wage and salary increases. For Australia this might be modified, on the lines of the 30:20 legislation for insurance companies, to give a tax rebate to those companies which conform to the wage and salary guidelines. The rebate should be substantial, perhaps 20 per cent of company tax, for the object is to secure conformity; it should be tapered so that those who only slightly exceed the norm pay only a slight penalty, "it should be based on total wage and salary payments in each job classification and grade divided by the number of man hours worked in the respective categories and combined into a

6 Sidney Weintraub, "An Incomes Policy to Stop Inflation" *Lloyds Bank Review*, January 1971, pp. 1-12. Henry Wallich and Sidney Weintraub, "A Taxed Based Incomes Policy", *Journal of Economic Issues*, Vol. 5, 1971, pp. 1-19.

weighted index of wage increases".[7] The data are available for such calculations but the administrative burden would be substantial. It would not be worth considering if the problem were thought to be temporary. But if, as I believe, this is a long term problem and the alternatives are substantial unemployment and loss of output or rapid inflation, then the burden of this tax rebate system is well worth shouldering.

Since the penalty will fall on company income it is less likely to be passed on in higher prices than a levy on units produced or labour employed. There is at least a good chance that most companies would try hard to earn the maximum tax rebate by resistance to demands for wage and salary increases above the norm. It is, of course, essential that such a policy in the company sector be buttressed by strict adherence to the norm in the public sector. Of course there will be hard cases, but hard cases make bad law. It is surely fair overall that one norm be applied to all increases in incomes. It is possible, I think, for the taxing power of the Commonwealth Government to be used to restrain inflation in this way. So this is one suggestion for a long term policy.

I am very glad that the Federal Treasurer has now joined in the discussion of income policies in a most interesting address on 18th November. He said, "it has yet to be demonstrated that such a shift has occurred here that our problems are not now amenable to the normal range of policies" and points out that prices incomes policies will seem like unwarranted interference to companies, professional people and wage earners alike.

I suggest that the situation is rather like that which obtained in the 1930s when Keynes was advocating that the government should assume responsibility for maintaining the general level of demand and output in the economy by counter-cyclical fiscal policy. There was strong opposition to that for many years. We have now reached the next phase of development in which, after 30 years of high employment, additional government measures, which do involve interference with the decisions of individuals and companies, are required in order to restrain inflation to an acceptable pace while maintaining a high level of employment and output. I hope we shall not have to wait for a major disaster before we learn this lesson.

7 Wallich and Weintraub, *op. cit.* If this is not done salaries of higher executives can be raised without penalty if some more charwomen are hired to keep down the average wage paid.

35

Political economy and the problems of our times: In defence of general economics

John Vaizey[1]

Despite the eminence which is accorded by our profession (if such it be) to the abstract theorist, it is the general economist who in the long run decides what is the significant theoretical innovation, or points to the inadequacy of accepted theoretical formulations.[2] It is his needs and problems which ultimately determine the shape of the theoretical structure. It is my thesis that we are witnessing today the culmination of some fifty years of radical restructuring of economic theory in the light of radically different problems that the general economist has had to deal with. And while fifty years may seem a long time, it is only the lifetime of one academic, it may be that a long working life is the necessary perspective in which to see the full working out of a new system of ideas. I am not claiming continuous victory for those ideas; a young revolutionary of 1789 looking back on his lifetime in 1848 – a revolutionary year seen as the logical culmination of 1789 – from one point of view would see the Terror, Napoleon, Waterloo, the restoration of the Bourbons and the reign of the Citizen King. That it was a series of uninterrupted victories from any one point of view, only a man who turned his coat as often as Talleyrand could say; most people would be content to say, with the Abbe Sieyes, "*J'ai vécu.*" But, sir, we have come through, and 1789 *did* mark the end of the *ancien regime.*

1 Thirty-fifth Joseph Fisher Lecture, 18 September 1974.

2 This lecture is not intended to be a contribution to the history of economic theory, that is a task I am doubly disqualified for by a lack of reputation as a theorist, and only a partial knowledge of the manuscript sources which would be necessary for an historian. The job that I am particularly trying to do is a different one. It is the need of a general economist, like myself, who is interested now in one thing, and now in another, to judge the state of economic science as a whole.

As general economists we may lock ourselves into one field, as I did with the economics of education, but our claim to competence cannot arise from our specialism alone. A general economist requires a general theory which in some sense must preside over the works of different specialists, whether in industrial or monetary economics, in the economics of transport or econometrics. The training of a general economist, and his function, is neglected at our peril, and those who have done most to advance our discipline – Marshall and Keynes, or Schumpeter and Myrdal – have not only carried economic reasoning to a higher point; they have also been interested in the history of their own subject, its links with the other disciplines, and above all, with the world as it really is and as people have to deal with it. And just by standing a little on tiptoe, by neglecting for a moment the latest article in the latest journal, and looking back at our own professional lifetimes, we may see how the world has changed while we have been looking after our particular interest; it is as though, sleeping on some aircraft, we were to awake and see below us some strangely unfamiliar landscape. In my view, this landscape is the new subject of political economy which has claimed to replace the so-called economic "science" which is now past. It is my view that a false analogy with physical sciences has led us and the world up the garden path. What I shall discuss is the nature of the general theory of economics that links the different parts of our subject. I shall argue the concept of general equilibrium is elegant but unhelpful; and that political economy is inelegant but helpful.

Consider, briefly, the disarray that our subject is in. I will not refer to the hostility that the world bears us for events, like falls in share prices, over which we have as much control as the doctor does over the onset of senility or a meteorologist over the weather. (We can, admittedly make things worse.) I will merely list a few of the topics where a general economist, hired by a government, or a firm, or a newspaper, or by a co-operative of adult students, has to fly by his own bootstraps because the high theorists disagree and hope he will do less harm than another might. I do not denigrate the achievements of our subject; I merely list the problems where the answers are in dispute.

What causes inflation and where will it go to next? Is the Common Market a Good Thing or a Bad Thing? How far can the redistribution of income go without adversely affecting economic growth? Ought school teachers to be paid more or less than skilled carpenters? What ought to be the price of bread? We don't know the answers, or we deny that they are appropriate questions. Yet to all these, and to many other questions, there would have been virtually unanimous replies at the time of Marshall's death, fifty years ago, in the English-speaking world. The exceptions would have been the Marxists, a tiny handful, tenuously in power in Russia; some Thomists, busily providing an ideology for Mussolini; and the German and American historicists. But "true" economists, especially Marshall's slightly less than best pupils, and through them the overwhelming majority of English-speaking economists, would have known all the answers to my questions.[3] Indeed, the test of their professional status would have been to know the answers, as you would expect an anatomist to know where the kneecap is, or a navigator to get to Tasmania rather than New Guinea, if he wishes to. I say "slightly less than best pupils" because Keynes and Sir John Clapham – the only economic historian to have students queueing up to attend his lectures and to be cheered to the echo at the end (how times have changed!) – shared Marshall's doubts, expressed in his appendices, and by small quibbles in the footnotes, about the system, or at least large parts of it.[4]

In the 1930s and 1940s specialists in a range of peripheral subjects, like the theory of wages and of distribution, and various topics in applied economics, including industrial and agricultural economics – peripheral, that is, to the central theoretical topics to which the journals and the ambitious young men addressed themselves, but far from peripheral to general economists and to those who sought their aid – carried on as though nothing had happened. Keynes had put everything into the melting pot, and the process of sorting it all out was – is – still going on. Came the war and the incidental suspension of all free-market economic laws, by rationing, direction of labour, and forced egalitarianism, and after the war the Bourbons returned, to write their textbooks, as though the

3 There were then very few economists. And there were substantial numbers of currency reformers tariff advocates, and socialists, whom Marshall dealt with faithfully in his enormous footnotes. The case for free trade, *laissez-faire* and the gold standard, with Jevon's supply and demand curves, was economics. The rest was heresy.

4 And, two years after Marshall's death, Sir John Clapham's doubts were expressed in his empty economic boxes metaphor. Sraffa prompted Joan Robinson into the overthrow of the theory of competition. Sraffa and Richard Kahn – and above all three million unemployed – had stimulated Keynes into the overthrow of the theory of money and employment. Kalecki and Joan Robinson had done away with distribution theory. All that was left of the economic consensus was the theory of value, increasingly under the assault of those who had doubts about utilitarianism, so Hicks and Allen tried to put economics on a "positive" basis.

Revolution had never been, having learned nothing and forgotten nothing. In the 1950s tranquillity reigned, along with Eisenhower, whilst once more the world economy transformed itself, neglecting to obey economic laws the while. Now, why was there this strange experience?

The answer to this is, I suggest, not a simple one. It is certainly not enough to suggest (what is undoubtedly historically true) that the brand of general equilibrium theory which the fervently anti-statist theorists took to the United States in the late thirties, which missed the Keynesian revolution[5], was successful because it then suited a particular political ideology. Too many socialists, like Anthony Crosland, share it for that to be wholly true. And there are conservatives on the other side, too, including Sir John Hicks. Rather, it seems to me, that in the field of the social sciences there is an almost inextricable welter of ideology and technique, of ends and means. Not only are these disciplines relatively under-developed, but they draw not only upon mathematics, but upon history and philosophy for their techniques, and they are inescapably policy-oriented. To try to abstract from this in a quest for "intellectual purity" seems to me to be understandable but erroneous. Lacking the methods of experimental science, we have no real way of building up a stock of accepted results. But that is, surely, not to say that all non-natural science is not intellectually valid? It is surely possible to have integrity, to try not to fake results, but to be eclectic, as historians are; to blinker your vision as though you were a horse in a classic race is to speed up the attainment of the goal, but to leave the question whether the goal is right or wrong out of consideration. And really, it is the goal which is interesting, as well as the way to it.

I think to identify economics with the present set of techniques is to ignore the fact – for it is a fact – that the bases of our subject are still in dispute, especially as many of us hold that the question of – for example – the measurement of capital, and hence of the concept of capital (and capitalism) is still (to put it mildly) open. To suggest that we hold the views we do is because we are either badly trained or politically committed (or both) may be partly but it cannot be

5 Sir John Hicks in *Value and Capital* broke with Marshall and embraced Walras, which was a major revival of old ideas which fitted, however, American theory in the 1950s, with its assumption that flexible prices guaranteed full employment.

wholly true. The question of what economics is about is not yet settled, nor in my view ever will be. Yet we still refer to ourselves on both sides as "professional economists".

The model of economics that is still widely taught is a fully-employed economy with steady money prices; where there is pure *laissez-faire,* and no government, where competition between small artisans determines supply, and roughly equal and informed consumers – who are immortal, for Time has been abolished, and single because they are solipsists – carefully weigh up their needs, and settle prices by haggling outside the carpenters' huts or the hen runs.[6]

In the 1950s there was a major revulsion, in Cambridge especially, against those ideas because the real problems arose from growth and change – that is time – and the notion of who should get what – that is ethics and justice. In the 1960s the real facts of the real world broke into the academy, and it is this revolution of ideas which is my theme.

Here we are, then, once more at the barricades of our discipline. Even the most reactionary of Bourbons have packed their things for fear of the *sans-culottes*. Professor Hahn so rightly says,

> " . . . the achievements of economic theory in the last two decades are both impressive and in many ways beautiful. But it cannot be denied that there is something scandalous in the spectacle of so many people refining the analysis of economic states which they give no reason to suppose will ever, or have ever, come about . . . It is an unsatisfactory and slightly dishonest state of affairs".[7]

Some may think it is indeed scandalous, and though the achievements of that economic theory are still taught, in many universities it has now been replaced by a new political economy. What is it that has caused this? It is, I suspect,

6 The Keynes theory of employment was, initially at least, accepted. But his theory of money, wages and prices was not. "Pure" theory was revived on the basis of a Walrasian system of general equilibrium, with no time, and with perfect knowledge. This cut it off automatically from real problems of society – which is what the subject is about, according to the political economists.

7 Professor Frank Hahn, quoted in John Kenneth Galbraith's *Economics and the Public Purpose*, p. 27, footnote 4. It is from Hahn's Presidential Address to the Econometric Society.

the return of commonsense as it was found that the conclusions of neo-classical economics seemed increasingly paradoxical to ordinary intelligent citizens. It is also a theoretical consolidation of a high order, which I shall attempt to spell out.

But before we get to that point I must deal with the Bourbon restoration, and for that story I must turn to some recent extraordinarily interesting publications by Professor Harry Johnson. It is perhaps easier to take these lesser, casual publications as a topic for discussion than Professor Johnson's assuredly more technical articles, because they raise directly what the technical articles only raise by implication, namely what subject it is that Professor Johnson says we are all professing. I have no doubt that Professor Johnson represents precisely and fairly the point of view of a large group of economists, who regard what they do as economic science and what the others do as drivel. "Economics has been undergoing a research revolution", Professor Johnson writes[8], and he refers to the "demonstrable superiority" of "the new techniques of mathematical analysis and econometrics, as contrasted with the social wisdom and philosophizing that characterised the older style of 'political economy'." "Economics shifted from an orientation towards 'political economy' to an orientation towards 'economic science'; and the essence of science is research . . . the application of known . . . techniques to the solution of suitable problems . . . which . . . may not be of general social interest." Johnson attributes this shift to a dominance of the US graduate schools. That dominance was due to the vast availability of graduate awards in the US for American and foreign students, in the late 1940s and early 1950s; the coherence and rationality of graduate training programmes in the US; and the exhaustion and demoralisation of postwar Europe.

In his Encounter article Johnson describes his own departure from Cambridge as he "began to appreciate the difference between scientific and ideological motivations for theoretical work." "Keynesian economics", in Cambridge, "was not a theoretical advance . . . it was only a tool for furthering left-wing politics". This is an extremely serious charge, and one that is often made. It is that "the intellectual poverty of English economics" is due to "a mistaken belief that to prove capitalism to be logically impossible is sufficient to dispose

8 "Cambridge in the 1950s", *Encounter*, XLII, I January 1974.

of its existence."[9] In contradiction to this group of Lysenko-ish ideologues, squabbling in an environment of intellectual and physical poverty – "no coal, and they managed also to contrive a shortage of bread" . . . "English public licensing hours are rather barbarous" . . . "bitterness" . . . "you can be as incompetent as you want to be" . . . "material poverty" . . . and so on – Johnson describes a group of competent, hardworking scientists who are using known techniques to advance the truth. In the United States, we are told, "a professor is not a member of the national élite" (Kissinger?), he lives in "a fairly self-contained world, within which entry and promotion are fairly strictly governed by academic standards." The United States has "a long tradition of explicit and organised programs of graduate instruction . . . in which the program adapts itself . . . to the incorporation and transmission of new developments in the field . . . an orientation towards techniques and research comes more naturally to the US than to the European scholar" and so on. In the US economists share "the general freedom of the public to disagree with its government"[10] – a freedom presumably lacking in the United Kingdom and Australia – and "as a result of this freedom, the most impressive characteristic of the economic profession in the United States is its consistently high quality." Johnson correctly points out that a concern with "research is an extremely modern phenomenon in the history of the academic community . . . up to modern times, what was valued was knowledge or 'scholarship'."

Towards the end of his article Johnson concedes that "the possibilities of acquiring useful knowledge by further research along scientifically respectable. . . lines will play out, and . . . the world will discover that what it needs, after all, are political economists and not economic scientists."

9 This belief he attributes to a Marxist, Maurice Dobb, and to Joan Robinson – who "was not recognisable as a female of the species and did not behave like one" – and Richard Kahn, who conspired against the "shy and gentle" Dennis Robertson, who was "incapable of standing up in public and defending himself." Robertson was a sophisticated academic, who, far from being incapable of standing up in public, had been President of the Union, President of the ADC, a senior civil servant, an army officer on active service, who at first regarded Harry Johnson as a sinister influence. What Robertson was frightened of was poverty, and, most clever and charming of men, he lived frugally.

10 Paul Sweezy's comments would be relevant at this point. There have been no "loyalty" oaths in England since the abolition of the laws against dissenters, Catholics and Jews over a century ago, which even then were rarely enforced, and only applied to the House of Commons and Oxford and Cambridge.

That is, indeed, the point of this lecture. I think social wisdom is as important as equations. Let me at once concede that, despite the unfortunate tone and factual errors of Johnson's article, there is much in what Johnson says. It is easier for clever people to debate than to do research. And there is a degree of absolute ignorance about so many matters that is inexcusable. If I may I will give three instances from my own autobiography. The first concerns education, the second the Irish famine and the third the British steel industry. I shall try to show how various interpretations are possible, but that the facts tend to suggest extremely complex answers to difficult questions.

Education first. Perhaps I should explain the points at issue. In the early 1950s the perennial problems of the British economy were attributed by the *Economist* newspaper, by economists like John Jewkes and Lionel Robbins, and by H. G. Johnson (in *The Overloaded Economy*), as due to excess demand, partly due to the welfare state with its substantial increase in public expenditure. Abel-Smith and Titmuss, in a report to the Guillebaud Committee on the Cost of National Health Service, showed that the NHS had not added greatly to the proportion of the GNP devoted to health, but had redistributed its benefits and economised in its use of resources. In *The Costs of Education* (London 1958) I showed that the same was true of education and, moreover, that the benefits of the public education system went proportionately more to the better-off. It was also necessary to refute the theory held by the more sophisticated – that education expenditure was demographically determined. (This heresy is now returning. It seems to be a feature of economic crises and the reactions to them.)

At the same time, Chicago sought to argue that people chose different sorts of education because of their evaluation of their discounted life-time earnings. This ignored much sociological research. But it was necessary for them to (a) prove that the labour market "worked", and (b) that "human capital" – a central part of the new neo-classical formulation – was not a mere metaphor (as Marshall had asserted). These matters are examined in Vaizey, Norris and Sheehan, *The Political Economy of Education* (London 1972).

I was also concerned to examine the actual role of education in economic and social change and development. This could not be argued a priori, but had to be examined case by case. Chicago, on the other hand, took the view that "investment in man" could be subjected to the same criteria as capital projects – the cost of educating a person being equivalent to buying a machine. The trouble with all this was an absence of facts.

When I took up the economics of education nobody knew how many British children were at school – the official estimates were half a million out – and the accepted view was that the slump of 1931 had caused disastrous cuts in expenditure. Laborious research, including the calculation of outlays and the construction of price indices, showed that from 1931 to 1934 a combination of falling prices and a reduction in the number of children caused per capita real expenditure on education to rise. In my view, the "human capital" argument was unnecessary, on the principle of Occam's razor.

Ireland next. The accepted explanation of the Irish famine of 1845 to 1850, 20 years ago, was that the English landlords extracted the surplus from their Irish tenantry in specie and spent it in London. By months of going through dusty and uncatalogued documents in the basements of Guinness's brewery I was able to show that this was not the case. The famine was the result of the collapse of a virtually moneyless economy in the interior of Ireland as a direct result of the post-Napoleonic war deflation, consequent upon the revaluation of the Irish pound, in the maritime sector. This is now the "accepted" explanation of the Famine which the clever young men are attacking. My argument, it will be seen, rests upon simple supply and demand. So much, I hope, for the charge that we eschew ordinary economic tools. In the Irish case, the error was nationalism. The accepted view was that the Union of the Parliaments in 1801 was designed to kill Ireland's nascent industries, condemning the Irish to a marginal, subsistence economy. The Guinness documents showed a great growth of prosperity between the mid-1790s and 1815. This coincided with the devaluation of the Irish pound. The postwar slump coincided with (a) a reduction in military expenditure in Ireland and (b) a very substantial revaluation of the Irish pound, as F. W. Fetter and F. G. Hall pointed out. At this time, the maritime sector contracted. In the view that Patrick Lynch and I took (*Guinness's Brewery in the Irish Economy*, 1859-1876, Cambridge University Press, 1962), the famine resulted chiefly from this fact and was – as a Marxist historian, Strauss, had suggested – the death throes of a subsistence economy which was contiguous to a commercial economy. The Irish emigrants added greatly to the reserve army in Scotland, England, America and Australia. Irish landlords, continuously hard up, were exploiters, but on a most petty scale. The Guinnesses were the first wealthy Irish family, and not until the late 1860s.

In this case, there were three "explanations" – nationalist, *laissez-faire* and Marxist.

Lastly steel.[11] The issues are indeed serious. In the Brewing Industry 1886-1951 (London 1960) I had already demonstrated that profit maximisation was not a realistic description of business motivation, and that the mix of political and economic considerations in industrial policy was inextricable. The issues in steel were: (a) the technological superiority of Germany and America; (b) tariffs; (c) location; (d) home based and foreign ores; (e) the level of investment. It is now clear that the joint-stock banks controlled the industry; that from 1929 the Bank of England had clear and strong policies; that agreement with the Bank's views was essential for promotion to the chairmanship of a major steel firm; that these steel firms had operated as a cartel from (at least) 1910. All this determined their approach to government, and to location and price policy. It does not make "supply and demand" wrong; but it utterly changes their context. The British steel industry has been nationalised twice and the debates between the free enterprisers – what Keynes called the lazy fairies – on the one hand and the centralisers on the other have been acrimonious, both at the political and the so-called scholarly level. As I read through literally thousands of forgotten documents about the steel industry in the past sixty years, I discovered that in 1930 an American consultant, Colonel Brassert, had written a six page secret report for Montagu Norman, the Governor of the Bank of England, which formed the basis of the next forty years' structure of the steel industry. The political and – more relevant to our purpose – the academic debates on pricing, location and investment were almost entirely irrelevant. It had all been decided by Colonel Brassert. The logic of inertia explained a great deal.

These three examples show that I emphatically agree with Professor Johnson on the need for research in our scholarly discipline. It seems to me that research may mean what I have just illustrated. Or it may mean a string of mathematical

11 *The History of British Steel*, London 1974.

theorems from *a priori* assumptions, which are not derived from any appropriate real problems. The assumptions are convenient for that particular mathematical reasoning. Now, it is far dirtier, and more difficult, to build up a plausible story, which makes some kind of sense, from the complexities and realities of the world as it is. This is what an historian means by research. In other words, we have to have the courage to be rough and ready if we are to try to tell the truth about reality.

Let all Johnson's claims be conceded. But a central question remains. What is this science that leads to all this research? This science that is clean and true, like the hero of some Edwardian novel. Why does Joan Robinson's remark that economic theory is difficult since economies which are not capitalist have come into being since it was invented still rouse Johnson's ire? And, if this clean and true discipline is indeed a science, why are all its results entirely predictable? There are two senses of predictable. If the scientists are right about the atom, then on a given day Hiroshima will blow up. But I can also teach my pet parrot to say "marginal productivity" every time it opens its mouth. Neo-neo-classical economics is just not predictable in the first sense, the sense in which a weather forecaster, with enough data to hand, can predict rain in the next few hours, but predictable in the second sense. One must pressingly ask why is *scientific* economics, as defined, so predictably pro-market, so predictably oriented to a particular set of policy prescriptions? If "intellectual purity" means a deductive axiomatic system, it is not a science, natural or historic a science requires (by definition) an empirical content. That is the reason, I think, why neo-neo-classical economics is widely regarded, not as a pure science, but as inherently apologetic: a dogma.

Now, then, is economics a "science"? This raises directly the question of what is a professional economist and what is not? I will not try to evade the question by the obvious positivist answer that an economist is somebody who is hired to be an economist, or recognised as such by the Royal Economic Society or the American Economic Association. I am trying to suggest a deeper question and answer. At any time those who study a subject may be divided into three: those – by far the greater number – who study the subject for an examination and then leave it; a second group who will carry on with the subject as practitioners, and as teachers and as researchers, whom we may call the professionals and who add to knowledge; and a third group who will ask really new questions. Now only in the second and third groups will an intellectual revolution be successfully achieved;

and since most people are intensely conservative about most things – from eating to sex – only a few even in the third group will question the bases of the subject. It is easy to see, therefore, why a subject carries on along railway lines, even when new discoveries are being made which suggest that a trek across country will be more interesting. Progress is bound to be fastest on railway lines. But occasionally the need for a reformation of the subject is so great that it affects all three groups. The need arises either from intellectual incoherence, or from pressures to answer questions that the subject refuses to acknowledge. These pressures have been present since the great slump, and are redoubled by the current economic crash.

Both intellectual incoherence, and new questions ignored, have been charges levelled at economics. We are obliged to answer many questions from the world of affairs by saying that a major part of the answer lies in the territory assigned to other disciplines. Take inflation as an example. There are two main sorts of explanations of inflation. One is the monetarist and the other is that it is ultimately the consequence of wage-fixing arrangements under full employment. Both sets of explanations are "economic", though the wage-fixing argument is suspect to "scientific" economists, and – *nota bene* – for its validity it depends upon a series of statements about the behaviour of trades unionists which are derived from what might be conventionally regarded as non-economic disciplines. But that is equally true of the "monetary" explanation, which is more orthodox in economic terms. If monetary mechanisms were to be effective in controlling inflation they would require quite specific political and social conventions – viz. that government did not seek to intervene in the economy in the way that governments have been intervening in the economy for the past 35 years, and that the trade unions did not seek to overthrow the political structure in order to force governments to resume their interventionist techniques, in the face of widespread unemployment. In other words, even the "purest" economic doctrine, that of the monetarists, not only assumes a given framework of social and political institutions, but is explicitly concerned with preserving them in a particular form.

This fact, for so I take it to be, is openly acknowledged by Professor Milton Friedman, whose stated – and in my view wholly praiseworthy – concern is with the need to avoid coercive relationships. He is an old-fashioned liberal with a highly specified moral and political position. His economics, for which I have a great deal of respect, is derived directly and explicitly from the Austrian general equilibrium school. This model is not in any sense value-free except when it is wholly formal. That is a point Professor Hahn has frequently made. There is no instance (that I have seen, at any rate) where the policy prescriptions are not predictable, in their general tenor, from the political and ethical predilections of the economist who undertakes the analysis. I do think this is an important point because if it is valid, the movement from a formal model to a situation where it is intended that a description of reality should be relevant, either to policy or to academic study, is inescapably "dirty". In that sense, then, a "clean" social science is impossible except in the wholly trivial sense that a formal model is bound to be neutral, since it assumes (explicitly) that it is neutral, in the sense of not being "about" anything. This is relevant to the notion of positive economics as a discipline that is "scientific" in the non-political sense. (I shall argue that it is possible to be "scientific" as historians and literary critics are – though the words "scholarly" and "dispassionate" may be better).[12]

Several questions immediately arise. The first is why a theory which some would claim has been discredited should not only have survived but still be flourishing. That might suggest that it has not been discredited. The second is whether or not it matters that theory and practice have so markedly diverged. That is a matter of common observation. The third is what the "correct" theory might be. In the 114 years since Soapy Sam Wilberforce was acidly rebuked by

12 Galbraith argues that one of the purposes of the preoccupation of the self-styled "pure" economists with this abstraction is in order to divert attention from the real world. He suggests that this diversion is not as unconscious as the amiable eccentricity of many of the economists concerned would lead us to believe; it serves the interests of those who wish their behaviour not to be thoroughly examined. He then begins a root and branch examination of the working of the modern American economy, pointing out that the consumer society depends for its functioning upon the subordinate role of the housewife, and that any change in the status of women would require a fundamental re-evaluation of the nature and process of consumption. He then points out that the major part of the economy is dominated by large firms which plan their own output and set their own prices at reasonably low levels, and that by a system of interlocking contracts they impose some degree of stability upon that part of the economy (predominantly the manufacturing sector) which they control. Furthermore, they exercise this power of planning partly through government agencies, with which they also have close and sometimes – though not necessarily – wicked relationships. The market sector consists of small firms in peripheral activities, chiefly in agriculture and the service industries, and as Professor Galbraith points out, in art. In this area of the economy, according to Galbraith, the level of wages, of conditions, is generally low. This reverses the normal findings of competitive theory that monopoly leads to inefficiency and competition leads to efficiency, and a great deal of his book is devoted to a survey of this particular paradox. Professor Galbraith says "The neo-classical model describes an ill that does not exist because it assumes a purpose that is not pursued." *Economics and the Public Purpose*, J. K. Galbraith (London: Andre Deutsch, 1974), p. 120.

Huxley for his vulgar attack on Darwinism, theology has ceased to be intellectually respectable in the great majority of the world's intellectual centres, and religious practice has become a fringe activity.[13] But religion has been a long time a-dying and since Joan Robinson's great grandfather, F. D. Maurice, was unseated for heresy, a great deal of water has flowed under the religious bridge. (The reflection is appropriate for it was at about that time that the theory of value began to go on the wrong road. His point was that he did not believe in eternal damnation; her point is that she does not believe in eternal economic truths.) For the purposes of exposition, I intend to take Joan Robinson's work as a basis of an interpretation of the present state of political economy, and to assume that there is an alternative view of economics to the neo-classical, that is intellectually respectable. The forty years of Mrs. Robinson's work touches on many themes; but constant among them is the view that neo-classical economics, and its offspring neo-neo-classical economics, has had bad practical and intellectual consequences.[14]

What, then is the new political economy? It arises from an increasingly critical view of the post-Jevons school, of general equilibrium, and proposes the establishment of a line from Ricardo, Marx and Marshall, through Keynes and Kalecki, to a modern economics which deals with genuine problems rather than with a series of simplified pseudo-problems, like those of Robinson Crusoe on his desert island dividing his time between fishing and picking up coconuts, or of a man faced with a series of choices between more rum and fewer cigarettes, or more cigarettes and fewer glasses of rum. The problems to which we want to know the answers are why tenant farmers earn more than milkmen; why so many people in Calcutta are starving and out of work; why modern governments

13 I refer to the 1860 meeting of the British Association where Huxley said he would rather be descended from the apes than degrade his intelligence by ignoring inconvenient truths.

14 It may be thought that because Mrs. Robinson is a woman, a vegetarian, a student of Marx (though not a Marxist), and an emeritus professor, her views are academic to the point of eccentricity, but any such patronising doubts, frequently expressed though they are, are designed to keep their students ignorant of the body of her work. She was the first British economist to show the irreconcilability of competitive doctrines with the facts of mass manufacturing industry with its economies of scale, she was a central person in the debates that led to Keynes's *General Theory* (as the recent Royal Economic Society volumes demonstrate) and her *Essays in Employment* drew attention to the implications of the new doctrines for inflation, international trade and regional policy. When Russia was all the rage and socialism on the up and up, she was the only serious intellectual critic of Marxist economic doctrines. She was first in the field in the now fashionable study of developing countries. She got to China before Kissinger. And now her views on wages and prices are the new orthodoxy. Not a bad record for relevance, it might be thought.

cannot control prices – all real questions, to which it is doubtful whether any a priori answers, couched in loose generalisations based on the accepted forms of Robinson Crusoe economics, will be adequate. The nature of the new economics is rooted therefore in relevance and direct observation of economic and social life, and not in the erection of formal models. Its central points are simple. An historical process cannot be understood in terms of mechanical equilibrium, and it is necessary to take account of the social, political and economic characteristics of the system to which the analysis is being applied.

It is perhaps not inappropriate to remark in parenthesis that the association of neo-classical economics with the defence of capitalism, and the identification of Cambridge economics with the defence of socialism, is accidental. Mrs. Robinson's socialist convictions have probably hindered the acceptance of her economics, even by socialists, who have felt that their hearts must not lead their heads into error. Paradoxically, therefore, a socialist like Anthony Crosland will embrace an old fashioned economics, out of intellectual puritanism. There is an historical link, of course, with the development of an ideology of the Cold War, on both sides, but (formally) the theoretical problems would arise in any case, and so would the practical questions as to what should be produced by whom and who should get it, and the basic reasoning of the neo-classicals is either faulty or not, regardless of whose side you are on.[15]

The answer to the first question, then – why should an empty theory flourish – may possibly be that it is at last ceasing to do so, and that it is common for theories to flower after their roots have died. But the second question is a more difficult one. Does it matter that theory and practice should diverge? Christian morality continues, after all, though God is dead. But surely it does matter, first, for the cause of rationality itself, for the cause of the cultivated intelligence, that a subject like economics, which is about something, should continue to be so, and secondly, for the world at large, it is better to act on an understood basis of what is the case than on hunch. The declared irrelevance of economic theory is obvious to

15 But the flourishing of the neo-neo-classical theory is undoubtedly deeply related to the political condition of the West; its present decline may also be associated with the faltering of the West. This would seem too simple an answer, which must surely lie far more in the sociology of thought; but it is probably not entirely incorrect.

a Marxist – it is part of its purpose to mask reality – but it must sadden those who prefer reason to unreason in human affairs. The important matter is not so much to get the correct answers but to find out where and how to look for the answers. What is the central feature of the new economics? We may take as a key text some concluding remarks of J. de V. Graaff in his Theoretical Welfare Economics:

> "any . . . 'objective' test . . . is itself in the last resort an act of faith, based on fundamentally ethical notions . . . it is sufficient to remark that more people would probably agree on the dividing line between the factual and the ethical, or on what constitutes an 'objective' test and what does not, than would agree on the ethical matters themselves . . .
>
> "No doubt many professional economists are reluctant to abdicate what they may like to regard as their traditional prescriptive role, and are uneasy at the prospect of becoming mere purveyors of information. If they are, it is up to them to show how welfare economics can be set upon a basis which is even reasonably satisfactory – or can be made to yield conclusions with which a significant number of men are likely to concur."[16]

At the level of high theory, the key assertion of the new synthesis lies in the denial of any general theory of value. It is argued that Sraffa has resolved Ricardo's puzzles, and put the rate of profits (a key element in economic theory) on a new basis. The reason why profits is the clue is simple. Profits are the petrol in the engine of the system. Without profits it won't go. But are profits a return for effort, ingenuity and so on (as some undoubtedly are), or a surplus, whose size depends upon certain social conventions which the Marxists would refer to as the degree of exploitation?

It is on this issue of profits that the argument stands or falls. "It destroys" Robinson argues "the presumption that the rate of profit measures the contribution of investment to national income" . . . "we must look somewhere else to determine the laws which regulate the distribution of the produce of each among the Glasses of the community."[17]

---

16 J. de V. Graaff, *Theoretical Welfare Economics* (Cambridge University Press, 1957), pp. 167-8, 170 and 171.
17 Joan Robinson, *Collected Economic Papers*, Volume IV (Oxford: Basil Blackwell, 1973), p. 120.

In the new world, there are technical relationships between land and labour (the subject is agriculture), and the distribution of the work and the crop depends on different kinds of ownership and custom, which in turn affects the kinds of technical relationships adopted. In industry, there are capital goods (instead of land), and the distribution of goods depends on the level of profits in relation to money wages. The point is the double nature of 'capital' as finance and as equipment. The general level of output (whose shares are determined by the property relationships and customs just discussed) is determined by effective demand. Technical change occurs, and affects demand. There is then a realistic description of the way prices are deter mined, in different markets, where prices of commodities like wool and minerals fluctuate according to supply, demand and expectations, while prices of manufactured goods tend to be fixed in respect of demand but to vary with costs, which output varies with demand. The argument is then able to return to the rate of profit, and to the determination of relative incomes.

There is an interesting series of studies that give some understanding of what actually determines the character of public expenditure. So, too, there are descriptions of financial institutions, and fascinating studies of the growth of firms, industries and nation states, in an historical (rather than a static) perspective.

As the third and final section of the recent textbook by Robinson and Eatwell[18] makes clear, the new economics is opposed to all-embracing attempts to explain the complexities of the real world in which time irresistibly moves onward. The chief complaint about the older system was its universality and timelessness. Each society, each age, has its economic system. Each system has its own contradictions and its own harmonies. The harmonies can be discovered and formulated. The error is to regard the necessary contradictions as transient flaws to be eradicated or patched up. Further, of course, economics is only a part of life, and it is what goes on in such matters as nationalism, race, social conflict, war, religion and the discussion of the good life which affects not only the way people think about economics, but the way economic agents actually act.

18 Joan Robinson and John Eatwell, *An Introduction to Modern Economics* (Maidenhead: McGraw-Hill, 1973).

"Cambridge" economics, the body of doctrine chiefly embraced by the attackers, derives from Ricardo, Marx, and Marshall, via Keynes and Sraffa. It has in turn been subject to three major assaults: first, from the neo-classicals because its value premises are often explicitly built into it; secondly, because it is thought to be wholly destructive, and "something has to be taught" – which is the equivalent of teaching people to count angels on pinheads when you no longer believe in the heavenly host; and, thirdly, because it has seemed to be socialist in tone, direction and intention. This last accusation is contingently true; almost all of those who now expound Cambridge economics would call themselves socialists. (But it is an accusation, or statement, which turns itself against those who use it, of course).

Certain major conclusions seem to emerge. The first is that in many respects this economics adopts the sort of position in the social sciences which has been adopted by analytical and linguistic philosophy in philosophy, that is to say, it has by a process of ruthless criticism, to the satisfaction of those who share its findings, destroyed a vast metaphysical construction. Its answer to those who enquire "what do we believe in?" is highly specified for the person who answers. But it will not present a body of agreed doctrines since it regards such a question as not being the sort of question that philosophy as such exists to answer. The parallel in economics is that the economist would be expected to have a general solution for every problem, drawn from a book of rules, whereas the political economist would say, "we have to proceed by the careful examination of individual cases, and it is improbable that there are many general principles that can be deduced. Certainly, it is unlikely that the general principles can be applied pure and simple to the complexities of real life."

The Cambridge theory, therefore, in a sense is a much more realistic and positive theory than that which it says it supersedes.[19] If economics were to be reconstructed around the central questions of a modern functioning economy, it presumably would have to be organised on the basis of first of all a pragmatic understanding of government activities, since government activities form a large part of the operation of a modern economy; secondly, the determination of relative prices and incomes in the context of modern fiscal policy; thirdly, the

19 See J. A. Kregel, *The Reconstruction of Political Economy* (London: Macmillan, 1973).

international monetary system and its connection with the domestic banking and financial system; and fourthly, a detailed consideration of the process of technological change and innovation; and fifthly, the relation of all this to individual consumption of all kinds in the field supplied by "private" industry and the social services. It is a form of sensible pragmatism, and in that respect closely resembles modern medicine before the invention of antibiotics. It indeed represents the position long held and strenuously advocated by Lord Balogh, for example, that you would start from an interpretation of government economic activity, and proceed with questions such as what determines the exchange rate and changes in the exchange rate, and carry on from there. Since this is what economists who work for the government and business and newspapers actually do, is there any real reason why this is where economic theory should not start?

36

Comparing the Industries Assistance Commission and Jackson Committee approaches to industrial development

G. Alf Rattigan[1]

Because the Jackson Committee states that its emphasis is on "procedural strategy as the means of progress on industry policy", I will first discuss the procedural aspects.

There are some basic issues which are of fundamental importance in determining any procedures for the formulation of advice on Government assistance for the development of industry.

The benefits provided by the assistance measures tend to be concentrated on "relatively small areas of industry" and on a relatively small number of people. On the other hand, the costs of these measures are widely spread throughout the community, and are difficult for individuals to assess. In fact, many taxpayers, consumers and users are not aware that they are contributing to assistance to particular industries. The concentration of the benefits and the diffusion of costs have resulted in the relatively small number of beneficiaries being better organised and more able to articulate their case than the much larger number of people who bear the costs. Furthermore, the provision of "discriminatory" industry assistance has important long term significance for the distribution of the community's income and for the efficiency with which the community's resources are used and consequently for the long term welfare prospects for the nation as a whole.

1 Thirty-sixth Joseph Fisher Lecture, 1 November 1976.

These considerations are often not considered by interests seeking – or opposing – "the provision of specific assistance measures" because these interests are usually concerned only with their own short to medium position, rather than with the long term welfare effects on the nation.

Because of the varying degrees of influence of the conflicting interest groups and of the long term welfare consequences of the specific assistance measures, formulation of advice on assistance for the development of industry should have the following characteristics: (1) the process should be independent, even-handed and impartial and "should be seen" to be so; and (2) the process should bring into account all the costs and benefits of the proposed assistance measures on the community as a whole.

I will now explain more fully the importance of each of these characteristics.

An independent, even-handed and impartial process

The large benefits which they can obtain through "measures of industry assistance" provide the incentive for particular interests to seek decisions in their favour by bringing strong – and usually non-public – pressure to bear on administrations. The problems inherent in expecting "non-independent government agencies" to tender impartial advice (or make impartial decisions) on such matters were described by the Hoover Commission in the United States in the following terms:

> "The wide latitude inherent in effective regulation opens the door to favoritism (and unfairness) in administration. The regulated interests are powerful and often politically influential. The privileges which the regulatory agencies can grant (or withhold) are often of great value, and the regulation will obviously have a tremendous impact on the profits, services and finances of the industry involved. This combination of wide discretion on the part of officials and strong motives 'for influencing the officials' on the part of the regulated industry, involve serious risks of corruption (and unfairness).
>
> "Thus, in the interests of fairness to the individuals concerned, the attainment of the public objectives and the maintenance of the integrity of government, there is a vital necessity for assuring that

such regulatory agencies are insulated from partisan influence (or control) to the maximum extent feasible."

The independence of the agency providing advice is thus a pre-condition to the impartiality of such advice.

Further pre-conditions to the independence (and impartiality) of such advice are that the process should provide the maximum opportunity for participation by all interested parties and that the whole process should be open to the maximum public scrutiny. Public scrutiny is essential to; (1) guarantee that all parties in the process enjoy parity, and that all interests represented are alike in influence and importance; (2) ensure that the views of particular groups are exposed to the critical scrutiny of all persons who may have an interest in the outcome of the inquiry; and (3) guarantee to the government (and the community) that the agency carrying out the inquiry (and providing the advice) is itself impartial and free from bias or favour.

Finally, public scrutiny has an important bearing on the qualitative nature of the advisory process. The government can only be assured that it is receiving the "highest quality analysis and advice" from its advisory agency if that analysis (and advice) is exposed to the critical view of all interested persons. Public "analysis and criticism" ensures that the advice given to government is accurate, based on correct premises and deals comprehensively with the effects of implementing that advice.

A comprehensive and well-informed process

The provision of advice on assistance measures must be based on an analysis of what long term effects the assistance measures would have, not only on the recipient industry and the people in it, but also on those groups who would have to provide the assistance, those industries which would have to compete with the recipient industry for resources, and the welfare of the nation as a whole.

It is, therefore, essential that advice to the government on industry assistance be provided, not only after independent and impartial public scrutiny of the various facts and arguments, but also within the framework of: (1) a programme of general research into factors likely to influence the future development of industries; (2) detailed "inter-industry studies" which show the effect of such assistance on other industries; (3) arrangements to facilitate adjustment to changes in assistance for the industries (and persons) affected by such changes; and (4) a clear (and unambiguous) set of assistance criteria based on generally agreed long term economic and welfare objectives.

Features of the IAC procedures

The IAC procedures have been carefully framed, in co-operation with a wide cross section of the community, to give independent, impartial and comprehensive advice to the government by means of a process which is as open as possible to public participation and to public scrutiny.

I will not detail the procedures[2] – most of you probably are reasonably familiar with them. I will simply emphasise two points: (1) the Commission extends the principle of public scrutiny to its own work. The opportunity is given to all interested persons to examine and comment on the analysis the conclusions and the recommendations of the Commission before the reports are finally settled. This is achieved by publishing draft reports and subsequently holding a public hearing; and (2) the Commission's inquiry procedures and its research programme are kept under constant review with a wide cross section of the community. This is achieved through regular meetings with a consultative group on which all sectors of industry and the trade unions, the welfare organisations and the consumer groups are represented.

Procedures proposed by the Jackson Committee

The principle on which these procedures are based is expressed in the Committee's report in the following terms:

> "In practice, it would plainly be best, when a major policy problem arises in a particular industry, for representatives of the union and the firms involved to confer with representatives of the governments concerned to devise an approach reasonably acceptable to all and to the public interest."

2 The important features of the IAC procedures are set out in the attachment.

The principle then is one in which problems would be dealt with as they arise and resolved in a way acceptable to the existing manufacturers and trade unions in the industry concerned. The public interest would be what the manufacturers, the trade unionists and the government representatives sympathetic to the manufacturers' point of view regard as in the public interest, not what the public might regard as "in its interest".

The proposal is to establish an Industry Council at the national level for each manufacturing industry, State Manufacturing Councils on the basis to be decided by the States concerned, and an Australian Manufacturing Council at the national level.

There would probably be some hundreds of Councils.

The report states: "Elements of the network (of Councils) would overlap, . . . cross organisational boundaries . . . would not be ordered in a hierarchy."

Discussions in the Industry Councils would be held behind closed doors because the Committee states: "*consensus . . . is more likely to be achieved without publicity*".

In the selection of members for all the Councils, the emphasis is on ensuring equal representation from manufacturers and trade unions. Quite clearly, the intention is that each Industry Council and the National Council (and therefore, the whole policy making process) should be dominated by the manufacturers and the trade unionists.

The report states that the recommendations of the Councils would be dealt with as follows:

> "Recommendations of each Council would be considered by the government in the manner appropriate to each recommendation. For example, a recommendation involving a new or varied government assistance would be subject to public inquiry by the IAC. If the recommendations affected other government policies, consultation with other Ministers . . . would be the normal course."

The only element of public inquiry in the procedures would mean that a recommendation included in a scheme – which had been drawn up by a Council dominated by the vested interests directly involved and agreed to by the civil servants who would be the final advisors to the government on the scheme and on any IAC report-would be referred to the IAC for inquiry and report.

The inquiry would obviously be a very restricted one and the procedures would guarantee a predominant influence to the existing manufacturing interests in determining the terms of reference and advising the government on the Commission's recommendations.

It will be apparent that the Jackson Committee's proposals do not have the characteristics I referred to earlier, namely that: (1) the process should be independent, even-handed and impartial, and should be seen to be so; and (2) the process should be well-informed (and comprehensive) and should bring into account all the costs and benefits of the proposed measures on the community as a whole.

It has been said that the Jackson Committee's proposed procedures reflect a "more participative" style of decision making and, therefore, will make for greater social cohesion. But, the proposals would give a decisive role, both to the individual industries and to the manufacturing industry generally in the determination of policies which impinge directly on the welfare of all Australians. How could such a process contribute to greater social cohesion within the community as a whole? Or is "social cohesion" a quality which has relevance between "employers and employees in a particular manufacturing industry", but not between these and other members of the community who may be directly affected by the process – such as farmers, miners, people working in tertiary industry and the consumers and taxpayers generally.

Policy for industry development

Before I outline the IAC's approach I want to comment on the relationship between the economic and social objectives.

An important part of the welfare of any community depends on the goods and services available to the community and the way those goods and services are distributed.

The objective of increasing the supply of goods and services to the community may appear to be essentially "economic" in character. But, in fact, it also is of vital importance for most of the government's "social" objectives.

These objectives are met by the provision of various services, such as education, health, social security, communications, improvement of the environment, and so on. The avail ability of such services to the community is just as much an output of the economic system as the more tangible goods that are produced.

Both "types of need" must be met from the resources available to the community; and any action which increases the efficiency with which those resources are used will increase the economy's capacity to supply the public and private goods and services considered necessary for increasing welfare. This will be so, regardless of what particular goods and services are preferred by the community; and what particular ratio of public to private goods is considered desirable.

The pursuit of efficient resource use in industry development is, therefore, "not competitive with or contrary to" the pursuit of the community's broad "social objectives" it is a pre-condition for achieving those objectives.

The objective of improving the general distribution of goods and services in the community is not formally dependent on the total supply of goods and services available. However, this objective is easier to achieve if the total supply of goods and services is rising. In other words, the government will have less difficulty in reducing inequalities in the community if there is a reasonable rate of economic growth.

There is an important distinction in the Commission's approach between the goal of industry development – which is to encourage greater efficiency in the use of Australia's resources – and its recommendations regarding the means by which and the speed with which the goal is approached. Change will occur gradually. But the Commission is aware that even changes which are small from an economy-wide viewpoint may impose significant adjustment costs on particular groups in the community. In every inquiry it under takes, in which some reduction in assistance is contemplated, the Commission takes into account the short term welfare costs of that reduction in terms of the adjustment costs it is likely to impose on individuals and firms as well as the more general and long term benefits the reduction is expected to bring to the community.

Every industry development policy will directly or indirectly involve the provision of assistance to some industries, and will, therefore, influence the movement of resources in the economy. The main reason why industries seek assistance from the government, and the principal basis on which it has been provided, is to help them to meet the competition in the markets for their products. But, more fundamentally, assistance helps individual industries to attract and hold resources. It helps them to obtain the inputs of materials, capital and labour which they require, and which they must bid for in competition with "other potential users" of those resources. If an industry is given a high effective rate of assistance, it is being helped to attract and hold resources at the expense of industries with lower rates of assistance.

The degree to which an industry strategy can discriminate in favour of some industries – and against others – is shown by the structure of assistance which has applied to manufacturing industries in Australia.

The average "effective rates of assistance" in 1969-70 ranged from "negative" amounts for 14 industries to over 100 per cent for 16 industries. There was an even wider dispersion of effective rates of assistance for activities within industries.

Another way of illustrating the degree of discrimination in the structure of assistance for Australian manufacturing industries is to compare the "average net subsidy equivalents of assistance per person employed" for different industries.

In 1969-70, these subsidy equivalents were negative for 14 industries, and over $4,000 per person employed for 13 industries – the average wage per person employed in manufacturing industries in that year was $3,023 – therefore, for 13 industries, the transfer payments from the community to the manufacturers were equal to a payment per employee of over 30 per cent higher than the average wage per person employed in manufacturing industries.

The dispersion of effective rates of assistance for manufacturing industries was reduced as a result of tariff reductions between 1969-70 and 1973-74 but it has been increased again as a result of the tariff and quota restrictions imposed on the imports in the last two years.

The figures I have referred to give some indication of the extent to which some manufacturing industries are helped – by transfer payments from the community – in bidding against other manufacturing industries for the use of resources.

Choices

In arriving at the IAC's approach to industry development, three major related decisions had to be taken. The choices were between: an inward-looking or an outward-looking approach; a narrow, "sectoral" approach or an economy-wide approach; and an approach which seeks to "insulate industries from change" or one which seeks to help adjustment to change.

An inward-looking or outward-looking approach

An inward-looking approach is characterised by a policy of encouraging "import replacement" industries. Such an approach can achieve its prime objective of discouraging imports, but it also discourages export industries because:

i. declining imports give rise to pressure for "exchange rate appreciation" which reduces the returns on exported goods and thus the profitability of export industries;

ii. the assistance given to import competing industries enables them to bid success fully (and higher than market circumstances would otherwise allow) against export industries for productive resources; and

iii. export industries and other consumers are obliged to pay more for their inputs when these are subject to tariffs or import restrictions.

An inward-looking strategy, therefore, tends to reduce both imports and exports and thus to impede trade with other countries. (It is worth noting that Australia's external trade, as a proportion of GDP, is lower than in most comparable countries. Furthermore, exports and imports, as a proportion of GDP, increased at a slower rate in Australia than in most comparable countries over the period 1960 to 1974; this, despite the very substantial increase in mineral exports – from 8 to 25 per cent of total exports.) The implications for economic growth are obvious; the higher the levels of protection a country affords its import competing industries, then the greater the difficulty it will face in achieving economic growth through international trade. In addition, such a strategy attracts productive resources into import replacement industries which could not attract them without high levels of assistance. This clearly results in an inefficient allocation of productive resources and reduces the scope for general welfare gains.

The approach recognises that, because resources are limited, it is impossible to en courage the development of low-cost industries without a concurrent, and gradual, reduction in the high assistance now being given to some industries which are competing for these productive resources.

The gradual lowering of high rates of assistance to "high-cost" import replacement industries will encourage imports of lower priced overseas products and facilitate the movement of resources into "low-cost" industries. This will be of benefit to Australian consumers, help to lower costs generally in Australia and encourage the growth of export industries. This approach is, of course, quite consistent with the objective of maintaining a high level of employment in the economy as a whole.

A sectoral or economy-wide approach

It is logical that an approach which explicitly recognises that resources are limited and mobile throughout the economy should be "economy-wide" in its scope. Equally, it is quite illogical that the community should continue to subsidise in the long term the use of resources in one industry or sector if those resources could be used "more efficiently" and with less subsidy (or no subsidy at all) elsewhere in the economy.

There are "low-cost" activities in all sectors of the Australian economy, including the manufacturing sector. "Low-cost" manufacturing industries have been disadvantaged by assistance to "high-cost" manufacturing industries in the same way that low-cost rural and mining industries have been disadvantaged by this assistance. Equally, "low-cost" manufacturing industries will be "encouraged to grow" as assistance to "high-cost" industries in all sectors of the economy is gradually reduced. The present approach recognises that the ultimate objective of industry policy is to improve the welfare of the whole community. It follows that those industries in all sectors of the economy which con tribute most to the welfare of the community as a whole should be encouraged – rather than "manufacturing" or "rural" or "mining" or "service" industries as such.

The fact that the present system is neutral between industries, in all sectors of the economy, in no way means that the government should do nothing to assist and en courage industry growth and development. What it does mean is that industry policy should provide a general climate in which all Australian industries that use the community's resources economically are encouraged to grow – rather than develop separate "climates" for manufacturing, rural, mining and tertiary industries. It means that an important result of having one approach to industry development (which is neutral between industries and sectors) is that it encourages individual producers to bring their own initiative, ability and experience to bear when making decisions about where to direct "their capital and enterprise". It also means a climate (or framework) for private decision-making and for industry development which involves a minimum of discrimination by the government between individuals, industries and sectors.

Insulation from change or adjustment to change

For the greater part of this century, assistance has been provided to many Australian industries on the basis of assessments of the amount of assistance "needed" to maintain their profitable operations in the face of foreign competition. Frequently, as protective needs have increased, assistance has been increased to a similar degree. Such a policy, not only maintains productive resources in activities which are becoming increasingly uneconomic, but also encourages a "hand-out" mentality which stifles the enterprise and initiative necessary for the vigorous growth of the private sector. When assistance from the government is "viewed as a right" and producers assume that assistance, which is, in their view, "necessary", will be provided, the incentive for producers to improve profitability and productivity by seeking out new markets, developing new production techniques or transferring resources to more economic operations is seriously weakened.

Such effects of a policy which gives assistance on a needs basis have long been recognised. In 1929, the Brigden Committee, reporting on the Australian Tariff, included the following passage in its report:

> "The most disquieting effect of the tariff has been the stimulus it has given to demands for government assistance of all kinds, with consequent demoralising effect upon self-reliant efficiency throughout all forms of production."

In a study of industrial development policy in six countries, sponsored by the World Bank, a few years ago, the conclusion states:

> "the continued sheltering of domestic industries from foreign competition and disincentives to exporting involve a dynamic cost to the national economy in the form of opportunities foregone for improvements in productivity. On the one hand, there is little incentive to improve production methods and product quality; on the other, discrimination against exports and objectives of industrial expansion on a broad front limit the scope of exploiting large scale economies."

When a firm's operations becomes unprofitable in the long term, assistance should be directed not at maintaining resources in the uneconomic activity but rather at inducing resources to move into other, more economic activities. Changes in the structure of industry are inevitable – as consumers' tastes change, new technologies are developed and new industries develop in other countries. Industrial policy should be directed not at assisting industries to resist such changes but rather at facilitating change and reducing any disproportionate burden which may fall on any section of the community.

It is fundamental to the IAC's approach to industry development that the rate at which high levels of assistance are reduced must take account of the ability of the economy to sustain any structural changes that may be involved.

Obviously, during the current recession in the economy, there is greater difficulty in absorbing "policy-induced" structural changes and the timing of changes should reflect this.

It is equally important to ensure that the long term development of import competing industries is not determined on the basis of assistance needed to achieve profitable production in a severe recession. (It is worth recalling that a substantial part of the emergency tariff measures introduced in the 1930 depression was in operation 40 years later – and this has contributed greatly to the inefficient use of resources and the high. rate of inflation in the post-war period.)

There is a strong relationship between encouraging adjustment to change and encouraging enterprise, invention and innovation.

To improve the standard of living of the Australian people, we need an "economic and social environment" which encourages enterprise, invention and innovation in the broadest sense in all sectors of the economy; which encourages adaption to change; which encourages Australian people in industry and commerce – investors, managers and workers – to live and work much more comfortably in a situation where change is a normal part of their lives.

The approach of the IAC will help create this kind of environment because it includes action aimed at:

i. providing the community generally with well-researched information about likely medium and long term effects of naturally occurring and policy-induced economic and social changes;

ii. ensuring that policy for development and industry is determined on an economy-wide basis;

iii. providing assistance to industries which is less exclusively directed towards supporting the prices of industries' outputs and more directed towards improving mobility, quality and productivity of resources; and

iv. ensuring that the form of government intervention to assist industry does not stifle enterprise and innovation.

I will illustrate the importance of each of these courses of action in creating the environment I have referred to.

Looking beyond the short term horizon

We need a situation where businessmen have the best possible information on which to base their investment decisions. The more information the decision-makers have about future movements in demand and supply of capital, labour and materials, about costs, prices, tastes and population changes the better will be their decisions. The need is greatest when the decisions relate to investment in the development and distribution of new products and services because the planning and establishment of production (and distribution) spans a time horizon of a considerable number of years.

At present, the only official predictions of expected change – even in the Australian economic situation – are those made by the Treasury for a short period ahead. The in formation is at a high level of aggregation and the basis on which the predictions are made is not known outside the government service. There is a need for well-researched "medium to long term" predictions to be made and for the details of these predictions, the basis on which they are made and the likely effects of the various options which are open to the government to be made available to all and to be given the widest possible publicity. A project called IMPACT, initiated by the IAC, and commenced in the middle of 1975, will do this. The project is unique in a world sense in that it will enable integrated projections (for example, of the future structure of industry and the labour force) to be made in greater detail than has been possible in projects of this type undertaken elsewhere in the world. IMPACT will give: (1) annual information for each of about seven years ahead tracing out the dynamic economic and social interactions of a large number of variables on 100 industry groups; and (2) also information in a less disaggregated form for future periods of 10, 15, 20 and 25 years ahead.

A number of government departments are combining with the IAC in carrying out this project. One great advantage which will flow from the combined work is that advice to the government on different aspects of economic and social policies from different departments and instrumentalities will be much more consistent (and co-ordinated) than it has been up to the present.

The first results of the IMPACT project will be available early in 1977. The project will be fully operational by 1978 and will, of course, be on-going.

Since the commencement of the project, papers relating to it have been made available to the consultative group I referred to earlier and discussions have been held with the group as an early part of the arrangement to ensure that the results are available to all and given the widest possible publicity.

The information available from the project will enable the government (and the public) to be aware of likely changes in the environment well ahead of the changes occuring – and to be aware of the policy options open to the government and the likely effects of adopting each of the options.

Consequently, everyone should be better situated to anticipate developments and problems rather than, as at present, react to them as they arise.

Policy for industry development on an economy-wide basis

If we are to make the best use of our resources, investors (and particularly prospective innovators) should be encouraged to consider investments in all sectors of the economy – and be able to compare the relative merits of the different potential investments. This, obviously, would be greatly helped by a long term "economy-wide" policy for the development of industries which uses "common criteria and reconcilable data" for all sectors of the economy. The establishment of the IAC and the development of its approach to assistance for industry has been an important step in this direction.

Government assistance should be more in the direction of improving the mobility, quality and productivity of resources

By far the major part of the government assistance to industry is for the support of prices of industries' outputs, that is, in the direction of protection against change.

I can illustrate this by referring to the situation revealed during the IAC inquiry into Consumer Electronic Goods. The Australian industry was producing a wider range of components than any other country in the world. All other countries imported some components from countries which specialised in their manufacture. Some of the components made in Australia were of 1950 technology despite the fact that there had been important changes in technology since the 1950s. To protect the Australian industry against changes, customs duties of up to 1,000 per cent were operating on components by 1973. The disastrous effects of this policy on innovation in the electronic industry in Australia and on the industrial application of the Australian innovations (and there have been some quite significant innovations) will be readily apparent.

Since the middle of the 1960s, the Tariff Board (and subsequently, the IAC) has been advocating the introduction of adjustment assistance measures, and it commenced research work, as soon as resources were available, to enable it to assess, foresee and explain the extent of adjustment costs.

A range of government measures are required including provision for training and re training, relocation of workers and families, income support and compensation for unusable assets. Quite generous provisions for adjustment would be far less costly to the community than protecting against change.

Let me give just one other example of the cost of protecting against change. Last year, the community subsidised each apple grower in Southern Tasmania at the rate of about $15,000 per annum, but the average income of the growers was something less than $6,000 per annum. The need for the high rate of assistance came from changes in the world trading situation (the development of the EEC and Britain's entry into the Community) and innovations in the methods of preserving fresh fruit. Both of these changes developed over a relatively long period during which adjustment should (and could) have been made.

The Labor government did introduce some adjustment measures in a piecemeal fashion and largely on a short term basis. The Fraser government recently introduced some measures to assist in the relocation of workers and their families. What is required is the introduction of a systematic (and comprehensive) system. Such a system would considerably reduce resistance to change and innovation.

An extensive and complex set of government measures is aimed at assisting research in Australian industry. These measures have been introduced in a piecemeal fashion over many years. For the last 18 months, the IAC has been pointing out the need to examine, on an economy-wide basis, the question of how best to encourage research and development and dissemination and application of research results.

Form of government intervention should not stifle enterprise and innovation

Perhaps I can illustrate this point by comparing the effect of providing assistance to industry in the form of a customs duty only with the effect of a local content scheme such as that used to protect the motor vehicle industry.

Where there is a customs duty only, the Australian manufacturers, the importers and the distributors can establish very clearly the landed duty paid cost of the imported article and they can then make all their commercial decisions in the normal way.

With the local content scheme applying to the motor vehicle industry, the government is involved in the normal commercial decisions affecting investment, specifications of the products and the distribution of motor vehicles and components. At a public inquiry in 1974, a leading company in the motor vehicle industry said that the rules had changed approximately every six months during the previous 10 years. This gives some idea of the difficulties any enterprising producer would have in trying to plan innovations. In the administering departments and in each of the motor vehicle manufacturers and in most of the manufacturers of components there has been built up a large bureaucracy which is necessary to maintain the consultations and negotiations continuously involved between the government and each of the manufacturers. All this is very costly. The protection now afforded the industry represents transfer payments from the community to the manufacturers equivalent to approximately $4,000 per annum for every worker in the motor vehicle and component industries.

The Form of government intervention is very important in determining the type of environment in which private enterprise functions. Intervention should be in a form which is as clear and administratively simple as possible. Without such an approach, enterprise and innovation will become increasingly stifled in the bureaucratic jungle which must be built up, both in the public service and in the business enterprises them selves.

Jackson Committee's policies for development of manufacturing industries

The general objectives referred to in the report are consistent with an outward-looking approach and one which encourages adjustment to change. But the actual proposals made by the Committee would have the opposite effect. They would result in: (a) an inward-looking approach; (b) an approach that is narrow and sectoral; and (c) an approach which would insulate against change and would stifle enterprise and innovation.

This difference between the objectives and the proposals has created considerable confusion regarding the report.

Inward (or outward) looking approach

The proposal for tariff reductions has been referred to as an indication of the Committee's adoption of an outward-looking approach. An examination of the proposal shows that the best which might be expected is that after a long time (probably 15 to 20 years in the majority of cases[3]), the tariff would be reduced on most industries (although the exceptions under the vague criteria of "capabilities for national independence" could be substantial) to benchmark levels which may be no lower than the present levels in a number of cases.[4] Thereafter, the benchmark levels would apply indefinitely-irrespective of the cost to the community or the

3 The proposal for tariff reductions appears to involve the following steps: (1) after holding a public inquiry, the IAC would recommend appropriate long term tariff benchmarks; (2) the government would allocate industrial activities to the benchmarks after reaching agreement with the industries; and (3) thereafter, tariffs would be reduced to thc benchmark levels by pre-determined installments over 5 to 15 years. There would be serious problems (and certainly a great deal of time required) to get agreement from each of the various industries and trade unions on: the benchmark level which should apply to their industry; the period for reduction to the benchmark level which should apply to their industry; and that any tariff reduction at all should apply to their industry, because the report provides the basis for each industry to disagree on each of these points with any proposal put forward.

4 The report states: "In respect of some industries recent tariff reductions will have already reduced tariffs to the appropriate benchmark levels." (p. 176.)

changes which may occur. But, it is also proposed that such tariff reductions as are made may be replaced with other forms of assistance (for example, subsidies, tax concessions, etc.) if the industries are covered by vague criteria such as "having desirable attributes".

Special assistance (including high protection) is proposed for activities required for "national independence". The Committee states that it is not specifically referring to attributes for defence. Therefore, the aim is to increase assistance for production for important replacement. As I have stated earlier, by concentrating on the development of import replacement industries, Australia has tended to insulate itself from international trade throughout the post war period. This proposal by the Committee would further insulate Australia.

The report proposes that manufacturing industry should be insulated from some of the effects from exchange rate adjustments when these tend to increase competition for the manufacturing industries (p. 122, 181). A two-tier system is referred to which apparently means the use of differential ex change rates: that is, a deliberately under-valued rate of imports of manufacturing pro ducts which would provide additional protection for Australian manufacturing industries, and a deliberately over-valued rate in relation to other sectors which would reduce their competitiveness in Australia and overseas. Therefore, the exchange rate proposal would mean that both imports and exports would be discouraged and Australia would be further insulated from international trade.

Sectoral approach rather than economy-wide

The Committee proposes: a massive injection of new capital into the manufacturing sector. This could only be done at the expense of capital for other sectors. Also, the total amount of capital available for all sectors would be reduced by some other proposals of the Committee, for example: "buying back the factory" and reduced reliance on overseas borrowings. Therefore, sectors other than the manufacturing sector would find it very difficult indeed to get capital.

The Committee also proposes a large number of measures for increased assistance (which would enable "high cost" industries in the manufacturing sector to outbid industries in other sectors for Australia's limited resources) are mentioned

– specifically referred to are grants, taxation concessions, concessional interest rates, subsidies and investment allowances – to be provided under vague criteria such as "socially responsible", "to encourage desirable attributes in industry" or "to influence investment in appropriate channels.

Thirdly the Committee proposes the management of the exchange rate, but also capital inflow and overseas reserves is proposed in a way which would assist the manufacturing sector and would transfer the burden of change to the other sectors of the economy.

This all adds up to a formidable list of assistance to manufacturing industries at the expense of the development of the other sectors, and the standard of living of the community generally. But no attempt has been made to analyse the likely effects of these proposals on industries in the other sectors of the economy or on the community generally.

Also, the only reach (which is substantiated in the report) as to why preferential treatment should be given to the manufacturing sector is that this sector needs to be restored to the relative importance in the Australian economy which it had in the 1950s.

But the decline which has occurred in the relative importance (not the absolute size) of the manufacturing sector should not be a cause for concern. The Australian experience parallels that of most other developed countries. As incomes rise, the consumers tend to spend an increasing share of their incomes on services and a falling share of their income on manufactured goods.

Insulation of industries from change

Although the Green Paper refers to the inevitability of structural change, the adoption of its recommendations would inhibit such change rather than promote adjustment to it. Indicative of this is the proposal that the manufacturing sector should be insulated from exchange rate adjustments which would disadvantage it, although the exchange rate adjustments would reflect changes in Australia's economic and trading environment. Additionally, the kind of policy machinery proposed in the report – in particular, the network of Industry Councils – would inhibit rather than facilitate the necessary structural change (and the adaptation) by industries.

The proposed Industry Councils would be dominated by established manufacturers and trade unions who have most to lose from structural change in the short term and the greatest incentive to obstruct it. Is it not more likely that these Councils would be pre disposed towards perpetuating (or increasing) levels of assistance, rather than towards policies which would subject them to the problems of structural adjustment? The need for structural adjustment would presumably be judged solely according to its effects within the particular industries rather than in terms of its effects on the community as a whole. Could this process encourage other than a "closed shop" approach, since potential new manufacturers would be excluded from policy formation? Would the rate of change in any manufacturing industry be other than the lowest common denominator accept able to the existing producers in that industry?

An impartial decision on whether the benefits of structural adjustment exceed the costs can only be made on the basis of an economy-wide approach to industry development which takes into account the effects of such change on all sections of the community – in the industry concerned, in other industries and on consumers and taxpayers generally – and which considers the effects of change on long term industrial development throughout the economy.

Discouraging enterprise, initiative and innovation

One very important general implication of the proposals in the Jackson Committee report is that they would discourage enterprise, initiative and innovation.

The proposals would result in a very wide range of business decisions – which are properly a matter of commercial judgement – being subject to concurrence by the government. Each Industry Council (on which the government would be represented and which would be "serviced and financed" by the government) would have the role of both developing proposals and seeing that they are put into effect in relation to such matters as promoting rationalisation, promoting mergers, altering the size of firms, improving the quality of products and altering the scale of operations.

Getting the government involved in these commercial decisions has been suggested by manufacturers from time to time. The advantages which some manufacturers see in this type of government intervention is that the government can later be called upon to underwrite the profitability of the operations because it (the government) must accept considerable responsibility for the commercial decisions which have been made.

The proposed network of Councils would result in a very considerable increase in the bureaucracy – in government departments, manufacturing firms and industry and trade union organisations – all of whom would be involved in the normal commercial decisions.

How could any enterprising, inventive or innovative manufacturer succeed when en meshed in "the tangled mess of bureaucracy" that would exist?

Social problems

In discussions about the report a lot has been said about the Committee's emphasis on the social aspects – on such matters as the conditions of work, the education (and living conditions) of the workers and their families and the relations between employers and employees. Existence of problems in these areas has been used to reinforce the need for "massive preferential treatment" for the manufacturing sector.

Undoubtedly, there is considerable room for improvement in these matters and this is cause for concern. But the problems are not restricted to the manufacturing sector. Similar problems exist in the other sectors of the economy. Relations between employers and employees are equally difficult in the mining, rural and tertiary sectors. Working conditions, education, the living conditions of families are problems relating to industries in all sectors.

Whilst these matters are very important, they are separate issues from "policy for industry development" and should be processed consciously and effectively as separate issues – in a way which applies to, and benefits, all sectors of the workforce.

If non-economic goals were introduced directly into the criteria for industry development – as a primary determinant – the resulting confusion of priorities and decline in efficiency of resources used would actually reduce the economy's capacity to achieve these non-economic goals. It would also reduce the scope for all sections of the community to have equal opportunity to share in the welfare gains.

We are only likely to make major progress in remedying the wide range of social problems throughout Australia when the level of real income of the community generally is rising at a reasonable rate.

To get a reasonable rate of increase in the level of real incomes, Australia must make better use of its resources. The Jackson Committee's proposals would certainly not achieve this because the proposals would:

1) stifle "enterprise and innovation" in the manufacturing sector through the operations of the network of Industry Councils;

2) hamstring development in the mining, primary and tertiary industries – by giving the manufacturing industries "massive preferential treatment" in obtaining resources; and

3) stimulate and protect uneconomic activities in the manufacturing sector which would be covered by vague criteria such as "capabilities for national independence", "socially responsible", "wisely conducted" or having "desirable attributes".

Appendix

Features of IAC Procedures

The IAC's inquiry procedures reflect the efforts made by the Commission to:

- explain clearly the assistance criteria, based on the policy guidelines in the IAC Act being used in the formulation of the Commission's advice, by setting out the criteria and the information and analysis supporting it in documents published by the Commission;
- encourage the participation in each inquiry of all the interested parties, by advertising widely the inquiry, by contacting parties likely to be interested and by the selection of suitable locations for the hearings;
- identify the main issues of each inquiry early in its life and promote worthwhile discussion of those issues at the Commission's public hearings, through the publication and distribution before the public hearings of the relevant statistical information and of staff papers on important issues;
- provide ample opportunities for both the presentation of all facts, views and arguments and also any rebuttal of information and arguments, by the timing of the stages of the hearings;
- ensure that all information provided by interested parties is accurate, by taking such information on oath and carefully analysing it for objectivity and consistency;
- record, clarify and publicise the arguments and factual evidence, through the public questioning of the submissions by the Commissioner(s) and through the publication of a transcript of the public hearings;
- give all interested parties an opportunity to examine and comment on the analysis, conclusions and recommendations of the Commission before the reports are finally settled, by publishing draft reports and subsequently holding a public hearing;

- carry out a continuing research programme into industry assistance and development, so that the recommendations which are made in specific inquiries are able to take into account the long term effects on all sections of the community; and

- keep under constant review with a wide cross section of the community the Commission's inquiry procedures and its research programme, through regular meetings with a consultative group on which all sectors of industry and the trade unions, welfare organisations and consumer groups are represented.

37

Australian economics, 1967 to 1977

Fred H. Gruen[1]

Judging from the statistics available from two major employers of economists (the Federal Government and Australian universities) Australian economics has been one of the pronounced growth industries over the last seven to ten years. The number of Federal public servants (third division) with economics degrees has increased by around 11.5 per cent per annum over the last eight years with considerably greater percentage increases in those holding Honours and higher degrees (14.6 per cent and 22.3 per cent respectively). The number of university students enrolled for a Bachelor's degree in economics, commerce and government, has increased by around 5.25 per cent per annum over the last ten years, with very much greater increases for Master's and Doctorate students (11 per cent and 9.75 per cent per annum respectively – since 1970 – the first year for which this information was available). The number of academic university staff in "economics, commerce and government" has also grown rapidly – by 9.25 per cent per annum, with the slowest rate of growth among professors – 7.65 per cent per annum, and the highest among assistant lecturers and teaching fellows – slightly over 10 per cent per annum (i.e. over the period 1967-77).

A large part of the increase in academic staff in these disciplines is the result of the expansion of academic staff generally. Economics, commerce and government attracted an increasing proportion of undergraduates from 1967 to 1971 (from 12.5 to 14.2 per cent); since then the proportion has again gradually declined to earlier levels (1977 – 12.9 per cent). On the other hand an increasing proportion of graduate students in Australian universities study economics, commerce and

1 Thirty-Seventh Joseph Fisher Lecture, 10 October 1978. The author is grateful for helpful comments on an earlier draft from his academic colleagues Bob Gregory Trevor Swan, Tom Valentine, Bryan Haig, Peter Scherer, Don Challen and from a number of his previous colleagues and friends in the "official family".

government. (In the case of Master's students the proportion has increased from 15.1 per cent in 1970 to 17.6 per cent in 1977 and for Doctorates from 4.4 per cent to 6.6 per cent over the same period.) How ever both universities and the Federal Public Service face a period of distinctly slower future rates of growth, if not actually declining numbers in some cases.

A further impression one gets is that a great deal of extra writing and research work is being done. At the first Conference of Economists in Melbourne in May 1970, 35 papers were read and discussed. At the Fourth Conference in 1974 the number had increased to 75, whilst at the most recent Conference in Sydney (1978) the number of papers fell one short of 100. Roughly two-thirds of the papers at all three Conferences were given by academics.

At the same time there has been a substantial up-grading of university staff in terms of professional qualifications. An examination of qualifications of tenured teaching staff in economics departments in six of Australia's largest universities (Adelaide, Queensland, Sydney, Melbourne, New South Wales and Monash) shows that the proportion without higher degrees has declined from 32 per cent in 1967 to 13 per cent ten years later, whereas the proportion with doctorates has increased from 32 per cent to 57 per cent. The United Kingdom remains the most important single post-graduate training centre for tenured academic staff, although it has slipped relatively, with an increasing proportion of such staff having US and Australian doctorates.[2]

Again an increasing number of Australian academic economists now frequently con tribute to the international literature – with Corden, Harcourt, Kemp, Ng and Turnovsky being perhaps the best known but by no means the only examples.

Partly because of this growth of the literature, because of pressures of time and partly, no doubt, because of my own limitations, I have not persevered with

2 Tenured staff in Economics Departments in these universities increased from 119 to 149 over this period (the figures for the University of NSW refer to 1975 rather than 1977). The number without higher degrees declined from 38 to 19, the number with PhD.s increased from 38 to 85 with particularly large increases in US doctorates (8 to 25) and Australian (4 to 12), whilst the U.K. Ph.D.s increased from 22 to 35.

my original intention of providing a Corden-type survey of Australian economic policy discussion[3] . Instead I have concentrated on three areas, areas where I am relatively more familiar with Australian economics.

The changing climate of Australian economic opinion, 1976-77

In spite of the impressive numerical growth in the profession (at least within universities and the Federal Public Service), and the increasing technical competence of at least these two important groups of economists, there has been a growing disenchantment both with the discipline itself and with such traditional indicators of economic success as economic growth, price stability and full employment. This disenchantment was evident both from outside and from within the profession and has occurred both in Australia and overseas. In this respect, as in others which we will be recording here, Australian views have been largely derived from overseas intellectual trends. Since this disenchantment pre dates the traumatic economic events of 1974-75 and of later years, it was largely rising expectations rather than falling standards of performance which were responsible. Groenewegen [9] has summarised the series of events and the intellectual trends in the late sixties and early seventies which led to this increasing disenchantment. The critics raised a long list of issues ranging from degradation of the environment and of the quality of life generally, to Vietnam and growing awareness of poverty and of discrimination against such groups as Aborigines, migrants and women. They regarded these as resulting inherently from the prevalent economic organisation of society. Further study of existing modes of economic organisation (without encompassing major institutional changes of such economies) was unlikely to be rewarding.

The radical critique ensuing from these issues has been equally wide ranging. Although, as Groenewegen points out, Australian radical left economists are a diverse group and often hostile to one another, there is agreement on one underlying, even if sometimes only implicit, proposition: whatever the issue under consideration, existing defects/problems could be alleviated, if not cured, by the abolition of the private ownership of the means of production, or at least by the substantial subordination of private interests to public guidance, regulation or dictation. Or, as some of the radicals would put it, in equality, alienation, discrimination and imperialism are inherent in the nature of capitalism. This view is, of course, the result of the Marxist intellectual heritage of the radical revival. To an outsider the attempted demonstration of the causal connection between capitalism and these evils is not very rigorous. Many non-radicals would argue that in equality, alienation and discrimination may be inherent in the minute division of labour which is common in all wealthy societies (whether capitalist, socialist or different degrees of "mixed"). Again these evils may be inevitable, though they can hopefully be mitigated, when an economy is characterised by decentralised decision-making and a reliance on economic incentives. Finally, they may be inevitable to some degree in any economy because of the limited changeability of human nature. "Maoist man" appears as much a myth as was "Soviet man" in the 1920s.

The radical emphasis is largely on critiques.[3] The inherent difficulties of their implicit or explicit solutions tends to be skated over (though this is a trait common to many critiques, not only to those emanating from radicals). Thus at least the newer radical groups, both in Australia and elsewhere, have tended to be critical of both markets and of co-ordination of economies through bureaucratic planning techniques, without suggesting any alternative coordinating mechanism which is known to be viable. The impact of radical critiques was probably at its greatest during the late sixties and early seventies, i.e. during the closing years of the Vietnam War, and before the election of the Labor government in December 1972.[4]

A good deal has been written about the Labor government's style and about its economic performance; here I shall be concerned with its impact on economic attitudes in the country. In this connection, the following aspects require reference here.

3 In terms of their wider impact, perhaps the two most important critiques of the economy emanating from Australian radical economists concern the piecemeal nature of planning by McFarlane (1968) and the growing importance (dominance?) of foreign ownership by Wheelwright (Wheelwright and Miskelly 1967; Wheelwright 1974).

4 On the other hand, in terms of conferences and radical magazines there is a good deal of continuing activity. Three Australian Political Economic Conferences have been held, each attracting large numbers. Two sizeable and active conferences have also been held by Labor Economists. Again there are a number of active journals such as the *Journal of Australian Political Economy*, *Arena*, *Intervention*; apart from papers by radical economists appearing in the non-radical literature.

First there was the liberating influence of the Labor government. This was especially felt by artists and writers, but also by many social scientists. A large number of academic and other "outside" economists became interested in using their skills for the solution of practical problems and were commissioned by the Labor government to re-examine the various economic and social issues confronting the country. The contrast was particularly great with the prevalent pre-Labor (and post-Labor?) practice of avoiding open (i.e. non public service) investigations of such problems whenever possible, or alternatively setting up "semi-amateur" committees of inquiry with no professional membership, or strictly minority representation of professional economists. Corden referred to this anti-intellectual tendency in his earlier survey [3, pp. 49-59].

Whether this plethora of Labor-sponsored enquiries, task forces and commissions contributed to better decision-making by government is another question, one gathers that some political scientists and students of public administration have some misgivings on this point [e.g. 14].

Only a small minority of the economists thus involved were committed ALP sup porters, of two dozen names of economists which readily come to mind, only about half a dozen stand out as committed ALP supporters.[5] The much beloved jobs-for-the-boys criticism applied to two or three prominent appointments which were probably relatively unrepresentative of the whole.

Secondly, there was the basic orientation of Labor's programme towards equality of opportunity. To quote a recent summary of it by Ralph Willis, MP, the present Labor Shadow Treasurer:

> " . . . we argued that people of all income levels should have the right to decent education, proper health care, efficient transport, adequate recreation facilities, and a non-polluted environment, and that the only way that such rights could be guaranteed was for the State to play a much greater role in their provision than hitherto" [38].

5 The names of those who were involved in government during this period include: Brennan, Brogan, Cochrane, Deeble, Gates, Gregory, Gruen, Hancock, Holmes, Ironmonger, Isaac, Karmel, Keating, A. G. Lloyd, Mathews, Mauldon, Parish, Pincus, Porter, Scotton, Selby-Smith, Snape, T. W. Swan, and Wheelwright.

But, as Edwards [5] pointed out:

> "Labor also arrived in office with an unresolved, almost unrecognised, conflict over the means by which it would promote equality."

On the one hand there was the increasing role for the State in the provision of services; on the other hand there was need for extra public revenue to finance transfer payments for more adequate social services; yet again, the trade union members of the government expected to greatly improve their members' real after-tax incomes and living standards, not to mention the share of GNP going to wage earners. Squaring this very round circle was an impossible task for any government. Critics, and perhaps even the electorate as a whole, may indulge in the luxury of espousing mutually inconsistent policies, but a government's inconsistencies are inevitably exposed publicly. After two and a half years in office Prime Minister Whitlam recognized some of these problems in his 1975 Chifley Memorial Lecture:

> ". . . In a sense the party of Reform in a democratic system carries a self-created handicap as a reforming Government. In Opposition, its essential task is to raise the public perception of the need for change, the need for reform. That is, its task is to raise expectations. The nature of politics, founded as it is on human nature itself, is that there will always tend to be a gap, a shortfall, between expectations aroused and expectations met.
>
> "A conservative Government survives essentially by dampening expectations and subduing hopes. Conservatism is basically pessimistic; reforming is basically optimistic. The great tradition which links the American and French revolutionaries of the Age of Reason with the modern Parties of Social Reform is the tradition of optimism about the possibility of human improvement and human progress through the means of reason. Yet inevitably there will be failures, and the higher expectations rise, the greater the likelihood of at least temporary failure to meet them."

In the event, even if there had been no world recession, these unavoidable conflicts would have needed to be faced, and would inevitably have led to some disillusionment among Labor supporters. As it turned out, the impossible task Labor set itself considerably aggravated subsequent levels of inflation and unemployment. Whilst high rates of inflation and unemployment were shared in part (though not to the same extent) by all other OECD countries, they were to provide a very potent impetus to the ensuing widespread disillusionment with Labor. This is not the place for a detailed discussion of the Labor government's economic policies, or of what we can learn from this particular episode.[6] The emphasis here is restricted to the effect of this period on the climate of economic opinion.

Paralleling the earlier history of American disillusionment with President Johnson's "Great Society", there has been a similar disillusionment with government here, coupled with a very rapid growth in libertarian economics, or what one might term, alternatively, the economic philosophy of Milton Friedman, George Stigler or Fredrich Hayek (if we can, for the purpose of broad-brush characterisation, ignore differences between their respective philosophies).

Both at ANU and at Monash (and perhaps at other universities) the libertarian stance has become, if not the new orthodoxy, at least the predominant intellectual movement among the younger members of the discipline. In addition a new libertarian organisation, the Centre for Independent Studies, sponsored an impressive professional conference on "What Price Intervention" at Macquarie University in April 1978 (e.g. the papers by McGregor, Parish, Porter and Sieper listed in the references).

The libertarians regard their basic stance as protective to the maximum extent possible of the liberty of the person. (In addition, there is a basic negative stance, i.e. against government, of which more below). Power over a person should be exercised only to protect others, not to protect man from himself or to achieve any other social goal. If freedom and the satisfaction of consumer wants are regarded as the most important ends which public policy should serve, the predominant prescription of the libertarians, rely on the market in practically every situation, follows logically. Those of us who believe that the world is more complicated, that government needs to bear in mind other considerations as well,

6 I have contributed elsewhere to this type of exercise [10].

find it less easy to endorse such universal remedies. Thus, to take one example, the health of the community is often regarded as a legitimate concern for governments which might, for instance, justify publicly financed anti-smoking campaigns, or discriminatory taxes on such products, or even the prohibition of tobacco advertising.[7] However, to the true libertarian this type of do-good public meddling is deeply suspect and, at least one prominent libertarian – Milton Friedman (in his *Newsweek* column) – has attacked both governmental anti-smoking campaigns ("Government has no business using the tax payer's money to propagandize") and prohibition of tobacco advertising as "hostile to the maintenance of a free society" [cited in 25, pp. 160-161].

Again, there is the awkward question: At what age does the individual become a sufficiently good judge of his welfare to make his freedom such a paramount goal? Perhaps of greater basic importance is Rawls' question, whether society (and by implication policy) can be adequately judged in terms of the fulfilment of given wants since society (i.e. the interaction of groups and individuals) has an important role in influencing and shaping these wants. The criterion of the maximum satisfaction of given wants is necessarily a partial criterion.

> "Everyone recognizes that the form of society affects its members and deter mines in large part the kind of persons they want to be as well as the kind of persons they are. It also limits people's ambitions and hopes in different ways, for they will with reason view themselves in part according to their place in it and take account of the means and opportunities they can realistically expect. Thus an economic regime is not only an institutional scheme for satisfying existing desires and aspirations but a way of fashioning desires and aspirations in the future" [33, p. 160].

7 For the economist who wants to maintain the supremacy of freedom and of consumer choice as goals, the externalities of smoking can be used as valid grounds for interfering with consumer's choice (i.e. the nuisance to others and the additional public health costs). But this does not meet the (paternalistic) argument that there is a case for discouraging patently impulsive and unwise choices which will often be regretted in the future when the consequences of the, often irreversible, choices become apparent (e.g. smoking, the non-wearing of seat belts or safety helmets on motor bikes).

The libertarians' deep suspicion of government is probably a useful antidote to the previous implicit view of many economists that governments could be relied upon to per form the role of Platonic guardians who, in a disinterested fashion, determined the best course amongst alternative possible outcomes for a particular economy.

Whatever one may think of the libertarians' suspicious (value) judgements about government, a great deal of valuable work on both the theory and the empirical consequences of governmental regulation of private economic affairs has resulted from this general orientation, though even here non libertarian economists will not follow them all the way.

Thus there is now a general consensus among (non-Marxist?) economists that nothing good can come of governmental attempts to regulate those competitive industries giving rise to neither externalities or informational deficiencies; but when confronted with such situations or with natural monopolies, we are in the realm of the second best. Here general principles remain elusive and case-by-case examination and (uncertain) judgements about optimal policies are still required.

As Joskow and Noll point out in their excellent and comprehensive overview of the US literature on regulation in theory and practice:

> " . . . the inherent inefficiencies of regulation that flow from these theories have no natural normative consequences, although one would not deduce that from the tone of the literature. That regulation fails to reach a Pareto optimum is fairly uninteresting if no institutions exist which can reach a point that Pareto dominates regulation. For regulatory interventions that deal with empirically important market imperfections, the departure of regulatory equilibrium from perfect competition is not normatively compelling" [18, p.61].

Wages policy

Over the period of our survey, Australian wages policy has passed almost full circle, from a fairly centralised policy enforced by sanctions to an almost completely decentralised policy of collective bargaining, and then back to the most centralised wage fixation system in our history: this time "enforced" or at least kept under central control by record levels of unemployment.

The 1967-1977 decade started with the Metal Trades work value decision which caused a spate of protest strikes and, indirectly within two years, eliminated the use of sanctions and fines to enforce Commission awards. By October 1971 Keith Hancock [13] felt that one could no longer reasonably speak of Australia having a wage policy

> "Although the market and the wage-fixing institutions have always been to some degree rival forces in the determination of pay levels and relativities, and the domination of either has never been absolute, the shift towards the market over the past two years has been so pronounced as to transform the relation. Control of wage movements has not been more slender at any time since before World War I."

This diagnosed loss of control was to be amply demonstrated within the next three years when, assisted by a variety of economic and political forces, Australia experienced a massive acceleration of nominal wage growth. Different observers have assigned differing relative importance to the economic, political and institutional forces responsible for the wage explosion. However this necessarily inconclusive debate need not detain us here.[8] What is important is that the Commonwealth Arbitration Commission gradually regained control over the growth of money wages after 1975, no doubt considerably assisted by the mounting level of unemployment. The current position is that the Commonwealth Commission has "managed to establish the most centralised system of wage determination ever to prevail in Australia" [36]

However, both highly centralised and completely decentralised systems of wage fixation possess different but possibly equally grave drawbacks. On the one hand the move towards decentralisation and allowing more room for collective bargaining is almost inevitably associated with increased wage pressure, followed by a more highly differentiated pay scale. This differentiation is not necessarily

8 See, for instance, J. P. Meuwenhuysen and J. Sloan [30], as an example of placing great emphasis on the role of the Labor government in the genesis of the wage explosion. I am on record for placing relatively more stress on the importance of economic factors and institutional trends in these developments [10, pp. 22-23].

in accordance with economic criteria but more in accordance with industrial bargaining strength. Although bargaining strength has some influence in any system of wage fixation, it looms much larger under free collective bargaining. On the other hand a completely centralised system has usually produced stresses and strains which tend to make the system fray at the edges at first and then to break down, perhaps especially under the weight of the odd inevitably unsustainable Arbitration decision.

The Australian profession discussed the respective merits and drawbacks of compulsory arbitration versus collective bargaining at some length fifteen to twenty years ago.[9] Intermittently, and in various forms, the discussion has continued to the present day. During the period under review here, a good deal of academic support built up for an incomes policy, perhaps as a kind of mid-way house between the market and compulsory arbitration with sanctions.

According to Hagger [11] between 1973 and 1974 Australian academic economists reached an impressive consensus on the desirability of a prices and incomes policy:

> ". . . accompanied by a variety of suggested 'carrots' and 'sticks'. The carrots proposed usually included a guarantee that wage restraint of the required degree would be rewarded by substantial tax concessions varying from a reduction in excise charges and sales taxes on essential items to personal tax indexation. Good examples are to be found in Sheehan and Ironmonger (1973) and Sheehan (1974). Among the suggested sticks one commonly found amendments to the company taxation arrangements designed to penalize firms which agreed to excessive wage increases, e.g Sheehan (1974), Nevile (1974), adoption of a modified form of the Wallich-Weintraub scheme for a tax-based incomes policy, e.g. Henderson (1972), and other such fiscal devices" [11, p. 175].

9 See, for instance, the three contributions by Hancock, Laffer and Isaac, in: *Australian Labour Relations, Readings*, J. E. Isaac and G. W. Ford (eds), Melbourne: Sun Books Ltd., 1966, pp. 442-470, and the literature referred to by the three authors.

At the time this consensus of publicly committed academics was reached, I had temporarily deserted academia and worked as Economic Consultant to the Prime Minister's Department on these and related issues. In particular I was one of six members of a Committee appointed by Cabinet in August 1974 to enquire into the possibility of penal taxes on excessive wage increases. Having served on that Committee, which I entered as a believer in such taxes, I am now much more doubtful, basically because of the administrative and "political" problems associated with such taxes. Let me summarise some of the points the Committee made:

> "It would of course be necessary for the government to lay down a norm for permissible wage increases. The Australian Bureau of Statistics estimates each month Average Weekly Earnings using payroll tax statistics and a similar method is used in the formula for Reimbursement Grants to the States.
>
> "But greater difficulties arise in an attempt to produce a corresponding figure for individual firms which might be used to determine what are "excessive" wage and salary payments. While such a figure could be produced for each firm there would be many anomalies and the Government would be en forcing penalties which in many instances would clearly be unjust. This is because it would be impossible from award determination, or from other sources, to determine how changes in *pay* rates, occupation by occupation, will affect *payrolls*, firm by firm and quarter by quarter. . . . Even if no wage rates increase, the average payroll might rise because of a different mix of skills and because of variations in overtime, holiday pay, etc. A firm could be penalised for a pay increase which did not arise from any excessive change in rates because of accidental factors such as weather, strikes, shortages of material or power, etc. . . .
>
> "No doubt some of these defects could be set right in the course of administration but it would be impossible to hope for more than the roughest of justice. It may be that rough and ready justice can be tolerated if it is the price of coping with the inflationary situation. But if the injustices were sufficiently common and glaring there would be widespread resentment against the scheme even if it would

help keep prices down. There might also be industrial unrest and unexpected failures of business . . .

"But it would be possible to give effect to such a measure, and if applied as part of a total programme it could help contain cost inflation. It would, however, be impossible to sustain such a plan for any considerable period of time. If employed it should be seen essentially as a short-term measure."

I have dealt at some length with the various considerations which were raised in the Committee to illustrate the kind of Hobson's choice which democratic governments the world over have increasingly faced in the last four or five years, and which have given rise to demands for tax-based incomes policies in other countries as well. On the one hand governments have been expected to reconcile (painlessly) irreconcilable income claims. On the other the community is becoming increasingly suspicious of government and less and less willing to back government in trials of strength with various sectional pressure groups. It would have been perhaps especially difficult for Labor. As Dr Barry Hughes observed recently, large sections of the Labor party believed that any restraint on the ability of trade unions to secure maximum wage increases represented high treason against the working classes.

If government cannot (or is not willing to) enforce fines or sanctions against trade unions, is there any reason to believe that it can enforce penal tax provisions against firms which agree to treat their workforce more generously than rival firms? Government also needs to consider not only the effect of proposed measures on inflation but also other aspects of the proposed changes, such as their effect on the acceptability of the tax system generally. My academic colleagues can and no doubt do retort that the alter native fiscal and monetary methods of coping with inflationary pressures and the horrendous cost and misery they imply in terms of greatly increased unemployment made it worth trying untested and possibly unworkable remedies and paying the price of administrative foul-ups and even of bringing the tax system into disrepute. These are judgements which different individuals will make differently. However, one got the impression during these years that the recommendations of outside economists were often made without a full awareness of all the possible pitfalls of the courses of action they were advocating. As Henry Kissinger once put it, comparing the policymaker and the outsider:

> "As an outsider you can paint the best consequences of your proposed actions and you are not responsible for its failure because it isn't being implemented. As a policymaker you are responsible not only for the best but also for the worst that can happen."[10]

The net effect of the last ten years of Australian wages policy is that we are now no nearer to a solution to the problem of securing wage restraint if tight labour markets should return. Our centralised wage fixation system is no more likely to survive a return to full employment now than eight or ten years ago. One possible way out of this dilemma favoured at one time by Mr Clyde Cameron, but subsequently repudiated by the 1971 Labor Party Conference, may be worth reviving. Cameron suggested that, provided a union-management agreement was ratified by the workers affected, it might include clauses providing for civil damages in the event of breach by either party. Such agreements might be more genuinely respected by both parties and could provide a more predictable industrial relations climate for the longer term. This is obviously desirable, partly for its own sake and partly to allow and encourage those longer-run investment and development decisions which determine a good deal of the growth in our living standards. Some more progressive private companies are attempting to negotiate agreements with their workforce which provide monetary incentives for continuing operation; this is obviously an example of private initiative in this direction.

Econometric modelling of the Australian economy

One important difference between Australian economic policy discussion when Max Cordon wrote ten years ago and the current position is provided by the operation and continuing refinement of sizeable econometric models of the Australian economy. Such modelling began with a series of individual academic efforts by Nevile (1962), Kmenta (1966), Zerby (1969), and Evans (1972). While academic modelling of the present Australian economy (Haig & Wood, 1977, Nevile, 1975) and of such relevant past periods as the 1930s depression

10 Interview with Henry Kissinger in the *London Observer*, 19 July 1977.

(Valentine, 1978) is continuing, particular attention is focussed here on the considerably larger and more elaborate models constructed by econometricians working either directly for government or for such statutory organisations as the Reserve Bank and the Industries Assistance Commission.

There are at least four such models. First the National Income Forecasting (NIF) model originally designed by Chris Higgins and Vince FitzGerald and now operated by a team from Treasury and the Australian Bureau of Statistics led by Neil Johnston. Then there are the Reserve Bank models, in particular RBA 1 originally designed by a team led by Bill Norton, and RBA 76 designed by Peter Jonson and his co-workers. Finally there is the IMPACT project, headed by Alan Powell and Peter Dixon and a group assembled under IAC auspices.

Developing and maintaining the larger models requires sustained team work as well as gifted individual research efforts. This type of research work is done more easily within governmental organisations than in universities, at least as presently structured. But it must be a source of regret that all regularly used and publicly documented models are operated by government and/or statutory organisations (though one should mention the Melbourne Institute's annual model – not as yet publicly fully documented but operated for some of its clients).

Models can, of course, be classified in a variety of ways. One obvious criterion is size, with the number of equations in the model being a common measure. By this criterion the IMPACT system is by far the largest, followed by the NIF model (with, at present, 14 around 130 equations); RBA 1 (with about 100 equations); while RBA 76 is the smallest, being in fact described as a "minimal" model with "only" 20-odd equations. However this is really a pretty unsatisfactory type of classification; by stressing numbers it ignores a lot, such as completeness of modelling, in particular whether the relevant interdependencies and relationships are adequately allowed for, etc.

More interesting questions about the models concern their characteristics, their uses and their limitations. Broadly speaking there are three major purposes of models; to increase understanding of the structure of the economy, to provide conditional forecasts and to evaluate the effects of possible proposed policy changes (including *ex post* assessments of actual policy changes). To some extent these aims may be conflicting; a model designed primarily for forecasting may have unsatisfactory features from the point of view of consistency or of economic theory; whilst a model for policy simulations may give relatively worse predictions. Like policy makers, model builders often have to choose between alternative ends and settle for trade-offs which can then be attacked by those with different aims and priorities. I will elaborate further on the various purposes and likely limitations below. It may be desirable first to continue with some further characterisation of the official and semi-official models although, for reasons of space, only sketchy characterisation is possible here.[11]

As one would expect, the Treasury and Reserve Bank model concern themselves particularly with short run macroeconomic questions they are quarterly models used both for forecasting and for policy analysis. New forecasts are produced every quarter as new sets of quarterly national accounts statistics become available. On the other hand the IMPACT system is designed basically for medium term (say 5-7 years) and longer term (over 10 years) policy analysis and projection. It focusses primarily on such longer term questions of resource allocation as tariff policy, manpower and immigration programmes. Since I will be concerning myself below mainly with macro-economic questions the remaining discussion will deal with these types of models.[12]

The NIF and RBA 1 models have strong Keynesian features, gross national product is mainly determined by effective demand, but there is considerable treatment of inventories in a buffering role and also of capacity constraints, especially in the longer run. As one might expect from a model developed within the central bank, RBA 1 has a more detailed modelling of the monetary sector than in the NIF model (at least so far, but see below). RBA 1 is also more "monetarist" in the sense that real wealth and price expectations tend to have more influence on expenditure than in the NIF model.

11 For a detailed discussion of the various models, the reader is referred to "Modelling the Australian Economy", by D.W. Challen and A.J. Hagger [1]. I am indebted to the authors for an early copy of their book in manuscript form.

12 For a short overview of the IMPACT project see P.J. Lloyd [22, pp. 274-5], for a more detailed description see First Progress Report of the IMPACT Project, vols. I & II, Australian Government Publishing Service, Canberra, 1977.

Comparisons of the predictive errors of the two models suggest that the predictive performance of the NIF model is generally superior.[13] There have been seven annual re-estimations (and partial re-specifications) of the NIF model so far which have no doubt added considerably to the realism and sophistication of the model. The model as it stands now is a good deal different from the original Higgins-FitzGerald model.

Some of the major changes made to the NIF model over the years include: (a) a more fully elaborated model of public-private sector interactions enabling fiscal policy changes to be analysed more adequately, (b) investment relationships have been studied intensively and probably modelled more satisfactorily, (c) the influence of real wage changes on unemployment has been included in the model in various forms since 1975, (d) expression of relevant flows at constant prices with the provision of the appropriate national accounts data, (e) the elaboration of a more fully developed incomes sector.

Work on a fully fledged model of the financial sector was reported at recent professional conferences and will be incorporated in the next (1978) re-specification of the model. Inadequate monetary-real sector interactions have been a subject of some past criticism [see 19, 20].

RBA 76 is, in many respects, a very different type of model to the successive NIF versions and RBA 1. It pays more attention to long-run consistency and is primarily de signed for medium and longer run policy analysis than for short-term (conditional) fore casting. RBA 76 is more "neo-classical" and monetarist. Demand for commodities and assets are modelled in two steps; equilibrium or long-run levels depend on relative prices and the relevant constraints, whilst actual demands gradually adjust to these (changing) long-run equilibrium levels. Buffer stocks, consisting of money in the case of households and of goods inventories in the case of firms, play an important role in the model and smooth the adjustment paths in the face of unforeseen disturbances. RBA 76 is estimated using more sophisticated full information maximum likelihood techniques than the models

13 D.J.P. Jüttner [201]. However, as Jüttner points out. His comparisons are not conclusive, partly because the NIF forecasts are wholly within the sample period whilst about 10 per cent of the RBA 1 forecasts are for an out-of-sample or post-sample period.

discussed earlier. It has been the subject of open discussion; for this discussion selected outsiders' experimentation with the model has been encouraged.[14]

Some effects of econometric modelling

It is probably too early to assess the full impact of official and semi-official econometric modelling of the economy, either on government or on policy, or on the economy itself. However, since I am one of the few academic economists who has had the regular opportunity over a period of 2 1/2 years or so to read the quarterly NIF model-based forecasts, some personal speculations on this topic may not be inappropriate. My impression is that the development and continuing operation of these models has considerably advanced understanding of the economy, in particular the understanding of those who operate the models and those who see the conditional forecasts and the policy simulations. This is basically because the models attempt in a systematic and precise way to trace through and to represent the relevant interactions and interdependencies within the economy. Regular quarterly operation continually throws up questions as to why certain unexpected events occur. This presents challenges and gradually improves understanding. The formal nature of the models means that this understanding can then be passed on to others, whilst the informal and intuitive knowledge of other "economy watchers" is less readily transmittable.

One should, of course, not overstate the advances in understanding which are possible as a result of the development and operation of these models. The available data often will not allow us to choose conclusively between rival models, models which might have very different policy implications. Model building will always contain a skill which is not wholly subject to scientific rules. As FitzGerald and Higgins [7] put it in their discussion of the RBA 76 model:

> "The nature of the data with which our profession must work requires the imposition of a high degree of prior specification if the facts are to be dis covered. On the other hand, if the imposition of specification is taken too far the modeller is in danger of 'discovering' only what he did."

14 Peter Jonson and the Bank should be commended for these endeavours. The papers and proceedings of a two-day conference on RBA 76 in December 1977 are published as "Conference in Applied Economic Research", Reserve Bank of Australia, December 1977.

Again official forecasting with models can never be complete or self-contained; the models can only predict how the economy is likely to behave once a large number of exogenous variables are specified and fed in to produce forecasts, forecasts which are then conditional on the values of the exogenous variables having been correctly specified. Every national econometric model forecast has to be based on some international trade and external price assumptions; normally the National Wage decision of the Arbitration Commission and farm output are also assumed to take on certain values.

In practice the number of variables to be thus specified is large, in the case of the NIF model there are over 100 exogenous variables. However, many of them are policy variables, e.g. the company tax rate, etc. In the case of some very large econometric models like the Norwegian MODIS IV, there are no less than 2,000 exogenous variables. Hence forecasting with econometric models is always conditional. Cynics might argue that since one can never get the future paths of so many variables right, one is never really likely to get the forecast right. Whilst it is true that the future is really unknowable, governments and other economic agents act (either explicitly or implicitly) on the basis of a likely future. Models then provide them with an explicit efficient information tool, a systematic storage and processing framework for the large quantities of information used by fore casters, whatever method they might wish to use.

The economic structure the model builders are trying to capture is a changing one, so that understanding can never be complete. There is a good deal of evidence that the Australian economic structure changed rapidly during the seventies, no doubt partly in response to the much higher rates of inflation and the much lower levels of economic activity experienced. To give just one example, Davis and Lewis [4] cite a good deal of evidence suggesting that the demand for money functions estimated with data of the 1950s and 1960s exhibited considerable instability during the 1970s. A change or evolution in the parameters creates considerable problems for statistical estimation. Also, the structure could change just because different policies are followed.[15]

15 Lucas has argued that these changing structures cannot in principle, be estimated sufficiently accurately to enable us to provide policy makers with useful information as to the actual consequences of alternative economic policies. (*Cf:* Robert E. Lucas, "Econometric Policy Evaluation: A Critique", in Volume I of *the Carnegie Rochester Conferences on Public Policy*, North Holland 1976). For one possible reply, see Robert J. Gordon's contribution in the same volume.

In spite of these drawbacks, the econometric models have firmly established their role both in forecasting and in policy simulation, both in Australia and in many overseas countries such as the United States, the United Kingdom, the Netherlands, Norway, and so on. According to Otto Eckstein, a leading US model builder and academic, virtually all serious national economic forecasting in the US is now done with the aid of large scale econometric models. Just as politicians rightly consult fallible public opinion polls as giving them the best available information, so economic policy advisers consult fallible econometric models before either making their own forecasts or recommending appropriate policy stances.

Partly as a result of the development and operation of these large scale models, I believe there is a substantial gap in understanding and expertise on the Australian economy between the economists in the central policy making departments (the members of the "official family" as they sometimes call themselves) and those outside who do not have regular access to these and other internal applied economic research and policy memoranda. I believe a good deal of this gap is unnecessary for protecting the formulation and the giving of confidential advice from senior public servants to Ministers. In fact, the gap may often be counterproductive for achieving a government's goal and for enabling the community at large to understand the limitations on a government's ability to manage the economy.

If I were to be thoroughly impractical and consider how best to run such a national econometric model, for the purposes of applying what intelligence and resources we can to the solution of our economic problems, I would place the model in a semi-autonomous organisation where its policy simulations could be carried out on behalf of not only those charged with giving macro-economic policy advice, but also on behalf of other groups. Other departments also have a need for such policy simulations (e.g. Environment, Housing and Community Development, Employment and Industrial Relations, etc.) as may others such as the Arbitration Commission, the ACTU, Employer's Organisations, the Opposition, etc. Of course, this is all very fanciful, naive speculation which neglects the realities and the intensities of both bureaucratic and party politics in this community. It only seems worth mentioning because other countries, not too dissimilar, have managed to order their affairs in such an apparently sensible fashion. In Norway, for instance, large scale public econometric models have been used to assist policy formulation for almost two decades (since 1960). Model development and operation is undertaken by a servant of Parliament and not of the executive, the Central Bureau of Statistics, with the Ministry of Finance as the largest but by no means the only user of the model.[16] Nor is Norway unique. The Netherlands Central Planning Bureau, though officially a government agency, is given a great deal of latitude in conducting and publishing applied economic research including model-based conditional forecasts.[17] In large economies, such as Britain and the US the question of access to officially operated models is less pressing, since resources devoted to such studies are greater and there are several alternative private, or at least non-official, models available. In fact, in these countries the private models may often be in the lead.

In popular discussion of models in Australia undue emphasis has been placed on getting the official forecasts going up to government published. It is probably one of the less important consequences of the 1975 Constitutional Crisis that the forecasts are not published. Under Treasurer Hayden's explicit instructions, a set of forecasts were pre pared for publication at the end of October 1975 and, but for the Senate's delay of Supply, it is likely that they would have been published in November 1975.

Although I attempted unsuccessfully during 1973-75 to get these forecasts published, other members of the "official family" put up a number of cogent counter-arguments. These were basically that the professional, non-political quality of the forecasts would probably suffer and thus government could be deprived of the best possible information for its decisions.

---

16 It was, and is, used for instance by all parties in centralised income negotiations, by other groups such as the Ship Research Institute of Norway to analyse the impact on the Norwegian economy of an expansion and a change in the product-mix of the shipbuilding industry (towards construction of oil and gas exploration platforms), etc.

17 Australian officials using the models are sceptical of their mechanical use without judgemental adjustments of models where the linkages are known to be weak (e.g. expectation linkages in the case of NIF). The Norwegians cope with this type of problem by having officials in their Ministry of Finance who have operated the model at an earlier time and who are thoroughly familiar with its strengths and weaknesses. In Australia, Treasury, Prime Ministers and the Reserve Bank have a number of senior policy advisers in an identical position.

Whilst I still believe that it would be desirable that sets of conditional forecasts be prepared and published, this should probably not be done by those charged with giving macro-economic policy advice, but perhaps by some more independent group (as it is in other countries). What is more important than such conditional forecasting is the public availability of policy simulations and of other applied economic research work. Whilst there has been a welcome increase in the publication of technical economic papers of professional public servant/economists at various professional fora, it is surely ironic that the only regular quarterly Commonwealth government publication of technical economic material for many years was the BAE's *Quarterly Review of Agricultural Economics*. A good deal of applied economic analysis and research work is done which could safely see the light of day without betraying confidential policy advice: in many cases it would aid public understanding and might even make acceptance of unpopular policy stances easier.

What the public studies with the models say – a modest sample

A great deal of information and applied research work has been done on the various models which one cannot hope to summarise within the space available. Comments here will be restricted to the more central economic issues of wages, taxes, inflation and unemployment and even within this broad area, the focus is on some of the more topical issues.

The comments refer mainly to three papers: (1) The Jonson-Taylor simulation of Australian inflation during 1971 to 1975 using RBA 76; (2) the FitzGerald-Higgins comparisons of alternative policy simulations with NIF7 and RBA 76; and (3) Paul Coghlan's recent simulations with the NIF7 model.

Jonson-Taylor used RBA 76 to ascertain the effects of "steadier" trend policies on inflation and unemployment over the 1971 to 1975 period. The alternative policies included a managed float of the exchange rate, tighter money, government spending growing at 1966 to 1970 average rates and award wages growing at the same rate as productivity. If these policies had been adhered to, the unsatisfactorily high levels of inflation and unemployment during 1971-75 could have been substantially avoided.[18]

18 According to the simulations, inflation would have averaged 5 per cent and unemployment less than 2 per cent with this bundle of policies over the period 1971-75.

Gregory has pointed out that while it is not possible, on the basis of the Jonson-Taylor simulations, to be certain, the simulations appear to indicate that the single policy change which could have made the greatest difference to the performance of the Australian economy during the early '70s was a lower path of award wages.[19]

Again, as shown in the FitzGerald/Higgins simulations with RBA 76 and NIF7, award wage increases lead both to output and to employment reductions, whilst Coghlan's NIF7 simulations suggest a wage pause for three quarters from May 1975 to February 1976 would have reduced registered CES unemployment by more than half over the next 2 1/2 years – i.e. by the June quarter of 1978.

None of these simulations are conclusive, in each case one can point to certain unsatisfactory features which cast doubts on the results.[20] But while academic economists can take the time to examine these and other puzzles regarding the real wage/employment nexus (such as the apparently slight female/male employment responses after the introduction of equal pay), policy makers do not have this luxury, they must act on the basis of the best information available, even when it remains uncertain.

19 R. G. Gregory [8, p. 232]. (I will put to one side whether such a lower path was politically or institutionally a possible option.)

20 Thus in the case of RBA 76, an aggregate production function is assumed (not estimated) with the demand for labour adjusting to close the gap between the marginal product of labour and the real wage rate. The speed of this adjustment is estimated empirically, but the assumption of a long-run decline in the demand for labour when its price rises .faster than labour productivity is not satisfactory for this type of policy simulation. In the case of the NIF model, Coghlan has pointed to the unsatisfactory nature of the output/employment response' in the present version of the model. Based on 1959-76 data the elasticity of employment with respect to product is about 0.9; but on the basis of 1974-78 experience, an elasticity of around half that level may be more correct at the present time (*cf.* Coghlan *op. cit.*, p. 7). There are other unsatisfactory features about the State and local government employment response to slower growth of award wages in the NIF model which need to be mentioned. State and local government outlays are fixed in nominal terms; thus any cut in inflation results in correspondingly higher real government outlays-with consequent effects on real output and employment. Thus of the increase in real GDP in the twelfth quarter of the simulation, no less than 45 per cent is the result of extra government output. Such modelling of State and local government expenditure seems unrealistic, at least in the second and third years. Some reduction in nominal outlays under these circumstances would probably model the real world more accurately.
On the other hand, as Coghlan points out, the NIF7 model probably does not fully reflect the monetary, expectational and balance of payments effects of reduced inflation. These would tend to increase the stimulatory effects of such a slower rate of growth of money wages.

It seems to me, therefore, that the Fraser government's attempt to argue before the Arbitration Commission for a substantially lower rate of increase in award rates is justified economically, both to reduce inflation and to gradually improve the employment position. This does not imply that other policy stances by the present Government could not also be used to improve the employment situation. For instance, the reduction of government expenditure and of personal income taxes has probably reduced employment appreciably. From an economic point of view, the best time to reduce the absolute or the relative size of the public sector is during a boom, not in the depth of a serious recession. According to the Coghlan simulations, the likely combined effects of a simultaneous decrease in current Federal government expenditure and in personal taxes is to reduce significantly the level of employment, whilst the price level is barely affected.[21]

Also there are other economic policy stances of the government which not only make no contribution towards alleviating the twin evils of inflation and unemployment but probably aggravate them. I refer particularly to two policy stances, first, the overwhelming preference for direct versus indirect tax reductions, and secondly the various attempts by government to reduce the price of capital relative to labour.

The Coghlan simulations show clearly that, according to the NIF model, indirect tax reductions have a more favourable effect on both inflation and jobs than direct tax cuts of the same magnitude.[22] In this respect, they confirm Nevile's simulations in November 1977 [29, pp. 32-39].

Coghlan's simulations enable us to compare tax cuts costing $100 million per quarter (in 1966-67 prices, or around $1,000 million annually in 1977-78 prices). An indirect tax cut of this size in the third quarter of 1975 would

21 Combining a decrease of $100 million (1966-67 prices) per quarter of personal tax collections and $122 million (1966-67 prices) of government expenditure (or around $1,000 million annually in 1977-78 prices) leaves the government deficit unchanged after three years, but reduces employment by between 66,000 and 78,000 over the three years and increases CES unemployment by some 27,000 to 36,000. The implicit consumption deflator as a result of such simultaneous reductions in taxes and government expenditure would be reduced by half a per cent after three years.

22 Here too it is necessary to enter a qualification about possible inadequate linkages in the NIF model. While there is a consumer price/money wage rate link in the model, there is no direct tax rate/money wage rate linkage.

have given us 2.5 per cent lower consumer prices by mid-1978 than a cut in personal income taxes costing the same, whilst the demand expansionary effect on employment would have given us about 50,000 extra jobs.[23] There are, of course, other reasons which can be advanced for preferring to reduce direct taxes, but it behoves an outside observer to point out that such a preference implies a relative downgrading of the inflation/unemployment objectives.

Recent work on the labour market sector of the NIF model by Johnston, Campbell and Simes suggests that relative capital/labour price movements "have resulted in sizeable amount of substitution of capital for labour" [16, p.16]. Relative capital/labour price movements depend not only on the movements in wage costs, but also on the cost of capital. The provision of the 40 per cent investment allowance and of accelerated depreciation allowances, not to mention the government's attempt to reduce interest rates have also played some part in encouraging such capital/labour substitution. One cannot therefore "blame" the current level of real wages for all the capital/labour substitution which seems to be taking place at present.

While I believe the models have given us some important order-of-magnitude estimates of a number of possible policy changes, one should not claim too much for them. For instance they are probably not able to shed much light as yet on one of the current central problems of economic management, namely whether traditional Keynesian pump priming methods would still predominantly stimulate output and employment or whether an increasing proportion of such a stimulus would be dissipated by higher prices, or again whether such a stimulus would set off unfavourable capital account movements. This is probably the most basic and contentious issue separating the expansionists from those who back the very cautious approach of the present government. But the mere fact that models are unlikely to answer all our questions is of course no justification for not using them to shed what light they can.

23 However the inflation rate is affected mainly in the first year (according to both the Coghlan and Nevile simulations). According to Coghlan the control inflation rate between the 1st and 4th quarters is 10.9 per cent; with indirect tax cuts this would be reduced to 8.8 per cent. In the second year, (i.e. between the 4th and 8th quarter) the inflation rate is reduced from a control 11 per cent to 10.8 per cent and in the third year (i.e. from the 8th to the 12th quarter) from 8.7 to 8.4 per cent. (I am indebted to Paul Coghlan for drawing my attention to an error on this point in an earlier draft.)

Conclusion

In my concluding comments I want to revert briefly to the disenchantment with economics referred to earlier. Originally this disenchantment was partly the result of rising expectations; growth of living standards, full employment and price stability became taken for granted; while lifting our horizons we managed to forget that these achievements could be lost if we didn't go on working at them.

Since then our unsatisfactory economic performance and the spectre of economists disagreeing about the solutions have no doubt accelerated this disenchantment. I believe some of the disenchantment is unjustified. Whatever may have been the mistakes of economists and of economic policy advisers, political and institutional failures have loomed large in recent inadequate economic performances. This inadequate performance started with the failure to appreciate in 1971, against the predominant professional advice at the time. The unduly expansionary fiscal policy stance in 1972-73 (essentially to avoid losing an election) and in 1973-74 (to keep election promises) set the stage for many of the subsequent difficulties.

On the other hand, inadequate economic growth rates, high levels of inflation and unemployment have been shared in greater or lesser degree by most if not all other OECD economies. Economic problems have become more threatening and are therefore more challenging than in the sixties. Can economic analysis come up with worthwhile solutions or are the political constraints too restricting? The dissatisfaction with the development of the discipline felt by many leaders of the profession internationally has been documented by Groenewegen [9, p. 31] . In a recent survey of the current state of economics, Thurow is agnostic about the future intellectual progress of economics. He believes that the development of the profession proceeds

> ". . . in a manner similar to gold mining. Some great, or lucky, prospector strikes a vein of high grade ore in the form of a new paradigm, technique or vision . . . ordinary miners go to work to mine much of the actual gold. Eventually the miners must work harder and harder . . . The intellectual rewards of further research along that line get smaller and smaller. In the last half century the great intellectual gold strikes have been the national income

accounts, Keynesian economics (a development that also allowed monetary economics to be rebuilt or rediscovered), mathematical economics and econometrics. Lesser gold strikes include the analysis of oligopoly, growth, human capital, and the random walk. Some of these strikes are still being worked in the last half of the 1970s, but most of them seem to have reached relatively low grade ore. The last decade has not witnessed a major or even a lesser gold strike. To rejuvenate its internal intellectual growth the profession needs a gold strike, but as with all actual gold strikes, no one knows where, or if, it will occur."[24]

Of course economists themselves could contribute to their professional standing by not being quite so opinionated and appearing certain on the basis of scanty and often inscrutable evidence. Let me close with Robert Solow's recipe for public statements by economists:

> "Can anything be done? Your guess is as good as mine. I would like to see us stick to fundamentals in public, and to robust, well-established empirical relationships. Understanding about supply and demand, and marginal cost and discounting, and the national income identity, and stocks and flows, and substitution, and the simpler macroeconomic models, and the limitations of those models – all that already gives us a comparative advantage over others. Why not stick to it? Tomorrow the world."[25]

24 Lester C. Thurow: Economics 1977, *Daedalus*, Fall 1977, p. 93/4.
25 *Challenge*, March/April 1978, p. 40.

References

D. W. Challen & A. J. Hagger, *Modelling the Australian Economy* (Melbourne: Longman-Cheshire, 1979).

P. L. Coghlan, "Simulation with the NIF Model of the Australian Economy", Paper presented to the Simulation Special Interest Group Conference, Canberra, September 1978, mimeo.

W. M. Corden, *Australian Economic Policy Discussion: A Survey* (Melbourne University Press, 1968).

K. Davis & M. Lewis, "Monetary Policy", *Surveys of Australian Economics*, F. H. Gruen (ed.) (Sydney: George Allen & Unwin, 1978).

J. Edwards, "Labor's Record" in *Australian Politics, A Fourth Reader*, H. Mayer & H. Nelson (eds.) (Melbourne: Cheshire, 1976).

H. D. Evans, *A General Equilibrium Analysis of Protection* (Amsterdam: North Holland, 1972).

V. W. FitzGerald & C. I. Higgins, "Inside RBA 76", Conference in Applied Economic Research, Reserve Bank of Australia, December, 1977.

R. G. Gregory, "RBA 76: Wages and the Balance of Payments", Conference in Applied Economic Research, Reserve Bank of Australia, December, 1977.

P. D. Groenewegen, "Radical Economics in Australia. A Survey of the 1970's", *Surveys of Australian Economics, Volume II.* F. H. Gruen (ed.) (Sydney: George Allen & Unwin, 1979).

F. H. Gruen, "What Went Wrong? Some Personal Reflections on Economic Policies under Labor", *Australian Quarterly*, December, 1976.

H. Hagger, "Inflation", *Surveys of Australian Economics*, F. H. Gruen (ed.) (Sydney: George Allen & Unwin, 1978).

Haig & M. P. Wood, "Tracing Price Changes Through Stages of Production: Australia, 1968-1977." Paper presented at the 15th General Conference of the International Association for Research in Income and Wealth, York, England, August, 1977. Forthcoming in Review of Income and Wealth, Yale.

K. Hancock, "The Demise of Australian Wage Policy" in J. R. Niland & J. E. Isaac (eds.) *Australian Labour Economics Readings* (Melbourne: Sun Books, 1975).

G. Hawker, "The Use of Social Scientists and Social Science in the Inquiries of the Labor Government". Paper presented to the Sociology Section of ANZAAS, 1977, mimeo.

R. F. Henderson, "Income Inflation in Australia", *Australian Economic Papers*, vol. 11, 1972.

H. N. Johnston, R. B. Campbell & R. M. Simes, "The Impact of Wages and Prices on Unemployment", Winter School, NSW Branch of the Economic Society of Australia & New Zealand, July, 1978, mimeo.

Peter Jonson & J. C. Taylor, "Inflation and Economic Stability in a Small, Open Economy: A Systems Approach" in *The Problem of Inflation*, vol. 8, Carnegie-Rochester Conference Series on Public Policy (North Holland, 1978).

Paul L. Joskow & Roger G. Noll, "Regulation in Theory and Practice: An Overview" *MIT Economics Working Paper* No. 218, 1978.

J P. Juttner, "Economic Policy, Inflation and Unemployment", *Economic Papers*, January, 1977.

J. P. Juttner, "An Evaluation of the Performance and a Critique of Econometric Models of the Australian Economy", 1978, mimeo.

J. Kmenta, "An Econometric Model of Australia, 1948-1961", *Australian Economic Papers* vol.5, 1966.

P. J. Lloyd, "Protection Policy", *Surveys of Australian Economics*, F. H. Gruen (ed.) (Sydney: George Allen & Unwin, 1978).

Robert E. Lucas, "Econometric Policy Evaluation: A Critique", *Camegie-Rochester Conference on Public Policy*, vol. 1 (North Holland, 1976).

Lacklan McGregor, "On the Rationale of Stabilisation Policy", Paper for Centre of Independent Studies Conference, "What Price Intervention", 1978, mimeo.

Ezra J. Mishan, "The Folklore of the Market: An Inquiry into the Economic Doctrines of the Chicago School", *The Chicago School of Political Economy*, Warren J. Samuels (ed.) (Michigan State University, 1976).

J. W. Nevile, "A Simple Econometric Model of the Australian Economy", *Australian Economic Papers*, vol. 1,1962.

J. W. Nevile, "Inflation in Australia: Causes and Cures" *Economic Papers*, March, 1974.

J.W Nevile, *Fiscal Policy in Australia, Theory and Practice*, second edition (Melbourne:Cheshire,

J. W. Nevile, *Tax Cuts as an Anti-Inflationary Weapon*, CAER Paper No. 3, November, 1977.

J. P. Nieuwenhuysen and J. Sloan, "Wages Policy", Surveys of Australian Economics, F. H. Gruen (ed.) (Sydney: George Allen & Unwin, 1978).

Ross Parish, "Industrial Censorship", Paper for Centre of Independent Studies Conference "What Price Intervention" 1978, mimeo

Michael G. Porter, "Stabilisation Policy and Misplaced Entrepreneurship", Paper for Centre of Independent Studies Conference "What Price Intervention", 1978, mimeo.

John Rawls, "The Basic Structure as Subject", *American Philosophical Quarterly*, vol. 14,1977

P. J. Sheehan & D. S. Ironmonger, "The Real Income Guarantee: A Fiscal Policy to Control Inflation", *Australian Economic Review*, October, 1973

Sieper, "Consumer Protection – Boon or Bane?" Paper for Centre of Independent Studies Conference "What Price Intervention", 1978, mimeo.

D. Whitehead, "Inflation versus Unemployment: a Non-Monetarist View". Paper presented to the 48th ANZAAS Congress, Melbourne, 1977. mimeo.

G. Whitlam, *The Road to Reform – Labor in Government*, Chifley Memorial Lecture, 1975, mimeo.

R. Willis, "Sound Economic Managers or Agents of Social Change?". Keynote Address to the Second National Conference of Labor Economists, 1978, mimeo.

T. Valentine, "The Battle of the Plans: An Econometric Analysis". Paper presented at the 7th Conference of Economists, 1978, mimeo.

J. A. Zerby, "An Econometric Model of Monetary Interaction in Australia", *Australian Economic Papers*, vol. 8, 1969.

38

Work and welfare in the years ahead

Robert G. Gregory[1]

Macro economic policy since World War II has been dominated by the notion of a Phillips curve, whereby the rate of inflation and the level of unemployment are linked together so that more of one implies less of the other. These two variables are among the six major objectives of economic policy as listed in the terms of reference to the Vernon Report [5].

It is interesting to look back over the Fisher Lectures since they began in 1904 to see the extent to which the role of these two objectives of present day governments were reflected in the choice of subject matter discussed.

Inflation has always had a presence. In his 1921 Lecture, Professor D.B. Copland included the following quotation in his first paragraph: "The rise and fall of the general price level is one of the greatest evils that can affect a commercial nation." [7, p. 5]

Such sentiments were expressed in other lectures between 1904 and 1944 and there was a much discussion of the relationship between inflation and gold, the money supply, national debt and government deficits in a vein similar to the discussions that are occurring today. In 1934, during the depths of the Depression,

1 Thirty-eighth Joseph Fisher Lecture, 9 December 1981. Since published in (1982) "Work and Welfare in the Years Ahead" *Australian Economic Papers*, 21(39): 219-43; (1983) "The Slide into Mass Unemployment: Labour Market Theories, Facts and Policies", Annual Lecture, The Academy of Social Sciences in Australia; and "Wages Policy and Unemployment in Australia" *Economica*, 1986, 53: 553-741. Much of the research reported was undertaken with W. Foster, P. Stricker and P. Sheehan of the Institute of Applied Economic and Social Research, University of Melbourne. The author is grateful for their help. The author also received comments from J. Pincus, F. Gruen, L. Edwards, A. Hall and M. Gray. The analysis of Parts III and IV is developed in more detail in Foster and Gregory [8, 9]. The research was financed in part by the Utah Foundation and the Bureau of Labour Market Research. Neither are responsible for the views expressed.

when trade union unemployment in Australia was about 30 per cent Sir Leslie Melville began his Fisher Lecture with the statement: "Today, in English-speaking countries, the price level has come to be the chief pre-occupation." [22, p. 5]

There is virtually no discussion of unemployment. A surprising omission given that throughout the pre-World War II period unemployment was generally much higher than it is now.

It is not until forty years after the first Fisher Lecture that an address is specifically directed towards employment and unemployment. In 1944 H.C. Coombs begins his lecture with the statement: "Governments of democratic countries during the war have accepted a new responsibility – that of maintaining a high, stable level of employment within their borders." [6, p. 5]

For those of you who may be starting to lose faith in the ability of governments to control the level of economic activity and who yearn for a simpler world, I recommend this lecture to you. It is a good lecture to read during these troubled times for it embodies the spirit of the brave new world that I remember when I was first taught macro economics. Coombs talks of how governments will manage the economy to maintain full employment and thereby increase human welfare. In the future "There will be a few more jobs available than men and women to fill them, (so) that there will be a slight but persistent shortage of labour". [6, p. 7]

Coombs mentions very briefly an inflation-unemployment link similar to that which made Professor Phillips famous and discusses the fact "that a high employment economy always carries within it the seeds of inflation" [6, p. 29]. However, little attention is given to this topic and he comments that the difficulties for macro economic policy that are presented by any inflation-unemployment link should not deter us. The emphasis is clearly on full employment and not on inflation. A new era seems to be beginning. Coombs comments upon the 10 per cent unemployment rate of 1940 and thought that full employment might mean 4 per cent unemployment for males and 2 per cent for females.

As we all know, after World War II and until very recently full employment policies appeared to be very successful. Recessions were short and unemployment was so low that three decades passed before unemployment of males rose above the level that Coombs called full employment.

After Coombs, inflation and unemployment disappeared from the Fisher Lectures until 1971 when Professor Henderson began his lecture by introducing the notion of stagflation: "the combination of a stagnant level of activity combined with a rapid rise in prices." [16, p. 1]

Like Coombs before him, Henderson focussed on what was to become the central issue of economic policy through the coming decade: low growth rates and high levels of unemployment and inflation.

I have drawn these lectures to your attention to help explain my choice of topic. Looking back over the Fisher Lectures in the period before World War II it is remarkable how little regard was given to unemployment. Not only was unemployment not in the centre of the stage but it also did not appear to be in the cast of players. In some respects we are stepping back towards a world more like that of pre World War II. The change in the price level is increasingly becoming the centre of attention and the degree of responsibility that governments feel for full employment, as measured by their policy actions, is gradually being reduced. Because I feel so uneasy about this transition process, most of this lecture is devoted to observations on the nature of employment and unemployment in Australia today. These observations are made in the hope that eventually they will make a small contribution towards the design of government policies that will lead to higher levels of employment and lower rates of inflation than we have experienced over the last six or seven years. They focus on the labour market, rather than the Australian economy as a whole: because of this and the complexity of achieving full employment and stability of costs and prices these observations do not offer a simple and clear panacea for the problems we now face. They are more in the nature of a beginning of an attempt to redirect the economic discussion away from the increasing emphasis that is being placed on the control of inflation by tight monetary policy, reduced government spending and deficits and slow economic growth. Disquiet with the current stance of policies in many western economies and similar ideas to those developed here can be found in Okun [25], Solow [30], Akerlof [1], Hicks [17], and Clark and Summers [4].

The basic themes of the lecture relate to a search for answers to the following two questions:

1) Why do real and nominal wage increases – and therefore price increases – appear to be only loosely related if at all, to excess demand and supply in the labour market?

2) How is employment and unemployment allocated among people in the Australian economy.

To a large extent these are relatively new questions, brought to the forefront by the very poor performance of the Australian economy over the last decade. Australia has shared this poor performance with other countries but as Gray and Gruen [11] and Norton and McDonald [23] have shown, the relative deterioration in Australia is among the worst in the OECD countries.

I have posed two questions because I want to suggest that to a significant extent the answer to the first is related to the answer to the second. Since most of the research to be described is new and possibly unfamiliar to you let me present a brief outline of the analysis to follow.

In section II I argue that real and nominal wages are only loosely related to excess demand and supply in the labour market, particularly in the long term. Then in sections III, IV and V the data are assembled which will be used to explain why the price of labour is less flexible than other prices in the economy.

The message of section III is that although many people experience unemployment, most of the unemployment weeks incurred are concentrated on a very small group. Thus, during 1980-81, the 4.6 per cent of all unemployment spells that lasted more than a year accounted for 32 per cent of all the weeks of unemployment during that year. This concentration of long unemployment spells upon a small group means that a lengthy period of unemployment is a rare event for most of the labour force.

In section IV I show that although job turnover is high (a new job lasts on average 2-3 years) most employed people are in jobs which last a long time. The expected length of a job for the currently employed is about twelve years.

Consequently for most of the employed labour force there is a small probability of leaving their current job and incurring unemployment.

In section V data are presented to show that at any point of time more than half of the unemployed have either not held a full time job in the last eighteen months or have held a job of short duration. The long term employee who works full time has a very small probability of becoming unemployed, even during a very slack labour market.

From these facets we develop two closely related themes. First, a steady but higher rate of unemployment does not offer firms a significant reserve army of unemployed persons from which they can draw good workers. Much of the unemployment is concentrated upon the long term unemployed who, as a result of a sorting process, appear to employers to have low productivity. Nor does a steady but higher rate of unemployment pose a serious threat to most of the employed work force. After one or two years in the job the probability of experiencing a long period of unemployment is very low. For these reasons a higher but stable level of unemployment will not significantly affect the rate of growth of money and real wages. It is suggested that the rate of growth of real wages is determined primarily by implicit long term agreements between the firm and its work force as to the allocation of productivity gains. The size of the unemployment pool is largely irrelevant for the striking of these agreements.

The second theme is more of an aside in tonight's lecture. If it is in the mutual interests of firms and employees to have long job tenure and implicit contracts are an efficient means of cementing career relationships between workers and employers then there is considerable scope for conventions, customs, fairness and equity in the wage determination process. It is a result of this view of labour markets that many economists have been recently expressing sentiments similar to the following from R. Hall [14]: "There is no point any longer in pretending that the labour market is an auction market cleared by the observed average hourly wage. In the extreme case, wages are just instalment payments on a long term debt and reveal essentially nothing about the current state of the market." [14, p. 120].

The Phillips curve

Figure 38.1 presents a Phillips curve[2] for the years 1967-1981. Since I am primarily interested in labour markets the vertical axis measures the rate of growth of average weekly earnings per employed male unit rather than the rate of increase of the price level. It is obvious that there is no stable relationship between wage increases and the level of unemployment. If a trade off between wage increases and unemployment exists then it has shifted to the right and become worse. Relative to the late sixties, and indeed the whole post World War II period, Australia is now experiencing both higher rates of inflation and higher rates of unemployment.

Figure 38.1: Unemployment and annual change of average weekly earnings

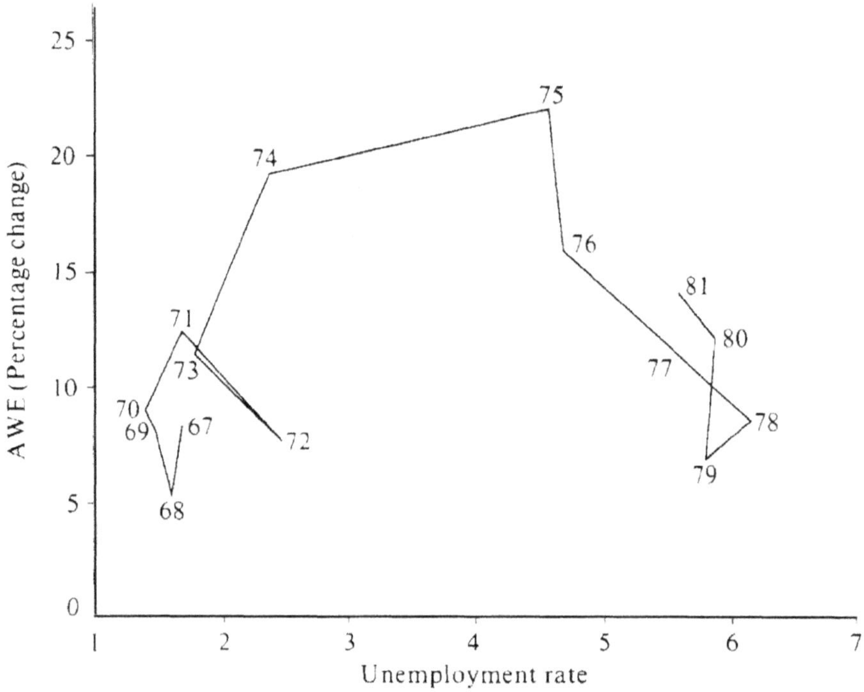

Source: ABS, *Average Weekly Earnings*, Cat. no. 6302.0. ABS, *The Labour Force*, Cat. no. 6204.0.

2 Phillips published his important article in 1958. He was Professor of Economics in the Research School of Social Sciences, Australian National University, between 1967 and 1970.

It does appear to be true, however, that initially an increase in unemployment is associated with some reduction in the rate of increase of money wages. The moderation of the wage increases during the 1971-72 and the 1975-78 period appear to be evidence of this. But when the labour market improves and unemployment begins to fall a new relationship appears to emerge with higher rates of wage inflation at each unemployment level. The period since 1979 is very marked in this respect. Unemployment, which is still at record levels for the post World War II period, has fallen slightly but the rate of increase of money wages during 1981 has been exceeded only in three of the last fifteen years.

A similar story may be told with respect to real wages (Figure 38.2). The initial rise in unemployment checked the rate of growth of real wages quite dramatically during 1975 but recently real wages have begun to increase again and at rates which are only slightly less than those of the pre 1975 period. There is an obvious move to the right of the real wage-unemployment relationship. The recovery of the rate of growth of real wages after each initial shock of an increase in unemployment is also evident.

Figure 38.2: Unemployment and the rate of increase of real wages

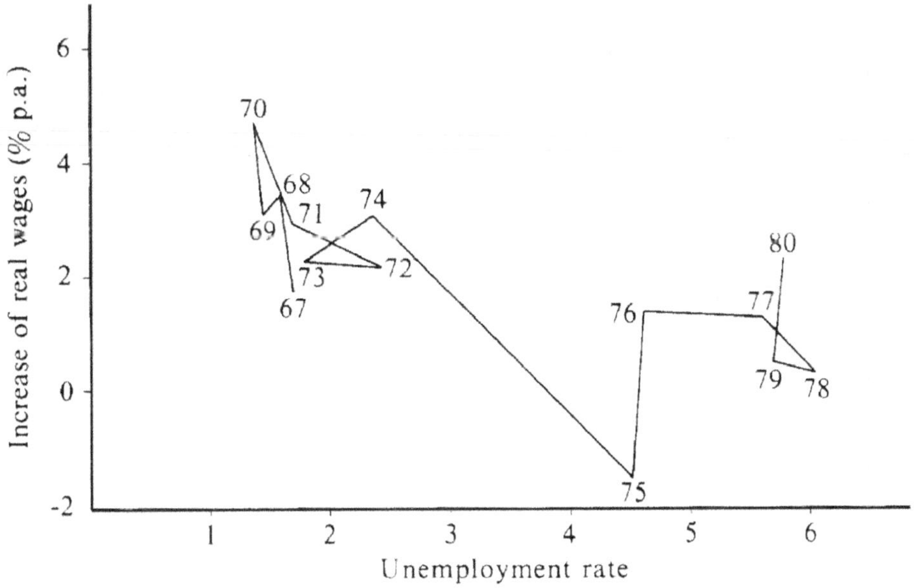

Source and Definitions: Average Weekly Earnings (male unit basis) deflated by the Implicit Price Deflator of Gross Non-Farm Product. Average Weekly Earnings, ABS, Cat. no. 6302.0. Australian National Accounts, ABS, Cat. no. 5201.0.

The original idea underlying the Phillips curve and the real wage-unemployment diagram is that the labour market is similar to a market for any other commodity in that the rate of change of the commodity price depends upon excess demand or supply. Unemployment is the measure of the gap between the demand and the supply curve. If this were an accurate description of the workings of the labour market the rate of increase of money wages should still be falling and real wages should not be increasing.[3]

Before we look more closely at the nature of the current levels of unemployment and some reasons why it is not affecting real and nominal wages to the extent that might be expected it is worth establishing the relative importance of demand and supply influences which have given rise to the increased level of unemployment.

Figure 38.3 plots the employment-population ratio (labour demand) and the labour force participation rate (labour supply) for the period 1966-81. It is evident that the rise in unemployment since 1973 has been the result of a collapse of labour demand. For seven of the last eight years the employment-population ratio has fallen. There has been no comparable drawn out recession since before World War II. In each of the previous recessions employment has recovered reasonably quickly. (OECD [24], Gregory and Duncan [12]). Between 1979 and 1980 the employment-population ratio increased at a rate comparable to the previous best years of employment growth but between 1980 and 1981 the decline has begun again.

A particularly depressing feature of Figure 38.3 is that the employment decline has not been concentrated in one or two bad years. Although the 1974-75 and 1977-78 recessions are evident the decline in the employment population ratio has been fairly steady and is beginning again.

3 The Phillips curve has generated a large literature. In that literature the shifting Phillips curve is 'explained' by adding additional variables to the equation that links wage increases to unemployment. The most important of these variables is the rate of increase of past consumer prices. We have placed this literature to one side in this paper. For an analysis of the Australian data in this tradition see M . G. Kirby [20].

Figure 38.3: Employment and labour force participation: All persons, 1966-1981

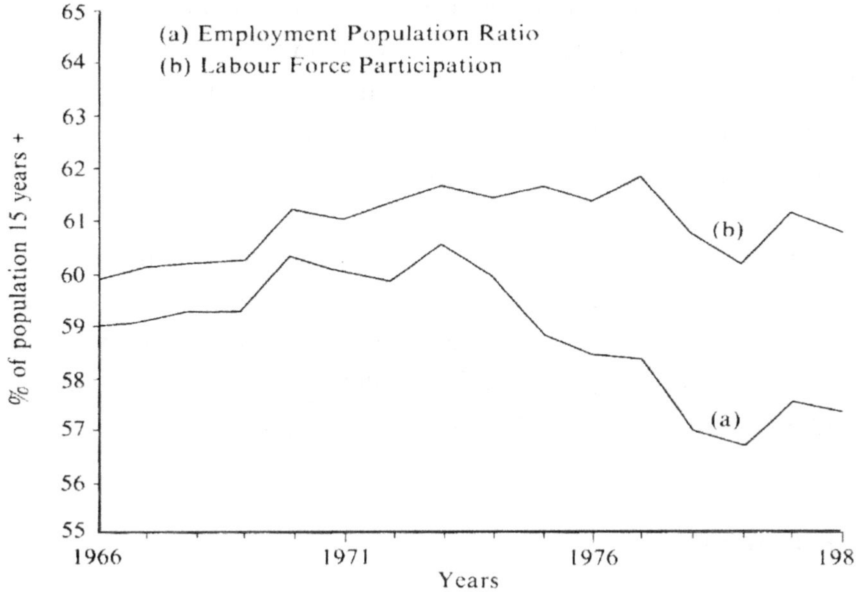

Source: ABS, *The Labour Force*, Cat. no. 6204.0.

It is especially interesting that the demand history over the recent seven or eight years is not faithfully reflected in the unemployment data. There have been unusual changes in labour supply. The 1974-75 employment falls were not matched by supply reductions and unemployment increased markedly as we saw in Figure 38.1. Since 1977, however, labour supply has varied closely with labour demand so that the employment declines of the employment-population ratio during 1978, 1979 and 1981 have not led to significant increases in unemployment.

The parallel movement of employment and labour force participation over recent years have led many economists to suggest that considerable hidden unemployment has been created in the Australian economy over the last few years (Stricker and Sheehan [29], Gruen [13], Gregory and Duncan [12]). If employment were to grow rapidly the hidden unemployed would return to the labour force. This phenomenon suggests that unemployment, as measured, is unlikely to fall quickly even if employment continues to grow quickly. Consequently in the absence of large falls in labour supply, it appears that there is little prospect for a significant decline in the high unemployment rates of recent years. For unemployment to return to 2 per cent of the labour force, three or four continuous years of employment growth would be needed at rates which have only been achieved in isolated good years over the post war period. The probability of three or four good years occurring together must be slight. Of course, the employment situation could continue to deteriorate as now seems likely and unemployment may increase further.

We now turn to consider how this higher burden of unemployment is allocated in our community and whether that allocation has any bearing on unemployment as a measure of excess demand and supply of labour? In considering possible answers to this question our focus will be primarily on unemployment as measured by the ABS. We put aside the concept of hidden unemployment.

Unemployment

Incidence of unemployment: 1981

Employment opportunities are not spread evenly in our society. It is common knowledge that the unemployment rate of teenagers is, on average, four times that of adults, that the unemployment rate of teenage girls is greater than that of teenage boys and that the unemployment rate of the low skilled and less educated exceeds that of the skilled and educated workers. Now that the unemployment rate is three times that of the sixties and appears likely to remain that way for some time, the incidence and concentration of unemployment looms more importantly as an economic and social problem.

It is usual to analyse the incidence and concentration of unemployment by documenting the dispersion of the unemployment rate across social, economic and demographic groups. I will adopt a different approach and analyse the incidence of unemployment by focussing upon the length of the unemployment spell that individuals experience.

Over the last few years the rate of unemployment has averaged about 6 per cent. Over a 12 month period this could mean at one extreme that 6 per cent of the labour force were without work for a whole year, or at the other, that every member of the labour force was unemployed for about 3 weeks and, as a result, incurred a loss of annual income of approximately 6 per cent. It obviously matters which situation more closely characterises the actual experience. Under most circumstances the more widespread a given level of unemployment the more equitable the burden of this unemployment[4] and certainly the greater the degree of understanding by society at large of the nature and ramifications of unemployment. The narrower the incidence of unemployment the more likely it is that society will generate a wide range of myths and general intolerance towards the unemployed. It is often useful therefore to think of the unemployment rate as the product of two factors – the rate of inflow to unemployment and the duration of the completed unemployment spell. Thus, the unemployment rate may increase because more people experience unemployment or because the unemployed remain without work for longer periods.

During 1981, 16.0 per cent of those who were in the labour force at some time experienced a period of unemployment.[5] The ABS does not publish information as to the completed duration of the unemployment spell of these people but there are a number of ways of estimating it.

The ABS publishes comprehensive data on the *interrupted* duration of unemployment of those measured as unemployed by the *Labour Force Survey*. The interrupted or current duration of unemployment is the number of weeks of unemployment experienced to date by those unemployed at the time of the sample. At August 1981, the average current duration of unemployment was 35.2 weeks. When these data are adjusted they can provide the foundation upon which a thorough and comprehensive analysis of the incidence of unemployment can be built.

For those in the ABS sample, duration refers to the length of the unemployment spell to date. They will have a further period of unemployment before their spell terminates. It can be shown (Salant [27]) that under steady state conditions these data will understate the average *completed* unemployment

4 The circumstances referred to relate to individual attitudes towards work and unemployment. The argument that equity is increased if unemployment is less concentrated presupposes that individuals experiencing unemployment are not those with the weakest preference for work.

5 *Labour Force Experience During 1981*. ABS, Ref. No. 6206.0.

experience of the currently unemployed by a factor of two because, on average, the currently unemployed will be halfway through their unemployment spell. Consequently for those measured as unemployed *at August 1981 the average completed spell of unemployment will be 70 weeks*. This is a very long time indeed and it suggests that the unemployment experience is very concentrated. The magnitude of the number is worth repeating: The 377,000 unemployed who represent 5.6 per cent of the labour force at August 1981 will, on average, be unemployed for between 16 and 17 months. This suggests a particularly serious unemployment problem.

You may be puzzled by this figure because it may be difficult to reconcile with your own experience of unemployment, or the length of the unemployment spell of those you know. I would guess that most of this audience believed that the average completed spell of unemployment was less than this. Further, you may ask the following question: if about 16 per cent of the labour force looked for work during a year and the average completed duration of unemployment, of those unemployed at August 1981 is 70 weeks, how is it that the unemployment rate is as low as 5.6 per cent? Should it not be much higher? These are good questions – the answers to which have only become clear quite recently (see the excellent article by Clark and Summers, [4]). The answers relate to the differences between the completed unemployment spell of those measured as unemployed at a point of time and the completed unemployment spell of all those who become unemployed during a year.[6]

The ABS survey measures the current unemployment experience at a point in time. It is a cross section sample and consequently not everyone who becomes unemployed during a year is included. Those who begin and end their unemployment between sample dates are excluded. In fact, the cross section is biased with respect to the length of all unemployment spells that occur during a year because the longer the spell of unemployment the more likely it is to be included in the cross section. The shorter the unemployment spell the greater

6 There are differences in definition involved in the measurement of the 16 per cent on the one hand and the 5.6 per cent and 70 weeks on the other. But these differences are not an important part of the answer to the question posed. The 16 per cent is taken from the *Labour Force Experience* where the unemployment concept used is "looking for work". This is a wider definition of unemployment than that used in *The Labour Force* which is the data source for the 5.6 per cent and the 70 weeks completed unemployment duration.

the under representation of spells of this length. This suggests that the length of the average completed spell of all who become unemployed will be less than the length of the average completed unemployment spell of those in the sample.

For our purposes of measuring the completed spells of unemployment there are two biases[7] at work in the ABS data. The first, as indicated above, is an "interruption bias" which states that for those in the sample the completed spell length is greater than the spell length to date. The second, is a "spell length bias" which states that the average completed spell length of those in the sample exceeds that of all those who become unemployed. The two biases operate in different directions. Is it possible to say which will predominate? Salant [27] has shown that the crucial factor is the relationship between the probability of leaving unemployment and the length of the unemployment spell. If the probability of leaving unemployment is unrelated to the length of the unemployment spell then the two biases exactly offset each other and the average length of the completed spell of unemployment is equal to the average length of the interrupted spells of unemployment as published by the ABS. If the probability of leaving unemployment declines as the duration of unemployment lengthens then the average completed spell of all who become unemployed will be less than the average interrupted spell of those in the cross section at the time of the survey.

In Figure 38.4 we plot the probability of leaving unemployment within the following month against spells of differing lengths, for August 1981. In the first month the probability of leaving unemployment is 0.29. After one year of unemployment the probability of leaving unemployment in the next month has fallen to 0.16. A similar relationship has been found in other western economies.[8] The probability of leaving unemployment declines as the length

7 These 'biases' are not to be taken to imply that there is something wrong with the ABS sampling procedure. It is only for our purpose of identifying the distribution of completed unemployment spells through time that the cross section data of incomplete spells at August 1981 is inappropriate

8 We are not sure why this phenomenon occurs. It is also evident in other countries and is thought to be the outcome of: (1) a sorting process – those who are most employable are employed first; (2) behaviour changes on the part of the unemployed – long periods of unemployment create either increasingly dispirited and unemployable people or people who adjust to their situation by reducing their desire for a job; and (3) the hiring policy of firms – the length of unemployment is used as a screening device. Hiring personnel believe that the long term unemployed are. on average. Less productive than the short term unemployed. For an analysis of the US, UK and Canadian data, see Clark and Summers[4], Main [21] and Hasanand de Broucher [15] respectively.

of the unemployment spell increases. Consequently the average length of the completed duration of unemployment will be less than the average length of the interrupted period of unemployment as published by the ABS.

Figure 38.4: Probability of leaving unemployment: All persons, 1981

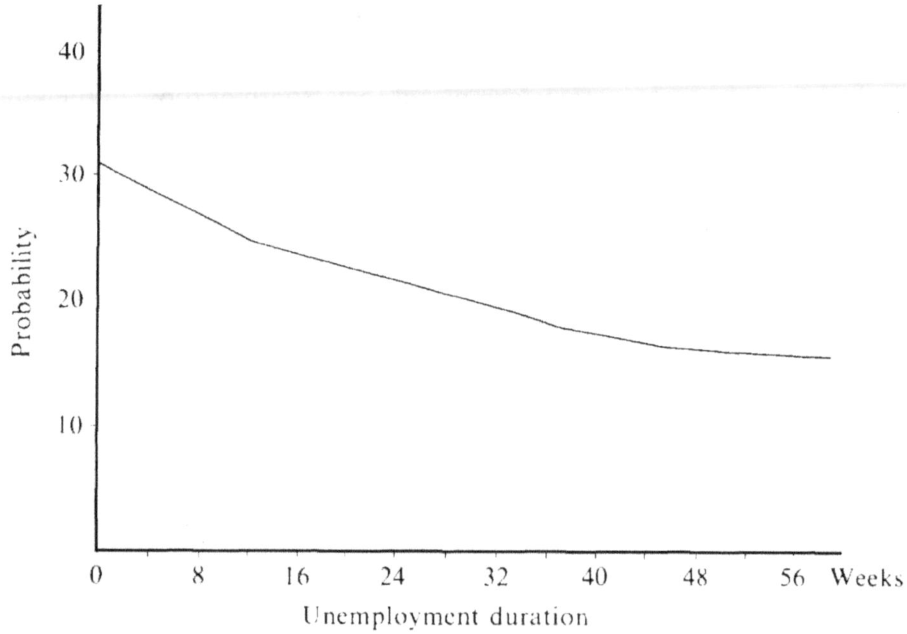

Source: Calculated from ABS, *The Labour Force,* Cat. No. 6204.0.

Table 38.1 presents the expected completed duration of an unemployment spell for all who entered unemployment during 1981. Upon entering unemployment the expectation was that the completed spell would be 16 weeks.

This is considerably less than the 70 weeks referred to earlier and is a reflection of the fact that the long term unemployed leave unemployment at a slower rate than the short term unemployed. It is the 16 weeks that should be closer to your experience of the unemployment duration rather than 70 weeks.

Table 38.1: Unemployment duration: All persons

Duration to date	1974	1978	1980	1981
0 weeks	5	15	17	16
26 weeks	10	24	30	32
65 weeks	nc	49	68	86

nc= not calculated
Source: Derived from *The Labour Force*, ABS Cat. No. 6204.0, see Foster and Gregory [8].

We also provide estimates of the expected number of weeks of unemployment yet to be experienced for those who have currently incurred spells of different lengths. Thus, after 26 weeks the expected number of additional weeks of unemployment is 32 weeks. This means, on average, that the completed spell will be 58 weeks long. After 65 weeks there is, on average, 86 weeks of unemployment yet to be served and, the completed spell will be 151 weeks long. There is a clear pattern. The longer a person remains unemployed the longer the period of unemployment yet to be served.

Another implication of the fact that the probability of leaving unemployment declines as the length of the spell increases is that there is a considerable difference between the distribution of completed spells of unemployment and the distribution of unemployment weeks attributable to spells of different lengths (Table 38.2). Thus, during 1981, when the expected duration upon entry to the unemployment pool was 16 weeks, 28.5 per cent of those who became unemployed left within 4 weeks and 63.6 per cent left within 13 weeks. For most people the completed unemployment spell is considerably shorter than the average. At the other extreme 4.6 per cent left after a completed spell of 12 months.

Table 38.2: Unemployment experience during 1981: All persons (per cent)

Completed spell length	Spells	Weeks
< 4 weeks	28.5	3.3
4 to less than 13 weeks	35.1	16.9
13 to less than 26 weeks	20.4	23.0
26 to less than 52 weeks	11.4	25.2
52 weeks and over	4.6	31.6

Source: Foster and Gregory [8].

We also present the distribution of unemployment weeks attributed to spells of different lengths. The distribution of unemployment weeks is the opposite to the distribution of spells. The 28.5 per cent of spells which terminate within 4 weeks account for 3.3 per cent of the total weeks of unemployment experienced during 1981, and at the other extreme of the distribution, the 4.6 per cent of spells which last for more than a year account for 31.6 per cent of the total number of unemployment weeks.

It is the declining probability of leaving unemployment as the spell increases that enables the following statements to be true at the same time. During 1981: 63.6 per cent of unemployment spells terminate within 13 weeks. But for all spells that occur the average length of a completed spell is 16 weeks; the average completed length of an unemployment spell of all who become unemployed is 16 weeks but the completed spell of the currently unemployed is, on average, 70 weeks; and 28.5 per cent of unemployment spells last less than 4 weeks but 31.6 per cent of all weeks spent in unemployment is accounted for by the 4.6 per cent of unemployment spells which last for more than a year.

Once these points are understood – and the concepts are difficult – a number of potentially important observations follow:

a) It is possible to have a very serious unemployment problem – 31.6 per cent of the total unemployment weeks that occur last more than a year – and yet the people you meet who have been unemployed will typically have experienced a very short unemployment spell. Consequently, the view that will be widely held in the community, based on experience, will be that there is no serious unemployment problem. After all, 28.5 per cent of the unemployment spells end within four weeks.

b) Welfare workers, and those who work with the unemployed will tend to meet the small proportion of all who become unemployed who account for most of the total weeks of unemployment that occurs in the community. The perception of unemployment shared by those who work with the unemployed will be different from the perception of the community at large. Consequently, as unemployment increases and the duration of unemployment lengthens we might expect a polarisation of views in society as to the seriousness of the unemployment problem;

c) Unemployment measured in terms of the number of people who experience unemployment is very concentrated in our society. As indicated earlier about 16 per cent of those in the labour force at some time during the year experience on average 16 weeks of unemployment during an unemployment spell.[9] However once allowance is made for the way in which the length of the unemployment spell is shared among the unemployed the concentration of unemployment is even more marked. Approximately three quarters of one per cent of those in the labour force at some time during 1980-81 will account for 31.6 per cent of the unemployment weeks that occur during the year. Two-and a-half per cent of those in the labour force at some time will account for half the unemployment weeks experienced in our society.

The changes since 1968

Between August 1968 and August 1981 the unemployment rate increased from 1.6 to 5.6 per cent of the labour force – a rise of 250 per cent. The number of people unemployed during the year as a proportion of those who were in the labour force at some time during the year increased by 120 per cent from 7.4 to 16.0 per cent. Consequently, although a wider range of people now experience unemployment during a year – one in six rather than one in fourteen – this change, in proportionate terms, is less than the increase in the rate of unemployment. As a result the duration of unemployment has lengthened and the unemployment experience has become more concentrated upon particular individuals. It is evident from Table 38.3 that those currently unemployed for more than 9 months have increased their share of unemployment from 4 per cent to 25 per cent.

It is not possible from the data available to calculate over all this time period the completed duration of unemployment of all those who become unemployed during each year.[10] We therefore utilise data as to the interrupted unemployment

9 We have not yet extended the analysis to encompass multiple spells of unemployment. As about 20 per cent of those who become unemployed incur more than one spell, the average length of time spent in unemployment per person will exceed the average length of a spell. Since delivery of this lecture this phenomenon has been analysed by Trivedi and Baker [31].

10 E. Khoo [19] attempted to measure changes in the completed duration of unemployment over the period 1962 to 1975. He uses data from the Commonwealth Employment Service.

duration of the stock of unemployed at August of each year. Over the period 1968-81 the average interrupted duration of unemployment for persons counted in the ABS *Labour Force* at August of each year, increased from 8.9 to 35.0 weeks – an increase of 290 per cent. If we use the doubling rule discussed earlier, the average completed spell for those counted as unemployed by the ABS has increased from 18 to 70 weeks. Furthermore, and this is particularly disturbing, although employment growth has been fairly buoyant since 1979 – and as a result the employment-population ratio has increased marginally – there is no sign of a reduction in the interrupted duration of unemployment. This disturbing fact should be investigated in a little more detail.

In Table 38.1 presented earlier, we calculate the expected completed spell of unemployment over the last few years. Although the expected completed spell upon entry to unemployment has not changed very much since 1978 the probability that the longer term unemployed will leave unemployment has continued to decline. For those unemployed 26 weeks the expected spell has increased from 50 to 58 weeks and for those unemployed 65 weeks the expected spell has increased from 104 to 151 weeks.

Table 38.3: Current duration of unemployment: All persons, 1972 to 1981[a] ('000)

Current duration of unemployment	1968	1972	1974	1976	1978	1981
Under 3 months	67	115	123	175	187	178
3 months and under 9 months	na	23	15	81	132	105
9 months or more	na	6	3	37	77	94
Total	**81**	**144**	**141**	**293**	**396**	**377**
Under 3 months	83	80	87	59	48	47
3 months and under 9 months	na	16	10	28	33	28
9 months or more	na	4	3	13	19	25
Total	**100**	**100**	**100**	**100**	**100**	**100**
Mean duration (weeks)	8.9	9.7	6.5	17.5	26.2	35.1
Unemployment rate	1.6	2.5	2.4	4.7	6.2	5.6

a) At 31 August
na= not available
Source: ABS, *The Labour Force*, Australia, various issues, Cat. No. 6204.0.

These results suggest that over the last few years as unemployment has marginally decreased the composition of unemployment is steadily changing towards an increasing number of long term unemployed.[11]

Employment

Employment can also be analysed in terms of inflows to employment ar completed employment spells. Interestingly we find the same kind of picture employment as of unemployment: although job turnover is high it conceals the fact that most jobs are held for very long periods of time.

It is often argued that the Australian labour force is extremely mobile. There are number of statistics that are often quoted to support this view. For example, the employment separation rates reported by industry indicate a very high degree (labour mobility. These typically show a turnover rate of labour of between 50 and 7 per cent per annum and an implied average completed job tenure of between one an two years. These data refer to job changes rather than to leaving employment.[12]

With respect to leaving employment the gross flow data recently published by the ABS[13] suggest that, on average, four per cent of those employed at the end of on month are no longer employed at the end of the next month, implying an annual rat of leaving employment of 47 per cent. These facts suggest a great deal of labour mobility, a very short job tenure and considerable scope for high incidence of new labour contracts between the firm and new hires. They raise the question as to why wages are not more responsive to excess demand or supply as measured by the unemployment rate. The answer lies, in part, in the nature of job tenure and the misleading impression that can be created by labour turnover and gross flow statistics.[14]

11 For a fuller analysis disaggregate by age and sex, see Foster and Gregory [8].

12 See ABS, *Labour Turnover*. Cat. No. 6210.0.

13 ABS, *The Labour Force*, August 1981, Cat. No. 6203.0.

14 There are very few studies of labour turnover in Australia. The most comprehensive is IAC [18].

For a number of years the ABS has collected the job duration to date of the employed. These data are available for a number of years since 1972 and from our perspective they indicate very little change in job tenure over the last decade.

These data are the job duration counterpart of the unemployment duration data and may be utilised in the same way to reveal the inflow into new jobs and the expected length of stay. It should be remarked, however, that the data refer to jobs and not t employment.[15] To the extent that job changes can occur without leaving employment they understate the length of continuous employment experience. The data for 1975 are given for all persons in column 1 of Table 38.4.[16] We could have chosen data from any of the other years for which they are available without any significant change in our conclusions.

The average current job tenure at the end of 1975 was 6.3 years but most people had held their job for less than 5 years (63 per cent). Only 20 per cent of those employed had been in their current job for more than 10 years. If we utilise the fact that on average the currently employed are sampled half way through their completed job tenure these data indicate an average completed job tenure of about 12 years – a statistic which at first sight is difficult to reconcile with the high employment turnover figures quoted earlier. The reconciliation lies in the changing probability of leaving the job as the job duration increases.

The probability of leaving a job of different current tenure can be derived from column 1 of Table 38.4. In a steady state the distribution of employment in column 1 implies the distribution of the probability of leaving a job of column 2. It is evident from column 2 that the probability of leaving a job within the next twelve months declines the longer the person has been in that job.[17] The probability that those employed in their current job for less than a year will leave

15 A job is defined with respect to a particular employer and locality. Consequently, a change in job locality without a change in employer is regarded as a job change. Thus employees can change their job but remain with their employer so increasing the length of continuous employment with one employer beyond that indicated by the data.

16 These data disaggregated by age and sex are analysed in detail in W. Foster and R.G. Gregory [9].

17 There are a number of ways of estimating the relationship between job tenure and the probability of leaving a job and each will involve some approximation. Our method is reported in Foster and Gregory [9]. Preliminary calculations suggest that the results of this method are likely to understate the rate at which people leave jobs of short tenure.

that job within the next 12 months is estimated to be 0.58. For those in the job duration category of 20 years and over the probability of leaving within 12 months is 0.10.

Table 38.4: Job tenure and the probability of leaving a job: All persons, 1975

Duration of job	Current job tenure (1)	Probability of leaving a job during the next year for a person employed at Dec. 1975 (2)	Completed tenure for new jobs (3)	Expected completed job tenure for persons employed at Dec. 1975 (4)
	Per cent	Per cent	Per cent	Per cent
<1 year	23	.58	60	9
1-less than 5 years	40	.20	24	23
5-less than 10 years	17	.16	10	24
10-less than 20 years	12	.13	5	23
20 years +	8	.10	2	20

Source: ABS, *Labour Mobility*, February 1976(1), Cat. No. 6.43. Foster and Gregory [8].

Since the probability of leaving a job is not constant as the length of tenure changes, considerations similar to those discussed with respect to unemployment arise. For example, job spells of short tenure will be under represented in the sample of the currently employed, the expected completed job tenure will change as the length of tenure increases and there will be a difference between the average length of time in the current job and the completed job tenure.

Column 3 of Table 38.4 presents the estimated job tenure for new jobs created during 1975. New jobs typically have a short life: 60 per cent of jobs begun in a year will terminate within 12 months.[18] Only 2 per cent of new jobs will last 20 years or more.

Column 4 presents the distribution of the expected completed job tenure of those employed at the end of 1975. It takes account of the fact that all those currently employed can expect to remain in their job for a longer period. The

18 It is likely that the population of new jobs that terminate within a year is even higher than this. See Foster and Gregory [9].

long length of expected job tenure may come as a surprise. Twenty per cent of the currently employed can, on average, expect to remain in their current job for more than 20 years and 43 per cent for more than ten years. Only 9 per cent of the currently employed will complete a job tenure of less than 12 months.

The data in column 4 indicate that the currently employed can expect a period of very long tenure and the particular definition of a job that is used by the ABS suggests that employees may in fact stay longer with their current employer. Furthermore, since it is possible to change jobs without experiencing unemployment the average length of continuous employment without unemployment will be even longer.

Table 38.5 is the job tenure counterpart to the distribution of unemployment duration in Table 38.2. It shows in column 1 the estimated completed tenure distribution of all those who began a new job in 1975, and in column 2 the proportion of completed employment years that will be associated with them.

Table 38.5: Expected completed tenure and years of further work associated with the existing work force and new jobs: 1975

	Completed job tenure	Years of work in new jobs	Completed tenure for persons employed at Dec. 1975	Extra years of work for persons employed at Dec. 1975
		Per cent	Per cent	Percent
<1 year	60	9	9	0
1-less than 5 years	24	23	23	7
5-less than 10 years	10	27	24	19
10-less than 20 years	5	27	23	36
20 years +	2	15	20	38

Source: Foster and Gregory [8].

These data indicate that the typical new job length is very short. During 1975 it was 3.2 years – a number which is larger than that calculated from labour turnover data. They also indicate that most work will be done by those employed in new jobs that will be of long duration. Thus, at one extreme of the distributions, 60 per cent of the new job starts will account for 9 per cent of the employment years worked and, at the other extreme, 2 per cent of the new jobs created will account for 15 per cent of the work years. In columns 3 and 4 we show comparable data for the currently employed. Here a similar phenomenon arises. The 32 per cent of the currently employed who will terminate their job within five years account for only 7 per cent of the work to be delivered by the current work force. Seventy-four per cent of the extra years of work to be delivered by the existing work force will come from those who will complete more than ten years of tenure.

These results suggest, where hiring costs are substantial and firm specific human capital is important, that firms will have a strong interest in their present work force relative to those newly hired. The existing work force will deliver in the future twice as many years work per worker as an average new hire. It will pay the firm to attempt to hoard its existing labour force during economic downturns and to develop employment contract terms and conditions that keep the existing employment stock intact.

The overlap between job tenure and unemployment

There is one more building block to construct.[19] Is it possible to relate job tenure to the probability of experiencing unemployment? If upon leaving a job the probability of experiencing unemployment were independent of job tenure then the results of the previous section would suggest that those with long tenure are unlikely to become unemployed because they are unlikely to leave their job.

Table 38.6 presents data that can be used to throw some light on the relationship between job tenure and unemployment. During May 1976, twenty-three per cent of the unemployed had not been employed in a full time job in the previous 18 months. Of those that had been employed the completed duration of their last job was typically very short. Forty-nine per cent of this group had held

19 Of course, if the building is to be grander we need more building blocks. One in particular would be very useful. Recent work in the USA, see Clark and Summers [4] and some of our earlier work, see Foster and Gregory [10] suggests that a considerable amount of unemployment ends not in finding a job but in leaving the labour force as defined by the ABS. We need data as to job finding success as unemployment duration lengthens rather than the data we have analysed here which refer to the rate at which people leave unemployment as unemployment duration lengthens.

their last job for less than 26 weeks and sixty-five per cent had held their last job for less than 12 months.

At any point of time, therefore, the unemployed come overwhelmingly from those who have not held a job or whose previous job was of very short duration. In the third column of Table 38.6 we have divided the number unemployed, classified by current job tenure by the number employed in each job tenure group. The approximate "unemployment rate" thus calculated diminished very quickly with job tenure, from 11 per cent for job tenures of less than 26 weeks to 0.78 per cent for job tenures greater than 5 years. Those with long tenure therefore face a very low probability of becoming unemployed.

Table 38.6: Completed duration of last job of the unemployed: All persons, May 1976

Completed job duration	Duration	Unemployment rate
	Per cent	Per cent
< 26 weeks	49	11
26-less than 52 weeks	16	5
1-less than 2 tears	13	3
2-less than 5 years	14	1
5 years +	8	

Note: The Table includes those persons unemployed at May 1976 who finished working in their last job in 1975 or 1976.
Source: ABS, *Persons Looking for Work*, Cat. No. 6.60.

Implications for the Phillips curve

The above description of the labour market stresses that the employment and unemployment experiences are very different for different groups of individuals.

With respect to the unemployed it was argued that as the level of unemployment increased and is now being maintained at a relatively high level, the nature of the unemployment pool has changed so that an increasing fraction of the pool consists of the long term unemployed. Over the period 1974 to 1981 those unemployed for more than 9 months have increased their share of the number unemployed, as measured by the ABS, from about 3 to 25 per cent. About 2 per cent of those who were in the labour force at some time during 1981 account for about 50 per cent of all the weeks spent in unemployment.

One outcome of the changing nature of the unemployment pool is that an increasing fraction of the unemployment pool is exerting very little influence on possible wage outcomes. On the demand side of the labour market the evidence suggests that the employability of the longer term unemployed is very low. In the employment stakes they certainly come a poor third behind the short term unemployed and those seeking employment from outside the labour force. In other words they do not serve as an effective reserve army. On the supply side of the labour market it is unlikely that the longer term unemployed are an important force acting upon the consciousness of the employed because (i) the long term unemployed represent such a small proportion of the labour force; (ii) the experience of the long term unemployed is atypical of all those who become unemployed; and (iii) those with current job tenures exceeding a few years have a low probability of becoming unemployed. Under these circumstances the employed are unlikely to have encountered those who have been unemployed for long spells.

With respect to the employed a picture of remoteness from potential unemployment has been built up. Forty-three per cent of the currently employed will remain in their current job for more than ten years. Long term job tenure buys advantages for both firms and employees. After an initial period, during which workers and the firm learn about each other and during which a high proportion of the newly employed leave, most of the remaining workers will stay with a firm a long time. By staying with the firm the risk of unemployment is reduced and the high probability of further costly job changes which are associated with beginning a new job is avoided. Furthermore after the initial learning period the worker may begin to reap the benefits of the specific skills that will have been acquired. For their part firms will want their workers to stay with them because of the high cost of hiring new workers. There is a very high probability that workers will leave during the initial phase of the job and the greater the degree of firm specific skills to be acquired the greater the cost imposed by this turnover. The interests of the existing work force and firms therefore mean that at any point of time the bulk of the employed are in the process of completing a job of long tenure. Even today when the average unemployment rate is about 6 per cent, the "unemployment rate" for the 40 per cent of the labour force that has been employed in their current job for more than 5 years is less than 1 per cent. A stable rate of unemployment of about 6 per cent is not a serious threat to these people.

These points can be put together to capture many of the important elements of the wage determination process and to throw some light on why real and nominal wage increases are loosely related, if at all, to excess demand and supply in the labour market. The existence of firm specific capital and the difficulties that workers experience in settling into a new job means that both labour and the firm have a stake in a stable, durable relationship. The long tenure that exists suggests that the firm and its work force will deal with each other on the assumption that there will be a long term relationship between them. The long term relationship and the efficiency gains that stem from this relationship will establish the preconditions for social customs and conventions to be important in the wage process. As Solow remarked in this context:

> "There is a difference between a long-term relationship and a one night stand, and acceptable behaviour in one context may be unacceptable in the other". [30, p. 10].

It is not surprising that under a long term relationship money or real wages are not flexible to clear markets and that customs, fairness and equity exert such an important role in the determination of wage levels and relativities. Under these circumstances it has been suggested that firms and workers will establish implicit contract or what Okun [25] has called invisible handshakes (see Hall [14], Okun [25], Solow [30], Hicks [17]). The implicit contracts that evolve become an understanding between the parties which, it has been argued by these authors, is to explain the following observed behaviour. Over the long term the firm will deliver a reasonable rate of growth of real wages and share the wealth that is generated. They will not reduce real wages during recessions or threaten tenured employees by hiring new workers during economic slumps under conditions which are less advantageous than those currently enjoyed. Bonnell [3], for example, has recently documented that real wages generally increased in the great depression of the thirties in the UK, USA, Sweden and Germany. The firm will attempt to hoard labour during the slump and as far as possible allow profits to absorb as much of the short run economic fluctuations, see Okun [25]. This behaviour generates the familiar pro-cyclical variation of labour productivity. For their part workers agree to moderate real wage demands during the profit slump and to allow their work effort to vary in the short run in a way that helps the firm. An analysis of the variability of average hours worked and labour productivity over the cycle suggests that most adjustments of labour input occur on the job rather than between employment and unemployment. See Hall [14].

As a result of these understandings there will not be a close relationship between the real wage and the value of the marginal product of labour in the short run.[20] Workers and firms build up a notion, based on past experience, as to what a reasonable rate of real wage increases should be in the medium and longer term and money wage increases are the mechanism to bring the real wage increases about. When there is a sudden fall in aggregate demand and a decline in firm profitability, the employed workers forego their real wage increases because the ability of the firm to pay real wage increases has been impaired. As a result, nominal wage increases are seen to be moderated at the same time as unemployment increases in response to the fall in aggregate demand. Hence, there appears to be a short run Phillips curve relationship and the rate of increase of real wages is reduced. But the change in the unemployment rate does not itself lead to the reduced rate of growth of real and money wages. The association is not causal. It is the profitability of the firm that matters.

If the labour market recession is a long one, as has been the case since 1974-75, firms are gradually able to re-establish their profitability by the continuation of productivity growth during the recession and by the adjustment of the capital stock that comes about by the reduction of investment during the slump. As a result of the restored profitability the elements of the implicit contract that relate to the understanding that real wages will increase when profits increase come back into play. Real and money wages begin to increase although unemployment is much greater than before. Some empirical support for this view was given in Figures 38.1 and 38.2 and is also discussed in Scherer [28].

20 These remarks are not to be interpreted as stating that market forces have no influence. If social customs and implicit contracts get too far out of line with the market for too long they will begin to break down. Throughout the text the term implicit contract has been used in a wider context than the class of models which have developed from M.N. Bailey [2].

From this view of the wage determination process a number of important conjectures may be made as to the current stance of macro economic policy.

First, short sharp shocks to aggregate demand will increase unemployment and moderate money and real wage increases. But it is not the unemployment per se that leads to the reduced rate of wage increases. Both are primarily the result of the reduced profitability of firms which invokes the implicit understanding between workers and firms that real wage increases will be moderated when firm profitability is low.

Second, long drawn out periods of unemployment and low real economic growth are not very effective anti inflation weapons. In the longer run the correlation between firm profitability and unemployment begins to breakdown. As unemployment is maintained through the years, less and less is gained in terms of lower wage claims (see Figure 38.1 and Figure 38.2). As soon as firm profitability is restored the real and money wage increases begin again.

The result is that a great danger stemming from long periods of sluggish output growth and high unemployment is a ratchet effect upon the unemployment pool. The number of long term unemployed and their expected period of completed unemployment duration increases. This analysis suggests that with respect to moderating nominal wage increases the crucial period is the beginning of the recession. It is during this time that the largest possible range of policy instruments should be brought to bear on nominal price increases. As the period of slack in the labour market lengthens the effect of excess supply on wage and price increases is reduced.

Third, it seems inevitable that a solution to the current crisis of low economic growth and high inflation must involve a change of attitude on the part of firms and the currently employed. The major thrust of the analysis of the labour market developed above suggests that the pursuit of low economic growth and the creation of large scale unemployment will not be sufficient to change these attitudes.[21] The economic position of most of the employed work force is

21 The world is more complex than that. To underline this point Solow explains why individual employers do not want to cut wages during recession "if employers know that aggressive wage cutting in a buyers market may antagonise the remaining work force. and make it harder to recruit high quality workers when the labour market tightens. they will be less inclined to push their short run advantage" [30, p. 8].

not seriously undermined by high and stable unemployment Consequently it is not useful to think of price and output effects of macro economic policy as the outcome of a two person game between a monolithic wage setting union and a central bank. The key players are the firms and their workers, most of the members of which have long job tenure. Therefore, despite the difficulties associated with income and wages policies of various sorts, perhaps we have to go down that road even if we are not optimistic as to the outcome. Income and wages policies cannot substitute for managing aggregate demand but given the insensitivity of nominal wages to high unemployment in the longer term it is likely that they must be a part of good economic policy. The more than can be done to affect the attitudes that are built into implicit contracts the better.

Fourth, there is probably a special need for policies that reallocate jobs towards the long term unemployed. Given that the long term unemployed are to be with us for quite some time, that their numbers are swelling and, if as I have argued above, they do not contribute significantly to the reduction of inflation or to the moderation of real wage increases there is a case for policies that do nothing more than reallocate job opportunities towards this group. As the level of unemployment and the expected length of unemployment increases, the welfare objectives of manpower policies should increasingly come to dominate the efficiency objectives.

Further, it might be argued that policies which widen the incidence of unemployment by reducing its duration may even contribute to the ability of macro policy to impinge on wage settlements. We have manpower policies that discriminate in favour of long term unemployed youth. Perhaps they should be extended to encompass adults.[22]

22 These programmes primarily reallocate jobs. There are two important facts which should be known. Who gets a job as a result of the programme (the target group) and who loses a job as a result of the programme. It needs to be shown that those who lose a job. in turn, do not join the long term unemployed.

Concluding remarks

The performance of the Australian economy since 1974 has been the worst for thirty-five years. The fall in the growth rate has been considerable. Between 1966-67 and 1973-74 the growth of real GNP averaged 5.4 per cent. Between 1974-75 and 1980 81 the average rate has been 2.2 per cent. No-one appears to believe that the restoration of a fast rate of economic growth is likely in the near future.

The negative effects of this slow growth have been large. I have focussed upon the increase in unemployment but I could also have drawn attention to the very large numbers of people now receiving sickness, invalid and service and widows pensions which in many respects act as a substitute for unemployment benefits. (See Stricker and Sheehan [29].) To date, on the positive side, the slow economic growth has brought us only a temporary respite from inflation. Since 1978 the inflation rate has begun to steadily increase and the forecasts are for no significant improvement.

In this lecture I have attempted to explain why the employed will not be aware of the seriousness of the unemployment problem and why restrictive policies, leading to low economic growth and unemployment, can only be expected to have a major effect on the wage bargaining process in the short run. In the longer run the effectiveness of restrictive policies is reduced as 'normal' behaviour is re-established on the part of both firms and the employed.

In sketching out the behaviour of the labour market with respect to job tenure and unemployment duration I have not had the time to tie down all the loose ends. Only a start has been made on the integration of the labour market flows material with the inflation process, good economic policy and the generation of attitudes towards wage increases in our society. The theory of implicit labour contracts is also not well developed nor is its empirical relevance fully established. Nevertheless, it seems clear that the history of the seventies indicates that a steady level of excess supply in the labour market will not lead to a substantial reduction in the rate of increase of money and real wages. Nor does it appear that the creation of excess supply by government policy is the obvious way back to a fully employed economy with a low rate of inflation within a measurable time scale. There is a need for a better economic policy.

We must not abandon the objective of full employment even though there will be a strong temptation to do so. That temptation stems from the difficulties inherent in the achievement of full employment and low inflation, the natural unwillingness to face the failure of current macro policies, and from the fact that most of us, being employed, belong to the group that can expect long job tenure. We are insulated from the worst effects of low output growth. Under these circumstances it is all too easy for most of us to shrug off the consequences of attempting to fight inflation by the application of restrictive policies alone.

References

G. Akerlof, "The Case Against Conservative Macroeconomics: an Inaugural Lecture", *Economica,* vol. 46. 1979.

M.N. Bailey, "Wages and Employment under Uncertain Demand", *Review of Economic Studies,* vol. 41, 1974.

S. Bonnell, "Real Wages and Employment in the Great Depression", *Economic Record,* vol. 57, 1981.

K. Clark and L. Summers, "Labor Market Dynamics and Unemployment: A Reconsideration", *Brookings Papers on Economic Activity,* (1), 1979.

Commonwealth of Australia, *Report of the Committee of Economic Enquiry,* (Vernon Report), Canberra, AGPS, 1965.

H.C. Coombs, "Problems of a High Employment Economy", The Joseph Fisher Lecture, University of Adelaide, 1944.

C. B. Copland, "Currency and Prices in Australia", The Joseph Fisher Lecture, University of Adelaide, 1921.

W.F. Foster and R.G. Gregory, "Unemployment Duration in Australia", IAESR (Mimeo), 1982.

W.F. Foster and R.G. Gregory, "Job Tenure and Labour Mobility", IAESR (Mimeo), 1982.

W.F. Foster and R.G. Gregory, "The Contribution of Employment Separation to Teenage Unemployment". *Economic Record,* forthcoming.

M.R. Gray and F.H. Gruen, "Economic Stabilisation in Australia: Inflation and Unemployment", Discussion Paper No. 32, Centre for Economic Policy Research, ANU, August, 1981.

R.G. Gregory and R.C. Duncan, "Wages, Technology and Jobs", Australian Economic Review, (1), 1979.

F.H. Gruen, "The Future of Work: An Economic Perspective", Discussion Paper No. 22, Centre for Economic Policy Research, January, 1981.

R.E. Hall, "Employment Fluctuations and Wage Rigidity", Prookings Papers on EconomicActivity, 1980.

A. Hasan and P. de Broucher, "Turnover and Job Instability in Youth Labour Markets in Canada", Economic Council of Canada (Mimeo), 1981.

R.F. Henderson, "Income Inflation in Australia", Australian Economic Papers, vol. 11, 1972. 17. J.R. Hicks, The Crisis in Keynesian Economics (London: Basil Blackwood, 1973).

Industries Assistance Commission, "Structure and Mobility of the Australian Labour Force", (Mimeo), 1976.

E. Khoo, "Estimates of the Full Term Duration of Unemployment in Australia, 1962- 1975", Working Paper No. 15, Institute of Labour Studies, Flinders University, February, 1976.

M.G. Kirby, "An Investigation of the Specification and Stability of the Australian Aggregate Wage Equation", *The Economic Record,* vol. 57, 1981.

B. Main, "The Length of Employment and Unemployment in Great Britain", *Scottish Journal of Political Economy,* vol. 28, 1981.

L.G. Melville, "Gold Standard and Goods Standards", The Joseph Fisher Lecture, University of Adelaide, 1934.

W.E. Norton and R.M. Donald, "Implications for Australia of Cross Section Comparisons of Economic Performance", *The Economic Record,* vol. 57, 1981.

OECD, *Economic Surveys: Australia*, April, 1978.

A. Okun, *Prices and Quantities: A Macroeconomic Analysis.* The Brookings Institution, Washington DC, 1981.

A.W. Phillips, "The Relation Between Unemployment and the Rate of Change of Money Wage Rates in the United Kingdom 1861-1957", *Economica*, vol. 25, 1958.

S.W. Salant, "Search Theory and Duration Data: A Theory of Sorts", *Quarterly Journal of Economics*, vol. 91, 1977.

P. Scherer, "Changes in the Distribution and Composition of Earnings and Wage Indexation, 1975-1980", Australian National University (Mimeo), 1981.

P. Stricker and P. Sheehan, *Hidden Unemployment, The Australian Experience,* IAESR, University of Melbourne, 1981.

R. Solow, "On Theories of Unemployment", *American Economic Review*, vol. 70, 1980.

P.K. Trivedi and G.M. Baker, "Unemployment in Australia: Duration, Experience and Recurrent Spells", Discussion Paper No. 45, Centre for Economic Policy Research, Australian National University, March, 1982.

39

Japan faces affluence

Martin Bronfenbrenner[1]

I am grateful to be invited to your country a second time – forty years after my first invitation was withdrawn. That earlier invitation was from the US Navy, in which I was a language officer with the exalted rank of Lieutenant Junior Grade and an urgent invitation to report to beautiful Brisbane. But before I left the US, the Navy withdrew that invitation and invited me somewhere else instead. Perhaps they noted that my linguistic qualifications did not extend to "Strine".

In preparation for this present visit, I read the new Brookings Institution study of the Australian economy and became an instant expert. That volume left me certain, that I would find Australia suffering, consciously or otherwise, from a serious brain drain of many sorts of talent. As has been said of many American States, "Many good men come from there, and the better they are, the faster they come". But I have now been here for ten full days, and the people who stayed in Australia – and some who have come here from abroad – have been assuring me that they are every bit as good as those who have left! Perhaps your way of life – including your climate and the Adelaide drinking-water supply – outweighs the aggressiveness of your tax system, the inefficiency subsidised by your protectionism, and the power of your trade-union movement. And so I am quite confused, Mr. Chairman – the usual plight of the "airport economist" who remains as long as I have – and had best revert to the topic of my remarks this afternoon.

As the subject of these remarks, I hesitated between "Japan faces Affluence" and "Japan and the Affluence *Disease*". The question is this: Can Japan, in its rise to the position of first-class economic power, manage to avoid certain difficulties

1 Thirty-ninth Joseph Fisher Lecture, 14 March 1985.

which have plagued other world economic powers like Britain and America – and perhaps Australia as well?

I want to begin by describing the symptoms of what used to be called "the English disease" or "the Anglo-American disease" and which I propose to call "the affluence disease". (Syphilis, you may know, was earlier called "the Spanish disease" and "the French disease".) I wish I might have created a title which combined stagnation-near-aspiration level disease" with "more-to-lose-than-to-gain-by-change disease", but it is less pedantic and more manageable than either. (The trouble with "affluence disease" is that far-from affluent medieval guildsmen and contemporary Welsh and Scottish coal miners have suffered it as acutely as anyone else.) I hope nobody uses "Bronfenbrenner's disease" as the title for the ailment I have in mind.

One of the great books of development economics in the early 1960s was Walt Whitman Rostow's *Stages of Economic Growth*. Of this volume little remains a generation later beyond the catch-phrase "take-off into self-sustained growth", but I want to talk about the other (later) end of the development process according to Rostow. Antiquarians among you will recall that "take-off" was followed by a rather mechanical "drive to maturity." Once "mature", however, Rostow's country came to a tri-furcation in the development highway; the choice among the three forks was presented as a matter of free political will rather than Marxian-type determinism. One fork was military expansion *à la* Third Reich or Greater East Asia Co-Prosperity Sphere. A second fork was the population explosion along the lines of all too many Latin American countries of today.[2] Rostow's third and last fork is "high mass consumption", which seems to be his economic equivalent for "living happily ever after" and the choice all developing countries should make.

Our disease, whatever we call it – let us be content with "affluence disease" – is a set of conditions which leads many "high mass consumption" societies to a fate more like arthritis or arteriosclerosis than "living happily ever after".

2 The problem is not the level of such countries' population, but its rate of growth. As a non demographer, I incline to accept the proposition that the world may eventually be able to support at present levels two or three times its present population. At the same time, I fear that "eventually" is further off than the optimists suppose. And meanwhile, the most pressing problem is one of growth rates rather than absolute numbers (as I have said).

The set of conditions comprising the "affluence disease" I classify unsatisfactorily under six overlapping heads. These are, in a language which I hope will become clearer as we proceed: (1) restrictions in general; (2) credentials in particular; (3) entitlements; (4) underclasses; (5) attenuations of property rights; and finally (6) retaliations from abroad. A couple of examples may explain the terms, their inter-relations, and some distinctions between them.

Illustration 1: Physicians in Japan, as in many other countries, claim to be facing a "doctor glut", meaning that the present real prices of doctors' services will increasingly exceed market-clearing levels. To become a medical practitioner in Japan, the aspirant must both graduate from a Medical University and pass a national examination. A panel of physicians has recently recommended to the Welfare Ministry not merely that the examinations be made more difficult but that only the top *n* candidates pass each year, regardless of high scores obtained by others. This entire system of professional licensure I consider credentialist. The addition of the *numerus clausus*, which now seems likely, I consider restrictionism pure and simple.

Illustration 2: American textile manufacturers may not lease machines for installation in workers' homes for piecework. This is because factory work rules and safety regulations may be violated, minimum wage laws evaded, and "unqualified persons" permitted to operate the machines. I should classify this prohibition, good thing or bad thing, as an attenuation of property rights in machinery, although the oppression of an underclass – housewives and hirees excluded from part-time home work – can be read between the lines, and although the concept of "unqualified worker" suggests credentialism.

Restriction and restrictionism are portmanteau words, including "practices not elsewhere classified". I need not tell this audience that real income and real growth are measured as nearly as possible in physical quantities, so that reduction of physical output in order to raise or maintain money prices is injurious to economic progress however profitable or even "necessary" it may seem to the restrictionists themselves. Nor need I add that the fixing of a price too high to clear a market, with production or sales quotas fixed to avoid any visible surplus, is equally restrictive – just as contraception may have the same demographic effects as abortion. But it is hard to convince even the most intelligent of audiences that if they and their organisations are "good guys", their "raising of standards" and policing of "price chisellers" can be just as restrictive as similar activities of "bad guys" and just as decelerative of economic growth.

Let there be no mistake about this. Trade associations, farm organisations, labour unions, and professional bodies all can be (and usually are) agencies of restriction, along with their other activities. Public ownership makes no difference either; consider OPEC with its "socialist" members. My own profession (academia) is no exception either. Our "academic freedom and tenure" rules are restrictions, at least in their American form which includes an "up-or-out" provision designed to prevent accumulation of untenured full time instructors and lecturers at the bottom of the pyramid. During my Graduate School days in the "hungry thirties", a labour economist from one of our best-known universities proposed to alleviate unemployment among older academicians by suspending all fellowships and assistantships for youngsters like myself!

Except perhaps in my examples, I have told you little that is new. What may be less hackneyed is its relation to the basic question of why even high-mass-consumption nations decline. On this topic, I owe a debt to Professor Mancur Olson, whose *Rise and Decline of Nations* has received much less attention than I think it deserves. Please pardon me for paraphrasing, compressing, and perhaps even distorting his argument.

Olson's starting point, developed in earlier work on *The Logic of Collective Action*, is that to establish and maintain an effective restrictionist (or credentialist) pressure group is not easy. (Labour historians among you can bear this out from the history of the trade union movement in your own country.) One important obstacle is the "free rider" who seeks to share the advantages of restriction without joining the organisation, paying dues, going on strike and in general avoiding the costs and opprobria of the restrictive effort. Britain and Mexico, for example, may be classified as OPEC "freeriders". Another obstacle is the "chiseller", the ostensible member of the cartel who shades prices down or output up, as Nigeria and Iran have apparently been doing within OPEC. The historical record indicates that, despite these obstacles, restrictionism can be established over long periods in economies which are relatively stable and fundamentally placid while operating at levels close to the membership's aspiration levels of prices and incomes. Once a union or a set of unions fastens closed-shop or union-shop tentacles upon an industry, this octopus position can be maintained for however long the members' wages and incomes are good – when compared with what they were last year, with what similar workers are making in other industries, with what similar unions achieve abroad, and so on in so-called "compulsive comparisons".

But let the fundamental stability or placidity be shattered, as by a lost war and/ or a foreign occupation, and "things fall apart". Most or all of the organising activity must be done over again, often under a new set of "rules of the game". With nearly all of the country's pressure groups weakened and some fatally wounded, the competitive market is free to operate, and the economy enjoys a period of "miracle" growth as compared with other economies which, whether they have won the war or remained neutral, return to or remain at something like the status quo, restrictive pressure groups included. Such is the Olson explanation of both the West German and the Japanese cases in the post-1945 – and to a lesser extent of the "British", "American" and "Australian" diseases as well. In Schumpeterian terms, what we have called the shackling of the pressure groups appears as the unleashing of the entrepreneur. (There is no conflict, so far as I can see, between Schumpeter and Olson on these points.)

Miracles, however, seldom last very long. Japan, in particular, was officially concerned with something undefined but called "excessive competition", as early as 1960, and was providing special treatment for "recession cartels". The pressure groups reorganise, or perhaps emerge in new forms. In Japan again, the pre-war *zaibatsu* is dead but long live the *keiretsu* – which is much the same thing with one or more giant banks replacing the old ruling-family and holding-company structure. And sometimes more pressure groups are added to the new witches' brew. In Japan once more, the union of farmers' co-operatives called *Nokyo*, whose political clout closes the market to both American and Australian grain and beef, was of no pre-war importance. Once the pressure groups recover their strength, in the Olsen view, restrictionism takes over and miracles fade. The country enters into a relative decline, either in a position of affluence (the Japanese case) or without ever attaining affluence (as in Italy). Not that this is not a business-cycle theory in the usual short-term or medium-term sense, where a recession carries within it some bases for recovery. It is rather a theory of long-term decline broken by occasional revivals.

So much for restrictions in trade in general. Credentialism is the special set of restrictions which prevents people directly from using their human capital most effectively. Here the academic community is a favourite accessory where it is not a major culprit. One cannot teach full-time at most US universities without a Ph.D. degree (or equivalent), although that level of scholarship can be and often is an impediment for elementary teaching.[3] One cannot teach in an American public school system without a certain number of education courses of questionable value. (To extend Bernard Shaw's epigram *from Man and Superman*: He who can, does; he who cannot, teaches; he who cannot teach, teaches how to teach.) Nor can Americans practice law without law degrees, which themselves have come to require university training – even when legal secretaries with no degree at all can and do perform all the routine tasks of the law office with only the pretence of supervision. And these remarks about the schools and the law apply likewise to medicine, engineering, accountancy: "And other professions in which men engage, The Army, the Navy, the Church and the Stage."

But the allegedly-learned professions have no monopoly on credentialism. The apprenticeship rules of the skilled trades do equally well or badly without formal academic degrees. So far as I am aware from American experience, the building, printing, and entertainment trades are the worst offenders. On the one hand, none may perform the simpler tasks of a trade unless his ability to perform more complex ones has been certified by completion of formal training or apprenticeship, with trainees limited in numbers by one or another craft union. And on the other hand, the skills of the master craftsman are squandered in dismantling or replicating work done by outsiders – non-union men, members of other locals, or with the aid of unsanctioned machinery.

I await the day when we may not touch up the paint on our houses without Art School certificates, and when our children may not annoy the neighbours by practice on musical instruments (or the human voice) without guarantees from a Conservatory of Music that their performances qualify for them for the

3 I know much more English than my Japanese-born wife does. She began learning English seriously only after our marriage, and has had little formal university education of any kind. But in teaching English as a second language, the fact of her having learned it that way makes her much better than I am, or (I suppose) than I ever could be, no matter how many courses I might take or how many degrees I might accumulate.

Musicians' Union. But I rejoice that the railroad preceded the canal Boatman's Union, the telephone the messenger boys' union, the automobile the rickshaw pullers' union.

Our next symptom is *entitlement.* In developed societies, and also in some less developed ones, a minimal living level is supposedly guaranteed by public authorities, both for those who cannot or will not work and for those who want more time to search out good jobs, without the necessity to accept whatever may be offered. I know of no proposals to scrap these "safety nets", although proposals to privatise or localise them may come close. Four substantial problems are: *how high* the support level should be; *how long* one should be protected from forced acceptance of low-paid, low-status, dead-end jobs; *what forms* subvention should take – money income, cheap food, cheap housing, or the Roman "circuses"; and finally, what obligations the recipient must accept – conscript labour, subsequent repayment, confinement, disenfranchisement, even sterilisation have been proposed.

I must confess no personal experience of anything approaching real poverty. It therefore seems hard-hearted, to me as well as to you, when I call your attention to the dangers inherent in entitlements becoming too generous even for countries as advanced as yours or mine. The danger is not that the price of "dirty work", is raised, or that some "superior" people like ourselves are underemployed when forced to do it. The danger is the tendency of the definition of "dirty work" to expand over time to include an increasing proportion of the humble, low-skill, but essential (and difficult to robotise) jobs that need doing if the society is to keep running. The eventual amount of such work can itself fall below an acceptable social minimum. The garbage and rubbish accumulate; the sewers overflow; the inmates of prisons and hospitals are uncared for; the army, navy and police are "all officers and no privates"; nothing is serviced or repaired efficiently. Already no "real American" will accept "stoop labour" on farms or personal service jobs in households – our famous "servant problem". Also, the enlisted ranks of the American military, particularly the US Army, are turning black.

Meanwhile, it may be objected, the dirty work does get done, and sometimes even at "reasonable" economic prices. But who does it, if "real Americans" do not? Members of one or another under-class, whose presence raises the social cost of getting that work done at the same time that it lowers the private cost. In American colloquial one finds the revealing phrase "nigger jobs" applied to what I have called dirty work. Indeed blacks do occupy such positions and do such work – along with Puerto Ricans, immigrants legal and illegal from other Latin-American countries, and various persons whose common denominators are poor English or low I.Q. Who does not do them? Real Americans, meaning white Anglo-Saxon Protestants, sometimes call WASPs, take increasing pride in their immunity. In Britain, the Indian sub-continent and the West Indies now supply the dirty workers, having replaced the Irish; in France, Africa, both Arab and black, supplies them; in much of western Europe, the "guest workers" came from Turkey, the Balkans and the Iberian Peninsula.

In all these "underclass" cases, there is resentment. Less resentment, I suppose, when the "greenhorns" like my parents and their children like myself can do better merely by learning a majority language like English, French, or German. More resentment, I am sure, when linguistic disability is not the basic problem. The social cost of fostering and depending on an underclass, and of controlling its resentments, is greatest when, as in South Africa, the underclass comprises the majority of the whole society. It is high enough in America, where several underclasses now add, or soon will add, to a full third of the population. (The estimate depends on one's guesstimate of the stock of our illegal immigrants.) Also, to hear certain feminists talk, housewifery and motherhood include a number of the dirtiest jobs of all, making women the largest underclass segment of both the American and the Japanese labour force.

There is another underclass too, not associated with dirty jobs or indeed with any regular employment whatever. These are largely age-segregated, barred (or enticed) from employment by high minimum wages, high school-leaving ages, high relief standards (the entitlement problem), and broad definitions of the terms "students" and "trainee". Most are either "too young" or "too old". Some are handicapped, as by injury, by illness physical or mental, by some form of addiction, or by a criminal record. Some are beggars, some are "layabouts", some are tramps, hoboes, and bums, and a minority are active criminals. All are alienated from society and "the system". During my stay in Britain, some sought to organise a Conference Against Youth Unemployment (CAYU) which called itself a second or alternate trade union movement. But they stopped short of opposing the restrictionism of the "first" trade union movement (and splitting the working class). I believe their movement has petered out into mindless terrorism.

Our fifth major symptom of affluence disease is a continuous attenuation of people's rights as property owners, meaning primarily their rights to retain and to enlarge the income streams they can obtain from the physical assets which they own. The attenuation process has been called "socialisation of the flow" by Dr. Shigeto Tsuru – who favours its acceleration. The label is apt, since he wants the income flow generated from these assets to go to others than the owners, who still retain what lawyers call "bare legal title" to these assets – plus, I presume, some obligation to maintain those assets in trust for society.

The main points under the "attenuation" head were pointed out most effectively in Joseph Schumpeter's *Capitalism, Socialism and Democracy*. They have included progressive taxation, price controls under a broadened "public utility" concept, co-management by union representatives, and competition with subsidised governmental agencies. I shall not dwell on these; we all know about them; many of us have made up our minds in particular instances how far we support or oppose them. (I am afraid that some of us favour each and every instance that comes up, while opposing the process "by and large and on the whole".)

The subset of attenuations which concerns me particularly in 1985 are connected with rights to shift resources from one business to another, from one locality to another, from employment of one input (usually labour) to another (usually machinery), or to discontinue a business operation altogether. At their worst, these extensions hold enterprises and their assets for ransom to a given line of business, a given country or town, and of course a given set of trade unions. The stakes transcend the quantitative issues of severence pay by a footloose company to a work force it leaves stranded in a community it deserts. They encompass the qualitative issues of whether the firm has any right whatever to move, or whether the workers have the right to occupy the plant to keep it doing what it does, where it does it, and with the same labour force. An Englishman will in this connection think immediately of Mr. Arthur Scargill and the Coal Board – already a socialised agency whose economic losses taxpayers have unconsciously undertaken to subsidise "from here to eternity". As an American, I think rather of the defence, by the President of the US Steel Corporation, of that company's decision to buy an oil company in Ohio rather than renovating steel plants in Western Pennsylvania: is US Steel in business to make steel or to make money?

Among Western economies West Germany, Israel, and the Scandinavian countries have travelled furthest along the attenuation highway. German Mitbestimmung in its more extreme forms gives to labour, meaning elected union representatives, veto power over enterprise decisions in general. Sweden's Meidner Plan of Entrepreneurial *hara-kiri* provides for a percentage of each year's profits to be transferred to unions and public representatives – not to individual workers! – to buy shares of profitable concerns, thus bringing about socialisation by the stock market! Meanwhile, if I may quote a Stockholm report of November 1984 as reported by the *London Financial Times*:[4]

> "The Swedish government launched a new scheme of compulsory corporate investment funds aimed at forcing companies to increase investment in employee training and research and development.
>
> Companies will have to transfer an amount equivalent to 10% of 1985 profits into so-called "renewal funds". The capital will be placed in non-interest bearing accounts at the Swedish central bank.
>
> The scheme will give Swedish trade unions an increased say in the allocation of companies' financial resources, as the funds will only be released for R and D and training projects that have received *the prior approval of the individual company's work force.*" (my emphasis)

This means, if I read correctly between the lines, that labour-displacing R and D will not pass. Neither will the skilling of enough youngsters in skilled trades to threaten established differentials. The report goes on to claim that the Swedish companies think they got off easy, because they will get their unspent funds back after only five years at negative real interest rates (given Sweden's inflationary economy). A certain cynicism compels me to add, although I know Sweden only as a tourist, the suspicion that this "eventual return" feature may not last long.

4 Reprinted in *Japan Times* (Tokyo), 16 November 1984.

Let me put the issue raised by this passage – the mundane macroeconomic issue, not the ethic or the politics – in elementary Keynesian terms. Here we are, modifying institutions in ways which lower the marginal efficiency of investment, at least the marginal efficiency of domestic investment "above ground". (Marginal efficiency is a potential investor's estimate of the annual post-tax net income over the lifetime of the investment, discounted back to the present time, as a percentage of the investment's cost.) We are doing nothing to lower marginal propensities to save, to export capital by purchase of foreign assets, or to "invest" in tax "sheltering". The Keynesian result, other things equal? Planned investment now equals planned saving at a lower income level and a higher measured unemployment rate than would prevail otherwise.

More generally, I believe, following Schumpeter, that the attenuation of property rights tends to be overdone in affluent economies – not only in Sweden. It produces either Keynesian under-employment or what Schumpeter himself called "capitalism in an oxygen tent" of public deficit financing of make-work and make-profit projects of all kinds, decidedly including the military.

Our sixth and last symptom of affluence disease is the foreign resentment and retaliation the affluence attracts. Both the resentment and the retaliation are consequences of affluence, possibly inevitable ones, although the ethical responsibility of the affluent country is questionable and envy is not regarded as a virtue.

In past ages, before the vogue of formal trade and immigration laws, retaliations took obvious forms like raiding, piracy, and invasion. ("The Assyrian came down like a wolf on the fold"; "From the fury of the Northmen, O Lord, deliver us!".) Sometimes invasion was quick and complete, as with the First "Frankish" Crusade, the Mongol Tartars, or the Spanish Conquistadores. At other times, it seems to have begun with trading in harbour of frontier areas, spread to immigration and residence in the affluent country's underclass, and expanded only later to the full-fledged seizure of power and loot. The original "barbarian invasions" of the Roman Empire followed some such pattern. So did that branch of the Viking raids which conquered Normandy and then, from Normandy, England.

But now we have immigration restrictions and international cartels, while the volume and variety of protective devices in international trade and capital movements increase without visible bound. The affluent countries may be hobbled for decades by arbitrary increases in the prices of their basic imports, as OPEC has shown the Western world and Japan since 1973. An interesting feature of the two oil crises has been the attitude of the non-affluent oil-importing LDCs. Many of them suffered more, proportionately speaking, than any industrial country did. In 1973-74 I expected them to make common cause with the West against OPEC, shattering the LDC "united front" in such United Nations agencies as UNCTAD. Instead they made common cause with OPEC, and the "North-South" controversy has increased in intensity.

One could explain such irrationality at first by these countries' hopes of achieving for coffee or cocoa or copper the same advantages OPEC was achieving for crude oil. But after these hopes faded for a variety of reasons, the continuing non-oil LDC attitude could hardly be explained without reference to satisfaction at the discomfiture of the so-called First World. Such pervasive resentment, coupled with ability to express it in some meaningful way, illustrate the international aspect of the affluence disease.

In addition, a country can only import if it can export, attract foreign aid, or attract foreign capital. An import-dependent affluent country can be unhinged as readily by discrimination against its exports as by raising the prices it pays for imports. As we shall see, this may become the major problem for Japan.

Beyond these legitimate concerns is a popular view, supported by much journalistic economics, that a country can decline from a position of opulence by reason of nothing more than foreign competition (and foreign imitation) under an essentially free-trade regime. But this is almost, although not quite, 100 per cent wrong. The so-called "British climacteric" of 1870-1914 is a supposed example. But is actually meant only that Britain's new rivals, primarily Germany and the US, grew more rapidly than Britain and surpassed Britain's own affluence. It did not make Edwardian Britain a poor country in any sense. Britain's absolute decline, insofar as it has been more than relative, can be traced to the human-capital and foreign-asset losses of two World Wars plus the "English disease".

What can competition-plus-emulation do to an affluent country? As we have said, they can lower its relative ranking. They can also wipe out whatever gain it has achieved from a position of monopoly in the sales of its exports or monopsony in the demand of its imports, either worldwide or within some trading bloc. (Free trade in petroleum, for example, would end whatever affluence countries like Kuwait and Abu Dhabi may have achieved). There may also be entire broad classes of factor incomes, for example even wages, which free trade can lower: suppliers of such inputs can lose as the result of competition, although the remainder of society gains. Thus there is not doubt that maintenance of the present American real wage level in manufacturing requires protection – but not the real per capita income of the US population.

Before passing from general principles to the Japanese case, perhaps I should digress sufficiently to assure some of you that Japan really is an affluent society, although probably not the "welfare superpower" that Professor Yatsuhiro Nakagawa once called it. It is far from the unhappy collection of "workaholics in rabbit-hutches" that OECD critics of 1979 vintage claim to have observed.

The casual visitor to Japan is usually confined to a couple of touristic enclaves and the transport arteries that connect them. The largest enclave is the Ginza and Shinjuku districts of Tokyo, with tentacles extending to Mt. Fuji, the Izu peninsula, and the ski country around Nikko. Another enclave is the temples of Kyoto, with one tentacle extending to Nara and another through Kobe or the Inland Sea to the Peace Park in Hiroshima. The first venture outside these glittering enclaves can be a shock. The venturesome tourist often sees urban Japan as one vast slum, or semi-slum at best, broken by occasional specks and streaks of something better. It is easy to make this mistake about "household Japan", but I shall try to convince you that it reflects the peculiarities of the country's price and tax structure rather than its real income.

Population density and mountainous geology have combined to make land scarce in Japan, and to raise its price and rental relative to the general price level. The profits from selling land are also taxed at high rates, which express the common resentment of the general populace against the passive land speculator. However, the pecuniary savings and psychic incomes which result from holding land out of use (or in economically-inferior uses) are not offset significantly by real-property taxes. So land is held in small parcels; block after block of single-family houses, mama-papa stores, parking-lots, even (alleged) farms. This raises still further the price of land transferred to more efficient uses – and also the tax penalties for transferring it there.

Given the high price of land, the Japanese use less of it (relative to other things) than Australians or Americans of similar real incomes would do. And at the same time, they spend more for its use, either as rent or as mortgage payments, both absolutely and as proportions of their incomes. They also have less income (or assets) to spare for improving whatever real estate they own. (In economists' language, the ordinary price elasticities of both the demand for raw land and the demand for improvements are low, but the cross elasticity of the demand for improvements with respect to the price of unimproved land is high). The result of all these elasticities and inelasticities is the aforementioned prairie of semi-slums which shock and disappoint so many visitors to Japan. A shabby house on a postage-stamp lot any passer-by can see. What the passer-by often misses are the contents of the house, the occupant's life-style, and the sizes of the occupant's bank account and investment portfolio.

We can now consider at long last our half-dozen symptoms of affluence disease in their Japanese environment, and attempt prognoses of their future "progress".

Restriction and *restrictionism* Japan certainly has, most substantially, in its agricultural sector and (to a decreasing extent, perhaps) in credit rationing by its financial sector. These are, however, offset by two freedoms which Japan's rivals do not share. One of these is the weakness of its trade union – particularly its craft union – movement. The other is its low defense burden, most of the "Japanese" defense expenditures being paid by the US.

For 20 years after 1945, I thought the second offset the more important. I accordingly believed both South Korea and Taiwan to be developmentally hopeless, because so high a percentage of each country's prime-age human capital was absorbed in the country's armed services and police forces. The record, I fear, has proved me wrong; it may be worth noting that in both these countries organized labor is even weaker than in Japan. I am compelled to believe, therefore, that Japan's resistance to restrictionism, at least outside agriculture, is stronger on balance than the resistance of other affluent countries, and that Japan is unlikely to dissipate its advantages to the care and feeding of an organized-labor aristocracy. (I wish I could say the same for its organized-agriculture aristocracy).

Some Japanologists of eminence will tell you that the peculiar Japanese "enterprise union" structure, and indeed the entire Japanese industrial-relations system, has almost mystical roots in Japanese feudalism, in the philosophy of Confucius as interpreted by Chu Hsi, and in the racial homogeneity of the Japanese people. All of this implies that Japanese advantages in the labor area cannot be exported to or imitated by other countries to any significant degree.

Without venturing too far beyond my shallow depth in cultural anthropology, let me suggest that this view may be only a half truth. Japanese racial homogeneity seems to be a relatively recent matter, since the country's proto-history and legend can be interpreted in terms of centuries of conflict (and intermarriage) between Ainu aborigines and rival waves of later invaders from Korea, China, Southeast Asia, and the East Indies. Much later, in the first generation of light-industry mechanization (1870-1905 approximately), the Japanese of the Meiji Era replicated the horrors of the European industrial revolution, being brought up short mainly by the scarcity of the labor skills needed to progress further. Later still, after the end of American supervision in 1952, Japan experienced a wave of long private industry strikes. In these strikes Leftist-led unions sought to infuse something like German or Scandanavian co-determination into the adolescent enterprise unions. These strikes failed; two famous ones were in the Mitsui coal mines and the Nissan automotives works. Similar strikes succeeded in other countries; in the form of slow-downs, they also succeeded in Japanese public enterprises like the National Railways and the Post Office. I wonder how much of the "miraculous" growth of Japan's private sector could ever have occurred had the Mitsui, Nissan, and other strikes come out the other way – and whether it might not have been duplicated in Europe and America, and their postwar strike waves ended as the Japanese strikes wave did.

We pass on to *entitlements*. These are already a live issue in Japan, affecting both the youth and the elderly at both ends of the range of working ages. The problems are expected to get worse as time passes. As a university lecturer, I think

I encounter the entitlement psychology among my own students. Affluence has opened both senior high schools and universities to academically under-qualified and uninterested youth, who could not previously have afforded the tutoring and coaching required to squeeze them through demanding entrance examinations on the basis of brute memory without understanding. And as a reward for surviving "examination Hell", they feel entitled to university degrees after four years of *Ike-nuki* (or "breaking room") – forgetting whatever they had learned in high school or crammed for examinations.[5]

Many students also talk as though their entitlement is for life. With "good" degrees, they are entitled to white-collar "salary-man" jobs in "good" companies. Once employed, they are further entitled to ride up a corporate escalator as years pass, to positions of power and prestige. They need not work nearly so hard as their fathers and elder brothers worked, and they need not become "company men". Some students even profess entitlement to public support at whatever artistic, creative, or meditative endeavor or non-endeavor they choose to pursue, without becoming salary-men or housewives at all! A question I cannot answer on my own, and about which I get varying answers from sociological investigators, is this: How serious is this "lifetime-entitlement" bluster and bravado in the newly-affluent Japanese middle-class youth, and what are its chances of surviving in the world off campus? Perhaps we can get reliable answers to such questions before the end of the present decade.

Entitlements for the aged to live without working, if they so desire, may be an even more substantial problem. Such people's post-retirement "second jobs" not only pay much less than the jobs they held before retirement at 55 or 60 or 65, but account for a considerable fraction of the routine, menial, and part-time work done in Japan – even at the purely physical level! If the old-age

5 An alternative explanation of students' academic lassitude stresses screening by companies over entitlements of students. For a respectable white-collar job, the new graduate must satisfy employers than he or she is not too dumb to learn the business, and simultaneously, that he or she is not likely to become any of the 57 varieties of trouble-maker (*yakkaimono*). One should particularly avoid seeming a potential political militant or psychiatric problem child. To satisfy the first requirement, the entrance examinations have been relied upon; to satisfy the second, one engages in a wide range of meaningful or meaningless collective activities – clubs, teams, etc. Assiduous devotion to one's studies, on the other hand, is a danger signal, especially in an isolate or "loner", as in Julius Caesar's comment on Cassius: " He thinks too much; such men are dangerous".

pension entitlements increase sufficiently, thanks to the voting power of the aged, the consequences will be some choice between and among higher taxes, higher interest rates, accelerated inflation, and reduction of public services other than pensions – along with reductions in both human capital input and final product output. It lies within the prospect of belief that technology can again come to the rescue more rapidly than resource exhaustion and the welfare state sink society into the mire. The mid-1980s however, find the Japanese population aging faster than any other population I know about, and the Japanese public deficit already higher than the Finance Ministry and the Bank of Japan would wish, so that the mainstream factions of the ruling Liberal Democratic party are resisting the pension lobby even as the aging process accelerates.

A way out of any future human-capital crisis arising from excessive entitlements would be the build-up of a substantial economic underclass of cheap immigrant labor. Western Europe did this in the first quarter-century after 1945. As we have said, Japan has no large economic underclass, and the great bulk of its dirty work is done by ethnic Japanese. Japan has thus been spared the social conflict and disruption such an underclass produces, not to mention the increased inequality in the distribution of wealth and income.

Japan's existing minority problem, small but noisy, is Korean. The Korean community in Japan is indeed a small underclass. Most Japanese "Koreans" were born in Japan of Korean parents, but Japanese birth does not confer Japanese citizenship, and many Japanese-born Koreans have no desire for such citizenship. Resident aliens in Japan are fingerprinted as special protection against the criminal proclivities of transient foreigners like myself; the Japanese-born Koreans are presently campaigning against this alleged infringement of their human rights. Another quasi-underclass, the *burakumin*, are ethnic Japanese whose ancestors engaged in activities considered unclean in Buddhist theology – butchering, leather-work, sandal-making, funerary trades, and so on. They are more numerous than the Koreans, especially in the Kansai area around Kyoto and Osaka, but their economic assimilation is progressing better than that of the Koreans.

Japan is now under humanistic pressure to create another potential underclass by admitting substantially more than the current trickle of Indochinese refugees. Japan is passively resisting on nationalist, not to say racist, grounds.

This resistance makes economic sense, however (taking Japanese nationalism and racism as givens), if one agrees that potentially long-term economic underclasses are undesirable things to foster or cultivate.

Our summary thus far makes it seems at least premature to diagnose Japan as suffering the early symptoms of affluence disease on the British or American model. But the problem of *foreign reaction* may reverse this tentative decision.

Let us begin with some counterfactual economic history. Suppose that, in the period 1955-1970, Japanese exports had been barred as effectively from the North American market as they were in fact from the Western European one. The question is, just as we have seen it for the great strikes of the 1950s, could the Japanese miracle have occurred under these counterfactual conditions? And again my answer is no, because without easy access to the US market for Japanese exports, Japan could not have financed the raw materials and capital equipment imports needed for rapid growth, while simultaneously feeding a population which was then growing more rapidly than it now is.

The broader implications of this negative conclusion still apply. The main threat to Japanese affluence still comes from abroad. To put the matter differently, the principal "disease" of Japanese affluence seems to be its capacity to stir up resentment and envy overseas, particularly in the other industrialized countries.

And what of the "squeeze" from Korea, Taiwan, Singapore, and the other NICs of the Third World? What will happen when and if the Chinese mainland "comes on line?" Is not Japan's main overseas problem an Eastern and Southern rather than a Western one? I think not – unless the "affluence disease" of entitlement psychology eventually prevents the necessary adjustments to competition from low-wage countries. (These adjustments, I admit, will involve unwelcome shifts away from higher wages, shorter hours, and easier jobs in the interest of higher productivity. There may also be a declining labor share in the national income, and a rising non-accelerating-inflation-rate-of-unemployment, known in Britain as NAIRU). None of this is pleasant, but it is quite consistent with rising affluence for the remainder of the population and a firmer safety net for the unemployed and under employed.

And so I think foreign protectionism – in which I include raw material OPEC-ism – is the main direct threat to Japanese opulence. And if this is not enough, perhaps low-age LDC competition may trigger the latent "entitlement" symptoms of a purely domestic "affluence disease".

What can Japan do about this foreign threat, either in advance or as it materializes? Reactions thus far have taken three contradictory and I think effectual directions: liberalization, import-substitution, and the export of capital.

Liberalization has been grudging, spotty, and slow here and there on the market. It has aimed at pacifying, or rather postponing, American protectionism at the rate of five minutes per concession. This runs counter to the specific interests injured by the concessions, and more importantly, to the national interest as seen by the Japanese man in the street, especially if the "street" is a rice paddy! Japanese are as instinctively xenophobic and mercantilistic as anyone else – possibly more so, echoing Tokugawa-era isolation, wartime experience of the consequences of dependence on foreign food supplies, and resentment of American postwar occupation and continuing military presence. In its minimal, attenuated, and frequently-sabotaged forms, recent Japanese liberalization measures have accomplished little to offset either foreign protectionism as a whole or American "Japan-bashing" as its most acute manifestation.

The second Japanese reaction has been to insure the viability of key industries and whole economic sectors, even after the outside world does its worst, by import-substitution and high protection – quotas rather than tariffs. Such a policy may also involve an increase in Japan's convertible-currency reserves for insurance purposes, but I am not sure either that this has been done or that such accumulation would be an optimal use of Japan's international receipts. I do know that import-substitution and market-closing have proved excellent ways to lose friends, alienate people, and enhance foreign protectionism. At the same time, unfortunately, they have been good domestic policy for the government party, securing the so-called Liberal Democrats the crucial support of rural regions which are over-represented in the Japanese Diet.

The third Japanese expedient, and the most important in recent years, has been first the permission and then the encouragement of capital exports. These balance payments, but not trade and not the current accounts.[6] Capital exports are purchases of foreign assets, including "tariff factories" operating behind the back of local protectionists. They have sometimes been costly to domestic industry in Japan, since funds have gone abroad which the MITI of the 1950s would have directed into expansion and modernization of Japanese plant and equipment, the acceleration of Japanese productivity growth, and the maintenance of low Japanese interest rates. They might be used advantageously for the same purposes today. Furthermore, at least three factors have prevented the capital export from burnishing the Japanese image internationally.

Insofar as the capital flows are speculative – in land, in bonds, in commodities, any employment effects outside Japan are too distant and too indirect to offset Japanese trade surpluses with their accompanying "exports of jobs".

When the capital flows do increase employment directly, it is often in the "wrong" places, the "wrong" industries, and under conditions which menace employment or working conditions elsewhere in the capital-importing country. Japanese automobile companies, in exporting capital to found American subsidiaries, have sought to avoid the United Auto workers' strongholds in metropolitan Detroit, where unemployment is concentrated. And the Nissan plant in Britain was delayed by the fears or organized labor that its efficiency might displace more workers at older plants of other companies than Nissan would itself provide.

Foreign purchases of domestic assets, land, and natural resources are almost sure to be resented. They may, for example, raise the price of farm land for ambitious rural youth. In Southeast Asia, and perhaps also in Australia, they result in ore shipments to Japan in raw or semi-processed states, for much less than its potential and undiscounted future value had it been processed fully in the host

6 A country's balance of trade includes only exports and imports of goods. It has the most direct bearing on employment. The country's balance on current account adds the exports and imports of services like shipping and tourism, factor payments like interest and dividends, and international transfers like aid. The country's balance of payments goes even further, to include the balance on private capital accounts. Here a capital export represents a demand for foreign assets and is a negative item, while foreign demand for domestic assets is a capital import and a positive item. In the Japanese-American bilateral case, Japan has a large trade surplus, a smaller current account surplus, and a large deficit on capital account.

country. Truth to tell, the export of raw or semi processed resources is resented under almost any terms whatever. Since it obviously benefits the foreigner, it must hurt us. (This illustrates what has been called the zero-sum fallacy, one of the most important, and at the same time most intuitive and most popular, fallacies of pop economics).

Before taking leave of Japan's foreign economic relations, I want to ask a hypothetical question and give a pessimistic answer. Suppose that in some sequence of miracles, Japan's Ministries of Agricultural and Forestry, Posts and Communications, and "notorious MITI" were to roll over and play dead, together with their networks of supporting lobbyists. Suppose that, as a result, Japanese markets were to become as free and open to American, European and Australian exports as even Senator Danforth could desire.[7] My question is, would "Japan-bashing" movements in American, Europe, and Australia be satisfied by such exemplary and possibly sacrificial Japanese behavior?

The answer must, I am afraid, be a resounding No, since in fact the "fair trade" arguments and the calls for opening for the domestic Japanese market are largely smokescreen and red herrings. The reason can be stated simply. The disemployed auto workers in Detroit or steel workers in Cleveland have no desire to grow rice for export, to work for Nissan in Tennessee, or even to subject themselves in their own home towns to retraining in new skills or for multiple jobs. No matter what Japan does or does not do, it will remain much easier for them, and their political spokesmen, to campaign for more and more protection, wreck more Japanese cars on the streets and parking lots, and beat up more Oriental looking people in neighbourhood bars.

How to end a disjointed ramble of this kind? Well, Japan is not yet suffering seriously from the affluence disease. But neither has Japan yet manifested immunity to the purely domestic strains of this disease. Should I remain alive, active, and Japanological five or ten years hence, I might be able to offer you a better estimate of Japan's resistance than I can today. But when it comes to the indirect, international strain of the affluence disease, five or ten years will not suffice.

7 Senator John Danforth (Republican of Missouri) is the leading Congressional advocate of "reciprocity" in American commercial treaties, to replace the standard most favoured-nation clause".

Protectionism and cartelization are ordinary if not inevitable causes of shocks and "growth recessions" in the countries victimised. Japan remains particularly vulnerable to both foreign protectionism and foreign cartels, to both demand shocks and supply from abroad. Japan may continue to withstand with relative ease the next (m-1) such demand shocks and the next (m-1) supply shocks, only to fall victim to the nth or the mth. This is why there is no single number of years after which one can be positive that Japanese prosperity is (or is not) secure enough for the guard to be let down. All I can do is admit to being worried, especially on the demand or export side, about the reception permitted Japanese products.

In present-day, mildly euphoric Japan, this makes me a pessimist and indeed I have been a pessimist on Japan for most of the last generation, and usually have been wrong. But having warned you of my fallibility, must admit to being back in my old pessimistic groove. And, again as usual, I must admit that Mrs. Bronfenbrenner who is Yokohama-born, is substantially less pessimistic than myself.

40

What do we really know about monetary policy?

David Laidler[1]

I

To be successful, economic ideas must satisfy two audiences. They must convince academic economists of their *a priori* theoretical reasonableness, and of their empirical content as well. They must also persuade those concerned with the formulation of economic policy of their relevance and usefulness. Since the latter group contains many individuals who have little or no academic training in economics, a successful economic idea must be simple and easily grasped by the intelligent layman. In the light of these formidable requirements, it is hardly surprising that successful economic ideas are few and far between. Moreover, to be successful is not necessarily to be correct. It is one thing to convince academic economists of the logical coherence of an idea, and of its explanatory power over past events, and to persuade policymakers of its usefulness; it is quite another to have policies based on it work out as expected.

This lecture is concerned with one particular economic idea that was, beyond any shadow of a doubt, successful by the above mentioned criteria, but whose correctness has been opened up to question by recent experience with its policy application. The idea to which I refer is Milton Friedman's proposition that the aggregate demand for money is a stable function of but a few arguments, and the policy application in question is the last ten years experience with those

1 Fortieth Joseph Fisher Lecture, 16 July 1986. The first draft of this essay was prepared during a visit to the Stockholm School of Economics in the spring of 1986, the final version being written while visiting the Flinders University of South Australia prior to the Fisher Lecture. The author is grateful to Johan Myhrman and Staffan Viotti for helpful discussions of many of the issues dealt with, and to Milton Friedman, to Peter Jonson and Peter Howitt, for reading and commenting on earlier drafts.

monetary policies more or less related to it.[2] In this lecture, I shall set out the idea in question, ask how well it has held up in the face of sustained contact with reality, and draw some tentative conclusions about the future conduct of policy. I shall not attempt specifically to relate my argument to current Australian conditions. This audience is far better equipped than am I to do that. Rather I shall put it in general terms, though the listener and reader will readily discern the influence of the recent histories of Canada, Britain and the United States on my thinking.

II

The theoretical ingredients of Friedman's propositions about the nature of the demand for money are to be found in his celebrated (1956) paper "The Quantity Theory of Money – a Restatement". There he argues, first of all, that the aggregate economy can be modelled "as if" made up of individuals, any one of whose behaviour may be treated as "representative" of the economy as a whole. Second, he argues that any such typical individual will desire to keep on hand a certain stock of money. Third, he argues that the size of this desired stock will depend upon just a few easily observed economic variables. Specifically, it will vary with: the individual's income; the costs to him of holding assets in the form of money rather than other assets, which can be represented by the level of nominal interest rates; and in proportion to the general price level.[3] Finally, and crucially, he argues that in the real world, the quantitive nature of the dependence of the demand for money upon these few variables is stable over time; that there are no other factors systematically affecting the demand for money; and that random variations in the demand for money are very small relative to those variations attributable to fluctuations in the above mentioned variables.

2 Of course Friedman's propositions about the demand for money from the basis from his case for a monetary policy "rule" as set out in a *Programme for Monetary Stability* (1960) This matter is discussed below pp 13 *et seq*

3 The reader who is familiar with Friedman's essay will recognise that I am simplifying its content a little here I am not mentioning its analysis of the subtle interrelationship of income and wealth, and I am ignoring the role of an array of interest rates on various assets both real and nominal, as well as expected inflation, as separate measures of the opportunity cost of holding money. Instead I refer only to nominal rates in general. In the present context, I hope it will be agreed that these simplifications are harmless.

The theoretical coherence of these ideas of Friedman's was never contentious. Economists were reasoning in terms of the behaviour of "representative agents" long before Alfred Marshall (1890) made them self-conscious about doing so. Furthermore, in formulating monetary theory as a particular aspect of the theory of asset choice, Friedman was developing an already well established line of enquiry whose roots can readily be traced to the Marshallian tradition in monetary economics. This, however, does not mean that his ideas were uncontroversial. The pre-Keynesian Quantity Theory, which Friedman invoked in the title of his article, had indeed treated the quantity of money as an economic variable of strategic importance, particularly for the determination of the general price level, but the Keynesian revolution had shifted the focus of macroeconomics, and by the 1950s economic orthodoxy attached little significance to this variable.[4] To argue as Friedman did that money mattered was, in the 1950s, a radical step in and of itself. Moreover, neither Keynesian monetary economics, nor the earlier Quantity Theory tradition, had ever suggested that the demand for money function could be treated as stable over time. The second radical element in Friedman's work lay in his controversial empirical assertion that it could be so treated.

Until the 1930s, the very idea of any economic relationship being empirically stable was regarded as highly unlikely. However the success of Keynesian economics, based as it was on the idea of an empirically stable consumption function, combined with the development of econometrics as a sub-branch of the discipline, meant that by the 1950s there could be no objection on grounds on principle, as there would have been in the 1930s, to Friedman's contentions about the demand for money. Their truth or falsity was open to econometric testing, and by the end of the 1960s, the empirical issue seemed to have been settled in Friedman's favour, Test after test for a wide variety of times and places appeared to confirm the stability of the demand for money function, and hence to establish the importance of the quantity of money.[5]

4 The relationship between Friedman's work, the Quantity Theory tradition and Keynesian monetary economics is contentious Relevant contributions to the discussion of this issue include Patinkin (1969), (1986), Parkin (1986) and sections of Gordon (1974).

5 Lionel Robbins' (1935) *Nature and Significance of Economic Science* expresses great scepticism about the stability over time of empirical relationships in economics, a scepticism which was widespread (though not universal) among his contemporaries. The first (1969) edition of my own *Demand for Money . . .* gives, I hope, a reasonable account of how the evidence on the demand function for money appeared at that time.

By the end of the 1960s, then, Friedman's fundamental idea about the demand for money had become academically successful, but in the course of the academic debate it had also developed in a particular direction. During the course of the debate, notions about the importance of money as a determinant of the behaviour of the general price level that came directly from the Quantity Theory tradition became more prominent than they had been in Friedman's original (1956) essay, (though this idea had been central to the other essays of the volume to which it formed an introduction). The relationship between the demand for money and interest rates was downplayed, so that real income and prices (or their product money income) were presented as the critical variables determining the demand for money. Moreover, Friedman argued that, as a first but frequently empirically relevant approximation, real income was determined by factors on the supply side of the economy. Thus, the general price level was left as the principal variable in the demand for money function that could change in order to maintain equilibrium when the supply of money varied.[6]

By about 1970 an academically successful proposition about the demand for money had thus been transformed into the notion that price level fluctuations were to be attributed to variations in the money stock too great to be absorbed by real income growth. In this form it had acquired the simplicity required to make it successful in the policy arena too; and this at the very time when inflation was becoming the central problem for macroeconomic policy. The early 1970s saw a number of attempts to cure what was widely thought to be "cost push" inflation, by a combination of wage and price controls and expansionary demand side policies designed to reduce the social conflicts that were believed to underly that cost push inflation. When they failed, "Monetarist" notions, derived from Friedman's work, were already available to underpin the design of alternative policies based, as everyone knows, on the implementation of target rates of growth for the money supply. In short Friedman's monetary economics had become a thorough success, in the sense described at the outset of the lecture, in a little less than two decades.

6 This is not the place to write a history of the development of Friedman's monetary thought Nevertheless, the interested reader will find the role of interest rates downplayed in (1959), the emphasis shifted from the demand for money per se to money – money income relationships in Friedman and Meiselman (1963), and the suggestion that holding real income constant is often a useful first approximation, in Friedman's contribution to Gordon (1974). It should be pointed out explicitly that the revival of interest in money was not solely the result of Friedman's efforts In this context, the work of Karl Brunner and Allan Meltzer, e.g. (1963) is also particularly worthy of notice.

As I remarked earlier, to be successfully is not necessarily to be right, and many would argue that the ideas under discussion here have not fared too well over the last decade. On the policy front, a worldwide economic slowdown more or less coincided with the implementation of monetary policy regimes based on money growth targets, and critics of such policy regimes have been quick and persistent in attributing this slowdown to them. On a more fundamental level, the stability of the demand for money function, which provided the scientific basis for the policy regimes in question, has proved to be a good deal less robust than many would have believed possible fifteen years ago. As a result, the close linkage between the behaviour of money and prices upon which "Monetarist" policies rely has been opened to question; and, closely related, widespread doubts about the ability of the authorities to control the money supply accurately enough to exploit such a linkage have also arisen. Policymakers, who were never too comfortable in the first place with the degree of pre-commitment implicit in the adoption of money growth targets, have offered this instability and its apparent implications as reasons to downplay money growth targets or to abandon them outright. This reason has appeared to be a good one to many academic commentators, because previously stable empirical demand for money functions in many countries have been shifting around. This is a well established result coming from a wide variety of studies. It is not just a claim advanced by those who were uncomfortable with the new ideas about money from the outset, however pleased they may be to see their discomfort apparently vindicated.

All in all, the stable demand for money function has given many signs of suffering the same fate as another successful post-war economic idea, the stable inflation unemployment trade-off. Like the Phillips curve the demand for money function began to disappear the moment it was made the basis of real world economic policy. If this interpretation of the evidence is the whole story, then the only answer that we could give to the question "What do we really know about monetary policy" would have to begin with some such phrase as "Precious little . . ." My own preferred answer, however, begins "Not a much as we thought we did ten years ago, but still quite a lot that is useful . . ." and I shall devote the balance of this lecture to explaining why.

III

I noted earlier that, somewhere in the process of becoming thoroughly successful, the idea of a stable demand for money function became simplified and transformed into proposition about the relationship between money and inflation. Though the transformation in question may well have been necessary for the idea to make an important impact in policy debate, that simplification was nevertheless an oversimplification. This fact lies a the root of much popular disenchantment with "Monetarism".

In economic analysis, the purpose of a demand function is to enable us to predict the consequences of supply curve shifts. If the demand for money depends only on the price level, the highly appealing result that reducing the rate of growth of money will reduce the rate of growth of prices is immediately implied. If the demand function takes the form originally proposed by Friedman, the likely implied effect of a slowdown in the rate of monetary expansion is some combination of rising interest rates, falling real income growth, and falling inflation. Just what combination however, and with what timing, cannot be deduced from consideration of the demand for money function alone. It must be derive, from an analysis of a complete model of the economy in which all the factors determining the interaction of these four variables (at least) are specified.[7]

Perhaps some of the advocates of a monetary attack upon inflation were overoptimistic about its capacity to work without significantly affecting interest rates, real income, and employment, because of their beliefs about the nature of these other interactions. Beyond doubt any such overoptimism was undermined by events. Even so, the fact remains that the behaviour of interest rates, real income, and prices in the last ten years has been quite compatible with the existence of a stable demand for money function of the type originally proposed by Friedman. Furthermore, it is now possible to argue that the lasting effects of the monetary slowdown have indeed been concentrated on the inflation rate. Its influence on interest rates has proved temporary, though long lasting enough to be a matter for

7 The reader's attention is drawn to the use of the word "likely" in this discussion. I have described here a response in which each argument in the demand function moves in the direction that it would have to take if it alone was to restore equilibrium to the supply and demand for money. Of course a richer array of possible responses than this is logically conceivable. For a further discussion see Ch. 1 of the (1985) edition of my *Demand for Money* . . .

serious concern, and recently there has been a considerable resurgence of economic growth. Even though unemployment rates have remained uncomfortably, and from the point of view of Monetarist economics, inexplicably, high, this evidence suggests that even the simplified version of Friedman's idea has some long run validity. The monetary cure for inflation did after all work, though at a greater cost than many of its advocates expected. Moreover, it was much more effective than the earlier medicine of demand expansion combined with price controls. That treatment actually made the disease a good deal worse.

Popular reasons for disenchantment with "Monetarism" do not, that is to say, stand up very well to scrutiny. The experience of the last few years has taught us a few things about the conduct of monetary policy, which I shall discuss in due course, but it has not demonstrated that money does not matter. On the contrary, manipulation of the quantity of money has been shown to be a powerful, perhaps a dangerously powerful, policy tool. However these popular reasons for disenchantment are not the only or indeed the main ones which we must discuss. The fragility of empirical demand for money functions, even quite complex ones, provides a much more serious challenge to the ideas which I am discussing in this lecture.

Empirical tests of demand for money functions carried out in the 1960s seemed to establish a quite remarkable stability in the relationship, not only over time in specific economies, but across economies as well. By the late 1970s, however, beginning with Steven Goldfeld's (1976) paper on the United States function, things were seen to be going wrong. As with the success of the relationship, so its breakdown was not confined to one country. In country after country in the late 1970s, it appeared that the demand function for whatever particular aggregate had been chosen as the basis of monetary policy had begun to shift around. Goodhart's law – that any monetary aggregate chosen for policy manipulation will immediately become unreliable for that purpose – began to give every indication of becoming a successful economic idea in its own right.

There have, I believe been three sets of reasons for this problem.[8]

First, there is a simple matter of myopia. The original studies which seemed to establish the stability of the demand for money were carried out with long time series of data. Though the goodness of fit of the relationships in question was high it was by no mean perfect. All studies produced occasional runs of data that did not lie on the predicted functions. The latter were right on average, but not year by year. If the demand for money function had been used as a basis of policy in the past (which of course it was not) policy would have been in considerable trouble in those badly predicted years. Such errors do not matter with the hindsight that the econometrician brings to them, but they do to the policymaker who lives through them. To put it simply, in going from the econometrics of the demand for money to its policy application, too many people forgot about the error term. They should not have been surprised when it reminded them of its existence.

There is, though, a second matter to discuss. A significant number of recently observed shifts in the demand function have been of a once and for all type. The culprit here seems to have been institutional change in the financial sector which has changed the economic significance of the aggregates treated as dependent variables in studies of the demand for money, and used as policy tools. This change, as Jonson and Rankin (1986) have argued, in turn, seems to have three interconnected causes. In part it is a spontaneous development in the private sector of the economy, in part it is the response of the private sector to particular regulatory environments, and in part it is a result of policy induced changes in those environments. Whatever its cause, that institutional change could affect the demand for money is an intuitively obvious idea, and yet early studies of the relationship seemed to demonstrate its stability independently of any consideration of this factor. In this respect it is now clear that they were misleading.

8 The law is named after its originator Professor Charles Goodhart, now of the London School of Economics but formerly of the Bank of England. It represents a special case of Robert E. Lucas' (1976) general scepticism about assuming the stability of empirical relationships in the face o changes in the conduct of policy. For recent discussions of the stability of the demand for money function see Judd and Scadding (1982) and Laidler (1985).

To begin with, the data which they used were constructed, with benefit of much hindsight, after the period to be studied. Those who constructed the data took into account the effects of evolving institutions in deciding which financial assets should be included (and when) in a consistent-over-time series for money.[9] Thus, the early studies to which I have referred *did* after all make allowance for institutional changes. They did so, however in the construction of the data they utilised, and not by including variables measuring such developments in regression equations. In interpreting the results of these studies economists overlooked the role played by institutional change in generating them. It was predictable, then, (but not predicted) that in policy experiments based on measures of money selected *ex ante* rather than *ex post*, the ongoing fact of such change should make its presence known.

Recent studies have shown that not all of the effects of institutional change on the demand for money were in fact incorporated in the process of data construction. Such change is a continuing process, and because studies of the demand for money carried out for lengthy time periods are dominated by trends in both money and income data, those of its effects on the demand for money, not already incorporated in the relevant data, tend to be attributed to the income variable by regression equation. Bordo and Jonung (1981) have made an extensive study of this matter using data from five countries, and have been able to show, in each case, that the demand for money is indeed a stable function of a few arguments. According to Bordo and Jonung however, among those arguments are variables measuring institutional developments. Moreover, quantitative measures of the parameter linking the demand for money to income are erroneous if these factors are ignored.

Now we must be careful how we interpret this evidence. It does appear to show that, once institutional change is allowed for, it is still possible to maintain the idea of a stable aggregate demand for money function. But that does not mean that earlier views about the relationship between the demand for money and monetary policy need no alteration. Institutional change is hard to predict; it

9 The relevant source to consult for details of the construction of US money statistics is, of course, Friedman and Schwartz (1970).

can, and sometimes probably does, occur as a response to policy measures.[10] These two factors in turn imply that the route from the postulate of a stable demand for money function to the derivation of principles for the conduct of monetary policy is a good deal less direct and easily navigated than most of us through ten or fifteen years ago. I shall take up the implications of all this for policy issues in more detail below, but, before doing so, I must discuss a third source of demand for money instability.

The theory of the demand for money tells us about the relationship between the quantity of money demanded and the factors determining it; but the quantity of money demanded is not itself a directly observable magnitude. The quantity of money in circulation is observable, however; conventional empirical studies of the demand for money have assumed that all money in circulation is willingly held, and hence have used the supply of money to measure the demand for it. Now to obtain satisfactory results with empirical demand for money functions, it is necessary to postulate the existence of time lags in the relationships, and much recently observed instability in demand for money relationships has occurred in the parameters measuring those time lags. One possible resolution of this problem, which I find appealing, is cast in terms of the so-called "buffer-stock" approach to analysing the demand for money.[11]

This "buffer-stock" approach notes that agents hold money as an inventory of readily available purchasing power, and that they permit the size of that inventory to vary as it acts as a buffer between fluctuations in the value of their receipts and outlays. The "quantity of money demanded" on this interpretation is the average or target value which agents attempt to maintain over time for their money holdings. It is not an amount which they ensure they have on hand at each and every moment. In this view, fluctuations in the quantity of money in circulation will, in the first instance, simply be absorbed into temporary buffer stocks of money, and will only slowly affect expenditure as agents attempt over time to move their cash holdings back towards their long run average target

10 That is to say, if Goodhart's law is not universally true, it certainly is sometimes.

11 A number of Australian economists and economists who have worked in Australia, notably at the University of Adelaide have made important contributions to this strand of monetary analysis. See Artis and Lewis (1976j, Lewis (1978), Jonson (1976a) (1976b), Jonson *et al.* (1976) for examples. I have attempted to survey its salient features in (1984).

value. Moreover, though the individual can get rid of money by spending it, the economy as a whole cannot do so if the money supply is indeed under the control of the monetary authorities. Hence, when the money supply fluctuates, the economy will be "off" its demand for money function until the arguments of that relationship, interest rates, income and prices, move to re-equilibrate the supply and demand for money.

All this, however, means that, in studies which treat the quantity of money in circulation as an accurate measure of the demand for money, fluctuations in the supply of money induced by policy will erroneously be interpreted as fluctuations in the quantity of money demanded. Moreover, if the lag effects picked up by such conventional studies are in fact the result of interest rates, real income, and prices responding to the efforts of agents to restore their cash holdings to some target level in the wake of supply induced disturbances, these lag effects too might be expected to show instability when the quantity of money in circulation is itself fluctuating by a significant amount. In fact the monetary contractions of recent years have been far from smooth processes. Money growth has varied a great deal around a downward trend. According to the buffer stock approach, this very fact ought to have been responsible for the appearance of instability in conventionally measured demand for money functions.

As in the case of institutional change, we must be careful with the interpretation of this argument. If it is true, it does imply that the demand for money function is not as unstable as the results of conventional studies would suggest. However, it also implies that the relationships, between the supply of money and the variables upon which the demand for money depends, are more complicated than straightforward supply and demand analysis would lead one to believe. Since it is precisely these relationships that must lie at the heart of any monetary policy experiment, the "buffer stock" interpretation of the apparent instability of the demand for money function does require us to modify our views about what is and is not a feasible set of tasks for monetary policy to undertake. I will now turn to a discussion of these policy issues.

IV

Though the 19th century Quantity Theory treated money as of critical importance for the determination of the general price level, and though its adherents attached great importance to price level stability, they did not advocate that the quantity of money be actively manipulated by some policy authority with the aim of achieving such stability. In part this was because 19th century economists had a healthy scepticism about the willingness of anyone in authority to act in the public, as opposed to his own private, interest; but it was also due to their belief that the velocity of circulation was an unpredictably unstable parameter. They preferred a policy regime in which the price level was stabilised by other means and the quantity of money enabled to fluctuate in order to meet the public's, as they saw it, volatile demand for money (though 19th century economists would not have used this phrase): hence their support for the gold standard.

The First World War effectively destroyed the gold standard, though its final demise was not to come until 1931. Even so, proposals to place control of the quantity of money at the centre of things were rather rare in the 1920s and early 1930s. The literature of this period typically discussed the means whereby the rate of interest could be manipulated in order to maintain a stable price level by ensuring that (to put it in modern language) the full employment level of investment was kept equal to the full employment level of saving.[12] A by-product of the successful implementation of such a policy would be a time path for the behaviour of the money supply compatible with the economy's demand for money. In this sense, money mattered to the contributors to this literature, but not as a policy instrument. The importance of money was further downgraded as a result of the intellectual revolution which followed the (1936) publication of Keynes' *General Theory*, which replaced the price level by the level of employment as the central concern of macroeconomic policy. Keynesian analysis, to the extent that it accorded any importance at all to monetary policy, always treated it as subsidiary to fiscal policy as an income stabilisation device.

12 American quantity theorists working in the tradition of Irving Fisher (1911) are something of an exception here. It is in comparison with this type of policy analysis that Friedman's work has its strongest claim to continuity with the Quantity Theory tradition.

When the revival of interest in the quantity of money began in the 1950s, it was, as we have seen, accompanied by the radically new idea that the demand for money was a stable function of just a few arguments. This new idea implied that the velocity of circulation, though not constant, was reliable enough to provide a basis for a monetary policy which did indeed involve controlling the money supply with a view to achieving price level targets. Along with the new theoretical idea, went a new policy idea also developed by Friedman (1960): namely that price level (and indeed general macroeconomic) stability could be greatly enhanced by putting the quantity of money on a predetermined growth path from which it would not be allowed to deviate. This policy idea, the "money supply growth rule", provides a useful focus for any discussion of the policy implications of the evidence about the demand for money generated over the last ten years.

The first thing to be clear about here is that policies of setting medium target growth rate ranges for the money supply, the actual form in which the new ideas about money discussed in this lecture found their way into the policy arena, were somewhat removed from Friedman's proposals completely to replace discretionary policies by a rule. Such policies were, by their very nature, open to change in the future, and because they involved target ranges for money growth, instead of a *well defined path*, they left considerable room for short term manipulation of the money supply into the bargain.

That "Monetarist" ideas should be translated into policy actions in this way had a great deal to do with the state of the economy at the time at which those ideas became fashionable. When Friedman proposed a money supply growth rule permanently binding upon central bankers, the economy (or at least the US economy about which he was writing) was to all intents and purposes inflation free. His proposal was thus one for ensuring continued stability in an already stable economy. By the time his ideas became popular, the economy was in an altogether different condition. In the mid-1970s inflation was both high and rising in the US and elsewhere. The policy problem was not to maintain, but to restore stability; and an immediate move to a rate of monetary expansion compatible with long run price stability would have had devastating effects on real income and employment. That rate of expansion had to be approached gradually from above, and for this purpose medium term growth targets, open to revision in due course, seemed to be required. Nevertheless, now that inflation is on the verge of acceptable ranges in a number of countries, it is not inappropriate to ask what the implications of the evidence generated over the last decade might be for the pursuit of a monetary growth rate rule.

As we have seen, even what was at least supposed to be a gradualist policy seems to have had serious effects on interest rates and real income, and the straightforward hypothesis of a stable demand for money function has been badly battered. Though I shall not end up defending a simple growth rate rule in this lecture, l shall argue that the evidence referred to above is less damaging to such a proposal than is often imagined; and I shall argue that medium term growth rate targeting is still both feasible and desirable. Though such a policy regime stops far short of a rule, it is still a good deal closer to it than to any monetary policy regimes that were thought desirable before the 1950s.

My basic reasons for taking this position are to be found in my interpretation of the evidence on the outcome of monetary policy over the last ten years and on the instability of the demand for money function in particular. I readily agree that much of the real slowdown that we have seen, particularly in the early 1980s, should be attributed to monetary policy; but surely this argues for avoiding the kind of monetary policy which produced the problem. Two properties characterise money growth between the mid 1970s and 1983. Its rate was on average below the growth rate of nominal income, and it was also very volatile. If we are to avoid further real contractions induced by monetary factors (and I would not wish to rule out the possibility of contractions traceable to other sources) it would seem that a falling and volatile money growth rate is to be shunned. To set money growth targets within rather narrow ranges, and with a positive trend roughly equal to the economy's underlying long-run real growth rate, would accomplish this.

But what about instability in the demand for money? If the money supply behaves itself, cannot demand fluctuations nevertheless have disruptive effects? In principle they certainly can. I have argued above that some of the apparent instability we have observed in the demand for money function has been attributable to the kind of random fluctuations that are present in any real world economy. I have also argued that some of it has been due to instability in the behaviour of the money supply. Such sources of instability in the demand function as these are very damaging indeed to the case for using monetary policy as an active tool of short run stabilisation policy, such as advanced by Modigliani (1977), but not the case for gearing monetary policy to medium term objectives.[13] Random errors do tend to cancel out over time, and if money growth is not volatile, then money supply fluctuations cannot disturb the relationship between the quantity of money and the variables affecting the demand for it.

If random errors and supply of money shocks were the only causes of recent instability in empirical estimates of the demand for money function, it would still be possible to make the case for basing policy on a simple money growth rate rule. However, they are not.

There is still the matter of institutional change to consider. New financial assets do get created, old ones do change their signficance in the structure of the economy, and such changes are difficult enough to recognise as they happen, let alone to predict. A money growth rule that was supposed to be binding ever afterwards on the authorities would have to embody a particular definition of money in its formulation. If it didn't, the authorities could evade the discipline of the rule by changing that definition as it suited their purposes. But, in the presence of institutional change, someone somewhere has to have the freedom to make such changes, otherwise the effects of the rule on the time path of the economy will deviate from its framers' original intentions as the institutional background changes. If they are to maintain a stable monetary environment by controlling the "money supply", the relevant authorities must as Jonson and Rankin (1986) argue, have discretionary power. Binding rules are not technically feasible, but medium-term targets, which permit a little discretion in the short run, and more in the long run as they are updated and revised, are.

13 In the Keynesian tradition, to attempt to use monetary policy for short run stabilisation purposes is almost entirely an American idea. British Keynesians, and those working in other countries with parliamentary systems, have accorded monetary policy the rather minor role of accommodating fiscal policy so as not to get in its way. The difference here stems from the fact that, given United States political institutions, it is impossible to vary fiscal policy fast enough to make it a credible tool of short run stabilisation policy. It is a sad commentary of economics as a discipline that this almost exclusively American problem has been allowed to colour a world-wide debate about monetary policy.

This implication of recent experience has caused a number of commentators to go one step further, and to argue for gearing monetary policy to the pursuit of a stable target range for the growth rate of *money income* rather than the money supply *per se*.[14] On an abstract and purely technical level, these two proposals amount to very much the same thing. After all, the purposes of choosing a particular target for money growth is to attain a more distant, but a nevertheless ultimately more important, goal for the behaviour of the price level; and hence, if real income is supply-side determined, of money income. Jonson and Rankin's (1986) discussion of the use of a "check list" of variables in the conduct of monetary policy shows this procedure to be more closely related "targetting" than may appear at first sight. They argue that, at times of rapid institutional change, the growth rate of any monetary aggregate is an unreliable indicator of the stance of policy, and that information about the likely future behaviour of money income is available in current data on such variables as interest rates, the exchange rate, inflation rate, and so on. They then argue that such information can be used in the design of policy intended to stabilise money income growth without the need to specify targets for the behaviour of any specific intermediate variable.

There can be no strong arguments against these procedures on ground of theoretical principle. However in practice, l still prefer policy targets to be set in terms of the quantity of money rather than money income or as a function of some "check list". The time lags between policy actions and their effects on money income are long and badly understood, as are the relationships among income growth and any "check list". Also money income is susceptible to shocks from sources other than monetary policy. A policy geared either directly to money income growth, or indirectly through a check list, is therefore more difficult for outsiders to monitor and criticise on a continuing basis than one based on money growth. Given that policymakers must be given discretion over monetary policy, and given the many pressures to act irresponsibly to which they are inevitably subjected by political processes, the more easily monitored and criticised they are, the better. This argument does not, of course, preclude the authorities from using a "check list" of

14 Among the proponents of stabilising money income growth as opposed to money supply growth are Sam Brittan (1982) and Robert Gordon (1983). For a penetrating survey of the theoretical issues involved here see McCallum (1985).

variables in choosing where, within their target range, money growth should actually be; nor does it preclude the deployment of data on the behaviour of other variables in the defence of a change in policy towards money growth, should that be deemed desirable. Its intent is to ensure that policy goals are stated clearly in advance, and that any change in policy be quickly visible and subject to public debate. The simplicity of using money growth targets as the centrepiece of policy has much to recommend it in this respect.

Now not everyone reads the evidence in this way. Some commentators, while agreeing that institutional changes make it impossible to take discretion away from monetary policy makers by imposing a monetary growth rule upon them, note that there are alternative ways of tying them down which do not suffer from this defect. In particular, requiring the monetary authorities to stand ready to convert money at a fixed price into some stable valued item – some non-inflationary foreign currency for example, or some commodity, of which gold is of course the archetype – would take away their discretionary powers. It would also effectively tie down the behaviour of the price level and permit the money supply to fluctuate in whatever way is necessary to satisfy the demand for it. Therefore, they propose that we return to a regime very like that which ruled in the international economy before the First World War. Though well enough conceived in principle, I believe that there are important practical objections to these proposals.

To begin with, to remove the authorities' freedom of action, an exchange rate would have to be really fixed. An adjustable peg system would simply open up the possibility of discretionary policy by another route. Bearing this in mind, and even setting aside the problem of finding some currency or commodity stable enough to make a desirable standard, we must not forget that real shocks as well as monetary shocks impinge on the world economy. Adherence to a fixed exchange rate requires an economy which suffers an adverse terms-of-trade shift to adjust by forcing down domestic money wages. The alternative, under a money growth target regime, is to allow the depreciation of a flexible exchange rate not offset by money wage increases, to bear the brunt of adjustment. Of course the ultimate real consequences of either adjustment must be the same, and of course, in a fully rational world, one form of adjustment would be as easy as the other. However, we should design monetary policy institutions with the real world in mind, and an exchange rate depreciation, which indirectly affects everyone at once, is more likely to be absorbed by an economy without disruptions than the alternative of a series of piecemeal and unco-ordinated money wage reductions.[15]

Second, for a fixed exchange rate regime to be viable for the world economy as a whole, or for a substantial segment of it, macro-economic policies in general, and monetary policies in particular, would have to be co-ordinated among participating countries. I have nothing against the international co-ordination of policies, quite the contrary; but policy authorities with sufficient self-discipline to co-ordinate their policies with those of other countries so as to maintain their exchange rate fixed on some stable valued currency or commodity, could surely also be trusted with the more modest task of setting and sticking to sensible domestic money growth targets. To put the same point in another way, the first task is to induce discipline in domestic policies. If this is accomplished, stability of exchange rates will take care of itself. If it is not, then a fixed exchange rate regime will prove impossible to implement and sustain. It is not, therefore, a viable alternative to money growth targeting as a basis for policy.

This is not, though, to argue that the international monetary system imposes no discipline on the conduct of domestic policy. The theoretical ideas of Russel Boyer about "currency substitution" under flexible exchange rates, first written up in 1973 (but not published until 1978) have been amply borne out by recent experience. As Melvin (1985) has shown, using European data, a country whose domestic monetary policy is volatile will make agents engaged in international trade unwilling to hold its currency, and hence will find its international transactions complicated by a weak and fluctuating exchange rate. International monetary mechanisms, that is, encourage the pursuit of stable domestic monetary policy even in the absence of fixed exchange rates.

15 I emphasize the effect of deteriorating rather than improving terms of trade here for the simple reasons that one cannot have a terms of trade change in the world economy without it adversely affecting some country; and it is the adversely affected country that faces the greater adjustment problems. The literature on the monetary approach to balance of payments theory, particularly the earlier literature abstracted from terms of trade effects, and hence gave a misleadingly simple impression of the case for permanently fixed exchange rates.

The question of whether the domestic money supply is indeed controllable does, of course, still arise, and there is not space to discuss it in detail here. Suffice it to make the following observations. First, the experience of the 1970s and early 1980s does show that attempts to control the money supply, by first monitoring income and prices, and then directly manipulating interest rates in the hope that the economy's efforts to stay "on" its demand for money function will keep the money supply on track, are misconceived. As Howitt and Laidler (1979) argued, such a policy package ignores the links between interest rates and the behaviour of credit markets, and the strategic role of bank credit creation in the generation of money, independently of the demand for money *per se*.

Second, and more generally, it is impossible to lay down mechanical formulae whereby the money supply can be controlled without referring to the institutional framework. However, if this is variable, the discretion which must be accorded the authorities in setting money growth targets will also have to extend to their choice of monetary control techniques. My own preference would be for some type of monetary base control applied to a rather broad aggregate, but precise operating procedures for its successful implementation must inevitably depend upon the structure of any particular financial system. Given the degree of discretion for the authorities implied here, and given the many pressures to which they are subject, the need for constant monitoring of their actions, already referred to above, is all the more pressing. The case for money, as opposed to money income, targeting is thus further strengthened by questions about the controllability of the money supply.

V

What then do we really know about monetary policy? As a matter of logic, we know that, if the time path of real income is, in the long run, driven by supply side factors, the interaction of the supply and demand for money determines the behaviour of the general price level. We know, also as a matter of logic, that, if the demand for money is indeed a stable function of but a few arguments, then keeping the money supply on a stable growth path will stabilise the behaviour of the price level. Shocks induced by the money supply itself would clearly be ruled out in this case, and steady money growth will act as a useful built in stabiliser against the effects of other shocks. The trouble, as we have seen, is that logic does not tell the whole story in this particular case. There are a few awkward facts to be considered too. Though the evidence does seem to be bearing out the prediction that money affects mainly prices in the long run, experience has been less kind to the postulate of a stable demand for money function.

The existence of random fluctuations in the demand for money is not in and of itself an insuperable difficulty. They do imply that steady money growth will not deliver perfect price stability on a quarter by quarter or even year by year basis, no matter how carefully its rate is calibrated to the rate of growth of real output. However, their influence will tend to cancel itself out over time. As to fluctuations, in the relationship between the quantity of money and other variables, which are the results of variations in the quantity of money itself, these can obviously be no problem in the context of steady money growth, toublesome though they may be for the interpretation of historical data generated when policy was unstable.

Institutional change, however, does present real difficulties. It has long been a complaint of the critics of "Monetarism" that, in modern economies, with their complex financial systems, it is far from clear just what is and is not "money" for purposes of designing policy. It used to seem possible to answer such criticism by conceding its logical validity while denying its empirical importance. It no longer is, and this fact has important implications for monetary policy, as I have argued. Its conduct must either be placed in the context of a set of constraints involving fixed exchange rates and some form of commodity convertibility, or must permit a good deal of discretion to the relevant national monetary authorities both in their choice of which aggregate to control, and the means whereby that control is achieved. Since I do not believe that the former alternative is viable, we seem to be left with the second.

How then should the monetary authorities use their discretion? I have suggested that they should do so in such a way as to keep whatever shifting definition of money may be appropriate to a given time and place on a time path that is consistent with the pursuit of long run price stability. Such a policy would appropriately be implemented in terms of a public commitment to target ranges for "money" growth, revised at regular intervals. I make this second suggestion not because of the potentially stabilising effects of money growth targeting on agents' expectations. These effects have surely been shown to be of minor importance in the last few years. Rather I advocate medium term money growth targeting because it seems to me to provide the best way to expose the authorities to monitoring and criticism.

Real economic variables do get subjected to troublesome shocks. There is, and will remain, a political demand for "effective" short-run stabilisation policy. Though monetary policy clearly can have powerful real effects in the short run, so that there is always a temptation to use it for such stabilisation, I have argued in this lecture that the timing of these effects is too uncertain for it successfully to be used in this way. A key problem, then, is to prevent the monetary authorities responding to demands for stabilisation measures and, in attempting to meet them, rendering the economy less, rather than more stable. If binding rules are not viable, then continuous public monitoring presents an alternative way of attempting to constrain the authorities to behave responsibly. Providing for it, therefore, is no light matter. A policy regime that forces them to state their intentions for money growth *ex ante* and hence permits their performance to be continuously observed and criticised in the light of those intentions, will make it more difficult for them to succumb to the temptation to aim at more ambitious goals.

Another defence against the misuse of monetary policy, complementary to this one, would involve the availability of alternative means for stabilising the real economy. Here one's mind naturally turns to fiscal measures. I would be willing to argue that these are useful tools of short run stabilisation, provided they are used against the background of a monetary policy regime that is unequivocally devoted to the pursuit of price level stability. Moreover, in parliamentary systems, such tools can be deployed and implemented quite rapidly. In the United States it is another matter, and it is surely no accident that so much of the opposition to abandoning the idea of using monetary policy for short run stabilisation arises in a country whose institutions render fiscal weapons unsuitable for this purpose.

There is not time now to enter into a detailed discussion of fiscal policy. Suffice it to say that there are, as I have said, good reasons why there should be a political demand for short run stabilisation policy; and my purpose in this lecture is not to argue that this demand should not be met, but only that it should not be met by monetary means. As should by now be apparent, I say this because my one sentence answer to the question "How much do we really know about monetary policy?" boils down to "Enough to prevent it doing harm, but not enough to use it to do good". I hope for all our sakes that this answer does not prove to be too complicated to be politically successful.

References

Artis, M. and Lewis M. (1976), "The Demand for Money in the United Kingdom: 1963-1973," *Manchester School*, vol. 44.

Bordo, M. D. and Jonung, L. (1981), "The Long-run Behaviour of the Income Velocity of Money in Five Advanced Countries 1879-1975: An Institutional Approach," *Economic Inquiry*, vol. 19.

Boyer, R.S. (1978), "Currency Mobility and Balance of Payments Adjustment" in B. Putnam and D.S. Wilford (eds.), *The Monetary Approach to International Adjustment*, New York: Praeger.

Brittan, S. (1982), *How to End the 'Monetarist' Controversy*, London: IEA.

Brunner, K. and Meltzer, A.H. (1963), "Predicting Velocity: Implications for Theory and Policy," *Journal of Finance*, vol. 18.

Fisher, 1. (1911), *The Purchasing Power of Money*, New York: Macmillan.

Friedman, M. (1956), "The Quantity Theory of Money – A Restatement," in *Studies in the Quantity Theory of Money*, Chicago: University of Chicago Press.

Friedman, M. (1959) "The Demand for Money – Some Theoretical and Empirical Results," *Journal of Political Economy*, vol. 67.

Friedman, M. (1960), *A Programme for Monetary Stability*, New York: Fordham University Press.

Friedman, M. and Meiselman, D. (1963), "The Relative Stability of Monetary Velocity and the Investment Multiplier in the United States 1898-1958" in *Commission on Money and Credit Stabilization Policies*, Englewood Cliffs, NJ: Prentice-Hall.

Friedman, M. and Schwartz, A.J. (1970), *The Monetary Statistics of the United States*, New York: NBER.

Goldfeld, S. (1976), "The Case of the Missing Money," *Brookings Papers on Economic Activity*, vol. 3.

Gordon, R.J. (ed.) (1974), *Milton Friedman's Monetary Framework*, Chicago: University of Chicago Press.

Gordon R.J. (1983), "The Conduct of Domestic Monetary Policy," NBER Working Paper 1221.

Howitt, P.W. and Laidler, D. (1979) "Recent Canadian Monetary Policy – a Critique," in R. Wirick and D. Purvis (eds.), *Issues in Canadian Public Policy* (11) Kingston, Queen's University (Mimeo).

Jonson, P.D. (1976a), "Money and Economic Activity in the Open Economy: The United Kingdom 1880-1970," *Journal of Political Economy*, vol. 84.

Jonson, P.D. (1976b) "Money, Prices Output – an Integrative Essay," *Kredit und Kapital*, vol. 4.

Jonson, P.D., Moses, E. and Wymer, C. (1976), *The Structure of RBA 76*, Reserve Bank of Australia (Mimeo).

Jonson, P.D. and Rankin, R.W. (1986), "On Some Recent Developments in Monetary Economics," Reserve Bank of Australia Research Discussion Paper 8605.

Judd, J. and Scadding, J. (1982), "The Search for a Stable Money Demand Function: A survey of the Post-1973 Literature?" *Journal of Economic Literature*, vol. 20.

Keynes, J.M. (1936), *The General Theory of Employment Interest and Money*, London: Macmillan.

Laidler, D. (1969), *The Demand for Money – Theories and Evidence*, Scranton PA: International Textbook Co.; (1985) 3rd ed, New York, Harper Row.

Laidler, D. (1984), "The Buffer-Stock Notion in Monetary Economics," Conference Papers supplement to the *Economic Journal*, vol. 94.

Lewis, M.(1978), "Interest Rates and Monetary Velocity – Australia and the United States," *Economic Record*, vol. 54.

Lucas, R.E. Jr. (1976), "Econometric Policy Evaluation" in K. Brunner and A.H. Meltzer (eds.), *The Phillips Curve and the Labor Market Carnegie-Rochester Conference Series*, vol. 1, Amsterdam: North-Holland.

Marshall, A. (1890*), Principles of Economics*, London: Macmillan.

McCallum, B.T. (1985), "On Consequences and Criticisms of MonetaryTargeting," *Journal of Money, Credit, and Banking*, vol. 17.

Melvin, M. (1985), "Currency Substitution and Western European Monetary Unification," *Economica*, vol. 52.

Modigliani, F. (1977), "The Monetarist Controversy or, Should We Forsake Stabilization Policies," *American Economic Review*, vol. 67.

Patinkin, D. (1969), "The Chicago Tradition, the Quantity Theory, and Friedman," *Journal of Money, Credit, and Banking*, vol. 18.

Patinkin, D. (1986), "A Reply," *Journal of Money, Credit, and Banking*, vol. 18).

Parkin, J.M. (1986), "*Essays on and in the Chicago Tradition* a Review Essay," *Journal of Money, Credit, and Banking*, vol. 18.

Robbins, L.C. (1935), *An Essay on the Natural Signficance of Economic Science* (2nd ed.), London: Macmillan.

41

Pacific challenges to the United States

Paul R. Krugman[1]

In a sense any US issue is a Pacific issue, and indeed almost any world economic issue is largely Pacific. More to the point, the principal counterpart of the US trade deficit lies in the surpluses of Asian Pacific nations – primarily Japan but also Taiwan and Korea. In that sense the issue of international payments imbalances is largely one of imbalances across the Pacific.

It is also true that if we ask about the possible consequences of the US trade deficit. The potential effects on the Pacific as an economic community loom large. The biggest danger of the persistent US trade deficit, as I think is now widely appreciated, is that it will lead to a protectionist reaction in the United States. Whatever the real economic evaluation of the effects of the US trade deficit, the persistence of a situation in which Imports exceed exports by 50 per cent or more makes preservation of a more or less open US market a constant rear-guard action. The forces in favour of a liberal economic system are weak relative to those in favour of protection, simply because more producers face import competition than those that perceive export opportunities. (Consumers, as always in trade policy, do not get anything like an equal voice.)

What would happen if the United States were to experience a protectionst reaction? The most likely answer is that the world would break up into trading blocs. And one of these trading blocs would almost surely be a Western Pacific bloc, centered on Japan, and including Australia. So the protectionist threat from the US trade deficit is very much a Pacific issue.

1 Forty-first Joseph Fisher Lecture, 29 July 1988. Revised version published as "The Persistent US Trade Deficit", in *Australian Economic Papers*, 27 (51): 149-58, December.

Also, there is another growing issue that is an indirect consequence of the US trade deficit that is, in its way, largely Pacific in character. This is the growing role of foreign investment in the United States. Increasingly, the US accumulation of foreign debt that is the counterpart of persistent trade deficits takes the form not simply of paper debts – treasury bills owned by Japanese pension funds – but direct foreign investments. US corporations, factories, land, and office buildings are increasingly being controlled by foreign corporations. again very largely Japanese. In the great scheme of things there may be nothing wrong with extensive foreign investment in the US, but in the current political context this growing foreign role raises all kinds of issues of nationalism. If and when the United States reacts against the feeling of growing dependence on foreign investors, all the rest of the world including especially the Pacific rim will feel the consequence.

Finally, there is an issue which is a little subtle but very important. The efforts to do something about the US trade imbalance and the counterpart surpluses on the part of Japan and other Asian countries have been the centrepiece of recent movements toward international economic cooperation. The one piece of serious forward motion that the governments of advanced industrial economies have made on cooperation has been the series of meetings on exchange rate policy from the Plaza in September 1985, when they agreed that the dollar needed to fall, to the Louvre in early 1987, when they agreed that the dollar should stop. These meetings have probably not had nearly as much effect on the world economy as has been claimed, but they have had great political importance as a demonstration that governments really can get together and thus as a precedent for cooperation in other areas. If the effort seems to fail, if progress grinds to a halt on rectifying the enormous imbalances among the Pacific economies, then this will poison the atmosphere for all future cooperative actions Pacific or otherwise.

I hope that I have managed to make the case that the US trade deficit really is a Pacific issue, or at least has a strong Pacific aspect. Let me now turn to the issue of the trade deficit itself.

The puzzle of the persistent US trade deficit

The important thing about the US trade deficit since 1985 is not what has happened, but what hasn't. What hasn't happened is a convincing reversal of the great surge in the deficit between 1981 and 1985. In the last year we have finally begun to see some downward movement in the trade deficit, which is currently running at an annual rate of about 130 billion dollars. This is better than the $170 billion annual rate of 1987, but it is still a number that would have been inconceivable in the 1970s. Indeed, the 1987 trade deficit was six times as large as any deficit we ever had before 1981.

Now the persistence of the US trade deficit poses not only political and economic problems but also analytical ones, because it wasn't supposed to happen. The rise of the trade deficit in the first half of the 1980s was no mystery because it was clearly caused in large part by the rise of the dollar. This persistence of the deficit, however, has occurred in spite of one of the greatest currency movements in history – the great fall of the dollar from its peak in 1985. While the numbers keep on shifting – the yen went from 121 to 137, then back to 121 between the time I was asked to give this lecture and the time I revised the final draft – the round number is that the dollar has fallen about 50 per cent in terms of its major counterpart currencies, the yen and the mark, since its peak (or, equivalently, the yen and the mark have doubled in terms of the dollar), currency depreciation is supposed to lead to an improvement in the trade balance, especially when the depreciation is that large.

One way to put this in perspective is to realize that we are dealing not with a run-of-the-mill currency movement, but with a depreciation that makes all the textbook cases, the famous currency realignments around which one builds university education look trivial by comparison. Consider when John Maynard Keynes inveighed against the economics of Mr. Churchill, by which he meant the foolishness of returning to the gold standard after the First World War, he calculated that the resulting overvaluation of the pound sterling was perhaps 10 per cent – which he regarded as a terrible thing. In 1967 Britain, after much turmoil and after years of desperate measures to avoid the awful step, decided to devalue sterling from $2.80 to $2.40 – a 14 per cent devaluation. When the Bretton Woods international monetary system was broken up in 1971, it was because the United States felt that the dollar had become overvalued and the US resorted to extreme actions (an illegal tariff) to force other countries to realign their currencies upward – by 10 per cent.

Now look at recent events: in the two months following the October stock market crash the dollar fell 20 per cent against the yen and the mark. During 1988 the dollar rose 13 per cent against the yen, then fell back to its previous level. We have been accustomed to eat for breakfast every day exchange rate changes of a magnitude that it used to take years for nations to swallow. And the overall change in the value of the dollar since 1985 is just unprecedented. No major country has ever reduced the relative prices of its goods, services and labour as far and as fast.

Yet the trade deficit remains, and is drifting downward only slowly. So the key issue, or at least the key starting point for a discussion of where the world economy is headed, has to be the question of why more has not happened, why this unprecedented depreciation has not done more to reduce America's trade deficit. In the course of discussing this issue we will, I hope, also gain some insight into some broader aspects of the world economy.

Some incorrect explanations of the persistent deficit

Before I discuss what I believe to be the correct explanations of the persistence of the US trade deficit, I want to begin by discussing some popular but incorrect explanations. This may be a bad pedagogic style – you may end up remembering the wrong explanations instead of the right ones – but there has been so much misguided and often deliberately misguiding discussion about the US trade deficit that it is important to spend a little more time on what isn't right before turning to what is.

There are three important false stories that have been circulating in the last two years about why dollar depreciation isn't working. The first is that the dollar's depreciation never happened; the second is that the problem is that foreign economies haven't grown enough; the third is that dollar depreciation is irrelevant anyway.

The argument that the dollar hasn't really declined remains surprisingly influential, in spite of years of careful refutation. The argument goes like this: although the dollar may have gone from 260 yen to 120 yen, there are many Third World countries whose currencies have depreciated against the dollar over the same period. Put these currencies into the basket, and the average hasn't changed much. A great deal of attention was given two years ago to the publication by the Federal Reserve Bank of Dallas of a broad-based index of the US dollar against 130 countries that showed a depreciation of only 4 per cent from its peak instead of 50 per cent depreciation that we've had against the mark and the yen. I still find myself encountering businessmen and journalists who cite that index arguing that the dollar is still wrong.

The reasons why such comparisons are nonsense should, of course, be clear as soon as one thinks about which countries have continued to depreciate against the dollar. The list includes Brazil, Mexico, Bolivia, Ecuador, the Philippines – it includes, in other words, countries that have high rates of inflation. But because of the high rates of inflation in these countries the large decline in their currencies has not produced any comparable improvement in their competitiveness against the US. There has been some change in real exchange rates – Mexico, in particular, has had a depreciation of the peso that makes it more competitive in manufacturing than it wad five years ago – but it is simply misleading to use the uncorrected number. On a real exchange rate basis adding developing countries changes the numbers slightly, so that the dollar may appear to have depreciated by say 40 per cent in real terms instead of 50 per cent but the basic point of a massive and indeed historically unprecedented exchange depreciation remains.

We might also want to notice that to the extent that developing countries have depreciated their currencies in real terms the appreciation of the yen and mark are even larger than the comparison with the dollar suggests. We should always realize that the puzzle of the persistent US deficit has as its counterpart the puzzle of the persistent surpluses elsewhere especially in Japan: this counterpart puzzle becomes even worse once one allows for the role of developing countries.

The second false story about the persistence of the US deficit is one that Americans, and especially government officials, tend to like, because it makes the trade deficit a badge of success instead of failure. This is the argument that the trade deficit is persisting because of the relative strength of the US economy, that because of the growth of demand in the US we are pulling in imports, while because of slower growth in the rest of the world there has not been a counterpart expansion in our exports. Leave aside the fact that faster growth in Japan and Germany this year has still not delivered the anticipated trade turnaround. This is an argument that should have been obviously wrong from the beginning.

Not that the argument is completely without validity. It is right in principle, but just wrong on arithmetic. It is true that since 1982 the US economy has on average taken up its slack capacity faster than the rest of the world so that the US is probably operating closer to full capacity than most other industrial countries. This differential growth has contributed to the US trade deficit. But even a simple back of the envelope calculation will tell you that growth cannot be much of either the cause of the deficit or of its solution. Suppose that we could somehow persuade all of the rest of the world to expand their economies by 5 per cent over and above their trend rate of growth. This would be a very large number, since it would be possible only if they had 5 per cent usable excess capacity. Since nobody believes there is that much usable excess capacity in the rest of the world as a whole (as opposed to the few most depressed economies), looking at this thought experiment will give us a very high upper bound on what growth can do.

Suppose then that we could get this unlikely 5 per cent excess growth in all US export markets. Then this would indeed increase the demand for US exports. Since in general a country's exports rise more than in proportion when its economy expands, the expansion in US exports would be more than 5 per cent – say 10 per cent. But US imports have been exceeding US exports by about 60 per cent in recent months. So even if we had a massive and totally unlikely improvement in growth performance in the rest of the world. The US trade deficit would fall only modestly probably less than 20 per cent. This would help, but it is clear from this sort of example that differential growth can't be much of the explanation of why cutting the value of the dollar in half hasn't done much for our trade deficit.

Finally let me turn to the third argument which is a somewhat insidious one, because it is hard to explain what's wrong with it. It is a familiar proposition that a trade deficit is not simply the difference between what a nation imports and what it exports; it is also the difference between what a nation spends and what it earns, which is in turn equal to the difference between investment and saving.

The insidious argument runs as follows: since the trade deficit is the difference between investment and savings, the exchange rate has nothing to do with it. Savings in the US are at historic lows in part because of the budget deficit while investment remains reasonably high. So why, this view asks, should one expect the trade deficit to decline?

The problem with this view is that it fails to acknowledge that while the trade deficit is indeed the difference between savings and investment, it is also the difference between what we buy and what we sell. No appeal to the amount of capital we need to import can explain why a tremendous cheapening of our goods has not increased the demand for these goods. That is, how can it be that US goods are half the price in foreign currency that they were three years ago, yet the demand for these goods has not increased? If the demand for US goods had increased without a rise in our savings, then that would be a different issue; I'll come back to that in a little while because one of the problems we may have is that when our trade deficit does begin to come down we won't be ready for it. But that hasn't happened yet; the US is still a long way from a situation where the world is clamoring for our goods but we are unable to supply the demand. Instead despite the enormous cheapening of US goods and services, we have so far seen only a moderate increase in demand.

These, then are the easy explanations of the persistent US trade deficit all of them false. The dollar really has declined despite some claims to the contrary. Slow growth abroad is only a minor factor in the persistence of the deficit. And the argument from the savings investment balance while important doesn't explain why making US goods cheaper doesn't seem to make them more attractive.

The persistence of the US trade deficit: The truth (maybe)

I have now argued that the dramatic fall in the relative prices of US goods and services that appears in exchange rate indices is indeed a real fact, not something that can be defined away; that differences in growth rates don't explain much about the trade deficit; and that appeals to capital flows are a diversion from the central issue. So why hasn't the dollar's decline worked?

I reject out of hand the idea that relative prices don't matter – that US goods are so shoddy that nobody will buy them no matter how low the price, or that world markets are so protected that prices are irrelevant. The US trade deficit emerged suddenly in the 1980s, when the dollar rose, there was no sudden loss of quality or technology that explains this deterioration. I do not regard elasticity pessimism, the belief that prices don't matter in international trade, as a sustainable position in the modern world.

That logically leaves two possibilities. One is that these things take time: purchasers who shifted away from US goods and services when the dollar was strong will not shift back until it has been weak for an extended period. The other is that something has made US goods and services permanently less attractive to buyers both at home and abroad than they used to be. That is, we may be experiencing the effects of long lags with substantial trade improvement still in the pipeline: or there may have been a decline in the equilibrium dollar so that the declining dollar has in fact been chasing a moving target. A case can be made for either view.

The case for lags starts with the observation that the US appears at current exchange rates to be a low-cost place to produce. Real exchange rate indices all show the US at a historical low. Some attempts have also been made at absolute unit labour cost comparisons: these seem to suggest that the US is a dramatically cheaper place to produce than the rest of the OECD. The assertion is that this must eventually show up in a relocation of manufacturing production lo the US.

Now econometric estimates of trade equations do not show this. They typically find lags of only two years or so, and by and large predict that the US current account deficit will begin to widen again in the near future. However the lags allowed for in standard trade equations are much shorter than seems reasonable if one considers the underlying economics of trade adjustment. The fall in exports and the rise in imports associated with the strong dollar were not simply a matter of consumers switching from US goods to foreign goods that were already available. Much of the deterioration in trade involved longer-term actions: construction of new capacity abroad and scrapping of capacity in the US. Long term changes in sourcing decisions, development of distribution networks etc. Given the long-term nature of the decisions involved in adjusting to an exchange rate change, we would expect the full response to take a number of years. Yet econometric trade estimates seldom allow for more than a two-year lag. There are good reasons why it is difficult to capture the longer-term effects based on historical data, yet it is unlikely that the short lags in standard equations measure the full effect. Almost certainly there is still considerable US trade adjustment in the pipeline. Thus a reasonable case can be made that the puzzle of the failure of US trade to improve will disappear in a couple of years, even at current exchange rates.

On the other hand, a case can also be made that the equilibrium dollar has in fact declined sharply since the beginning of the decade. There are four developments in particular that can be used to justify the need for a lower dollar. First, the Third World debt crisis has forced both substantial real depreciations and sharp cuts in domestic demand on the part of a number of developing countries. This tends to worsen the US current account, other things equal. It is important to note however, that the debt crisis affects industrial countries other than the US as well. While debt problems thus help explain part of the puzzle of persistent US external deficits, they make the persistent German and Japanese current surpluses even more puzzling. Second the 1980s have been marked by somewhat slower growth than the 1970s in industrial countries other than the US, especially in Europe. "Eurosclerosis" has presumably had some effect in depressing the demand for US exports. Third, there is the broad issue of US "competitiveness", in terms of such matters as technological leadership and the perceived quality of US goods. The 1980s have been marked by an unmistakable decline in US technological leadership, as well as increased competition in traditional goods from newly industrializing countries. In the 1960s the US was able to maintain external balance with much higher unit labour costs than other industrial nations due to superior technology and quality, while in the 1970s the US was compelled to have rough parity. If this represents a trend rather than a one time convergence the US may now need lo have a labour cost advantage in order to sell competitively on the world markets. Finally, the series of current deficits since 1981 have made the US a net debtor, with an adverse effect on overseas investment income. In the early 1980s the US could offset trade deficits of $20-30 billion with net earnings from overseas investments: now the investment account is in deficit. This means that the US must run a smaller trade deficit to achieve any given current account target, and thus that the dollar must be low enough to give US producers an extra cost advantage.

These four effects combined can be used to argue for the need for a considerably lower dollar in real terms than in 1980 and perhaps lower than the current level.

My own guess is that while there has been some secular decline in the equilibrium dollar, there is still a lot of trade adjustment in the pipeline. I would not be surprised if the current level of the dollar were to turn out to be sustainable for a long time. Indeed, I would expect the most immediate strains on the US – and hence on the world economy – to come from a trade deficit that declines rapidly, rather than a persistent trade deficit that refuses to go away.

The risks of a declining US trade deficit

No discussion of the US trade deficit can be complete without a scenario for a "hard landing" in which US chickens come home to roost with a vengeance. The usual hard landing story begins with a crisis of confidence that sends the dollar into a tailspin, followed by sharply rising interest rates and a hair-raising recession. I'd like to conclude his lecture by offering a different scenario.

This scenario starts from the proposition that the loss of confidence that provokes the crisis is not something in the future – it is something that has already happened. The hard landing is the result of the working through of forces that are already in motion.

As a starting point it is important to realize that financial markets do not actually determine the rate of capital inflow into the United States at any given point in time. The rate of capital inflow is by definition equal to the current account deficit, and the current account reflects the decisions of firms and households – not financial markets – that is, it reflects decisions about which products to buy where to source, supply or locate production, and so on. Furthermore, as the experience since 1985 has shown, the real decisions that underlie the current account are not changed quickly. For the most part, the decisions that will determine the US current account over the next two years have already been made. Even if financial markets become very pessimistic about the United States. They cannot do much to make the US current account decline faster over the next two years, and thus they cannot reduce the rate of capital inflow very much. Conversely, optimism about the United States cannot do much to increase capital inflow in the near future.

This may seem like a paradox: capital markets cannot determine capital movements. What keeps it from being paradoxical is the role of the exchange rate. Suppose that foreigners decide that US assets are a poor investment at current prices. What will happen in the short run is not that foreign investment in the United States stops, but that the dollar falls until US assets appear to be good bargains. Or to put it another way the dollar must fall until it is cheap enough to induce foreigners to invest enough there to cover our current account deficit.

This is, of course, not the end of the story. If foreigners lose confidence in the United States, and the dollar falls as a result, this will lead over time to a reduction in the current account deficit, and therefore to a fall in the rate of capital inflow. Over time, then, a fall in confidence will be reflected in a decline in capital inflows. The process is, however, one that takes place over time. An unwillingness of foreigners to invest here shows as a decline in the dollar, and only much later as a decline in foreign investment. Putting the issue this way casts recent experience in a very different light from the usual.

Many people have wondered when foreign investors will become unwilling to finance the US external deficit, and have marvelled at the fact that large capital inflows have continued in recent years. But in fact the loss of confidence has already occurred – and it shows in the value of the dollar. We all too easily forget that the decline in the dollar since its 1985 peak represents one of the largest real exchange rate declines ever experienced by an industrial country. Four years ago some economists were arguing that the dollar had moved to a permanently higher plateau than its levels of the 1970s, now the dollar is, in real terms weaker than at any time in history.

Arguably, the improvement in the US trade position that we have seen since 1987 is only the beginning. If the dollar is really weak enough to make the US a highly favourable place to produce then there should be large trade improvements still in the pipeline. Some evidence can be found to support this view. US trade improvement, according to anecdotal evidence, has been increasingly limited by capacity constraints: but high capital goods imports show that domestic firms are increasing their capacity and further declines in the trade deficit will follow when this capacity comes on line. Foreign direct investment in the US will add considerable capacity in many import-competing and some export industries; when this capacity comes on line, if the dollar remains weak the result will be more an improvement in trade than a displacement of US-owned firms. Although econometric models do not suggest dramatic improvement in US trade from here on, many economists – myself included – think that the lags in these models are far too short and that a large further decrease in the US trade deficit is in prospect even at the current exchange rate.

We now come to the basic problem: US domestic demand is too high to be consistent with any large closure of the trade gap. During the 1980s US domestic demand has risen rapidly considerably outstripping the rate of growth of domestic productive capacity. This was not inflationary precisely because the movement of the US into external deficit prevented this rise in demand from being translated into an excess demand for domestic goods. In effect, the trade deficit provided a safety valve that let out the steam created by rising domestic demand, preventing the economy from overheating.

The problem now is that if the dollar has indeed fallen to a level that will bring about a substantial further reduction in the trade deficit this safety valve will be closed off. Thus there is a substantial risk of inflationary pressures arising ironically from too much success on the trade front.

The point may be made almost as a syllogism. From 1980 to 1985 there was a sharp rise in US domestic demand relative to productive capacity, but this was accompanied by a rise in the dollar that insured that the excess demand was diverted to foreign goods and services. Since 1985, the dollar has fallen sharply, to below its 1980 level, but demand has not. Thus the economy is now in a region that should ordinarily be associated with excess demand, and thus an inflation problem.

There have been some signs of growing inflationary pressures this year, and the US economy is arguably operating at an unemployment rate below the level consistent with price stability. However, thus far the effects of the dollar's decline have been mild. The reason is precisely that the declining dollar has had only mild effects on the trade deficit, presumably because of the long lags discussed above. In fact, we have been lucky not to have had the results we hoped for from a declining dollar: had the dollar had a quicker effect there would have been an early confrontation between external adjustment and the problem of excessive domestic demand.

I have argued however that there may well be substantial further trade adjustment in the pipeline even as the current value of the dollar. If this is right, this means that the immediate problem is going to be how to cope with the inflationary risks posed by a falling trade deficit. If the US economy is not going to risk throwing away the hard-won reduction in inflation achieved during the 1980s, domestic demand will have to be restrained to make room for the trade improvement in progress.

How will this restraint of domestic demand be accomplished? The sensible answer is through fiscal restraint. But unfortunately that does not look likely. The President-elect has pledged in the crudest of terms not to do anything sensible – not to raise taxes, not to rethink the structure of military spending. He will eventually probably break these promises, but only under duress, and in the atmosphere of crisis. So the burden will fall on monetary policy.

So here is my unconventional hard landing scenario: a crunch brought on by the need to restrain the effects of a trade deficit that falls too fast, using monetary policy alone. The point is, or course, that this would mean high interest rates – easily several percentage points higher that the current rates, pushing nominal rates into double digits.

At this point we can again invoke the problem of US internal debt. In an environment of much higher interest rates, how will the highly leveraged corporate sector of the late 1980s fare? A financial crisis is certainly not outlandish.

It is important to note, however, that this particular hard landing does not necessarily involve a recession. Domestic demand would be hard hit by high interest rates, but net exports would be high, indeed it is an overheated economy that causes the problem, and it would be peculiar if overheating should translate into reduce employment. Individual groups – notably those sectors closely tied to construction – but on average the employment picture would remain strong. If there is a financial crisis, it might be peculiarly divorced from the real economy – we might have workers performing on overtime for companies that are being administered by the courts.

For what it is worth this is my own guess at the most likely hard landing scenario. It could be a difficult situation financially, and if mishandled could be turned into a recession, but it is not as unambiguously a catastrophe as the speculative attack scenario that has dominated popular discussion.

Some concluding remarks

I'm not sure if this talk has a moral. I've tried to describe and explain as best I can one of the key problems – perhaps *the* key problem – of the current world economy. I can only hope that the discussion I have provided helped to make some sense of an issue that is often surrounded by fog.

Let me conclude, however, on an upbeat note. If there is a silver lining to the US trade deficit, it is the fact that it has given the world a crash course on interdependence. In 1980 few important politicians in the US thought hard about international economics: few Japanese leaders took seriously the need form Japan to op-en itself to the world and to take on a leadership role comparable to its economic importance. The huge and persistent trade imbalances have changed all that – forcing the US to realize that it does not live alone in the world, forcing Japan to open its markets for capital and manufactures. We will probably face a good deal more economic stress as we try to work our way out of this situation, but I don't expect that the results will be very bad in the long run. Meanwhile, with some luck the policy mistakes of the 1980s will have inadvertently created the climate for a more cooperative world in the future.

42

How convincing is the evidence linking education and income?

Orley Ashenfelter[1]

In recent years the value of our expenditures on schools and colleges has become a source of considerable controversy. At one level every politician expresses a belief in the importance of the American system of education as an investment in the future. For example, Senator William Bradley introduced his recent proposal for "Self-reliance Scholarships" by stating (in the *Congressional Record*, July 25, 1991) ". . . a college graduate will earn about 60 percent more than someone with just a high school diploma. Our economy rewards college graduates because we need their skills so deeply."

But there is nothing that brings out education's detractors like proposals to spend more money. The most famous recent critic of school expenditures has been William Bennett, who was quoted (in *USA Today*) when he was US Secretary of Education three years ago as saying that "Money doesn't cure school problems. We cannot show a strong, positive correlation between spending more and getting a better result." Bennett's comments were based on a survey article by economist Eric Hanushek who concluded, " . . . increased expenditures by themselves offer no overall promise for improving education. Further, the components of these expenditures offer little promise. Thus, a simple recommendation: Stop requiring and paying for things that do not matter." Such controversy suggests that a review of the evidence on the link between education and income may be of more than academic interest at this time.

1 Forty-second Joseph Fisher Lecture, 12 October 1993. Reprinted in his *Labour Economics and Productivity*, Vol. 6, 1994. The author is indebted to David Card, Alan Krueger, Tom Lemieux, and David Zimmerman for discussions and assistance in the preparation of this paper.

I must also admit at the outset that I have an ulterior motive in selecting this topic. The recent research on the link between schooling and income provides a fascinating example of the new emphasis on credibility in empirical economics. This new research style began with the study of problems in the labour market, but it has also influenced other social scientists and even some policy makers. As we shall see, this research style emphasises the importance of collecting new data and of finding and creating actual or natural experiments that will permit us to make some credible inferences about the effect of public policy changes.

Schooling and income: The simple relationship

No one doubts that college graduates earn more than high school graduates, or that high school graduates earn more than high school dropouts. In 1987, for example, the average weekly earnings of white males between the ages of 26 and 65 who had 16 years of education was some 40 per cent to 50 per cent greater than the average weekly earnings of those with exactly 12 years of schooling.

Figure 42.1 shows the relationship between weekly earnings and age for high school graduates (H) and college graduates (C) in 1987. It is obvious that college graduates earn more than high school graduates at all ages, but this difference is especially great in the years of middle age.

Figure 42.1 The relationship between weekly earnings and age of high school and college graduates

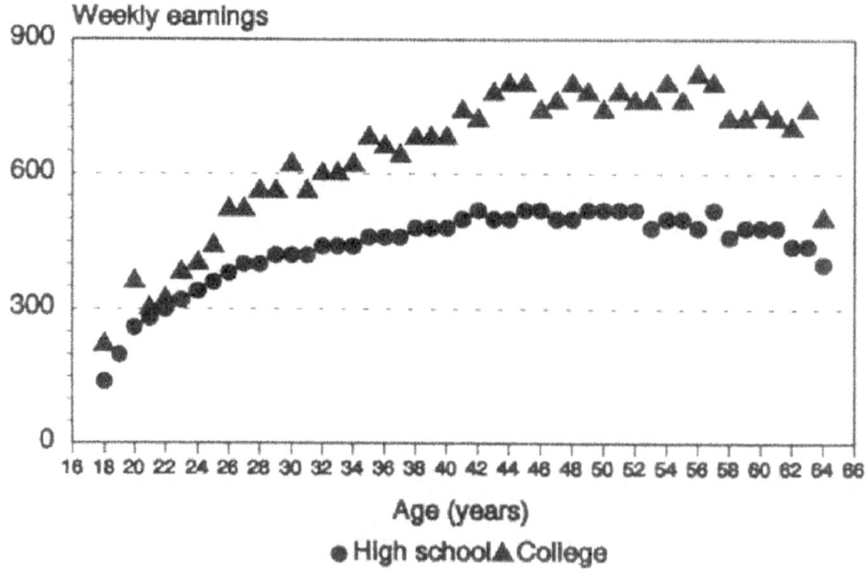

But how are we to interpret these differences in earnings? Is it not possible that those who obtain high school or college degrees would earn more than other workers even if they had not taken the time and spent the money to obtain them?

Schooling and income: The ideal experiment

In principle the only way to answer this question definitely is to perform an experiment. In such an experiment different groups of students would be randomly assigned to different educational levels without regard to their ability or general background. Years later we would compare the incomes of these students. On average the only differences among the students would be the level of their schooling. Contrasts of the earnings of the various groups would, with a large enough sample, provide an entirely credible estimate of the effect of schooling on earnings.

Of course, the experiment I have described has not been performed, and so we do not have any entirely credible estimates of the effect of schooling on earnings. Some people will object that such an experiment would, even in principle, be morally objectionable because it would deny a potentially valuable education to those who might otherwise have obtained it. The way to meet this objection, of course, is to make sure that no one is denied access to anything. For example, in most developing countries inadequate finances make it impossible to educate all those students who wish to attend secondary schools. If students were admitted to secondary schools, in part, on a randomised basis it would be possible to perform a credible experiment that would not be objectionable. When people must be denied access to educational opportunities in any case, why not use a randomised allocation system so that we may learn from their experiences?

Although many people are not aware of it, there has been a quiet revolution in the extent to which randomised trials have been used to evaluate the role of education and training in the determination of earnings in the US. The National Supported Work Demonstration in the mid-1970s showed that worker training programs could be implemented using a classical randomised design and that the resulting data provided very credible evidence of the success (and failures) of these programs. Indeed, the results from these classical experiments have served as an impetus to develop more credible econometric methods for evaluating the impact of training programs on worker earnings.[2]

Despite these advances, however, we do not yet have any evidence on the role of education in the determination of earnings that is based on the classical experimental methods. Instead, we must necessarily look elsewhere for convincing non-experimental evidence. One way to look for this evidence is to use comparisons between workers who have similar genetic and family backgrounds, but who differ in educational levels. A systematic correlation between the educational differences and income differences of such workers is one place to look for evidence of the link between income and schooling.

Intra-family schooling-income relations: Fathers, sons, brothers

In some recent research David Zimmerman and I have studied differences in the schooling level of fathers from the schooling levels of their sons and the relationship of these schooling differences to income differences between fathers and sons. Figure 42.2 is a scatter diagram that shows this relationship. On the vertical axis is a measure (in ratio or logarithmic scale) of the difference between the hourly wage rate of each father and his son. On the horizontal axis is the difference between the years of schooling of the father and his son. Each point on the diagram represents one father-son pair, and there are 232 such pairs in the National Longitudinal Survey that we have used.

As one would expect in an economy where the average schooling level has been growing, fathers have about four fewer years of schooling than sons. As one would also expect in a society which has imperfect generational mobility, fathers with higher education levels tend to have sons with higher education levels. (The correlation coefficient is about .4.) This suggests the possibility that the simple correlation between the income and schooling of the sons may be the result of the fact that better educated sons also have better connected fathers. If this were the only reason for the correlation between the income and schooling of sons we would know that the returns to schooling were negligible.

2 See Robert Lalonde (1986), "Evaluating the Econometric Evaluations of Training Prams with Experimental Data", *The American Economic Review*, 76 (4): 604-620, September.

Figure 42.2: The relationship between the difference in wages & the difference in schooling of fathers and sons

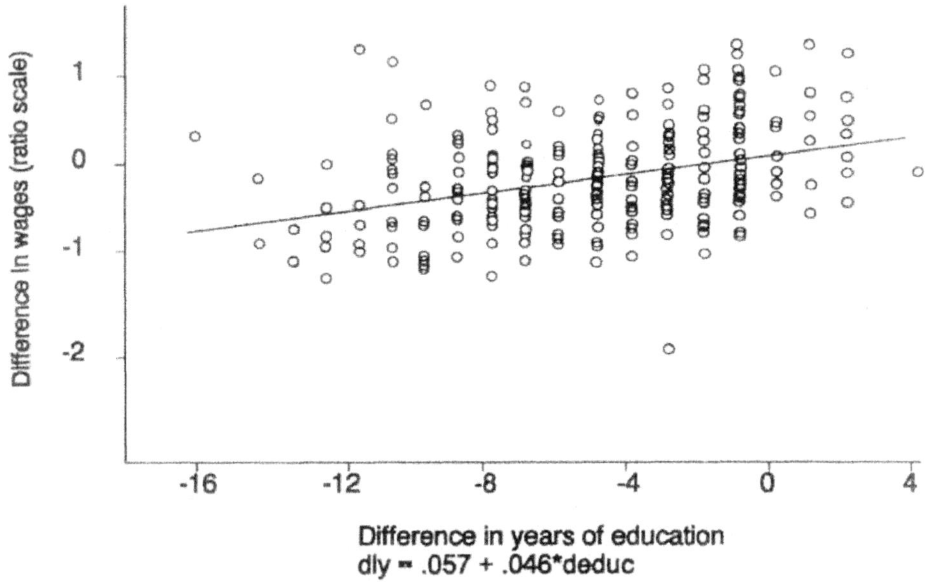

As Figure 42.2 indicates, however, this cannot be the entire story. After all, the diagram indicates that there still remains a substantial correlation between the difference in the education level of the father from the son and the difference in their incomes. If we compare two sons who both have well educated fathers, the son who is better educated has the higher income. In short, more education for the son increases the son's income regardless of the father's education level. (The slope of the best fitting line in these data indicates that a one year difference in the education levels of father and son translates into about a 5 per cent difference in wages rates.) This implies that the returns to schooling are not simply a result of the fact that sons with more schooling have fathers with more schooling too.

Zimmerman and I have also studied the correlation of differences in the incomes of brothers with differences in the schooling level of brothers. When we compare two brothers from the same family we find that the better educated brother's income averages about 5 per cent more for each extra year of schooling he has. In short, although some part of the correlation between income and schooling may be due to family background characteristics, the intra-family correlation between income and schooling indicates that most of the relationship between income and schooling must be due to something else.

Intra-family schooling-income relations: Identical twins

Although there have been surprisingly few attempts to measure the returns to schooling by the comparison of education and income differences within families, there is one study of identical twins which remains the most important effort to date. In this work Behrman, Hrubec, Taubman, and Wales find that the simple relationship between schooling and income in their data suggests that each additional year of education adds about 8 per cent to the income of a twin. However, a comparison of the twins alone indicates that the better educated of two twins earns no more than 2 per cent extra for each additional year of schooling. In short, Behrman, Hrubec, Taubman, and Wales find that the differences in education levels between identical twins are virtually uncorrelated with the differences in their income levels. This finding, if correct, is the single most important piece of empirical evidence suggesting that the observed relationship between schooling and income may be a result of genetic or family background differences and is not a result of any real increase in the skills of better educated workers.

The Behrman, *et. al.* research has been criticised on the grounds that schooling differences between twins are likely to be very small. As a result, the measured schooling differences between twins may be a result of measurement error.[3] To see the effect that this will have on the results of a comparison of schooling differences with earnings differences, consider the case where all twins have identical education levels. In this situation any measured differences in the education levels of twins will be entirely a result of measurement error. The result will be that measured schooling differences will be unrelated to earnings differences. Instead of indicating that true schooling differences are unrelated to earnings differences, this result would only indicate that the data on twins do not provide the right natural experiment for examining the issue. In sum, the Behrman, *et. al.* results may be consistent with a considerable effect of schooling on earnings, but this issue cannot be resolved at the present time because there is no independent measure of the error in the Behrman, *et. al.* survey data.

3 This point is due to Zvi Griliches (1979), "Sibling Models and Data in Economics: Beginnings of a Survey", *The Journal of Political Economy*, 87(5): 537-564, October.

It appears that the only way to resolve this issue is to obtain new data on twins and to attempt some independent validation of the reliability of the measured education data. During the past summer my colleague Alan Krueger and I organised a team of graduate students to collect new data on twins in order to settle this issue. To do this at reasonable cost we participated in the research group that gathered data from the twins who assemble each year for the National Twins Festival in Twinsburg, Ohio. Much to our surprise we are able to administer the Current Population Survey to nearly 500 twins in a brief, but intensive, three day period. In order to validate the data on the education level of each twin we separated the twins for the purposes of our interviews and asked each twin about his (or her) own education level as well as the education level of his (or her) twin.

Our main findings are displayed in Figure 42.3. As before, this is a scatter diagram where each point represents a single pair of twins. The vertical axis represents the difference (in ratio terms) between the incomes of identical twins, while the horizontal axis represents the difference between the schooling levels of the twins. As one would expect, the diagram indicates (by the concentration of observations at zero on the horizontal axis) that in the most typical case the twins have the same education level. The diagram also makes clear that there is a considerable correlation between income differences and schooling differences. In these data the better educated twin earns about 7 per cent more for each extra year he (or she) attains compared to his (or her) twin.

We also find considerable evidence of measurement error in the data on education levels. (Overall, the schooling level reported by one twin has a correlation of about .9 with the schooling level reported by the other twin.) Using a standard procedure, Krueger and I find that the return to schooling estimated by a comparison of intra-family education differences for twins may be as small as one-half the return that would be estimated with data that contained no measurement error. In short, the results of our new study of twins indicates that, on average, an additional year of education has a very sizeable effect on the earnings of twins and may be as large as 14 per cent for each additional year.

Figure 42.3: The difference in the LN wage versus the difference in education: Identical twins

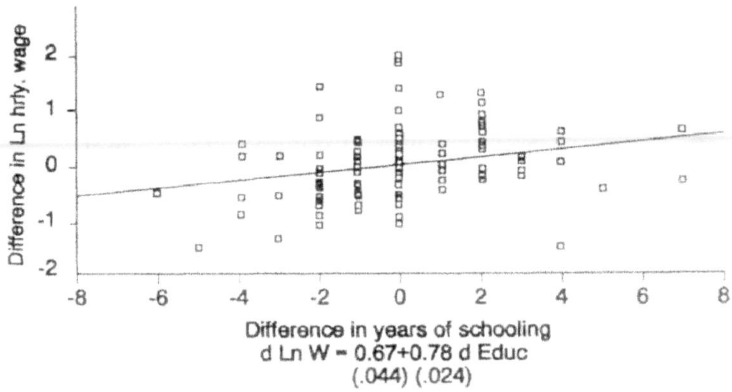

Schooling and income: Natural experiments

The evidence from the study of intra-family differences in education and their correlation with intra-family differences in income strongly supports the hypothesis that additional schooling is responsible for increases in worker earnings. Despite the consistency of this evidence, none of it represents the equivalent of an ideal experiment. In the past few years Joshua Angrist and Alan Krueger have attempted to find a natural experiment that would provide the kind of information that an ideal experiment would provide. To do this they have attempted to locate exogenous events that might be expected to alter the schooling decisions of some people, but which would not be expected to independently alter their income. Naturally, finding such events is difficult.

In one paper Angrist and Krueger[4] observe that there is a relationship between the quarter in which an individual is born and the mean level of schooling that the individual attains. Angrist and Krueger argue that compulsory schooling laws are a natural explanation for why individuals born in the first quarter of the

4 Joshua Angrist and Alan Krueger, "Does Compulsory School Attendance Affect Schooling and Earnings?" *The Quarterly Journal of Economics*, November 1991.

year attain fewer years of education than individuals born later in the year. They observe that school districts typically require that students turn age six by January 1st of the year they enter school. Thus, students born early in the year enter school at an older age. Since compulsory schooling laws permit students to drop out as soon as they attain age 16 students born early in the year may drop out of school with fewer years completed than is the case for those born later in the year.

In fact, Angrist and Krueger find that workers born in the first quarter of the year typically average about one-tenth year less schooling than workers that are born in the other three quarters of the year. Remarkably, these same workers also typically earn about one per cent less per week than other workers. In short, the accident of being born in the first quarter of the year is typically associated with a lower schooling level and a lower earnings level. The implied return to schooling is about 10 per cent per additional year of education attained.

Conclusion

Of course, compulsory schooling laws affect primarily high school completion rates and may be of little assistance in evaluating the returns to a college education. In a subsequent paper Angrist and Krueger[5] explore the role that the Vietnam era draft lottery had on education levels. During the Vietnam era a public lottery was used to randomly assign eligibility status for the draft to different birth dates during the year. Individuals were thus eligible for the draft according to their birth dates. Angrist and Krueger find that the relationship between birth date and schooling level is the same as the relationship between birth date and earnings. Again, it appears that an event likely to be independent of the determination of earnings (an individual's date of birth) has influenced both worker schooling levels and worker earning levels in the same direction. This is still further evidence that the relationship between schooling and income results from a casual connection between education and the determination of earnings.

5 Joshua Angrist and Alan Krueger, "Estimating the Payoff to Schooling using the Vietnam-era Draft Lottery", unpublished paper, August 1991.

I began this paper with the question, how convincing is the evidence linking education and income? Here is my answer: Pretty convincing. If I had to bet on what an ideal experiment would indicate, I would bet that it would show that better educated workers earn more.

There is, however, a great deal more to be learned about the role of education in the determination of income. For one thing, relatively little is known about how the quality of education determines earnings. This is an area were the experimental method can be used extensively to study the role of class size and other educational innovations on learning. Indeed, it already has been used in Tennessee, where students (and teachers) were randomly assigned to different class sizes within the same schools and then differences in the scores of these students on standardised tests were studied.[6] The results of this experiment, which are strikingly credible in an area dominated by work that is not very credible, indicated that class size was clearly linked to test performance. Whether this result can be duplicated elsewhere, and whether the costs of such alterations are worth the benefits, are important topics for further research.

6 See Project Star, Final Executive Summary Report, June 1991, Tennessee State Department of Education, Nashville, Tennessee.

43

The role of the NAFTA debate in US trade policy

Anne O. Krueger[1]

One of the main driving forces in the economic history of the past millennium has been the increasing integration of the world economy. Not only have technical discoveries and innovation led to greatly reduced costs of transport and communication, but those reduced costs have in turn led to an increasingly global market place. Further integration has permitted increased productivity in a wide range of industries: specialised parts and components can reduce assembly costs in many lines of activity; when specialised parts can be made for a wider market, costs of production fall; and increased competition in a larger market spurs many firms on to greater technical and economic efficiency.

The subject of this paper is US trade policy, and the role of the NAFTA debate in it. While that subject might seem far removed from long-term trends in world economic growth, it is not. Economic growth and productivity increases have depended, and will continue to depend, on an open multilateral trading system. And, the United States is important enough in the world economy that American trade policy is crucially important to the viability of the entire trading system.

My thesis is that the world economy (in part because of American schizophrenia, but also in part because other countries are insufficiently convinced of the importance of commitment to the open multilateral system) is dangerously close to the brink – the open multilateral trading system is in danger, and the

1 Forty-third Joseph Fisher Lecture, 7 October 1994. Reprinted in *Australian Economic Papers*, 34(65): 5-16, June. The author is indebted to Professor Richard Snape for valuable discussions on many of the issues raised here, and also for comments on a draft of this lecture. She is also grateful to the American Enterprise Institute which financed some of the research on which this lecture is based.

threat is protectionism, hiding behind regionalism. Should the threat become reality, all will be losers, and an engine of growth that has served the world very well, especially for the past half century, will be lost. But the biggest losers will be the smaller trading countries, whose bilateral bargaining power with the large trading nations will be small.

One of the propositions on which there is most unanimity among economists is that, in almost all circumstances, interventions with trade do not increase economic efficiency or well-being. Many of the cases for which protection (or support of export industries) is advocated are self-serving pleas by vested interest groups. Even when there is a legitimate purpose – such as national defence – being advocated, measures (such as storage of critical materials or mothballing factories) are usually found to be low-cost in comparison with the costs of maintaining ongoing production.

Despite the continuing validity of that proposition, the GATT (whose Articles were written largely by economists), which has underpinned the open multilateral trading system for the past half century, was founded on brilliant principles of political economy, but relatively poor economics. That is, the GATT has operated to liberalise the world's trading system by facilitating rounds of multilateral tariff negotiations in which each country reduced its own tariffs in order to gain 'concessions' from other trading nations.

This was brilliant political economy because the promise of reduced tariffs in other countries put pressure on each country's export interests to provide political support for the results of each round. It was poor economics, because tariff reductions benefit most those in the country where the tariff is being reduced. However, the rhetoric of multilateral tariff negotiations was and is that of 'concessions': each country is said to 'gain' insofar as markets for its exports are open. Unfortunately, over time, people – including trade negotiators themselves – began to believe it.

The simplest approach to an understanding of the present situation and current dangers confronting the open multilateral trading system is to start with the Great Depression, and review the evolution of the system from that point through the establishment of the GATT, and successive rounds of trade liberalisation, to the present.

Although it is certainly true that nineteenth century economic progress was spurred by the liberalisation of trade (with the adoption of free trade first by England and then by France), for present purposes I can start with the Great Depression. After the recovery from the First World War and the economic growth of the 1920s, the world plunged into the Depression of the 1930s. The Depression was certainly intensified, if not caused, by 'beggar-thy-neighbour' policies of increasing tariffs and competitive devaluations. In the United States, the infamous Smoot-Hawley tariff act of 1930 raised tariffs in the United States to extremely high levels contrasted with tariffs earlier. And, as country after country abandoned the gold standard, currency devaluations 'exported' depression from one country to another.

When those British and American economists charged with providing a blueprint for the post war economic system set to work during the Second World War, their memories of the Great Depression were vivid, and they viewed their task in large part as ensuring that there could not be a repeat of the 1930s. Their vision, as set forth in Bretton Woods documents,[2] was that an international organisation[3] would serve to coordinate trade and other policies in such a manner that the competitive devaluations and 'beggar thy neighbour' policies of the 1930s could never happen again.

The GATT system was to be one in which all signatories would adhere to the principles of an open multilateral trading system. The system was to be non discriminatory (although 100 per cent preferential trading agreements 'across substantially all' sectors of the economy were to be countenanced). Countries agreed in almost all circumstances (the exceptions being short-term emergencies and developing countries' difficulties) to avoid quantitative restrictions on trade; tariffs were to be virtually the only form of intervention with imports except

2 The Bretton Woods conference in fact produced blueprints for the International Monetary Fund (to coordinate exchange rates and the international monetary system) and the International Bank for Reconstruction and Development (to provide an institution to support international capital flows). The ITO charter was not completed until a later date, but it was certainly contemplated at Bretton Woods, and it (and GATT) was regarded as essential for maintaining an open trading system.

3 This was initially intended to be the International Trade Organization, but in fact only part of the ITO charter was used. The GATT – General Agreement on Tariffs and Trade – was approved to deal with the trading system; its articles were a subset of the ITO charter, which covered a much wider range of issues than the final GATT.

in exceptional circumstances. Countries would come together to negotiate reciprocal tariff reductions, and then 'bind' those reductions under international law, agreeing not subsequently to raise tariff rates except in unusual circumstances.

The United States was the pre-eminent economic power in the immediate post-war years, with an estimated 43 per cent of world GDP, and a quarter of the world's trade. As such, American leadership and support for the open multilateral system was crucial to the emergence of the system. And US policy was entirely supportive. Motivated in part by foreign policy concern especially the belief that recovery of the economies greatly damaged by war was essential for Cold War reasons, America supported the GATT and led successive rounds of multilateral trade negotiations. Although foreign policy was the dominant motive, however, there was little domestic opposition to free open liberal trading policies in the United States. Indeed, the US had the most open trading system in the world, one of the very few convertible currencies, a relatively low tariff contrasted with other countries in the decade after the Second World War.

A first round of multilateral tariff reductions took place almost immediately after GATT was established. Thereafter, seven successive rounds of tariff reductions gradually reduced tariffs among all the industrial countries. From an estimated average level of 40 per cent in the late 1940s, the average tariff rate on imports into developed countries is estimated to have dropped around six per cent by 1980. Regrettably, until the 1980s, trade liberalisation was confined largely to the developed world, as the developing countries initially chose to attempt to promote the economic development through inward-looking policies and protection of domestic industries against competition from imports. It was only in the 1980s that developing countries in large numbers began reversing trade policies and started reintegrating with the world economy.

Starting in the late 1940s, there followed a 'golden era' of expansion and growth in income and living standards enjoyed by much of the world. Despite their failure to liberalise their own economies, developing countries benefitted from the buoyant state of the world economy and their own efforts to increase educational attainments and social welfare so that their growth accelerated. Meanwhile, industrial countries' growth reached rates never before witnessed over a sustained period. The quarter century from 1948 produced a rate of growth of real world GNP faster than the rate estimated to have been realised in the single most rapidly growing country in the nineteenth century!

There was under way a 'virtuous' circle. Rapid economic growth created an atmosphere in which further trade liberalisation was politically relatively easy and economically painless; further trade liberalisation in turn spurred further economic growth.

Before turning, to subsequent developments that paved the way for the present difficulties, it is useful for later reference to note the evolution of preferential trading arrangements during the 'golden era'. The international trading system evolved almost entirely along multilateral lines. Although, as noted, there was a GATT provision for 100 per cent preferential trading arrangements, most efforts at such arrangements met with little success. The only exception was the European Community (and EFTA). The United States, which staunchly opposed most preferential arrangements, supported the formation of the EC and European integration on the theory that economic integration would reduce the likelihood of further hostilities among European nations. Moreover, as trade barriers among the EC members were reduced, the US also supported tariff reductions through GATT rounds, so that tariffs on imports of manufactures from outside the Community were falling as internal trade barriers were falling even more rapidly. And it was not until the 1980s that the protectionism inherent in European agricultural policies became highly visible and costly in the world economy. Other preferential trading arrangements basically failed. Latin America, East Africa, and a number of other preferential groupings commenced, but some were disbanded and others languished. Consequently, the open multilateral trading system appeared secure and academics and policy makers alike turned their attention to aspects of the international system other than preferential arrangements.

Turning then to the 1980s, the decade began with a highly integrated economy. Although the first and second oil price increases had been major shocks to the system, economic growth had resumed in the late 1970s, albeit with high rates of inflation, and when the second oil price increase occurred, most developed nations took anti inflationary measures (in contrast to policies after the first increase).

The world entered the decade with a degree of integration between national economies much greater than at any earlier time in history. As already mentioned, tariffs had averaged around 40 per cent in the immediate post-war years, while transport costs had averaged around 25 per cent of the f.o.b. value of exports. In all, this amounted to an average level of protection for each country's import-competing industries of around 65 per cent. By 1980, average tariffs were around ten per cent (and still falling), while transport costs had fallen to an average of eight per cent. Adding the two together, the total insulation averaged around 18 per cent, representing a drop of more than two thirds over three decades.

That drop had, of course, facilitated the growth in trade and productivity. It also, however, made producers in national economies much more sensitive to developments in the global economy.

Two critical changes had already begun to take place, which had strong effects on American trade policy. America had been entirely successful in her post-war goals, in that Europe and Japan had achieved very rapid growth and re-established their place in the global economy. Their very rapid growth, however, had naturally meant the declining relative importance of the US, to which there was already some degree of political reaction. Although America was still the pre-eminent economic power, the degree of pre-eminence had greatly diminished, as Japanese and German exports were almost as large as the American, and the US share of world GNP had dropped from the 40 to the 20 per cent range. Related to that change, the fixed exchange rate system, which many had termed a 'dollar-standard' system, had been abandoned in the early 1970s, as differential rates of inflation made it impossible to maintain the fixed-rate system.

When the 1980s began, these events had several interrelated consequences. First, there was a severe worldwide recession which began after the second oil price increase. Second, the US dollar began to appreciate significantly in both nominal and real terms *vis-à-vis* major trading partners. Dollar appreciation put tremendous pressure on US tradeable industries, while at the same time, employment was rising rapidly.

The major factor leading to appreciation of the dollar was the fiscal-monetary mix of US macroeconomic policies after the Reagan tax cuts of 1981.

Those cuts had left a large fiscal deficit, while at the same time monetary policy was tight. The result was a sizeable capital inflow (so that the fiscal deficit was in effect financed in large part by foreigners through the current account deficit).

With the severity of the recession, surging imports and high interest rates, many Americans clamoured for protection, instead of recognising the situation for the macroeconomic phenomenon that it was. At first, this increase in protectionist pressure went largely unheeded because the Reagan administration was widely believed to be supportive of free trade.

However, many members of the American Congress were under severe pressure from their constituents and genuinely distressed at the burgeoning current account deficit. Believing the Reagan administration unwilling to counter the flood of imports, and viewing increase protection as the logical answer, they began seeking ways in which they could address the problem.

Like other countries, the US had long had a trade law which provided for the imposition of duties in cases where other countries' exporters were deemed guilty of 'dumping' or where foreign governments were subsidising exports. Anti-dumping (selling below cost) and countervailing duty (against subsidised exports) law was referred to as 'administered trade' law and there were provisions within GATT for anti-dumping and countervailing duty processes. In the American case, individual firms, industry representatives, or the government itself could register a complaint, under which the US Department of Commerce[4] entered into an investigation of the 'dumping' allegation while the US International Trade Commission had the responsibility of ascertaining whether imports had been the 'major cause' of material injury to the import competing industry.

Administered trade law had been occasionally, but infrequently, used in the 1950-80 period. Congress, in its impatience with imports, and believing that foreign competition must be 'unfair', began amending the law to make the standard of proof for injury weaker, while simultaneously the procedures used to ascertain foreign firms' costs came to be regarded as biased.

4 The US Treasury had been charged with investigating costs. However, perhaps believing that the Treasury was 'too sympathetic' to foreign producers. Congress shifted that responsibility to the Department of Commerce when it was seeking to make anti-dumping and countervailing duty procedures more restrictive.

The threat of administered trade law was sufficient to make firms in other countries willing to seek other solutions, while the US administration also viewed the trade remedies with suspicion. What resulted was a series of 'voluntary export restraints' (VERs), under which foreign governments agreed to restrict the volume of their exports of automobiles, steel, machine tools and other products to the US market in exchange for the withdrawal of the administered trade complaint.

Over time during the 1980s, US trade law was further modified. In addition to negotiating VERs, the administration began negotiating – especially with Japan, Korea and Taiwan – with respect to market opening, demanding that there be a designated target share of imports in that country's market. In 1988, Congress enacted a trade law in which USTR was instructed to examine other countries' trading practices, to ascertain whether countries were systematically 'unfair'. When they were, USTR was to designate the country an 'unfair trader', indicating the objectionable practices. Were those practices not changed within a specified time period, USTR was instructed to impose retaliatory trade barriers against imports from the offending country. Congress also asked USTR to examine other countries' treatment of intellectual property rights, and to designate countries with unsatisfactory and inadequate protection for intellectual property.

These moves, it should be noted, diverged further and further from the notion of an open multilateral trading system. Anti-dumping and countervailing duty procedures might be administered with something of a bias, but they were authorised within the GATT charter. Voluntary import expansion agreements were bilateral, and there were a number of factors (including the US's ability to choose the industry it wanted to support) that resulted in the process being tilted toward favouring American over other countries' exports. Bilateral bargaining with Japan and Korea was clearly outside the GATT arrangement, and Super-301 was of highly doubtful GATT legality and certainly bilateral in its approach.

Thus, the US was increasing its protection and diverging further from GATT norms throughout the 1980s. A widespread popular belief that there were 'unfair' trading practices on the part of America's trading partners gave political support for these actions. While that was happening, another set of events was also to have important ramifications for the evolution of trade policy. Late in 1982, there had for long been scheduled a Ministerial meeting of GATT. The new United States

Trade Representative and his delegation went to that meeting advocating a new round of multilateral trade negotiations, without having previously persuaded other countries' representatives of its desirability and of an appropriate agenda. The rebuff received by the US delegation led the USTR to announce that the US would proceed with other 'like-minded' countries further to liberalise trade, and form a club of 'Super-GATT' members who would openly support the GATT but engage in further integration among themselves. It was his stated belief that the benefits of further liberalisation would be evident to all, and would result in pressures for other countries to join. This proposal was seen as a way around the roadblock perceived at GATT to further negotiations through that forum.

USTR therefore enunciated US policy as consisting of a 'two-track' approach, under which the US would work through and support the open multilateral system as much as possible, and then go further with countries wishing to enter into free trade agreements with it. At the time, little attention was paid to this pronouncement, although, virtually unnnoticed by the rest of the world, Israel did sign a free trade agreement with the US in 1985.

Finally, in 1986, delegates met in Montevideo, and agreed upon an ambitious agenda for a new round of trade negotiations – the Uruguay Round. A number of items not previously considered by GATT were to be included in the negotiations – a protocol for trade in telecommunications, all services, and, indeed, even agriculture (which had long been neglected in trade negotiations, after the important initiative of Australia and the Cairns group).

There were, thus, three strands to US trade policy by the late 1980s. On one hand, there was the stated commitment to the open multilateral trading system and the Uruguay Round. There was also the enunciated principle of willingness to negotiate free trade agreements with 'like minded' free traders. Finally, there was the protectionist pressure that was increasingly manifest in bilateral trade negotiations.

As these three, somewhat conflicting, strands were evolving, the Canadian and American authorities agreed to negotiate a bilateral free trade agreement. Such an agreement certainly appeared consistent with the USTR notion of 'Super-GATT', and at any event appeared to be between two countries with a long common border, already very low tariffs, and very complimentary trade patterns. Seventy per cent of Canada's exports were destined for the US, and most were primary commodities for which American tariffs were in any event very low. A major Canadian motive for seeking an FTA with the US was to avoid the damages of the administered trade remedies in US law – an objective which was at best partially achieved under the agreement. But an FTA agreement with Canada did not appear at all inconsistent with the Uruguay Round and the strengthening of the GATT.

Then came the surprise! Mexico had until the mid-1980s had inward-looking trade policies like many other developing countries. Starting around 1985, however, the Mexican government undertook a series of major and dramatic policy reforms, including the elimination of quantitative restrictions, joining GATT, reducing tariffs, and overhauling incentives and government interventions in the domestic market. For years, the official (and unofficial) attitude toward the United States had been one of deep suspicion, and it had been unthinkable that Mexico might seek closer trading ties.

However, for a variety of reasons, President Salinas reversed that position, announcing the desire of the Mexican government to enter into negotiations with the US and Canada to join the free trade area. For foreign policy reasons, the US immediately agreed.

To understand what followed, it is necessary first to review some of the underlying economics. From a Mexican perspective, more than 70 per cent each of exports and imports were with the United States, and there was no doubt it would be to Mexico's advantage to join the FTA, in large part because it would 'lock in' the policy reforms already made. The average height of remaining Mexican tariff protection was around ten per cent. Additional Mexican motives for seeking membership in the FTA included the desire to attract more foreign direct investment at a time when investors appeared to be paying more attention to the economies in transition in Eastern Europe and the former Soviet Union.

From the US perspective, about five per cent of US trade was with Mexico. Although Mexico has a much greater population than Canada, with about 80 million people, the low per capita income in Mexico meant that the Mexican market was about the same size as the Canadian one. The average US tariff on

Mexican goods was around four per cent, so there it was difficult to believe that there could be any serious 'threats' to US industries from an FTA with Mexico.

Based on the observed average tariff rates on each others' goods – ten per cent for Mexico and four per cent for the US – it appeared that there could be little additional competition for American goods in the US market, while American producers would gain somewhat more in Mexico. Comparison of unit labour costs (wage rates divided by productivity) showed US costs to be about five per cent lower than Mexican. While quite clearly there would be some differences across industries, there was little reason to believe that Mexican competition could in any macroeconomic sense give US firms major adjustment problems.

Moreover, if as the Mexicans expected, foreign direct investment into Mexico was spurred by the FTA, then the US current account vis-a-vis Mexico should have turned more positive – with positive impetus to the US macroeconomic balance. To the extent that the rate of Mexican economic growth would be accelerated by joining the FTA, it could be expected that that additional growth would be a net benefit for US industries.

Thus, economic analysis strongly suggested that the net impact of an FTA with Mexico on US industries would be positive, but probably relatively small.[5] When, after the NAFTA agreement was negotiated, it was to be ratified by Congress, a heated political debate of major proportions arose.

From the viewpoint of international economists, the proper subject of debate should have been the consistency of NAFTA with the open multilateral trading system. The desirability of a preferential trading arrangement within the western hemisphere might have been questioned, unless assurances were given and there was a clear understanding that such an arrangement was well embedded within the GATT.[6]

5 Many Americans had been concerned by the presence of many illegal Mexican immigrants in the United States. It could be argued that the true American choice was between permitting Mexican goods into the US, or having large continuing flows of migrants. In fact, this fundamental choice was never well articulated during the NAFTA debate. Thus, while it probably should have been the compelling issue, it is ignored for present purposes.

6 There were a number of reasons for there to be misgivings on this score, including the ways in which certain sectors were exempted from the FTA and also the way in which rules of origin were negotiated.

In fact, however, the political protest to NAFTA arose from those same protectionist pressures that had resulted in Super-301, the relaxation of criteria for anti-dumping and countervailing duty findings, and bilateral bargaining with Japan, Korea, and other countries. Opposition to NAFTA was strong among those in the labour movement (despite the fact that all except one of over 200 studies of the impact of NAFTA showed net – small – employment gains in America), those concerned with the US current account deficit and who thought that the US 'could not compete against low wages', those who believed that there would be 'unfair' trade, environmental groups, and others.

Instead- of constituting a debate over the desirability of an open multilateral system relative to preferential (and therefore more bilateral) trading arrangements, therefore, the NAFTA debate became one in which those supporting open multilateral trade were in support of NAFTA. In the final analysis, the NAFTA debate was the first time in the post-war period that there had been a major, head-on, confrontation between free traders and protectionists. And, as you know, the free traders won by a small margin, although President Clinton conceded some key issues to protectionist lobbies (especially in Florida) in order to obtain the necessary support.

Having debated the free trade-protection issue, rather than the preferential trading arrangement issue, there still remains the key question as to how NAFTA will evolve. Will it be the GATT plus arrangement that the USTR envisaged in 1982? Or will it be a preferential trading arrangement in which the US diverges further and further from its commitment to an open multilateral trading system?

Before addressing that issue, however, the second strand in the complex evolution of the trading system must be considered. That is, the conclusion of the Uruguay Round. Even as the NAFTA agreement was being debated, and finally passed, by the American Congress, the Uruguay Round of trade negotiations was finally concluded late in 1993.

There can be little question but that the NAFTA negotiations were at the least a distraction to the Round. And the American Congress' passage of 'Super-301' certainly signalled the ambivalence of the American government to the GATT. Nonetheless, in the end, the results of the Round provide much promise for the future of the world trading system. It is estimated conservatively that world GNP will be increased by $500 billion annually by 2002 as the effects of the Round's agreements are felt in international markets.

Further tariff cuts are to bring the average tariff level among the industrial countries to 3.8 per cent (from the present six per cent level). Agriculture is for the first time to be brought under GATT discipline, and agricultural subsidies are to be constrained. A number of services agreements were reached. Agreements were reached covering trade-related investment measures and intellectual property rights. Dispute settlement procedures within the GATT were streamlined and strengthened. Finally, a World Trade Organization, with a strengthened Secretariat, is to be established, encompassing GATT and also the other agreements reached in the Uruguay Round.

An optimist could, therefore, conclude that the reassertion of the importance of the open multilateral trading system embodied in the Uruguay Round documents provided the basis for optimism that world economic growth could resume the virtuous circle that was witnessed in the 1950s and 1960s.

That is certainly a possibility. NAFTA and the EU could evolve along outward-looking lines, becoming 'GATT-plus' organisations along the lines initially envisaged by USTR. But there are dangers that events could proceed in different directions. There are fears, for example, that any significant surges of imports from Mexico might be met by the application of administered trade law to imports from East Asia and other countries. In that case, increased trade with Mexico, especially when it occurred in sensitive products, would be offset by reduced trade with other countries. Aside from the economic inefficiencies that would result, such trade diversion would surely be a source of friction between the US and East Asian traders, and would increase their motivation to form a regional trading bloc as a defensive measure against US protection.

Aside from such an outright protectionist scenario, there are also dangers that the existence of NAFTA – especially if it is widened to include more Latin American countries – would serve as a 'diversion of attention' for the United States from the open multilateral system. US frustration with trading partners who no longer feel impelled to placate the US at every turn could lead to the false conclusion that the US could 'go it alone' in the Westem hemisphere. That, of course, cannot happen overnight, but the risk of gradual erosion over time should not be overlooked.

There are also concems about the future evolution of NAFTA. Questions have been raised about the emergence of a 'hub-spoke' system, whereby each new potential entrant to NAFTA must negotiate a deal with the United States, with even less bargaining power than the preceding entrant. In that scenario, the US would become the 'hub' country, with free trade agreements with Canada, Mexico, Chile, Colombia, Caribbean countries, and potentially many others. But if each of those countries had a bilateral agreement with the US,[7] the effects would be significantly different than if an extended NAFTA is multilateral. Confusion would result for the US (with different rules of origin and conditions of access for imports from each of many countries) but the rest of the world would also lose. Each prior 'concession' to the US would become less valuable as new entrants were accepted, although presumably each new entrant's terms of access would be less favourable than earlier entrants.

There is also concern about the protective effect of some NAFTA provisions. Rules of origin were a focal point of contention during the negotiations, and can be used to restrict imports from the rest of the world and favour imports from union members. This certainly seems to be the case with autos and auto parts, and textiles and apparel, in the NAFTA agreement.

There is no danger that the world will split immediately into trading blocs. Rather, the risk is one of continued gradual erosion of the multilateral trading system, as East Asian and Pacific countries respond to trade diversion to Mexico and other NAFTA members by forming their own regional agreement. Such an agreement would doubtless be launched within the context of GATT, but it is plausible that, over time, trade disputes with NAFTA members would become increasingly acrimonious. If disputes of ever-increasing intensity, with threats, counter threats, and occasional imposition of retaliatory tariffs, were to start, it is not unthinkable that a mounting history of disputes could eventually lead

7 Some Latin American countries, such as Chile and Mexico, have already concluded bilateral agreements with each other.

to miscalculation and possibly trade war. Certainly, those supporting efforts to create or strengthen regional trading blocs should be alert to this danger.

There is also a question as to whether the existence of NAFTA and the Uruguay Round Agreement can stop the American tendency toward increased bilateralism. The bilateral demands for quantitative 'indicators' for Japan and continued bilateral 'demands' on other countries offer no reassurance. President Clinton's reinstatement of 'Super-301' was likewise discouraging. Even more worrisome, perhaps, is that US trade disputes with Canada do not seem to have lessened despite the FTA. Not only are Americans contesting imports of Canadian wheat, but the US placed Canada on the 'watch list' in connection with 'Super-301' in September 1994.

Meanwhile, in order to obtain Congressional approval of the NAFTA agreement. President Clinton bowed to Congressional pressure and sought 'side agreements' on labour and the environment. Even after the completion of the Uruguay Round, the US insisted that, as a condition for its signature on the agreement, future consideration would be given to environmental and labour codes within the GATT/WTO.

There are, to be sure, legitimate environmental concerns, although many in developing countries believe that, given the history of despoilation of its own environment as a route to riches in the nineteenth century, the west is now attempting to prevent developing countries from taking the same route to development. Labour standards constitute a similar threat, in that developing countries' comparative advantage understandably lies in labour-intensive goods. To insist upon measures that raise labour costs (either by raising wages, or, equivalently by raising costs of safety equipment or otherwise of hiring labour) is to deny developing countries of their comparative advantage and therefore of the opportunity in many cases for rapid economic growth. Experience in East Asian countries, as well as others, has demonstrated that a period during which unskilled workers are working in low-productivity labour intensive industries may be a prerequisite for 'learning' and experience to move up the scale to more highly productive types of employment. If opportunities for exporting labour intensive products are greatly reduced, growth of other poor countries will be greatly inhibited.

Advocates of 'labour standards' assert that there is deliberate suppression of wages in developing countries. If that were correct, we ought to observe excess demand for labour as employers queued for the available workforce. What we observe instead is a rapidly growing labour force, with lengthy queues of young people seeking work. Their existence is simply inconsistent with the view that wages are suppressed and that there is 'exploitation'.

Even when it comes to questions of 'child labour', the question is by no means clear. Parents do not want their children to work, but in many developing countries, they are so poor that the alternative is a family income so low that chronic malnutrition would result. In some countries, the opportunity for factory employment provides young girls with an alternative to an early marriage, or worse – an altemative that some eagerly accept.

Whether labour standards are an appropriate response or not, there are surely legitimate desires for children in all countries to be enabled to attend school and avoid long hours in factory jobs, although that may not be the relevant alternative to their employment. Past history indicates that, as soon as incomes rise, parents enter their children in school and the incidence of child labour falls. Choking off opportunities for growth may, therefore, serve to increase, rather than decrease child labour.

One fears that much of the support for 'labour standards' and environmental standards originates, not from environmentalists or those concerned with labour practices, but as an appeal for public support for protection. A highly restrictive labour or environmental code attached to the Uruguay Round agreement could in fact be highly protectionist and exclude especially the developing countries from the benefits of the open multilateral trading system.

When there are environmental spillovers, there are legitimate grounds for international concern. But whether these should be tied to trade policy is a much more difficult matter. Certainly, means need to be found to insure that measures taken in the name of the environment are truly environmental in their effect and, in addition, represent economically effective and low cost mechanisms for achieving the desired environmental results.

There are, then, a large number of conflicting cross currents in the international trading system today. On one hand, the passage of the Uruguay Round offers the promise of further strengthening of the open multilateral system. On the other hand, tendencies toward regionalisation, reinforcing protectionist pressures, present threats to the system.

The Uruguay Round has now been ratified and the World Trade Organisation has commenced operations. With the scope that that offers for bringing additional aspects of international exchange of goods and services under an open multilateral regime, and the gains to be exploited with the liberalisations already agreed to in the Uruguay Round, there are good reasons for optimism. The attention of the world, and especially of trade officials, should be focussed on doing everything possible to strengthen the organisation and its prospects for success.

To strengthen those prospects will be to resist pressures for protectionism and regionalism. It is to be hoped that smaller nations will eschew bilateral or regional approaches and emphasise the importance of multilateral solutions to trade difficulties. Efforts to strengthen the WTO, and move the US away from bilateral pressures on Japan and other trading partners and toward reliance on the WTO may have very great rewards.

For the smaller trading nations, expressions of disapproval at bilateral approaches, and efforts to support the multilateral system are clearly called for, both in the interest of the system as a whole, and in the individual interest of small countries that are clearly better off with a system than in bilateral bargaining with large countries.

This conclusion has clear implications for APEC. An APEC without Japan and the United States makes no sense as a free trade area: it simply creates another regional arrangement, but this time one in which the countries involved even taken together are sufficiently small that their bargaining power as a group is minimal with respect to the large trading nations. Formation of such a group would reinforce the tendencies toward regionalism and bilateralism – the very factors it is in the interest of the countries to avoid.

If, on the other hand, the US and Japan were willing to join into an FTA, almost all of the barriers to increasing multilateral liberalisation would disappear. An effort on the part of APEC countries to induce the US and Japan to resolve their trade differences through the WTO, rather than in bilateral bargaining, is surely much in the interest of the smaller countries in APEC.

While the temptation to enter regional arrangements is understandable, if the very nations that have gained the most from the open multilateral trading system in the past now fail to support it vigorously, just when it is at a crossroads, the prospects for a resumption of the virtuous circle that served the world so well in the 1950s and 1960s will greatly diminish. The rewards for a resumption of the virtuous circle are potentially enormous. It is greatly to be hoped that the lures of much smaller, but more immediately visible, accomplishments do not detract political attention from the crucial issues.

44

Protection and liberalization in Australia and abroad

W. Max Corden[1]

I have the honour of being only the second person so far who has been invited to give the Joseph Fisher Lecture twice – not the same lecture, of course. My subject twenty eight years ago was "Australian Tariff Policy". It was a lecture that attracted much attention at the time, both in the press and in official circles. I reviewed Tariff Board reports and tariff changes that had taken place in the preceding two years and various possible principles for tariff-making, ending with proposals of my own. In re-reading this lecture now, I am amazed at my pragmatism and moderation, which no doubt helps to explain why the lecture was influential at the time. In the present lecture I want to compare the situation in 1967 with that in 1995, to review changes in Australian trade policies that have taken place during these 28 years – noting especially the motivations for these changes – and to put all this in an international perspective. This is an opportunity to look back on developments in which my writings played a role, so that at various points I shall be somewhat autobiographical here.

1967 and 1995 compared

The position in 1967 was that Australian protection was primarily in the form of tariffs. Quantitative import restrictions were removed in 1959. Tariffs protecting manufacturing industry were in significant cases very high, and also varied greatly between products, so that the tariff structure was thoroughly non-uniform. This was true in terms of nominal rates and even more in terms of effective rates.

1 Forty-fourth Joseph Fisher Lecture, 26 September 1995. . Reprinted in the *Australian Economic Review* June 1996: 141-54, and as chapter 8 in Corden, W. M. (1997) *The Road to Reform: Essays on Australian Political Economy*, Sydney: Addison-Wesley.

My 1967 lecture cited many nominal tariff rates of over 40 per cent and far higher effective rates. Rattigan (1986), drawing on Tariff Board reports, notes that "the average rates of effective protection available to individual Australian manufacturing industries in 1967-68 ranged from 0 to 120 per cent, and the average rate for manufacturing industry as a whole was 46 per cent." Because of the local content scheme for motor cars, the average effective rate for motor vehicles and components was 67 per cent. The Industry Commission has calculated effective rates for 1971 averaging 35 per cent for all manufactures but much higher for particular categories (See 44.1). Times have certainly changed. By 1995 all nominal tariffs were on a predetermined downward path, with many to reach 5 per cent by 1996. In the year 2000 the general level of nominal tariffs will be 5 per cent for most products, with motor vehicles and most textiles and footwear getting 15 per cent, and clothing 25 per cent. The average *effective* rate of assistance will be about 5 per cent.

It is certainly interesting to reflect how this remarkable change – one that I would have welcomed but never forecast twenty eight years ago – came about. It is also worth examining to what extent there has been anything special about these and related changes in Australia when they are compared with the trade liberalization process in other countries.

Looking back

In order to pursue this matter, one must really go back further, at least back to another Joseph Fisher lecture. In 1936 L. F. Giblin, the Ritchie Professor of Economics at the University of Melbourne, lectured on "Some Economic Effects of the Australian Tariff". He had been a member of the Committee which produced the famous Brigden Report, and in his lecture he discussed its calculations of the cost of protection and how these were borne by different sectors of the economy. It is an interesting lecture to reread. It certainly raised or expounded important issues, though it does remind one how much our understanding of these topics has advanced.

Table 44.1: Average effective rates of assistance for manufacturing – selected years (per cent)

Subdivision

		1971	**1974**	**1977**	**1983**	**1989**	**2000**
ASIC	**Description**	**-72**	**-75**	**-78**	**-84**	**-90**	**-01[a]**
21-22	Food, beverages and tobacco	19	21	10	6	4	2
23	Textiles	45	39	47	69	53	17
24	Clothing and footwear	86	87	141	227	113	34
25	Wood, wood products and furniture	23	18	18	18	15	4
26	Paper, paper products, printing and publishing	52	31	24	16	9	2
27	Chemical, petroleum and coal products	32	23	19	12	8	3
28	Non-metallic mineral products	14	11	5	4	4	2
29	Basic metal products	29	16	10	10	9	4
31	Fabricated metal products	58	39	30	25	19	4
32	Transport equipment	50	45	48	65	37	13
323	Motor vehicles and parts	49	54	73	129	52	19
33	Other machinery and equipment	44	24	20	22	19	6
34	Miscellaneous manufacturing	32	27	30	26	20	7
21-34	Total manufacturing	35	27	23	22	15	5

a Projection based on 1989-90 base year production. *Source:* Industry Commission (1995).

Giblin's practical attitude to protection, as that of the Brigden Report, was somewhat ambiguous. It is worth quoting one passage from his lecture. "There is, then, little disagreement about the necessity of the protective policy today. The general principle is admitted, but its application is still controversial. How hard should the policy be pushed? And in what directions? How can we get the greatest advantages at the least cost?" He did not answer these questions, but the questions posed the key issue that faced Australian policy makers in the early sixties when, owing to the removal of quantitative import restrictions (which had been imposed for balance-of-payments reasons), tariff policy became important again.

The conventional view in the fifties and early sixties was that the Brigden report had provided a justification for Australian protection. It is certainly true that there was "little disagreement about the necessity of the protective policy." The Brigden argument is well known, so I shall not expound it here. It did not explain why tariffs were imposed or raised at various times in Australia's history, especially in Victoria before Federation, and then, particularly, in 1908 and 1920. Rather, it provided an *ex-post* rationalization. But Professor Giblin did focus on the huge intellectual gap that remained. The Brigden argument provided no guidance at all on the criteria for the details of tariff-making. Which industries or sections of industries should be protected and, how much?

It thus provided no help at all to the Tariff Board which had the responsibility of advising on this very matter.

The Tariff Board did state its criteria ("economic" and "efficient"), but these were quite empty of content, at least as stated. In my own studies of Tariff Board reports and tariff practices (Corden, 1962), I deduced more thoroughly what "the logic" must have been concluding that the "existence principle" (my term, not that of the Board or the government) seemed to govern the choice of which industries to protect, while the "made-to-measure principle" determined how high a tariff rate to provide. But even to suggest the existence principle was to highlight the nature of the problem. Which industries or activities should come into existence? And what protection could such new activities expect? The language of the Tariff Board seemed to have no relation to standard economic theory. It is this gap that my 1967 lecture sought to fill, though actually the story goes further back. This brings me to the Vernon report.

Once the tariff had again become the principal or almost only means of protection, namely, from 1960, some members of the Tariff Board became gradually aware that their existing principles – insofar as there were any – were unsatisfactory and that decisions were being made on a piecemeal basis. There is quite a long story here about different points of view on the Board and the conversion of the celebrated Alf Rattigan (who became Chairman of the Board in 1963) to the view that new, more rational principles needed to be adopted. I shall not repeat this story here, but just note that a key role was played by the Vernon Committee's report on the Australian economy.

The Vernon Report (1965) contained a key chapter on tariff policy (possibly the only chapter that eventually had any influence), and a pioneering appendix where effective rates and subsidy equivalent calculations were made. In this field the Committee was much influenced by my own work and submissions. In particular they developed the idea of a tariff "benchmark" – a rate of tariff of about 30 per cent which would be provided readily, and towards which existing higher tariffs would gradually be moved.

This "benchmark" approach harked back to a lecture I had delivered – also in Adelaide and published as Corden (1958) – where I proposed first that import restrictions should be replaced by tariffs (as they were in 1960) and then that there should be a gradual movement to a uniform *ad valorem* tariff rate. To cut a long story short, the Tariff Board, and especially Mr. Rattigan and his right-hand man, Bill Carmichael, were much influenced by the Vernon Committee report, which thus played a key role in the conversion of the Tariff Board both to use of the effective protection rate as a criterion for tariff policy – broadened later to the effective rate of assistance (ERA) – and, more generally to the application of what would now be called economic rationalism to tariff policy. This conversion process was just underway when I wrote my 1967 Fisher lecture. In particular, several members of the Board, and subsequently Mr. Rattigan, were much attracted by the benchmark approach.

In this 1967 lecture I aimed to sort out and explain the policy choices. I chose to assume a fixed exchange rate and rule out overnight changes. I was definitely not a shock therapy man. I shall come back to discussing the exchange rate assumption later.

What were my concluding recommendations? I should mention here that, while my writings on tariffs were quite widely read, many real-world practical down-to-earth people regarded me as a typical, somewhat unrealistic, academic and (dirty word) a free trader. This last characterisation was correctly deduced from my 1958 uniform tariff paper, since I had made it clear there that the movement to a uniform tariff should be an intermediate or second-best step, free trade (with appropriate exchange rate adjustment and some exceptions) being first-best. In the 1967 lecture I proposed two benchmarks. There should be a benchmark in nominal rate terms *of 30 per cent for new activities* and another benchmark *of 45 per cent for existing activities.* Of course, "the benchmark for existing activities would involve lopping of the substantial high protection areas, an operation which would have to be gradual, perhaps in steps announced precisely in advance." Let me repeat these figures: 30 per cent for new activities and 45 per cent for existing activities. So these were this free trader's very radical recommendations. (Laughter).

Progress and some retreat: 1967-75

The developments which I shall now summarize very briefly all happened after I had left the Australian National University for Oxford, though I really have to go back to 1965 or even earlier. Essentially there were three developments.

First, the Tariff Board under Mr. Rattigan asserted its independence – or, more precisely, Mr. Rattigan asserted his independence, a process that involved some conflicts within the Board. There was a well-known conflict between the powerful Minister for Trade, John McEwen, and Mr. Rattigan on the role of the Board and on Mr. McEwen's attempt to by-pass it, to limit its scope for independent assessment, or to ignore it in various ways.[2] This story has been written up in various places.[3] Mr. Rattigan's commitment to transparency, his courage, and his political skills were impressive. The matter was resolved with the election of the Whitlam government, Gough Whitlam proclaiming himself "a Rattigan man".

At this point I should like to mention that a South Australian Liberal member of the House of Representatives, Bert Kelly, had been a prominent but lone parliamentary critic of high tariff policy from well before 1967. This did not make him popular with the government or other members of his own party, but by his persistence he contributed to greater awareness of the issue. Mr. Kelly was in my audience at the 1967 Fisher Lecture, and I am happy to note that he is here, in the front row, now (applause).

2 John McEwen, the leader of the Country Party and therefore Deputy Prime Minister, was Minister for Trade, and later for Trade and Industry, from 1956 to 1971. He was succeeded in these positions by Doug Anthony, who had a similar attitude towards the Tariff Board.

3 See Glezer (1982), Anderson and Garnaut (1987), Capling and Galligan (1992), and Bell (1993). By far the most thorough and fascinating account, at least of the "inside" politics, is that by the star actor, Rattigan (1986). All these accounts go back to 1963, and sometimes earlier.

It is worth noting that the issue of the role of the Board relative to the government was an old one. In his 1936 Fisher lecture Professor Giblin complained that the government had taken certain trade policy action (protection of textiles from Japanese competition and the protection of motor car manufacture) without referring "these highly technical questions" to the Board. In my 1967 lecture I dealt with the same issue, remarking in my usual cautious way that, if decisions are made in a political way: "it becomes at least possible that contributions to party funds would have some effect on actual policies" (Surprise, surprise!). I stressed the value of the Tariff Board system of public enquires. I proposed that the Tariff Board be attached to the Prime Minister's Department, rather than, as it was at the time, to the Department of Trade (which represented the interests of secondary industry). This proposal was later implemented by the Whitlam government.

The second major development in the period was the 25 per cent uniform tariff cut of the Whitlam government in 1973.[4] This was motivated, or at least influenced, by the macroeconomic situation at the time – inflation and a balance-of-payments surplus. An increased supply of imports was expected to reduce inflation. I shall come back to discussing the relevance of the balance-of-payments situation later. The decision came as a great surprise and was, of course, heavily criticised, especially later. Quite wrongly, it was blamed for the increase in unemployment that came with the recession of 1974-75 (though it must have had some localised effects). The recession actually led to the reimposition of quotas on imports of textiles, clothing, and footwear (the so-called TCF group) and of passenger motor vehicles and parts (PMV), this being the "retreat" to which I referred in the heading.

The third development of the period was, in a long-run perspective, the most important. Thanks to Mr. Whitlam and the initiative of Mr. Rattigan, the Tariff Board was replaced by the Industries Assistance Commission (IAC), with Mr. Rattigan the chairman of the new IAC. Its mandate was much wider than that of the Tariff Board, and it was conceived on a much more ambitious scale. This was the beginning of an important and remarkable organization, one which

4 See Gruen (1975), and also Rattigan (1986, pp. 162-71). A 25% tariff cut meant that, for example, a 50% tariff would be cut to 37.5%.

acquired a world reputation and which, through its careful empirical work and strong and consistent "economic rationalist" analysis, undoubtedly influenced informed thinking and policy-making in the broad area of industry assistance subsequently. There is really a remarkable contrast between the Tariff Board reports of the early sixties (and some of the reports reviewed in my 1967 lecture) which were empty of serious economic analysis, and the highly professional reports of the IAC, backed up with effective rate and subsidy equivalent measures and the use of general equilibrium modelling resulting from the IMPACT project.

An international perspective up to 1975

Right through the sixties and up to the world recession of 1974-75, developed (OECD) countries other than Australia and New Zealand went through a reciprocal trade liberalization process. The most important trade liberalization exercise was the establishment, in stages, of a European customs union through the European Economic Community and the associated European free trade area. In the case of manufactures (but not agriculture) there is little doubt that trade creation far outweighed trade diversion. In addition, there was world-wide reciprocal trade liberalization of manufactures under the auspices of the GATT through the various multilateral negotiating rounds.

Australia and New Zealand did not take part in these rounds. Our government saw Australia as essentially a developing country with an infant manufacturing industry. Furthermore – and this was the main reason for Australia not participating – given that Australia was an exporter of agricultural products (with no immediate prospects of significant exports of manufactures), it was perceived that we had nothing to gain from reciprocity when the rounds excluded agriculture. Of course, since the tariff reductions were on a most-favored-nation basis, so that they applied to all members of GATT, Australia was still a potential beneficiary. (Australia was a member of GATT even though we did not participate in the rounds). Thus, we opted out of the whole postwar trade liberalization process.

From the point of view of protection policy, the more relevant comparison for Australia is not with advanced industrial, but with developing countries. Almost all of these – notably India, Indonesia, and the major countries of

Latin America – were highly protectionist, with levels of nominal and effective protection (implicit and explicit) higher – sometimes far higher – than those of Australia. More important, most of the developing countries used quantitative import restrictions and the associated licensing of imports as the main method of protection. Incidentally, this also was true of New Zealand which, unlike Australia, maintained its quantitative restrictions for many years after 1960. The histories, motivations and popular arguments for protection in many of the developing countries, notably in Latin America, were quite similar to those applying to Australia. But there were two differences.

The first I have already mentioned. In almost all developing countries the primary method of protection was through quantitative import restrictions. While Australia did reimpose some quotas at the end of the period (1974-75), it was, in fact, the only country (so far as I am aware) which was high protectionist but from 1960 used tariffs as the main instruments of protection. Of course, the developing countries did all have tariffs, mostly very high ones, but the protective effect was dominated by quantitative restrictions.

Second, only Australia had a semi-independent advisory institution like the Tariff Board – an institution which was designed from its beginning in the nineteen twenties to put some distance between the politicians and the tariff-making process, and which, above all, was designed through its public enquiry process and its published reports, to ensure transparency. The concept and process were always under attack and governments often by-passed the Board, but to a considerable extent the system worked. All this meant that in developing countries there was no counterpart to the Australian debate or battle over Tariff Board independence. Certainly no other country had an independently-minded and highly *professional* advisory institution in this field like the IAC.[5]

5 I have to be a little cautious in generalizing here. As far as I know, none of the developing countries have had such bodies dealing in detail with protection measures and having some degree of independence. Of course, the United States has an independent economic advisory body of high professional quality in the Council of Economic Advisers, and Germany and Canada also have such bodies. None of them are comparable with the IAC.

The extensive discussion about the optimal level and – more important – optimal pattern of protection was at this time (up to 1975) unique to Australia. In Australia the focus was on unilateral liberalization or (more precisely) second-best optimization subject to constraints, while the other OECD countries were focused on reciprocity. Most developing countries (with the notable exceptions of Korea and Taiwan) were still very comfortable with their import-substituting industrialization and not concerned very much with the pattern-of-protection issue.

The rest of the story: 1975-95

I base (and paraphrase) the following account primarily on Industry Commission (1995). See also Table 44.1, from that report. The main point is that the period from 1975 can clearly be divided into two parts by the landmark year 1988. The radical Australian trade liberalization process really began with the Hawke government's decisions announced in that year.

As I have already noted, import quotas on the textiles-clothing-footwear (TCF) and passenger-motor-vehicles-and-components (PMV) categories were reintroduced in 1974 and the result was that the implicit effective rates on these greatly increased. On the other hand, there were widespread tariff reductions in 1977 on other categories following an IAC report on the multilateral trade negotiations (in which Australia was now participating) and in response to the devaluation of the Australian dollar at the end of 1976. But mostly, these tariff reductions involved the removal of unused assistance (water in the tariff). The net result of these and some further changes resulting from IAC reports on particular industries, was that the average level of protection for manufacturing (in terms of effective rates) fell somewhat in 1977 and then stayed fairly constant, while the degree of non-uniformity of the structure of protection greatly increased. (The Industry Commission measured non-uniformity – or "disparities" – by standard deviations).

The very important *May 1988 Economic Statement* announced a general program of phased reductions in nominal tariff rates for most imports (excluding TCF and PMV), tariffs above 15 per cent to be brought down to 15 per cent, and tariffs between 15 per cent and 10 per cent to be brought down to 10 per cent by 1992. The *March 1991 Industry Policy Statement* announced the continuation of this program of tariff reduction with most tariffs to be phased down to 5 per cent by 1996. It is remarkable that the 1991 Statement came in the midst of a recession. Quotas for PVM were ended in 1988 and for TCF in 1993. In 1991 tariffs protecting TCV and PMV were substantially reduced.

By July 2000 PMV and most textile and footwear industries will be protected by tariffs of 15 per cent, while clothing imports will have tariffs of 25 per cent. All these figures refer to nominal tariff rates. Average effective rates of assistance are given in Table 44.1, and more detailed information and calculations of these remarkable changes can be found in Industry Commission (1995).

It is certainly interesting to reflect on the reasons for these developments. The motives for changes in Australian protection up to 1988, and especially for the imposition of TCF and PMV quotas in the seventies, have been discussed in Anderson and Garnaut (1977). They stress the importance of pressure groups. The background and motives of the liberalization since 1988 are discussed in Garnaut (1994)[6]. Garnaut underlines the importance of political leadership when the government is in a strong electoral position, and that Mr. Hawke "was predisposed to internationally oriented and market-oriented solutions" (something that is also evident from Hawke's memoirs).

Here one should note that the biggest reductions in Australian tariffs have taken place under the Whitlam and Hawke Labor governments. Is that a coincidence? It is true that the 1973 uniform tariff cut and the 1988 Statement came at a time of boom, but the 1991 Statement which ensured a continuation of the tariff reduction program came in a recession, suggesting that by that time, the direction of policy was firmly set. I have hypothesized that Labor governments are generally prepared to be more radical, once in pursuit of more interventionist or welfare-oriented policies, and now also in pursuit of policies which they have come to believe would raise national efficiency or productivity, and thus also make both higher real wages and improved welfare provision feasible. But it is also relevant that the 1988 and 1991 programs were undoubtedly helped by the fact that the Opposition was in general sympathy with the policy direction.

6 See also Keating and Dixon (1989), Capling and Galligan (1992), and Bell (1993), for discussions of motives for Australian trade liberalization since 1988.

At this point, the important role of the IAC (which is now, with a broadened mandate, the Industry Commission) must again be noted. Quite apart from the specific recommendations, usually involving reductions in tariffs, that came out of particular IAC reports, its information and educational role must have been immense. All these changes have taken place in Australia in a quite exceptional context of transparency. Of course, the IAC has not been a decision-making body, its recommendations have often not been accepted, and it has had to cope with its unpopularity with various politicians (including Prime Minister Malcolm Fraser and his Deputy, Doug Anthony). It is only an advisory, and not a regulatory agency. Nevertheless, for many years its work and status have depended primarily on the existence of an elaborate tariff (and subsidy) system, so one might expect, on the basis of Stigler's generalization based on US experience of "regulatory capture" that it would have been captured by the protectionists. But, quite to the contrary, it has been a consistent proponent of orthodox ("rational") economics, with an emphasis on maximizing national (Pareto) efficiency).[7]

An international perspective again: The new liberalization

The Australian unilateral trade liberalization process since 1988 has close parallels with many developing countries. This is by contrast with the Australian developments of the sixties and early seventies, which were unique. The arguments against import-substituting industrialization and high protection were spread in the seventies and gradually influenced elite thinking in developing countries, notably Latin America. Nevertheless, the reaction to the shocks and the debt crisis of the early eighties were in some cases still protectionist. When there was a balance-of-payments crisis it had been a traditional reaction (as also in Australia) to increase protection – usually by imposing or tightening quantitative import restrictions. But already in the 1981-83 recession it was noticeable that many countries did not react in this way.

7 As in all countries, the Australian government department or office that is specifically responsible to advise on industry policy and maintain contact with industrialists (carrying various names during the period) has always been more than sympathetic, and sometimes has been completely captured, by the protectionist interests. This is evident particularly from Rattigan (1986) and other references cited earlier.

Subsequent to the recession, many developing countries started on a process of unilateral trade liberalization. In some cases this was very sharp, and the parallel with Australia was quite close. In particular three major oil-exporting countries – Indonesia, Mexico, and Nigeria – reacted to the severe 1986 drop in the price of oil, leading to balance-of-payments crises, with adjustment programs that included drastic trade liberalization. In historical terms it was certainly unusual for countries to react to balance-of-payments crises with trade liberalization. In Little et. al.(1993) this has been called "the new liberalization", and episodes are fully documented there. Of course, such policies were part of broader structural adjustment programs that, above all, included exchange rate devaluations.

Chile, Sri Lanka and Turkey already were "new liberalizers" in the seventies. I have already cited the three oil exporters, Indonesia, Mexico, and Nigeria. Argentina and Brazil followed later, more in reaction to hyper-inflation than to balance-of-payments crises. India is the most recent case, clearly reacting again to a balance-of-payments problem, and still having a long way to go. By the early nineties, unilateral trade liberalization had become quite conventional in almost all developing countries. This audience does not need to be reminded of New Zealand, a country which was still imposing widespread quantitative import restrictions at a time when every other OECD country had abandoned them. Its Labor government reacted to its inflation, growth and balance-of- payments crises in the "new liberalization" way.

What were the reasons for the new liberalization? First, there was the possibility of exchange rate adjustment. I shall come back to this later. Second, the view had spread (influenced by the crises of the early eighties, and sometimes before) that the old model of import substituting industrialization, leading to heavy dependence by uneconomic domestic industries on imported components and materials, had not worked, or at least had reached its limit. Third, the growth success of the East Asian, especially Korean, export-oriented outward-looking model, was contrasted with the apparent failures of the import-substitution model. Fourth, crises made countries ready for change. Fifth, countries that received assistance from the International Monetary Fund (IMF) and the World Bank had usually to accept conditions ("conditionality") that included some trade liberalization. Sixth – and this was undoubtedly important – the staff of the IMF and the World Bank had vigorously and successfully spread the same "economic rationalist" message that economists had been spreading in Australia, so that it was not just conditionality but also the convictions of key policy makers that help to explain the new trend. Finally, in the case of Latin America, the increasing number of US-educated "technocrats" (often with Ph.D's in economics from leading US universities) began to attain positions of power, and were naturally inclined to free-market approaches, sometimes in extreme, at other times in moderate, ways.

When one goes through this list, one can see that the explanations for Australian liberalization in the eighties were quite similar. Our "technocrats" were not necessarily US-educated, and the educational or conversion process did not depend on the IMF or the World Bank, but came from within Australia. I shall also come back to this later. Furthermore, while our terms-of-trade deterioration of 1985-86 was perceived as a kind of crisis (the "banana republic" crisis), its impact and magnitude were not comparable with the crises of many developing countries. Hence we could embark on more gradual reforms. Unlike New Zealand, we did not need shock treatment. But we also looked to the success of East Asia, comparing ourselves unfavorably, and a view gradually developed in Australia that our protectionist model had not worked, as reflected in our relatively low measured long-term per capita growth rate.

The crucial role of exchange rate policy

Substantial trade liberalization needs, in general, to be associated with depreciation of the exchange rate if unemployment and a deterioration in the balance of trade are to be avoided. I say "in general" because there are assumptions and qualifications to be noted. A key assumption is the essentially Keynesian – and realistic – one that, normally, the general level of nominal wages is inflexible downwards, and that the rate of labor productivity growth is not so high as to allow a sufficient decline in unit labor costs even with constant nominal wages.

Another qualification is illustrated by the uniform tariff cut of 1973. The balance-of-payments situation had improved owing to a striking terms-of-trade improvement, and there were domestic inflationary pressures. Hence, a broad tariff cut was possible even with a fixed exchange rate (and the Australian dollar had actually been appreciated).[8] I foreshadowed this kind of circumstance in my 1967 lecture. In that lecture I simply assumed a fixed exchange rate, and then remarked: "Thus some significant downward movement in existing tariffs would be practicable only when (with a given tariff level and full employment) balance-of-payments trends were favorable. Such an opportunity would result from an improvement in the export situation."

I have already noted that tariff reductions in 1977 were associated with devaluation. Of the greatest importance for Australia was the decision to float the Australian dollar in 1983. One cannot say that an explicit decision was made to reduce tariffs and induce an associated depreciation. Rather, the market sharply depreciated the dollar in 1985 and 1986 owing to the decline in the terms of trade. This made import-competing and export industries much more competitive, and thus made possible and politically acceptable the phased tariff reductions initiated in 1988 and later. The depreciation came first and tariff reductions followed. Some import-competing activities have no doubt come under greater pressure as a result of the tariff cuts, but this has been offset both from a balance-of-payments and political pressure-group point of view by the striking boom in manufactured exports and in services that has been caused, at least in part and with a lag, by depreciation.

The evidence adduced in Little et. al. (1993) clearly shows that almost all major trade liberalizations in developing countries have been associated with devaluations of the exchange rate. The "new liberalizations" have usually involved very sharp devaluations sufficient not only to deal with the consequences of balance-of-payments crises but additionally sufficient to counteract the balance-of-payments effects of trade liberalization. In Corden (1993) I have stressed that it is undesirable for a developing country to commit itself to a fixed nominal exchange as an anchor against inflation when there is still a need for trade liberalization.

8 See Gruen (1975).

Coming back to Australia, it is clear that any determined commitment to a fixed exchange rate in the early nineteen-eighties would not only have led subsequently to a balance-of-payments crisis of Latin American proportions but also – as long as the exchange rate was indeed kept fixed – would have been an overwhelming obstacle to any large-scale program of trade liberalization. Even if the balance of payments and employment effects of liberalization had been minor – as is quite possible, given that the tariff reductions have been implemented gradually and given that some real depreciation might have been brought about by wage restraint combined with modest productivity growth – substantial liberalization as has taken place would not have been politically acceptable. Of course, there might have been a real crisis in 1986, and then a big devaluation associated with trade liberalization.

The exchange rate issue always played a big role in my own writings on Australian tariff policy from 1958 to 1967. In various places, notably Corden (1958, 1966), I stressed the need for devaluation if tariffs were to be removed or reduced. When it came to practical proposals I regarded the fixed exchange rate commitment as given, and thus worked out proposals of a second-best nature which inevitably involved maintaining a general level of positive protection. This led me to the uniform tariff idea and, later, its several "benchmark" variants discussed in detail in the 1967 Fisher lecture. Thus, in that lecture I was not a "free trader". Rereading this lecture, I find that it is not only very protectionist but also that it goes into second-best complications which appear quite irrelevant now. A single assumption explains this. "I shall assume a fixed exchange rate and rule out "overnight" changes." Then followed a footnote. "To assume a fixed exchange rate is not, of course, to advocate that it should be fixed. But for various reasons it seems a reasonable assumption."

Political economy: Role of economists, climate of opinion

I have already referred to the motivations for unilateral trade liberalizations both in Australia and in developing countries. Notably, there were shocks, and there was the sense that protectionist policies had failed and had just led to low growth rates and contributed to rigidities which had made adjustments to crises more difficult. Exchange rate flexibility was important. Then there was the changed international climate of opinion in this field. Here I want to discuss more fully the role of professional economists, or as they are called in Australia, "economic rationalists" and in developing countries, "technocrats".

Over a long period the climate of informed or "elite" (that is, politically and economically interested and active) opinion on free trade and protection changed in Australia. I am referring to politicians, bureaucrats, the financial and business community, officials of trade (lobbying) organizations, and trade union officials. The case against protection – or at least high and variable protection – came to be more widely understood. Particularly important have been financial journalists. A crucial explanation of this change is, in my opinion, the boom in economics training in Australia. Academics have complained about the large numbers in their classes, but this has borne fruit in producing a more economically-literate community. The pass economics degree has indeed been a passport to success, and the basic messages of our profession (even when taught often with unnecessary complications) have become widespread through teaching and textbooks. Economics has indeed played a key role in Australia, similar to that of law in many other countries, and this has certainly raised the economic literacy of our community. I hope that, with the ascent now of business studies, this situation will not change.

A particularly important role has been played by senior bureaucrats in key departments, notably the Treasury and Prime Minister's Department, who have (almost all) been qualified professional economists. I suspect that they were the key initiators of the tariff reduction programs of recent years. They are the equivalents of the "technocrats" in many developing countries whose role has been widely discussed internationally (Williamson, 1994). The technocrats have usually been ministers deep in politics (as in Indonesia, India, Mexico and Argentina) or central bank governors, and in this respect there has been a contrast with Australia.

Academics acting as temporary advisers have also had some role in Australia, but because of the high professional quality of the senior bureaucrats, I think the academic-on-leave role here is much less than in many other countries. In the field of tariff policy, the two names that come to mind are Fred Gruen, who played a key role in (indeed produced the idea of) the 25 per cent tariff cut while economic adviser in the Department of the Prime Minister under Mr. Whitlam, and Ross Garnaut, who influenced policy as economic adviser to Mr. Hawke, 1983-85.[9]

Going back to 1958-67, my own role in influencing tariff policy was quite different. Primarily, leaving aside technical advice, I operated as a straightforward academic in the public arena. I wrote my articles, published them, and they were read and had influence. It helped that they were pragmatic. In this way I influenced my academic colleagues, who then passed on these ideas in their classes and through their reading lists, and later officials with economic training who fed them into the policy arena. In the same way my writings influenced the staff of the Vernon committee, and also Sir John Crawford, the Deputy Chairman, who was the author of the Committee's tariff chapter. My personal contact with persons of importance was near-zero, aside with Sir John.[10] I gave technical advice about the various new measurement concepts (effective rates, subsidy equivalent) to the Vernon Committee staff, and subsequently to Mr. Carmichael of the Tariff Board.

Did it matter: What are the costs of protection?

The standard analysis of protection is concerned with the costs of resource misallocation – the costs of departure from Pareto-efficiency. This can be called the standard orthodox approach. The costs that used to be emphasized were the misallocation between import-competing and actual and potential export production, as well as the costs of distorting the pattern of consumption between importables and exportables. The Australian discussion brought in additionally the costs of distortion within the import-competing sector – that is, the costs of non-uniformity of the tariff structure.[11] In the nineteen sixties this latter emphasis

9 His subsequent published report, Garnaut (1989), has also been influential. This report proposed (among other things) a movement to complete free trade. These remarks should not be understood to underplay Mr. Hawke's own outward-looking and free trade-inclined views developed over the years.

10 The exception was my friendship from 1959 with the late Dick Boyer, who was already a member of the Tariff Board (representing the rural community) before Mr. Rattigan became Chairman and who stayed right into the early seventies. He was a solid "free trader", reluctant, possibly excessively so, to make compromises. When Mr. Rattigan joined the Board in 1963, he asked members how they approached their work. "Boyer, however, differed from his colleagues; he was interested in the underlying economic issues" (Rattigan 1986, p. 12).

11 There are complications here about effective and nominal tariff rates, and qualifications to the uniform tariff approach when the exchange rate is fixed that I have analyzed in various publications.

was new by international standards. My various proposals were all concerned with reducing these costs, and this approach formed the basis of the Tariff Board and IAC advocacy of a level playing field both between exportables and importables, and within the import-competing sector. Of course, the orthodox approach is subject to qualifications which have to do with externalities, terms-of-trade effects, and constraints that call for second-best policies. In partial equilibrium analyses, the costs are expressed by the familiar Marshallian triangles.

On the basis of many back-of-the-envelope calculations, these costs calculated for various countries have turned out to be only a small proportion of the gross national product (GDP), say 1-2 per cent. Similar calculations for Australia would lead to rather larger figures, but still a relatively small proportion. In any case, they would not explain a relatively low growth rate. One has to bear in mind, in particular, that in the sixties the protected manufacturing sector accounted for about 15 per cent of the Australian workforce.[12]

Supposing that protected manufacturing value-added also made up 15 per cent of GDP when calculated at free trade prices, that the average effective tariff protecting the sector was 50 per cent, and that the excess resource costs were 50 per cent of the production subsidy equivalent (the other 50 per cent being producer surplus), we get a production-distortion cost of 3.75 per cent of GDP. That is a generous back-of-the envelope estimate, since a part of the protected sector would no doubt have survived under free trade, so that for that part there would be no excess cost. Hence, the excess cost might be well below 50 per cent of the producer's subsidy equivalent, say 40 per cent. Furthermore, the average effective rate for all manufacturing was estimated by the IAC as 35 per cent for 1971 (before the uniform tariff cut), and perhaps it might be a better figure to use. Using these two lower percentages, the production-distortion cost of protecting manufacturing at the time comes out at 2.1 per cent of GDP. In any case, there may be much better estimates available, and these figures are plausible but purely illustrative.

12 This was my estimate in Corden (1963, p.174).

Using this type of approach, one might conclude that the cost of protection was not really very large and that the emphasis on protection as a cause of Australia's rather modest economic performance has been overdone. Protection did not matter so much. But there are some important qualifications here, even while adhering to the orthodox static resource allocation approach. First, there are also the familiar consumption-distortion costs of protection, including here the distortion in usage of protected inputs by industries, whether manufacturing or otherwise. Second, the distortion costs of non-uniformity of tariffs, which I tended to emphasize and on which the IAC has focussed so much, are not included. Third, economies of scale (including potential economies of scale resulting from expansion of exports of manufactures) are likely to raise the costs – that is, increase the gains from free trade. Finally, it has to be emphasized that 2-3 per cent of GDP is not a small amount and is well worth having. It is, after all, 2-3 per cent of GDP every year.

When I used to talk about these matters to students and in various public or business forums, I would say that you can build plenty of schools and hospitals every year with 2 per cent of GDP. An additional motivation for seeking reform was, simply, that the tariff system as it existed in the sixties and early seventies was fundamentally irrational, other than as explainable in political or pressure group terms. There was really no sound basis from a *national* interest point of view for protecting one industry, or particular activity within an industry, relative to others, for favoring sales to the home market over export sales, and for providing such a non-uniform structure.

Looking back, it is true that the effects of the tariff system must be put in perspective. Moving to near-free trade for manufacturing will not necessarily transform the economy, but only limited parts of it. This is particularly true because the importance of manufacturing relative to services has, in any case, declined, not because of tariff reductions but because of well known worldwide trends. Trade liberalization represents one significant element in a microeconomic reform process that has been much needed. In recent years attention in Australia has shifted in other directions, and this is as it should be. But yes, tariff policy reform did matter, both for its own sake and as a precursor of more general microeconomic reform.

In addition to the standard resource misallocation costs just discussed, there are also the costs of rent-seeking. These have been emphasized in the more recent theoretical literature. Resources, especially labor-time, are used up in the process of potential gainers trying to obtain import licences, getting tariffs imposed or increased, or preventing their decrease. Potential losers from tariffs – especially industries using inputs protected, produced by protected industries, also need to engage in such activities designed to avoid losses. Costs of this type have certainly arisen in Australia, especially because the tariff system was made-to-measure, though they may not have been large. Since 1960, import licensing has fortunately been limited to a few cases. It is worth stressing that, if tariff rates were firmly fixed, with no potential increases or decreases (and if formulae for allocating licenses were immutable), this kind of rent seeking would disappear. The more flexible the system, the greater the scope for rent seeking. Currently, the main costs of this type are associated with anti-dumping cases.

There is another aspect of rent seeking. A flexible tariff system based on no firm principle provides an inducement for interested parties to contribute to political parties with the expectation of rewards. I hesitate to call this corruption (though many would) since parties must be financed and since the money need not go to individuals. But it leads to *corrosion* of the political system. Of course, there are many possible rewards other than the ones that governments can give through the tariff system. Undoubtedly, in the McEwen era this was a significant effect of the system, and it is generally accepted that the Country Party was a principal beneficiary. Interest group pressures on governments and the Tariff Board were quite blatant. It is this consideration, and not only a concern with the orthodox resource allocation effects, which particularly influenced both Mr. Rattigan and Mr. Whitlam. They wanted to reform the system, to ensure independence and thus freedom from pressure for the Tariff Board and IAC, and to make the processes transparent. Of course, the resource allocation motive was there: they wanted tariff-making to be guided by principles focused on the national interest and not sectional interests.

The case for free trade is often put as a case for making the country more competitive (especially in exporting manufactures) and for raising its growth rate. Certainly arguments for trade liberalization in the nineteen-eighties were often put in broader terms than the orthodox resource allocation argument that was used in the sixties and seventies and that the Rattigan Tariff Board, the IAC and I focused on. In particular, it has often been suggested that Australia's relatively low growth rate is at least partially explained by its protectionist policies. I cannot discuss this in detail here, but, while there are broader issues, one can to some extent relate the orthodox approach to these other approaches.

First, removing tariffs and devaluing will indeed make manufactures (and other exports) more competitive in world markets. Domestic resources will thus be reallocated within the manufacturing sector from selling in the home market to selling abroad, and on orthodox grounds this yields a net gain. Such an emphasis on improving the competitiveness of exports of manufactures is simply another way of putting the standard resource allocation argument. On the other hand, industries that were previously highly protected become less competitive on the home market. Second, reducing protection will increase import competition on the Australian market and thus will reduce domestic monopoly or oligopoly power. This, in turn, may raise incentives for productivity improvements which will eventually also benefit exporting and possibly raise the growth rate. Third, improving resource allocation in the static sense will improve the productivity of investment and thus raise the growth rate.

The position now

As noted earlier, in five years protection for most Australian industries will be negligible. This assumes that the tariff reduction program as planned will indeed continue. There is no reason to expect otherwise since both the Government and the Opposition are committed. There are three exceptions. First, there will still be 15 per cent tariffs protecting motor vehicles and components (PMV), with no quotas. This is a vast drop from earlier protection. Second, clothing, textiles and footwear (TCF) will still be protected, most textiles and footwear at 15 and clothing at 25 per cent. Clearly, clothing protection will have to be further reduced in time. Finally, there is an active anti-dumping system which is really a loophole in the tariff reduction process and certainly the biggest potential threat to effective trade liberalization.[13]

13 I have not discussed the anti-dumping issue here. Australia has been one of the biggest users of anti-dumping measures. Fortunately, the requirement for a five-year "sunset" clause somewhat reduces their impact. On the other hand, threats of anti-dumping action can be a powerful restraint on competition from imports. Contingent protection can be as effective a protective device as actual protection. The impact of anti-dumping legislation cannot be measured just by looking at actual tariffs imposed. Annual Industry Commission reports contain relevant information on anti-dumping activity. Incidentally, the 1993 report notes that the chemical and petroleum products industry has been the dominant initiator of anti-dumping and countervailing action; this brings back memories, since a huge Tariff Board report on the then highly protected chemical industry received much attention in my 1967 Fisher lecture.

Let me conclude. The protectionist instinct is universal, and opinion polls suggest that Australian public opinion is by no means fully won over. Nevertheless, one would like to think that the issue is settled now in Australia, and that the battles must not be fought over and over again. Perhaps we are approaching the end of a chapter in Australian political and economic history, and this is the last of three Fisher lectures on the Australian tariff.

References

Anderson, Kym, and Garnaut, Ross (1987) *Australian Protectionism: Extent, Causes and Effects*. Sydney: Allen and Unwin.

Bell, Stephen (1993) *Australian Manufacturing and the State: The Politics of Industry Policy in the Postwar Era*. Cambridge: Cambridge University Press.

Brigden, J. B. *et al.* (1929) *The Australian Tariff: An Economic Enquiry*. Melbourne: Melbourne University Press.

Capling, Ann, and Galligan, Brian (1992) *Beyond the Protective State. The Political Economy of Australia's Manufacturing Industry Policy*. Cambridge: Cambridge University Press.

Corden, W. M. (1958) 'Import Restrictions and Tariffs: A New Look at Australian Policy,' *The Economic Record* 34(69), pp. 331-346. Reprinted in Arndt, H. W. and Corden, W.M. (eds.), *The Australian Economy: A Volume of Readings*. Melbourne: Cheshire, 1963.

Corden, W. M. (1962) 'The Logic of Australian Tariff Policy' in *Planned and Unplanned Development* (Economic Papers No. 15). Sydney: Economic Society of Australia and New Zealand. pp. 38-58.

Corden, W.M. (1963) 'The Tariff,' in A. Hunter (ed.), *The Economics of Australian Industry*. Melbourne: Melbourne University Press, pp. 174-214.

Corden, W.M. (1966) 'Protection' (Review article of the Vernon Report), *The Economic Record* 42 (97), March, pp. 129-48. Reprinted in G. McColl (ed.), *Overseas Trade and Investment*, Penguin Readings in Australian Economic Policy, 1972.

Corden, W.M. (1967) 'Australian Tariff Policy,' Joseph Fisher Lecture at the University of Adelaide. Reprinted in *Australian Economic Papers* 6, December 1967, pp. 131-54, and in G. McColl (ed.), *Overseas Trade and Investment*, Penguin *Readings in Australian Economic Policy*, 1972.

Corden, W.M. (1993) 'Exchange Rate Policies for Developing Countries.' In 'Policy Forum,' *The Economic Journal* l03, January, pp. 208-222.

Garnaut, Ross (1989) *Australia and the Northeast Asian Ascendancy*. Canberra: Australian Government Publishing Service.

Garnaut, Ross (1994) 'Australia: The Political Economy of Policy Reform,' in John Williamson (ed.), *The Political Economy of Policy Reform*, Washington DC: Institute for International Economics.

Giblin, L. F. (1936) *Some Economic Effects of the Australian Tariff* (The Joseph Fisher Lecture). Adelaide: At the Hassell Press, for the University of Adelaide.

Glezer, Leon (1982) *Tariff Politics: Australian Policy-Making 1960-1980*. Melbourne: Melbourne University Press.

Gruen, F.H. (1975) 'The 25 Per Cent Tariff Cut: Was It a Mistake?', *Australian Quarterly* 47(2), June: 7-20.

Industry Commission (1995) *Assistance to Agricultural and Manufacturing Industries*, Information Paper. Canberra: Commonwealth of Australia.

Keating, Michael and Dixon, Geoff (1989) *Making Economic Policy in Australia 1983-88*. Melbourne: Longman Cheshire.

Little, Ian, Cooper, R.N., Corden, W.M., and Rajapatirana, S., (1993) *Boom, Crisis and Adjustment: The Macroeconomic Experience of Developing Countries*. New York: Oxford University Press for the World Bank.

Rattigan, Alf (1986) *Industry Assistance. The Inside Story*. Melbourne: Melbourne University Press.

Vernon, J. *et al.* (1965) *Report of a Committee of Economic Enquiry* (the Vernon Report). Canberra: Commonwealth of Australia.

45

Population, food and trade

D. Gale Johnson[1]

The past two centuries and especially the last half century have witnessed dramatic improvements in the wellbeing of the world's population. The positive changes have been unparalleled in human history. The increases in per capita food consumption may have been greater than in all previous human history. Other measures of wellbeing, such as life expectancy and freedom from famine have shown great improvement. Yet during recent years claims have been made that the world was overpopulated or soon would be. Some have claimed that the growth of world demand for food will soon outpace the growth of supply. The fact that such claims made over the past three decades have all proved to be false seems always to be forgotten.

The competent professional studies of prospective food supply and demand conclude that there will be continued improvement in per capita food consumption, especially in the developing countries (Islam 1995). Yet projections of doom and gloom receive headlines and media attention. The potential accuracy of such projections seems irrelevant, notice depends solely on the emphasis on possible disaster. The sober and well documented studies have received little attention in the world's press.

What did Malthus really believe?

The above point is well illustrated by how Thomas Malthus is remembered. He is remembered for his illustrative statement that food production increased in an arithmetic ratio while population, if unchecked, increased at a geometric rate and thus population always had the potential to outrun the food supply.

1 Forty-fifth Joseph Fisher Lecture, 18 September 1996. Reprinted as "On the Resurgent Population and Food Debate", *Australian Journal of Agricultural Economics*, Vol. 41 (1): 1-17, March 1997.

Population could only be held in check by vice and misery – starvation, disease or war. This is the Malthus of the first edition. But Malthus very soon revised his views but hardly any one noticed or remembers. After noting the recent growth of population in Europe, he wrote: "....fewer famines and fewer diseases arising from want have prevailed in the last century than in those that preceded it. On the whole, therefore, though our future prospects respecting the mitigation of the evils arising from the principle of population may not be so bright as we could wish, yet they are far from being entirely disheartening and by no means preclude the gradual and progressive improvement in human society which, before the late wild speculations on the subject, was the object of rational expectations." (Malthus, pp. 330-31) In other words, he came to agree with those who, before the first edition of *An Essay on the Principle of Population*, believed that there could be and would be continuing improvement in the wellbeing of people.[2] Thus my paper is Malthusian, but Malthus of the revised editions. The fact that the conclusions of the revised editions have been remarkably perceptive, in contrast to the lack of congruence between the pessimism of the first edition and the actual experience of the last two centuries, has had absolutely no effect on what Malthus is remembered for.

2 The principle of population is that, if unchecked, population will grow faster than the means of subsistence. After noting that "...everything depends upon the relative proportion between population and food, and not on the absolute number of people" he adds that he believes "...that countries which possessed the fewest people often suffered the worst from the effects of the principle of population..." (p. 330)
The fundamental change introduced in the revised editions was that Malthus added a check to population growth; vice and misery were not the only checks. The preface to the 1803 and all subsequent editions included the following: "Throughout the whole of the present work, I have so far differed in principle from the former, as to suppose another check to population growth, which does not come under the head either of vice or misery; and in the latter part I have endeavored to soften some of the harshest conclusions of the first essay." (p. 9)
The new preventive check to population was due to a combination of laws and institutions and self-love or self-interest: "To the laws of property and marriage, and to the apparently narrow principle of self-love (or self-interest), which prompts each individual to exert himself in bettering his condition, we are indebted for all the noblest exertions of human genius, for everything that distinguishes the civilized from the savage state. A strict inquiry into the principle of population leads us strongly to the conclusion that we shall never be able to throw down the ladder by which we have risen to this eminence; but it by no means proves that we may not rise higher by the same means." (p. 331)

Population and wellbeing since Malthus' first edition

It is nearly two centuries since Malthus' first edition was published in 1798. In no other two centuries has the wellbeing of mankind been so enhanced as in the two centuries since his first edition appeared. In fact, we can say that there has been more improvement in wellbeing, as indicated by a large number of conventional measures, than in all of prior history. Choose whatever objective measure you wish – life expectancy, infant mortality, the incidence of famines and plagues, per capita food consumption, per capita real incomes or per capita levels of real consumption, or biological measures such as height or weight or ratios of weight to height – improvements during the past two centuries swamp those of the previous millennia, not just by a little bit but by a lot.

While the Nineteenth Century followed the path laid out in the revised editions, that century saw much less progress than the current century. That was due, in considerable part, to the rapid growth of urbanization which brought with it diseases that caused great suffering and loss of life. The large increase in human migrations that came with the industrial revolution resulted in the spread of disease on a scale seldom seen before in the world. Even so, there were modest improvements in wellbeing, at least among significant segments of the population (Fogel 1996). But it was the steps taken near the end of the Nineteenth Century in providing clean water and improving sanitation and the beginnings of knowledge concerning the transmission and prevention of disease that made possible the spectacular gains in life expectancy that have occurred in the current century.

It was also during the Nineteenth Century that the discoveries of labor saving farm implements made possible the transfer of labor out of agriculture and into other pursuits that converted cities into productive enterprises and permitted their rapid growth. At the end of the 18th Century the United States had no city with a population of more than 75,000 while London and Paris, two of the three largest cities in Europe, had populations of 861,000 and 547,000, respectively (Chandler 1987). The improvements in wellbeing that came in the last century were intimately related to the agricultural revolutions in North America and Europe.

All this has been accomplished while population grew at the most rapid rate in the recorded history of the world. It is seldom recognized that world population growth was less than 0.2 per cent annually from about 500 B.C. to about 1400 A.D. and didn't exceed 0.5 per cent until the middle of the 18th Century (Kremer 1993). World population grew very slowly through the Seventeenth Century, with the most rapid rates of economic growth generally occurring in the countries with the highest rates of population growth. Throughout the Nineteenth Centuries and until about World War II, population growth rates in the industrial countries were greater than in the developing countries (Table 45.1). Only after World War II did the developing countries have the higher rates of population growth and only then did their per capita income growth exceed that of the industrial countries. From 1850 to 1920 population in the developing countries grew approximately 0.5 per cent annually. Subsequently the rate exceeded 1 per cent, but remained at less than 1.5 per cent until 1950.

Table 45.1: Expectations of life at birth for six European countries and Massachusetts in the US, 1840-1955

Year	Expectation of life at birth, years	Ave. annual increase, per cent per year
1840	41.0	-
1850	41.5	0.05
1860	42.5	0.07
1870	43.5	0.17
1880	45.2	0.13
1890	47.1	0.20
1900	50.5	0.34
1910	54.3	0.38
1920	58.3	0.40
1930	61.7	0.34
1940	64.6	0.29
1955	71.0	0.43

Source: United Nations, Population Bulletin, no. 6, table IV.1, 1962.

The period of rapid population growth in the developing economies began in 1950 when growth exceeded 2 per cent for three decades. It was also during this period, from 1950 to 1980, that the rate of growth of real per capita incomes were greater in the developing than in the developed countries and the highest ever achieved in the developing countries or in the developed countries as a group. In the years from 1750 to 1920, population grew more rapidly in the developed than the developing countries and per capita income growth was greater in the developed countries. Contrary to the implicit model of the relationship between population growth and economic growth of those who favor slow or zero population growth, historically economic growth as measured by the growth of real per capita incomes has been highest during periods of rapid population growth.

Let me give you some of the data that lie behind what I have just said. Maddison (1995) provides estimates of per capita GDP for most major countries starting with 1820. He provides estimates for 11 Asian countries, which may be used to indicate the experience of the developing countries for 1820 to 1950. Over that period of more than a century, it is estimated that the 11 Asian countries increased their per capita gross domestic product by only 25 per cent – from $609 to $863 while their population increased by 84 per cent (or an annual rate of less than 0.5 per cent). From 1950 to 1992 the Asian countries increased per capita income to $5,300, increasing by five times while population increased by 128 per cent (an annual rate of almost 3 per cent).

Data for the 12 Western European countries show an increase in real per capita income of $1,228 in 1820 to $5,513 in 1950, with population increasing by 131 per cent (an annual growth rate of approximately 0.65 per cent) while the real per capita income of the United States grew from $1,287 in 1820 to $9,573 in 1950. For this period the annual rate of increase in per capita income in the United States was 1.56 per cent, much less than the growth rate in developing economies from 1950 to 1980.

The 11 Asian countries included Taiwan, South Korea and Japan. It may be useful to review the data for the two large Asian countries, namely China and India. Magnusson estimates the two countries had essentially the same per capita incomes in 1820 – $523 and $531, respectively. And they had almost the same incomes in 1950 – $614 and $597. These data indicate the absence of a significant increase in real per capita income for more than a century. From 1950 to 1992, China and India followed quite different paths, with the Chinese average increasing to $3,098 and India's to $1,348, with most of the difference arising in the past 15 years.[3] But even at India's much slower pace of growth in a period of 42 years, India more than doubled its per capita income after an increase of a tenth in the previous 130 years. And its population grew much more rapidly in the recent than the earlier period – by a factor of approximately four.

A measure of improvement in wellbeing that merits serious attention is change in life expectancy as well as various measures of infant and child mortality. Mortality or life expectancy probably was roughly constant throughout history until 1650 when, according to Bogue (1969, p. 566), the average expectation of life was 25 years or less. The infant mortality rate was about 30 per cent. Data from Roman tombstones indicated that life expectancy was about 20 to 30 years during the period of the Roman empire, giving some support to the view that for a millennia there had been little or no change in life expectancy. Data for six European countries and Massachusetts indicate that as of 1840 life expectancy in high income countries was 41 years (Bogue 1969, p. 567). Sixty years later life expectancy had increased to 50.5 years, an increase of less than 10 years. In the next fifty five years – to 1955 – life expectancy increased to 71 years, an absolute increase twice that achieved in the previous sixty years.

Swedish data are available on infant mortality starting in 1750 (Bogue 1969). Until the beginning of the Nineteenth Century infant mortality exceeded 20 per cent, in some years exceeding 25 per cent. Infant mortality did not go below 15 per cent until 1850 and reached 10 per cent only at the beginning of this century. At the present time the available data indicate that there is now only one country with infant mortality rates exceeding 15 per cent – the Swedish level as of 1850 and many developing countries are now at or below 5 per cent which was reached in Sweden about 1940 (World Bank 1996, p. 198). The average infant mortality rate for all low income countries is now less than 6 per cent.

3 In 1978, the year before the start of the Chinese economic reforms, the per capita GDPs were $1,352 for China and $972 for India – a difference of only 39 per cent in China's favor. In 1992 the difference was 130 per cent in China's favor. India's population grew by 36 per cent over the period while China's grew 22 per cent. Even if we assumed that the additional population contributed nothing to GDP and we subtract their consumption, the difference in population growth rates, the difference in population growth rates would account for less than about 15 percentage points of the increase in the ratio of Chinese to Indian per capita incomes.

The rapid world population growth after World War II was due almost entirely to a sharp decline in mortality rather than an increase in fertility. In fact, fertility has declined almost everywhere. I have long found it incongruous that there has been so much concern about rapid world population growth during the last half of this century since it has been due primarily to improvements in health and thus the length of life, something that mankind struggled for centuries to achieve. I can think of nothing that reduced suffering more than reducing infant mortality from when one out of every three children died before a year of age of one to now when most mothers in the world are confronted with a loss of less than one in 20 (a rate of 50 per 1,000 births) and this is continuously changing rapidly for the better.

Population an unimportant factor in determining wellbeing

I believe that the evidence is now overwhelming that the rate of population growth is a relatively unimportant factor in determining the wellbeing of a nation's people. As I wrote earlier "...population is but one among many factors that determines wellbeing and that it is far from the most important factor. National policies that adversely affect the efficiency with which the human and natural resources of a country are utilized are far, far more important than population growth." (Johnson 1990, pp.29-30). I would not rule out that within reasonable limits (say 1 to 2 per cent annual growth rates), population growth may have a positive influence on per capita income growth. This view is supported by Kremer (1993) who argues that technological change has been a function of population size and thus population growth has not had a deleterious effect on economic growth. He does not, for this reason, argue for pronatalist policies, nor do I. But he does conclude "...that economists should conduct further research to measure the growth and welfare effects of population growth under nonrival technology, rather than simply following conventional wisdom and concentrating on the negative effects of population growth." (p. 713).

Recent evidence from world developments should have created doubts that population growth rates have been a major factor in determining per capita incomes. Evidence points strongly to the importance of policies and institutions and the unimportance of population growth rates. The economic experience of the socialist countries where we have a real world test in the different rates of economic growth in socialist and market economies that were once part of the same countries constitutes one set of evidence. The role of population growth can explain little or nothing of the differences in per capita income growth that occurred in North and South Korea, East and West Germany, Czechoslovakia and Hungary and Austria. Or for that matter, in China, before and after 1979 when major economic reforms were undertaken. It may be noted that population growth rates were lower in the socialist than in the market economies in Europe, but this seemed not to matter. Olsen (1996) has argued persuasively that policies do matter, that most countries have not come close to achieving maximum efficient use of their resources. The recent large body of empirical work on the effects of openness to world markets, political stability, and education on economic growth support that conclusion.[4, 5]

Will we like negative population growth rates?

We are likely to see a real world test of whether negative rates of population growth lead to more rapid growth of real per capita incomes than moderate positive rates. Every country in Western and Central Europe now has fertility rates below the replacement level and will face absolute declines in population over the next decade or two unless fertility increases or immigration is substantially increased (World Bank 1996). Given the

4 The body of such work is now very large and only two representative studies are noted – Levine and Renelt (Levine 1992) and Barro and Sala-i-Martin (Barro 1995).

5 Please not that I do not argue that the rate of population growth has no effect on the rate of per capita economic growth. I do not know for sure what the effects have been or are under all circumstances and conditions. What I believe is that there are many factors that affect people's welfare and that even if population growth has a negative effect on per capita real income growth, it is very small and much less important than many other factors, such as investment in schooling or the extent of governmental intervention in markets. I do say that one cannot and should not derive a negative relationship between population and economic growth rates from neoclassical growth models. True, diminishing returns to labor cannot be avoided, but the relationships between population and economic growth are far more complex than implied by diminishing returns alone or any of the other variables normally included in such models. Factors such as innovation and discovery, total investment including investment in human capital, increasing returns to scale and the rate at which new methods of production are adopted appear to be positively related to population density and numbers. Because population growth can be and probably is to some degree endogenous in its relationship to real per capita incomes, empirical analyses that indicate a positive relationship between the two variables must be interpreted with caution. But the same must be said for the few empirical studies that have found a negative relationship between population and real income growth rates.

changes in age distribution that accompany declining populations, I anticipate that the population problem that will attract the public's attention in these countries is that of too low a rate of fertility rather than one that is too high.

Those who place emphasis on natural resource scarcity and environmental degradation will have difficulty accepting the conclusion that negative population growth can have adverse long run consequences. What needs to be recognized is that many environmental problems people of the world face are ameliorated or solved as real per capita incomes increase. I refer here to the important environmental problems in the developing countries of unclean water and unsafe disposal of human excrement. But other forms of pollution abatement also respond to higher incomes, such as reducing air pollution or the creation of parks and reduction of the rate of deforestation occur once the level of real per capita incomes reach a relatively low level (World Bank 1992, p. 54; Antle 1995).

Recent world food developments

The recent increases in world grain prices following an extended period of slow growth in world grain production has led to some degree of alarm concerning the continued improvement in per capita food supplies in the developing countries. An outlandish argument has been made that China may starve the world due to an actual decline in grain production and rapid increase in grain use over the next three or four decades. Given the proclivity of the world's press to revel in disaster, this argument, if it can be so designated, has received considerable attention. But before turning to my own view of what the future may hold, let us briefly summarize the developments of the past three or so decades.

Table 45.2 presents data on the daily per capita supply of calories for major world regions for 1961-63 to the most recent period for which FAO data are available. For the developing regions as a whole the daily caloric supply increased by 28 per cent in approximately three decades. The average availability is well above the average daily requirements for the developing countries, though this in no way assures every one or even most persons in a given region an adequate diet. This is particularly true in Africa which has seen little increase in calories over the three decades. The improvement in calorie availability for developing regions has been a significant decline in the percentage of the population classified as malnourished. The per cent so classified declined from 36 in 1969-71 to 20 in 1988-90 and is projected to decline to 11 by 2010 (Alexandratos 1995a, p. 33). The absolute number of individuals malnourished fell from 941 million in 1969-71 to 781 million in 1988-90 and is projected to decline to less than 650 million by 2010 (Alexandratos 1995a, p. 33). It is generally recognized that poverty rather than the absence of food has been and will continue to be the primary cause of malnutrition.

The data on the increases in life expectancy and the declines in infant and child mortality in developing countries since 1960 signal a significant improvement in the availability and effective utilization of the food supply. Increased access to clean water and improved sanitation have contributed as much as, or perhaps more, than increased availability of food to the declines in infant and child mortality. But whatever the relative contributions, these changes have benefited millions of the world's poorest people.

Table 45.2: Daily per capita supply of calories for major world regions, 1961-63 and selected years to 1988-90

	1961-63	**1969-71**	**1979-81**	**1988-90**
Developing, all	1940	2117	2324	2473
Africa	2117	2138	2180	2204
Latin America	2363	2502	2693	2690
Near East	1825	2029	2245	2442
Other, ROW	2116	2292	2425	2626
Developed, all				
North America	3054	3235	3330	3603
Europe	3088	3239	3371	3452
Oceania	3173	3287	3157	3328
Former USSR	3146	3323	3368	3380
Other, ROW	2545	2722	2812	2975

Source: FAO, *Production Yearbook*, various issues.

It has been repeatedly called to our attention that world per capita grain production peaked in 1984 and has failed to regain that level. Is this a cause for concern? It is not, however, the case that world per capita food production failed to increase during the 1980s and the 4.6 per cent growth was only slightly below the 5.7 per cent for the prior decade. But in the developing regions, per capita food production increased by 13 per cent in the 1980s, significantly more than the 8 per cent increase for the previous decade. The growth of per capita food output for the developing countries was dominated by the three most populous countries – China, 28 per cent(16); India, 20 per cent (2), and Indonesia, 32 per cent (18).[6]

Per capita grain production in the developing countries did increase during the 1980s – by 9 per cent. The slowdown in world grain production occurred in the industrial countries of Western Europe, North America and in the former socialist countries. During the 1980s the European Union, the United State and Japan followed policies designed to limit the production of grain.

Even if world grain production grew slowly during the 1980s and early 1990s, the supply of grain grew more rapidly than did the world's demand for grain during the period.[7] How do we know? Because international market prices for grain between 1980-82 and 1990-92 fell by about 40 per cent for wheat and maize and almost 50 per cent for rice (Table 45.3). Why should grain production have grown at a significant rate under these conditions? It is something of a miracle that world per capita grain production was approximately maintained. Nor should it have been too much of a surprise that world grain stocks, excluding China, declined. There was, first of all, a concerted effort on the part of the U.S. and EC to reduce governmentally held and subsidized stocks.

And, second, given the declining trend of prices, there seemed little prospect that private stockholding would be profitable. As it turned out, as sometimes is the case, the market may have gone a little too far, but this is uncertain. The real annual

6 The numbers in parenthesis are the per cent increases in per capita food production during the 1970s. Data on per capita food production increases for the most recent decade for which FAO data are available – for 1982-84 to 1992-94 differ little than those given for the decade of the 1980s. The increases in per capita food output for China was 27 per cent, for India 16 per cent and Indonesia, 36 per cent.

7 I refer to supply and demand in terms of the shifts in the functions over time. The decline in real grain prices occurred because the rightward shift of the supply function was greater than the shift in the demand function.

cost of holding stocks is high – close to 20 per cent of the value of the grain – so price would have to double to provide a normal return on holding grain four years.[8]

Prospects: Future supply and demand for food

I believe that the supply of food over the next two to three decades will increase at least as fast as the demand for food and probably somewhat faster, leading to a continuation of the long run decline in real grain prices. The basis for this belief is that there is strong evidence that the rate of growth of demand for food in the three decades from 1990 to 2020 will be significantly less than the growth from 1960 to 1990. The primary reason for the slower demand growth is that population growth rate is now slower than it was for the previous three decades and demographers predict that there will be a further reduction in the growth rate for the period to 2020. The population projection is the medium UN projection and over the past quarter century the UN projections have been remarkably accurate for the world population as of 2000.

Table 45.3 presents a projections of world grain use for 1990-2020 in terms of annual rates of growth, with comparisons to actual developments for 1960-1990; this is the "B" projection. The only difference between the two periods affecting the growth of grain use is the reduction in population growth rates. The annual rate for 1960-1990 was 1.895; the UN medium projection is 1.3. The income elasticity of consumption is assumed to be unchanged in the "B" projection as is the growth rate for per capita income. The resulting projections of grain use indicate a significant decline of a fourth in the annual rate of growth. The worst is over.

8 The data in Table 45.3 make it clear that the recent increases in international grain prices are modest blips on the long term declining real price trends. The real price of wheat for January through June 1996 is lower than any annual price from 1970 through 1985 and the recent maize price is lower than any price save one for the same period. Rice prices have increased relatively little in the last eighteen months – the real price for the first half of this year was less than in 1989 and lower than in 1994. It is difficult to understand why quite minor deviations from the long term trends in real prices have caused so much excitement. What nearly everyone failed to notice was how the low prices of grain have been since the mid-1980s and especially in the first four years of this decade.

The world food supply can more than keep pace with world food demand in the years ahead according to the conclusions of three independent studies presented in early 1994 at a conference at the International Food Policy Research Institute (IFPRI). These were studies done by researchers at FAO, the World Bank and IFPRI. There was a remarkable degree of consistency in the results, which are summarized in a book edited by Islam (1995). The studies indicate a range in the growth rate of grain use for 1990 to 2010 of 1.4 to 1.6 per cent per annum and the midpoint is included in Table 45.3 as projection "A" as applying to 1990 to 2020. In doing so, I assume that the third decade will have the same rate of population growth – it will be lower – and income growth and variables affecting use as the first two. Consequently, the "A" projection is likely to be on the high side. As indicated, most of the increase in consumption will be due to population change.[9]

Table 45.3: Growth rates of key variables and alternative projections of growth of world grain utilizAtion, 1990-2020

	Actual 1960-90	Projected 1990-2020 1979-81	
		A[b]	B[c]
Population (per cent)	1.90	1.30	1.30
Income per capita (per cent)	1.8	n.a.	1.8
Income Elasticity [a]	0.31	n.a.	0.31
Per capita growth of grain use (per cent)	0.56	0.15	0.56
Total growth of grain use (per cent)	2.46	1.55	1.86

Notes: [a] Since price changes were ignored, this is the elasticity of world per capita use of grain for all purposes with respect to world per capita income. Estimates for 1960-90 are trend, rather than annual point to point rates.
[b] Projection A takes the projected average rate of per capita grain use growth from three studies surveyed by Islam (1995).
[c] Projection B adopts the rate of per capita grain use growth observed over 1960-90.
Sources: 1960--1990 for growth rates: World Bank, *World Development Report* 1992, and FAO, *Production Yearbook*, various issues.

9 The annual increase in world per capita grain use in the consensus projection is very small – the range of 0.1 to 0.2 per cent. But this figure is largely irrelevant. What is relevant is the rate of increase in the developing countries. The annual growth is projected to be 0.5 per cent for a total increase of 16 per cent. And I believe that it can be argued that this growth will be demand constrained since real prices are projected to decline much as they have in the past.

Concern has been expressed that further improvements in agricultural output may be subject to greater technical constraints than has been true in the past.

Two comments seem relevant. The first is that the rate of growth of demand for food will be significantly slower over the next three decades than for the past three. Consequently even if it proves somewhat more difficult to increase output in the future than in the past, this does not mean that either real farm prices must increase or that supply will grow more slowly than demand. The second is that so far there is no evidence of a slowdown in the rate of growth of per capita food production in the developing countries. The growth of per capita food production in the developing countries in the 1980s was 13 per cent, significantly higher than the 8 per cent in the previous decade (FAO 1991). Some put great emphasis on the fact world per capita grain production has declined since 1984. People do not live by grain alone and as the diets of people of the developing countries have improved, other foods have been given increased emphasis in diets. In any case, per capita grain production in the developing countries increased by 9 per cent during the 1980s (FAO 1991).

Implications for world trade

World trade in grain showed little growth after 1980, following a doubling during the 1970s. Since 1980 world trade moved in a range of approximately plus or minus 20 million tons from a rough average of 200 million tons. Even when the USSR imported 40 million tons annually in the late 1980s, world grain trade could not break out of a narrow range. I see little prospect for a significant growth in world grain trade during the next decade.[10] Trade will not be supply constrained; it will continue to be constrained by demand growth.

Much attention has been focussed on the possibility of very large grain imports by China. While some outlandish claims have been made that imports night be as much as 200 million to 300 million tons, responsible projections put the level of imports at 40-45 million tons over the next two or three decades (Lin, Huang and Rozelle 1996; Huang, Rozelle and Rosegrant 1995, Koo, Lou and R.G. Johnson 1996).

10 The three studies project increases in world grain trade of from 80 million to more than 100 million tons for 1990-2020 (Islam 1995, pp. 86-87). In the text I consider only the next decade.

Scenarios leading to both higher and lower levels of grain imports have been developed by Lin, Huang and Rozelle, but some of the higher ones require serious policy errors by the Chinese government if the scenarios were to materialize. While such policy errors cannot be ruled out, given recent counterproductive grain market and price policies, large grain imports would be likely to finally convince policy makers that it was at long last necessary to do something to increase agricultural productivity rather than just talk about doing something, as has been recent behavior. Agricultural research has been an important factor in the success of Chinese agriculture over the past 15 years; if the government neglects it as it did during much of the 1980s, grain imports could increase significantly. But there is evidence that the benefits of agricultural research are being recognized and there have been modest increases in funding in recent years.

An increase in China's annual grain imports to 40 or 50 million tons could be readily supplied, even at real prices as low as or lower than those of the early 1990s. In fact, there is a possibility that so far as the traditional grain exporters are concerned, they will see rather little expansion in demand for their exports. This will be the case if grain production in the territory of the former USSR returns to the amount of grain *in the fields* to the level of the late 1980s when the grain harvest ranged from 180 million to 200 million tons (clean basis).[11] Reductions of waste in harvesting, transportation, and marketing and in seed use combined with increased yields of forage crops (hay, silage and feed roots) and improved efficiency in feed conversion into meat and milk could increase the available supply of grain by at least 55 million tons (Johnson 1993, pp. 27-28).

Of nearly equal importance is the reduction in the internal demand for grain due to the decline in livestock output. In the USSR the production of meat and milk were heavily subsidized by large consumer subsidies – in the late

11 While returning to the same level of grain production as occurred in the late 1980s may seem to be an objective that can be easily reached. It needs to be noted that under the socialist system grain may have been produced where it will not be profitable to do so in a market system. For example, the geographic pattern of grain prices deviated significantly from those in a market system – the prices did not reflect differential costs of transportation and market but were influenced by costs of production. This meant, for example, that the prices of grain in Kazakhstan were higher than in the Ukraine. It is probable that once the grain market is a competitive one, the grain sown area will decline and some yield increases will be required to achieve the same level of grain output as in the late 1980s.

1980s such subsidies equalled 10 per cent of GNP.[12] The production of meat has already declined sharply – by more than 40 per cent – and the adjustment is not yet complete, especially for beef (ERS 1996, p. 20). The former USSR has sharply reduced its grain imports and perhaps as early as this year, the area will become a net exporter of grain if crops continue to develop well. As real incomes recover, there will be some recovery in meat and milk demand, but it is probably optimistic to assume that total meat consumption will recover to much more than two thirds of its level of approximately 20 million tons in the late 1980s. I have estimated that system change would increase grain availability by 55 million tons and the reduction in feed use due to decreased livestock consumption would amount to 35 million tons (Johnson 1993). If these are realistic estimates, then the territory of the former USSR would shift from being a net importer of nearly 40 million tons of grain in the late 1980s to a net exporter of 40 million to 50 million tons, perhaps soon after the turn of the century.[13] The productivity gains from system change have so far been less than I have assumed but the decline in consumption of livestock products has been significantly greater. Consequently, grain imports have nearly disappeared sooner than most observers expected. The significant grain exports may also emerge sooner than expected. I can think of nothing else that could contribute more to the development of a profitable agriculture in the former USSR than the emergence of substantial grain exports in the early years of the next century.

Consequently in viewing the future of international trade in grain and food, it is clearly inappropriate to concentrate our attention on China to the exclusion of another area that has a great potential for influencing international

12 In the USSR retail prices of meat and milk products in the late 1980s and early 1990s covered less than half the cost of bringing these products to the retail store. Consequently, when the subsidies were removed, there was a sharp decline in the profitability of livestock production and output fell sharply. Consumer subsidies also existed in the socialist economies of Central Europe, though generally at not quite as high rates as in the USSR. Livestock production has also fallen in the Central European economies with an effect on their grain utilization.
The future consumption for livestock and poultry products will be significantly less than it was in the 1980s, with a decline of a third as a possibility once livestock production returns to profitability and consumers must bear the real costs of what they consume.

13 If this were not enough bad news for the traditional grain exporters, there is a reasonable prospect that the former socialist countries of Central Europe will have significant grain exports within the decade. A recent study (ERS 1996) projects that these countries will export almost 12 million tons by 2005 (p. 13). This is a shift from a net import position of several million tons in the late 1980s.

trade. Major changes affecting grain trade are underway in Central and Eastern Europe and these changes are large relative to what I consider to be reasonable projections of China's grain imports.[14]

Concluding comments

My message is a simple one – there is little prospect that the factors affecting world food supply and demand can either stop the decline in real market prices for grain or result in more than a modest increase in world grain trade. While China may emerge as a significant importer of grain, it is at least as likely that Central and Eastern Europe will emerge as a major grain exporter and become an important competitor for the traditional exporters. While the probable future path of real world grain prices represents good news for urban consumers, farmers in the developing countries will be under continuous pressure to adjust to the declining prices.

14 This paper has not reflected any of the difficulties of projecting future supply and demand for grain due to known and possible inaccuracies in China's agricultural data. The cultivated area and yield data used in all of the projections have been based on data currently published by the government even though it is now admitted that instead of the cultivated area being about 95 million hectares it is about 125 million hectares. If one accepts the official grain output estimates, this means that grain yields have been overestimated by about 30 per cent leaving a larger margin for further increases in yield than has been assumed to be likely. On the other hand, there is some reason to believe that grain output has been underestimated in recent years, perhaps by as much as 10 per cent (Johnson 1994; OECD 1996, p.163). My conclusion that grain output may have been underestimated is based on the results of the rural household surveys. To add further uncertainty, the data on meat production and on meat consumption differ by as much as 50 per cent. If one accepts the meat production data, per capita consumption was more than 35 kilograms in 1994 while the per capita consumption data indicate an average of no more than 17 kilograms though this estimate may include only meat consumed in the home (SSB 1995).

References

Alexandrotos, Nikos (1995), "The Outlook for World Food and Agriculture to the Year 2010," in Islam (1995), pp. 25-48.

Antle, John and Gregg Heidebrink (Antle 1995), "Environment and Economic Development: Theory and International Evidence," *Economic Development and Cultural Change*, Vol. 43, No. 3, pp. 603-25.

Barro, Robert J. and Xavier X. Sala-i-Martin (Barro 1995), *Economic Growth*. New York: McGraw-Hill, Inc.

Bogue, Donald (1969), *Principles of Demography*. New York: John Wiley and Son.

Chandler, Tertius (1987), *Four Thousand Years of Urban Growth*. Lewiston, New York: The Edwin Mellen Press.

Economic Research Service, U.S. Department of Agriculture (ERS 1996), *Former USSR: Situation and Outlook Series*. International Agriculture and Trade Reports. WRS-96-1.

Fogel, Robert (1992), "Egalitarianism: The Economic Revolution of the Twentieth Century," the 1992 Simon Kuznets Memorial Lectures, Yale University, April 22-24. 1992.

Food and Agricultural Organization (FAO), *Production Yearbook*, various annual volumes. Rome: FAO.

Huang, Jikun, Scott Rozelle and Mark W. Rosegrant (Huang 1995), "China's Food Economy to the 21st Century: Supply, Demand and Trade," IFPRI's 2020 Vision Paper. Washington, D.C.: International Food Policy Research Institute.

Islam, Nurul, editor (1995), *Population and Food in the Early Twenty-First Century: Meeting Future Food Demand of an Increasing Population*. Washington, D.C.: International Food Policy Research Institute.

Johnson, D. Gale (1990), "Population, Food and Wellbeing," Office of Agricultural Economics Research, The University of Chicago, Paper No. 90.13, July. Revised version published as "Can There Be Too Much Human Capital? Is There a World Population Problem?" in Sisay Asefa and Wei-Chiao Huang, editors, *Human Capital and Economic Development*. Kalamazoo, Michigan: W. E. Upjohn Institute for Employment Research, 1994.

Johnson, D. Gale (1993), "Trade Effects of Dismantling the Socialized Agriculture of the Former Soviet Union," *Comparative Economic Studies*, Vol. 36, No. 4.

Johnson, D. Gale (1994), "Does China Have a Grain Problem?". *China Economic Review*. Vol. 5, pp. 1-14.

Koo, Won W., Jianqiang Low and Roger G. Johnson (Koo 1996), "Increases in Demand for Food in China and Implications for World Agricultural Trade," Agricultural Economics Report No. 351,North Dakota State University.

Kremer, Michael (1993), "Population Growth and Technological Change: One Million B.C. to 1990," *Quarterly Journal of Economics*, August.

Levine, Ross and David Renelt (1992), "A Sensitivity Analysis of Cross-Country Growth Regressions." *American Economic Review*, Vol. 82, No 4, pp. 942-963.

Lin, Justin, Jikun Huang and Scott Roselle (1996), "China's Food Economy: Past Performance and Future's Projection." China Center for Economic Research, Peking University, Working Paper Series, No. 1996001.

Malthus, Thomas R. (1992), *An Essay on the Principle of Population: or A View of its past and present Effects on Human Happiness: With an Inquiry into our Prospects representing the future Removal or Mitigation of the Evils which it Occasions*. Cambridge: Cambridge University Press.

Maddison, Angus (1995), *Monitoring the World Economy 1820-1992*. Paris: OECD.

Organisation for Economic Co-operation and Development (OECD 1996), *Agricultural Policies, Markets and Trade in Transition Economies: Monitoring and Evaluation 1996*. Paris: OECD.

State Statistical Bureau of China (SSB 1995), *China Statistical Yearbook 1995*. Beijing: China Statistical Publishing House.

World Bank (World Bank 1992), *World Development Report 1992: Development and the Environment*. New York: Oxford University Press.

World Bank (World Bank 1996), *World Development Report 1996: From Plan to Market*. New York: Oxford University Press.

46

Strengthening intellectual property rights in Asia: Implications for Australia

Keith E. Maskus[1]

In 1900, Korekiyo Takahashi, the first president of the Japanese Patent Office, announced during a visit to the U.S. Patent Office:

> "We have looked about us to see what nations are the greatest, so that we can be like them. We said, 'What is it that makes the United States such a great nation?' and found that it was patents and so we will have patents."[2]

Indeed, Japan adopted a comprehensive patent system, though it was distinctive from the American and major European systems. Loosely stated, it was designed to promote industrial development through emphasising technology acquisition from abroad, domestic diffusion, and incremental invention, as befits a technology follower. On behalf of perceived economic and social interests, it placed serious limits on patent scope and coverage, including a refusal to provide patents for pharmaceutical products until the 1970s. How important the system was in Japan's becoming a "great nation" is a matter for continuing debate, but in my view it played a positive role. As Japan matured into an industrial power and technological leader, features of its patent regime became the subject of increasing complaints by both foreign and domestic firms, prompting its re-examination.

This example illustrates several cross-currents characterising intellectual property rights (IPRs), the catch-all phrase encompassing provision and enforcement of patents, trademarks, copyrights, legal protection of trade secrets, and many related devices. First, IPRs can markedly assist a nation's efforts to

1 Forty-sixth Joseph Fisher Lecture, 17 November 1997. Reprinted in *Australian Economic Papers*, 37(3): 346-361, September 1998.

2 Quoted in Heath (1997, p. 305).

encourage its own technological, industrial, and cultural development and a failure to provide some protection can be costly for inventive domestic firms. Second, the terms on which a country may wish to protect IPRs depend on its position on the global technology ladder and on social concerns, among other things. The demand for protection rises with the level of economic development and the character of technology, making IPRs dynamic in nature.

Third, Japan adopted its patent system at the end of the last century, during an era of considerable change in global IPRs. The two international treaties that codified the classical conceptions of intellectual property rights – the Paris Convention (1883) covering industrial property (1883) and the Berne Convention (1886) covering copyrights – were negotiated, in part because of frustration over alleged infringements in the "newly industrialising countries" of the day, such as the United States and Japan.[3] Thus, that period provided an interesting parallel to the recent outpouring of attention lavished on this most arcane of policy areas.

Still, no period in history compares with the last 15 years for the evolution of global IPRs. Recall that in 1982 the United States was alone in calling for developing GATT disciplines against trade in counterfeit products, an idea that was viewed as an irritation by most countries. In contrast, many of the developing countries were engaged in a long-running attempt to revise the Paris Convention to tilt the global balance further in the direction of uncompensated international dissemination of new technologies. This effort resonated with the import-substitution commercial policies of the day.

The United States (joined shortly thereafter by the European Union and Japan) won this battle, sweeping the field before it. By 1986 a commitment was reached at Punta del Este to include trade-related IPRs on the agenda of the new Uruguay Round negotiations. This was simply the beginning of a tidal wave of lawyers and negotiators working feverishly to promote exports of intellectual property. Economists largely have sat and watched this happen, sometimes cheering it on and sometimes raising fundamental concerns about it, albeit rather feebly.

3 In fact, the United States did not join the Berne Convention until a century later because its manufacturing requirements for publishers were inconsistent with the convention.

How successful has this wave been? Since 1987, we have witnessed sharply increasing levels of legal protection for intellectual property, surely among the most significant changes in recent international commercial policies. In that period, over 40 developing countries have unilaterally undertaken significant strengthening of these rights, both because of external pressure from the United States and the EU to do so, and because of changes in their own perceived domestic economic interests. Regional trade agreements now routinely include provisions for protection of intellectual property rights, with distinctive approaches adopted that may have implications for regional trade and investment flows, an issue that is completely unstudied in the literature (Maskus, 1997a).

The culminating achievement is the adoption of the Agreement on Trade-Related Intellectual Property Rights (TRIPs), a founding component and pillar of the World Trade Organisation (WTO). This agreement requires minimum standards for IPRs that are, in many instances, far stronger than current norms in developing countries. Countries that join the WTO in the future must adhere to these standards. Therefore, as the agreement is implemented over the next several years the global system will move toward a considerable degree of IPRs harmonisation and higher levels of protection.

For their part, developing Asian economies, among the main targets of the tidal wave, have been at the center of intense efforts to upgrade protection for intellectual property. The most visible complaints still are directed at the copying of foreign compact disks, movies, books, and computer software and at the passing off of counterfeit consumer goods under unauthorised use of trademarks. Such activities, colourfully and pejoratively referred to as piracy, continue largely unabated in China, Thailand, the Philippines, and elsewhere, though significant enforcement activities have cleaned up much of the problem in Hong Kong, Korea, Taiwan, and Singapore. More subtle complaints arise over limits on protection for potentially patentable technologies, including medicines, seed varieties, and biotechnological inventions. In addition to external pressures for change, it became successively clearer in rapidly growing Asian economies that their own innovative firms were disadvantaged by weak IPRs.

In consequence, major legislative changes were introduced over the last decade in Korea, Singapore, Hong Kong, Taiwan, Thailand, Indonesia, Malaysia, and China (see Table 46. 1), among other countries.[4] Even Vietnam recently passed a law extending copyrights to software, though its requirement that software be produced locally has attracted criticism and must be relaxed before the country can join the WTO (Heath, 1997). Further, ASEAN members signed the Framework Agreement on Intellectual Property Cooperation in December 1995, which aims to enhance cooperation in reducing piracy in the area and to create ASEAN standards and practices that are consistent with international norms. Moreover, APEC documents exhort regional economies to enhance their IPRs systems, a fact that at a minimum will complement the implementation of TRIPs requirements. Taken together, these new laws and institutions represent a marked strengthening of the region's structure of IPRs, though aspects of several national systems still come short of TRIPs standards. The effective strength of regional IPRs will intensify as enforcement efforts are expanded and regularised and as further legislation is enacted in accordance with the requirements of TRIPs.

While the conclusion of TRIPs and the adoption of new laws in Asia may have dissipated some of its energy, the wave rolls on. Countries are currently choosing mechanisms by which they will protect geographical indications for wines and spirits, an area that before now has been neglected outside Europe but is clearly significant for Australia. Many developed economies continue to adopt ever-stronger standards of protection for biotechnological inventions, computer programs, electronic databases, and other new technologies. Moreover, the United States is pushing for stronger international protection by asking foreign governments to adopt new approaches that are questionable under standard IPRs. One example is the current request that Australia extend its pharmaceutical patents to eliminate "springboarding," or testing by rival firms of generic drugs during a patent period in anticipation of the lapsing of protection. And the TRIPs accord itself is subject to further revision in the year 2000.

4 The Philippine Congress has not yet enacted proposed new copyright and trademark legislation.

Table 46.1: Selected recent IPRs legislative changes in developing East Asia

P.R. China	Joined Madrid Agreement on Trademarks, 1989 Enacted Copyright Law, June 1991 Joined Universal Copyright Convention and Berne Convention, 1992 Enacted Unfair Competition Law, December 1993 Joined Patent Cooperation Treaty, 1994 US-China Bilateral IPRs Enforcement Agreement, March 1995 Joined Madrid Protocol on Trademarks, 1996
Hong Kong	Enacted Copyright Bill, June 1997 Enacted Patent Bill, June 1997
Indonesia	Adopted amendments to Copyright Law, 1987 Implemented Trademark Law, 1993 Action Plan to combat copyright piracy, 1996 Enacted TRIPs-consistent Patent, Trademark, and Copyright Laws, 1997
Rep. of Korea	Enacted Korea Patent Act of 1995 Enacted new copyright, software, and customs laws in 1996 Trademark Law of 1996 is under review
Malaysia	Enacted Copyright Act of 1987 Joined Paris Convention, January 1989 Amended Patents Act of 1983 to remove bar against software patents, 1997
Singapore	Enacted Copyright Act of 1987 Enacted Trademarks Act of 1991 Enacted Patents Act of 1994
Taiwan	Enacted Copyright Law of 1992 Adopted amendments to Trademark Law, December 1993 Enacted New Patent Law, 1994 Enacted Integrated Circuits Protection Law, 1995 Agreed with US to 18-Point Action Plan on enforcement, 1996
Thailand	Enacted Trademark Act of 1992 Recognised drugs and agricultural chemicals as patentable, 1992 Enacted revisions to Copyright Law, 1994

To stretch my analogy, tidal waves can have two opposing effects. On the one hand, they can raise many boats to higher levels of activity. These recent policy changes constitute a major achievement for technology and entertainment developers, the vast majority of which reside in a small number of developed countries. Those firms will be significant winners from the system. Advocates of the new rules point to potential gains in innovation, product development, and technology transfer as firms have to worry less about losing their informational advantages to free-riding copiers and imitators in different nations. Further, countries with strong emerging innovative capacities could gain from the new system, particularly if they manage it appropriately.

On the other hand, waves can leave considerable destruction. Strong concerns arise in technologically lagging nations about the potential for tighter IPRs to encourage firms to act more monopolistically and to limit international access to their inventions and creations. Firms and consumers in the poorest countries could be made worse off unless they benefit from the more open trading regime that the WTO represents generally.

Between these extremes lies a continuum of national and industry interests that must accommodate themselves to the new global reality. Within East Asia, the high-income service-oriented and industrialising economies of Hong Kong, Singapore, Republic of Korea, and Taiwan already have strong domestic interests in IPRs. China, Malaysia, Thailand, Indonesia, and the Philippines also are experiencing rising preferences for IPRs, though the benefits for them will be longer in coming and there will be transitional costs.

For its part, Australia may be characterised roughly as a net importer of technology through trade in high-technology goods, FDI, and licensing, though it also has strong and growing interests on the export side. Table 46.2 provides some basic indicators. In all of the four categories of IP-intensive manufactures, imports continue to exceed exports. However, exports have grown at significantly faster rates than imports, suggesting a shift in comparative advantage toward Australian production. This is especially true in beverages (including wines), pharmaceutical products, and professional and scientific instruments. Both imports and exports of these goods have risen faster than aggregate merchandise trade, indicating their growing relative importance in Australia's trade structure. More generally, Australia's growing export strength in high-technology products and services, including elaborately transformed manufactures, computer software, and pharmaceuticals, has attracted considerable attention.[5] Much of this rising trade is with East Asia. Over the period 1990-1996, the highest growth rates of Australian exports were to China, Korea, Hong Kong, New Zealand, and Taiwan, while exports to ASEAN as a group doubled.[6]

5 See Australian Financial Review (May 17, 1995).

6 *Source:* Australian Bureau of Statistics.

Table 46.2: Basic indicators of Australia's trade in intellectual property

Panel A. Trade in selected IP-intensive goods (A$ million and growth rates)

	1990		1996	
	Imports	**Exports**	**Imports**	**Exports**
Beverages	300	266	341(14)	676(154)
Pharmaceutical products	901	293	1933(115)	942(222)
Electrical machinery	7851	1339	14696(87)	3784(183)
Professional and scientific instruments	1941	473	3126(61)	1174(148)
Total merchandise	48705	46169	77608(59)	70008(52)

Panel B. Technology balance of payments ($A million)

	1986			1992	
Payments	**Receipts**	**R/P**	**Payments**	**Receipts**	**R/P**
281	102	0.36	479	276	0.58

Panel C. Royalties and license fees ($A million)

	1990			1995	
Debits	**Credits**	**D/C**	**Debits**	**Credits**	**D/C**
1070	210	5.1	1362	322	4.2

Note: Nominal growth rates in parentheses.
Sources: Australian Bureau of Statistics, OECD Basic Science and Technology Indicators, IMF Balance of Payments Statistics

The data in Panels B and C demonstrate that, while Australia continues to be a substantial net importer of technology, as measured in its technology balance of payments and its net royalties and license fees, receipts (credits) are rising faster than payments (debits). Indeed, the increase in the ratio of receipts to payments in Panel B continues a long-run trend; this ratio was 0.10 in 1981.

Australia already has a strong IPRs regime, which has contributed positively to its technology development. Its status as a growing exporter of intellectual-property intensive products and technologies means that it also has important interests in the emerging system of protection in Asian developing economies. However, these policy changes present Australia with both problems and opportunities. Australia has a small but sophisticated and outward-looking high-technology sector, and a successful record of product and trademark development. These are significant advantages that should be enhanced by regional IPRs. It is also open to foreign direct investment and technology imports, both of which might become relatively scarcer as regional economies converge on Australia's already-strong IPRs.

The challenge for Australia is to maintain the attractiveness of its market to foreign investors while ensuring that there is sufficient coherence between IPRs and broader regulatory systems to maintain open and dynamic competition in the economy. Indeed, Australia could be in the vanguard of nations that maintain a pro-competitive counterweight to emerging over-protection of intellectual property in the United States and Europe. In this regard, it is positioned to be a leader in subsequent multilateral negotiations over IPRs.

The evolving international system

There are no universally applicable guidelines about IPRs from economic theory. Intellectual property rights operate in inherently second-best markets and are crude attempts to address the potential market failures arising from the conflict between finding adequate incentives to innovate and ensuring effective knowledge diffusion. Depending on one's point of view, various aspects of the system may provide inadequate protection or excessively strong protection.

Thus, it is no surprise that policies on IPRs, which, with few exceptions, are taken at the national level, vary greatly over time within each country and across countries (David, 1993). For example, Japan and Italy only began offering pharmaceutical product patents in the 1970s. Canada eliminated its compulsory licensing procedures in medicines in 1993 and retains the right to review and control patented drug prices (Torrens, 1996). Significant differences persist between the United States and the European Union over geographic indications, biotechnology patents, fair-use exceptions in copyrights and patents, parallel imports, and misappropriation of trademarks, among other issues. Moreover, there are substantive and controversial differences of opinion within countries about the optimal scope and even wisdom of some forms of rights.

The essential dynamic behind changes in IPRs is that they rise with levels of economic development (Rapp and Rozek, 1992; Sherwood, 1997). As a stylised fact, as poor countries begin to develop significant capacities to imitate foreign technologies and to copy artistic products, their IPRs actually become effectively weaker as they find it more advantageous to free ride in the "technology draught" (Maskus and Penubarti, 1995; Evenson, 1992). Only as countries develop innovative capabilities and a capacity to purchase and use new technologies effectively under license do economic interests emerge in favour of strong rights to deter local imitation. Put loosely, technology developers and exporters prefer stronger and more harmonised IPRs, while technology users and importers prefer weaker and more variable IPRs.

Thus, the stronger system of rights embodied in TRIPs and in Asian legislative changes reflects a recent and dramatic shift upward in the demand for globally consistent IPRs and a perhaps grudging willingness of developing nations to supply them. This shift may be traced to three fundamental changes. First, a system of highly variable national rights became increasingly incompatible with expanding integration of markets through the reduction of government and natural barriers to trade, investment, and technology flows. In this globalising economy, the creation of knowledge and its adaptation to product designs and production techniques are increasingly essential for commercial competitiveness and economic growth. As has been amply demonstrated, since the early 1980s international trade in intellectual-property-intensive goods has risen faster than trade in other goods (Maskus, 1993) and FDI in high-technology sectors has risen at roughly twice the rate of merchandise trade (Markusen, 1995). International technology licensing has also risen rapidly (Mansfield, 1995).

In this environment, firms wish to exploit their technical and product advantages on an international scale. This is made easier with strong international standards on IPRs, which markedly expand the strategic options for firms, allowing them less-constrained choices among inter-firm and intra-firm trade, FDI, setting licensing conditions, and pricing to segmented markets. For their part, the process of globalisation has convinced governments in many developing countries that access to investment resources and technology are critical for growth and that stronger IPRs can play an important role in attracting them. Considerable anecdotal evidence suggests that limited IPRs frustrate domestic entrepreneurs seeking to conclude licensing deals and joint ventures with international firms (Mansfield, 1994; Sherwood, 1993).

A second factor is that technologies for copying software, entertainment products, books, transmissions, and certain technologies have become cheaper and more reliable, expanding opportunities for international free riding. This fact has markedly raised the profile of copyright and patent protection on the international policy agenda as innovative firms perceive substantial losses in export markets from unauthorised copying.

Finally, the area of intellectual-property law itself remains in considerable flux because of the advent of new technologies that do not lend themselves easily to protection by standard industrial-property or artistic-property devices (Barton, 1993; Reichman, 1994). For one example, computer programs are widely protected as literary text, yet many of them have industrial utility, novelty, and non-obviousness, suggesting that patent protection is warranted. In general, patent protection is considerably stronger than copyrights, because the former does not admit fair-use reverse engineering for purposes of employing the idea in related programs. Related legal ambiguities relate to computer chip topographies and to electronic databases available over integrated networks.

For another, the proper scope of patents for biotechnological inventions is widely debated on legal grounds, even ignoring the ethical issues it raises. Biotechnological research is expensive but the therapeutical and genetic results it achieves are easily copied. Thus, patents are considered crucial for the development of the industry. However, some question the applicability of standard patents in that products stemming from recombinant DNA techniques may be more the result of luck and patience than of originality. Thus, it is not clear whether particular products are "inventions" (and therefore patentable) or "discoveries of nature" (and therefore not patentable in the classical approach). National systems of protection for micro-organisms reflect several approaches to this question. At one extreme, many developing economies provide no protection at all. At the other, the United States Patent and Trademark Office recently has moved decisively toward providing broad patents covering all potential products from genetic engineering of a particular plant or a critical research tool such as a genetic sequence developed for one drug but that could be required in developing numerous pharmaceutical products, all of which would be subject to the initial patent (Barton, 1995).[7]

The largest differences in intellectual property protection occur between developed and developing economies. From the standpoint of the industrialised (and, increasingly, the industrialising) countries, there are several primary shortcomings in the regimes of many developing countries. Inadequate copyright and trademark protection promotes extensive copying of entertainment and software products and misappropriation of well-known trademarks. Pharmaceutical products and agro-chemicals are widely excluded from patent protection. Neither is there patent protection for biotechnological inventions or patents or *sui generis* rights for plant varieties. Compulsory licenses are issued with inadequate compensation to firms that are seen to be exercising their rights insufficiently to achieve desired technology transfer or consumer benefits. Rules protecting trade secrets are weak or absent and procedures for administrative and judicial enforcement of IPRs are deficient.

The most significant response to these problems is the TRIPs Agreement, which introduces the concept of MFN treatment into IPRs (Primo Braga, 1996; Maskus, 1997a). While TRIPs mandates dozens of significant changes in legal and institutional norms and practices, it is worth mentioning major requirements that fundamentally alter the IPRs landscape. The standards discussed are minimum requirements in all WTO members but nothing precludes countries from adopting stronger practices.

Computer programs and databases must be protected with copyright protection for at least 50 years. In most countries this obligation means that literal copying must be ended, while the scope for fair-use decompilation and reverse engineering may be determined in each member.

7 See U.S. Patent 5,159,135, 7 December 1994, Agracetus cotton patent covering genetic engineering of cotton plants and lines; and U.S. Patent 5,328,987, 12 July 1994, Maliszewski (Immunex) IgA FC receptors.

Countries must protect well-known trademarks and rights must be extended to service marks and collective marks. Compulsory licenses of trademarks are prohibited.

WTO members must protect geographical indications of origin and prevent producers from misleading the public about the geographic origin of goods.

Integrated circuits designs must be protected for a minimum of ten years. Rights owners have the right to prevent imports and sales of products that incorporate the unauthorised devices, even if the merchants are unaware of the infringement.

WTO members no longer may exclude any area of technology, such as pharmaceutical products, from patent eligibility and the burden of proof in process infringement cases is placed on the accused. Patent protection must extend for at least 20 years from the application filing date. Patent holders cannot be obliged to work their patents with local production (imports are sufficient). Compulsory licenses are subject to severe limitations and must bear adequate compensation.

Countries must protect new plant varieties, either within their patent systems or with a separate system of breeders' rights.

Countries must develop a system for protecting trade secrets from unfair competition, according to specified minimum standards.

WTO members must develop effective enforcement measures, including border controls, to prevent international and domestic transactions in counterfeit goods and unfair competition. Such measures must include the potential for paying damages to rights-holders and for criminal sanctions against wilful counterfeiting and copying.

The agreement recognises the potential for abusive practices in the exercise of IPRs and gives countries wide latitude to control such abuses. The competition rules used for this purpose must be consistent with other provisions of TRIPs and the agreement also calls for opportunities for consultation in this area.

Developed countries were given one year to introduce TRIPs-consistent laws.[8] Developing countries and countries in transition must meet the detailed obligations by January 1, 2000 and least-developed countries must meet them by January 1, 2006. Countries may choose to accelerate their implementation of TRIPs and, indeed, many Asian members have done so.

Disputes in the treatment of intellectual property will be subject to the integrated dispute settlement mechanism agreed in the WTO. However, there is a five-year moratorium on the use of dispute settlement against indirect violations of TRIPs, allowing nations to select implementation strategies without interference.

Regarding this last point, one of the primary benefits of TRIPs is that it will move conflicts over IPRs into an established multilateral forum for settling disputes. These conflicts likely will become frequent given the high administrative expenses of IPRs and institutional resistance to strong enforcement that will emerge in many developing countries.

Policy guidelines for East Asia

A curious aspect of the debate over IPRs is that while economists devote nearly all their attention to issues of innovation, technology diffusion, and growth, the international policy arena has been driven largely by questions of trademark and copyright pirating. The latter area generates the most visible damages to firms operating in Asia and is the proximate source of political pressures on trade negotiators.

Thus, in the short to medium-term, the primary task for East Asian developing economies and newly industrialising economies is to devote more resources to administration and enforcement efforts. This will require some time because of the significant costs of training intellectual property officials, judges, and customs authorities and because effective enforcement will encounter considerable opposition from interested parties. For example, a common complaint about China is that, despite its modernised national IPRs laws, infringement

8 Australia did so at the end of 1994.

takes place at regional levels, often with the acquiescence of local governments (Oksenberg, Potter, and Abnett, 1996). As one observer puts it, "While the legal instruments may all be in place, rampant pirating has highlighted the dire state of enforcement. Lack of enforcement is one reason why China has not yet been admitted to the WTO."[9]

It is fair to expect that over time levels of piracy will subside considerably in major East Asian developing countries. While this change would require absorbing some adjustment costs, open, dynamic economies could experience several benefits from the effort. Consider two examples. First, tentative evidence indicates that many firms engaged in piracy are capable of profitable production under license and also of developing incremental innovative gains themselves. For example, generation of indigenous trademarks for culturally distinctive apparel and processed foods is an elastic process in developing countries and there are considerable consumer gains from the quality guarantees inherent in trademarks (Maskus, 1997b). Development of applications software for local markets is also frequently a rapid and dynamic response. There is scope for benefiting from the designation of local geographic appellations, though building international markets for such products is expensive.

Second, econometric evidence suggests strongly that countries with effective IPRs and enforcement attract significantly greater amounts of international trade (Maskus and Penubarti, 1995). The essential reason for this is that as pirating activities are reduced the market for legitimate products expands, more than offsetting any tendency toward higher monopoly prices. Such monopolisation is rare in open markets in any event. Thus, there are allocative efficiencies from limiting the trade-distorting impacts of weak IPRs. Note that because of both its geographical proximity to the region and its natural complementarities in comparative advantage, Australia will earn a considerable share of the rising trade that results.

While markedly reducing counterfeiting will go a long way toward satisfying rights-holders in the developed countries, the important long-term issues relate to how stronger IPRs might affect technical innovation, international diffusion,

---

9 Heath (1997), p. 306.

and growth in the region. Economic theory is surprisingly uninformative on this question because of its limited conception of what IPRs are and how they operate internationally. For example, if the sole effect of stronger patents is to raise imitation costs, then as Asian nations strengthen their patent systems they would suffer from lower technology transfer and growth (Helpman, 1993). However, if we recognise that well-established patent rights can raise the certainty and lower the costs of licensing, the opposite conclusion is supported (Yang and Maskus, 1997). Survey evidence indicates that both the amount and the quality of technologies transferred depend positively on the strength of local intellectual property rights (Mansfield, 1994). Finally, weak IPRs can discourage local firms from engaging in innovative activity, a factor that takes on increasing salience as countries develop.

What seems clear is that for countries to maximise any net gains from stronger IPRs they must devise appropriate systems that interact coherently with other policies. Given the need to implement new laws under TRIPs, the time is ripe for Asian countries to establish norms that promote effective, dynamic competition on their markets and in the region, which is of direct relevance for Australia. For this purpose, simply following highly protective American and European IPRs standards is neither necessary nor desirable. Indeed, I share the view of many scholars that the emerging structure of Asian practices could serve as an effective counterweight to the excessive standards evolving in the major industrial countries, which involve ever more extensive forms of protection and relaxed treatment of horizontal collaboration in applied research.[10]

If they consider the issue carefully, Asian developing economies may be expected to implement IPRs that meet the TRIPs requirements but maintain a balance in favour of diffusion and incremental innovation. It is important to recognise that a critical source of technical change and growth is competition among followers seeking to improve inventions and to develop specialised applications without infringing the original terms of protection (Scotchmer, 1991). Clearly, such possibilities are determined by both the scope of protection and broader competitive factors.

10 Reichman (1996) effectively develops this argument.

Regarding scope of protection, it is not widely recognised that there is considerable room within the mandates set out by TRIPs to promote such competition and to achieve other goals (UNCTAD, 1996). Because this is another complicated area, I only highlight key points. Countries may wish to establish or extend protection for small inventions through utility models. Countries are free to set liberal policies on exemptions to exclusive rights in patents and software copyrights in order to promote reverse engineering aimed at developing non-infringing inventions. Fair-use exemptions in copyright for purposes of scientific research and education may also be pursued.

Managing the TRIPs obligations to provide patents in biogenetic engineering and rights in plant varieties is critically important in countries with substantial agricultural sectors and plant resources. This is a delicate issue because it requires striking a balance between needs of users of improvements in agricultural technologies and opportunities for developing local research opportunities. In biotechnology, countries may wish to establish strict standards for disclosure in patenting and set a higher bar in identifying novelty and an inventive step than the weak one that has emerged in the United States. In protecting plant varieties, governments could take full advantage of exemptions for farmers' privilege and for research needs, as spelled out in the International Union for the Protection of New Varieties of Plants (UPOV). More broadly, recent experience in Latin America suggests that establishing plant breeders' rights can generate considerable local research activity (including in public research institutes) and improve access to foreign germplasm supplies, without markedly raising seed costs to farmers (UNCTAD, 1996). How effectively such benefits could be transferred to poor countries with limited research capabilities remains to be seen. Finally, new legislation covering plant varieties may be devised to help conserve biodiversity and share rents from exploitation of products developed from native species.

Another critical issue relates to impacts of patent protection on pharmaceutical output and prices. These anticipated effects depend strongly on competitive aspects of the industry and may be relatively small (Maskus and Konan, 1994). Moreover, patents will be phased in over a lengthy period, moderating such effects. Nevertheless, in countries with uncompetitive markets that have developed local pharmaceutical sectors behind the absence of patents, such as India, Thailand, and China, new protection will destroy companies that do not arrange licenses with major international pharmaceutical firms and could also increase drug prices. The TRIPs agreement does not prevent the use of public monitoring and control of prices in the pursuit of public-health goals. Governments that take recourse to such controls must weigh their advantages against costs of deterring technology transfer and local production, however.

Perhaps the most significant issue in establishing new IPRs regimes is the need to develop complementary and appropriate competition rules for deterring abuse of property rights. Like IPRs, interests in competition policies varies across countries for many reasons and their harmonisation into a global anti-trust code is unlikely.[11] Nonetheless, each country needs to consider its policies in three key areas relevant to the exercise of IPRs. First, because patents, copyrights, and trademarks provide protected market positions, it makes little sense to reinforce that market power by sustaining limits on competition at the distribution level. Thus, exclusive representation and licensing laws may need reform and countries must take a decision on whether to allow parallel imports under the doctrine of international exhaustion. Second, countries need to develop anti-monopoly guidelines for the terms of licensing contracts, particularly as these terms conspire to limit horizontal competition. Third, the judicious use of compulsory licenses under the TRIPs guidelines still provides scope for limiting severe pricing abuses and for effectuating technology transfer in cases of refusals to license.

On a broader scale, the effectiveness of IPRs in promoting innovation, diffusion, and growth depends on related policies. For example, competitive pressures associated with open trade and investment policies tend to spur local innovation and technology acquisition. Gould and Gruben (1996) report econometric estimates indicating that growth induced by patent protection among developing nations is approximately 0.66 per cent higher per year in open economies than in closed economies. One reason for this is that access to imported high-technology inputs improves under patent protection. This finding bears the important implication that as countries liberalise their commercial

11 The extent of disagreement even among developed countries is remarkably wide. One noted legal scholar analysed three issues in patent abuses – monopoly pricing, contracts to limit parallel imports, and refusals to trade – and found that European and American laws would support quite different court rulings (Fox, 1996).

policies, accompanying strength of IPRs provides a more affirmative path to growth. Moreover, recent econometric evidence supports a growing consensus that countries with stronger IPRs attract significantly more FDI than do countries without them, other things equal (Mansfield and Lee, 1996; Maskus, 1998). Such evidence seems especially relevant for East Asian economies with relatively open economies and sustained liberalisation programs associated with ASEAN and APEC.

Asian countries will also find it advantageous to improve their national innovation systems in order to maximise the potential gains from tighter IPRs. Much promising research goes on in universities and government research institutes, the results of which often are not commercialised effectively. Here, promoting effective markets for venture capital and linkages to domestic and foreign private firms who would undertake applications R&D can be valuable. Note also that liberalisation of telecommunications markets improves access of researchers to the internet and other sources of technical information.

Implications for Australia

Imagine that this optimistic scenario comes to pass in East Asia over the next five-to-ten years. The results should include a significant reduction in piracy in the region, considerably stronger minimum standards for rewarding technological innovation and protecting trade secrets, and complementary regulatory systems that promote diffusion and competition. Such a systemic reform would be valuable in preparing Asian economies for a shift from labour-intensive manufacturing with lagging technologies to more innovative technological and service-based economies. What would be Australia's gains and losses from this change? It is impossible to assess such impacts quantitatively but important qualitative factors are worth discussing.

Potential gains and losses

As mentioned earlier, Australia is a largely open economy that, at least among developed economies, is particularly dependent on trade and foreign direct investment as sources of competition, exports, and technology. At the same time, Australia unmistakably has a growing comparative advantage in particular high-technology goods and services that are sold extensively in Asian markets. These characteristics suggest that Australia faces a complex set of tradeoffs in the emerging Asian IPRs regime.

The advantages of stronger Asian property rights include the following. The first, and probably most significant effect, is indirect. If the new system sets the stage for more rapid economic growth and structural change in Asia, it will directly expand demand for imported products and services. Australia is well suited to realise a significant share of this rising demand because of its trading ties to Asia, its proximity, and comparative advantages. For example, additional income growth should elastically expand demands for Australian food and meat products as diets become richer. To the extent that stronger IPRs accelerate Asian structural transformation, they will also expand demand for Australian natural resources, capital goods, and business services.

To gain an idea of how much merchandise trade might be affected by this factor alone, consider that Australian exports to ASEAN rose by approximately 15 per cent per year from 1990-1996, suggesting an income elasticity of import demand of around 2. At current trade levels, if stronger IPRs in ASEAN were to raise its growth rate by 0.5 per cent per year, annual Australian exports to the region would be one per cent higher, or some A$116 million higher than otherwise.[12] Similar computations suggest a gain in exports to China of A$57 million, to Hong Kong of A$37 million, A$110 million to Korea, and $34 million to Taiwan. These are crude calculations and should not be assigned normative content, but they indicate the potential significance of the regime change.

Stronger IPRs would also have beneficial direct impacts in various sectors. Perhaps most evident is that protection of Australia's geographical indications, especially important to the wine industry, should support higher export prices and additional export growth. Already there seems to be growing recognition in Asia of the names Barossa, Margaret River, Hunter Valley, and Coonawarra.[13]

12 Recall the Gould and Gruben (1996) estimate that stronger IPRs tend to raise growth rates by 0.66% in open economies. These computations are based on trade data from Australian Bureau of Statistics and recent GDP growth rates.

13 Australian Financial Review (May 17, 1995).

More generally, stronger protection of Australian trademarks and copyrights should be to the advantage of the sporting goods, fashion, food products, and entertainment sectors, among others. This may be of particular significance to Australian film producers and software developers as they find greater legitimate markets in Asia.

Further, to the extent that Australia's comparative advantage lies in its intellectual property with respect to Asia, its position will strengthen with additional Asian compliance and enforcement of the TRIPs standards. An Australian firm's contribution to a joint venture is likely to be knowledge-based technology, design, and services, while the Asian firm's contribution is more likely to be labor, capital, and land. Evidence noted earlier suggests that stronger IPRs should expand Australian firm's willingness to share technologies in this manner because of the additional certainty of retaining proprietary control over them. Returns to foreign investment and technology licensing in Asia should be higher as a result. Plant breeders in Australia might benefit particularly from additional Asian technology protection.

Australia should also experience some gains on the import side. As noted earlier, it is expected that additional trademark protection in Asia will be instrumental in encouraging local trademark development and product differentiation, some of it bound for export markets, such as Australia. In turn, Australian consumers should benefit from greater product variety and quality in imports, with attendant gains in competitive pressures on Australian producers.

Stronger Asian IPRs are not an unambiguous gain for Australia, however. One problem particularly facing small, open economies that already have comprehensive IPRs in place is that as Asian systems become more protective their markets become relatively more attractive to foreign investors and licensors. That is, there may be a substitution effect in investment away from Australia toward Asian economies to the extent that local economic characteristics do not otherwise discourage it. Similarly, Australian firms will face greater competition in trying to gain access to protected foreign technologies. This effect is completely unstudied and it is not clear how significant it might be. It does point to the importance of Australia improving its attractiveness to foreign investors on other grounds in the future.

A second factor is that strengthened IPRs in the region will place upward pressure on the prices of protected goods, such as pharmaceuticals. This effect may be slight in Australia because it already protects patents and copyrights. However, as the availability of generic drugs and pirated copies dries up in the region, rights-holders will feel less constrained to maintain competitive prices. In economic terms, regional import demand curves will become less elastic while rights-holders will find it easier to segment markets. Thus, there may be some rise in prices, suggesting the need to pay some attention to pharmaceutical markets in particular. This factor also supports consideration of further import deregulation in areas where distributional monopolies exist, which is advisable in its own right.

Australian policy responses

It is impossible to assess accurately the net balance of these various factors, though I expect Australia to experience net gains from the emerging system of Asian IPRs. However, the potential gains would be enhanced and the potential problems would be attenuated to the extent that Asian countries pursue the pro-competitive regulatory approach sketched earlier and Australian negotiators might be advised to advocate such an approach.

Australian negotiators have at least one other relevant concern in the IPRs area. It will be important to voice the country's interests in any attempts to push for even stronger global standards. Australia has already followed the U.S. lead in declaring computer software and algorithms patentable, which is of dubious value for the local software industry and might sacrifice long-run competitive advantages in favour of firms operating in more open Asian systems. It is unlikely that similarly choosing to adopt broad scope of patent protection in biotechnology would make competitive sense, nor would tighter restrictions against software decompilation. The United States also advocates low standards of creativity in protecting electronic databases, which promises to limit information diffusion on the internet without commensurate social gain.

As an open economy that remains sensitive to terms of competition in acquiring key technologies, products, and services, Australia is in a unique position to argue against this emerging system of over-protection. This could be done by working to see that the TRIPs revision exercise in 2000 is more devoted to consolidating its gains than to extending protection to new fields of endeavour.

In the short term, one highly visible means of making Australia's case is to declare that the market is open to effective competition even as regional IPRs are upgraded. This declaration could be made through additional import deregulation, in particular allowing parallel imports in copyrighted goods. It is also important to remain vigilant in its competition policy.

Ultimately, Australia has a variety of complicated interests in the international system of intellectual property rights. The evolving Asian regime presents both challenges and opportunities that must be deliberated carefully by both Australian firms and policy makers. Maintaining an effective system of rights in the region with due regard for competitive balance is in the mutual interests of the countries involved.

References

Barton, John H., 1993, "Adapting the Intellectual Property System to New Technologies," in M. B. Wallerstein, M. E. Mogee, and R. A. Schoen, eds., *Global Dimensions of Intellectual Property Rights in Science and Technology*, Washington: National Academy Press, 256-283.

Barton, John H., 1995, "Patent Scope in Biotechnology," *International Review of Industrial Property and Copyright Law*, Vol. 26, 605-618.

David, Paul A., 1993, "Intellectual Property Institutions and the Panda's Thumb: Patents, Copyrights, and Trade Secrets in Economic Theory and History," in M. B. Wallerstein, M. E. Mogee, and R. A. Schoen, eds., *Global Dimensions of Intellectual Property Rights in Science and Technology*, Washington: National Academy Press, 19-61.

Evenson, Robert E., 1992, "Intellectual Property Rights for Appropriate Invention," in James A. Roumasset and Susan Barr, eds., *The Economics of Cooperation: East Asian Development and the Case for Pro-Market Intervention*. Boulder: Westview Press, 51-78.

Fox, Eleonore, 1996, "Trade, Competition and Intellectual Property – TRIPS and Its Antitrust Counterparts," *Vanderbilt Journal of Transnational Law*, Vol. 29, 481-505.

Gould, David M. And William C. Gruben, 1996, "The Role of Intellectual Property Rights in Economic Growth, *Journal of Development Economics*, Vol. 48, 323-350.

Heath, Christopher, 1997, "Intellectual Property Rights in Asia: An Overview," *International Review of Industrial Property and Copyright Law*, Vol. 28, 303-309.

Helpman, Elhanan, 1993, "Innovation, Imitation, and Intellectual Property Rights," *Econometrica*, Vol. 61, 1247-1280.

Lee, Jeong-Yeon and Edwin Mansfield, 1996, "Intellectual Property Protection and U.S. Foreign Direct Investment," *Review of Economics and Statistics*, Vol. 78, 181-186.

Mansfield, Edwin, 1994, *Intellectual Property Protection, Foreign Direct Investment, and Technology Transfer*, International Finance Corporation, Discussion Paper no. 19.

Mansfield, Edwin, 1995, *Innovation, Technology, and the Economy: The Selected Essays of Edwin Mansfield, Volume II*, London: Edward Elgar.

Markusen, James R., 1995, "The Boundaries of Multinational Enterprises and the Theory of International Trade," *Journal of Economic Perspectives*, Vol. 9, 169-189.

Maskus, Keith E., 1993, "Trade-Related Intellectual Property Rights," *The European Economy*, no. 52, 157-184.

Maskus, Keith E., 1997a, "Implications of Regional and Multilateral Agreements for Intellectual Property Rights," *The World Economy*, Vol. 20, 681-694.

Maskus, Keith E., 1997b, "Intellectual Property Rights in Lebanon," unpublished report for the World Bank.

Maskus, Keith E., 1998, "The International Regulation of Intellectual Property Rights," *Weltwirtschaftliches Archiv*, forthcoming.

Maskus, Keith E., and Denise E. Konan, 1994, "Trade-Related Intellectual Property Rights: Issues and Exploratory Results," in R. M. Stern and A. V. Deardorff, eds., *Analytical and Negotiating Issues in the Global Trading System*, Ann Arbor: University of Michigan Press, 401-446.

Maskus, Keith E. and Mohan Penubarti, 1995, "How Trade-Related Are Intellectual Property Rights," *Journal of International Economics*, Vol. 39, 227-248.

Oksenberg, Michel, Pitman B. Potter, and William B. Abnett, 1996, "Advancing Intellectual Property Rights: Information Technologies and the Course of Economic Development in China," The National Bureau of Asian Research, *NBR Analysis*, Vol. 7, No. 4.

Primo Braga, Carlos A., 1996, "Trade-Related Intellectual Property Issues: the Uruguay Round Agreement and Its Economic Implications," in Will Martin and L. Alan Winters, eds., *The Uruguay Round and the Developing Countries*, Cambridge: Cambridge University Press, 341-379.

Rapp, Richard T. and Richard P. Rozek, 1990, "Benefits and Costs of Intellectual Property Protection in Developing Countries," *Journal of World Trade*, Vol. 24, 75-102.

Reichman, J. H., 1994, "Legal Hybrids Between the Patent and Copyright Paradigms," *Columbia Law Review*, Vol. 94, 2415-2485.

Reichman, J. H., 1996, *Intellectual Property Rights and the Dissemination of Technical Knowledge: A Pro-Competitive Strategy for Compliance with the TRIPS Agreement*, Geneva: UNCTAD, Division of Science and Technology.

Scotchmer, Suzanne, 1991, "Standing on the Shoulders of Giants: Cumulative Research and the Patent Law," *Journal of Economic Perspectives*, Vol. 5, 29-41.

Sherwood, Robert M., 1997, "Intellectual Property Systems and Investment Stimulation: The Rating of Systems in Eighteen Developing Countries," *IDEA: The Journal of Law and Technology*, Vol. 37, 261-370.

Sherwood, Robert M., 1993, "Why a Uniform Intellectual Property System Makes Sense for the World", in M. B. Wallerstein, M. E. Mogee, and R. A. Schoen, eds, *Global Dimensions of Intellectual Property Rights in Science and Technology*, Washington: National Academy Press, 68-88.

Torrens, Paul L. C., 1996, "Compulsory Licensing of Pharmaceutical Products in Canada," *International Review of Industrial Property and Copyright Law*, Vol. 27, 316-331.

United Nations Conference on Trade and Development, 1996, *The TRIPS Agreement and Developing Countries*, UNCTAD/ITE/1, Geneva.

Yang, Guifang and Keith E. Maskus, 1997, "Intellectual Property Rights, Licensing, and Economic Growth," Seminar Paper no. 97-09, Centre for International Economic Studies, University of Adelaide.

47

Human behaviour and the transmission of infectious disease: An economist's perspective

Mark Gersovitz[1]

No one whom I have met likes to be sick. Illness has all sorts of costs. Avoiding illness through various preventive activities also has its costs, however, as do activities designed to effect a cure or other mitigation of an infection. So compromises have to be made about activities that affect health. People make these compromises individually and the government does so for people taken together.

It is the goal of this lecture to delineate some of the considerations in these decisions by individuals and governments as they affect infectious diseases. These diseases are either transmitted from person to person, as with HIV, the virus that causes AIDS, or tuberculosis, or transmitted by vectors, such as mosquitos in the case of malaria or yellow fever. Among other things, a discussion of these diseases establishes one role for governments in the health sectors of their societies, and thereby defines one meaning of public in the phrase public health.

When most non-economists such as medical professionals first think about what an economist can contribute to understanding health, they focus on the measurement of costs. A typical question might be: What are the costs of treating tuberculosis? And the medical professional would expect an answer of so much money based on an accounting of all the very specific components of the costs of treating a case of tuberculosis in the usual way. The economy-wide costs of treating

1 Forty-seventh Joseph Fisher Lecture, 3 June 1999. A modified version has been published as "A Preface to the Economic Analysis of Disease Transmission", *Australian Economic Papers*, 31(1): 68-83, March, 2000.

the disease would then be the costs per case multiplied by an estimate of the number of cases. If a new treatment becomes available that is equally efficacious as the old, its costs could be estimated in the same way and compared with the old method to see which is cheaper and therefore better. In fact, however, most economists are not particularly adept at such an accounting and leave the details of these calculations to cost accountants.

While economists' concept of costs is much less specific than a cost accountant's, it is the implications of the concept of cost and the different types of costs that interest economists. At the most general level, economists are interested in how different types of costs affect the choices of individuals and governments, in short, their behaviour. Thus economists bring a way of looking at decision making by individuals and governments to the discussion of health and infectious diseases. This economist's perspective is based on the notion of rationality at the individual level and the notion that a role for governments arises when rational behaviour by individuals does not lead to the best outcome for individuals taken together. Economics tries to provide criteria to decide between two treatments when one costs less but is also less efficacious; at the least, it tries to warn about the shortcomings of proposed methods that purport to do so. It includes decision making in situations of imperfect information and uncertainty.

By way of final introduction, many of the examples of decisions about infectious diseases in this lecture come from the experience of poor countries and, in particular, from the instance of HIV/AIDS. Infectious diseases are much more widespread in poor countries both because their climates are more conducive to these diseases and because individuals and governments have taken many fewer of the actions that control infectious diseases in the richer countries.

Table 47.1 provides information on the percentage of the adult population that is infected with HIV in two regions of the world, Africa where the situation is worst and Asia and Oceania where some countries may be moving in the direction of Africa. An important question is whether the present desperate situation of parts of Africa is the future for large parts of Asia.

As is typical of much information on infections in general and HIV in particular, the statistical basis for understanding is weak. Almost without exception, data on the percentage infected with HIV, that is its prevalence, are not based on national censuses or representative random surveys of infection but rather on samples of convenience of unknown representativeness. As is conventional, high risk groups include prostitutes and their clients, sexually-transmitted disease (STD) patients or other groups such as intravenous drug users who are infected early in the epidemic and may play a strategic role in its propagation. Low risk groups include pregnant women and blood donors, people thought to represent the general population of adults.

In Sub-Saharan Africa, it is generally accepted that the main mode of infection is heterosexual with secondary infections passed from mother to baby either before or during birth or during breast feeding. Table 47.1 contains rather chilling information. Witness the percentages for the African countries in the first column of Table 47.1 which reports the prevalence for low-risk groups in the capitals of Botswana, Burundi, Malawi, Rwanda, South Africa, Zambia and Zimbabwe among others. By contrast, the prevalence for these groups in Asia is still low, but ominously, the rates among high risk groups in the capitals of such countries as Burma, Cambodia, India, Malaysia and Vietnam have reached the levels of Sub-Saharan Africa. In India, in particular, the main mode of infection seems to be heterosexual and with high rates among high risk groups there is beginning to be significant spread into the general population (Bentley, 1998).

Because Table 47.1 only shows data across countries around 1998, it does not show how rapidly HIV can spread in a population. The West African country of Côte d'Ivoire provides an example of rapid spread: In Abidjan, the capital, rates of infection in pregnant women may have reached 15 per cent by 1992 from just 3 per cent six years earlier (US Bureau of the Census, February, 1999). AIDS was the leading cause of adult death in Abidjan by the early 1990's (De Cock *et al*, 1989, 1990 and 1991) and infection has spread to both urban and rural areas (Ouattara, 1988, 1989a and b, Soro *et al*, 1990 and 1992). By contrast, there are such countries as the Democratic Republic of Congo (former Zaire) in which infection, while significant at 3-5 per cent in low-risk populations, has remained stable.

Table 47.1: Estimates of HIV prevalence, by region and risk factor, about 1998

	Sub-Saharan Africa	Capital/major city		Elsewhere	
	Country	Low	High	Low	High
1	Angola	1.2	-	0.5	-
2	Benin	1.2	48.9	4.2	58.1
3	Botswana	42.9	60.0	31.7	39.2
4	Burkina Faso	9.7	56.8	5.7	-
5	Burundi	23.2	-	3.4	-
6	Cameroon	4.5	16.0	6.7	9.0
7	Central African Rep.	11.7	18.3	15.3	33.3
8	Chad	2.0	13.4	-	-
9	Congo	5.8	17.5	4.0	-
10	Congo, Dem. Rep.	3.1	29.0	6.3	-
11	Côte d'Ivoire	15.9	51.9	8.1	-
12	Djibouti	2.4	28.2	-	-
13	Equatorial Guinea	1.8	5.7	0.3	2.2
14	Eritrea	3.0	-	-	25.0
15	Ethiopia	17.6	43.0	12.7	-
16	Gabon	4.7	16.7	1.2	-
17	Gambia, The	1.0	13.6	2.4	-
18	Ghana	3.6	72.6	3.0	-
19	Guinea	1.5	36.6	1.4	-
20	Guinea-Bissau	2.6	-	3.4	-
21	Kenya	15.9	53.5	9.1	33.6
22	Lesotho	31.1	35.6	8.7	16.2
23	Liberia	4.0	-	-	-
24	Madagascar	0.1	-	-	1.0
25	Malawi	30.8	-	-	-
26	Mali	2.5	-	-	52.8
27	Mauritania	0.5	-	-	1.7
28	Mozambique	2.7	7.6	1.5	-

Table 47.1: Estimates of HIV prevalence, by region and risk factor, about 1998 cont.

	Sub-Saharan Africa	Capital/major city		Elsewhere	
	Country	**Low**	**High**	**Low**	**High**
29	Namibia	18.1	18.2	10.3	-
30	Niger	1.3	23.6	1.7	33.6
31	Nigeria	6.7	30.5	2.3	60.6
32	Rwanda	32.7	54.5	10.2	13.2
33	Senegal	0.3	1.4	0.1	14.0
34	Sierra Leone	-	26.7	-	-
35	South Africa	27.0	50.3	18.1	-
36	Sudan	4.5	6.6	-	-
37	Swaziland	26.3	35.2	26.5	42.6
38	Tanzania	13.7	2.4	16.6	34.3
39	Togo	6.8	78.9	4.6	7.3
40	Uganda	14.7	35.1	6.9	-
41	Zambia	27.0	58.0	12.7	36.0
42	Zimbabwe	28.0	86.0	29.3	71.8
	Asia and Oceania	**Capital/major city**		**Elsewhere**	
	Country	**Low**	**High**	**Low**	**High**
1	Australia	0.3	0.4	-	-
2	Bangladesh	0	1.2	-	-
3	Bhutan	0	0	-	-
4	Burma	1.5	36.0	1.5	8.0
5	Cambodia	3.8	61.3	2.5	28.0
6	China, Hong Kong	0	0.1	-	-
7	China, Mainland	0	73.2	-	-
			0.4		
8	China, Taiwan	0	0	-	-
9	India	1.2	32.0	0.8	12.2
10	Indonesia	0	0.2	-	-

Table 47.1: Estimates of HIV prevalence, by region and risk factor, about 1998 cont.

	Sub-Saharan Africa	Capital/major city		Elsewhere	
	Country	**Low**	**High**	**Low**	**High**
11	Korea, South	0.8	0	-	-
12	Laos	0.4	1.2	-	-
13	Malaysia	0	29.5	0.1	0.1
14	Mongolia	0	0	-	-
15	Nepal	0	20.4	-	2.0
16	Pakistan	0.6	3.7	-	-
17	Papua New Guinea	0.2	1.9	0	0
18	Philippines	0	0.5	-	-
19	Singapore	0	3.7	-	-
20	Sri Lanka	0	0	0	0
21	Thailand	2.0	15.9	-	-
22	Vietnam	0.2	44.8	0	7.0
			3.8		0.5

Source: US Bureau of the Census (February, 1999).

The requisites and consequences of individual rationality

To answer questions about people's behaviour, economists postulate that individuals are rational in that they make the best choices as they see them from the options that they face subject to the information they have. At a general level, many people may find this rationality postulate to be innocuous and perhaps even without content because whatever anyone is observed to do could be defined after the fact to be the individual's best choice. Other people may bristle at the very notion that individuals understand and choose what is best for them or that they even have any options among which to choose. The proof of this pudding will be in its eating: Does the starting point of rationality lead to deductions about how individuals behave that are confirmed by evidence?

For the postulate to be useful in making predictions, it is necessary to specify two things: First are the options that the individual actually faces as determined both by the disease environment in which the individual operates and the information the individual has about this environment, termed the constraints that the individual faces. Second is how an individual ranks different choices among these options, termed the objectives of the individual. Once an analyst specifies the constraints and objectives, hypotheses about choices follow from the rationality postulate that individuals take the best option as defined by their objectives that is available to them as defined by their constraints.

The biology of a disease is the first determinant of the disease environment that people confront. Working backward after a person is infected, do they recover to become either susceptible again or immune, or do they suffer chronic ill health or death, and how are these conditions evaluated by the person? The answers to these questions determine part of the costs of being infected. Can individuals know when they are infected and infectious, and when others are infectious, either through symptoms or through a medical test? Can the course of the disease be altered by therapy? If so, the costs of the disease are the costs of illness as mitigated by therapy plus the costs of the type of therapy that is chosen.

Now moving backward to the point at which a susceptible person is exposed, is the disease transmitted easily or with difficulty and in which ways? What preventive actions can a person take to lessen the risk of exposure to infection and how much do these preventive actions cost? In particular, is a vaccine available? Is a vector such as a mosquito involved and how can it be combatted? To what extent is the risk of infection determined by the overall rate of infection and hence stage of the epidemic? Are the infectious people who put a particular susceptible at risk relatively anonymous as would be the case with influenza or plausibly identifiable to the susceptible, as with an STD?

Information that is relevant to individuals' decisions about preventive and curative or palliative actions are of two main types. The first type of information is general. It includes information about the existence of a disease, how it is (and is not) transmitted, whether infectious individuals can be asymptomatic, and the availability of preventive, curative and palliative options and their associated costs. The second type of information is specific to the individual. It includes information about whether a person is infected or infectious and about whether the people with whom the person consorts are infectious.

An important question is whether information of the first, general type is the real constraint on people's decisions. If people already have this type of information, it is likely to be of little value to provide it over and over again. Many economists share an instinct based on experience that there is often too little willingness to believe that people may take seemingly dangerous choices because they face other considerations than merely a lack of information. People may see offsetting benefits in risky choices.

Table 47.2 provides information on the diffusion of general knowledge about HIV/AIDS in the adult population of Tanzania based on a representative random survey, the Demographic and Health Survey (DHS) of 1996.[2] As Table 47.1 reports, Tanzania has a high prevalence of HIV, perhaps 15 per cent throughout the country. The top panel of Table 47.2 provides the respondents' answers to some questions on the general nature of HIV/AIDS. Just about everyone has heard of the disease and knows that it cannot be cured. In answering five questions about ways to avoid HIV that are generally believed not to be efficacious, the majority of people answer in the way that would be conventionally correct, although significant numbers do not. More importantly, the vast bulk of people know that HIV is sexually transmitted, can be avoided by condom use, is transmitted from mother to baby, and can be asymptomatic so that carriers are not known to potential partners.

2 A representative random sample is not the only requirement for useful data on behaviour relevant to the HIV epidemic. Another requirement is that respondents answer accurately about some of their most private activities. Caldwell *et al* (1994) doubt that surveys with large random samples can elicit accurate answers. One troublesome inconsistency in surveys of sexual behaviour is that women typically report less (heterosexual) activity than men, whether measured by partners or sexual acts. Wadsworth *et al* (1996) and Gersovitz *et al* (1998) discuss this issue.

Table 47.2: Responses to the Tanzanian Demographic and Health Survey, 1996
(Weighted by population probabilities)

Question	Men			Women		
	Yes	No	D.K.	Yes	No	D.K.
A. Information on AIDS of a general nature:						
Ever heard of AIDS?	99	1		97	3	
Can AIDS be cured?	2	96	2	2	95	3
Avoid AIDS by good diet?	13	73	14	16	65	18
Avoid AIDS by avoiding urine or stool?	24	57	20	18	57	25
Avoid AIDS by not touching person with AIDS?	17	67	17	15	63	23
Avoid AIDS by not sharing eating utensils?	22	61	16	18	59	23
Avoid AIDS by avoiding insect bites?	30	54	16	21	52	27
Avoid AIDS by staying with one faithful partner?	83	10	7	79	11	10
Avoid AIDS by using condom?	70	13	18	65	14	22
Avoid AIDS by using clean needles for medical injections?	84	8	8	73	13	14
Apparently healthy person have AIDS?	79	11	10	70	16	14
Woman pass AIDS to baby?	77	9	14	75	10	15
B. Person-specific information and AIDS strategies:						
Ever tested for AIDS?	11	89		4	95	1
Like to be tested for AIDS?	74	23	3	70	26	4
Advise partner when had STD?	60	40		91	9	
Tried to avoid infecting partner?	80	15		52	7	
Memo: Partner already infected?	6			41		
Behavioural change: Did not start sex.	15	85		13	87	
Behavioural change: Stopped all sex.	7	93		7	93	
Behavioural change: Started using condoms.	9	91		2	98	
Behavioural change: Use condoms more often.	5	95		1	99	
Behavioural change: Only one partner.	45	55		49	51	
Behavioural change: Reduced number of partners.	24	76		15	85	
Behavioural change: Man avoids prostitutes, woman asks spouse to.	18	82		4	96	

Source: DHS (1997)

The first step in judging how much of the misinformation should be corrected by further information campaigns would seem to be to establish if the misinformed have any use for improved information. Presently, there is no such analysis which would be best undertaken by seeing if people who increase their knowledge change their behaviour. That relatively uneducated and rural respondents in Tanzania disproportionately answer incorrectly combined with the widespread epidemic does suggest that there still may be groups who could benefit from further information campaigns in this country.

Turning now to the second type of information that is specific to individuals, Table 47.2 shows that Tanzanians know that in the case of HIV infectious people may be asymptomatic and that there is therefore no way to tell without a test whether a prospective partner is infectious. This fact naturally leads to the question of access to tests, the choice to be tested, and the choice to reveal test results to prospective partners. For a number of biological reasons, medical tests for HIV infection are not perfectly accurate, but nonetheless provide highly important information. Before turning to the determinants of the decision to be tested, which raise many strategic questions for individuals that fit well within the rationality paradigm, it is worthwhile to consider the range of objectives that people have.

Individuals have many objectives in making decisions that affect their health. Although a list of these objectives is commonsensical, many of the pitfalls in the analysis of health arise from neglecting some of these objectives so it seems worthwhile to list them. People are concerned about the direct costs of illness to themselves: pain, fear, the loss of income and other opportunities, and early death. They want to minimize the money costs of prevention and curative or other therapeutic activities insofar as they pay these costs. They value physical intimacy of all sorts with other human beings including sexual relations whether for pleasure or for procreation. But physical intimacy promotes the spread of infection whether with a classic STD, new ones such as HIV, or diseases of proximity such as influenza, tuberculosis or leprosy. Individuals may also value the costs paid by people whom they infect, such as their sexual partners; to the extent they do so, they are termed altruistic. At the same time, individuals may want their sexual partners to believe that they are sexually faithful and they may want their partners to be sexually faithful independently of their becoming infectious. Furthermore, in the case of vector-borne diseases such as malaria, yellow fever, and bubonic plague, among others, people value doing activities and being in environments that risk infection. So a lot of considerations are in play and objectives are often in conflict, depending on the particular disease. In the case of the heavily HIV-infected parts of Africa, it looks like a fundamental conflict is between avoiding AIDS and having a family, two fairly basic objectives.

All these considerations are irrelevant if individuals lack choices. In the case of HIV in Tanzania, the DHS provides information on some of the strategies people have adopted. Their main strategy seems to be to change the type of partner: avoid prostitutes, reduce the number of partners or, for almost a majority of respondents, restrict oneself to only one partner. A large proportion of people, 22 per cent of men and 20 per cent of women, report having chosen sexual abstinence, either by not starting to have sexual relations or by stopping relations. The knowledge requirements and cash costs to adopt a strategy of abstinence are particularly simple, nothing more than the knowledge that HIV is a deadly STD. Of course, with better information, say about prospective partners, these people will have better options, including the opportunity to form partnerships and have families. By contrast, relatively few people report starting to use condoms or using them more frequently. Indeed, in this survey, only 16 per cent of men and 6 per cent of women report ever using a condom to avoid HIV on even one occasion (data not shown in tables).

Although these results on the relative adoption of abstinence and condoms as preventive strategies may seem implausible, they are consistent with other less representative samples. In a study of people tested at a centre in Kampala, Uganda that comprised several groups of respondents, 16 per cent of one sample said they would abstain from sex if they were to receive a negative test result, while 25 per cent of another sample reported that they had actually abstained since receiving their test results (Muller et al, 1992). In a study of two areas of rural Zimbabwe, 24 per cent of 1093 women aged 15-49 reported that they abstained, while only 10 per cent of this group reported using condoms with their regular partner (Gregson et al, 1998). Fifty per cent of these women claimed to want fewer children since hearing about AIDS while only 3 per cent wanted more, consistent with the substantial adoption of abstinence which respondents report. By contrast, a study of urban Uganda reports both a significant increase in condom use and decrease in sexual activity, accompanied by a decrease in HIV infection (Asiimwe-Okiror et al, 1997).

If the picture of substantial abstinence is accurate, it means that the costs of the epidemic are not just measured by infection but also by what must be important sacrifices of happiness by these people who see physical intimacy and childbearing as just too dangerous. Although people who adopt abstinence as a precaution will contribute to lower population growth, there may be people who form monogamous partnerships earlier than they would in the absence of AIDS, with the opposite effect on overall fertility. These people also pay a cost if they form partnerships with individuals whom they would not choose except for the fear that otherwise more suitable partners might be infectious.

The generally low level of condom adoption is widely seen as a troublesome puzzle. But there are some good reasons expressed by African respondents in a number of studies (Cohen and Trussell, 1996 and Pool et al, 1996). First, an important reason these people have sexual relations is to have families. Second, the use of a condom would seem to presuppose that one or the other partner is unfaithful or suspicious, and this process of inference is one people want to avoid, especially with their regular partners. By contrast, there are a number of misunderstandings about condoms, such as that they are porous, that could possibly be overcome through information campaigns.

Against this background, it seems time to turn to the role of a test for infection in the dynamics of the epidemic. Testing and the associated behaviour are particularly useful in gaining information about whether people care only about themselves (termed egoists) or also about some or all of their partners (termed altruists). Presumably if people are altruists, they will test to avoid infecting their partners, and such action will tend to slow the epidemic. Philipson and Posner (1993) in their book Private Choices and Public Health: The AIDS Epidemic in an Economic Perspective argue for an important qualification to this view: They emphasize that egoists who test positive may increase their level of activity because they personally have nothing to lose while they do not care about the consequences for their partners. Furthermore, some people who were thought by moderate-risk people to be at too high risk to be acceptable as partners will test negative, thereby making themselves eligible for partnerships that will sometimes infect them. In general, therefore, these authors (p. 84) argue that "testing may increase the incidence of AIDS rather than being sure to decrease it."

As for other reasons than deciding about sexual activity, testing in poor countries can inform decisions about the future in all sorts of ways such as making provision for children who will be orphaned or planning fertility especially because without intervention about a third of all children born to infected mothers are infected. In a study of men and women clients of a testing centre in Kampala, Uganda (Muller et al, 1992), reasons for taking the test were a planned marriage or new relationship (27 per cent) suggesting altruism, to plan for the future (35 per cent), distrust of a partner (14 per cent) or illness or death (not HIV specific) of a partner (20 per cent). In rich countries an important reason to test is to begin life-prolonging therapy in the case of a positive test but these expensive therapies are not available in poor countries. And there are costs to being tested such as abandonment by partners who become aware of a positive test. Finally, there are the costs of coming back for test results which may not be negligible because the recent provision of same-day testing at a centre in Kampala, Uganda has led to 100 per cent of people learning their test results compared to the 79 per cent who learned their results at the same clinic when the technology of testing required a return visit after two weeks (Kassler et al, 1998). On the other hand, it may be that the additional 21 per cent who learned their results had no use for the knowledge, and that costs were not a deterrent.

The first thing to be learned from the DHS about testing in Tanzania is that a not insignificant number of people have done so, 11 per cent of men (though a lower 4 per cent of women). In comparison to men who have not been tested, almost twice as many men who have been tested report stopping sexual activity to avoid HIV (6.7 per cent versus 12.3 per cent). Furthermore, almost three-quarters of men and of women who have not been tested would like to be. So testing is a real issue for these people. On the other hand, in the survey only one woman and no men report that they have AIDS. Either the people who are tested are a self-selected group of people at low risk or there is something anomalous about the survey or the estimates of national HIV seroprevalence in Table 47.1. In any case, there is little scope for observing egoistical behavior by people who test positive for HIV in this data set.

Among the people in the DHS survey who reported having had a classic STD in the last 12 months, Table 47.2 shows that the majority (vast majority in the case of women) claim to inform their partner and take precautions to avoid infecting them if they are not already infected.[3] Thus these people seem to be broadly altruistic in their admittedly self-reported behaviour. But testing for a conventional STD has very different benefits from testing for HIV because conventional STDs are curable and once people are cured they would not want to be re-infected by their regular partners. So the framework of rational behaviour leads to the possibility of very different behaviour between conventional STDs and HIV.

In addition to a representative random survey like the DHS for Tanzania, there are small scale studies of HIV testing and associated behaviour based on samples of convenience. Some of the findings from these studies provide important hints about how people see their strategic situation, in some cases suggesting egoistical motivations for many.

First, these studies show that a significant number of people who are tested do not return for their test results. Furthermore, a survey of 12 HIV testing centres in poor countries (Cartoux et al, 1998) found that in 9 centres women who tested HIV positive were less likely to return for their tests than women who tested negative. These results suggest that either these women can guess the answer based on what they know about their past histories or that their circumstances mean that they have much less use for knowing their results than women who test negative. Maybe they do not care about their partners perhaps because their partnerships are casual ones that put them at greater risk in any case.

Second, these studies show that significant numbers of people who are tested do not tell their partners about their test results and that they are less likely to do so if their test results show that they are infected with HIV. In a study in Kinshasa, Congo, 97 per cent of 238 HIV-positive women were unwilling to inform their partners of their HIV status (Ryder et al, 1991). In a study in Kigali, Rwanda (Van der Straten et al, 1995), 95 per cent of HIV-negative women reported discussing their test results with their partner, but only 77 per cent of

3 Petry and Kingu (1996, pp. 267-268) report that almost all people with a classic STD in their sample were aware of it, although only 25% of patients who reported STD-like symptoms had a classic STD.

HIV-positive women did so. In another study in Kigali (Ladner et al, 1996), 71 per cent of HIV-negative women chose to learn their tests results in contrast to 64 per cent of the HIV-positive women. Of the women who learned their results, 92 per cent of HIV-negative women in contrast to 85 per cent of HIV-positive women told their partners that they had been tested prior to getting their results. After learning their results, however, only 51 per cent of HIV-positive women intended to tell their partners the results, in contrast to 95 per cent of the HIV-negative women.

Third, discordant partnerships in which one partner is HIV positive but the other is HIV negative provide an important window on whether behaviour is egoistical or altruistic once infection has occurred.[4] In a study of discordant partnerships in Uganda (Serwadda et al, 1995), 17 per cent of men used condoms when the woman was the infected partner whereas only 10 per cent of men used condoms when they were the infected partner. The number of partnerships in the study was too small, however, to be confident that the results were not due to chance. Furthermore, most of the members of these partnerships had not requested their test results despite having the opportunity to do so. Consequently, interpreting these results as suggesting that men protect themselves more than they do their partners presupposes that it was not easier for these men to infer when their partners were more at risk of being infected than when they themselves were. In 28 discordant partnerships in Kigali, Rwanda (Van der Straten et al, 1995), 84 per cent of men used a condom in the 16 partnerships in which they were negative while only 57 per cent of the men did so in the 12 partnerships in which they were positive, but again these are very small numbers.

In a study of 149 married discordant couples in Kinshasa, Congo who were intensively counseled (Kamenga et al, 1991), 18 per cent of 80 couples in which the woman was positive practiced abstinence while the remaining 82 per cent used condoms. By contrast, in 69 couples in which the man was positive, 25 per

4 The ratio of male-positive to female-positive discordant partners was close to one in these studies: 69 versus 80 in Kamenga et al (1991); 12 versus 16 in Van der Straten (1995) and 44 versus 35 in Serwadda et al (1995). Carpenter et al (1999) present evidence that the incidence of women in discordant partnerships is twice that of men. Even taking account of this finding, the numbers on the ratio of male-positive to female-positive discordant partnerships suggests that a model in which men become infected by very high-activity women and then infect their regular partners/wives cannot be the whole story; too many women in the discordant regular partnerships are the infected partner.

cent practiced abstinence but only 62 per cent used condoms, so that on balance 13 per cent of the couples engaged in unprotected sexual relations. Of the 13 men in this study who had extramarital partners after learning their test results, 11 did not use condoms with their extramarital partners although 11 of the 13 either abstained from or used condoms during relations with their wives. By contrast in Kigali while fewer women who tested positive told their partners of their results, those who did tried harder than the women who had tested negative to persuade their partners to adopt safer practices (Van der Straten et al., 1995). Seventy-nine per cent of HIV-positive women who told their partners of their results reported discussing condom use with their partner while only 61 per cent of HIV-negative women did so; 63 per cent of these HIV-positive women asked their partner to use a condom while 43 per cent of HIV-negative women did so; and 39 per cent of these HIV-positive women tried to convince their partner to use a condom while 18 per cent of HIV-negative women did so (Van der Straten et al, 1995).

Externalities and public health

The foundation of rational behaviour and individual decision making provides a basis for public policy. The central concept is the externality. Usually, if individuals are not compensated for benefits that they generate for others outside of family and friends, they do not take these consequences into account in making their decisions. Similarly, if individuals do not pay for costs that they impose on others, they do not take them into account. In either case, they generate externalities, respectively good and bad effects on the welfare of others, people whose benefits and costs are external to their decision making.

From society's perspective, however, all benefits and costs should be included in the weighing of decisions, no matter whether they enter into the decisions of the people whose actions lead to the benefits and costs or not. For this reason, when there are externalities, there is a divergence between the benefits and costs as seen by individuals who take decisions and the benefits and costs that concern governments. Such a divergence provides one of the classic rationales for intervention by governments. Thus the concept of an externality is central to much of economics and has application to the case of infectious diseases.

A good example of an externality is environmental pollution that affects public health although without necessarily involving an infectious agent. Left to himself, a factory owner who pollutes a lake shared by many others reaps the full benefit from avoiding the costs of pollution abatement but only suffers a small fraction of the total costs of water pollution as one among many members of the community. On the presumption that the factory owner does what is in his own personal interest, he will choose levels of pollution higher than the community as whole would find desirable when it weighs the costs of pollution abatement against the total costs of water pollution to the community. A role for the government is then to communicate the larger social costs of pollution to the factory owner by charging him a pollution fee that represents the full costs of pollution to the community. Such a fee will induce the factory owner to reduce pollution to the level that the community finds desirable. Of course, if the factory owner is an altruist who bases decisions on the community's best interest, then there is no need for government intervention; but this assumption is implausible.

In some ways, individuals take decisions that affect the prevalence of infections without fully incorporating the effect of their actions on the community's costs and benefits, just as the hypothetical factory owner. Diseases that involve transmission from vectors to humans and back to vectors would seem to fit the externality model well. For example, a farmer who is infected with schistosomiasis (bilharzia) and voids one stage of the parasite into an irrigation canal where it can mature into another stage that infects other farmers probably does not incorporate these costs fully into his decision, if he does so at all. For this type of infectious disease, the people who are put at risk of infection are often neither friends nor family; in any case, the way the farmer provides the next link in the chain of infection is not transparent. The same situation would seem to prevail in the case of diseases that are transmitted directly from person to person, but relatively anonymously, perhaps before the infected person is even aware that they are infectious. Influenza is a good example, and one that killed millions of people in 1919. STDs would seem to allow more scope for altruism because a sexual partner is rarely anonymous and is often included among people whose interests an infected person wants to take into account. The discussion of behaviour associated with testing, however, suggests that many people who test positive behave egoistically. Different views of the scope for altruistic behaviour seem to have been part of a contentious interchange between two Australian economists (Lloyd, 1991 and 1992 and Parish, 1992) on the relevance of the concept of externality to policy on AIDS, so not all economists agree. Finally, infectious diseases of any sort may be contrasted with cardiovascular disease or cancer, for which there is no externality caused by an individual's becoming ill and, correspondingly, there is not an externality rationale for government intervention, although there may be other rationales.

While the notion of externalities is straightforward, situations characterized by externalities can lead to seemingly paradoxical results. For instance, consider a situation in which a disease spreads among a population comprising two groups, one with a high exposure to infection and one with a low exposure. For concreteness, the first group may be identified with people with many sexual partners and the second with people with relatively few partners, while the disease is AIDS. From an individual's perspective there is no doubt that lowering the number of their own partners will lower the probability of that individual's becoming infected, other things equal. But what about the infection rate in the population as a whole?

For sake of argument, assume initially that the low-activity people are not active at all. In this case, the epidemic may spread rapidly among the high-activity people. Now consider an increase in the activity level of the low-activity group, perhaps to one contact. Some of these contacts will be with high-activity people and some will result in infections of low-activity people. But if the low-activity people have only one contact they will not infect anyone else. In the meantime, some of the high-activity people who are not yet infected will be less likely to meet infected high-activity people and will be less likely to be infected. This effect may even lead to the extinction of the epidemic among high-activity people and therefore among the population as a whole, although at a cost to the low-activity people who become infected during the transition. To put the lesson of this analysis in the opposite way, the observation of an increased prevalence among high-activity people need not reflect an increase in risky behaviour by them. Instead, it may reflect decreased risky behaviour by low-activity people. Indeed, high-activity people may even be decreasing their risky behaviour somewhat.

So much for a theoretical possibility as presented in a stark and simplified example. Spurred by this type of example, two economists, Kremer and Morcum

(1998), have looked for this effect in a more realistic model of HIV transmission calibrated to data from the United Kingdom. They estimate that 80 per cent of the heterosexual population has sufficiently low activity levels as measured by partner change that an increase in their activity would decrease the national prevalence level. Thus the theoretical result may not be a curiosity.

While understanding this phenomenon may be important to the interpretation of the dynamics of an epidemic with different groups (Whitaker and Rentin, 1992), its policy implications are less clear. Few people would want to encourage low-activity people to take risks with their health for some notion of the greater good. Nonetheless, such a finding would seem to suggest the need to find policies to lower infection rates among high-activity groups who may actually be made more vulnerable by campaigns that decrease activity levels among low-activity groups.

In the context of infectious diseases, it is useful to distinguish two types of externalities that arise, the pure infection externality and the pure prevention externality (Gersovitz and Hammer, 1999). The pure infection externality arises if individuals do not take into account the fact that their becoming infected affects the risks of others' becoming infected. The discussion of externalities in sexual behaviour and the transmission of HIV has focused on this type of externality, both negative and positive in the case of the Kremer-Morcum example. In contrast, the pure prevention externality operates whether or not the individual becomes infected himself. An example would be spraying for malarial mosquitoes which lowers others' risks of becoming infected regardless of whether the person who pays for the spraying becomes infected or not.

This distinction between different types of externalities helps to provide some qualitative guidance for government interventions. Consider a quintessential infection externality: a disease transmitted from person to person and in which people are either infected and infectious or well but susceptible to infection; a person once cured does not become immune but is once again susceptible. In offsetting the externality, it is equally desirable to prevent someone from becoming infected as to cure them; the main thing is to keep more people out of the infectious group than would otherwise be the case. As a consequence, prevention and cures should be subsidized at exactly the same rate. This result is not general; it depends on the structure of the disease as defined by what happens to an infected person. Recovery to susceptibility, recovery to immunity, or death all imply different types of intervention as between prevention and cure. By contrast, many of these issues of policy design do not arise in the HIV epidemic because there is very limited scope for government intervention. While HIV transmission raises complex questions in terms of individuals' decisions, the governments of poor countries have relatively few options and exclusively preventive ones: provision of information, and subsidization of condoms and tests. There is no cure and even interventions that mitigate the effects of the infection are generally far too expensive to be available in the very poor worst-affected countries.

Vector-transmitted diseases provide further complications in the design of an intervention package. Interventions are not restricted only to those that either prevent people from infecting each other or cure the infected; there are also interventions that affect the population of the vector and its ability to infect people. In the case of vector control, pure prevention externalities arise to an extreme degree. The government may often have to pay for the whole program of vector control because control at the individual level may be entirely impractical; the infiltration of vectors from outside a single individual's perimeter of control may be overwhelming. For instance, spraying in one's own compound may have little effect on the probability of getting malaria if one's neighbours do nothing. Absent a method of co-ordinating large groups of people, the definition of a government, the result will be that no one bothers to spray.

Formulation of policy using the concept of an externality requires an estimate of the discrepancy between benefits and costs at the individual and community levels. While the rationality postulate provides a basis for prediction it is also closely related to most economists' solution to another problem: how to evaluate what happens as an outsider or policy analyst. Having started with the view that individuals choose what is best for them individually, it is not a long step to assert that what happens should be evaluated the way individuals do. In the context of infectious diseases, this position means that the evaluation of an epidemic is not based solely on infection rates, but must take into account that individuals also value doing those risky activities that lead to infection. When there are externalities, however, individuals' actions taken together do not lead to the best overall outcome as seen by them so that there is a role for government in public health. Thus just because one uses the same method of valuing costs and benefits as do individuals does not mean that the world as it exists is the best possible.

Estimation of the costs imposed on others by the person who is infectious is a difficult but unavoidable problem in establishing the extent of an externality: What is the monetary equivalent of the pain of illness or the loss from a death? Economists have some answers. For example, there are studies that derive individuals' valuation of risk to health and life from the wage premium that they require to do jobs that pose these kinds of risks (Viscusi, 1992).

An alternative that is sometimes used to avoid the valuation of illness and death, especially in the field of health policy, is the cost-effectiveness approach. The idea is to calculate the costs of an intervention divided by a given outcome, usually lives saved, cases prevented or life years saved (Hammer, 1993). For example, the cost-effectiveness calculation could produce a result with the meaning of dollars per life saved. Advocates of this approach would then choose to spend the health budget on those interventions that have the lowest cost in terms of lives saved. But this methodology can be severely misleading and for a number of reasons. Hammer (1993, p. 20) gives the following example which is sufficiently telling that it deserves to be quoted:

> Consider a situation in which two drugs are available to treat a particular disease. Drug 1 changes the probability of avoiding death from 0.2 to 0.3 and costs $5 per treatment. Drug 2 changes the probability from 0.2 to 0.25 and costs $2 per treatment. The cost per life saved by drug 1 is $50 ($5/[0.3-0.2]), while lives saved by drug 2 cost $40 ($2/[0.25-0.20]), making drug 2 more cost effective.

Most people probably would opt for drug 1, though, provided they are willing to pay more than $60 to save their life. For any imputed value of life greater than $60, the value of the increased probability of recovery outweighs the extra cost of the drug Cost-effectiveness ratios, while seeming to avoid the contentious issue of deciding on a monetary value of life, merely disguise an implicit valuation that may not reflect people's preferences.

Furthermore, cost-effectiveness abandons the principle of intervention to offset an externality as a motivation for government policy. It may be that the greatest cost-effectiveness is realized in cancer therapy, but if this therapy would be paid for by a rich private citizen on his own behalf, there is no obvious reason to raise tax dollars to pay for such a therapy through the government and certainly no reason based on externalities.

So far government intervention has been restricted to subsidizing extant prevention or cures. Governments also fund research to develop new preventive and curative methods. The economist's justification here again derives from a concept similar to an externality, namely a public good. Because knowledge is costly to produce but relatively inexpensive to disseminate, it is difficult for private businesses to recover the costs of generating new knowledge. In some cases, such as pure science, government plays an important role in directly funding the activity to generate knowledge. In other cases, such as the application of pure science to produce a specific drug, government creates property rights through the patent system to enable private businesses to obtain a protected return on their investments for a fixed period of time. Finally, the same sort of rationale justifies government information campaigns about the risks of diseases; these are activities that the private sector will find hard to make profitable because it is difficult to charge people for the service that they get. For instance, neighbours talk to neighbours who have heard information but no one is going to take up a collection to pay a private business for the costs of the initial radio broadcasts.

Conclusions

The economic approach to infectious diseases is in its infancy, somewhat oddly because many economists have long had the intuition that epidemics and infectious diseases are quintessential manifestations of the principle of an externality, itself a central concept in economics. Yet only recently have economists begun to look at these questions in a formal way with some surprising results, such as the consequence of increased activity by people with low-activity levels for overall prevalence. There is controversy among economists over such basic issues as whether the choice to vaccinate involves an externality or not (Brito *et al*, 1991, Francis, 1997, Geoffard and Philipson, 1997 and Kremer, 1997) and therefore whether there is justification for public vaccination campaigns based on offsetting an externality. Nonetheless, the principles of rational behaviour at the individual level and interventions to offset externalities provide a powerful framework for thinking about infectious diseases and public health.

References

Asiimwe-Okiror, G. *et al*, "Change in Sexual Behaviour and Decline in HIV Infection among Young Pregnant Women in Urban Uganda," *AIDS*, vol. 11 (1997), pp. 1757-1763.

Bentley, M. E. et al, "HIV Testing and Counseling Among Men Attending Sexually Transmitted Disease Clinics in Pune, India: Changes in Condom Use and Sexual Behavior over Time," AIDS, vol. 12 (1998), pp. 1869-1877.

Brito, D. L., E. Sheshinski and M. D. Intriligator, "Externalities and Compulsory Vaccinations," Journal of Public Economics, vol. 45 (1991), pp. 69-90.

Caldwell, J. C. et al, "The Social Context of AIDS in Sub-Saharan Africa," in Sexual Networking and AIDS in Sub-Saharan Africa, eds. I. O. Orubuloye et al (Canberra: Health Transition Review, 1994).

Carpenter, L. M. et al, "Rates of HIV-1 Transmission within Marriage in Rural Uganda in Relation to the HIV sero-status of the Partners," AIDS, vol. 13 (1999), pp. 1083-1089.

Cartoux, M. et al, "Acceptability of Voluntary HIV Testing by Pregnant Women in Developing Countries: An International Survey," AIDS, vol. 12 (1998), pp. 2489-2493.

Cohen, B. and J. Trussell, Preventing and Mitigating AIDS in Sub-Saharan Africa (Washington: National Academy Press, 1996).

de Cock, K. M. et al, "Rapid Emergence of AIDS in Abidjan, Ivory Coast", The Lancet, August 19 (1989), pp. 408-411.

de Cock, K. M. et al, "AIDS – The Leading Cause of Adult Death in the West African City of Abidjan, Ivory Coast", Science, vol. 249 (1990), pp. 793-796.

de Cock, K. M. et al, "Mortality Trends in Abidjan, Côte d'Ivoire, 1983-1988", AIDS, vol. 5, (1991), pp. 393-398.

DHS (Demographic and Health Surveys), Tanzania: Demographic and Health Survey 1996 (Calverton, MD: Macro International Inc, 1997).

Francis, P. J., "Dynamic Epidemiology and the Market for Vaccinations," Journal of Public Economics, vol. 63 (1997), pp. 383-406.

Geoffard, P.-Y. and T. Philipson, "Disease Eradication: Private versus Public Vaccination," American Economic Review, vol. 87 (1997), pp. 222-230.

Gersovitz, M. et al, "The Balance of Self-Reported Heterosexual Activity in KAP Surveys and the AIDS Epidemic in Africa," Journal of the American Statistical Association, vol. 93 (1998), pp. 875-883.

Gersovitz, M. and J. S. Hammer, "The Economical Control of Infectious Diseases," mimeo, The Johns Hopkins University (1999).

Gregson, S. et al, "Is There Evidence of Behaviour Change in Response to AIDS in Rural Zimbabwe," Social Science Medicine, vol. 46 (1998), pp. 321-330.

Hammer, J. S., "The Economics of Malaria Control," The World Bank Research Observer, vol. 8 (1993), pp. 1-22.

Kamenga, M. et al, "Evidence of Marked Sexual Behavior Change Associated with low HIV-1 Seroconversion in 149 Married Couples with Discordant HIV-1 Serostatus: Experience at an HIV Counselling Center in Zaire," AIDS vol. 5, (1991), pp. 61-67.

Kassler, W. J. et al, "Rapid HIV Testing with Same-Day Results: A Field Trial in Uganda," International Journal of STD & AIDS, vol. 9 (1998), pp. 134-138.

Kremer, M., "Integrating Behavioral Choice into Epidemiological Models of AIDS," Quarterly Journal of Economics, vol. 111 (1996), pp. 549-573.

Kremer, M. and C. Morcum, "The Effect of Changing Sexual Activity on HIV Prevalence," Mathematical Biosciences, 151 (1998), pp. 99-122.

Ladner, J. et al, "A Cohort Study of Factors Associated with Failure to Return for HIV Post-Test Counselling in Pregnant Women: Kigali, Rwanda, 1992-1993," AIDS, vol. 10 (1996), pp. 69-75.

Lloyd, P. J., "AIDS: An Economic Approach to the Choice of Policies," The Economic Record vol. 67 (1991), pp. 126-138.

Lloyd, P. J., "AIDS and 'Market Failure'; a Reply," The Economic Record, vol. 68 (1992), pp. 281-282.

Muller, O. et al, "HIV Prevalence, Attitudes and Behaviour in Clients of a Confidential HIV Testing and Counselling Centre in Uganda," AIDS, vol. 6, no. 8 (1992), pp. 869-874.

Ouattara, S. A. et al, "Blood Transfusions and HIV Infections (HIV1, HIV2/LAV2) Ivory Coast", Journal of Tropical Medicine and Hygiene, vol. 91 (1988), pp. 212-215.

Ouattara, S. A. et al, "Compared Prevalence of Infections by HIV-1 and HIV-2 during a 2-Year Period in Suburban and Rural Areas of Ivory Coast", Journal of Acquired Immune Deficiency Syndromes, vol. 2 (1989a), pp. 94-99.

Ouattara, S. A. et al, "Prevalence of HTLV-I Compared to HIV-1 and HIV-2 Antibodies in Different Groups in the Ivory Coast (West Africa)", Journal of Acquired Immune Deficiency Syndromes, vol. 2 (1989b), pp. 481-485.

Parish, R., "AIDS and 'Market Failure'," The Economic Record, vol. 68 (1992), pp. 278-280.

Petry, K. U., and H. Kingu, "HIV Infection among Pregnant Women in Lindi, Tanzania, 1989-1993," International Journal of STD & AIDS, vol. 7 (1996), pp. 265-268.

Philipson, T. J. and R. A. Posner, Private Choices and Public Health: The AIDS Epidemic in an Economic Perspective (Cambridge, MA: Harvard, 1993).

Pool, R. et al, "The Price of Promiscuity: Why Urban Males in Tanzania are Changing their Sexual Behaviour," Health Transition Review vol. 6 (1997), pp. 203-221.

Ryder, R. W. et al, "Fertility Rates in 238 HIV-1-Seropositive Women in Zaire Folowed for 3 Years Post-Partum," AIDS, vol. 5. (1991), pp. 1521-1527.

Serwadda, D. et al, "The Social Dynamics of HIV Transmission as Reflected Through Discordant Couples in Rural Uganda," AIDS, vol. 9 (1995), pp. 745-750.

Soro, B. N. et al, "Seroprevalence of HIV Infection in the General Population of the Côte d'Ivoire, West Africa", Journal of Acquired Immune Deficiency Syndromes, vol. 2 (1990), pp. 1193-1196.

Soro, B. N. et al, "The Present and Future Course of the AIDS Epidemic in Côte d'Ivoire", WHO Bulletin OMS, vol. 70 (1992), pp. 117-123.

US Bureau of the Census, HIV Surveillance Data Base (Washington: February, 1999).

Van der Straten, "Couple Communication, Sexual Coercion and HIV Risk Reduction in Kigali, Rwanda," AIDS, vol. 9 (1995), pp. 935-944.

Viscusi, W. K., Fatal Tradeoffs: Public and Private Responsibilities for Risk (Oxford: Oxford, 1992).

Wadsworth, J. et al, "What's in a Mean? – an Examination of the Inconsistency between Men and Women in Reporting Sexual Partnerships," Journal of the Royal Statistical Society, A, vol. 159 (1996), p. 111-123.

Whitaker, L. and A. M. Rentin, "A Theoretical Problem of Interpreting the Recently Reported Increase of Homosexual Gonorrhea," European Journal of Epidemiology, vol. 8 (1992), pp. 187-191.

48

Public policy and higher education

Peter H. Karmel[1]

The invitation to deliver the Joseph Fisher Lecture this year has given me great pleasure not only because of the honour of the invitation itself but because of my close association with the University of Adelaide during the 1950s and 1960s. I well remember the first Joseph Fisher Lecture in which I was involved. It was in 1952 and the lecturer was J. G. Crawford speaking on "Australian Agricultural Policy". In those days the lecture was held at night in the Bonython Hall and the platform party wore black ties. The official party arrived on the platform at 8.00 pm to discover a virtually empty hall – the University authorities had neglected to advertise the event! Embarrassed, the 15 or 20 persons present adjourned to the Staff Club where Jack Crawford conducted an informal but well informed seminar. I hope that we will do better this evening!

Purposes of higher education

The main purposes of universities have recently been described in a report of the Commonwealth Minister for Education, Training and Youth Affairs (Kemp, December 2000) as:

- to inspire and enable individuals to develop their capabilities to the highest potential throughout their lives (for personal growth and fulfilment, for effective participation in the workforce and for constructive contributions to society);
- to advance knowledge and understanding;
- to aid the application of knowledge and understanding to the benefit of the economy and the society;

1 Forty eighth Joseph Fisher Lecture, 30 April 2001. I wish to acknowledge the help of Mr R. H. Arthur in the development of the ideas set out in this paper and his assistance in spelling out details.

- to enable individuals to adapt and learn, consistent with the needs of an adaptable knowledge-based economy at local, regional and national levels; and

- to enable individuals to contribute to a democratic, civilised society and promote the tolerance and debate that underpins it.

Few would disagree with this list, although the manner in which a particular institution pursues these purposes depends on the priorities or weights it attaches to them.

Most would also agree that public policy relating to higher education should aim at facilitating these purposes by:

- promoting access to higher education;

- pursuing excellence in the work of students and in the scholarship and research of academic staff;

- providing an environment to enable universities to fulfil their purposes.

My purpose in this paper is to discuss the implications of the current arrangements for policy setting and management of our university system, in particular government/institution relations and funding mechanisms. These unquestionably impinge on the universities' capacity to fulfil their purposes and on the efficacy of public policy in meeting its objectives.

There is general agreement that our universities are in need of a substantial financial boost. (This has been recognised by the Commonwealth Government in the leaked 1999 Cabinet Submission and by the Opposition in its statements on the *Knowledge Nation*.) But the arguments for reform that I shall advance are deeper and the longer-term consequences of inaction more serious than simply a claim for more money. At stake is the nature and quality of our universities, their independence, their international competitiveness and their capacity to serve Australia in the 21st century.

The 1990s have seen significant changes in the relationship between universities and government. While some have been clearly beneficial (for example, the Higher Education Contribution Scheme (HECS)) the trend has been towards an increasing level of government and bureaucratic involvement with, and influence over, the way our universities function. Unless significant changes are made in the way governments interact with universities, the principles of institutional autonomy and academic independence will cease to have any real meaning, public higher education policy will falter and our universities will fail to meet our expectations.

Centralisation versus decentralisation

The present government involvement in the administration of higher education in Australia is highly centralised with a concentration of authority over the system in the hands of a government department under a Commonwealth Minister. The degree to which the system of higher education is currently subject to a single point of view is well illustrated by a reading of the Commonwealth Minister's current report on *Higher Education for the 2001 to 2003 Triennium* (Kemp, 2000). The document is not a report on the state of the universities but rather a specification of plans (resources and student numbers) for individual institutions and a declaration of policies for universities including a range of requirements that are to be met. There is no analysis of student demand, quality of intakes, adequacy of resourcing, staff numbers and quality, or quality of outcomes. Nor is there any discussion of options or trade-offs between numbers of students, quality and resources.

The flavour of centralised planning that imbues current higher education policy is in contrast to the emphasis currently being given to open and free markets in the economic world. In the economic world, centralised planning has seldom proved successful: decentralised markets are a much more effective mechanism for producing and distributing goods and services. The presumptions favouring a more decentralised system of universities are powerful.

The highly centralised perspective of higher education policy places emphasis on the pursuit of national objectives laid down by the Commonwealth Government. But in a free society national objectives are often imprecisely defined and are subject to controversy and change. Universities must prepare students for life in a world the characteristics of which are necessarily imperfectly foreseen. A university that geared its activities to known requirements could hardly provide an education or conduct research appropriate to meet as yet unknown problems. Moreover, one of the roles of a university in a free society is to be the conscience and critic of that society; such a role cannot be fulfilled if the university is expected to be an arm of government policy. There is thus a strong case for a plurality of priorities among universities whereby each institution determines its own priorities in the light of its circumstances and its assessment of the current and future environment.

The independence of the universities from direct government control or influence, i.e. institutional autonomy, is one pillar of a truly democratic society. Institutional autonomy is a necessary, if not a sufficient, condition for academic freedom – itself an essential element of the kind of society in which we live. The universities are among those institutions that should operate at arm's-length from government if they are properly to fulfil their role. In this they are not dissimilar to institutions such as the Reserve Bank, the Australian Broadcasting Corporation and other independent statutory bodies. Indeed, from 1959 when the Australian Universities Commission (AUC) commenced operations until 1987 when the Commonwealth Tertiary Education Commission (CTEC) was abolished the universities were largely, if not entirely, insulated from political pressures and their autonomy protected to a significantly greater degree than has recently been the case. This is not widely appreciated, either within or beyond the universities.

Decisions on public policy relating to higher education need to be informed by objective analysis unaffected by political/electoral considerations. The Commonwealth is unlikely to receive advice of this kind from a government department subject to ministerial direction and the lobbying of individual institutions. Above all, the advice should be based on sound knowledge and an understanding of how universities operate and their role in society.

The standard of public debate on higher education in terms both of knowledge of facts and sophistication of argument reflects a serious deficiency in our capacity for objective analysis. This is well illustrated by several policy proposals that have recently emerged. The first example is the proposal for a large-scale on-line university – a proposal made apparently without detailed consideration of the extensive involvement of some existing universities with distance education, including on-line delivery, and the not very encouraging experience of the Open

Learning Agency. Another is the suggestion that regional universities (somewhat eccentrically defined) should receive special support for the enrolment of research students (Aitkin, 2001) without regard to any rationale relating to research training itself. A third example is the Commonwealth proposal to create more science places, apparently without considering whether the putative shortfall of science graduates is due to a lack of places or a lack of appropriately qualified students.

For these reasons, and to enable the universities better to achieve their purposes, I am advocating:

(a) the establishment of an independent body to monitor higher education in Australia, to advise the Commonwealth Government through objective analysis of higher education issues and to act as an intermediary between the government and the institutions; and

(b) the decentralisation of the funding of teaching within universities.

Furthermore, the highest levels of scholarship, research and research training need to be concentrated, for any given discipline, in a limited number of locations in order to provide a critical mass of inputs and achieve excellence in outcomes. The alternative is for these activities to be a by-product of undergraduate student numbers, since these determine staff numbers in the individual institutions. This would hardly be a rational way of allocating scarce research resources. Consequently I am also advocating:

(c) some concentration of resources, in each discipline, for advanced teaching, scholarship and research.

Issues

Before proceeding with details of these reforms, I want to examine a number of issues arising from current policies and practices. They illustrate how higher education policy has evolved in recent years with little critical and objective analysis of its implications and without a proper regard for its consequences. They underline the need for reform. I shall discuss them under four headings: student numbers; resources; quality and; management.

Student numbers

Over the past decade university enrolments have shown considerable growth, increasing by almost 60 per cent. (Over the longer run, the expansion of Australian university education has been truly remarkable – when I was an undergraduate in 1940 there were only about 14,000 students in the whole country, and when I came to Adelaide in 1950 there were under 31,000: now the figure is close to 700,000 – a 50-fold increase over my working life during which time the Australian population has multiplied 2½ fold).

All Students – Australian universities

	1989	2000	Increase
	000	000	per cent
Non-overseas			
Research	12	33	171
Graduate course work	53	91	74
Undergraduate	355	476	34
Overseas	21	96	353
Total	**441**	**695**	**58**

Source: DETYA (2000b).

The increased participation in higher education is partly a reflection of a lengthening of the time people spend enrolled as students: research and graduate course work enrolments have increased much more than undergraduate enrolments and double degrees have become common. Thus while enrolment figures reflect the increased *participation* of the Australian population in higher education, they do not give a precise indication of *access* to higher education.

Access is measured in terms of numbers of students enrolling in higher education for the first time. If the numbers of first time commencers are related to the size of the relevant age groups, the lifetime probability of a person enrolling in higher education can be calculated. Thus, on the basis of current experience, some 47 per cent of an age cohort will enrol in a university either on leaving school or shortly after or at some later stage in their lives. (Incidentally, there is a marked gender differential: the probabilities being 40 per cent for men and 55 per cent for women).

The figure of 47 per cent indicates a high level of access to higher education in Australia. It is high absolutely and relative to comparable countries. The overall figure does, of course, conceal some differential access, particularly in relation to socio-economic status and to the situation of indigenous Australians.

	First-time commencing non-overseas students	**Probability of enrolling in higher education**
	'000	**per cent**
1989	103	37
1995	124	46
2000	127	47

Source: DETYA data base and author's calculations

Moreover the figure of 47 per cent should be considered in the context of access to all tertiary education, i.e. to vocational education and training as well as to higher education. When access to vocational education and training is added to access to higher education, and double counting is eliminated, the life time probability of accessing tertiary education comes out close to 90 per cent (Aungles, Karmel and Wu, 2000). This must be near to saturation. Of course, for a given level of access, participation in tertiary education may still increase if students take longer courses or more courses or endure more failures.

Over the past ten years or so policies have promoted access and the growth of the higher education system, but there has been virtually no discussion as to what an appropriate level of access or size of the system might be. The fact is that trade-offs between student numbers and entry standards, and between student numbers and the resources available for teaching each student, have been ignored.

An examination of tertiary entrance scores reveals that some universities have relatively low entry standards. This can be illustrated by analyzing the tertiary entry scores in 2000 for the eighteen campuses located in New South Wales. Most universities admit some students with very low scores, probably because of special circumstances. To eliminate these the Universities Admissions Index (UAI) rank at the ninth decile for each campus has been calculated. These indicate the index above which 90 per cent of those newly enrolled in 2000 ranked. It can be seen that these vary between 75.2 and 46.4 – a wide disparity in standards of entry. The overall State average is 64.0.

Entry standards are inversely related to numbers of enrolments. Enrolments are largely determined by the number that the Commonwealth is willing to fund – a number fixed apparently without regard to standards – and by the desire of institutions to grow. Thus standards are determined by the number of students universities manage to enrol, and by the general view that the more students the better, rather than the number being the result of standards set by the institutions. If entry standards become too low the quality of work that can be expected of students will fall and degree standards decline. This is not to say that some variation in entry standards might not be desirable or that less demanding courses do not have a place, but decisions in relation to standards ought to be made deliberately.

New to higher education enrolments universities admission index

New South Wales 2000

Campus	**Ninth decile**	**Campus**	**Ninth decile**
A	75.1	J	55.8
B	62.5	K	53.3
C	70.7	L	54.7
D	52.9	M	75.5
E	61.0	N	67.0
F	55.6	O	75.2
G	74.3	P	70.2
H	54.4	Q	67.8
I	46.4	R	47.1

All Campuses: 64.0

Source: New South Wales Admissions Centre data base and author's calculations

Over the past decade, with enrolments expanding faster than funding, the resources available per student for teaching have declined. As a result the quality of the university experience offered to students has deteriorated, also compromising standards.

The size of the higher education system to be supported by government funding should be the result of a deliberate decision taken after an objective analysis which considers the interrelationships among the level of access, the standards of entry, the resources (cost) per student, student demand and the accessibility of other forms of post-school education and training. This has not happened over the past twelve years or so.

Resources

Over the past twenty years public funding for higher education institutions has not risen as rapidly as enrolments. This reflects the Commonwealth Government's view that the institutions should improve their efficiency so that the burden imposed by the universities on Commonwealth finances can be reduced.

In 1989 the Commonwealth Government transferred some of the public funding burden to students, requiring them to contribute a portion of the cost of their courses either up-front or through income contingent loans. In 1996 the Commonwealth raised the charges under HECS and differentiated them among courses. Allowing for forgone interest and defaults, HECS charges are tending towards covering around 25 per cent of base operating grants.

Commonwealth outlays on higher education in real terms, net of HECS receipts, are now 5 per cent lower than they were in 1995 despite an increase of 10 per cent in non-overseas student load and an increase of 25 per cent in the size of the economy as measured by gross domestic product. Virtually the whole expansion of domestic enrolments since the early 1990s, as reflected in base operating grants, has been funded by a combination of students' contributions and increased teaching loads. Public funding of universities has been significantly compressed.

Commonwealth Government funding for higher education in year 2001 prices[a]

	1988	1993	1995	2000
	$m	$m	$m	$m
Base operating grants[b]	3,624	4,294	4,763	4,886
HECS receipts	-	250	499	917
Base operating grants, net of HECS	3,624	4,044	4,264	3,969
Other Commonwealth funds	313	762	921	939
Net Commonwealth funding	3,937	4,806	5,185	4,908

a current funding adjusted for cost increases by Commonwealth's cost adjustment factor;
b including HECS liabilities.
Source: AVCC (2001).

The serious deficiency in funding that the universities have faced in the last five or six years is mainly the result of two factors: the introduction of enterprise bargaining into university industrial relations in 1993 in relation to which the Commonwealth no longer fully funds salary increases, and the Commonwealth decision in 1996 to reduce its funding of base operating grants by a total of 6 per cent over the years 1997-2000.

To maintain real funding per student at 1995 levels in the light of salary and other cost increases an increase in government base operating grants of around $¾ billion would be required. In the light of the decline in Commonwealth funding of universities that has taken place since the mid-1990s, such an increase would not in itself appear to be unduly burdensome for the Commonwealth.

Universities have responded to the above financial pressures by shedding staff and/or by enrolling additional students so as to attract marginal funding at rates well below the average cost of teaching students. Either way, academic staff /student ratios have grossly deteriorated.

Student/staff ratios

1975	11.7
1980	11.7
1989	14.2
1995	15.0
2000	18.7

Source: TEC (1985); DETYA (2000b).

During the 1970s the ratios were around 1 to 12. By 1989 they had fallen to 1 to 14 and by 1995 to 1 to 15. These declines were a response to pressures for improved efficiency and may have reflected an element of substitution of technology for face-to-face teaching. However by the year 2000, the institutions' reduced command over resources forced a further decline to 1 to 18.7 – a decline of over 20 per cent in five years. As a result many classes are now far too large; staff/student contact has diminished; academic staff have inadequate time for preparation, study and their own scholarship and research; and morale is low. In the international market for top quality staff, salaries and working conditions are making the Australian universities increasingly unattractive.

During the 1970s and early 1980s considerable improvements were achieved in teacher/pupil ratios in schools. By and large, in spite of budgetary pressures, these improvements have been maintained through Commonwealth and State Government support for both government and non-government schools, with only a slight deterioration in government schools in some States. (Harrold, 2000). This is in striking contrast to the treatment accorded the Commonwealth funded higher education sector.

Decisions about the government's resourcing of the universities need to be made in the context of the consequences of these decisions in terms of student numbers and the quality of the work of the institutions. Again, objective analysis is essential.

The universities have been active, and in many cases very successful, in seeking alternative sources of revenue. However major elements of the revenue from new sources are dedicated to particular activities (especially research and consultancies), and fees from overseas students are largely absorbed by teaching those students. The fact is that the teaching of Australian undergraduates and the training of Australian research students has been and remains virtually 100 per cent dependent on the Commonwealth Government. It must be remembered that the Commonwealth determines the level of HECS payments for undergraduates just as it determines the level of its grants; thus, the universities remain almost 70 per cent dependent on the Commonwealth with its highly centralised mode of dealing with the institutions.

Universities revenue by source

	1981	**1989**	**1998**
	per cent	**per cent**	**per cent**
Commonwealth Government grants	89	77	51
HECS	-	-	17
Fees and charges	-	6	16
Other	11	17	16
	100	100	100

Source: AVCC (2000).

While there has clearly been a welcome diversification of the sources of university revenue, it should not be assumed that all diversification is desirable. As already pointed out, diversification may not produce resources which are available for discretionary use. Moreover the thrust towards the commercialization of university activities (especially research), apart from carrying high risks, raises the questions of whether commercialization is not a distraction from the universities' core business of teaching and research and whether the skills available in universities and the culture that imbues them are generally appropriate for commercial enterprises. Enthusiasm for commercialization should not lead us to assume that these are settled questions, however desirable commercial operations might be in particular instances. Again, objective analysis is needed.

Quality

One of the positive consequences of the changes in higher education initiated by John Dawkins in 1987 (Dawkins, 1988) (I hasten to interpolate that there were a number of negative ones) was an increased emphasis on outcomes and a growing consciousness of the importance of institutional efficiency and effectiveness. Indeed, concerns about efficiency and effectiveness in education had surfaced earlier and reviews of school and higher education efficiency and effectiveness had been conducted in the mid-1980s (Karmel, 1985; Hudson, 1986), but within the universities serious attention to these matters did not surface until the 1990s.

The abolition of the binary divide in higher education in 1988, which resulted in a doubling of the number of universities, and the subsequent large increase in enrolments, stimulated concerns about the quality of the work of the universities and resulted in the establishment of the Committee for Quality Assurance in Higher Education (CQAHE). The Committee conducted inspections and published reports on the institutions in the three years 1993 to 1995. Universities were given gradings and rewards for good performance. The exercise involved elements of both quality assessment and quality assurance. To date there has been no attempt to assess its value or effectiveness.

Recently (March 2000) the Ministerial Council on Education, Employment, Training and Youth Affairs (MCEETYA) endorsed the establishment of the Australian Universities Quality Agency (AUQA) as an independent body to conduct quality audits of higher education institutions on a five yearly basis. The emphasis is on the quality assurance processes employed by institutions and the audits will be conducted on a whole-of-institution basis (Kemp, 2000).

The issue of quality is bedevilled by the complexity of what is meant by "quality" in a university setting. Clearly, quality is multi-dimensional. For the range of courses offered by a university there are questions of quality in relation to course content, teaching, lecturers, graduate outcomes, the environment for students, and so on. Quality of research activities or community services raises an equally large range of issues.

Discussions of quality in universities seldom specify quality characteristics in ways capable of precise definition or measurement. Moreover, the benefits that a university education may be expected to confer on graduates (and which reflect the quality of that education) accrue not on graduation but over a lifetime and therefore are difficult to assess at any given point of time.

In the production and distribution of most goods and services in the market economy, quality is able to be more or less precisely defined and assessed. Mechanisms for quality control, quality assurance and quality improvement can be devised and applied in a relatively straight forward manner. This is not the case in the field of education and the application of techniques established for ordinary business purposes may be of little practical benefit and be wasteful of effort. This is not to say that concerns about quality are unimportant, but the special characteristics of educational and research processes need to be taken into account.

The conceptual difficulties in defining what is meant by quality in higher education and in assessing it have lead to an emphasis on quality assurance mechanisms. Indeed this was the emphasis of the CQAHE in 1993-95 and is the remit of the newly formed AUQA. There is a risk that quality assurance procedures will be set up in institutions which will absorb considerable resources and be little more than rituals pursued to conform with the requirements of bodies external to them. A "whole-of-institution" approach seems likely to reinforce this risk, since the heterogeneity of a university's activities makes variability of quality within the institution probable. Moreover, the existence of quality assurance mechanism is relatively unimportant if quality outcomes are in fact being achieved; if they are not being achieved the existence of quality assurance rituals is no guarantee of quality improvement. In all considerations of quality in universities the fundamental role played by academic staff needs to be emphasized: the surest route to high quality outcomes is high quality staff.

The alternative approach to quality assurance reviews of whole institutions is peer review on a course or field of study basis; for example, a review every so many years of a given course or field of study across all institutions, involving quality assessment and an audit of processes to achieve quality improvement. Such reviews rely on the expertise of people with years of experience in the activities that they are assessing. The Quality Assurance Agency for Higher Education in the United Kingdom appears to be operating along these lines (QAA, 2000). In fact discipline reviews of law, engineering, accounting, teacher education in mathematics and science, agriculture and computer science were conducted in the late 1980s through CTEC, with some positive results. The contrast between such an approach and that likely to be followed by the AUQA underlines the need for a capacity for objective analysis of policy options in this important area.

Management

I shall refer to two separate aspects of management in universities: the first relates to the internal management arrangements of the institutions; the second to the influence exerted by current government policy on these arrangements.

I have already pointed out, in respect of quality issues, that the provision of education services is different from the ordinary business of supplying goods and services in the market place. Universities are not driven by the motive of maximising profits: there is no bottom line in the private enterprise sense. Instead there is a whole range of outputs – course offerings, graduations, research results, publications, community services – that cannot be added together to give a profit and loss statement or a balance sheet. Moreover the executive of a university cannot exercise the same degree of control over the operations of the institution as the executive of a corporation of comparable size, because "authority" in the university is necessarily disseminated among the professors who are the authorities in their own fields. In addition, universities, as currently operating, have only little control over the quantities of services they provide and the prices they charge for them. In brief, universities are *sui generis* and the application of management practices which work in private businesses will not necessarily work in them.

Many decisions within universities need to be made on a collegial basis – although the definition of the "college" is variable and is not necessarily inclusive – in particular, appointment of academic staff, admission of students, course structure, examining, research evaluation. However, there is no simple dichotomy between collegial and managerial styles of governance. The resources available to universities are limited; they have to be managed. Decisions on their allocation need to be made strategically, and this may require executive action. In short, universities require a style of management that is, at least, consultative in process even if firm in final decision-making.

In recent years government policy has been not to attempt to micro-manage the universities but to induce universities to become more "business like" by requiring them to conform to certain practices and to pursue government priorities by offering inducements through special programs. These requirements and inducements have, in practice, resulted in considerable government intervention.

The former include the submission of quality assurance and improvement plans, guidelines for the preparation of annual financial reports, equity plans, capital management plans, research and research training plans, mission statements and strategic plans. These plans absorb considerable resources. They are usually of little operational use either within the institutions or for policy formulation. Their development seems little more than a ritual. Thus research plans have to be expressed in very general terms since a university's research activities are so many and varied, developments are often quite unpredictable and progress serendipitous. The application of business techniques to universities may, in some cases, turn out to be counter-productive. This appears not to be understood by government authorities.

As far as special programs are concerned, the Minister's recent report (Kemp 2000) lists 37 programs, projects and schemes which are managed by the Higher Education Division of DETYA. Many of these involve providing universities with grants earmarked for specific purposes. This procedure reduces the discretion universities can exercise in the allocation of their funds and their capacity to determine their own priorities. It reflects the interventionist flavour of government policy towards higher education over the last twelve years or so, during which additional funding has been provided only in ways circumscribed by the Commonwealth. This has been accepted by universities, apparently with little questioning.

A prime example of conditional funding is the Commonwealth's funding for its Workplace Reform Program for universities, involving the payment of an additional 2 per cent of the notional salary component of operating grants. Twenty one criteria have been laid down and universities are expected to conform to at least a number of these. Some of these criteria will significantly affect the detailed internal management arrangements of the institutions, and are highly interventionist.

Since universities have no bottom line by which to measure performance, government policy has supported DETYA in developing a range of performance indicators (a practice which has become common in many public sector operations). Performance indicators can provide useful information, but they need to be interpreted with caution. Some do little more than describe the characteristics of particular institutions (e.g. student numbers, range of courses); others are influenced by many independent variables which the indicator cannot take into account (e.g. pass rates, students' course experience questionnaires). Great care must be taken in comparing the performance of institutions or in constructing league tables. The precise meanings of indicators need explication. Objective analysis of performance indicators is essential if conclusions are to be drawn from them.

The Commonwealth Government in allocating funds has made a good deal of use of formulae. The distribution of operating grants has been based on a formula since the relative funding model was established in 1990. As a consequence of the White Paper on research funding (Kemp 1999), the allocation of funding for research training, as well as the allocation of the research quantum (now institutional grants) and the research infra-structure block grants, is formula based. Many universities have themselves adopted the formulae (sometimes in a modified form) for internal allocation purposes – a practice which places internal allocation procedures in a straitjacket and greatly reduces managerial discretion in funding.

As far as allocation among institutions is concerned, the use of publicly known formulae almost always produces unintended, but perfectly predictable, consequences. Universities feel they have little choice but to play the formula, incentives are affected and undesirable consequences emerge (e.g. researchers may be encouraged to produce numbers of small, quick and superficial publications rather than a major piece of work, universities may engage in wasteful competition and misleading advertising to attract students, diversity among institutions may be reduced as they attempt to profit from a common formula). On the whole publicly known and automatically applied formula funding ought to be avoided.

Universities have been under pressure for some time to improve efficiency. Productivity, as crudely measured, has certainly risen substantially over the past decade. Thus, course completions rose by over 80 per cent over the decade 1989-99, while full time equivalent academic staff rose by less than 20 per cent – a productivity increase (completions per academic worker) of over 50 per cent or 4 per cent per annum. Superficially this is a creditable performance. However, this is a quite misleading conclusion because the services rendered by academics to students, their research activities and their community services have almost certainly diminished. University staff are in the business of rendering personal services in much the same way as doctors, lawyers and other professionals. A greater throughput of clients inevitably affects the quality of the services rendered. Again, objective analysis of this and other management issues is needed.

Productivity (???)

	1989	1999	Increase
Course completions	90,477	164,423	82 per cent
Academic staff (FTE)	24,919	29,748	19 per cent

Source: DETYA (2000a,b).

Reforming higher education[2]

The matters that I have just discussed illustrate the need for major reforms in the arrangements for higher education in this country as well as for additional public resources. Without these reforms and without additional resources, Australia's higher education system is likely to regress towards a uniform mediocrity. I now turn to the question of reform. I shall deal with it under four headings: government/institution relations; funding undergraduate courses; funding research training and; funding research.

2 What follows is based on the proposals set out in some detail in my paper "Reforming Higher Education" recently published as an Occasional Paper by the Academy of Social Sciences in Australia (Karmel, 2000).

Government/institution relations

An independent statutory body standing between the universities and the government, along the lines of the commissions which operated successfully from 1959 to 1987, should be established. The Australian Research Council (ARC) recently constituted as a statutory body with advisory, policy and operational responsibilities also provides an appropriate model. The body should:

(a) advise the government publicly on all higher education matters;

(b) report publicly, say triennially, on the state of higher education in Australia;

(c) accredit institutions for eligibility to receive public funding for undergraduate higher education, subject to appropriate conditions;

(d) accredit institutions for eligibility to enrol holders of research training awards in particular disciplines;

(e) advise on the number and value of publicly funded undergraduate places and research training awards;

(f) advise on institutional research grants (research block funding);

(g) advise and report on quality assurance mechanisms both within and across institutions;

(h) administer programs arising from the foregoing.

The statutory body should have operational responsibilities, i.e. it should administer policies and programs and not be purely advisory. Limiting the responsibilities of such a body to offering advice and publishing reports is a recipe for irrelevance. This was clearly demonstrated in the case of the National Board of Employment, Education and Training and its Councils.

The statutory body should be chaired by a respected senior person with academic and management experience (of vice-chancellorial status or the equivalent) and include eight members: two academics, two practitioners of the professions, two business persons and two members from the wider community. The members should be persons of high standing, who are well informed on how universities work and what they do. The membership should not include current vice-chancellors or senior university executives. It should certainly not be representative: the arrangements need to guard against capture by interest groups.

The proposed body would be able to address objectively those issues, to which I have referred, relating to the size of the higher education sector, its resourcing, its quality and its management and provide the Commonwealth with advice on them, indicating the consequences of various courses of action. Such advice would be public and would lead to more transparent decision making. Moreover, the existence of a buffer body between the institutions and the government would greatly reduce, if not eliminate, political pressures on the institutions as well as protect the government from lobbying by the institutions. Universities would be freer to express their views on policy issues affecting them without the concern currently obtaining that they cannot afford to criticize or embarrass their paymaster. The low level and quality of the public debate on the issues that I have canvassed is proof enough of the reluctance of senior university officers to make statements for which their institutions might be disadvantaged.

Funding undergraduate courses

The Commonwealth should move to the funding of undergraduate courses through students rather than through direct government grants to institutions. To achieve this, the Commonwealth should offer annually some 120,000 scholarships (almost the current number of first time commencing university students – I am assuming a slight tightening of standards). This number would support a university system of around the present scale – the number would need to be adjusted from time to time in relation to demographics and standards. A scholarship would entitle the winner to, say, up to five years of subsidised full time equivalent undergraduate or coursework graduate education at a university to which he/she can gain entry. Enrolling a scholarship holder would entitle the university to an annual subsidy from the Commonwealth for the duration of the course. The subsidies would need to vary according to the cost level of the student's enrolment.

At present funding levels the subsidies would need to average around $6,500 per annum. To the extent that the erosion of operating grants of the past five years is restored in real terms they would need to be higher. Universities would charge higher education contributions on top of the subsidies. On average they would need to be around $4,000 per annum. Courses or course work extending beyond the five years of subsidised tuition would carry full fees.

Some institutions would compete for students by charging less; others might charge more to cover the cost of special services. Some might charge the same for all courses; others might take into account differential costs or the relative demand for courses. In order to allay fears of the charges being pushed too high, it might be necessary for the government to mandate an upper limit to the contributions.

Both the subsidies and the upper limits to the contributions would need to be indexed to take account of movements in the cost of the resources universities employ. The salaries component should be indexed by movements in average weekly earnings and the remainder, as at present, by the Consumer Price Index. It would be essential for the students' contributions to be subject to the present HECS arrangements.

The 120,000 scholarships should be divided into three tranches. About 80,000 should be allocated on the basis of students' tertiary entrance (TE) scores; State and Territory rankings would need to be converted to a national ranking, but there is a standard procedure for doing this. About 30,000 should be available for mature age entry. These could be allocated on the basis of candidates' results in the Special Tertiary Admissions Test (STAT) administered by the Australian Council for Educational Research (ACER) and already widely used for admitting mature age entrants. The remaining 10,000 scholarships should be allocated to institutions for special entries to be awarded at the institutions' discretion.

The 120,000 scholarships annually represent about 45 per cent of an age cohort. The number of scholarships, and hence the number of subsidised enrolments, would need to be determined by the Commonwealth Government from time to time after careful analysis, taking account of demographic factors, entry standards, student demand, workforce considerations, the availability of alternative vocational education and training opportunities, and costs. The analysis, and the public advice to the Commonwealth flowing from it, would be a major responsibility of the statutory body proposed earlier.

The suggested reform will meet opposition from staff and student bodies, partly because of objections to student charges on principle and partly because of fears that universities will push up charges. The former are countered by the continuation of the patently equitable HECS arrangements (and by a recognition that universities are, in any case socially selective and charging students a contribution serves to promote equity in the distribution of costs and benefits between those who do and those who do not receive a higher education); and the latter are countered by the previously suggested ceiling on student contributions.

The proposals will also be opposed by some universities because they fear that the stronger institutions will admit increasing numbers of students leaving them with too few. This is especially a fear of regional universities. In my view, these concerns are exaggerated. In the current active competition for students most regional universities experience strong demand. If anything the above arrangements should advantage them as they could compete by lowering their higher education contribution charges. However, if necessary, the Commonwealth could impose limits on the number of scholarships tenable at individual universities. Such a move should allay concerns. Alternatively, lump sum annual subsidies of, say, $5m or $10m might be paid to regional institutions.

The proposed reform has many advantages. Entry standards would be determined on educational grounds rather than in response to political, regional and institutional pressures as at present. The allocation of student places would be determined through a combination of education testing and student choice, thus avoiding arguments about States' shares of enrolments. Funding would be decentralized and political pressures and bureaucratic intervention would be greatly reduced as would bilateral dealing between institutions and government officials. The grant assessment and profile negotiation functions of DETYA would no longer be required; the number of enrolments, subject to possible upper limits, would be a matter for each institution to determine. The universities' independence would be enhanced and they would become patently responsible for their own affairs. They could determine their own priorities, and diversity in course offerings, teaching methods and student services would be promoted. The Commonwealth Government would not be directly involved in assessing/monitoring the quality of institutions. There would be economies in public administration.

At the same time, the Commonwealth would be in a position to control its expenditure on higher education teaching through the quantum, value and length of tenure of scholarships and through the conditions under which HECS operates. The Commonwealth could still influence the development of higher education through the quantum of scholarships and their value, and through the provision of capital to establish and foster new institutions. The quantum of scholarships and entry standards would be clearly linked. Governments could also expand access for special groups by special scholarship schemes. It would remain open to the Commonwealth to provide funding to particular institutions for specific purposes under contractual arrangements.

Funding research training

The funding of research training has thus far been built into the operating grants of universities. The Commonwealth Government is currently proposing to separate out this funding and to attach it to some 21,500 research training places to be allocated to universities by a formula based on their research degree completions, their publications and the research funds they attract. The research training places will bring with them funding to the universities at two rates according to cost, and averaging about $23,000 per equivalent full time place per annum.

These new arrangements will cap the number of Commonwealth funded higher degree research places and encourage some concentration, but overall they will reinforce the emphasis on quantity rather than quality. Institutions will tend to play the formula and compete aggressively with each other by enrolling as many research students as possible, in order to ensure that they at least maintain their relative share of a fixed quantum of funding.

The allocating of research training awards to the students themselves rather than to the universities would be a significant advance. Thus the Commonwealth should offer annually some 6,000 postgraduate research training awards. This number of new awards would support a total enrolment of about 21,500 awardees, which corresponds to the present level of funded research enrolments. An award would entitle the winner to, say, two years of equivalent full-time research training for a master's degree or four years for a PhD at a university willing to enrol him/her. The award would carry a subsidy to the university to cover the full cost of training. There ought to be, say, three levels of subsidy according to the cost of training: at current funding levels these would average about $23,000.

Candidates for the awards should apply through the university of their undergraduate degree or through a university willing to give them status. The individual universities would place their candidates in order of merit. Candidates would be required to sit the Graduate Skills Assessment Test administered by the ACER. Their results in this would be used to calibrate university rankings so as to obtain a national ranking of the candidates.

Candidates successful in obtaining awards would select the institution at which they wished to train (not necessarily the university nominating them) and, if acceptable to the institution, would enrol there. Students should be encouraged to undertake their research at institutions other than those at which they were enrolled for their undergraduate studies. Funding them for an additional semester of study might be an effective way of achieving this. A width of experience is important. In Australia there has been far too little movement of research students. Students who do not obtain awards could be enrolled by universities on a fee paying basis. For these, access to HECS arrangements would be desirable.

The arguments in favour of concentrating the research activities of particular disciplines in a limited number of locations (see below) apply equally to research training, that is, the need for appropriate physical infrastructure and sufficient senior research staff. There has been a tendency over the past ten or twelve years to enrol excessive numbers of research students either to attract funding or for reasons of prestige: evidence of this is the great rise in research student numbers from 14,600 in 1989 to 37,300 in 2000; of the latter, 9,200 are at institutions which were not universities at the beginning of the period.

Concentration of research training would raise research quality generally and enhance students' training experiences. Such concentration could be achieved by restricting the tenure of research training awards in a particular discipline to those locations which are rated at higher levels in the research assessment exercise proposed below.

Final year studies for honours bachelor degrees are akin to research training: they usually involve a research project and are often preliminary to undertaking postgraduate research. Such studies need supervision by senior scholars and researchers. For these reasons a case can be made for concentrating final year honours studies in particular disciplines in those institutions eligible to enrol research training awardees.

Funding research

The provision of block funding to universities for research is essential to provide physical infrastructure, a staff base on which research activity can be built and a capacity to undertake long-term fundamental research unlikely to attract project funding.

Present block funding (the research quantum, research infrastructure block grants and the ARC small grants scheme), apart from being inadequate in amount, is spread too thinly across institutions. Funds are distributed by formulae which give insufficient weight to quality and which encourage institutions to expand higher degree enrolments, irrespective of their research capacity, and to foster research activity, irrespective of its intrinsic merit. The Commonwealth is proposing to increase research funding, but the changes currently being implemented through the Government's White Paper on research funding maintain the formula based approach to block funding.

In any given disciplinary field, research ought to be concentrated on those research teams whose members and facilities have the appropriate strengths; for example, in say 10 or so locations rather than spread over up to 38 universities. The concentration should be on a discipline not an institutional basis. Such concentration would unquestionably raise productivity and research quality.

Australia should move to an assessment of research strengths in universities along the lines of the Research Assessment Exercise which has been conducted in the United Kingdom for some years (RAE, 2001). The research activities of the universities would be classified on a discipline basis into units of assessment. Every five years a committee of senior researchers for each unit of assessment would review the relevant research activities in those universities seeking assessment in that unit. The committee would rate the quality of the activities. Institutional research grants (i.e. block funding to individual universities) would be calculated in relation to numbers of active research staff and research costs in each assessed discipline weighted by a quality index on, say, a five point scale. There would be no predetermined distribution of the quality ratings for a given unit of assessment; the classification would be based purely on absolute research quality. Some research groups might rate no support; some minor support; others might rate considerable support. Once the institutional research grant was determined for a particular institution (based on the ratings of its assessed disciplines) the allocation of the grant would be at the institution's discretion – support for disciplines not assessed could be provided.

The Research Assessment Exercise in the UK is a complex operation and is by no means universally popular, but it has been working effectively for 15 years and has recently been favourably reviewed. It concentrates research funding among the most productive and promising researchers. It does not aim at nominating particular institutions to be research universities, but concentrates on disciplines within universities. The allocation of institutional research grants along the lines proposed would concentrate activity in the most promising locations and enhance quality. All research groups would have the opportunity of being assessed.

The suggested reform will probably run into opposition because it will expose weaknesses as well as strengths. However, the concentration of research on a discipline rather than an institution basis should make it more acceptable. All universities would have research strengths in some disciplines. Moreover, the assessment of research would be regularly revisited, and institutions would be able to use institutional research grants to support any research considered worthwhile.

Conclusion

The proposed reforms, involving the funding of most university courses through scholarships to students and the concentration of research activity on a discipline basis, have been canvassed by myself and others over the past decade (see, for example, Miller and Pincus, 1995). They have not received wide support. More surprising is that the proposed re-establishment of a statutory body to advise on higher education policy, administer higher education programs, and stand between the institutions and the government, has not been discussed to a significant extent; indeed its possibility was not even mentioned in the Review of Higher Education (West, 1998). In my view this is, perhaps, the most important of the reforms that I am suggesting.

Much of the opposition to the funding reforms stems from fears of rising fees, of unequal resourcing of institutions, of doctrinaire deregulation, marketisation and commercialisation and of barriers to access to university education. Most of these fears are unjustified: fees and higher education contributions will be moderated by competition and can be capped by government; institutions will be resourced in relation to the activities taking place within them; the elimination of direct involvement by government in universities' affairs is essential to the promotion of institutional autonomy, academic freedom and a diverse system of higher education, and, in any event, the government can set the ground rules, provide broad guidelines and determine the aggregate level of public financial support for higher education; access will be promoted by funding a sufficient number of scholarships, by maintaining and extending the HECS arrangements, by special programs for disadvantaged groups (especially in schools) and by promoting greater social and economic equality.

One of the arguments commonly used in supporting the provision of public funds to universities *via* students rather than directly is that this will create a competitive market for university services which will bring with it the efficiency and effectiveness benefits that flow from competitive arrangements. There is some force in this argument, but I am not relying too much on it for the reforms I am advocating. My justification for them has more to do with the maintenance of the independence of the universities and the pursuit of excellence than with the benefits flowing from market economics.

Students are not and cannot be well informed consumers in the same way as those who are operating in the market for detergent or automobiles or other ordinary goods and services. Ordinary goods and services have characteristics that are more or less well known. But the benefits to be rendered by a university course cannot be known with any precision to the intending student, nor can there be any symmetry in knowledge between student and academic. Also in any given locality there are necessarily relatively few university suppliers and certainly not a perfectly competitive market. Thus the optimum properties of competitive markets cannot be expected to hold in the market for educational services. Moreover universities, as non-profit and publicly assisted bodies, must respond to public interest considerations; for example, in the maintenance of scholarship and research in basic disciplines or in areas of national concern, even if student demand in these areas is low. It should be obvious from my proposals on funding and on research assessment that I am not advocating a free-for-all deregulated market for higher education, although this appears to be a common misinterpretation of what I am suggesting.

The reforms I have outlined will ensure quality higher education for a high proportion of the Australian population – in the long run about one half of the population will have attended university and more than one third will possess degrees of high standing. The reforms will also create numerous concentrations of scholarly and research activity at the forefront of the natural sciences and technology and in the humanities and social sciences. Thus the objectives of widespread access to higher education, of nurturing the most intellectually able and of providing an environment in which higher education can flourish will be served.

Higher education reform needs to be developed through an objective analysis of what is wrong with the present arrangements and how they might be improved for the benefit of Australia and Australians. Public policies should be judged by their consequences. It is a matter of what will work best, not of being bound by ideological predilections of whatever persuasion.

References

Aitkin, Don (2001), "Definition of regional universities sure to annoy," *Monitor*, University of Canberra, 27 February.

Augles, Phil, Tom Karmel and Tim Wu (2000), "Demographic and Social Change: Implications for Education Funding," in *School Resourcing: Models and Practices in Changing Times* edited by Peter Karmel, Australian College of Education: College Year Book.

AVCC (2000) (Australian Vice-Chancellors' Committee) (2001), *Key Statistics*, Canberra, July.

AVCC (2001) (Australian Vice-Chancellors' Committee) (2001), *Funding Tables*, Canberra, March.

CTEC (1985), Commonwealth Tertiary Education Commission (Chaired by Hugh Hudson), *Report for 1982-84 Triennium*, Canberra, September.

CTEC (1986), Commonwealth Tertiary Education Commission (Chaired by Hugh Hudson), *Review of Efficiency and Effectiveness in Higher Education*, Canberra, September.

Dawkins, Hon. John S. (1988), *Higher Education, A Policy Statement*, Canberra, July.

DETYA (Department of Education, Training and Youth Affairs) (2000a), *Selected Higher Education Statistics – Staff*, Canberra.

DETYA (Department of Education, Training and Youth Affairs) (2000b), *Selected Higher Education Statistics – Students*, Canberra.

Harrold, Ross (2000), "The Economic and Political Context of School Resourcing: 1985-2000," in *School Resourcing: Models and Practices in Changing Times* edited by Peter Karmel, Australian College of Education: College Year Book.

Karmel, Peter (2000), "Reforming Higher Education," *Occasional Paper, Series 2/2000*, Canberra: Academy of the Social Sciences in Australia, December.

Kemp, Hon. David (1999) *Knowledge and Innovation, A Policy Statement on Research and Research Training*, Canberra, December.

Kemp, Hon. David (2000), *Higher Education, Report for the 2001 to 2003 Triennium*, Canberra, December.

Miller, Paul W and Jonathon J. Pincus (1988), "Financing Higher Education in Australia: the case for Super HECS," *Journal of Higher Education Policy and Management* 20 (2), November.

Quality Assurance Agency for Higher Education (2000), *About QAA*, Canberra http://www.qaa.ac.uk/aboutqaa/aboutQAA.htm

Report of Review Committee (Chaired by Peter Karmel) (1985), *Quality of Education in Australia*, Canberra: April.

Research Assessment Exercise (2001), *What is the RAE 2001*? http://www.rae.ac.uk/AboutUs/

Review of Higher Education Financing and Policy (Chaired by Roderick West) (1998), *Learning for Life*, Canberra, April.

49

The role of natural resources in economic development

Edward B. Barbier[1]

Compared to some other academic disciplines, economics is not known for being particularly tolerant of revisions to its "mainstream" core concepts or paradigms. Yet, today a major change is occurring in the economic view of the world, and it is likely to have profound implications for many years to come.

Surprisingly, however, contemporary economists appear to be largely unaware that their "worldview" is undergoing such an important change. Perhaps one reason is that, unlike previous major innovations in economic thinking, there is no one person responsible or associated with the new doctrine, such as a Karl Marx with "Marxism", a John Maynard Keynes with "Keynesian economics", a John Nash with "Nash equilibrium", or a Milton Friedman with "monetarism". Perhaps another reason is that the change in economic thinking has been fairly gradual and unheralded. Just as it is hard to pinpoint a single individual, or even a group of like-minded individuals, as being responsible for this changing worldview, it is difficult to find a particular body of work, journal articles or books that has instigated this change. Instead, in this instance economic thinking is evolving more as the result of outside influences and pressures, such as the need for economics to be "relevant" to contemporary policy issues and problems.

So what exactly is this gradual, largely unnoticed, yet possibly profound change in the economic worldview? Simply put, the age-old concept of the "economic system" has been irrevocably changed. No longer do we consider the

1 Forty-ninth Joseph Fisher Lecture, 30 September 2002. Since published in *Australian Economic Papers* 42(2): 253-72, June 2003.

economic process of producing goods and services and generating human welfare to be solely dependent on the accumulation of physical and human capital. That is, an increasing number of economists now accept that there is a third form of "capital" or "economic asset" that is also crucial to the functioning of the economic system of production, consumption and overall welfare. This distinct category consists of the natural and environmental resource endowment available to an economy, which is often referred to generally as *natural capital.*

The rest of this lecture is devoted to elaborating further on the "new thinking" concerning the relationship between natural resources and economic development, and in particular, on the key issues and debates that are emerging from this thinking. As a useful starting point, I will characterize briefly how physical, human and natural capital are now thought to contribute to the functioning of an economic system. What becomes immediately clear is that the services provided by natural capital are unique, and in the case of the ecological services and life-support functions of the environment, are not well understood. As a result, there has also been considerable debate over the role of natural capital in "sustainable" economic development. That is, does the environment have an "essential" role in sustaining human welfare, and if so, are special "compensation rules" required to ensure that future generations are not made worse off by natural capital depletion today? A further debate has emerged over whether environmental degradation in an economy may initially increase, but eventually declines, as per capita income increases. Empirical verification of this *environmental Kuznets curve* hypothesis has occasionally been cited as evidence that economies will be able to overcome certain environmental problems through further economic growth and development. Finally, recent economic theories and empirical evidence have questioned whether poorer economies that are endowed with abundant natural resources develop more rapidly than economies that are relatively resource poor. It is often argued that resource-abundant economies are not reinvesting the rents generated from natural resource exploitation into productive assets, or that commodity price booms actually divert economic resources from more productive and innovative sectors.

In sum, our understanding of the role of natural resources in economic development has advanced considerably in recent years, although there is still much more to learn. In the rest of this lecture, I will try to convince you that what we do know about this role is sufficient to recognize that efficient and sustainable management of natural resources is a critical policy objective for the economic process. We can no longer exclude natural capital from any meaningful discussion of the factors determining economic development. Our concept of the "economic system" has indeed changed irrevocably.

Natural capital and the economic system

Figure 49.1 depicts the basic relationship between physical, human and natural capital and the economic system.

Figure 49.1: Human, physical and natural capital and the economic system

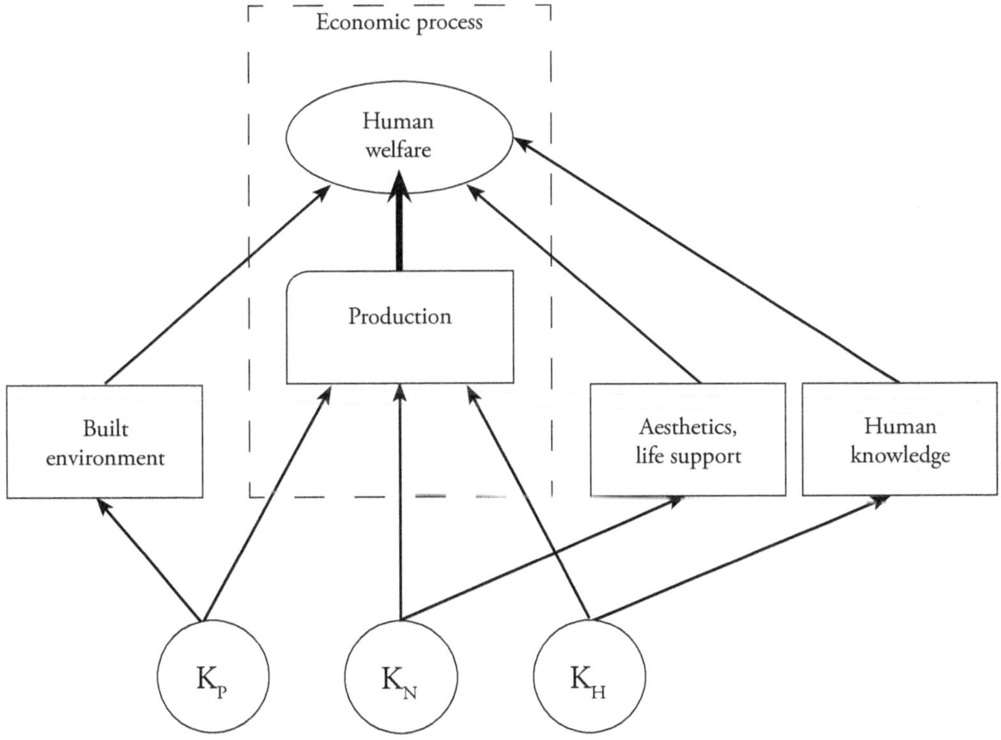

Source: Adapted from Pearce and Barbier (2000).

Person-made, or physical, capital (K_P), natural capital (K_N), and human capital (K_H) all contribute to human welfare through supporting the production of goods and services in the economic process. For example, K_P, consists of machinery, equipment, factory buildings, tools and other investment goods that are used in production; K_N is used for material and energy inputs into production, acts as a "sink" for waste emissions from the economic process, and provides a variety of "ecological services" to sustain production, such as nutrient recycling, watershed protection and catchment functions, and climate regulation; and K_H includes the human skills necessary for advanced production processes and for research and development activities that lead to technical innovation. However, all three forms of capital also contribute directly to human welfare independently of their contributions through the economic process. For instance, included in physical capital, K_P, is fine architecture and other physical components of cultural heritage; K_N includes aesthetically pleasing natural landscapes, and provides a variety of ecological services that are essential for supporting life; and increases in K_H also contribute more generally to increases in the overall stock of human knowledge.

One way of illustrating how unique are the various "goods and services" produced by natural capital is to examine the various economic values that arise through the functioning of a natural ecosystem. For example, most natural ecosystems generate multiple benefits, or values. Table 49.I illustrates this with the example of an aquatic ecosystem. As shown in the table, the concept of *total economic value* (TEV) is one framework that economists have developed for categorizing the various multiple benefits arising from natural systems such as an aquatic ecosystem. Total economic value distinguishes between *use* values and *non-use* values, the latter referring to those current or future (potential) values associated with an environmental resource which rely merely on its continued existence and are unrelated to use. Typically, use values involve some human 'interaction' with the resource whereas non-use values do not.

Table 49.1: Classification of total economic values for aquatic ecosystems

	Use values	**Non-se values**
Direct use values	**Indirect use values**	**Existence values** **Bequest values**
Fish	Nutrient retention/cycling	Biodiversity
Aquaculture	Flood control	Culture, heritage
Transport	Storm protection	
Wild resources	External ecosystem support	
Potable water	Shoreline/river bank stabilization	
Recreation		
Genetic material		
Scientific/educational		

Source: Adapted from Barbier (1994).

Use values are also grouped according to whether they are *direct* or *indirect*. The former refers to both *consumptive* and *non-consumptive* uses that involve some form of direct physical interaction with the resources and services of the system: harvesting of fish and wild resources, transport and use for recreation and tourism. It is also increasingly being recognized that the livelihoods of populations in areas neighboring aquatic ecosystems may be affected by certain key *regulatory ecological functions* (e.g. storm/flood protection, water purification, habitat functions, etc.). The values derived from these functions are considered to be "indirect", as they occur through the support and protection of economic activities that have directly measurable values (e.g. property and land values, drinking supplies, commercial fishing, etc.). Many unique natural environments are considered to have substantial existence values, in that many individuals do not make use of these environments but nevertheless wish to see them preserved "in their own right". Other important non-use values are bequest and cultural/heritage values. The Everglades in Florida or the Great Barrier Reef off the coast of Australia are unique ecosystems that we may wish future generations to enjoy in a fairly "intact" state and that are also considered important components of national and cultural heritage.

Natural capital and sustainable development

The importance of the total capital stock concept to sustainability is illustrated in Figure 49.2, which summarizes broadly the economic view of sustainable development. Most economic interpretations of sustainability take as their starting point the consensus reached by the World Commission on Environment and Development (the WCED, or Brundtland Commission). The WCED defined sustainable development as "development that meets the needs of the present without compromising the ability of future generations to meet their own needs" (WCED 1987).

Economists are generally comfortable with this broad interpretation of sustainability, as it is easily translatable into economic terms: an increase in well-being today should not have as its consequences a reduction in well-being tomorrow.[2] That is, future generations should be entitled to at least the same level of economic opportunities – and thus at least the same level of economic welfare – as currently available to present generations. Consequently, economic development today must ensure that future generations are left no worse off than present generations. Or, as some economists have succinctly put it, per capita welfare should not be declining over time (Pezzey 1989).

As noted in Figure 49.2, it is the *total* stock of capital employed by the economic system, including natural capital, which determines the full range of economic opportunities, and thus well-being, available to both present and future generations. Society must decide how best to "use" its total capital stock today to increase current economic activities and welfare, and how much it needs to "save" or even "accumulate" for tomorrow, and ultimately, for the well-being of future generations.

2 Although as Bishop (1993) has pointed out, the objective of "sustainability" is different from that of the standard economic objective of "efficiency." That is, there are potentially an infinite number of development paths for an economy, only some of which are sustainable. Efficiency therefore does not guarantee sustainability, as some efficient paths are not sustainable. At the same time, there is no reason why an economy could not be both efficient and sustainable.

Figure 49.2: Sustainable economic development

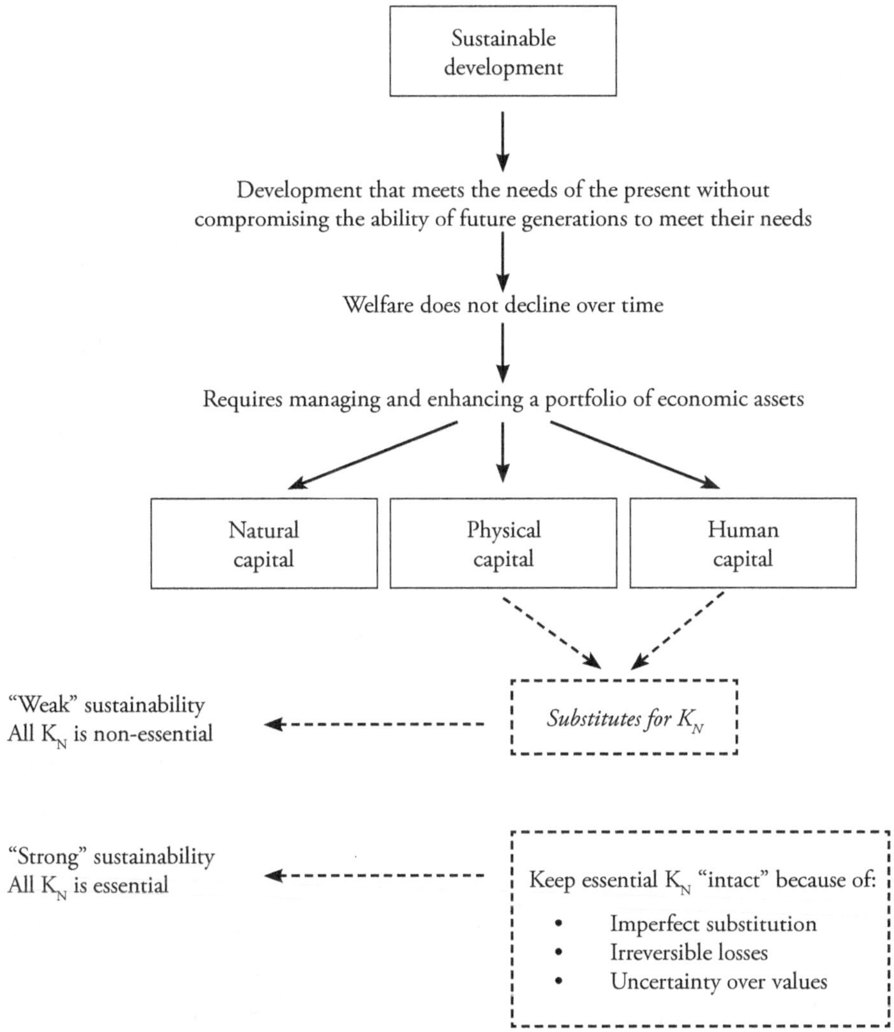

Source: Adapted from Pearce and Barbier (2000).

However, it is not simply the aggregate stock of capital in the economy that may matter but also its composition, in particular whether present generations are "using up" one form of capital to meet the needs of today. For example, much of the recent interest in sustainable development has risen out of concern that current economic development may be leading to rapid accumulation of physical and human capital, but at the expense of excessive depletion and degradation of natural capital. The major concern has been that, by depleting the world's stock of natural wealth irreversibly, the development path chosen today will have detrimental implications for the well-being of future generations. In other words, according to this view, current economic development is essentially unsustainable.

While it is generally accepted by most economists that economic development around the world is leading to the irreversible depletion of natural capital, there is widespread disagreement as to whether this necessarily implies that such development is inherently unsustainable. From an economic standpoint, the critical issue of debate is not whether natural capital is being irreversibly depleted, but whether we can compensate future generations for the current loss of natural capital, and if that is possible, how much is required to compensate future generations for this loss (Mäler 1995).

However, economists concerned with this problem appear to be divided into two camps over the special role of natural capital in sustainable development. The main disagreement between these two perspectives is whether natural capital has a unique or "essential" role in sustaining human welfare, and thus whether special "compensation rules" are required to ensure that future generations are not made worse off by natural capital depletion today (see Figure 49.2). These two contrasting views are now generally referred to as *weak sustainability* versus *strong sustainability*.[3]

According to the *weak sustainability* view, there is essentially no inherent difference between natural and other forms of capital, and hence the same "optimal depletion" rules ought to apply to both. As long as the natural capital that is being depleted is replaced with even more valuable physical and human capital, then the value of the aggregate stock – comprising human, physical and the remaining natural capital – is increasing over time.[4] Maintaining and enhancing the total stock of all capital alone is sufficient to attain sustainable development.

3 For further discussion of this distinction between weak and strong sustainability see Howarth and Norgaard (1995), Pearce, Markandya and Barbier (1989), Pearce and Barbier (2000), Toman, Pezzey and Krautkraemer (1995) and Turner (1993).

4 Note, however, that rapid population growth may imply that the value of the per capita aggregate capital stock is declining even if the total value stays the same. Moreover, even if the per capita value of the asset base were maintained, it may not imply non-declining welfare of the majority of people. These considerations also hold for the 'strong sustainability' arguments discussed below.

In contrast, proponents of the *strong sustainability* view argue that physical or human capital cannot substitute for all the environmental resources comprising the natural capital stock, or all of the ecological services performed by nature. Essentially, this view questions whether, on the one hand, human and physical capital, and on the other, natural capital, effectively comprises a single "homogeneous" total capital stock. Uncertainty over many environmental values, in particular the value that future generations may place on increasingly scarce natural resources and ecological services, further limits our ability to determine whether we can adequately compensate future generations for irreversible losses in essential natural capital today. Thus the strong sustainability view suggests that environmental resources and ecological services that are essential for human welfare and cannot be easily substituted by human and physical capital should be protected and not depleted. Maintaining or increasing the value of the total capital stock over time in turn requires keeping the non-substitutable and essential components of natural capital constant over time.

The two sides in the debate between weak and strong sustainability are not easy to reconcile. Recent extensions to the economic theory of sustainable development have not so much resolved this debate as sharpened its focus. It may take several generations before we know for sure which view of the role of natural capital in sustainable development is the correct one. Unfortunately, by then it may be too late to correct many of the costly mistakes of the past.

Growth, environment and environmental Kuznets curves

A new area of enquiry has emerged in environmental economics that also has important implications for sustainable development. This recent literature is concerned with the analysis of *environmental Kuznets curves* (EKC), that is, the hypothesis that there exists an "inverted U" shaped relationship between a variety of indicators of environmental pollution or resource depletion and the level of per capita income.[5] The implication of this hypothesis is that, as per capita income increases, environmental degradation rises initially but then eventually declines. Figure 49.3 shows a typical EKC estimated for sulfur dioxide (SO_2). Although estimations of such EKC relationships began in the early 1990s, interest in these studies is likely to continue for some time. There are several reasons for this.

Figure 49.3: An environmental Kuznets curve for sulfur dioxide

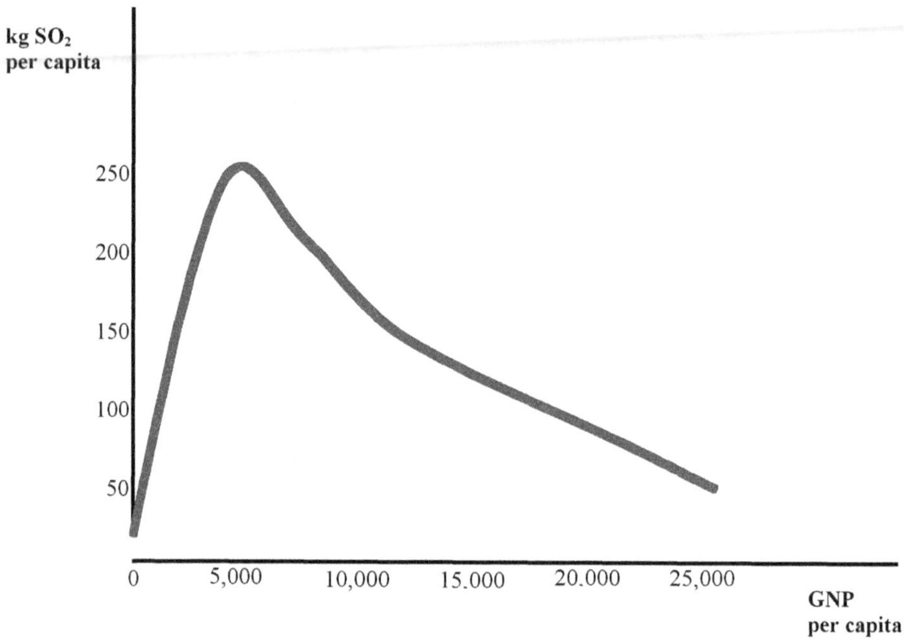

The above curve is the environmental Kuznets curve for sulfur dioxide (SO_2) estimated across the world's rich and poor countries. The "peak" or "turning point" level of per capita income where SO_2 levels start to fall is around $5,000.
Source: Adapted from Panayotou (1995).

5 The concept of an environmental Kuznets curve (EKC) relationship draws its inspiration from the income distribution theory developed by Kuznets (1955), who hypothesized that there is an 'inverted U' relationship between an indicator of income inequality and the level of income. However, the exact origins of the EKC hypothesis are somewhat ambiguous, and appear to be the product of numerous studies conducted simultaneously in the early 1990s. Most sources point to the analysis by Grossman and Kreuger (1995) of air quality measures in a cross-section of countries for different years, which was part of a wider investigation into whether the claims that the economic growth accompanying the North American Free Trade Agreement might foster greater environmental degradation. Similarly, the study by Shafik (1994) was originally a background paper for the World Bank's enquiry into growth and environment relationships for the World Development 1992 (World Bank 1992). Finally, Panayotou (1995) offers perhaps the earliest and most detailed explanation of a possible "Kuznets type U-shape relationship between the rate of environmental degradation and the level of economic development" in analysis conducted for the World Employment Programme of the International Labour Office in 1992.

First, the EKC is a falsifiable hypothesis that can and will continue to be tested through empirical investigation. Thus an increasing number of studies are attempting to determine whether the EKC hypothesis holds for various indicators of environmental degradation, both over time and across countries, regions, states, districts and even cities.

Second, the EKC hypothesis poses an important intellectual challenge. Explanations as to why environmental degradation should first increase then decline with income have focused on a number of underlying causes, including:

- the effects of structural economic change on the use of the environment for resource inputs and to assimilate waste;
- the effects of increasing income on the demand for environmental quality; and
- the types of environmental degradation and ecological processes.

It is not yet clear which of these factors, if any, explain why we might observe an EKC relationship. For example, many of the original explanations of the EKC hypothesis focused on changes in the composition of goods and services due to structural shifts in the economy, the efficiency of resource use, the composition of inputs, and technological innovation. However, increasingly it has been recognized that the effect of such changes on environment-income linkages are not "exogenous" processes – determined by factors outside the economy – but are influenced by policy choices (Andreoni and Levinson 2001; Lopez 1994; Panayotou 1995 and 1997; Stern *et al.* 1996; World Bank 1992). Similarly, previous conjecture that environmental quality is simply a "luxury good", and thus the demand for improved environmental quality increases more than proportionately with income, is proving difficult to substantiate (Lieb 2002; McConnell 1997). Finally, it is possible that EKC studies are providing misleading information on environment-income linkages (Stern *et al.* 1996). As discussed earlier in this lecture, there is much that we do not know about key ecological processes and functions, as well as the valuable services that they provide. Even if we observe EKCs for certain indicators of pollution and resource depletion, it does not necessarily follow that the overall health and functioning of ecosystems will also improve as income increases.

Third, and perhaps most importantly, the EKC hypothesis has revived interest in the long-standing debate over the environmental implications of economic growth (Ansuategi *et al.*1998). One important interpretation of such estimated curves is that economies will eventually "grow out of" many environmental problems (Beckerman 1992). Taken to its extreme, this argument suggests that we do not have to regard the environment as anything special. As people get richer they will increase their demand for the environment and improve it, initially with public health legislation, then clean air, then conservation generally.

However, other commentators have been more cautious, noting that conclusive evidence of an EKC relationship applies only to a few pollutants, thus making it difficult to use this evidence to speculate more generally about growth-environment linkages (Arrow *et al.* 1995). Still others have pointed out that, even for those pollutants displaying EKC characteristics, aggregate global emissions are projected to rise over time, demonstrating that the existence of an EKC does not necessarily imply that, at the global level, any associated environmental damage is likely to disappear with economic growth (Selden and Song 1994; Stern *et al.* 1996). Policy makers are following this renewed debate with interest. From their perspective, the critical policy issue is whether economic growth should continue to be the main priority, with protection of the environment as a secondary consideration to be addressed mainly in the future, or whether explicit policies to control environmental degradation at the local, national and global level are required urgently today.

To date, the empirical evidence suggests that EKC relationships are more likely to hold for certain types of environmental damage, e.g. pollutants with more short-term and local impacts, versus those with more global, indirect and long-term impacts such as carbon dioxide and other greenhouse gases (Arrow *et al.* 1995; Barbier 1997; Cole *et al.* 1997; Selden and Song 1994). In terms of types of "localized" environmental damage, the EKC hypothesis seems mainly to be valid for air pollution, in particular sulfur dioxide (SO_2) and to a lesser extent solid particulate matter (SPM). The evidence for other localized forms of environmental damage, such as water pollution, deforestation, urban waste and toxic metals, is more mixed (Barbier 1997; Cole *et al.* 1997). Moreover, environment-income relationships appear to vary across individual countries. For example, a study for Malaysia found SPM to be increasing with income (Vincent

1997), whereas a study for the United States indicated that SPM and other major air pollutants decline with increasing levels of income (Carson *et al.* 1997).

However, even when an EKC relationship is estimated, often the turning point on the curve, where environmental degradation starts to decline with per capita income, proves to be very high relative to the current per capita GDP levels of most countries of the world (Barbier 1997). For example, the turning point for sulfur dioxide in Figure 49.3 is just under $5,000 per capita. In another recent analysis, none of the estimated EKC turning points for various environmental indicators are below the minimum income level of the sample of countries analyzed, and the turning points for nitrates, carbon dioxide, energy consumption and traffic volumes are well above the maximum income of the countries in the data set (Cole *et al.* 1997). In the case of those EKC estimates for tropical deforestation that are robust, the per capita income levels of most developing countries are also well to the left of the estimated turning point peaks (Cropper and Griffiths 1994; Barbier and Burgess 2001; Koop and Tole 1989).

Overall, such results suggest that most countries have not yet reached levels of per capita income for which environmental improvement is likely to occur. The implications are a worsening global problem of environmental degradation as the world economy and populations expand, even for those environmental indicators that display EKCs (Selden and Song 1994; Stern *et al.* 1996). This can be seen clearly in Figure 49.4. This figure shows the future trend in global sulfur dioxide emissions based on the estimated EKC for SO_2 depicted in Figure 3 and employing aggregation of individual country projections of population and economic growth over 1990 to 2025. The resulting projections show a rise in global sulfur dioxide emissions throughout this period. For example, total global emissions of SO_2 rise from 383 million metric tons in 1990 to 1,181 million metric tons in 2025, or from 73 to 142 kg per capita (Stern *et al.* 1996).[6]

6 Selden and Song (1994) conduct similar projections for the four air pollutants for which they estimate an EKC relationship, SO_2, SPM, nitrogen dioxides (NO_x) and carbon monoxide (CO). Their results show world emissions increasing for all four pollutants through 2025, and for SPM and NO_x, emissions rise through 2050.

Figure 49.4: Projected trends for global SO_2 emissions

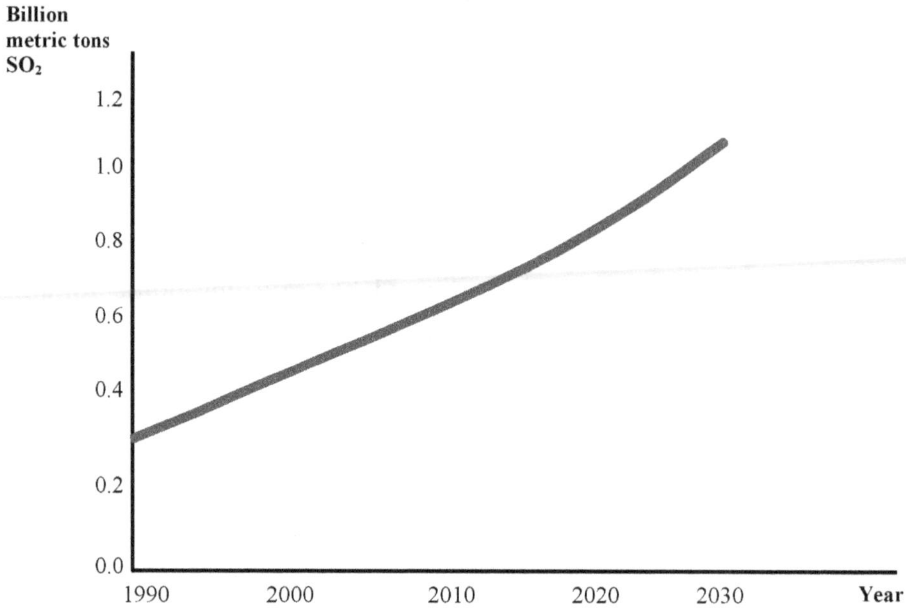

Source: Stern *et al.* (1996).

Where the EKC relationship does appear to hold, especially for certain air pollutants with localized or short-term effects, there is evidence that the eventual reduction in emissions associated with higher per capita income levels may be attributable to the "abatement effect" that arises as countries become richer (Andreoni and Levinson; Lopez 1994; Panayotou 1997). Also, both the willingness and the ability of political jurisdictions to engage in and enforce improved environmental regulations, to increase public spending on environmental research and development, or even to engage in multilateral agreements to reduce emissions may also increase with per capita income levels (Carson *et al.* 1997; de Bruyn 1997; Komen *et al.* 1997).[7] However, it is a great leap of faith to conclude from these results that economic growth on its own will foster environmental improvement automatically. As Panayotou (1997) has concluded, "when all effects are considered, the relationship between growth and

7 On the other hand, corruption and bureaucratic inefficiency may also explain why EKCs "break down" for certain countries. See López and Mitra (2000).

the environment turns out to be much more complex with wide scope for active policy intervention to bring about more desirable (and in the presence of market failures) more efficient economic and environmental outcomes."

This conclusion may be particularly relevant for low income and rapidly industrializing developing countries, whose current per capita income levels are well below the turning points of most estimated EKCs. In the absence of national and multilateral policy interventions, environmental degradation will continue in these countries as per capita income increases, at least over the medium term. In this regard, the observation of Vincent (1997) from his analysis of Malaysia is very apt: "The lack of evidence of EKCs in Malaysia does not prove that EKCs do not exist anywhere. It does indicate, however, that policy makers in developing countries should not assume that economic growth will automatically solve air and water pollution problems."

In sum, the implications of the EKC literature for sustainable development are fairly straightforward. Regardless of whether one is an adherent of the weak sustainability or strong sustainability view, estimated EKC relationships on their own do not help us determine what actual policies are required in the economy to manage its total capital stock, including its stock of natural capital. Although recent EKC studies appear to have revived the wider "growth versus the environment" debate, these studies offer very little support for the view that economic growth alone is the solution to all environmental problems. Rather, it is clear from the EKC literature that specific policies to protect the environment are necessary to reduce environmental damages that are imposing real welfare losses. As Arrow *et al.* (1995) have succinctly put it: "Economic growth is not a panacea for environmental quality; indeed it is not even the main issue."

Natural resource abundance and economic growth

So far, we have examined how management of environmental and natural resources, i.e. the *natural capital stock*, of a country is important for achieving sustainable economic development. We have also reviewed the recent findings of the EKC literature to make the case that the causal relationship is from improved environmental management to enhanced economic development and welfare, and not the other way around.

It is therefore tempting to conclude that, if natural capital is so important to sustainable development, then more of a good thing must be even better. That is, economies that have a greater endowment of natural resources must surely have a much better chance of attaining higher economic growth rates and prosperity than relatively resource-poor economies. This must be particularly true with respect to low and middle-income countries, whose economies are generally more dependent on exploiting their natural capital stock in the transition to developing industrial and service sectors and the "take off" into higher and more balanced rates of long-run growth.

However, if per capita income is to be sustained or increased in these economies, especially with population increases, then any depreciation of natural resources must be offset by investment in other productive assets. This implies managing natural resources so as to maximize resource rents and channeling those rents into productive investments elsewhere in the economy. Although it would seem that the windfall profits generated by resource price booms would be beneficial to this process, this may not be the case for resource-abundant developing countries.

In fact, recent evidence suggests that resource-abundant countries, especially developing economies, may not be benefiting economically from this apparent comparative advantage. Many low-income and lower middle-income economies that can be classified as highly resource dependent today also currently display low or stagnant growth rates (Barbier 1999). Cross-country analysis has confirmed that resource-abundant countries – i.e. countries with a high ratio of natural resource exports to GDP – have tended to grow less rapidly than countries that are relatively resource poor (Sachs and Warner 1997). Economies with a high ratio of natural resource exports to GDP in 1971 also tended to have low growth rates during the subsequent period 1971-89 (Sachs and Warner 1995).

Such evidence might be considered surprising, given the commonly held view that abundant natural resources ought to be the basis for economic expansion for those countries fortunate to have such a rich endowment. For example, the origins of rapid industrial and economic expansion in the US over 1879-1940 were strongly linked to the exploitation of abundant non-reproducible natural resources, particularly energy and mineral resources (Romer 1996; Wright 1990). In particular, during 1880-1920, the intensity of US manufacturing exports in terms of non-reproducible resources grew both absolutely and relative to the resource-intensity of imports. However, there is also evidence that were other factors that made this historical situation in the US unique. For example, Wright (1990) maintains that, over this era:

- the United States was not only the world's largest mineral producing nation but also one of the world's largest countries and markets;
- high international transport costs and tariff barriers for manufactured goods compared to highly efficient and low cost domestic transportation meant that the United States was a vast free trade area for internal commerce and industrial expansion that benefited from "economic distance" from the rest of the world; and
- because of the quantities of resources that were available combined with the large internal markets for goods, increasing investment in basic technologies for extracting and processing natural resources was highly profitable.

As Wright (1990, pp. 665 and 661) suggests: "the abundance of mineral resources, in other words, was itself an outgrowth of America's technological progress," and in turn, "American producer and consumer goods were often specifically designed for a resource-abundant environment".

However, it is doubtful that the unique circumstances over 1879-1940 that allowed the United States to achieve "congruence" between intensive resource use and basic processing and manufacturing technologies, and thus attain rapid economic expansion, are applicable to resource-abundant developing economies today. For one, after 1940, this unique "congruence" had clearly ended for the United States, largely due to changes in the international economy, even though the US still had abundant resources. As Wright (1990, p 665) points out: "the country has not become 'resource poor' relative to others, but the unification of world commodity markets (through transportation cost reductions and elimination of trade barriers) has largely cut the link between domestic resources and domestic industries ... To a degree, natural resources have become commodities rather than part of the 'factor endowment' of individual countries." As some researchers have pointed out, the changed international conditions during the post-war era may have also affected the role of primary-product export promotion as the "engine of growth" for developing economies.

During this era, the main source of economic growth in developing countries has not been primary-product based exports but labor-intensive manufactured exports (Findlay 1996; Findlay and Wellisz 1993).[8]

Not only are the conditions for "congruence" between resource abundance, technological progress and industrial expansion lacking in most developing economies today, but it is also possible that increased economic dependence on resource exploitation may be detrimental to innovation and growth. For example, recent explanations of the limitations of resource-based development have focused on the poor potential for such development in inducing the economy-wide innovation necessary to sustain growth in a small open economy. Matsuyama (1992) has shown that trade liberalization in a land-intensive economy could actually slow economic growth by inducing the economy to shift resources away from manufacturing (which produces learning-induced growth) towards agriculture (which does not). Sachs and Warner (1995) also argue that the relative structural importance of tradable manufacturing versus natural resource sectors in an economy is critical to its growth performance, i.e. when a mineral or oil-based economy experiences a resource price boom, the manufacturing sector tends to shrink and the non-traded goods sector tends to expand. This phenomenon is often referred to in the literature as the "Dutch disease" effect.[9]

---

8 From their case study analysis of five open developing economies, Findlay and Wellisz (1993) conclude that over the post-war era it was economies with relatively no resources, such as Hong Kong, Singapore and Malta, which were among the earliest and most successful exporters of labor-intensive manufactures. In contrast, resource-rich Jamaica and the Philippines have done relatively poorly, whereas Indonesia and Malaysia have done comparatively better by balancing primary exports with rapid expansion of labor-intensive manufactures.

9 Originally, the "Dutch disease" phenomenon was associated with the macroeconomic implications of an economy's over-dependence on a single, traded natural resource sector (e.g. oil), which emphasized the enclave character of the sector as the predominant source of foreign exchange availability (Neary and van Wijnbergen 1986). As the consequence of a resource price boom (e.g. oil price shock), expansion of the resource-based sector would be accompanied by a change in the real exchange rate, and the rest of the economy would decline relatively. The more recent treatments of the "Dutch disease" phenomenon, such as by Matsuyama (1992) and Sachs and Warner (1995) discussed here, focus less on the economic implications of a resource boom via real exchange rate movements but via internal economic distortions caused by the shift of resources from a more innovative sector (e.g. manufacturing) to a less innovative sector (e.g. agriculture, minerals). This latter representation of the "Dutch disease" is more appropriate for characterizing a small open economy, in which real exchange rate determination is not considered.

Sachs and Warner (1999) have recently examined evidence over the period 1960-94 for eleven major Latin American economies to test the hypothesis that any natural resource booms occurring in these countries may have had a positive impact on their growth performance.[10] First, the authors note that the main structural feature of these economies is that they have remained by and large exporters of primary commodities or manufactured products based on these commodities. Second, they suggest that a significant resource boom occurred in only four of the eleven countries (Bolivia, Ecuador, Mexico and Venezuela), and mixed evidence of a boom in another three (Chile, Colombia and Peru). However, Sachs and Warner conclude that in only one of these seven countries (Ecuador) did a resource boom have a positive and lasting effect on GDP per capita. In two countries (Chile and Colombia) there appears to be no effect of a resource boom on economic development, and in the remaining four cases (Bolivia, Mexico, Peru and Venezuela), the resource boom actually produced a negative impact on GDP per capita. On balance, resource booms appear to frustrate economic growth in Latin America, most likely through a Dutch disease effect.

If natural resource booms are not important catalysts for economic development in poorer countries, then perhaps the process of resource exploitation occurring in these economies is not as economically beneficial as it could be. That is, the structural economic dependence of a small open low or lower middle income economy on exploiting its natural resource endowment may not be leading to sustained and high rates of economic growth. This may be occurring because natural resource assets, including land, are not being managed so as to maximize rents and/or whatever rents are being generated in the economy are not being channeled into productive investments elsewhere in the economy.

Brander and Taylor (1997 and 1998) provide some theoretical support for this perspective. They note that over-exploitation of many renewable natural resources – particularly the conversion of forests to agricultural land – occurs in developing countries if property rights over a resource stock are hard to define, difficult to enforce or costly to administer. They demonstrate that opening up trade for a resource-abundant economy with an open access renewable resource

10 The countries are Argentina, Bolivia, Brazil, Chile, Colombia, Ecuador, Mexico, Paraguay, Peru, Uruguay and Venezuela.

may actually reduce welfare in that economy. As the resource-abundant country has a comparative advantage in producing the resource good, the increased demand for this good resulting from trade openness leads to greater resource exploitation, which under conditions of open access leads to declining welfare in the long run. Brander and Taylor conclude that, as the problem lies with the "open access" nature of exploitation in the resource-abundant economy, then the first-best policy would be for the developing country to switch to more efficient resource management policy through simply establishing property rights.[11] However, as they acknowledge, there are many policy and institutional distortions that currently work against such solutions in developing countries. Consequently, Brander and Taylor (1997, p. 550) argue in favor of "second best approaches", such as the imposition of "a modified 'Hartwick's rule' (see Hartwick 1977) under which an exporting country that experienced temporary gains from selling a resource good on world markets might re-invest those proceeds in an alternative asset."

Current policies in resource-abundant developing economies appear not to be ensuring that any resource rents earned are re-invested efficiently into other productive assets in the economy (Pearce and Barbier 2000). Such an outcome may be reinforced by corruption, bureaucratic inefficiency and misguided policies that benefit special interests that gain from short-term resource exploitation (Ascher 1999; Barbier and Damania 2000; Deacon 1994). If this is the case, then irrespective of what may happen to a country's terms of trade or commodity prices, any initial "economic boom" associated with land conversion or increased resource exploitation is invariably short-lived as the extra rents generated are eventually dissipated. Once the land expansion and increased exploitation of new resource "reserves" comes to an end, or poorer quality land and resources are brought into production, then some economic retrenchment is inevitable. What we should therefore observe is that economic development in a resource-dependent small open economy displays an inherently "boom and bust" pattern.

11 In a recent analysis of land expansion in Mexico, Barbier (2002) demonstrates that institutional constraints, such as the *ejido* common-property land management regime, may have slowed down the pace of land conversion and deforestation in pre-NAFTA Mexico. However, increased trade liberalization under NAFTA combined with the widespread relaxing of the land management rules of the *ejido* regime could accelerate land clearing in Mexico.

Again, Brander and Taylor (1997) show that a small, open and resource-abundant economy that produces both a resource and a manufacturing good in the long run will have such a pattern of development. That is, the economy will experience early gains from trade, followed by a period of declining utility. With the specific case of Latin America in mind, in which raw materials are often inputs into semi-processed or processed exports, López (1989) also develops a two-good model of a resource-rich open economy in which the open access renewable resource serves as an input into an "enclave" export processing sector. López demonstrates that improvements in the terms of trade increases the rate of open access resource extraction and causes real income to rise in the short-run, but inevitably permanent income falls in the long run.

As mentioned above, the classic case of open access resource exploitation in many developing countries is conversion of forest to agriculture (Barbier and Burgess 2001). If agricultural land expansion in these small open economies is associated with a "boom and bust" pattern of economic development, then there are two possible consequences. First, economies that have increased their agricultural land base significantly over the long run are likely to have lower levels of GDP per capita then economies that have tended to reduce their dependence on agricultural land expansion. For the latter countries, a shrinking agricultural land base may be evidence that tradable manufacturing and other dynamic sectors have become structurally more important in the economy relative to natural resource sectors and that agriculture itself has become a more capital-intensive, productive and innovative sector.[12] Second, for those countries that are dependent on agricultural land expansion, further increases in agricultural area will tend to produce only modest increases in GDP per capita. Beyond a certain point, additional increases in land expansion will be associated with lower GDP per capita, because of the "boom and bust" pattern of resource-dependent development described above.

A fairly straightforward way of empirically verifying the above phenomenon is to estimate a relationship between GDP per capita and some measure of long-run agricultural expansion. For example, if the latter indicator was some index,

12 In the small open economy model of Brander and Taylor (1997), if the country specializes in the manufacturing good in the long run, it gains unambiguously from trade.

$\forall_{it}$, then the above hypotheses suggest that there may be a cubic relationship between per capita income, Y_{it}, and this indicator of long run agricultural land change:

$$Y_{it} = b_0 + b_1 \ _{it} + b_2 \ ^{2}_{it} + b_3 \ ^{3}_{it} \qquad (1)$$

Table 49.2: Panel analysis of per capita income and long run agricultural expansion for tropical developing countries, 1961-94

Dependent variable: GDP per capita (PPP, constant 1987 \$)[a]		
Parameter estimates:[b]		
Explanatory variables	**All countries** (N = 1135)	**Lower income countries[c]** (N = 867)
Constant	14393.37 (23.69)**	9560.07 (7.03)**
Long run agricultural land area change index (☒$_{it}$)[d]	-24293.31 (-19.04)**	-16645.71 (-5.30)**
☒$^{2}_{it}$	15217.53 (11.18)**	11013.18 (4.58)**
☒$^{3}_{it}$	-2896.32 (-6.59)**	-2330.33 (-3.87)**
F-test for pooled model	168.01**	126.05**
Breusch-Pagan (LM) test	6576.23**	3614.50**
Hausman test	6.85	44.02**
Adjusted R^2	0.368	0.937
Preferred model	**One-way random effects**	**Two-way fixed effects**

Notes: [a] Mean for all tropical developing countries over 1961-94 is \$2,593, and for lower income countries \$1,539. PPP is purchase power parity.
[b] t-ratios are indicated in parentheses.
[c] Countries with GDP per capita (PPP, constant 1987 \$) less than \$3,500 over 1961-94.
[d] Mean for all countries over 1961-94 is 1.150, and for lower income countries 1.149.
** Significant at 1% level, * significant at 5% level.
Source: Author's estimation.

In the above equation $b_0 > 0$, $b_1 < 0$, $b_2 > 0$, $b_3 < 0$ and $|b_1| > b_2$ would imply that countries with increased long run agricultural land area would have lower levels of per capita income than countries with decreased agricultural land area, and per capita income would tend to fluctuate with long run agricultural land expansion.

The above relationship was estimated through employing a panel analysis of tropical developing countries over 1961-94. Per capita income, Y_{it}, is represented by gross domestic product (GDP) per capita in constant purchasing power parity (1987 \$). The indicator $\forall_{it}$ is an agricultural land long run change index, created by dividing the current (i.e. in year *t*) agricultural land area of a country by its land area in 1961.[13]

The results of the analysis for all tropical countries and for low and lower middle income countries (i.e. those economies with real per capita GDP less than \$3,500 over 1961-94) are shown in Table 49.2. For both regressions, the estimated coefficients are highly significant and also have the expected signs and relative magnitudes.[14] Thus the estimations provide some empirical evidence that agricultural land expansion in developing countries conforms to a "boom and bust" pattern of economic development. This is seen more clearly when the regressions are used to project respective relationships between long run agricultural land expansion and GDP per capita, which are displayed in Figure 49.5.

As indicated in the figure, an increase in agricultural land expansion in the long run is clearly associated with a lower level of per capita income than decreasing agricultural land area. For all tropical countries, the turning point is a long run agricultural change index of just under 1.2. For lower income countries

13 The data used in this analysis is from the World Bank's *World Development Indicators*.

14 Although only the preferred models are indicated in Table 1, the panel analysis was performed comparing OLS against one-way and two-way random and fixed effects models. Alternative versions of these models also employed White's robust correction of the covariance matrix to overcome unspecified heteroskedasticity. However, heteroskedasticity proved not to be a significant problem in both regressions. In the regression for all tropical developing countries, the F-test for the pooled model and Breusch-Pagan LM test were highly significant, suggesting rejection of the OLS model due to the presence of individual effects. The Hausman test was significant only at the 10% level, suggesting that random effects specification is preferred to the fixed effects model. The one-way model tended to outperform the two-way effects model. In the regression for lower income countries, the F-test for the pooled model, the LM test and the Hausman test were all highly significant, suggesting that the fixed effects model is preferred. The two-way model tended to outperform the one-way effects model.

the turning point is 1.3. Although continued agricultural land expansion beyond these points does lead to a slight increase in GDP per capita, this impact is short-lived. For all tropical countries, per capita income starts to fall once the land area index reaches 2.3; for lower income countries this occurs sooner at an index of 1.9. Note as well that for lower income countries, there is very little increase in GDP per capita associated with expansion of land over the 1.3 to 1.9 range.

Figure 49.5: Projected trends in agricultural land expansion per capita income for tropical developing countries

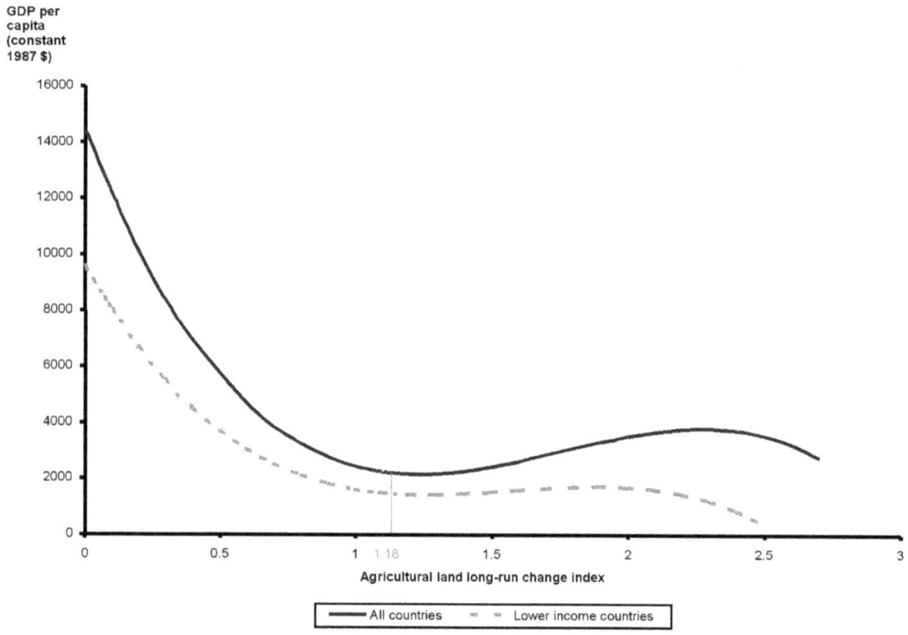

Source: Author's estimation.

To conclude, even though a developing economy is endowed with abundant natural resources, the country may not necessarily be exploiting this natural wealth efficiently and generating productive investments. Or, as Wright (1990, p. 666) suggests: "there is no iron law associating natural resource abundance with national industrial strength." It is clear that the open access conditions and ill-defined property rights under which many resources, and especially land, are exploited in developing economies is partly to blame. It is also the case that in many countries natural resource assets, including land, are not being managed so as to maximize rents and/or whatever rents are being generated in the economy are not being re-invested productively elsewhere, especially in tradable manufacturing and other dynamic sectors.

Final remarks

Although our understanding of the role of natural resources in economic development has improved markedly in recent decades, there is still much to learn. Nevertheless, as I have argued in this lecture, the view that environmental and natural resources should be treated as important economic assets, which can be called natural capital, is becoming more accepted. Armed with this concept, economists are now able to show the conditions under which depletion of this natural capital stock may or may not lead to more sustainable economic development.

However, the services provided by natural capital are unique and, in the case of the ecological and life-support functions of the environment, are not well understood. Improving our knowledge in this area is a critical task. It is also one in which economists must learn to work more closely with scientists from other disciplines, particularly biologists, ecologists and other natural scientists. Such inter-disciplinary efforts are especially relevant for a host of complex environmental management problems facing the world today, such as biodiversity loss, climate change, and the spread of biological invasions and infectious diseases (Barbier *et al.* 1994).

Better understanding of these complex environmental problems and of the value of ecological services may also help eventually to resolve the "weak" versus "strong" sustainability debate in economics. As I have noted in this lecture, the heart of this debate concerns whether the environment has an "essential" role in sustaining human welfare, and if so, whether special "compensation rules" are necessary in order to ensure that future generations are not made worse off by natural capital depletion today. These issues are unlikely to be resolved in the near future, and I have not attempted to do so here. Nevertheless, it is clear that the *very minimum* criterion for attaining sustainable economic development is ensuring that an economy satisfies *weak sustainability* conditions. That is, as long as the natural capital that is being depleted is replaced with even more valuable physical and human capital, then *the value of the aggregate stock* – comprising human, physical and the remaining natural capital – should be increasing over time. This in turn requires that the development path of an economy is governed by principles somewhat akin to Hartwick's rule (Hartwick 1977). First, environmental and natural resources must be managed efficiently so that the welfare losses from environmental damages are minimized and any resource rents earned after "internalizing" environmental externalities are maximized. Second, the rents arising from the depletion of natural capital must be invested into other productive economic assets.

The conclusion that efficient environmental resource management is the minimum condition necessary for sustainable economic development may surprise those who believe that the causality might run in the other direction. Proponents of the latter view argue that the environmental Kuznets curve literature provides evidence that environmental problems are likely to lessen as economies grow and develop. However, as I have sought to clarify in this lecture, the EKC literature does not support such a conclusion. Rather, many EKC studies suggest that specific policies to protect the environment are necessary for curbing certain forms of pollution and resource depletion, both currently and in the future. How key environmental indicators change with rises in per capita income is an important issue, but what is of more fundamental concern is how different policies can affect this relationship. Specifically, we need to determine what environmental policies are required to ensure that the needs of the present are met without compromising the economic opportunities to meet the needs of the future. With regard to these bigger policy issues, estimating EKC relationships for various indicators of environmental degradation is instructive of likely trends under current policies, but is perhaps less helpful in indicating what additional policies and instruments should be implemented.

Finally, this lecture has also considered a recent paradox concerning the role of natural resources in economic development: if natural capital is important for sustainable development, why is the economic performance of many resource-abundant developing countries lagging behind that of comparatively resource-poor economies? The answer to this paradox seems to be fairly straightforward. Simply because a developing economy is endowed with abundant natural resources, it does not necessarily follow that the country will exploit this natural wealth efficiently and reinvest resource rents in other productive investments. Ill-defined and lack of enforcement of property rights that create "open access" conditions for exploiting land and other natural resources in developing countries are part of the problem. In addition, rather than ensuring that any resource rents earned are re-invested efficiently into other productive assets, current policies in resource-abundant developing economies appear to work against this outcome. Corruption, bureaucratic inefficiency and polices biased in favor of special interests that gain from excessive resource extraction or conversion also exacerbate these policy failures. The result is that land expansion and increased exploitation of new resource "reserves" in many resource-dependent developing economies are not fostering a "takeoff" into sustainable development but rather a "boom and bust" pattern of economic growth and development.

In conclusion, the importance of natural resources to economic development is now well-established. How a country manages its natural capital stock is critical for achieving sustainable economic development. Moreover, misinterpretations of the EKC literature aside, the causal relationship is clearly from improved environmental management to enhanced economic development and welfare, and not the other way around. On the other hand, poor policies and the inefficient mismanagement of natural resources can also be detrimental to growth and development. Of course, it will always be difficult to determine what exactly is lost when we deplete natural resources and degrade the environment. But at the very least, economic policies should be in place to ensure that welfare-damaging environmental externalities are corrected, the rents generated from the depletion of natural capital are maximized, and that these rents are reinvested into dynamic and innovative sectors in the rest of the economy.

References

Andreoni, J. and Levinson, A. 2001, 'The Simple Analytics of the Environmental Kuznets Curve', *Journal of Public Economics* 80: 269-286.

Ansuategi, A., Barbier, E.B. and Perrings, C.A. 1998, 'The Environmental Kuznets Curve', pp. 139-164 in J.C.J.M. van den Bergh and M.W. Hofkes (eds.) *Theory and Implementation of Economic Models for Sustainable Development*, Amsterdam: Kluwer Academic Publishers.

Arrow, K., Bolin, B., Costanza, R., Dasgupta, P., Folke, C., Holling, C.S., Jansson, B-O., Levin, S., Mäler, K-G., Perrings, C.A. and Pimentel, D. 1995, 'Economic Growth, Carrying Capacity, and the Environment', *Science* 268: 520-521.

Ascher, W. 1999, *Why Governments Waste Natural Resources: Policy Failures in Developing Countries*, Baltimore: Johns Hopkins University Press.

Barbier, E. B. 1994, 'Valuing Environmental Functions: Tropical Wetlands', *Land Economics* 10(2): 155-173.

Barbier, E.B. 1997, 'Introduction to the Environmental Kuznets Curve Special Issue', *Environment and Development Economics* 2(4): 369-382.

Barbier, E.B. 1999, 'Poverty, Environment and Development', pp. 731-744 in van den Bergh, J.C.J.M, ed. *The Handbook of Environmental and Resource Economics*, London: Edward Elgar.

Barbier, E.B. 2002, 'Institutional Constraints and Deforestation: An Application to Mexico', *Economic Inquiry* 40(3): 508-519.

Barbier, E.B. and Burgess, J.C. 2001, 'The Economics of Tropical Deforestation', *Journal of Economic Surveys* 15(3): 413-421.

Barbier, E.B., Burgess, J.C. and Folke, C. 1994, *Paradise Lost? The Ecological Economics of Biodiversity*, London: Earthscan Publications.

Barbier, E.B. and Damania, R. 2002, 'Lobbying, Trade and Resource Conversion', Paper Presented at the Workshop on 'Trade, Renewable Resources and Biodiversity', University of Tilburg, The Netherlands, 5-6 September.

Beckerman, W.A. 1992, 'Economic Growth and the Environment: Whose Growth? Whose Environment?' *World Development* 20: 481-496.

Bishop, R.C. 1993, 'Economic Efficiency, Sustainability and Biodiversity', *Ambio* 22(2-3): 69-73.

Brander, J.A. and Taylor, M.S. 1997, 'International Trade and Open-Access Renewable Resources: The Small Open Economy', *Canadian Journal of Economics* 30(3): 526-552.

Brander, J.A.and Taylor, M.S. 1998, 'Open Access Renewable Resources: Trade and Trade Policy in a Two-Country Model', *Journal of International Economics* 44: 181-209.

Carson, R.T., Jeon Y. and McCubbin, D.R. 1997, 'The Relationship Between Air Pollution Emissions and Income: US Data', *Environment and Development Economics* (*Special Issue on Environmental Kuznets Curves*) 2(4): 433-450.

Cole, M.A., Rayner, A.J. and Bates, J.M. 1997, 'The Environmental Kuznets Curve: An Empirical Analysis' *Environment and Development Economics* (*Special Issue on Environmental Kuznets Curves*) 2(4): 401-416.

Cropper, M. and Griffiths, C.W. 1994, 'The Interaction of Population Growth and Environmental Quality', *American Economic Review* 84(2): 250-254.

Deacon, R.T. 1994, 'Deforestation and the Rule of Law in a Cross-Section of Countries', *Land Economics* 70(4): 414-430.

de Bruyn, S. 1997, 'Explaining the Environmental Kuznets Curve: Structural Change and International Agreements in Reducing Sulphur Emissions', *Environment and Development Economics (Special Issue on Environmental Kuznets Curves)* 2(4): 484-504.

Findlay, R. 1996, 'Modeling Global Interdependence: Centers, Peripheries and Frontiers', *American Economic Review*, vol. 86(2), 47-51.

Findlay, R. and Wellisz, S. eds. 1993, *The Political Economy of Poverty, Equity and Growth: Five Small Open Economies,* New York: Oxford University Press.

Grossman, G.M. and Kreuger, A.B. 1995, 'Economic Growth and the Environment', *Quarterly Journal of Economics* 110(2): 353-377.

Hartwick, J. 1977, 'Intergenerational Equity and the Investing of Rents from Exhaustible Resources', *American Economic Review* 67: 972-974.

Holtz-Eakin, D. and Selden, T.M. 1995, 'Stoking the Fires? CO_2 Emissions and Economic Growth', *Journal of Public Economics* 57: 85-101.

Howarth, R.B. and Norgaard, R.B. 1995, 'Intergenerational Choices under Global Environmental Change', pp. 111-138 in D. Bromley, ed. *The Handbook of Environmental Economics*, Oxford: Basil Blackwell.

Komen, M.H.C., Gerking, S. and Folmer, H. 1997, 'Income and Environmental R&D: Empirical Evidence from OECD Countries', *Environment and Development Economics (Special Issue on Environmental Kuznets Curves)* 2(4): 505-515.

Koop, G. and Tole, L. 1999, 'Is There an Environmental Kuznets Curve for Deforestation?' *Journal of Development Economics* 58: 231-244.

Kuznets, S. 1955, 'Economic Growth and Income Inequality', *American Economic Review* 49(1): 1-28.

Lieb, C.M. 2002, 'The Environmental Kuznets Curve and Satiation: A Simple Static Model.', *Environment and Development Economics* 7(3): 429-448.

López, R. 1989, 'Exchange Rate Determination in Natural Resource-Rich Economies', *Revista de Análisis Económico* 4(1): 91-105.

López, R. 1994, 'The Environment as a Factor of Production: The Effects of Economic Growth and Trade Liberalization', *Journal of Environmental Economics and Management* 27: 163-184.

Lpez, R. and Mitra, S. 2000, 'Corruption, Pollution and the Kuznets Environment Curve,' *Journal of Environmental Economics and Management*, vol. 40(2), pp. 137-50.

Mäler, K.-G. 1995, 'Economic Growth and the Environment', in Perrings, C.A., Mäler, K-G, Folke, C., Holling, C.S. and Jansson, B-O, eds., pp. 213-224 in *Biodiversity Loss: Economic and Ecological Issues*, Cambridge: Cambridge University Press.

Matsuyama, K. 1992, 'Agricultural Productivity, Comparative Advantage, and Economic Growth', *Journal of Economic Theory* 58: 317-334.

McConnell, K. E. 1997, 'Income and the Demand for Environmental Quality', *Environment and Development Economics (Special Issue on Environmental Kuznets Curves)* 2(4): 383-400.

Neary, J. P. and van Wijnbergen. S., eds. 1986, *Natural Resources and the Macro Economy,* Cambridge MA: MIT Press.

Panayotou, T. 1997, 'Demystifying the Environmental Kuznets Curve: Turning a Black Box into a Policy Tool', *Environment and Development Economics (Special Issue on Environmental Kuznets Curves)* 2(4): 465-484.

Panayotou, T. 1995, 'Environmental Degradation at Different Stages of Economic Development', in I. Ahmed and J.A. Doeleman, eds., *Beyond Rio: The Environmental Crisis and Sustainable Livelihoods in the Third World*, London: Macmillian.

Pearce, D.W. and Barbier, E.B. 2000, *Blueprint for a Sustainable Economy*, London: Earthscan Publications.

Pearce, D.W., Markandya, A. and Barbier, E.B. 1989, *Blueprint for a Green Economy*, London: Earthscan Publications.

Pezzey, J.C.V. 1989, 'Economic Analysis of Sustainable Growth and Sustainable Development', Environment Department Working Paper No. 15, The World Bank, Washington, DC.

Romer, P.M. 1996, 'Why, Indeed, in America?" Theory, History, and the Origins of Modern Economic Growth', *American Economic Review* 86(2): 202-212.

Sachs, J.D. and Warner, A.M. 1995, 'Natural Resource Abundance and Economic Growth', National Bureau of Economic Research Working Paper No. 5398, December.

Sachs, J.D. and Warner, A.M. 1997, 'Fundamental Sources of Long-Run Growth', *American Economic Review* 87(2): 184-188.

Sachs, J.D.and Warner, A.M. 1999, 'The Big Push, Natural Resource Booms and Growth', *Journal of Development Economics* 59(1): 43-76.

Selden, T. M. and Song, D. 1994, 'Environmental Quality and Development: Is There a Kuznets Curve for Air Pollution Emissions?' *Journal of Environmental Economics and Management* 27: 147-162.

Shafik, N. 1994, 'Economic Development and Environmental Quality: An Econometric Analysis', *Oxford Economic Papers* 46: 757-773.

Stern, D., Common. M.S. and Barbier, E.B. 1996, 'Economic Growth and Environmental Degradation: The Environmental Kuznets Curve and Sustainable Development', *World Developmen, vol.* 24(7), pp. 1151-1160.

Toman, M.A., Pezzey, J.C.V. and Krautkramer, J. 1995, 'Neoclassical Economic Growth Theory and 'Sustainability", pp. 139-165 in D. Bromley, ed., *The Handbook of Environmental Economics*, Oxford: Basil Blackwell.

Turner, R.K. 1993, 'Sustainability Principles and Practice', pp. 3-36 in R.K. Turner, ed., *Sustainable Environmental Management: Principles and Practice*, 2nd ed., London: Belhaven Press.

Vincent, J.R. 1997, 'Testing for Environmental Kuznets Curves within a Developing Country', *Environment and Development Economics* (*Special Issue on Environmental Kuznets Curves*) 2(4): 417-432.

World Bank (1992), *World Development Report 1992*, New York: Oxford University Press.

World Commission on Environment and Development (WCED) 1987, *Our Common Future,* New York: Oxford University Press.

Wright, G. 1990, 'The Origins of American Industrial Success, 1879-1940', *American Economic Review* 80(4): 651-668.

50

Globalization

Mike Moore[1]

The globalisation debate and how nations, businesses, cultures and individuals cope is one of the defining issues of our day. In the absence of other issues it has joined imperialism, colonialism and communism and can be wielded like a club in any ideological direction. It's not new, it's not a policy hatched by some secret cabal, it's a process that has been under way ever since the first person climbed down from a tree. Indeed some historians suggest trade as a percentage of GNP is lower now than in 1900, and the movement of people is certainly lower now than then. Those who revisited the crusaders fought with swords cast in India from ore mined in Tanzania. The French saw King Louis XIV drink Yemen coffee served on Chinese porcelain, sweetened with sugar from Sao Tome, and smoke Virginian tobacco.

China had great trading ships, twice the size of Columbus' tiny fleet, and its sailors traded with India, Africa and the Islamic world. One fleet had a crew of 20,000 men. This was centuries before Columbus. Opponents accuse globalisation of favouring big business and concentrating wealth, yet Bill Gates owns a smaller percentage of America than Rockefeller did. Look at the Fortune 500 companies: most of the leading companies ten years ago have disappeared, as did the great Royal fortunes in most of Europe earlier. Company taxes as a percentage of revenue in OECD countries have marginally grown over the past decade.

It is the speed of change that destabilises people, but is this all bad? No one complains about the speed of change in medical research. Prince Albert died of Typhoid from the Thames. The richest man in the world died 150 years ago of a disease that could be solved by simple antibiotics that are now cheaply and

1 Fifty-first Joseph Fisher Lecture, 18 June 2003

readily available to the poorest people in most countries. Life expectancy has increased by 20 years, infant mortality has fallen by two-thirds, and literacy has exploded over the past 50 years. Hundreds of millions have been lifted from extreme poverty, especially in China and other economies that have adopted open economic strategies.

Technology and science are man's best friend. Norman Borlaug won the Nobel Prize for Peace for breeding dwarf rice and wheat varieties, saving millions of lives. Nowadays protestors would try to stop him. Agricultural production in the US has gone up by nearly 800% in 75 years. Most American farmers did not have electricity in 1990 and their life expectancy was 49 years. Railways in the US cut freight costs by as much as 95% between 1815 and 1990. Refrigeration changed forever economies such as Australia, New Zealand and the Argentine, but now 40% of the world's manufacturing exports by value go by air. A three-minute phone call between New York and London cost $300 as recently as 50 years ago.

In my youth it took a year's pay to purchase the Encyclopaedia Britannia; now it costs a few dollars for a copy on CD. Thirty years ago Ghana had the same living standard as Korea, now Korea is as rich as Portugal, even though Portugal's living standards have exploded since she embraced democracy and joined the EU. North Korea was richer than South Korea at the time of partition. Now North Korea's people starve and live in fear. Burma and Thailand's living standards were the same after the war, now Thailand is 25 times richer per person. Thirty years ago Japan was a developing country, the Baltic States and the Czech Republic had living standards closer to France and Denmark before the Soviet experience. Their income per person were just half that of their previous equals by the time the Soviet empire imploded. A Taiwan factory owner paid his workers U$7.50 a month 45 years ago, now it is $7.50 per hour. The Argentine arguably had a higher living standard than Australia or New Zealand in 1900. What went wrong? What are the common denominators?

Open economies and societies do better. Globalisation is not a threat to the world's poor. Marginalisation – the denial of what the world offers – is the threat. There are still grave injustices. Free trade in agriculture would return to Africa 4 to 5 times more than all the overseas aid put together, and ten times more than all the debt relief offered so far. EU and US consumers pay 50% more for their sugar than they need to. This robs jobs from poor countries. Abolishing cotton subsidies would return $250 million a year to West Africa alone. The Cairns Group of Ministers led by Australia should be praised by the NGOs because no other political group offers a better, more immediate, permanent and effective way of assisting the poorest producers in the world. Globalisation should not be demonised or idealised. It offers the gift of opportunity, but if politicians, bureaucrats and phoney capitalists wish to plunder and protect their narrow interests, there is little that can be done to prevent such economic suicide.

Quite a good living is being made by people like Naomi Klein writing against global corporates in books such as her bestseller 'No Logos'. Please, there's no bitterness because she outsells my books.

The world is not being taken over by great companies. In fact their share of world trade is smaller now than 200 years ago when the great imperial protected, privileged companies carved up India and other colonies. Their shareholding is now much more diverse, even democratised. Peter Drucker, the management guru, recently pointed out that, through their pension funds, employees of US businesses today own at least 25% of US equity capital. If socialism is defined as the ownership of the means of production then the US is more socialist than Poland ever was. The funds of the self-employed and public employees own at least another 10%, giving workers ownership of more than one-third of the equity capital of US businesses. Business can no longer trick Governments into guaranteeing profits by promising local monopolies. In most cases, the finished product has inputs now from many sources and countries.

Anyhow, what is a brand name but a reputation? All that represents is the goodwill and trust stored up over years of success. I think the opposite will and is happening in spite of what some activists claim. A reputation is vulnerable, hard won and easily lost. Corporates live in a world of free information, investigative journalists, NGO's, and opportunistic politicians on the prowl for a headline all now need to conduct business in a more ethical and transparent manner. Nike has been at the end of protests over ripping workers off in poor countries. In Vietnam, Nike pays their workers five times the average wage, and in Indonesia three times the average wage. In Vietnam this is causing real problems with doctors leaving hospitals and professors leaving universities to work on the factory floor.

The International Labour Organisation did a survey in developing countries and found that multinationals paid higher wages, had better safety and health records, and were more likely to recognise trade unions. It's local businesses that are more likely to treat their workforce badly. The big corporates are vulnerable and must respond to public and shareholders opinion. And this is healthy: it's the trust people have in well-known brands, because they know what they will get, that opens up all sorts of possibilities to effect social change and improvements in the way people work and live in poor counties. The world is interdependent, as is obvious from the SARS scare and the aids pandemic. It's a bit like Victorian England when the rich discovered they were not safe in their mansions and great estates if their servants and workers were sick and poorly educated. When that impacted on them and their families, the idea of public goods, municipal socialism, public sewerage, clean water, and education came of age. Now corporations in poor countries understand that they must provide for their workers and they live in a wider society. If they dig up an ounce of gold in Southern Africa, companies must calculate a cost of over 10 pounds because of aids. If you are employing a worker in parts of Africa you must employ three, because two will die of AIDS. Therefore many companies are now investing heavily in AIDS prevention. They need to because if they don't they will get taxed to do it and that money will be used ineffectively, often stolen.

I've been in countries where nothing works but you can always get a cold glass of Cola Cola. There's a trial under way for coke to service condom machines.

Due to public embarrassment and grotesque rip offs in the past, the giant petroleum companies like BP and Shell have adopted strict policies of ethical behaviour and now refuse to pay bribes. They are working with the United Nations and its global compact to provide new transparent standards of behaviour and public/private partnerships to alleviate poverty. It's good business to be a good citizen. Virtue gets a real reward. What's encouraging also is the movement in developed countries for consumer to take power and not purchase products that damage the environment or are produced in an unethical manner.

I've made my case that in the main globalisation is a good thing. It's morally neutral. What governments do with the wealth a modern and open economy can deliver is up to them.

How, though, do we manage a world that has become interdependent but not yet integrated, where 2 million people cross borders every day? Let's look to our parents, the greatest generation for inspiration. Even before the 2nd World War had finished, great minds and men were thinking of what the new world would be like based on the lessons of the 1st World War and the Great Depression (which was made deeper, more lethal and prolonged by protectionist measures that halved world trade). That depression gave rise to the twin tyrannies of the last century. Fascism and marxism were tribal, vicious and protectionist, and from this came World War II, which in turn gave birth to the UN, World Bank, IMF, and what became the WTO. The words of President Wilson should haunt us even now when he failed to convince the US senate to adopt the League of Nations. 'Reject this and you will break the heart of the world', he argued.

We should not forget that one of the key reasons for establishing the GATT (now the WTO) was to stop the possibility of the world dividing into rival, possibly hostile trading blocks.

What makes the WTO different?

The WTO is the only international organisation that has a binding dispute system. Therefore Costa Rica or New Zealand can take on the greatest economic power and win under its rules. If civilisation can be defined as the rule of law, then this system is the jewel in the crown of the WTO. Unique also in the WTO is that all decisions must be unanimous and final agreements must be ratified by all the members' legislatures and Parliaments.

You are aware that we failed to launch a new round in Seattle and later succeeded to launch a round in Doha. Seattle failed, not because of process or protest. Governments could not agree in the substance. Europe and Japan could not move enough on agriculture, the US had problems on anti-dumping, developing countries had problems with investment, competition, trade facilitation and government procurement. We succeeded in Doha because all sides made compromises. Agriculture was the key issue. We made it a development issue. Rich countries spend a billion dollars a day to make food dearer for working families. A deal in agriculture would return four to five times more than all the overseas assistance to Africa. Agriculture is always a deal breaker or a deal maker.

The so-called new issues are also good governance issues, anti-corruption programmes. Everyone gains out of trade facilitation. APEC studies show that our region would gain more out of trade facilitation than abolishing all remaining import tariffs. For example, it costs four times more to get a container from North Africa to New York than from Hong Kong.

A new WTO round could return nearly three billion to the world economy. A deal in cotton alone would return over $250 million to the poorest African Nations. It would lift over 300 million people out of extreme poverty. The cost of Europe's Common Agricultural Policy (CAP) is equal to Spain's total economic output. The CAP devours half of all the money sent to Brussels. Now Europe is enlarging the expenditure is exploding. That's why there is hope. For the first time Europe is talking about decoupling, that is, paying farmers NOT to farm.

The cost of failure is high. The big players have other options. Regional and bilateral deals will expand in direct relationship with progress in the WTO. This hurts the smaller and poorer players.

Having said all this, I now want to indulge myself as a Kiwi, a Pacific Islander, and talk a bit about our region, where globalisation has passed too many people by, where too many people sit with their faces pressed against the window or TV watching and waiting for a train that may not arrive. Those marginalised are in an arc of poverty and instability that stretches from Indonesia across the Pacific to the Cook Islands. Ours is not a safe neighbourhood. What to do? Bismark famously said that talking of a moral foreign policy was like walking down a narrow forest path with a large stick between your teeth.

A damning paper on the Pacific Islands and Australia's aid was recently released by Professor Helen Hughes (2003). A similar study of New Zealand's aid programme would, I suspect, come to similar conclusions. Aid has failed the Pacific, Hughes argues. Per capita income has grown by less than 1% a year in the

Pacific during the past 30 years. In some islands it has declined, while population has grown at more than 3% per year.

Over the past 30 years the Pacific has received $200 billion in aid. Why haven't the associated policies worked? It's a tired story repeated in so many developing countries. Aid is not an earned income and creates 'rents' that distort economies, and because the projects are frequently chosen by the 'beneficiaries' it mainly goes on consumption and not on investment. Often on island economies' balance sheets, aid from Australia and New Zealand appears as income, allowing governments to avoid and hide from their real and precarious financial position.

AusAID pays for 85% of PNG's road maintenance. PNG and the Solomon Islands could soon achieve a unique Pacific status, that of being its first failed states. As I am writing this Lecture, bad and dangerous information is coming in from the Solomon Islands. PNG and Fiji 30 years ago enjoyed a higher living standard than Mauritius and Botswana. Now Mauritius and Botswana have a living standard twice that of our Pacific neighbours. Mauritius has a similar ethnic breakdown as Fiji, so these outcomes are not pre-ordained. It is economic and political strategies that made the difference.

Hughes goes further, and suggests that with PNG's population reaching 10 million by 2025, unless there is a sharp change of direction they face the prospect not merely of being a failed state but of becoming a rogue state like that of Mobutu and Mugabe. The ingredients are there. Urbanisation, crime, tribal gangs, failing education and health policies, and urban employment haunt the region. The elites collect the 'rents' from generous 'aid packages', implement economic policies that benefit mainly the few, and sent their children off to schools in New Zealand and Australia.

The King of Tonga is now seeking power to overrule any legislation and control the media. A free press is a human right, it's also a pre-condition for development. The London School of Economics studied governments in India and found those provinces with the highest newspaper readership enjoyed the best results, and they responded quicker to droughts and floods, and were less corrupt. Democracy works. Perhaps that's why there's never been famine in a democracy.

Much can be blamed on the colonial past, but that doesn't account for appalling choices now being made. In Tonga, the King and his mates apparently followed the advice of the King's Court Jester and lost nearly 30 million US dollars. In 1965 Nauru achieved independence and each person was worth half a million Australia dollars, giving them the second highest income in the world. Yet Canberra and Wellington were seen in New Zealand and Australia as imposing a new form of colonialism. Let's face it, we were wrong. It has not worked. The Hughes report was brought to my attention by a Kiwi journalist, who in an email seeking comment, referred to a little book I wrote over 20 years ago entitled "A Pacific Parliament". He cheerfully admitted he rubbished the book then, but now thinks I was a 'tad ahead of my time!' It is wrong to be right too soon. I guess that's the closest you ever get to an apology from a Kiwi journalist. The book is a little embarrassing to read now, but the basic argument about political cover for regional integration, common values, the creation of a professional civil service, free media, entrenching principles of good governance by property rights, honest courts, effective tax systems, police and military personnel properly trained working within legal constraints, remains valid.

The Pacific Parliament was not to be elected but consist of existing MPs in the regions, who would also serve as members of the Pacific Parliament, similar to the Nordic Council, not like the European Parliament.

To build common values needs patient, long term thinking. Still, my idea is more than 20 years old. The concept needs polishing but there is ample economic evidence that such pillars and institutions act as external anchors to drive up standards. IMF and World Bank studies show countries preparing for entry to the European Union have done better than those who have no external pressure and objectives. This is true also of countries who wish to join and enjoy the benefits of the World Trade Organisation. It forces the creation of transparent institutions, and property rights, and all those things that make a modern society work. Croatia, Poland, Hungary, and now China and Chinese Taipei, have gone through this strict process as economies in transition. These are globalized rules, standards, rights and obligations.

Mexico was a one-party state, corrupt and inefficient. Joining NAFTA forced it to comply with rules of engagement. This economic discipline brought with it economic growth, social progress, better governance, and democracy.

There are certain economic, legal and social conditions that successful countries take for granted. They are the rule of law, property rights, accountable politicians, an independent judiciary, free media, trade unions and an active, engaged civil society. Are these institutions a result of a modern successful economy or are economies successful because of the quality of these institutions? We need to revisit the ideas of the founders of modern economics and the enlightenment upon which our civilization is based.

Immanuel Kant more than 200 years ago wrote in his essay Perpetual Peace: "Durable peace could be built upon the tripod of representative democracy, international organisations and economic dependence." He first coined the phrase a League of Nations. For those who think globalisation is new, listen again to Mill, Hume and Adam Smith who all argued that expanded commerce produced good government and thus reduced the prospect for war and enhanced individual liberty.

Adam Smith in 1976 wrote "commerce and manufacturing can seldom flourish in any state in which there is not a certain degree of confidence in the justice of government." Money is a coward, so investment will go where it can get the best most-secure results. Guess why huge Arab investment funds buy property in London and New York and not Syria, Egypt or the Gaza Strip? This idea was recently revisited by a group of economists at the IMF. Their report suggested that if Cameroon could somehow build political institutions as good as these in the average country, its per capita income would rise nearly five-fold, from $600 to $2760. To make an economy work and reward its citizens takes more than capital, labour and technology. Institutions, property rights and transparency are crucial. If Bangladesh could lift the quality of its institutions to the level of Uruguay, that would give it a 5% lift in GNP.

We are correctly proud of what we have tried to do in the Pacific. But it has failed. The deadly prospect of communal violence, corruption, money laundering, aids, drugs, refugees, rich politicians, wealthy bureaucrats, phoney capitalists and poor angry people in a population getting younger, more angry, and alienated looms at our doorstep.

It doesn't have to be like this, and our failures are not born from meanness or lack of commitment. This has been a costly, honest mistake in policies and direction. We shall all pay sooner or later. And we will pay more the longer we fail to take leadership. These stories rate a small mention on page 5 of newspapers. They will be front-page news soon.

For the virtues of the market, both economic political and civil, to work we need institutions and laws that provide predictability that protect property rights and ensure liberties and disciplined pluralistic market structures.

I am optimistic. Freedom is growing. Never in the history of our species have so many people been free to choose in the political and economic market place. Just 20 years ago half of Europe, Latin America, South Africa were imprisoned. In our time, think of these photographs and TV clips: Mandela free, Berlin Wall collapsing, girls at school in Afghanistan, Tienamen Square.

Can I share my most inspiring moment? Cambodia was as bad as it gets. Millions murdered. Phnom Penh had a population of about a million. Pol Pot got it down to 30, three zero people. I went to this great capital at night. There were only a few hundred lights. What were they? They were cyber-cafes, with queues of people standing in line for their turn. If we give these hungry, eager-to-learn people the opportunity then they will seek prospects, peace and freedom. They fear marginalisation, they like young people everywhere seek the best the world has to offer. We must not betray them or let them down. They are the hope of the future.

Reference

Hughes, Helen (2003), *Aid Has Failed the Pacific*, Issues Analysis No. 33, Sydney: Centre for Independent Studies, May.

51

Paying for the past: Economics, cultural heritage, and public policy

C. David Throsby[1]

Joseph Fisher was not only a successful businessman but also a citizen with a strong sense of obligation to the public interest. The combination of private and public in Fisher's curriculum vitae suggests to me that he would approve of a lecture in his name being devoted to the matter of cultural heritage, given that heritage, as we shall see, combines elements both of widespread private ownership and of ubiquitous public benefit. Furthermore, my conjecture that Fisher would be favourably disposed towards this topic is reinforced by reference to his interest in art. He showed great generosity towards the Art Gallery in Adelaide, described handsomely in the inaugural Joseph Fisher Lecture given in 1904 while its benefactor was still alive; the lecturer, Henry Gyles Turner, Esq., praised Fisher's munificence in bringing "a fine selection of the world's masterpieces ... (to) ... this far-away corner of the earth". So here was a man with a clear sense of the importance of keeping the past alive for the edification and enjoyment of present and future generations.

To begin, we need to understand what is meant by the term "heritage". As its dictionary definition indicates, heritage is something inherited from the past. Attaching the adjective "cultural" to it defines its scope more precisely – it means we are talking about inherited things that have some cultural significance, where the term "cultural" is used both in its anthropological or sociological sense and also in its more specific artistic or aesthetic interpretation. Thus inherited rituals that help to define Australian identity – like Anzac Day, for example – are just as much a part of our cultural heritage as are historic buildings, artworks and so

1 Fifty-first Joseph Fisher Lecture, 16 August 2006.

on. Indeed it is helpful to distinguish clearly between *tangible* cultural heritage, existing as buildings, locations, precincts etc. or as paintings, sculptures or other artefacts, and *intangible* cultural heritage, comprising traditions, customs, beliefs etc. as well as artworks existing as public goods like literature or music.

Thinking about cultural heritage inevitably draws us into contemplation of some of the most fundamental emotional and spiritual aspects of human experience – the power of place, for example, or the sense of continuity with the past provided by our cultural traditions, or the transcendental qualities of art – all these are essential ingredients of different items of heritage that make them relevant to our contemporary lives. And none of this seems to have anything much to do with economics. So what can economics contribute to an understanding of cultural heritage? Let us focus for purposes of illustration on the urban built environment.

A city like Adelaide has a rich urban heritage, comprising many nineteenth and twentieth century buildings and patterns of public and private land use that form essential ingredients of the urban fabric and help to give the city its distinctive identity. But Adelaide is also a modern city that is growing and changing. Decisions must constantly be made as to which old buildings are worth preserving and, for those to be kept, what sort of restoration, renovation or adaptive re-use is appropriate? Arguments for heritage preservation are generally based on historical, archaeological, artistic and cultural assessment; hence conservation decisions have in the past been largely the province of art historians, archaeologists, architects, urban planners, cultural theorists and others, either in their own right as cultural workers on heritage projects or as expert advisers to governments or other agencies. Yet it is undeniable that there are significant economic dimensions to heritage decisions, even if one uses the word "economic" simply to denote "financial". Resources for the maintenance of heritage buildings and sites are by no means unlimited. Choices must often be made where the demands of cultural conservation conflict with those of economic development. Whatever financial revenues are brought in by new uses for old buildings, for example, must be offset against possible damage to culturally significant property. Such trade-offs are familiar territory to economists, so there are likely to be concepts and tools in the economist's armoury that will be useful in looking at cultural heritage decisions.

What sorts of concepts can economists contribute to a discussion of heritage? To begin with, as any first-year student knows, the science of economics highlights the phenomenon of scarcity and the choices it necessitates. Accordingly, economists are inclined to point to the sobering fact of the scarcity of material and human resources available for allocation to heritage conservation. We cannot conserve everything and so choices must be made. Furthermore, resources are costly; if they are used for the maintenance and preservation of heritage they are not available for other uses, so they incur opportunity costs. The range of tangible and intangible costs that may be implicated in heritage decisions is extensive and multifaceted. And, in addition, economists are good at pointing out that the preferences of consumers matter; experts and enthusiasts may value a building or monument highly, but if it is to be restored using public funds, an economic analyst will pose the question as to whether those who pay (taxpayers) are willing to do so. A problem arises when taxpayers' preferences are out of line with those of the heritage experts who are making decisions and spending money on their behalf.

Yet despite the obvious relevance of these sorts of simple economic concepts to an understanding of cultural heritage decisions, the initial efforts by economists a decade or so ago to enter the heritage arena were resented by heritage professionals, who feared a process whereby their "cultural" decisions would be inexorably transformed into "economic" decisions. These experts preferred in any case not to have to be worried by financial concerns, and were quite content to go on making their decisions on purely cultural grounds. Two things happened to change this state of affairs. First, shrinking budgets and tightened financial constraints on heritage managers around the world during the 1980s and 1990s meant they could no longer afford the luxury of assuming that money didn't matter. Secondly, after a while conservationists began to realise that not all economists were the insensitive philistines of legend, but that they could bring to the table analytical methods that could actually help to achieve better conservation outcomes.

When applied to cultural heritage decisions, economics does what economics is good at: it lays out the dimensions of a decision problem, identifying who the stakeholders are and how their interests are affected by the decision; it insists on defining objectives and constraints, in particular identifying potential trade-offs when multiple objectives are involved; and it identifies the data needed to quantify the relationships between variables and to animate the economic discussion. All this it purports to do without imposing its own values; objective economic analysis accepts tastes and preferences as given and would not presume to assert preferences of its own.

But wait a moment. Doesn't this raise the old debate about whether or not economics is a value-free science? When an economist looks at heritage and analyses it in the above terms, isn't she unconsciously imposing a set of values, the most obvious of which is that in assessing the value of alternative proposals before the decision-maker, a monetary yardstick is the appropriate one by which to calibrate the decision? In short, isn't the cultural professional's fear justified after all, that the economic agenda will finally dominate? This is an issue that has been addressed directly in the economic theory of heritage. The question has been posed in the following terms: Is it possible that some values associated with culture generally, and with cultural heritage in particular, cannot be adequately captured within standard neo-classical economic models? In the discussion surrounding this question a new concept has emerged in economics, that of cultural capital.

Economists look upon capital both as a store of value and as a long-lasting asset that produces a stream of services over time. An item of cultural heritage, such as a historic building, can be thought of as just such an asset. But its distinguishing characteristic as a specifically *cultural* capital good is that it embodies or yields not only economic value through its financial worth and through the economic services it provides, but also cultural value through its historical or aesthetic significance and the cultural experiences it provides for the community. It is becoming increasingly apparent that the concept of cultural capital can be helpful in analysing heritage and in formulating heritage policy. This is so for at least four reasons.

First, the phenomenon of "capital" is, as noted above, an important one in economics; defining heritage as capital enables the related concepts of depreciation, investment, rate of return etc. to be applied to the evaluation and management of heritage. In so doing one can open up a dialogue between heritage professionals whose job it is to care for cultural assets and economists who are concerned with the formulation of economic and cultural policy.

Second, the idea of cultural capital depends on articulating specific forms of value. In particular it draws attention to cultural value as something distinct from (though not altogether unrelated to) economic value. I return to the question of cultural value in more detail later.

Third, since capital assets are long-lasting, the notion of cultural capital leads naturally to thinking about sustainability. We are now accustomed to speaking of environmentally or ecologically sustainable development as being a growth path for the economy that preserves the natural resources of the planet for future generations; in exactly the same way it is possible to speak of culturally sustainable development, meaning ways of safeguarding our cultural heritage for the benefit of our children and our children's children. Neglect of cultural capital by allowing heritage to deteriorate, by failing to sustain the cultural values that provide people with a sense of identity, and by not undertaking the investment needed to maintain and increase the stock of both tangible and intangible cultural capital, will place cultural systems in jeopardy and may cause them to break down, with consequent loss of welfare and economic output.

Fourth, it is usual to apply economic appraisal methods such as cost-benefit analysis to public investment in capital assets. Defining heritage as cultural capital opens up possibilities for looking at heritage projects in similar cost-benefit terms. For example, an intervention involving expenditure of public or private funds can be seen as a capital investment project. In such a case, if the asset is a historic building or location and the "project" is the restoration, re-use or re-development of the site, we can suggest that treating the cultural resource as an item or items of cultural capital enables the familiar tools of financial investment appraisal to be applied. But there is an important difference from "ordinary" cost-benefit analysis: it is (or should be) the time stream of *both* economic *and* cultural value that is being evaluated and assessed. In other words, the identification of cultural value alongside the economic value generated by the project means that the economic evaluation can be augmented by a cultural appraisal carried out along the same lines, i.e. as an exercise comparing the discounted present value of the time-streams of net benefits with the initial capital costs.

Let us look more closely at these various dimensions of value when applied to a particular heritage project, beginning with the different types of economic value the project might generate. Economic analysis applied to cultural heritage has drawn increasingly on concepts and methodologies developed by economists studying the economics of the environment. As with natural phenomena such as wilderness areas or marine parks, cultural heritage gives rise both to direct use values – reflected, for example, in the fees tourists pay to visit heritage sites – and indirect or passive use values. These non-use values may relate to the asset's *existence* value (people value the existence of the heritage item even though they may not consume its services directly themselves); its *option* value (people wish to preserve the option that they or others might consume the asset's services at some future time); and its *bequest* value (people may wish to bequeath the asset to future generations). These non-use values are not observable in market transactions, since no market exists on which the rights to them can be exchanged, so they have to be measured by special-purpose studies designed to gauge people's willingness to pay to preserve the heritage asset in question using techniques such as contingent valuation methodology or choice modelling. Such methods allow us to gain some insight into the monetary values people place on these non-market benefits. For example, they provide data on the basis of which it is possible to estimate how much revenue might be raised if in fact the hypothetical willingness to pay were able to be converted into a real payment, or how much expenditure of public funds might be justified to secure these benefits for the community.

In a full-scale assessment of the economic value of a particular heritage project, these non-market effects are likely to be especially important. In many cases they may overshadow in monetary terms the direct revenue generated by the project, providing a justification in their own right for proceeding with it. For example, a recent willingness-to-pay study of the heritage benefits of preserving views of Stonehenge in England by building a tunnel under it instead of a surface road around it found that the heritage benefits alone justified the building of the tunnel because they exceeded the present value of construction and maintenance costs. Similarly a World Bank study of the non-market demand for the preservation of the historic town centre in Fez in Morocco found significant willingness to pay, sufficient to rationalise a tax on tourists to Morocco, including on those who do not actually visit Fez themselves.

The above economic values, both direct and indirect, are relatively easy to measure, at least in principle, because they can all ultimately be expressed in monetary terms. Cultural value, on the other hand, has no ready-made unit of account. In ordinary discourse, people often refer to the "cultural value" of a painting, a piece of music, or a historic building; by this they generally mean some notion of the cultural worth of the item which transcends a financial measure. But this vague notion is not much help for analytical purposes. So is it possible to be more precise?

In fact, we can suggest that the composite notion of cultural value can be disaggregated into several constituent elements. Not all of them may be present in any particular case, and their significance may vary from one situation to another. Let us think of the cultural heritage item under consideration simply as "the site". The principal components of cultural value can be listed as follows.

- *Aesthetic value*: The site may possess and display beauty in some fundamental sense, whether that quality is somehow intrinsic or whether it only comes into being in the consumption of it by the viewer. Under the general heading of aesthetic value we might also include the relationship of the site to the landscape in which it is situated, i.e. all the environmental qualities relevant to the site and its surroundings.
- *Spiritual value*: Spiritual value conveyed by the site may contribute to the sense of identity of the community as a whole and of the individuals living in or around the site, and of visitors to the site. It may provide them with a sense of cultural confidence and of connectedness between the local and the global, i.e. it may help to define the notion of human civilisation and the civilised society. The realisation that similar spiritual value is created by other sites in other communities may promote intercultural dialogue and understanding.
- *Social value*: The interpretation of culture as shared values and beliefs which bind groups together suggests that the social value of the heritage site might be reflected in the way in which its existence may contribute towards social stability and cohesion in the community. The site may impinge upon or interact with the way of living in the community, helping to identify the group values which make the community a desirable place in which to live and work.
- *Historical value*: This value, however it is received, is unarguably intrinsic to the site, and of all the components of cultural value it is probably the most readily identifiable in objective terms. Perhaps its principal benefit is seen in

the way in which historical value assists in defining identity, by providing a connectedness with the past and revealing the origins of the present.

- *Symbolic value*: The site may convey meaning and information which helps the community to interpret its identity and to assert its cultural personality. The value of the site as a representation of meaning may be particularly important in its educational function, not just for the young but for advancing the knowledge base and level of understanding of the whole community.
- *Authenticity value*: The site may be valued for its own sake because it is real, not false, and because it is unique. An important concomitant characteristic is integrity, variously defined in different circumstances; protection of the site's integrity, however interpreted, may be a significant constraint imposed on project decision-making when cultural value is taken into account.

To illustrate these various elements of cultural value, consider the case of Uluru in central Australia. The cultural value of Uluru to both indigenous and non-indigenous Australians can be seen to comprise all six of these characteristics: it is a unique, beautiful and spiritual place, providing a sense of identity to both the traditional owners and to other Australians, with strong historical links and deep symbolic value within Aboriginal culture.

Although these components of cultural value can be identified for a given site, measuring them or ranking them against alternative sites presents a considerable challenge. We urgently need clear and objective means of representing and measuring cultural value, so that it may be systematically taken into account alongside economic value in heritage decision-making processes.

What can we say about the relationship between economic value and cultural value when both are defined in the above-mentioned terms? Because as a general rule the more highly people value things for cultural reasons, the more they will be willing to pay for them, we would expect some relationship between some aggregated measure of cultural value and the assessed economic value of a particular heritage asset or of the services the asset provides. Indeed, an appeal to the standard neo-classical economic model of individual utility maximisation might suggest that the relationship should be a perfect one, thus rendering a separate account of cultural value unnecessary. But broadening our view to a more comprehensive notion of value would indicate that the correlation between economic and cultural value over a range of heritage items is not at all likely to be perfect, since there are some aspects of cultural value that cannot realistically be rendered in monetary terms. For example, it is simply not feasible to use a financial yardstick to express the value of a sense of cultural identity to individuals or communities, or the collective benefits of cultural diversity. So we must look to alternative metrics by which the elusive and multi-faceted concept of cultural value can be captured. It is pleasing to note that contemporary research in the economics of art and culture is beginning to throw some light on this question.

Let us turn finally to the matter of heritage policy in Australia at the present time. The rich diversity of Australia's cultural heritage takes many forms: the artefacts, traditions, rituals and stories belonging to the Indigenous people of this country; the significant repositories of moveable heritage contained in our art galleries and museums; the iconic buildings in our capital cities ranging from the earliest examples of colonial architecture to modern structures such as the Sydney Opera House; and modest houses, streetscapes, rural outbuildings and so on that define local community identities across the land. Some of this heritage is owned by Federal, State and local governments but much of it is in private hands. How can cultural policy help in its preservation, maintenance and enjoyment? As before, let us concentrate attention on the urban built heritage because, as it happens, this area has been the subject of a recent inquiry by the Federal Government's Productivity Commission, which was charged last year with the task of examining the benefits and costs of conservation of the built heritage and making recommendations for policy.

The Productivity Commission has a reputation for applying the rigorous principles of free-market economics to government policy formulation. For heritage advocates, the prospect of this Inquiry when it was announced raised the spectre of an uncompromisingly commercial attitude to heritage on the part of the Commissioners appointed to the Inquiry. Yet in the Discussion Paper released as the Inquiry's first step, full acknowledgement was made of the fact that substantial non-market benefits accrue to cultural heritage, and during the course of public hearings a sympathetic ear was turned to the many witnesses proclaiming the public benefits of heritage protection. Nevertheless, when the Draft Report was released in December 2005, the worst fears of the heritage sector were confirmed. Although the Draft reiterated much of the case for dealing with the public-good benefits of heritage, its principal policy recommendation was for a system of voluntary negotiated agreements to replace the compulsory listing process that for decades has been the main regulatory means by which Australia, in common with most other countries, has safeguarded its built heritage assets.

The Commission's proposal was based on the well-known Coase Theorem, that negotiated solutions over non-market effects will, under certain conditions, be economically efficient. The elegance and simplicity of the theorem, which helped win the Nobel Prize for Ronald Coase in 1991, appeals to economists. But like the theory of perfect competition, it depends for its application on a set of assumptions that are not often met in the real world. The Coase Theorem requires that: interested parties can be defined and property rights assigned; transactions costs are negligible or zero; and contracts can be monitored and enforced. As the chorus of dissent that greeted the Draft Report made clear, none of these conditions could be adequately met by the Commission's recommended course of action.

In the Inquiry's Final Report, released just last month, the Commission has retreated somewhat from its draconian stance, preferring now to rely on "unreasonable costs" as a basis for allowing private owners to opt out of a statutory listing process. This seems to me to be a rather slippery concept, strongly influenced by short-term financial exigency in circumstances where long-run considerations need to be taken into account. The owners of the Palace of Versailles, for example, could no doubt have pleaded "unreasonable costs" at various times in its history, had they been minded to replace it with something less expensive to maintain. This is not to deny the short-term hardships that may confront private property owners; rather it is to suggest a stronger assertion of the long-term public interest in providing appropriate assistance in such cases. I would suggest that a clearer understanding of cultural value would help in finding the right balance in heritage policy-making between the cultural and economic effects of heritage and hence between the public and the private interest. In fact the listing process implicitly recognises the primacy of cultural value as a basis for long-term heritage protection, and this is not something we should yield up to short-term economic pressures.

Indeed empirical evidence strongly suggests that any relaxation of present controls over heritage conservation would be quite contrary to the expressed preferences of the Australian population. Part of the documentation tendered to the Productivity Commission's Inquiry was a report from the Allen Consulting Group, who carried out a choice modelling study of the demand for the public benefits of heritage in Australia at the present time, based on a random sample survey of just over two thousand respondents. This pioneering research showed that people have a very strong perception of the existence, option and bequest values of heritage; the results also indicated that cultural rather than economic motives underlay the public's approval of government support for heritage conservation. In addition the study calculated willingness-to-pay estimates under a range of assumptions; these results suggested a significant demand for increased public funding for heritage protection over current levels.

I want to make just two final points in relation to the Productivity Commission's Report. First, criticism of the manner in which the Commission proposes to deal with "unreasonable costs" should not be allowed to obscure the reality of what this idea is trying to capture. As the Commission points out, much of Australia's built heritage is in private hands, owned by firms and individuals who respect the cultural value of the property in their care and who reap private benefits from restoring and maintaining it, without the need for government assistance. But for some owners the costs imposed by regulatory controls or simply by the physical task of restoration and repair are excessively burdensome in relation to the individual benefits the heritage bestows on them. In these circumstances – where in effect the benefits of preservation are substantially public rather than private – it is appropriate that public assistance should be provided if the size of the public benefit warrants it. The difficulty then is assessment of the extent of public benefit involved, since even with a more generous financial contribution from the public sector, not all old buildings can be preserved. Present processes for assessing public value lack common standards across jurisdictions, and their implementation is often inadequately resourced. Policy prescriptions could focus on improving these processes. Furthermore a stronger recognition of the precautionary principle is required, whereby irreversible decisions (e.g. demolition) are taken only under extreme risk-averse conditions. Again, the policy recommendation should be pointing to sharpened techniques of value assessment at all levels of government in the application of regulatory controls.

The second point concerns funding. The Productivity Commission declined the opportunity to recommend either increased funding or potential sources of extra finance. The Commissioners' unwillingness to engage in what is essentially a political matter is perhaps understandable. Nevertheless it needs to be pressed that a ready source of increased federal funding is in fact available, namely the Natural Heritage Trust. The Trust was set up by the Commonwealth in 1997 to help restore and conserve Australia's environmental and natural resources. Allowing cultural heritage projects access to the regional and national investment programs provided by the Trust could readily be accommodated without compromising the Trust's environmental activities and would, according to the Allen's survey results, be fully in line with consumer preferences.

To conclude, let me return to Joseph Fisher whose benign ghost haunts these scholarly corridors. What would he have made of the Productivity Commission's Draft or Final Reports? This is not an easy question to answer because, alongside his championing of the public interest, he was also impatient with unnecessary government interference; indeed he made his donation to the University of Adelaide four years before his death in order to avoid the 10 per cent succession duty which he described as "an unjust and unwise exaction … tending to check the flow of public spirited benevolence". But therein lies the clue perhaps. It is through "public spirited benevolence", whether exercised by enlightened philanthropists or by governments on behalf of all of us, that our cultural heritage can best be protected, preserved and enhanced, for the benefit of ourselves and of generations to come.

Further reading

Avrami, Erica, *et al.*, eds. (2000), *Values and Heritage Conservation.* Los Angeles: Getty Conservation Institute.

De La Torre, Marta, ed. (2002), *Assessing the Values of Cultural Heritage.* Los Angeles: Getty Conservation Institute.

Hutter, Michael, and Ilde Rizzo, eds. (1997), *Economic Perspectives of Cultural Heritage.* London: Macmillan.

Hutter, Michael, and David Throsby, eds. (2006), *Beyond Price: Value in Culture, Economics and the Arts.* New York: Cambridge University Press.

Navrud, Ståle, and Richard C. Ready, eds. (2002), *Valuing Cultural Heritage: Applying Environmental Valuation Techniques to Historic Buildings, Monuments and Artifacts.* London: Edward Elgar.

Peacock, Alan, ed. (1998), *Does the Past Have a Future? The Political Economy of Heritage.* London: Institute of Economic Affairs.

Rizzo, Ilde, and David Throsby (2006), "Cultural Heritage: Economic Analysis and Public Policy", Ch. 28 in Victor Ginsburgh and David Throsby, eds. *Handbook of the Economics of Art and Culture.* Amsterdam: Elsevier.

Schuster, J. Mark, John de Monchaux and Charles A. Riley, eds. (1997), *Preserving the Built Heritage: Tools for Implementation.* Hanover: University Press of New England.

52

Globalization and the Great Divergence in the long run

Jeffrey G. Williamson[1]

The economic impact of the industrializing core on the poor periphery during the century before 1870 was carried by four dramatic global events: a world transport revolution, a liberal policy move in industrial Europe towards greater openness, an acceleration in GDP growth rates associated with the industrial revolution, and colonialism. The transport revolution in seaborne trade connecting ports and in the railroads connecting ports to interiors helped integrate world commodity markets (O'Rourke and Williamson 1999, Ch. 3; Shah Mohammed and Williamson 2004; Williamson 2005, Chs. 2 and 3). While the previous literature may have exaggerated the impact of a transport revolution on ocean trade routes (Jacks 2006; Jacks and Pendakur 2007), it certainly did not overestimate the impact of the railroads on land routes (Keller and Shiue 2007). Since falling trade costs from all sources accounted for more than half of the trade boom between

1 This paper is a revised version of the Joseph Fisher Lecture presented at the University of Adelaide, 10 April 2008. A variant of it was also presented as the John Hicks Lecture, University of Oxford, 27 May 2008 which was subsequently published as "Globalization and the Great Divergence: Terms of Trade Booms and Volatility in the Poor Periphery 1782-1913," *European Review of Economic History* 12(3): 355-91, December 2008. I gratefully acknowledge help with the data from Lety Arroyo Abad, Luis Bértola, Luis Catão, David Clingingsmith, Aurora Gómez Galvarriato, Rafa Dobado González, Hilary Williamson Hoynes, Gregg Huff, Pedro Lains, Kevin O'Rourke, Leandro Prados de la Escosura, Amy Williamson Shaffer, Tarik Yousef, and audience responses at the University of Adelaide, the Australian National University and Oxford University. I also acknowledge comments from Albrecht Ritschl, as well as the excellent research assistance of Janet He and Taylor Owings, and financial support from the Harvard Faculty of Arts and Sciences. The sources of data are laid out in the Appendix to the NBER Working Paper version (Williamson 2008, see www.nber.org/papers/w13841).

1870 and 1914 (Jacks et al. 2008: 529), it must have accounted for even more than that before 1870 when the fall in transport costs was more rapid and the move to free trade was in full swing. In any case, it is clear that falling trade costs played a major role in fueling the trade boom between core and periphery, and that it created commodity price convergence for tradable goods between all world markets. By raising every country's export prices and lowering every country's import prices, it also contributed to a rise in every country's external terms of trade, especially, as it turned out, in the periphery. The move by the European industrial core toward more liberal commercial policy (Estevadeordal *et al.* 2003), a commitment to the gold standard (Meissner 2005) and perhaps even imperialism itself (Ferguson 2004; Mitchener and Weidenmier 2007) all made additional contributions to the world trade boom.

The accelerating growth in world GDP, led by industrializing Europe and its offshoots, was the second force driving the trade boom before 1870. The derived demand for industrial intermediates – like fuels, fibers, and metals – soared as manufacturing production led the way. Thus, as the European core and their offshoots raised industrial output shares, manufacturing output growth raced ahead of GDP growth. Rapid manufacturing productivity growth lowered their costs and prices in the core, and by so doing generated a soaring derived demand for raw material intermediates. This event was reinforced in the core by accelerating GDP *per capita* growth and a high income elasticity of demand for luxury consumption goods, like meat, dairy products, fruit, tea, and coffee. Since industrialization was driven by unbalanced productivity advance favoring manufacturing relative to agriculture and other natural-resource based activities (Clark et al. 2008), the relative price of manufactures fell everywhere, including the poor periphery where they were imported.

All three forces – liberal trade policy, transport revolutions and fast manufacturing-led growth – produced a positive, powerful and sustained terms of trade boom in the primary-product-producing periphery, an event that stretched over almost a century. As we shall see, some parts of the periphery had much greater terms of trade booms than others, and some reached a secular peak earlier than others, but all (except China and Cuba) underwent a secular terms of trade boom. Factor supply responses facilitated the periphery's response to these external demand shocks, carried by South-South migrations from labor abundant (especially China and India) to labor scarce regions within the periphery, and by financial capital flows from the industrial core (especially Britain) to those same regions. That is, countries in the periphery increasingly specialized in one or two primary products, reduced their production of manufactures, and imported them in exchange.

Let me rephrase these events in a different way. Whether culture, geography or institutions, western Europe launched modern economic growth first, carried by rising productivity growth rates, especially in manufacturing. The economic leaders had to share these productivity gains with the rest of the world by absorbing a decline in the price of their manufactured exports. To the extent that the leaders could retain some of the productivity advance for themselves, and to the extent that the productivity advance also took place in their big non-tradable sectors, the terms of trade effect was hardly a big enough transfer for the periphery to keep up with the core. Even though trade made it possible for the periphery to share some of the fruits of the industrial revolution taking place in the core, an industrialization-driven Great Divergence still emerged. To add to the forces of divergence, globalization fostered de-industrialization (e.g. specialization) in the periphery so that, according to modern theory, growth rates in the periphery fell behind those in the core still further. In addition, globalization-induced specialization in primary products must have meant greater price volatility in the periphery, and thus, according to modern theory, even greater divergence in growth rates.

Eventually all these global forces abated. A protectionist backlash swept over continental Europe and Latin America (Williamson 2006a). The rate of decline in real transport costs along sea lanes slowed down before World War I, and then stabilized for the rest of the 20th century (Hummels 1999; Shah Mohammed and Williamson 2004). Most of the railroad networks were completed before 1913. The rate of growth of manufacturing slowed down in the core as the transition to industrial maturity was completed there. As these forces abated, the resulting slowdown in primary product demand growth was reinforced by resource-saving innovations in the industrial core, induced, in large part, by those high and rising primary product prices during the century-long terms of trade boom. Thus, the secular boom faded, eventually turning into a 20th century secular bust during the interwar slowdown and the great depression of the 1930s. Exactly when and where the boom turned to bust depended, as we shall see, on export commodity specialization, but the terms of trade peaked somewhere between 1860 and 1913 throughout the poor periphery. Typically, that peak occurred very early in that half century, rather than late, most often between the 1870s and 1890s. To repeat, the terms of trade in the periphery peaked *long* before the crash of the 1930s, in some cases seven decades earlier.

This Lecture reports this terms of trade experience for 21 countries located everywhere around the poor periphery except sub-Saharan Africa (where the data are missing): the European periphery 1782-1913 (Italy, Portugal, Russia, Spain), Latin America 1782-1913 (Argentina, Brazil, Chile, Cuba, Mexico, Venezuela), the Middle East 1796-1913 (Egypt, Ottoman Turkey, Levant), South Asia 1782-1913 (Ceylon, India), Southeast Asia 1782-1913 (Indonesia, Malaya, the Philippines, Siam), and East Asia 1782-1913 (China, Japan). I focus on the 19th century secular boom since so much has already been written about the subsequent 20th century bust, the latter triggered by the writings of Raul Prebisch (1950) and Hans Singer (1950) more than a half century ago. Furthermore, I focus on the period from the 1780s to the 1870s, after which the boom had pretty much run its course. This focus is in sharp contrast with that of W. Arthur Lewis whose famous writings in the 1970s (Lewis 1978a, 1978b) dealt almost exclusively with the 1870-1913 period. I argue here that his new international economic order had been established long before the late 19th century. Indeed, there were signs of a *retreat* from Lewis's new international economic order between the 1870s and WWI. I also argue that the secular terms of trade boom must have contributed far more to the Great Divergence before 1870 than after. Having established that the secular terms of trade boom in the periphery led to de-industrialization, slow growth and GDP per capita divergence between it and the core, I then measure the extent to which terms of trade volatility did the same. Terms of trade volatility was *much* greater in the poor periphery than in the rich core between 1820 and World War I. Since modern development economists have established that volatility retards growth, and since external price volatility in the poor periphery was far greater before 1870 than at any time between 1870 and 1940, I argue that these forces must have contributed even more to the Great Divergence before 1870 than after.

The Great Divergence

All economic historians agree that a wide income gap between the rich European core and the poor periphery opened up before 1913. Economic historians do not agree, however, as to *when* it opened up, and *why*. My purpose is not to engage in the *when* debate, but rather only to remind us just how much the periphery lagged behind during this first global century, and to suggest how importantly globalization forces are likely to have contributed to it. Table 52.1 uses Angus Maddison's (1995) GDP per capita estimates to document the Great Divergence after 1820, and real wage data are used to extend his series backwards to 1775. Between 1775 and 1913, the economic gap between core and periphery widened greatly: Southern Europe income per capita fell from 75.2 to 47.3 percent of Western Europe, so the gap rose from about 25 to 53 percent; the Eastern Europe gap rose from 30 to 58 percent; Latin America from about 25 to 59 percent; Asia from about 44 to 80 percent; and Africa from about 54 to 85 percent. Note that the gap rose much more *before* 1870 than after: on average, the poor periphery gap rose by about 27 percentage points up to 1870, but only by about 5 percentage points thereafter. Thus, Table 1 informs us that the forces causing the Great Divergence were never constant, but rather that they were *much* greater before 1870 than after.

I stress the point that the Great Divergence was much more dramatic before 1870 than after since it is consistent with the fact that globalization-induced terms of trade forces in the poor periphery – to be discussed below – were also much more powerful before 1870 than after. Furthermore, the modern debate over 'fundamental' growth determinants like culture (Landes 1998; Clark 2007), geography (Diamond 1997; Sachs 2001; Easterly and Levine 2003), and institutions (North and Weingast 1989; Acemoglu, Johnson and Robinson 2005) in contributing to the Great Divergence cannot speak to variance in its intensity over time. Indeed, William Easterly and his collaborators (1993) pointed out some time ago that the contending 'fundamental' growth determinants – culture, geography, and institutions – exhibit far more historical persistence than the late 20th century growth rates they are supposed to explain. What is true for the late 20th century is even truer for the 19th century. Since globalization forces were variable between 1782 and 1913 while the fundamentals were not, the former have a much better chance of explaining the timing and magnitude of the Great Divergence than the latter.

Table 52.1: The Great Divergence: Income per capita gaps 1775-1913

	1775	1820	1870	1913
Western Europe	100	100	100	100
Southern Europe	75.2	62.4	52.7	47.3
Eastern Europe	70.0	58.1	48.8	42.0
Latin America	75.2	55.3	37.9	40.9
Asia	56.4	42.6	27.5	20.0
Africa	46.1	34.8	22.7	15.5
Poor periphery average	64.6	50.6	37.9	33.1

Notes and sources 1820-1913: The underlying data are GDP per capita in 1990 Geary-Khamis dollars, and from Maddison (1995): Table E-3.
Notes and sources 1775: The projection backwards to 1775 is based on unskilled real daily wages, and is an 1750-1799 average. The southern and eastern Europe trends 1775-1820 are assumed to be the same, and the African trend 1775-1820 is assumed to replicate Asia. For Europe and Asia (India); Broadberry and Gupta (2006): Table 1, Panel A; Table 6, Panel B. For Latin America (Mexico); Dobado, Gómez and Williamson (2008): Appendix Table. The poor periphery average is unweighted.

The secular terms of trade boom in the poor periphery 1782-1913

At the outset, a brief commentary is warranted on the heterogeneous character and limitations of the net barter terms of trade data that underlie the analysis. Twenty-one important regions in the periphery offer terms of trade estimates from points well before 1865, some deep into the 18th century, thus covering the era prior to the mid-late nineteenth century when, typically, the relative price of primary products reached their peak. In every case but Argentina and Mexico, these new series are taken up to 1913 and replace the 1865-1939 series used previously in my work with Chris Blattman and Jason Hwang (hereafter BHW; Blattman et al. 2007). For Argentina and Mexico, the new series are linked to the BHW series at 1870.

For the purposes of this Lecture, the best measure of the terms of trade is to construct a weighted average of export and import prices quoted in local markets, *including* home import duties, thus capturing the impact of relative prices on the local market. The weights, of course, should be constructed from the export and import commodity mix for the country in question. Unfortunately, the data are sometimes unavailable for such estimates – what I call in the worst case scenario.

It is easy enough even in those cases to get the export prices (and the weights) for every region in our sample. However, these prices are rarely quoted in the local market, but rather in destination ports, like London or New York. To the extent that transport revolutions caused price convergence between exporter and importer, export prices quoted in core import markets will understate the rise in the periphery country's terms of trade. On this score alone, any boom in a periphery country terms of trade, where it is based on the worst case scenario estimation, was actually somewhat bigger than that measured. However, since the terms of trade booms are, as we shall see, so big, these worst case scenario flaws on the export side are unlikely to matter much for the analysis. Things are a bit less accommodating on the import side in the worst case scenario. As with export prices in the worst case scenario, import prices are also taken from export markets in the industrial core. Since transport revolutions reduced freight costs on the outward leg from the industrial core much less (they were high value, low bulk products: see Shah Mohammed and Williamson 2004), the periphery import price estimates are less flawed in the worst case scenario than are the export price estimates. The more serious problem on the import side is the difficulty of documenting the import mix for many of the periphery countries, especially as we move earlier in the 19th century. The appendix to Williamson (2008) describes the proxies used to solve this worse case scenario problem. Having pointed out the flaws in the worst case scenario, it should be stressed that there are only 6 of these (out of 21).[2]

2 The following 15 are taken from country-specific sources which do an excellent job in constructing estimates which come close to the ideal measure: Argentina 1810-1870 (Newland 1998), Brazil 1826-1913 (Prados de la Escosura 2006), Chile 1810-1913 (Braun et al. 2000), Cuba 1826-1913 (Prados de la Escosura 2006), Egypt 1796-1913 (Williamson and Yousef 2008), India 1800-1913 (Clingingsmith and Williamson 2005), Indonesia 1825-1913 (Korthals 1994), Japan 1857-1913 (Miyamoto et al. 1965; Yamazawa and Yamamoto 1979), Levant 1839-1913 (Issawi 1988), Malaya 1882-1913 (Huff and Caggiano 2007), Mexico 1751-1870 (Dobado et al. 2008), Ottoman Turkey 1800-1913 (Pamuk and Williamson 2008), Portugal 1842-1913 (Lains 1995), Spain 1750-1913 (see Appendix to Williamson 2008), and Venezuela 1830-1913 (Baptista 1997). The worst case scenarios apply to Italy 1817-1913 (Glazier et al. 1975) and the remaining five (see Appendix to Williamson 2008): Ceylon 1782-1913, China 1782-1913, the Philippines 1782-1913, Russia 1782-1913, and Siam 1782-1913.

The big picture: Stability, boom and bust

Although the number of countries underlying the poor periphery average is limited for most of the 18th century[3], what we do have reveals no trend in the net barter terms of trade, that is, in the ratio of the poor periphery's average export price to its average import price. The averages are calculated so that the price of each commodity exported or imported is weighted by the importance of that traded commodity in the country's total exports or imports. Furthermore, the poor periphery average is calculated using fixed country 1870 population weights. The resulting series plotted in Figure 52.1 is waiting for the industrial revolution, the transport revolution, peace in Europe, liberal trade policy, and a world trade boom.

Figure 52.1: 18th Century terms of trade secular stability in the poor periphery

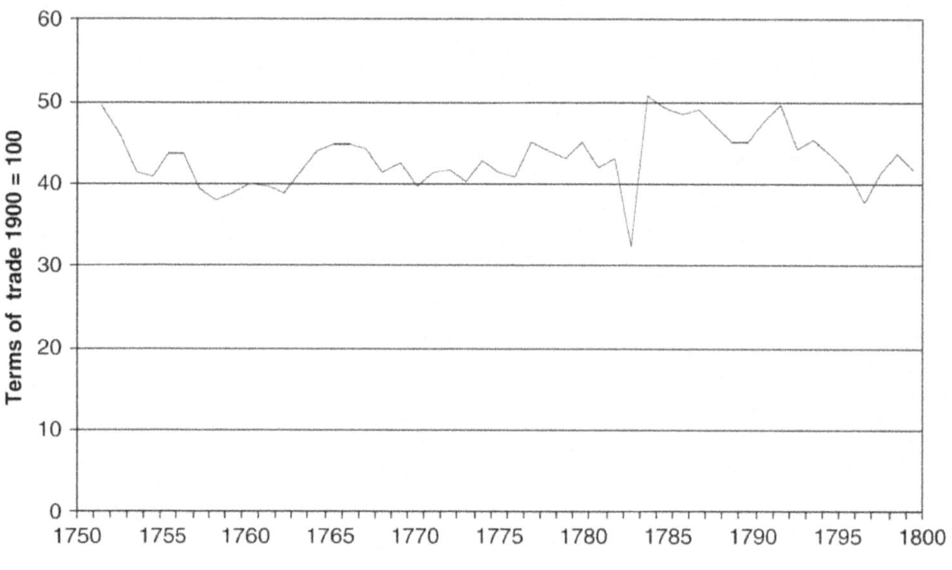

Figure 52.2 describes quite a different century. Excluding China and the rest of East Asia (more on that below), the terms of trade in the poor periphery soared from the late 18th century to the late 1880s and early 1890s, after which it underwent a decline up to 1913, before starting the interwar collapse about which so much has been written. The timing and the magnitude of the boom up to the

3 Until the 1780s, I have only been able to find long time series on the terms of trade in the poor periphery for Mexico and Spain. See Appendix to Williamson (2008), Part 2.

late 1860s and early 1870s pretty much replicates – but in the opposite direction – the decline in the British terms of trade over the same period. The secular price boom was huge in the poor periphery: between the half-decades 1796-1800 and 1856-1860, the terms of trade increased by almost two and a half times, or at an annual rate of 1.5 percent, a rate which was vastly greater than per capita income growth in the poor periphery (0.1 percent per annum, Asia 1820-1870; Maddison 1995: p. 24), and even greater than per capita income growth in Britain (1.2 percent per annum, United Kingdom 1820-1870: Maddison 1995; p. 23).

Figure 52.2: United Kingdom versus the poor periphery: Net barter terms of trade 1796-1913

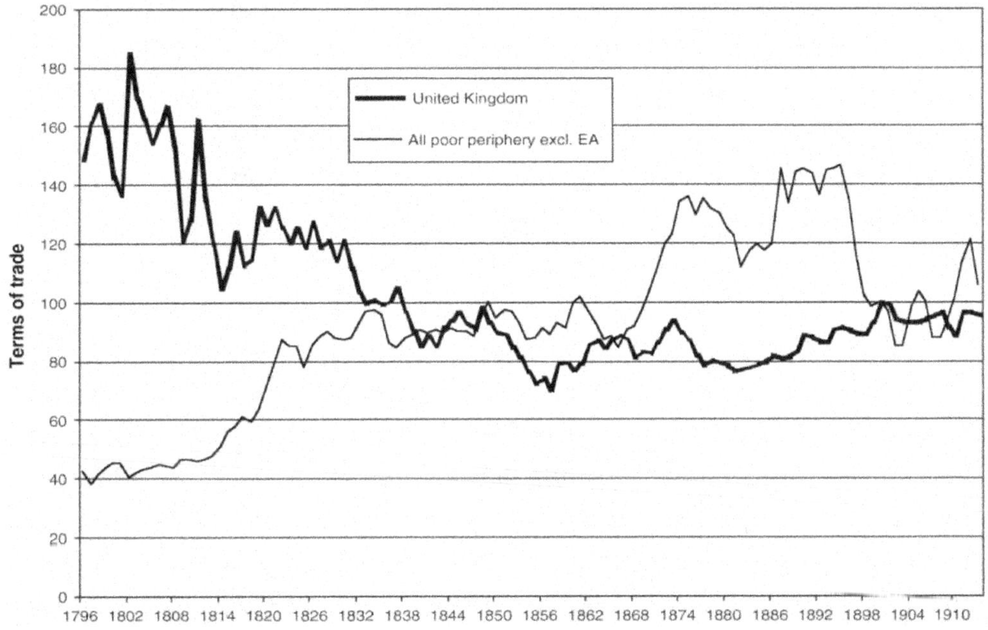

A rise in the primary-product specializing country's terms of trade implied, of course, a fall in the relative price of imported manufactures. And the decline in that price implied de-industrialization. When Lewis published his now-famous *The Evolution of the International Economic Order* in 1978 (based on his 1977 Janeway Lectures), he placed his emphasis on "the second half of the nineteenth century" (1978a: p. 14). But if we are looking for Dutch disease forces which caused de-industrialization in the poor periphery – the same forces that helped create Lewis' new international economic order, the century before 1870 is the place to look, not after.

Chinese and East Asian exceptionalism

Not every part of the poor periphery followed the average since what a region traded mattered.[4] The best example of this is the biggest country in our sample, China. Figure 52.3 plots the terms of trade for China, for the poor periphery with East Asia (and thus China [5]) included, and for the poor periphery without it. The difference is astounding. First, China did not undergo a terms of trade boom over the century before 1913, but rather underwent a secular slump. Second, as the rest of the periphery began the boom between 1796 and 1821, China underwent its first big *collapse*, with its terms of trade falling to one-fifth (sic!) of the 1796 level. Third, when China finally joined the boom taking place in the rest of the periphery, it was very brief since its terms of trade peaked out much earlier than the rest, in 1840 after only a two decade boom. Following the early 1860s, China underwent the same slow secular decline in its terms of trade that was common across much of the poor periphery.[6] China's terms of trade *exceptionalism* is, of course, driven by its unusual country-specific mix of imports and exports. On the import side, what distinguished China from the rest of the periphery was opium. The price of imported opium rose sharply from the 1780s to the 1820s and it maintained those high (but volatile) levels until the 1880s (Clingingsmith and Williamson 2008).[7] Since opium imports rose from about 30 to 50 percent of total Chinese imports over the period, the rise in the opium price helped push China's terms of trade downwards, and in a direction opposite to that of the rest of the periphery. Reinforcing that secular fall in China's terms of trade, was the fact that it also exported the "wrong" products since the price of silk, cotton and tea all fell dramatically over the century between the 1780s and 1880s, by 60, 71 and 79 percent, respectively (Mulhall 1892; pp. 471-8).[8] Chinese *exceptionalism* indeed!

4 Carlos Diaz-Alejandro (1984) made this point some time ago, and called it the "commodity lottery."

5 The other member of the East Asian sample is Japan, but it does not enter the sample until 1857. Thus, all of the differences between the series with and without East Asia can be attributed to China before the late 1850s. In the second half of the century, the population weight for China is so huge, China still dominates the East Asian terms of trade trends.

6 It should be noted that one other country, Cuba, showed "exceptional" terms of trade experience. The Cuban terms of trade are not plotted in Figure 6, but it *fell* by 49 percent between 1826 and 1860, and by 50 percent up to 1885-1890. The source of the decline lay, of course, with sugar prices.

7 I am not suggesting here that the price of opium was exogenous to the Chinese market. Indeed, rising Chinese demand helped account for the price boom.

8 To repeat the previous footnote, I am not suggesting that the price of silk and tea were exogenous to China. Indeed, China was a major supplier of both to world markets

Figure 52.3: Chinese exceptionalism: Net barter terms of trade in the poor periphery 1796-1913 with and without East Asia

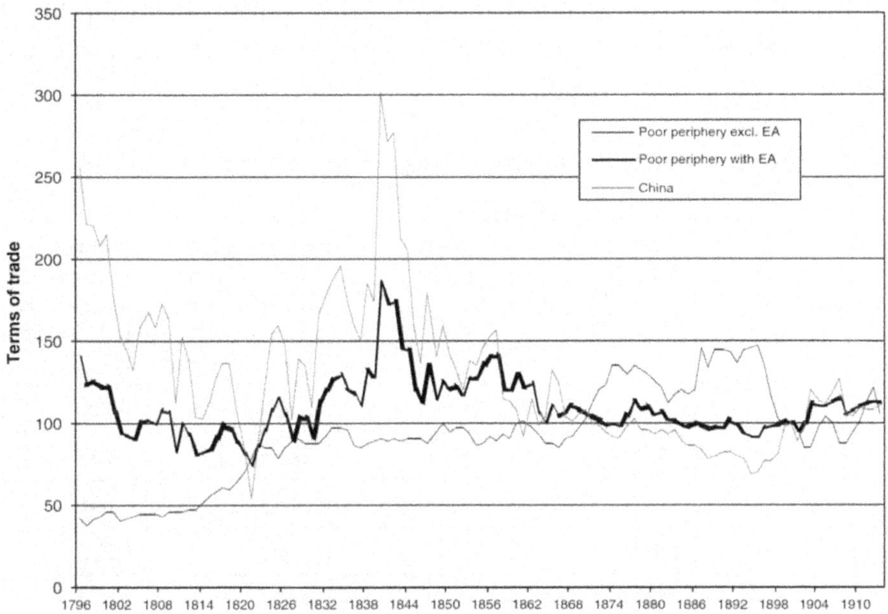

While China was certainly big enough to dominate East Asian trends, it should be pointed out that Japan was exceptional as well. First, it remained closed to world trade until 1857, so that there is no terms of trade trend worth reporting up to that time. Second, when Japan was forced to go open by American gunships, it underwent the biggest terms of trade boom by far, just when the rest of the poor periphery had pretty much completed its secular boom. East Asian *exceptionalism* indeed.

Poor periphery variance around the average

While each region in the poor periphery had much the same import mix (except for China and its opium), they had very different export mixes. Endowments and comparative advantage dictated the export mix, and different commodity price behavior implied different magnitudes during the secular boom, as well as different timing in its peak. Figures 52.4-10 document terms of trade performance in each of the six poor periphery regions, some starting as early as 1782. The regional time series are constructed as a fixed 1870 population weighted average of the region's countries (listed above: the European Periphery four, the Latin American eight, the Middle East three, the South Asian two, the Southeast Asian four, and the East Asian two). Table 52.2 and Figure 52.4 summarize the magnitude of the boom and its length (or peak) by region and by major country members, making a comparative assessment possible.

Table 52.2: Terms of trade boom across the poor periphery: Timing and magnitude

Region	Starting year in the series	Peak year	Annual growth rate between half-decades start to peak (%)	Annual growth rate between half-decades start to 1886-90 (%)
All periphery excl. EA	**1796**	**1860**	**1.431**	**0.726**
European periphery	1782	1855	2.434	1.234
Latin America	1782	1895	0.873	0.851
Middle East	1796	1857	1.683	0.872
South Asia	1782	1861	0.904	0.037
Southeast Asia	1782	1896	1.423	1.423
East Asia	1782	None	NA	-2.119
European periphery	**1782**	**1855**	**2.434**	**1.234**
Italy	1817	1855	3.619	0.697
Russia	1782	1855	2.475	1.335
Spain	1782	1879	1.505	1.264
Latin America	**1782**	**1895**	**0.873**	**0.851**
Argentina	1811	1909	1.165	1.284
Brazil	1826	1894	1.115	1.067
Chile	1810	1906	0.966	0.140
Cuba	1826	None	NA	-1.803
Mexico	1782	1878	1.096	0.989
Venezuela	1830	1895	0.692	0.677
Middle East	**1796**	**1857**	**1.683**	**0.872**
Egypt	1796	1865	2.721	1.571
Ottoman Turkey	1800	1857	2.548	1.233

Table 52.2: Terms of trade boom across the poor periphery: Timing and magnitude cont.

Region	Starting year in the series	Peak year	Annual growth rate between half-decades start to peak (%)	Annual growth rate between half-decades start to 1886-90 (%)
South Asia	**1800**	**1861**	**0.904**	**0.037**
Ceylon	1782	1874	0.670	0.366
India	1800	1861	0.932	0.024
Southeast Asia	**1782**	**1896**	**1.423**	**1.423**
Indonesia	1825	1896	3.294	3.335
Philippines	1782	1857	1.480	0.720
Siam	1800	1857	1.534	0.397
East Asia	**1782**	**None**	**NA**	**-2.119**
China	1782	None	NA	-2.342

Notes: The following countries are excluded from the table's detail since their series begin too late (starting date in parentheses): Portugal (1842); Columbia (1865), Peru (1865), Venezuela (1830); Levant (1839); Malaysia (1882); and Japan (1857). These country observations were used, however, when constructing the regional aggregates and the All Periphery aggregate. Where it says "start", the calculation is the average of the first five years. Where it says "peak", the calculation is for the five years centered on the peak year. The regional and all the periphery averages are weighted by 1870 population.

Figure 52.4: The poor periphery: Net barter terms of trade 1796-1913

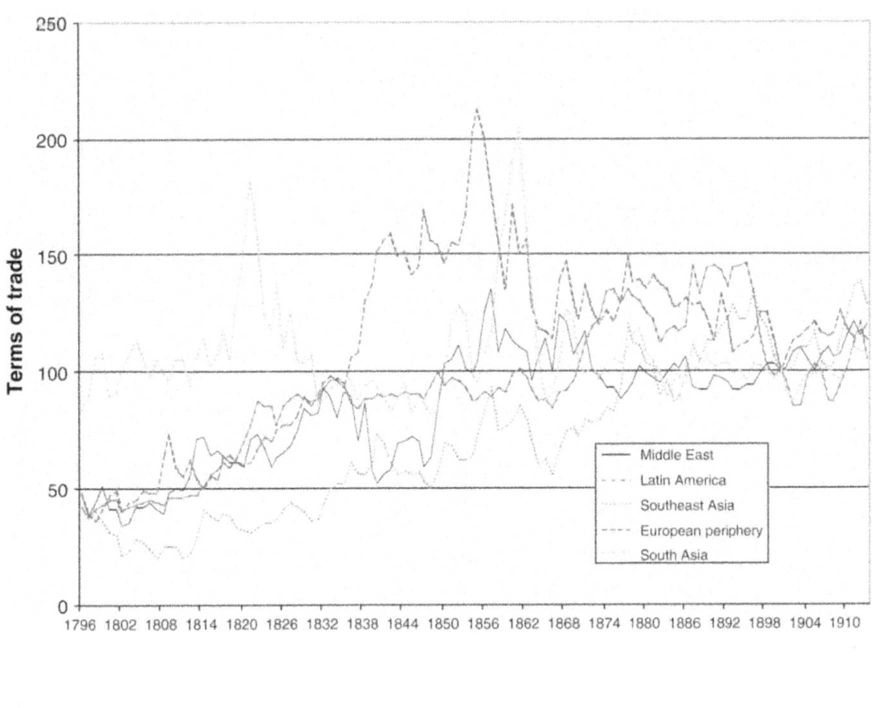

European Poor Periphery 1782-1913. Figure 52.4, Figure 52.5 and Table 52.2 suggest that the shape of the secular boom and bust in the European periphery was pretty much like that of the overall poor periphery average, with peaks very close together (1855 versus 1860). However, the *magnitude* of the booms certainly differed. The terms of trade boom in the European periphery was *much* greater than the average (2.4 versus 1.4 percent per annum), especially for Italy and Russia. This was also true of the century-long boom up to 1885-90 (1.2 versus 0.7 percent per annum). As we suggest below, these powerful Dutch disease effects may help explain why the industrial revolution was slow to spread from the core to the European east and south.

Figure 52.5: European poor periphery: Net barter terms of trade 1782-1913

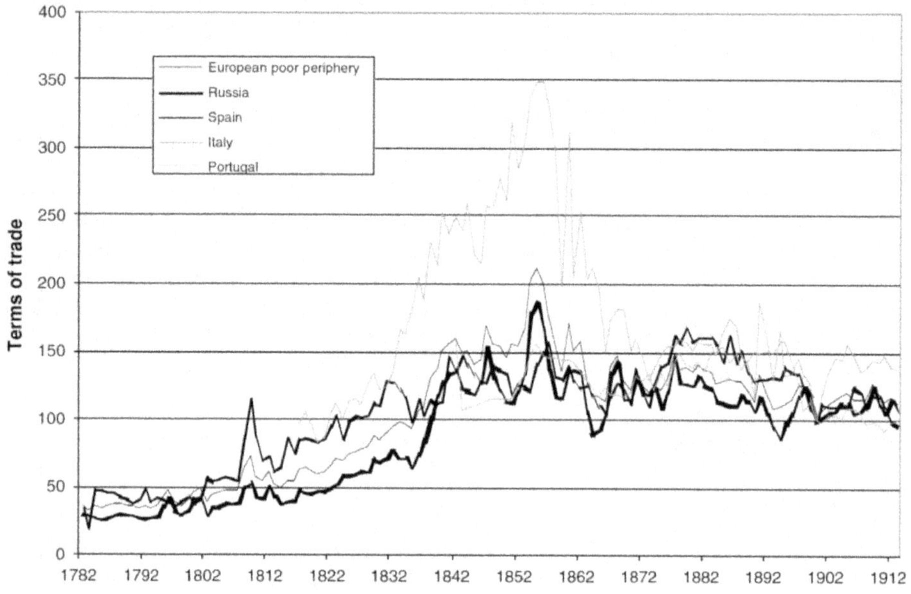

Latin America 1782-1913. Figure 52.4, Figure 52.6 and Table 52.2 report that Latin America also deviated significantly from the poor periphery average, but on the down side. The terms of trade boom up to 1860 was much more modest in Latin America. Indeed, there was very little change at all in the Latin American terms of trade between about 1830 and 1870. At least the new Latin America republics did not have to deal with global de-industrialization forces during their 'lost decades' of poor growth when violence and political instability was already doing enough economic damage (Bates, Coatsworth and Williamson

2007; Williamson 2007). Still, the Latin American terms of trade boom lasted far longer (1895) than was true for the average periphery region (1860), more than three decades longer. The more modest early boom in Latin America and its great length about balanced out, such that the century-long boom was much the same as in the average poor periphery region (0.9 versus 0.7 percent per annum up to 1885-90). To summarize, de-industrialization forces were very weak in Latin America during its *lost decades*, when they were strong everywhere else in the poor periphery; and they were very strong during its *belle époque*,[9] when they were weak everywhere else in the poor periphery.

Figure 52.6: Latin America: Net barter terms of trade 1782-1913

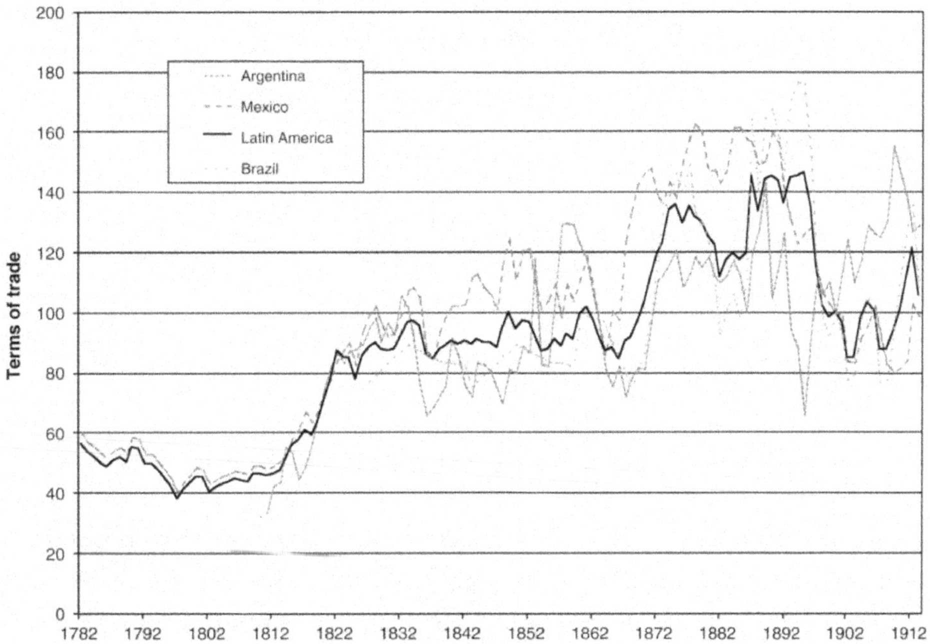

Middle East 1796-1913. Figure 52.4, Figure 52.7 and Table 52. 2 document that the terms of trade facing the Middle East was pretty much like it was for the average poor periphery: the peak was about the same (1857 versus 1860), and the magnitude of the boom was similar (1.7 versus 1.4 percent per annum), although it was much more dramatic for Egypt and Ottoman Turkey (2.7 and 2.5 percent per annum) than it was in the Levant.[10] The magnitude of the century-long boom

9 Mexico is an exception. See Dobado, Gómez and Williamson (2008 forthcoming) and Williamson (2007).

10 Levant is not shown in Table 2, since the series starts only with 1839.

to 1885-90 was also similar between the Middle East and the periphery average (0.9 versus 0.7 percent per annum). In terms of the globalization price shock, the Middle East therefore seems to have been the most representative of the poor periphery.

Figure 52.7: Middle East: Net barter terms of trade 1796-1913

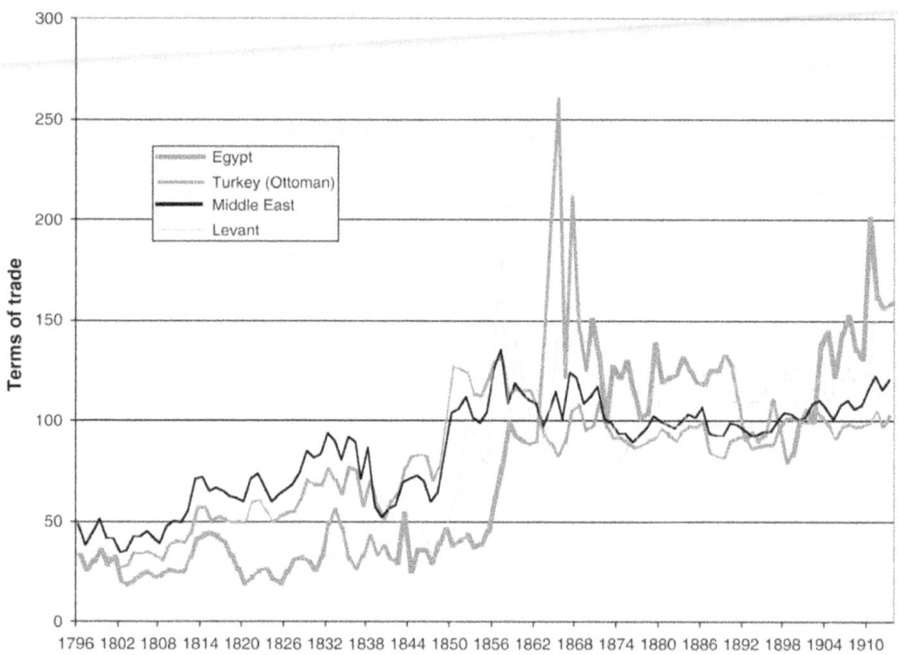

South Asia 1782-1913. Our South Asia sample has only two observations, Ceylon and India, but the latter is so large that the South Asian weighted average lies on top of the India series in Figure 52.8. Like Latin America, India (and thus South Asia) had very weak terms of trade boom up to mid-century.[11] The South Asian and the average periphery terms of trade (still excluding East Asia) peaked only one year apart (1861 versus 1860), but beyond that similarity there are only differences. The boom in South Asia up to 1861 was far weaker than the average (0.9 versus 1.4 percent per annum), and this was even more true over the century to 1885-1890 (no growth versus 0.7 percent per annum). Indeed, all of that early

11 One explanation for the weak terms of trade boom is that India remained a gross (but not a net) exporter of cotton goods even when British factory textiles flooded India's domestic economy. Since cotton textiles influenced India's export prices, and since the latter were falling dramatically up to 1850, P_X/P_M did not enjoy quite the same boom in India that it did in the rest of the poor periphery.

growth in India's terms of trade took place up to the 1820s; after that decade, India exhibited great volatility (like the spike up to 1861) but no secular growth whatsoever. And, to repeat, there was no growth at all in India's terms of trade between 1800 and 1890. Like China, India was exceptional, an especially ironic finding given that the literature on 19th century de-industrialization in British India has been the most copious and contentious by far, starting with the words of Karl Marx about the bones of the weavers bleaching on the plains of India (Roy 2000, 2002; Clingingsmith and Williamson 2008).

Figure 52.8: South Asia: Net barter terms of trade 1782-1913

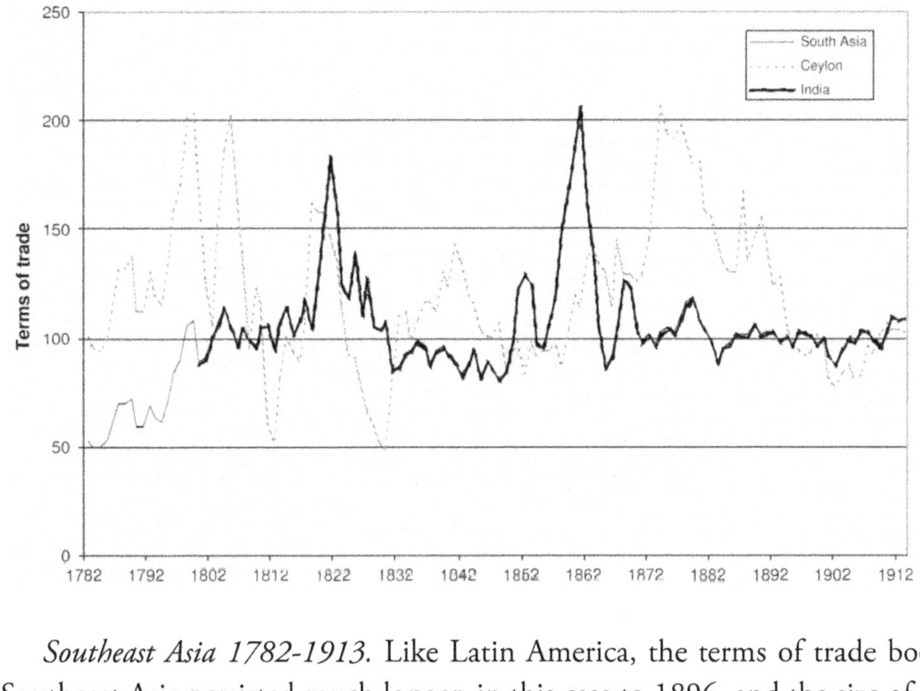

Southeast Asia 1782-1913. Like Latin America, the terms of trade boom in Southeast Asia persisted much longer, in this case to 1896, and the size of the century-long boom up to 1885-90 was much greater (1.4 versus 0.7 percent per annum). Yet, there was immense variance within the region (Figure 52.9), much more than elsewhere in the poor periphery. For example, the terms of trade for Siam grew at only 0.4 percent per annum over the century up to 1885-90, but it grew almost twice as fast in the Philippines (0.7 percent per annum), and more than eight times as fast in Indonesia (3.3 percent per annum). Due to its size, the latter dominates the regional weighted average.

Figure 52.9: Southeast Asia: Net barter terms of trade 1782-1913

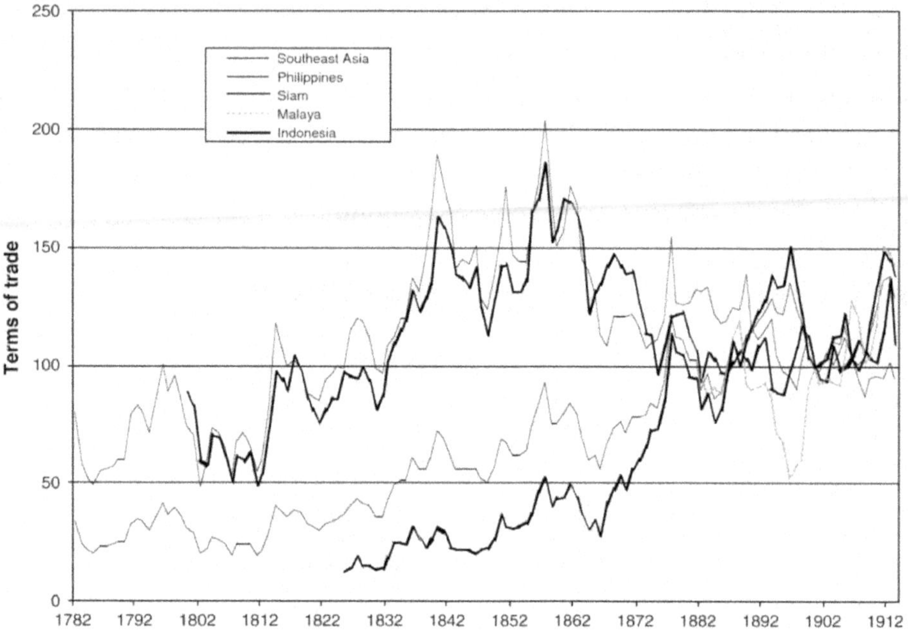

Figure 52.10: East Asia: Net barter terms of trade 1782-1913

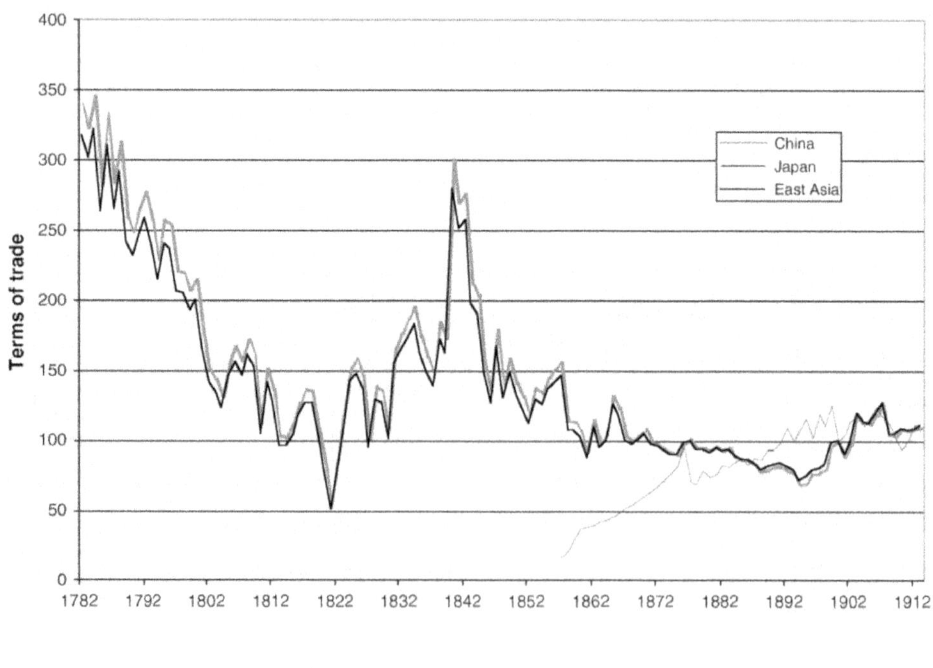

East Asia 1782-1913. We have already discussed Chinese *exceptionalism*, but Figure 52.10 also highlights Japan's unusual experience. That is, after being forced by American gunboat diplomacy to go open in 1857 – after centuries of autarchy, Japan underwent a textbook response (Bernhofen and Brown 2005): the price of importables collapsed, and the price of exportables soared. Thus, the terms of trade improved, and by a factor of six or more (sic!) between 1857 and 1913 (Huber 1971; Yasuba 1996).

The impact of the terms of trade on the Great Divergence: Argument and post-1870 evidence

How did secular change and volatility of the terms of trade impact economic growth before 1913? Was the impact asymmetric between rich core and poor periphery? Can the behavior of the terms of trade in the poor periphery help explain the GDP per capita divergence over the long 19th century?

Chris Blattman, Jason Hwang and myself (Blattman, Hwang and Williamson 2007) recently used a 35 country data base to explore these questions for the 1870-1939 period. The sample contained 14 from the rich core and 21 from the poor periphery, and it covered about 90 percent of world population in 1900. The impact of secular change and volatility in the terms of trade was reported separately for the core and periphery, making it possible to test for the presence of any asymmetric impact between them. Asymmetry regarding secular impact was predicted by the following reasoning. To the extent that the periphery specialized in primary products, and to the extent that industry is a carrier of development, then positive price shocks reinforced specialization and caused de-industrialization in the periphery, offsetting partially or totally the short run income gains yielded by the terms of trade improvement and the trade response. However, there should have been no such offset in the industrial core, but rather a reinforcement, since specialization in industrial products would have been strengthened there by any improvement in the terms of trade. Thus, the prediction was that while a secular terms of trade improvement unambiguously raised growth rates in the industrial core, it raised them less in the periphery, or not at all. The asymmetry hypothesis was strongly supported by evidence covering the seven decades after 1870. The core benefited from a secular increase in its terms of trade since it reinforced comparative advantage there, helped stimulate additional industrialization, thus augmenting growth-induced spillovers. That is, dynamic effects reinforced static effects. The fact that the periphery, in contrast, did not benefit when the terms of trade rose over the long term, or suffer when it fell, appears to confirm some dynamic offset to more conventional static gains from trade. The place to look for the source of dynamic asymmetry between secular impact on core and periphery is likely to be de-industrialization. However, since the secular terms of trade in the poor periphery had already reached its peak between the 1870s and the 1890s, there was hardly any terms of trade boom left to make a contribution to divergence in the half century before World War II. However, there was such a boom before 1870.

We expected the same asymmetry with respect to terms of trade volatility given that 'insurance' was cheaper and more widely available in the core. Modern observers regularly point to terms of trade shocks as a key source of macroeconomic instability in commodity-specialized countries, but, until very recently, they paid far less attention to the long run growth implications of such instability.[12] Most theories stress the investment channel in looking for connections between terms of trade instability and growth. Indeed, the development literature offers abundant modern microeconomic evidence linking income volatility to lower investment in both physical and human capital. Households imperfectly protected from risk change their income-generating activities in the face of income volatility, diversifying towards low-risk alternatives with lower average returns (Dercon 2004; Fafchamps 2004), as well as to lower levels of investment (Rosenweig and Wolpin 1993). Furthermore, severe cuts in health and education follow negative shocks to household income in poor countries—cuts that disproportionately affect children and hence long term human capital accumulation (Jensen 2000; Jacoby and Skoufias 1997; Frankenburg *et al.* 1999; Thomas *et al.* 2004).

12 For important early exceptions, see Mendoza (1997), Deaton and Miller (1996), Kose and Reizman (2001), Bleaney and Greenway (2001) and Hadass and Williamson (2003). I review the more recent (booming) literature below in the text.

Poor households find it difficult to smooth their expenditures in the face of shocks because they are rationed in credit and insurance markets, so they lower investment and take fewer risks with what remains. Poor firms find it difficult to smooth net returns on their assets, so they lower investment and take fewer risks with what remains. Perhaps most importantly, poor governments whose revenue sources are mainly volatile customs duties (Coatsworth and Williamson 2004; Williamson 2005, 2006a) and which also find it difficult to borrow at cheap rates locally and internationally, cannot, without serious difficulty, smooth public investment on infrastructure and education in the face of terms of trade shocks.[13] Lower public investment ensues, and growth rates fall. In short, theory informs us that higher volatility in the terms of trade should reduce investment and growth in the presence of risk aversion. In addition, the less-risky investment that does take place will also be low-return.

Modern evidence seems to be consistent with the theory. Using data from 92 developing and developed economies between 1962 and 1985, Garey and Valerie Ramey (1995) found government spending and macroeconomic volatility to be inversely related, and that countries with higher volatility had lower mean growth. This result has since been confirmed for a more recent cross-section of 91 countries (Fatás and Mihov 2006). Studies like these have repeatedly found that volatility diminishes long run growth, and we now know more about why it is especially acute in poor countries. In an impressive analysis of more than 60 countries between 1970 and 2003, Steven Poelhekke and Frederick van der Ploeg (2007) find strong support for the core-periphery asymmetry hypothesis regarding volatility, and with a large set of controls. Furthermore, while capricious policy and political violence can and did add to volatility in poor countries, extremely volatile commodity prices "are the main reason why natural resources export revenues are so volatile" (Poelhekke and van der Ploeg 2007: p. 3) and thus why those economies are themselves so volatile. While we have offered some reasons why poor countries face higher volatility and why that higher volatility

13 While greater volatility increases the need for international borrowing to help smooth domestic consumption, Catão and Kapur (2004) have shown recently that volatility constrained the ability to borrow between 1970 and 2001. It seems likely that the same was true between 1870 and 1901, a century earlier, and even more so before 1870 when a global capital market was only just emerging (Obsfelt and Taylor 2004; Mauro *et al.* 2006).

costs them so much more in diminished growth rates, Philippe Aghion and his collaborators (2005, 2006) offer more: macroeconomic volatility driven either by nominal exchange rate or commodity price movements will depress growth in poor economies with weak financial institutions and rigid nominal wages, both of which characterized all poor economies before 1913 even more than it characterizes them today. [14] Thus, "given the high volatility of primary commodity prices … of many resource-rich countries, we expect resources-rich countries with poorly developed financial systems to have poor growth performance" (Poelhekke and van der Ploeg 2007: p. 6).

What is true of the modern era was thought by Blattman *et al.* (2007) to be even more true of 1870-1939 when more undeveloped financial institutions and *more* limited tax bases made it even harder for poor households, poor firms and poor governments to smooth expenditures. Analysis bore this out: greater volatility diminished growth in the periphery, but not in the core. Strong support for the asymmetry hypothesis for the 1870-1939 years was especially welcome since that result raised the value of a research agenda that would explore its implications for the post-1870 years. Furthermore, the economic effects for 1870-1939 were very large: a one-standard-deviation increase in terms of trade volatility lowered output growth by nearly 0.39 percentage points, a big number given that the average per capita growth rate in the periphery was just 1.05 percent per annum.[15] These magnitudes suggest that terms of trade volatility was an important force behind the rising Great Divergence between core and periphery after 1870. The gap in per capita income growth rates between core and periphery in the 1870-1939 sample was 0.54 percentage points (1.59–1.05). Had the periphery experienced the same (lower) terms of trade volatility as the core, price volatility would have been reduced, adding 0.16 percentage points to average GDP per capita growth rates there. This alone would have erased about a third of the output per capita growth gap (0.16/0.54=0.3). In addition, had the core experienced the same

14 See also Aizenman and Marion (1999), Flug *et al.* (1999), Elbers et al. (2007), and Koren and Tenreyro (2007).

15 A contemporary estimate has it that a one-standard-deviation increase in output volatility in the Third World lowers annual GDP per capita growth by 1.28 percentage points (Loayza *et al.* 2007: 345-6). While this is certainly a bigger growth impact than that estimated for 1870-1939 (0.39), the modern estimate is an *output* volatility impact, not, as for 1870-1939, a price volatility impact. That is, this modern estimate does not identify *source* of the output volatility.

secular deterioration in its terms of trade that the periphery did (-0.28), instead of the observed positive 0.3 percent *per annum* growth rate, this would have reduced output growth there by 0.37 percentage points. Combined, these two counterfactual events would have eliminated nearly the entire gap in growth rates between core and periphery between 1870 and 1939.

At least for the seven pre-1940 decades, globalization seems to have had a bigger impact on the Great Divergence than did the so-called fundamentals. To put it more modestly, it appears that terms of trade shocks were an important force behind the substantial divergence in income levels between core and periphery during Lewis' post-1870 epoch. Note, however, that secular movements in the terms of trade contributed less to the growth gap between core and periphery after 1870 than did volatility (0.16 versus 0.37). The secular boom *before* 1870 ought to have contributed much more to the Great Divergence to the extent that the terms of trade boom in the poor periphery was so much bigger. And the contribution would have been bigger still if volatility was also bigger before 1870.

Impact of the terms of trade boom on the pre-1870 poor periphery

There should be no doubt that these global price shocks reinforced comparative advantage around the poor periphery, giving a powerful incentive to primary product export expansion while severely damaging import-competing manufacturing. That is, powerful de-industrialization (or Dutch disease) forces were set in motion everywhere in Latin America, Africa, the Middle East and Asia, helping contribute to Lewis's new international economic order. Just how powerful depended on the size of the export and import-competing sectors. Where trade was a big share of GDP, and where, conversely, non-tradable activities were a small share of GDP, the de-industrialization impact was also big. It depended as well on whether and the extent to which the non-tradable food sector was able to keep the cost of food low, and thus the nominal wage in manufacturing low and competitiveness high. It also depended, of course, on the extent to which the poor periphery could absorb and use effectively the new European industrial technologies. All of these factors mattered, but the main determinant was the size of the price shock itself. Where the secular terms of trade boom was greatest, de-industrialization should have been greatest, *ceteris paribus*. Lewis and most of the subsequent literature has argued that the big de-industrialization impact occurred between 1870 and 1913 (Lewis 1969, 1978a, 1978b; Tignor 2006: pp. 256-60). Based on the new terms of trade evidence just reviewed, it appears that Lewis was off by three-quarters of a century; the big impact must have been during the century before 1870 when the terms of trade boom was so much bigger.

So much for timing. What about *location* of de-industrialization? To make the comparative judgment, look at the annual growth rate in each country's terms of trade up to its country-specific 19th century peak (Table 2). According to this criteria, 19th century Dutch disease and de-industrialization effects must have been much more powerful in the European periphery than they were anywhere else in the periphery, even more so than the tropical periphery that Lewis stressed (1969, 1978a). It follows that part of the explanation for a lag in the spread of the industrial revolution to the European periphery (Gerschenkron 1966; Pollard 1981) might be blamed, at least in part, on these powerful terms of trade forces. The second strongest de-industrialization effect should have been in the Middle East and Southeast Asia, at least up to the late 1850s and early 1860s.[16] The weakest de-industrialization effects were in East Asia; indeed, since China's terms of trade *deteriorated*, it might be expected that industry was favored there, helping account for industrial success in Shanghai. The next weakest de-industrialization effects must have been in Latin America where the terms of trade boom was almost half that of the periphery average. Perhaps it is no longer a puzzle why Mexico and other parts of Latin America were so effective in fending off the global forces of de-industrialization up to 1870 (Dobado, Gómez and Williamson 2008; Williamson 2007). Nor was South Asia far behind since its terms of trade boom was not much bigger than that of Latin America. To the extent that India underwent one of the most dramatic rates of de-industrialization in the poor periphery (Clingingsmith and Williamson 2008), that experience must be attributed to domestic forces rather than to external price shocks.

16 Note that the Middle Eastern and Southeast Asian regional terms of trade growth rates to peak are not always bounded by the country rates reported for those regions in Table 2. One reason is that some countries embedded in the regional averages are not reported in Table 2: e.g. Levant and Malaysia. Another is that the regional averages are weighted, and are often extended backwards on the basis of a small country.

Table 52.3: Terms of trade volatility 1782-1913: Core versus poor periphery

Region	Starting year in the series	Before 1820	1820-1870	1870-1913
United Kingdom	**1782**	**11.985**	**2.91**	**2.006**
Europe periphery		**4.036**	**10.72**	**7.058**
Italy	1817	0.922	19.003	11.214
Russia	1782	3.226	10.722	6.104
Spain	1782	7.959	6.472	6.023
Portugal	1842	N/A	6.681	4.891
Latin America		**3.728**	**6.429**	**8.14**
Argentina	1811	4.409	6.961	8.303
Brazil	1826	N/A	2.174	10.283
Chile	1810	5.116	6.367	7.865
Cuba	1826	N/A	9.435	6.822
Mexico	1782	1.658	5.531	5.379
Venezuela	1830	N/A	8.108	10.185
Middle East		**2.902**	**13.611**	**7.316**
Egypt	1796	2.982	17.861	11.76
Ottoman Turkey	1800	2.821	6.549	3.289
Levant	1839	N/A	16.423	6.898
South Asia		**11.876**	**9.628**	**5.364**
Ceylon	1782	17.86	7.59	7.532
India	1800	5.891	11.666	3.196
Southeast Asia		**7.788**	**6.977**	**7.303**
Indonesia	1825	N/A	3.202	6.678
Malaya	1882	N/A	N/A	9.199
Philippines	1782	7.992	9.778	6.603
Siam	1800	7.583	7.951	6.732
East Asia		**15.554**	**10.527**	**4.952**
China	1782	15.554	19.752	4.311
Japan	1857	N/A	1.302	5.592
Average periphery		**6.46**	**9.176**	**7.089**

Note: Volatility measured using the Hodrick-Prescott filter with smoothing parameter 6.25, which is appropriate for annual observations (Ravn and Uhlig 2002: 375), as we have here. The periphery average is unweighted.

When the magnitude of the secular terms of trade boom is measured up to 1885-90, the regional ranking remains pretty much the same. South Asia drops farther down the list with even weaker terms of trade effects (indeed, close to zero), the relatively rapid terms of trade growth of Southeast and the European periphery persist, and East Asia continues its *exceptional* terms of trade decline. The Latin America boom keeps the modest middle ground, and the Middle East joins it. Thinking comparatively helps. Consider two examples. First, and to repeat, the South Asia result should surprise any specialist who is steeped in the enormous and contentious literature on Indian de-industrialization written by nationalist historians. However, the facts are that the terms of trade shock facing South Asia in general, and India in particular, were very modest, implying that much of the de-industrialization India underwent was of its own supply-side doing (Clingingsmith and Williamson 2008). Second, Latin American economic historians make much of export-led growth after 1870 during what they call the *belle époque*, implying that the region exploited these world market conditions better than the rest of the periphery (Bulmer-Thomas 1994: Chps. 3 and 4). Yet, the Latin American terms of trade boom was not much greater than the periphery average, and for Mexico it was much less (Gómez Galvarriato and Williamson 2008).

Impact of terms of trade volatility on the pre-1870 poor periphery

By 1870 and certainly by the end of the 19th century, most countries in the poor periphery had responded to the terms of trade boom by exploiting comparative advantage and increasing their specialization with the export of just a few commodities. The top two exports made up 70 percent of all exports from the average poor periphery country in 1913 (Bulmer-Thomas 1994: p. 59), while the figure was only 12 percent in the industrial core even two decades earlier (Blattman *et al.* 2007: Table 1). Furthermore, most countries in the poor periphery had raised exports so that they claimed a large share of GDP by 1890. Finally, while some of these commodities had prices which were a lot more volatile than others, primary products generally had much more volatile prices than did manufactures exported by the core.

Was the deleterious impact of volatility as powerful before 1870 as it was afterwards? While limited data make it impossible to estimate the impact, we can certainly calculate whether the volatility was as great or even greater before 1870, and infer the deleterious impact on periphery growth and thus its contribution to divergence. Table 52.3 summarizes the results using the Hodrick-Prescott filter, where the United Kingdom is taken to be representative of the core. That said, terms of trade volatility was much greater in the UK during the wartime years 1782-1820, than it was in the peacetime *Pax Britannica* century that followed. This result is hardly surprising given what we know about the volatility of the conflict itself and its stop-go impact on trade (Findlay and O'Rourke 2007). The peacetime years after 1820 were another matter entirely.[17] First, terms of trade volatility in the periphery was more than three times what it was in the UK, either in 1820-1870 (9.18/2.91 = 3.2) or 1870-1913 (7.09/2 = 3.5).[18] It is of some interest to note that the ratio of terms of trade volatility between industrialized economies and the periphery in the 1990s was 2.9.[19] Apparently, there has been a lot of historical persistence in the data, even though the difference between core and periphery was greater in the 19th than in the late 20th century. Second, terms of trade volatility in the periphery rose over the century, from 6.46 before 1820 to 9.18 between 1820 and 1870, and to 7.09 after 1870, a result consistent with evolving export concentration as the region exploited comparative advantage. Third, terms of trade volatility varied considerably around the periphery. Between 1820 and 1870, the highest volatility measures were recorded in the European Periphery (especially Italy and Russia), the Middle East (especially Egypt and the Levant), and East Asia (especially China), regions whose long run economic progress must have suffered accordingly. Latin America and Southeast Asia consistently recorded lower volatility than the rest of the periphery, but it was still more than twice that of the United Kingdom. South Asia was about average, but it was still more than three times that of the United Kingdom. If we are looking for countries

17 David Jacks, Kevin O'Rourke and myself are collecting monthly commodity price data 1750-1913 to explore more fully these volatility issues, one dealing with the impact of the world going open during *Pax Britannica,* and the other dealing with asymmetry between manufactures and primary products.

18 It may at first seem that the UK should have had the same terms of trade volatility as the periphery since it imported all those commodities with volatile prices. However, the UK imported a diverse market basket of primary products while each periphery exported just one or two.

19 Loayza *et al.* (2007: data underlying Figure 3, 346) where volatility is calculated as the standard deviation of the logarithmic change.

in the periphery where terms of trade volatility would have had an especially powerful deleterious effect on GDP growth performance before 1870, the places to look would be China, Cuba, Egypt, India, Italy, Levant, the Philippines, and Russia. But with the exception of Brazil and Japan, every periphery country had much higher price volatility than did the European core before 1870. There were no exceptions after 1870: every country in the poor periphery had higher price volatility than did the United Kingdom.

Given that terms of trade volatility was higher before 1870 than after, and given that this volatility contributed powerfully to the Great Divergence after 1870, it seems reasonable to infer that terms of trade volatility in the periphery contributed even more powerfully to the Great Divergence before 1870 than after.

Concluding remarks

W. Arthur Lewis (1978a, 1978b) and the literature that followed his pioneering work has argued that a new international economic order emerged between 1870 and 1913, and that global terms of trade forces induced rising primary product specialization and de-industrialization in the poor periphery. This paper has offered five revisionist findings that speak to the Lewis thesis. First, it has shown that the new order was firmly in place at the start of Lewis' epoch, and that the transition took place in the century before 1870, not after. Second, we know that terms of trade booms did not raise long run growth in the poor periphery 1870-1913, and may have lowered it. Given that the secular terms of trade boom in the poor periphery was much bigger over the century before 1870 than after, and given that de-industrialization and Dutch disease forces were much more powerful as well, it seems safe to infer that the Great Terms of Trade Boom helps explain the Great Divergence between core and periphery. Third, the terms of trade boom varied enormously across the poor periphery, and therefore its contribution to periphery performance must have varied as well. Over the century before the late 1880s, the boom was completely absent in East and South Asia, about average in the Middle East and Latin America, and powerful in Southeast Asia and the European periphery. Fourth, the terms of trade boom (with its de-industrialization impact) was only half the story; growth-reducing terms of trade volatility was the other half. Between 1820 and 1870, terms of trade volatility was *much* greater in the poor periphery than the core, in some cases six or seven times greater. In the post-1870 epoch, terms of trade volatility was still very big in the poor periphery and still much greater than the core, in some cases four to five times greater. We know that terms of trade volatility has lowered long run growth in the poor periphery in both 1870-1939 and 1960-2000, and that the negative impact has been big. Given that terms of trade volatility in the poor periphery was even bigger during the century before 1870, it seems plausible to infer that it helps explain the Great Divergence. Fifth, and finally, since the secular terms of trade boom in the poor periphery reached its peak in the mid-late 19th century, *de-industrialization* forces should have abated afterwards. Indeed, as the terms of trade started its long secular decline in to the 20th century, those prior de-industrialization forces should have become *re-industrialization* forces, that is, industrialization in the poor periphery should have been favored by secular terms of trade deterioration in the half century or more before 1930, an ironic finding given the rhetoric of Prebisch and Singer. Furthermore, the re-industrialization stimulus should have been strongest in locations where the terms of trade peak was earliest and the fall from it the steepest. These locations would have included East Asia (e.g. Shanghai),[20] the European periphery (e.g. the Italian triangle and Russia), Latin America (e.g. Brazil and Mexico), and South Asia (e.g. Bombay and Bengal). During the decades before 1913, early industrialization was taking place in all of these places, but how much of that is explained by a secular (pro-industrial) terms of trade slump, better pro-industrial policies, improved wage cost competitiveness in manufacturing, or getting the 'fundamentals' right?[21]

20 Meiji Japan is an exception: It underwent an improvement in its terms of trade right up to WWI (Figure 10), so it never reached a secular peak before 1913. However, like western Europe, it was a net exporter of manufacturers very early after opening up to trade, so those "exceptional" global price events (compared with the rest of the periphery) fostered industrialization there.

21 Aurora Gómez Galvarriato and I recently explored this question for Latin America (Gómez Galvarriato and Williamson 2008).

References

Acemoglu, D., S. Johnson, and J. Robinson (2005), "The Rise of Europe: Atlantic Trade, Institutional Change and Economic Growth," *American Economic Review* (June): 546-79.

Aghion, P., G.-M. Angeletos, A. Banerjee and K. Manova (2005), "Volatility and growth: credit constraints and productivity-enhancing investments," NBER Working Paper 11349, National Bureau of Economic Research, Cambridge MA.

Aghion, P., P. Bacchetta, R. Rancière and K. Rogoff (2006), "Exchange rate volatility and productivity growth: the role of financial development," CEPR Discussion Paper No. 5629, Centre for Economic Policy Research, London.

Aizenman, J. and N. Martion (1999), "Volatility and Investment: Interpreting Evidence From Developing Countries," *Economica* 66: 157-79.

Baptista, A. (1997), *Bases cuantitativas de la economía venezolana 1830-1995*, Caracas: Fundación Polar.

Bates, R.H., J.H. Coatsworth and J.G. Williamson (2007), "Lost Decades: Postindependence Performance in Latin America and Africa," *Journal of Economic History* 67 (December): 917-43.

Bernhofen, D.M. and J.C. Brown (2005), "An Empirical Assessment of the Comparative Advantage Gains from Trade: Evidence from Japan," *American Economic Review* 95 (March): 208-24.

Blattman, C., J. Hwang, and J.G. Williamson (2007), "The Impact of the Terms of Trade on Economic Development in the Periphery, 1870-1939: Volatility and Secular Change," *Journal of Development Economics* 82 (January): 156-79.

Bleaney, M. and D. Greenway (2001), "The Impact of Terms of Trade and Real Exchange Rate Volatility on Investment and Growth in Sub-Saharan Africa," *Journal of Development Economics* 65: 491-500.

Braun, J., M. Braun, I. Briones, J. Diaz, R. Luders, and G. Wagner (2000), *Economia Chilena 1810-1995: Estadisticas Historicas*, Santiago: Pontifica Universidad Catolica de Chile.

Broadberry, S. and B. Gupta (2006), "The early modern great divergence: wages, prices and economic development in Europe and Asia, 1500-1800," *Economic History Review* LIX(1): 2-31.

Bulmer-Thomas, V. (1994), *The Economic History of Latin America Since Independence*, Cambridge: Cambridge University Press.

Catão, L. and S. Kapur (2004), "Missing Link: Volatility and the Debt Intolerance Paradox," Mimeo, International Monetary Fund, Washington DC, January.

Clark, G. (2007), *A Farewell to Alms: A Brief Economic History of the World*, Princeton NJ: Princeton University Press.

Clark, G., K. H. O'Rourke and A.M. Taylor (2008), "Made in America? The New World, the Old, and the Industrial Revolution," *American Economic Review* 98(2) (May): 523-8.

Clingingsmith, D. and J.G. Williamson (2008), "Deindustrialization in 18th and 19th century India: Mughal decline, climate shocks, and British Industrial Ascent," *Explorations in Economic History* 45.

Coatsworth, J.H. and J.G. Williamson (2004), "The Roots of Latin American Protectionism: Looking Before the Great Depression," In A. Estevadeordal, D. Rodrik, A. Taylor and A. Velasco (eds.), *FTAA and Beyond: Prospects for Integration in the Americas*, Cambridge MA: Harvard University Press.

Deaton, A. and R.I. Miller (1996), "International Commodity Prices, Macroeconomic Performance and

Politics in Sub-Saharan Africa," *Journal of African Economics* 5: 99-191, Supplement.

Dercon, S. (2004), *Insurance Against Poverty*, London: Oxford University Press.

Diamond, J.M. (1997), *Guns, Germs, and Steel: The Fates of Human Societies*, New York: Norton.

Diaz-Alejandro, C.F. (1984), "Latin America in the 1930s," In R. Thorp (ed.), *Latin America in the 1930s: The Role of the Periphery in World Crisis*, London: Macmillan.

Dobado Gonzáles, R., A. Gómez Galvarriato, and J.G. Williamson (2008), "Mexican Exceptionalism: Globalization and De-Industrialization 1750-1877," *Journal of Economic History* 68 (September): 1-53.

Easterly, W., M. Kremer, L. Pritchett, and L.H. Summers (1993), "Good Policy or Good Luck? Country Growth Performance and Temporary Shocks," *Journal of Monetary Economics* 32: 459-83.

Easterly, W. and R. Levine (2003), "Tropics, Germs, and Crops: How Endowments Influence Economic Development," *Journal of Monetary Economics* (January): 3-40.

Elbers, C., J.W. Gunning and B. Kinsey (2007), "Growth and Risk: Methodology and Micro Evidence," *World Bank Economic Review* 21(1): 1-20.

Fafchamps, M. (2004), *Rural Poverty, Risk and Development*, London: Edward Elgar.

Fatás, A. and I. Mivhov (2006), "Policy Volatility, Institutions and Economic Growth," INSEAD, Singapore and Fontainebleau, unpublished.

Ferguson, N. (2004), *Empire: How Britain Made the Modern World*, New York: Penguin.

Findlay, R. and K.H. O'Rourke (2007), *Power and Plenty: Trade, War, and the World Economy in the Second Millennium*, Princeton NJ: Princeton University Press.

Flug, K., A. Splilimbergo, and A. Wachtenheim (1999), "Investment in education: Do economic volatility and credit constraints matter?" *Journal of Development Economics* 55(2): 465-81.

Frankenberg, E., K. Beegle, B. Sikoki, and D. Thomas (1999), "Health, Family Planning and Well-being in Indonesia during an Economic Crisis: Early results from the Indonesian Family Life Survey," RAND Labor and Population Program Working Paper Series 99-06, Rand Corporation, Santa Monica CA.

Gerschenkron, A. (1966), *Economic Backwardness in Historical Perspective*, Cambridge MA: Harvard University Press.

Gómez Galvarriato, A. and J.G. Williamson (2008), "Was It Prices, Productivity or Policy? The Timing and Pace of Latin American Industrialization after 1870," NBER Working Paper 13990, Cambridge MA, April.

Hadass, Y. and J.G. Williamson (2003), "Terms of Trade Shocks and Economic Performance 1870-1940: Prebisch and Singer Revisited," *Economic Development and Cultural Change* 51 (April): 629-56.

Huber, J.R. (1971), "Effect on Prices of Japan's Entry into World Commerce after 1858," *Journal of Political Economy* 79(3): 614-28.

Huff, G. and G. Caggiano (2007), "Globalization and Labour Market Integration in Late Nineteenth- and Early Twentieth Century Asia," mimeo, University of Glasgow.

Hummels, D. (1999), "Have International Transportation Costs Declined?" mimeo, University of Chicago, November.

Issawi, C. (1988), *The Fertile Crescent 1800-1914: A Documentary Economic History*, New York: Oxford University Press.

Jacks, D.S. (2006), "What Drove 19th Century Commodity Market Integration?" *Explorations in Economic History* 43(3): 383-412.

Jacks, D., C.M. Meissner and D. Novy (2008), "Trade Costs, 1870-2000," *American Economic Review* 98(2) (May): 529-34.

Jacks, D.S. and K. Pendakur (2007), "Global Trade and the Maritime Transport Revolution," presented at the *New Comparative Economic History: A Conference in Honor of Peter Lindert*, University of California, Davis, 1-3 June.

Jacoby, H.G. and E. Skoufias (1997), "Risk, Financial Markets, and Human Capital in a Developing Country," *Review of Economic Studies* 64 (July): 311-35.

Jensen, R. (2000), "Agricultural Volatility and Investments in Children," *American Economic Review* 90 (May): 399-404.

Keller, W. and C.H. Shiue (2007), "Tariffs, Trains, and Trade: The Role of Institutions versus Technology in the Expansion of Markets," mimeo, University of Colorado, October.

Koren, M. and S. Tenreyro (2007), "Volatility and Development," *Quarterly Journal of Economics* 122(1): 243-87.

Korthals, W.L. (1994), *Changing Economy in Indonesia: Volume 15: Prices (non-rice) 1814-1940*, The Hague: The Netherlands: Royal Tropical Institute.

Kose, M.A. and R. Reizman (2001), "Trade Shocks and Macroeconomic Fluctuations in Africa," *Journal of Development Economics* 65(1): 55-80.

Lains, P. (1995), *A economia portuguesa no seculo XIX*, Lisbon: Imprensa Nacional Casa da Moeda.

Landes, D. (1998), *The Wealth and Poverty of Nations: Why Some Are So Rich and Some So Poor*, London: Little Brown.

Lewis, W.A. (1969), *Aspects of Tropic Trade, 1883-1965: The Wicksell Lectures*, Stockholm: Almqvist and Wiksell.

Lewis, W.A. (1978a), *The Evolution of the International Economic Order*, Princeton NJ: Princeton University Press.

Lewis, W.A. (1978b), *Growth and Fluctuations, 1870-1913*, Boston: Allen and Unwin.

Loayza, N.V., R. Rancière, L. Servén, and J. Ventura (2007), "Macroeconomic Volatility and Welfare in Developing Countries: An Introduction," *World Bank Economic Review* 21(3): 343-57.

Maddison, A. (1995), *Monitoring the World Economy 1820-1992*, Paris: OECD.

Mauro, P., N. Sussman and Y. Yafeh (2006), *Emerging Markets, Sovereign Debt, and International Financial Integration: 1870-1913 and Today*, Oxford: Oxford University Press.

Meissner, C. (2005), "A New World Order: Explaining the Emergence of the Classical Gold Standard," *Journal of International Economics* 66: 385-406.

Mendoza, E. (1997), "Terms of Trade Uncertainty and Economic Growth," *Journal of Development Economics* 54: 323-56.

Mitchener, K.J. and M. Weidenmier (2007), "Trade and Empire," mimeo, August.

Miyamoto, M., Y. Sakudo and Y. Yasuba (1965), "Economic Development in Pre-industrial Japan, 1859-1894," *Journal of Economic History* 25(4).

Mulhall, M.G. (1892), *The Dictionary of Statistics*, London: Routledge.

Newland, C. (1998), "Exports and terms of trade in Argentina, 1811-1870," *Bulletin in Latin American Research* 17(3): 409-16.

North, D. and B. Weingast (1989), "Constitutions and Commitment: The Evolution of Institutions

Governing Public Choice in 17th Century England," *Journal of Economic History* 49(December): 803-32.

Obstfeld, M. and A.M. Taylor (2004), *Global Capital Markets: Integration, Crisis, and Growth*, Cambridge: Cambridge University Press.

O'Rourke, K.H. and J.G. Williamson (1999), *Globalization and History*, Cambridge: Cambridge University Press.

Pamuk, Ş. and J.G Williamson (2008), "Globalization and De-Industrialization in the Ottoman Empire 1790-1913," mimeo, Harvard University..

Poelhekke, S. and F. van der Ploeg (2007), "Volatility, Financial Development and the Natural Resource Curse," CEPR Discussion Paper 6513, Centre for Economic Policy Research, London, October.

Pollard, S. (1981), *Peaceful Conquest: The Industrialization of Europe, 1760-1860*, London: Oxford University Press.

Prados de la Escosura (2006), "The Economic Consequences of Independence in Latin America," in V. Bulmer-Thomas, J.H. Coatsworth and R. Cortés Conde (eds.), *The Cambridge Economic History of Latin America*, volume 1, Cambridge: Cambridge University Press.

Prebisch, R. (1950), The Economic Development of Latin America and Its Principal Problems, Lake Success NY: United Nations, Department of Economic Affairs. Reprinted in Economic Bulletin for Latin America 7 (1962): 1-22.

Ramey, G. and V. A. Ramey (1995), "Cross-country Evidence on the Link Between Volatility and Growth," *American Economic Review* 85(5): 1138-51.

Ravn, M.O. and H. Uhlig (2002), "On Adjusting the Hodrick-Prescott Filter for the Frequency of Observations," *Review of Economics and Statistics* 84(May): 371-5.

Rosenweig, M.R. and K.I. Wolpin (1993), "Credit Market Constraints, Consumption Smoothing, and the Accumulation of Durable Production Assets in Low Income Countries: Investments in Bullocks in India," *Journal of Political Economy* 101(2): 223-44.

Roy, T. (2000), *The Economic History of India 1857-1947*, Delhi: Oxford University Press.

— (2002), "Economic History and Modern India: Redefining the Link," *Journal of Economic Perspectives* 16 (Summer): 109-30.

Sachs, J.D. (2001), "Tropical Underdevelopment," NBER Working Paper 8119, National Bureau of Economic Research, Cambridge MA.

Shah Mohammed, S. and J.G. Williamson (2004), "Freight Rates and Productivity Gains in British Tramp Shipping 1869-1950," *Explorations in Economic History* 41 (April): 172-203.

Singer, H.W. (1950), "The Distribution of Gains between Investing and Borrowing Countries," *American Economic Review* 40 (1950): 473-85.

Thomas, D., K. Beegle, E. Frankenberg, B. Sikoki, J. Strauss, and G. Teruel (2004), "Education in a Crisis," *Journal of Development Economics* 74 (June): 53-85.

Tignor, R.L. (2006), *W. Arthur Lewis and the Birth of Development Economics*, Princeton NJ: Princeton University Press.

Williamson, J.G. (2005), *Globalization and the Poor Periphery before 1950*, Cambridge MA: MIT Press.

— (2006a), "Explaining World Tariffs 1870-1938: Stolper-Samuelson, Strategic Tariffs and State Revenues," in R. Findlay, R. Henriksson, H. Lindgren and M. Lundahl (eds.), Eli F. Heckscher, *International Trade, and Economic History*, Cambridge MA: MIT Press.

— (2006b), "Globalization, De-Industrialization and Underdevelopment in the Third World Before the Modern Era," *Journal of Iberian and Latin American History (Revista de Historia Económica)* 24(1): 9-36.

— (2007), "Lost Decades: Dealing with Independence and Globalization in 19th Century Latin America," Inaugural Lecture, *Third International Congress in Economic History*, Cuernavaca, Mexico, 29-31 October.

— (2008), "Globalization and the Great Divergence: Terms of Trade Booms and Volatility in the Poor Periphery 1782-1913", NBER Working Paper 13841, Cambridge MA, March.

Williamson, J.G. and T. Yousef (2008), "Globalization, Policy and Competitiveness: De-Industrialization in Egypt 1790-1913," mimeo, Harvard University

Yasuba, Y. (1996), "Did Japan Ever Suffer from a Shortage of Natural Resources before World War II?" *Journal of Economic History* 56(3): 543-60.

Yamazawa, I. and Y. Yamamoto (1979), *Foreign Trade and Balance of Payments, Volume 14 of Estimates of Long-Term Economic Statistics of Japan Since 1868*, Tokyo: Toyo Keizai Shinposha.

53

Globalization and the environment

Brian R. Copeland[1]

The world is facing serious environmental problems. Some are local or confined within countries or regions, such as poor urban air quality in rapidly growing economies, or poor water quality caused by either industrial effluent or poor urban sanitation. Others have implications that spill over national borders, such as threats to biodiversity caused by deforestation and the alarming pattern of fisheries depletion worldwide. And still other problems, such as the effects of greenhouse gas emissions on climate change, are truly global in scope.

At the same time, the world economy is becoming increasingly integrated. Globalization is not new, and the great migrations of the past, including those that led to the emergence of countries such as Australia and Canada are a reminder of the massive changes that globalization has induced over the years. But the pace of globalization seems to have sped up. World trade increased by a factor of 11 between 1950 and 2000; more than twice the increase in world income in the same period. The diffusion of information has accelerated with the development of the internet. And the speed with which the financial crisis spread across countries a year ago (late 2008) was a startling indicator of how interconnected the world economy has become.

Many people think it is no coincidence that environmental problems have become more serious as the pace of globalization has increased. This has led to much debate in policy circles, and it has stimulated a great deal of academic research. In this Lecture, I would like to review some of what I think we have learned from this work, especially during the past 20 years;[2] and I would also like

1 Fifty-third Joseph Fisher Lecture, 28 September 2009.

2 For more comprehensive reviews see Copeland and Taylor (2004), Frankel (2003) and Sturm (2003).

to talk about its implications for climate change. I will not focus exclusively on climate change and some of what I will say on climate change is speculative. The reason for this is that outcomes in this area are not pre-ordained – they depend on government policy responses. And while many governments have aggressively responded to some types of environmental problems (such as local air and water quality issues), there has not been the same level of systematic response to greenhouse gas emissions. As a result, we have only limited data available to assess the interaction between globalization, policy responses and greenhouse gas emissions. But what we have learned from studying other pollutants can provide lessons for thinking about climate change.[3]

Two key questions have dominated this debate. The first is whether or not globalization exacerbates environmental problems. Does freer trade and international investment accelerate the deterioration of environmental quality? Trade directly increases emissions via increased transport, but it may also indirectly generate more environmental problems by shifting economic activity to jurisdictions with weak policy regimes. Is there evidence for this?

The second key question is whether globalization makes environmental policy implementation more difficult. Do concerns about global competitiveness make it harder to introduce and tighten up environmental policies? And, once policies are in place, are they less likely to work well in an integrated global economy? Is it harder to achieve environmental quality targets if firms can shift their production to regions with less stringent policy?

Is globalization bad for the environment?

It is easy to come up with examples where trade or international investment has resulted in environmental damage. Images of toxic waste from rich countries being dumped in low income countries had a galvanizing effect on anti-globalization activists and led to the Basel convention on shipments of hazardous waste. There are several examples of renewable resource depletion – especially deforestation and fisheries collapse – that can be linked to trade. For example, fisheries off the

3 See also the recent WTO/UN Environment Programme report (WTO 2009) which provides an excellent overview of the interaction between trade, environment and climate change.

coast of Estonia collapsed shortly after export markets opened in the 1990's, the collapse of bison populations in the US was likely hastened by an export market for their hides, and evidence suggests that strong demand for wood in China has led to forest depletion in some neighbouring countries.[4] And of course trade has had direct negative effects on the environment. Trade has provided a conduit for invasive species, and shipping generates both air and water pollution.

On the other had, the news is not all bad. Globalization can be good for the environment too. An early example comes from Denmark in the 1700's, where there was an ecological crisis due to deforestation – excessive harvesting of trees for construction allowed sand dunes to encroach inland (see Kjaergaard, 1994). Two factors helped alleviate the crisis. German engineers (an example of trade in services) helped build dikes to stabilize the coast line and prevent further erosion; and imports of timber from neighbouring countries reduced pressure on local forests. In more recent times, technology transfer has meant that new factories in developing countries are often much more energy efficient than would be the case without foreign technology. And by outsourcing production to low cost suppliers new environmentally friendly products (such as hybrid cars) are cheaper to produce and are therefore adopted more quickly by consumers.

In short trade and investment have both good and bad effects on the environment, and in this respect it is not unlike any other economic activity – some aspects are harmful to the environment and others are benign or beneficial. Does this mean trade has environmental effects that are much like economic growth – or are there ways that trade may have fundamentally different effects on the environment?

To help sort this out, it is useful to decompose the effects of changes in economic activity on the environment into 3 different channels – scale, technique and composition effects.[5]

4 See Vetemaa (2006) on Estonian fisheries, Taylor (2007) on bison, and Ferreira (2004) on deforestation.

5 See Grossman and Krueger (1993) and Copeland and Taylor (1994, 2003) for more detailed development and measurement of these effects.

Scale effects refer to the fact that trade can have effects like growth – it can lead to a scaling up of economic activity. All else equal, one would expect this to be bad for the environment. A pure increase in the scale of the economy, without adjustments in the type of economic activity or the level of pollution abatement or conservation will be bad for the environment.

But as we know, growth is not always bad for the environment. Water quality in many rivers and lakes in Europe and North America is better now than it was 40 years ago, and air quality in major urban centres such as London and Tokyo has improved in the same time period. This is where the other two channels of change matter. Changes in methods of production and consumption can alter emission intensities and the use of environmental services. These "technique effects" can be driven by technical change, but in most cases they are driven by regulation. There is a great deal of evidence that as incomes have risen in industrial countries, environmental regulation has also tightened up.[6] Technique effects therefore act as a countervailing force against scale effects.

Finally, there are also composition effects. Growth and trade also lead to changes in the mix of production and consumption activities. At the macro level, countries may shift from agriculture to industry to services, all of which have different impacts on the environment. But also within any sector, changes in environmental impacts occur as specialization and innovation change the mix of economic activity. Consumption in the transport sector, for example, may shift from bicycles to cars (which raises pollution) or from cars to subways (which reduce pollution).

One line of argument is that trade causes growth, growth causes environmental degradation, and therefore trade is bad for the environment. There is a debate about whether growth is bad for the environment, and there is some debate about whether trade promotes economic growth.[7] But I don't want to pursue this here. Developing countries want to grow – and the interaction between economic growth and the environment is a subject for different talk. Instead, the question I want to focus on here is whether growth paths in countries

6 See Dasgupta et al. (2001).

7 Brock and Taylor (2006) provide a good review of this work.

that are more open to trade and investment are worse for the environment than growth paths in countries that are more closed. That means that I will not talk much about the scale effects of trade on the environment – it is via composition and technique effects that trade has the most potential to be different than economic growth.

Composition and technique effects of trade

Trade means that countries specialize more in doing what they do relatively well. Successful firms expand; less successful firms are squeezed out. Low cost industries expand; others contract. Consumption patterns change as the mix of goods available expands and relative prices adjust. All of this happens even in the absence of environmental policy – it is based on standard ideas of the gains from trade and comparative advantage dating back to Ricardo. But heterogeneity in policy regimes across countries raises the possibility that specialization and changes in patterns of production and consumption may also be caused by international differences in environmental policy.

The Pollution Haven Hypothesis is the idea that trade could cause polluting industry to shift to countries with relatively weak environmental policy.[8] This alone need not be a bad thing. We accept this on a regional basis all the time and think of it as good public policy. We have rules that say you can't have a garbage dump in the middle of a residential neighbourhood – this causes us to export our garbage to a designated area. Zoning regulations separate heavy industry from residential areas, and they also protect fragile ecosystems. Regulations tend to be tighter in a fragile estuary than on open coastline, and this shifts production locations. This can happen on an international scale as well: shifting polluting or environmentally threatening industry to a place where the environment has the capacity to handle it is not a bad thing. Trade driven by policy differences across jurisdictions can be a good thing if environmental policy reflects the sensitivity of the environment.

But environmental policy differs across jurisdictions for many other reasons – institutions are weak in some countries, and governments are pressured

8 See Copeland (2008) for a more detailed exploration of the Pollution Haven Hypothesis.

to weaken policy because of concerns about competitiveness in others. In the case of global pollutants such as carbon emissions, there are international free rider problems. In such cases, trade induced by environmental policy differences can be bad for the environment if it systematically shifts polluting industry from countries with tough regulation to countries with weak regulation. This is particularly troubling in the case of global pollutants because such trade can mean that efforts to reduce emissions can be undermined if trade simply induces a shifting of polluting industry to countries without emission regulations. In the context of climate change, this is referred to as carbon leakage.

So one way that trade can potentially have very different effects than growth on the environment is via composition effects, especially if these work to shift polluting industry to countries with weak environmental regulations. I'll come back to this and look at the evidence.

A second way that trade can have effects on the environment is via technique effects. Again, there are positive and negative effects, but there is reason to be optimistic that the net effects here will be positive. Policy stringency is positively correlated with real income per capita, so if trade raises real income, it is likely to increase pressure for more stringent environmental regulation. And trade can also lower abatement costs by increasing flows of technical information and by increasing competition in the market for environmental services. However, there could be adverse effects on policy as well. Exposure to international markets and increased mobility of people could disrupt traditional norms and institutions that have evolved to encourage conservation and community responsibility for the environment. Again, we need to look at the evidence.

Evidence on the effects of trade on the environment

The critical piece of information we need to determine whether trade is bad for the environment is how responsive trade and investment is to differences in environmental policy. We need to know this to determine whether the pollution haven hypothesis is correct; and we also need to know this if we want to address issues of carbon leakage and concerns that stringent environmental policy will undermine competitiveness.

Coming up with good evidence to address this question has been a challenge. We can't do experiments (we can't take a group of regions; tighten policy in one group, weaken it in others; and then wait ten years or so and see what happens to trade patterns and plant location), and so we have to infer evidence from changes in environmental policy over time and across jurisdictions. But for this to be fruitful, we need good data on the stringency of environmental policy for a large group of jurisdictions over a long period of time. And we don't have this. Environmental policy stringency is hard to measure – it is typically a mass of complex regulations, and there is usually not a simple index of stringency available. Many economists have used data on pollution abatement costs, but these are not available for most countries, and the reliability of such data is often in question. Even if we are prepared to accept that firms report abatement costs honestly, it may be difficult for them to isolate abatement costs from other costs if the entire design of a facility reflects environmental policy pressures. Moreover, there are selection problems. If the pollution haven hypothesis is correct, then stringent environmental policy will chase away the high abatement cost firms, and this can bias our sample if they are not around to respond to the survey questions.

The history of work in this area reflects these difficulties.[9] For a long time (up until about 10 years ago), most attempts to isolate the effects of environmental policy differences on trade and investment flows found nothing.[10] In fact, some found that more stringent environmental policy was associated with increased competitiveness. There is an argument (Porter and van de Linde 1995) that environmental policy can actually increase competiveness by encouraging innovation, creating new markets, and reducing waste. And some interpreted the evidence as supporting this view.

However, recent work using better data and improved statistical techniques has reversed this finding. Perhaps the most compelling evidence has come from studying the effects of the US Clean Air Act on trade and plant location. This Act forced tighter environmental regulations in some counties in the US (those not in compliance with air quality standards), but not in other counties (those that

9 See Copeland and Taylor (2004) and Brunnermeier and Levinson (2004) for reviews of empirical work in this area.

10 Jaffe et al. (1995) provide a comprehensive review of the literature up to the mid-1990s.

were in compliance). Becker and Henderson (2000) and others have found that the Clean Air had a significant effect on plant location within the US – tighter environmental regulations shifted polluting industry away from high regulation counties. Keller and Levinson (2002) found that foreign investment inflows were deterred in high regulation counties, and Hanna (2006) found that the Clean Air act encouraged multinationals in high regulation counties to shift some of their production out of the US.

Studies using abatement costs have found similar results. Levinson and Taylor (2008) and Ederington and Minier (2003) found that, all else equal, US imports are higher in industries subject to more stringent environmental policy, which is consistent with the view that environmental policy reduces competitiveness.

The evidence therefore confirms that environmental policy does indeed affect competiveness. The next question is whether this effect is big. Is there any evidence that trade is systematically causing polluting industry to shift from countries with stringent environmental policy to those with weak policy? That is, is the pollution haven hpothesis correct? While we can certainly find cases where this has happened, it looks like that this is not the case for many pollutants. For example, Ederington, Levinson and Minier (2004) find that the pollution content of US exports has been rising faster than that of US imports from developing countries as trade has been liberalized over the past 30 years. This is opposite to what the pollution haven hypothesis predicts. In my own work with Werner Antweiler and Scott Taylor (2001), we isolated the pure composition effect of trade liberalization on sulphur dioxide pollution. We found that this effect tended to raise pollution in rich countries and lower it in poor countries (the opposite of what the pollution haven hypothesis predicts). In many cases SO_2 pollution was in fact increasing in poor countries, but this was driven by growth and capital accumulation, not trade per se. In short, there is very little evidence in support of the pollution haven hypothesis.

Is this surprising? In most cases, the cost of complying with environmental regulation is low – in very few industries does it rise above 5% of costs; and in many others it is much lower. Production location is determined by overall cost conditions – labour costs, infrastructure, political stability, local expertise, supply lines, and so on. Consequently if environmental costs are relatively low, it is not surprising that they tend not to drive the pattern of trade.

If we put all this together, we can come back to our big question – is trade bad for the environment? The answer depends on the type of environmental problem, and on institutions. Several studies have looked at sulphur dioxide pollution – mine (with Antweiler and Taylor, 2001); Frankel and Rose (2005), and Grossman and Krueger (1993). These all have found that on average, trade appears to be good for the environment, even if we take into account scale effects. The reason for this is that compositional effects turn out to be small, and in many cases tend to shift polluting industry to rich countries (because SO_2 pollution comes mostly from capital intensive industry and rich countries are capital abundant); moreover, technique effects (more stringent policy) have tended to offset scale effects. So the net effect of trade has been small, and possibly positive. This is not to say that environmental quality is getting better everywhere – it is not. But growth and capital accumulation are much more important than trade for determining environmental outcomes.

The news is not all good, though. There is some evidence to suggest that trade is exacerbating renewable resource depletion in some countries. Fishery and forestry depletion has been exacerbated by trade in some countries.[11] However, institutions matter a lot and the impact of trade has varied across countries and even across different resources within countries.[12] A good example to illustrate the complexity of the issue comes from a couple of shell fisheries near my home off the coast of British Columbia in Canada. In the 1970's, the growth of the Asian market triggered an export boom in several west coast fisheries, including the geoduck and abalone shell fisheries.[13] Both were not subject to significant pressure prior to the export boom, and neither would have been sustainable in the face of a huge increase in fishing. In both cases, a transferable quota system was introduced to regulate the fishery. This is exactly what fisheries economists recommend, and it is the type of policy that has been highly successful in other jurisdictions, notably New Zealand and Iceland. The policy was successful in the geoduck fishery – that fishery prospered with the export boom and so far has been sustainable. On the other hand the abalone fishery collapsed – this was a fishery where the monitoring of the regulations was very difficult, poaching was rampant, and the regulatory apparatus was unable to cope with pressures induced

11 See, for example, Lopez (1997, 2000), Ferreira (2004), and Vetemaa (2006).

12 See Copeland and Taylor (2009) for a discussion and further references.

13 See Muse (1998) and Jones and Bixby (2003), as well as the discussion of these fisheries in Copeland and Taylor (2009).

by the export boom. There has not yet been a systematic study of the effects of trade on renewable resource depletion, but a number of case studies suggest that there is a complex interaction between trade and the effectiveness of institutions in determining outcomes.

What about climate change? Is globalization responsible for increasing carbon emissions? The fact that carbon emissions are a global pollutant means that the policy response has been different for carbon emissions than for other pollutants such as SO_2. SO_2 emissions have been regulated because the effects occur within the country (or its near neighbours) where emissions occur. Moreover the effects of SO_2 pollution are measurable and occur within a fairly short time horizon (although some effects such as acidification are delayed). In contrast, carbon emissions have not been systematically regulated to the same extent. Because it is a global pollutant and because the effects of climate change will occur far into the future, there are free rider problems and many countries have not imposed effective regulations. This means that we do not have good data to test for the effects of policy on trade patterns and firm location. And it also means that the scale effects of trade and growth have not been offset with technique effects, as in the case of SO_2.

One indication of how the lack of active policy response to climate change has led to different outcomes between SO_2 and carbon emissions comes from the Environmental Kuznets curve literature.[14] A number of studies have found an inverse-U-shaped relation between SO_2 and per capita income. Subsequent work indicates that the relation is not automatic and varies across countries, but one robust result from this literature is that while there are forces from economic growth that tend to increase pollution, these forces can be offset by the policy process; and the policy process has in many countries responded to increases in per capita income.

No such relation has been found for carbon emissions.[15] Similar forces are at work increasing emissions, but there has not been the countervailing policy response to control them. So there is no environmental Kuznets curve for carbon emissions.

14 Barbier (2002) provides a good discussion of this literature.

15 See the WTO (2009) for a discussion of the evidence on carbon emissions.

Consequently, it has not yet been possible to test for the pollution haven effect for carbon emissions because of a lack of data on policy interventions. There is some evidence that the net effect of trade on carbon emissions has been to increase them – this is because the scale effect of trade (which tends to raise emissions) has not been offset with strong policy responses. Attempts to measure the pure trade-induced composition effects on carbon emissions have been inconclusive, suggesting that the effect is likely small.[16]

In short, the potential crisis looming over carbon emissions has not been caused by globalization; other things, namely economic growth and a lack of policy response, are the major culprits. But globalization is likely making the policy response more difficult. That is what I'll turn to now.

Is environmental policy harder to implement in a more open economy?

Globalization increases interdependencies between countries, and this means the effects of domestic policy changes can spill over international borders. There are a number of ways that this can complicate the implementation of environmental policy; here I will focus on three major channels. First, governments may yield to pressure to be less aggressive on environmental policy because of concerns about international competitiveness. Second, some have alleged that international trade agreements have constrained the flexibility of governments to implement environmental policy – the argument is sometimes made that within the WTO, disputes concerns about free trade trump concerns about the environment. And finally, it is possible that once in place, environmental policies will be less effective in open economies because firms can avoid them by shifting production to countries with weaker policy regimes. I will consider each of these arguments in turn.

Competitiveness is more of a concern in an open economy than in one more closed off to trade and investment. Trade tends to concentrate production according to comparative advantage or firms' success in carving out a market niche. This means that production location decisions are more sensitive to cost in

16 See Cole and Elliot (2003).

open than in closed economies. Technically, supply elasticities tend to be larger in more open economies. Hence the heightened concern about the cost effects of environmental policy in more open economies.

It is important to note that from a pure national interest perspective (ignoring the role of interest groups), these stronger supply responses actually *strengthen* rather than weaken the case for good environmental policy. The costs of policy mistakes are higher in more open economies. If trade concentrates production of polluting industry in your region or country, then the environmental damage from bad environmental policy can be much larger in open than in closed economies (Copeland, 1994). The British Columbia shell fisheries I mentioned earlier are good examples of this – prior to the export boom, there was not really any serious regulation of these fisheries and they were not in any danger. Once the export boom happened, it was only strong and effective policy that saved the geoduck fishery; and it was difficulties in the enforcement of policy that led to the collapse of the abalone fishery.

However the distributional effects of environmental policy are also larger in open economies than in closed economies. If we focus on production-generated pollution, then in a closed economy, it is easier for firms to pass on to consumers the increased costs of complying with environmental policy. In an open economy, firms face more competition, and so (especially if their competitors do not face similarly stringent policy) it is harder to pass on costs. Hence those affected by stringent policy are more likely to pressure governments to weaken policy as economies become more open.[17] The key problem here is that while it is in the overall national interest to have strong policy in place, the costs of the policy tend to be concentrated on the producers directly affected, and so policy may end up being skewed.

This does not, however, apply to all sectors of the economy – not all producers are hurt by stronger environmental policy, and in some cases, strong policy can actually increase competitiveness. We have to distinguish between pollution generated by consumption (automobile emissions, packaging, household energy are examples) and that generated during production. Much of the concern about competitiveness is restricted to policies aimed at curtailing pollution generated

17 See McAusland (2003).

during production of tradable goods. This is because tighter regulation affects domestic producers but not foreign producers and therefore can give foreign producers an advantage when selling their goods in the domestic market.

However, when policy affects consumption-generated pollution, both foreign and domestic producers have to comply. If automobile emission standards are raised, then both locally produced cars and imported cars have to comply with the standards and so local producers need not be disadvantaged – in both cases, costs can be shared with consumers. In fact, it is possible that policy can be structured so as to give local producers an advantage – if it is easier for domestic producers than foreign producers to comply with tougher standards then local producers may actually lobby for tighter environmental policy.[18]

Another case where tighter policy can benefit local producers is policy designed to preserve natural capital – such as fisheries regulation. However such regulation typically raises costs (or reduces harvesting) in order to preserve natural capital for the future. Producers benefit in the long run, but in the short run costs rise (reducing international competitiveness in the short run) and this can generate resistance to tighter regulation.

Theory therefore suggests that if governments are responsive to narrow producer interests, then it may be harder to enact stringent environmental policy in more open economies. However, this effect is more likely to be found for production-generated pollution than for consumption-generated pollution. What does the evidence say about what governments actually do? There is a lot of anecdotal evidence, but not a lot of careful statistical analysis. The few studies that exist support the hypothesis. Ederington and Minier (2003) and Eliste and Fredrikksson (2002) study the US experience and find that pollution policy is somewhat weaker in industries subject to high level of import competition. In the case of policy aimed at dealing with climate change, governments have often created exemptions and loopholes that help to shield the tradable sector from the effects of carbon taxes, etc., which is consistent with the hypothesis that they are responding to concerns about competitiveness. This evidence is not conclusive

18 McAusland (2008) provides a detailed analysis of the distinction between consumption and production generated pollution.

because it compares the stringency of environmental policy in sectors more open to trade than others. It is possible that globalization has helped to ramp up the average stringency of environmental policy, as producers respond to concerns of green consumers, and as the influence of NGOs is amplified via globalization. Nevertheless, the evidence is suggestive of a problem.

The second channel through which globalization is alleged to make it harder to implement good environmental policy is via the constraints imposed by the WTO. Any trade agreement must confront the problem that once overt restrictions on trade (such as tariffs and quota) are eliminated, governments still face pressure from producers for trade protection and so they look for loopholes in the trade agreement. Subsidies, tax exemptions, regulatory exemptions, and so forth are all ways of helping out producers who are looking for protection. Consequently any trade agreement that is effective has to go beyond overt restrictions on trade and try to constrain governments from using domestic policy as a substitute for trade policy. These means that trade agreements, including the WTO, try to restrict governments from enacting policies that favour domestic producers or which favour some foreign producers over others. For example, it would violate WTO rules if a government imposed a more stringent emission standard on an imported car than on a domestic car. Also, recognizing that domestic producers may sometimes lobby for regulation that is harder for foreign producers to comply with than local producers, the WTO also requires that governments have some scientific justification for imposing an environmental or health and safety regulation.

This means that some domestic environmental policy is subject to scrutiny to ensure compliance with international trade rules, and this has sometimes led to trade disputes over environmental policy. But as a number of reviews of the relevant cases have concluded, there is little evidence that this has constrained domestic policy (as long as it is non-discriminatory). The major area where the WTO could be said to be making domestic policy harder to implement is with respect to competitiveness issues; and this comes back to the distinction between production and consumption generated pollution. The WTO allows governments to impose regulation and standards on goods that cause environmental problems after they come into our country as long as these rules are applied in a non-discriminatory way. That means we can impose the same emission standards on imported cars as we do domestic cars. However, the WTO does *not* generally allow us to impose taxes or regulations that target producers that generate pollution or environmental damage outside our country. So even though we may impose stringent regulation on domestic steel producers to offset the local pollution caused, we cannot tax or otherwise restrict imports from foreign steel producers who despite polluting their own countries may be subject to weak or non-existent regulation. That is, governments are not permitted by the WTO to try to level the playing field for production-generated pollution. And as discussed above, this can exacerbate the competitiveness problem, making environmental policy harder to implement.

There is one potentially, but as yet untested, exception to this prohibition on policies targeting environmental damage generated by foreign producers outside our country. This is in cases where the foreign environmental damage may affect the home country – threats to endangered species is one example and carbon emissions is another. In the famous Shrimp/Turtle case, the US restricted imports of shrimp from Southeast Asia because the harvesting techniques harmed endangered turtles.[19] This trade restriction was found to be inconsistent with WTO rules. However, the rationale for this ruling was not that the US did not have the right to use trade policy to try to protect the turtles. Rather, the US had applied the policy in a discriminatory way. The rules it imposed on Southeast Asian producers were more stringent than those imposed on producers in Latin America and the Caribbean, and so the US was violating the non-discrimination rule. In fact, the WTO ruling determined that the endangered turtles were trans-boundary resources and noted that trade measures were not necessarily inconsistent with WTO rules. This potentially opens the door to carefully designed (non-discriminatory) policies that target such environmental damage. This has implication for attempts to control carbon emissions, and I will come back to this.

The third way that globalization can make it harder to control environmental problems is that environmental policy may not be as effective in an open economy because firms may simply relocate to avoid tough regulations. If pollution has

19 Khalilian (2009) provides a good discussion of this and other cases and reviews the broader issues of the interaction between WTO rules, trade measures, and environmental policy.

only local effects, then the main concern is displacement – regulation may solve your environmental problems by passing them on to some other jurisdiction. This may or may not be reason for concern (depending in part on the sensitivity of the trading partner's environment, and the quality of their environmental policy), but at least in this case, the Home country's policy does improve Home's environment.

If pollution is global, then it is possible for policy to be ineffective and not improve the policy-implementing country's environment at all. If carbon emitting firms simply shift location in response to a carbon tax, then Home's carbon tax may be unsuccessful in improving Home's environment.

This is (as is well known) one of the major policy concerns in the debate on how to deal with climate change, and in that context it is referred to as carbon leakage. Given the evidence that environmental policy does affect firm location, trade and investment flows, some carbon leakage will occur. The question is how much.

We have two types of evidence. We have the results of computer simulation models that attempt to forecast into the future, and we have the evidence of past experience with other pollutants. Computer simulation models do predict carbon leakage. The predictions vary widely – from 5% to 20% of any reductions in Annex I countries are predicted to be offset by increases in emissions by countries not constrained by agreements to reduce emissions.[20] The predictions vary widely because they depend on how the computer models are specified. Such forecasts and should be treated cautiously.

The evidence from our past experience comes from mostly other pollutants, as discussed above. As discussed earlier there is pretty good evidence that more stringent environmental policy raises production costs and affects competitiveness. More stringent environment policy targeting production-generated pollution will deter investment in that sector and, all else equal, will shift some production to other jurisdictions. But the effects in the past have been rather small, and as Ederington et al. (2004) show, these effects have been dwarfed by other changes

20 See Frankel (2009).

in the economy over the years. In the case of SO2 regulations, the US imposed tighter environmental policy, but US imports became cleaner relative to US exports during the same time period. As Levinson (2009) notes, other changes – such as innovation, capital accumulation, growth, and preference changes have turned out to be much more important for determining trade patterns than the costs of complying with environmental regulations. We don't know if the same pattern will hold for carbon emissions. To the extent that the carbon content of production is higher than the SO_2 content, it is likely that competiveness effects may be larger. But past experience suggests it is going to be other unforeseen changes in the world economy that are going to matter more in the long run.

Implications for the design of climate change policy

In some ways, the policy needed to deal with greenhouse gases (for ease of exposition, I'll usually refer to these as carbon emissions, but obviously policy has to be directed at all such gases) is quite straightforward. Carbon emissions impose costs on others and need to be restricted. That is, the right to emit these gases should be thought of as a resource that is in limited supply. We live in a market economy where resources that are in limited supply are allocated through prices. So carbon emissions need to be priced. Prices simplify the decision process for producers and consumers – they don't have to try to figure out the environmental impact of each good when they try to decide which to buy. Good and services that generate a lot of carbon would have a high price to reflect their environmental impact. Moreover prices would encourage innovation to economize on carbon intensity.

While using prices to deal with pollution problems is usually quite complex, for carbon emissions the solution is actually quite simple. For most pollutants, the location of the pollution source matters. That is, generating water or air pollution in the middle of a densely populated city is more damaging than doing it far away from population centres. Polluting drinking water is more damaging than polluting the open ocean. Consequently, for most pollutants, the appropriate price for a unit of emissions varies with location; and the pattern of variation across locations is very complex to calculate. This is one reason why the use of pollution taxes is relatively rare. However, in the case of carbon emissions, it does not really matter where the emissions come from. Carbon emitted from a city is just as damaging from the countryside; and carbon emitted form Australia is just as damaging as from Canada. What this means is that in an efficient regulatory system, the appropriate price for carbon emissions is the same everywhere in the world. Ideally, there should be an integrated market for carbon emissions with a single global price, just as there is a world price for oil and other commodities. Carbon emissions is one of the very few pollutants for which the idealized textbook solution of a uniform pollution tax or tradable permit system applies.

Of course, the fact that the solution to the problem requires global coordination is also what makes achieving that solution elusive. Countries can't agree on what the target emission level (and hence the target price) should be; and they can't agree on how the burden of compliance should be shared. Hence the reality at least for the near future is that some countries will not regulate carbon emissions at all; and others will do so with varying degrees of effectiveness. This variation across countries in the stringency of environmental regulation in a regime where these same countries are becoming increasing integrated in other ways creates major challenges in implementing policy. As discussed above, trade makes the implementation of environmental policy more difficult.

What lessons can we draw from the previous work on trade and environment for policy design in such a world?

First, since policy stringency will vary across countries, competitiveness concerns are a major factor impeding the implementation of climate change policy. For those countries that are serious about meeting their emission targets, this heightens the need for policies that are cost effective (i.e. that minimize compliance costs); and this means that policies that create incentives to innovate and use prices to allocate scarce resources are desirable. Carbon taxes and cap and trade schemes both meet these criteria, with carbon taxes having the advantage of simplicity (especially with respect to achieving broad coverage of all polluters), but with cap and trade schemes being more politically attractive because governments have the option of awarding permits free of charge to polluting firms.

Second, the carbon leakage issue needs to be confronted. Although there is debate about how serious the carbon leakage problem will be, the perception that it will be significant will impede the implementation of policy unless it is addressed. This means that the world will likely move to a regime where carbon content taxes (or some equivalent remedy) are applied to imports from countries that are not adequately regulating carbon emissions. This will be a significant departure from the current regime under which it is illegal for countries to tax or restrict imports based on the pollution generated outside of their jurisdiction.

The WTO currently is somewhat inconsistent in the way it treats export subsidies. If countries have domestic policies that provide explicit subsidies that have the effect of subsidizing exports, then importing countries can legally impose countervailing duties to offset these subsidies. This acts both as a deterrent against such subsidies and helps address competitiveness concerns than could potentially undermine free trade agreements.

However, countries that do not adequately regulate pollution are also effectively subsidizing their firms by allowing them access to environmental services at a price below their true social cost. In principle there is no difference between this and an explicit production subsidy; and if polluting firms export, they are effectively receiving an export subsidy. However WTO rules and most trade agreements do not allow governments to impose countervailing duties to offset the implicit export subsidies arising from weak environmental policy in their trading partners.

The reason for this is because of concerns that such a system would be subject to abuse: governments could use it opportunistically to protect local producers. Moreover, while there is an obvious benchmark rule for explicit production or export subsidies – the rule is these subsidies should be set at zero – there is no such obvious benchmark for environmental regulation. Environmental regulation should ensure that producers and consumers bear the full social costs of their activities. But for most pollutants, these costs vary with location, income and other factors; and therefore there is no agreement on what the benchmarks should be. Consequently, determining when a countervailing duty could legitimately imposed to offset implicit subsidies arising from weak environmental policy would always be a subject of great controversy and litigation, making such a regime open to abuse and likely unworkable.

However, carbon is different because it is a global pollutant for which the location of the emission source is more or less independent of its environmental impact. This has a couple of implications which suggest that a regime allowing border taxes to offset weak policy in exporting countries might be workable. First, it is much easier to agree on what the benchmark price for carbon emissions should be. Ideally, in an international agreement there should be a common price across countries; and this would provide a clear benchmark. But even in the absence of such an agreement, those countries that adhere to binding targets will have their own implicit prices for carbon, and these could be used as an objective basis to calculate the import levy.[21] Second, there is some precedent for such an approach. The Montreal Protocol on ozone depleting gases contains trade remedies for enforcement purposes. And the WTO ruling in the Shrimp/Turtle case raises the possibility that trade remedies to deal with global environmental problems may be WTO-consistent.

Nevertheless any policy regime that opens more doors to import protection has the potential to be manipulated by governments responding to local pressures to protect producers; and it seems inevitable that this would occur. To minimize the potential for conflict, it would desirable for any such regime to be multilateral with established procedures such as those within trade agreements such as the WTO.

Conclusion

Environmental outcomes depend on individual behaviour of producers and consumers, social norms, and the environmental policy regime. Current environmental policy is not sufficient to ensure that individuals face the full social costs of their impact on the natural environment. Consequently, many types of economic activity, including international trade, can be harmful to the environment.

Research over the past few years has identified some cases where trade has been good for the environment and others where it has been harmful. But

21 McKibbin and Wilcoxen (2009), using a computer simulation model of the world economy argue that the benefits of using border tax adjustments to prevent carbon leakage would be rather small and may not be large enough to offset the administrative costs of such a system. Their work, however, does not take into account political constraints and so cannot assess the issue of how including a mechanism to deal with carbon leakage affects the scope of a climate change agreement and the stringency of emission targets.

the evidence does not support the view that growth paths of economies more open to trade are more damaging to the environment than those more closed to trade. Economic growth and capital accumulation, if not coupled with effective environmental policy, have a much more significant impact on the environment.

However, globalization can make the implementation of environmental policy more difficult. There is some evidence that concerns about the effects of policy on international competitiveness have restrained governments from implementing effective policy. The opportunity to shift production between countries can also hamper the effectiveness of policies aimed at trans-boundary and global environmental problems, such as climate change. Moving forward towards an effective policy on climate change will require that these issues be confronted.

References

Antweiler, W., B. R. Copeland and M. S. Taylor (2001), "Is Free Trade Good for the Environment?" *American Economic Review* 91(4): 877-90.

Barbier, E. (2002), "The Role of Natural Resources in Economic Development," Ch. 49 in K. Anderson (ed.), *Australia's Economy and its International Context: the Joseph Fisher Lectures, Volume II 1956-2009,* Adelaide: University of Adelaide Press.

Becker, R. and V. Henderson (2000), "Effects of Air Quality Regulations on Polluting Industries," *Journal of Political Economy* 108(2): 379-421.

Brock, W.A. and M.S. Taylor, (2006), "Economic Growth and the Environment: A Review of theory and empirics," in P. Aghion and S. Durlauf (eds.), *Handbook of Economic Growth,* Amsterdam: Elsevier.

Brunnermeier, S. and A. Levinson, (2004), "Examining the Evidence on Environmental Regulations and Industry Location," *Journal of the Environment and Development* 13: 6-41.

Cole, M.A. and R.J.R. Elliott (2003), "Determining the Trade-Environment Composition Effect: The Role of Capital, Labor and Environmental Regulations," *Journal of Environmental Economics and Management* 46: 363-83.

Copeland, B.R. (1994), "International Trade and the Environment: Policy Reform in a Polluted Small Open Economy," *Journal of Environmental Economics and Management* 26: 44-65.

Copeland, B.R. (2008), "Pollution Haven Hypothesis," in K.A. Reinhert and R.S. Rajan (eds.), *Princeton Encyclopedia of the World Economy,* Princeton NJ: Princeton University Press.

Copeland, B. R. and M.S. Taylor (1994), "North-South Trade and the Environment," *Quarterly Journal of Economics* 109: 755-87.

Copeland, B. R. and M.S. Taylor (2003), *Trade and the Environment: Theory and Evidence,* Princeton NJ: Princeton University Press.

Copeland, B.R. and M.S. Taylor (2004), "Trade, Growth and the Environment," *Journal of Economic Literature* 42(1): 7-71.

Copeland, B.R. and M.S. Taylor (2009), "Trade, Tragedy and the Commons," *American Economic Review* 99: 725-49.

Dasgupta, S., A. Mody, S. Roy and D. Wheeler (2001), "Environmental Regulation and Development: A Cross-Country Empirical Analysis," *Oxford Development Studies* 29(2): 173-87.

Ederington, W.J and J. Minier (2003), "Is Environmental Policy a Secondary Trade Barrier? An Empirical Analysis," *Canadian Journal of Economics* 36: 137-54.

Ederington, W.J, A. Levinson and J. Minier (2004), "Trade Liberalization and Pollution Havens," *Advances in Economic Analysis and Policy* 4(2), Article 6 (Berkeley Electronic Press).

Eliste, P. and P.G. Fredrikksson (2002) "Environmental Regulations, Transfers and Trade: Theory and Evidence," *Journal of Environmental Economics and Management* 43: 234-50.

Ferreira, S. (2004), "Deforestation, Openness and Property Rights," *Land Economics* 80(2): 174-93.

Frankel, J.A. (2003) "The Eenvironment and Globalization," NBER Working Paper 10090, National Bureau of Economic Research, Cambridge MA.

Frankel, J.A. (2009), "Addressing the Leakage/Competitiveness Issue in Climate Change Policy Proposals," in L. Brainard (ed.), *Climate Change, Trade and Investment: Is a Collusion Inevitable?* Brookings Institution Press.

Frankel, J.A. and A.K. Rose (2005), "Is Trade Good or Bad for the Environment? Sorting out the Causality," *Review of Economics and Statistics* 87(1): 85-91.

Grossman, G.M. and A.B. Krueger (1993), "Environmental Impacts of a North American Free Trade Agreement", pp. 13-56 in P.M Garber (ed.), *The Mexico-U.S. Free Trade Agreement,* Cambridge MA: MIT Press.

Hanna, R. (2006), "U.S. Environmental Regulation and FDI: Evidence from a Panel of U.S. Based Multinational Firms," Development Research Institute Working Paper No. 23, New York University, New York.

Irwin, W.A., (2002), "Long-run Trends in World Trade and Income," *World Trade Review* 1: 89–100.

Jaffe, A., S. Peterson, P. Portney and R. Stavins (1995), "Environmental Regulation and the Competitiveness of U.S. Manufacturing: What Does the Evidence Tell Us?" *Journal of Economic Literature* 33: 132-63.

Jones, L. and M. Bixby (2003), *Managing Fish: Ten Case Studies from Canada's Pacific Coast,* Vancouver: The Fraser Institute.

Keller, W. and A. Levinson (2002), "Pollution Abatement Costs and Foreign Direct Investment Inflows to US States," *Review of Economics and Statistics* 84: 691-703.

Khalilian, S. (2009), "The WTO and Environmental Provisions: Three Categories of Trade and Environment Linkage," Working Paper No. 1485, Kiel Institute for the World Economy, Kiel.

Kjaergaard, T. (1994), *The Danish Revolution, 1500-1800: An Ecohistorical Interpretation* (Studies in Environment & History), Cambridge: Cambridge University Press.

Levinson, A. (2009), "How Significant is the (Carbon) Pollution Content of Trade?" mimeo, Georgetown University, Washington DC.

Levinson A. and M.S. Taylor (2008), "Trade and the Environment: Unmasking the Pollution Haven Effect," *International Economic Review* 49: 223-54.

López, R. (1997), "Environmental Externalities in Traditional Agriculture and the Impact of Trade Liberalization: The Case of Ghana", *Journal of Development Economics* 53(1): 17-39.

López, R. (2000), "Trade Reform and Environmental Externalities in General Equilibrium: Analysis for an Archetype Poor Tropical Country", *Environment and Development Economics* 5(4): 377-404.

McAusland, C. (2003), "Voting for Pollution Policy: The Importance of Income Inequality and Openness to Trade," *Journal of International Economics* 61: 425-51.

McAusland, C. (2008), "Trade, Politics, and the Environment: Tailpipe vs. Smokestack," *Journal of Environmental Economics and Management* 55: 52-71.

McKibbin, W.J. and P.J. Wilcoxen (2009), "The Economic and Environmental Effects of Border Tax Adjustments for Climate Policy," mimeo, Australian National University, Canberra.

Muse, B. (1998) "Management of the British Columbia Geoduck Fishery," Alaska Commercial Fisheries Entry Commission Report No. 8-3N.

Porter, M.E. and C. van de Linde (1995), "Toward a New Conception of the Environment-Competitiveness Relationship", *Journal of Economic Perspectives* 9(4): 97-118.

Sturm, D. (2003), "Trade and the Environment: A Survey of the Literature," pp. 119-149 in L. Marsiliani, M. Rauscher and C. Withagen (eds.), *Environmental Policy in an International Perspective,* New York: Kluwer Academic Publishers.

Taylor, M.S. (2007), "Buffalo Hunt: International Trade and the Virtual Extinction of the North American Bison," NBER Working Paper No. 12969, National Bureau of Economic Research, Cambridge MA.

Vetemaa, M., R. Eschbaum and T. Saat (2006), "The Transition from the Soviet System to a Market Economy as a Cause of Instability in the Estonian Coastal Fisheries Sector", *Marine Policy* 30(6): 635-40.

WTO (2009), *Trade and Climate Change: A Report by the World Trade Organization and the United Nations Environment Programme,* Geneva: World Trade Organization.

54

Exploring the mysteries of trends and bubbles

Peter C. B. Phillips[1]

It is a pleasure to visit the University of Adelaide and an honour to present the Joseph Fisher Lecture. This lecture series has a long list of eminent economists as past speakers. It is a particularly welcome opportunity therefore to present what appears to be the first lecture in this series on econometrics.

Econometrics is a statistical tool that forces economic ideas to face the reality of observations. As Milton Friedman once remarked about economics, simple theories are the most powerful, like the power of rational decision making that underlies most economic models. What makes the subject of econometrics difficult is that simple theories of human behaviour like rationality are never right. Econometrics must simultaneously confront the reality that economic theories are inevitably wrong yet in many cases contain a powerful kernel of truth. Measuring these kernels of truth in the presence of near universal model misspecification is one of the challenges that make econometrics an exciting and relevant subject.

Trends and bubbles in modern econometrics

My subject in this lecture is trends and bubble phenomena. The primary focus is on economic activity. But as we all recognize, trends and bubbles occur in the natural and physical world. So their relevance extends well beyond economics and other matters of human affairs. To broaden its coverage this lecture draws upon examples of such phenomena in areas like climate change that are of pressing global concern in the modern world with their own concomitant economic

1 This paper is a revised version of the fifty-fourth Joseph Fisher Lecture presented at the University of Adelaide, 18 February 2010. The author thanks the School of Economics at the University of Adelaide for their hospitality and Jiti Gao for arranging this visit.

implications. Happily, one of the big export industries of econometrics is the novel and rapidly changing econometric technology of stochastic trends which has opened up many new areas of application in other disciplines over the last two decades

With the advent of the recent sub-prime financial crisis, we all know something about bubbles. The Asian financial crisis, the dot com bubble in the 1990s, and the latest global financial crisis have reawakened interest in this important and little explored field. It has alerted the new generation of economists as well as the public at large to the reality that bubbles intermittently occur in financial markets, that they have consequences on the real economy, and that we need methods to assist us in identifying them to avoid some of these consequences. Econometrics helps deliver such methods.

Trends are phenomena we like to think we know a great deal more about than bubbles, partly because they are omnipresent and have been studied so extensively. Macroeconomics, for instance, has had a long-time focus on modelling and explaining economic growth. Time series econometrics has produced a massive volume of research on nonstationarity and trends over the past three decades. And microeconometrics frequently focuses on changing behaviour over time. Yet in spite of the enormous attention, trends are phenomena about which we really know very little.

Trends and bubbles are mysteries. Trends are compelling mysteries to econometricians because they are a major characteristic of virtually all time series in economics and finance and they must be addressed in modelling. Bubbles are fascinating mysteries to economists because they are so difficult to anticipate, so difficult to model in terms of rational behaviour, and potentially tumultuous in their effects on human economic conditions and the course of human progress.

Trend is a simple five letter word whose modern dictionary meaning is 'a general direction or tendency, particularly over time'. The definition has appealing econometric implications and gives an astonishingly simple way of thinking about data – trending data go up, down, or stay constant. Public discussion and media commentary repeatedly rely on these simple characterisations in describing the world around us. We talk of trends in education, in health, in sociological characteristics such as crime, suicide and divorce, and in human characteristics such as body mass indices, obesity, senility, longevity, and sports performance. All these topics are discussed and analysed in terms of their trends. The discussion captivates interest because trends point to the future – where the data are going – and this inevitably rivets public attention.

Professional economic commentary has the same preoccupation. Prominent economists such as the Chairman of the Federal Reserve or Governors of Reserve Banks regularly pronounce on trends in economic phenomena. We hear comments like "if current trends continue then we will be out of recession by the end of the year", or "a newly emerging trend is the recovery in house prices", or "long term trends in performance show that stocks outmatch other financial assets". These pronouncements give the impression of scientific authority, especially when they appear in scientific presentations or as congressional testimony by a respected central bank authority. After all, central banks collect and publish data, have teams of economists on hand to analyse it, have public mandates to ensure price stability and economic growth, provide regular forecasts of key economic indicators, and their spokespeople are highly qualified professional economists. So the authenticity of central bank commentary on economic affairs often goes unquestioned.

But commonly used phrases such as "if current trends continue" do not stand up to the simplest scrutiny. What is meant by the word "current" – the last five days, five months or five quarters of data? How is the concept "trend" formalized and measured – a straight line through the data, a curve or some random drift? How are we expected to interpret and use quantities that are not properly defined? Once these questions are raised, the apparent precision of the statement vaporizes. In place of a clear message, we see something impressionistic – a hazy signal whose interpretation relies on some implicit understanding of the concept of a trend. The concept is so loosely defined and elusive that trend takes on a mysterious character. Like the inscrutable Hamlet, the protagonist in Shakespeare's most famous play, you never really know what it is going to do next. In short, no one really understands trends but everyone sees trends in data.[2]

2 This 'law' of econometrics was suggested in Phillips (2003). The analogy with Hamlet was given in Phillips (2010), on which some of the discussion in this paper draws.

Yet there is a basic human instinct that drives us all to look for trends in data. This instinct is a desire to bring order to disorder. Learning to understand the world around us (the seasons, the environment, topography and climate) is a basic human survival instinct. Bringing order to disorder is like creating a map to describe aspects of the territory which holds our interest. Maps can be very useful. But the territory is always more complex, just as living organisms are always more complex than the stylized diagrams of their component parts that we see in medical texts.

The same is true with data. The human instinct is to bring order to the disorder of data. When we see a cloud of points on a chart, we have an irrepressible urge to put a line through it – to show where it has been and where it is going. This human urge turns the observer into an eyeball statistician – a fellow who draws a line through a set of point based on unwarranted assumptions with a foregone conclusion.

One important characteristic of this human statistical instinct is that drawing a line through a set of points produces a smooth curve which has direction. That is how we usually see things and how we draw them. We don't take the pencil off the page. We draw a smooth curve or one with a kink if we really need to turn a sharp corner. Smooth curves are differentiable and curves with kinks are (one-sided) differentiable. A curve that is differentiable tells you where it's going at every observation. It's predictable. That is the outcome of this instinctive thinking – it reveals a direction vector for the future from a cloud of points. It is this characteristic, this limiting characteristic of the human statistical instinct, that is implicit in media and public scientific commentary about trends. It explains why public pronouncements about trends are so frequently accepted – people are by nature sympathetic to this form of trend analysis and they like to think they know what these pronouncements mean.

Modern econometrics has challenged this simplistic view. The biggest change in econometrics over the last three decades is the recognition in empirical research that trends are stochastic. Trends involve inherently random elements – like Hamlet we never know what to expect next – and yet the trend process may explore the whole sample space in a recurrent non-differentiable manner like a Brownian motion. With non-differentiability we lose the direction vector and no longer have the forecasting capability at any point in time that is delivered by a smooth curve. The modern dictionary definition of trend is no longer relevant. A more fitting characterisation is given by the middle English (circa 1590) verb "trenden", from which the word trend is derived and whose meaning is "to turn or roll about" like the wandering course of a coastline or a river. The recent usage of trend as a general direction or tendency originates from 1884 and that usage soon became dominant and was popularized in reporting economic statistics. By the 1960s the usage in statistical time series analysis and econometrics had narrowed further and trend had come to mean a simple deterministic function like a time polynomial or sinusoidal time polynomial. It is this perspective on trend that is presented in classic time series treatments such as the texts of Grenander and Rosenblatt (1957) and Anderson (1971).

Analysing trends that are inherently stochastic is a far more challenging task for the econometrician than drawing a line through a set of points, which partly explains why so much has been written on this subject over the past 30 years. A Google search (October, 2012) on "unit roots", which we often take as the simplest embodiment of a stochastic trend, produces 252,000 thousand hits, which exceeds "microeconometrics" (150,000 hits), "time series econometrics" (144,000 hits), and "ARCH models" (118,000 hits).[3] A vast amount of empirical evidence now supports the presence of unit autoregressive roots or near unit roots in economic and financial data. Theories of efficient markets and martingale-like phenomena in capitalist economies are consonant with this econometric notion of a unit root and the shock persistence that comes from temporal aggregation. The best predictor of tomorrow's price is typically still today's price.

Bubbles differ from trends because the general tendency during an upswing contrasts with the general tendency during collapse. During an upswing we have sub-martingale behaviour where the conditional expectation is a price rise tomorrow whereas, during a collapse, the conditional expectation is a price fall, giving super-martingale behaviour. The silent elephant in the room, of course, is that we don't know when the behavioural mechanism will shift from martingale to sub-martingale or sub-martingale to super-martingale. With financial asset prices, the upswing uncertainty stems from doubts over the continuation of a

3 "Cointegration" – the sister subject of "unit roots" – records 901,000 hits.

rally and whether or when a correction or collapse will begin. During the 1990s Nasdaq bubble, the Federal Reserve Chairman Alan Greenspan articulated this type of uncertainty as a loaded question in his famous 1996 dinner speech with:

> "How do we know when irrational exuberance has unduly escalated asset values?"

Greenspan's remark underscores the fact that we usually don't know when an asset price bubble begins and, even after a collapse, academic disputes arise over whether a bubble has actually occurred. Such disputes are often ridiculed in the press and popular writing.[4] These are some of the many issues that modern econometric methodology can address and clarify.

In view of the ubiquity of trends across the business, social and natural sciences, methodology for analysing and interpreting trend behaviour has wide applicability. In consequence, the rapidly developing technology of stochastic trend analysis in econometrics has been imported by other disciplines and many new applications have emerged. Two areas that bear particularly on the present discussion are planetary climate change and biodiversity (the number of different species or genera of life forms). Data sets for these phenomena are the longest to which econometric methods have ever been employed. The time frames involve hundreds of millions of years in the case of fossil records in counting genera and hundreds of thousands of years in the case of climate change based on ice core samples and sea sediment data. These long range data embody planet-wide trends that call out for analysis which can help us understand the course of Earth's climate and life forms over time.

Long term trends in climate

To illustrate, we look at climatological data based on ice core samples that extend over geologic time frames and are measured in thousand year (kyr) or million year (myr) units. Against this time frame economic time series are extremely

4 See the article by Pástor and Veronesi (2006) and the biting critique in Cooper (2008, p. 9): "People outside the world of economics may be amazed to know that a significant body of researchers are still engaged in the task of proving that the pricing of the Nasdaq stock market correctly reflected the market's true value throughout the period commonly known as the Nasdaq bubble. … The intellectual contortions required to rationalize all of these prices beggars belief."

short, especially when it comes to studying trend behaviour. Yet many of the same problems (such as the inherent random elements in trend, shortfalls in theory guidance, and ambiguities between trend and cycle) continue to manifest themselves. Having more data, in effect, does not always lead to an improvement in analysis or understanding. Sometimes, especially with trending time series, the advent of more data simply means that the investigator has more to explain. In this event, trends appear endogenous to the sample. Then, as in economics, it is the synergy of good theory, data, and statistical methodological that is most likely to enhance understanding.

The graphs shown in Figure 54.1 are based on (linearly interpolated) data constructed from ice core samples at the Vostok station in Antarctica (Petit et al. 1999). These data cover the past 420kyrs with time measured from right (past) to left (present) on the horizontal axis. The figure contains four (slightly overlapping) panels that show the time paths of different variables over this historical period, each series having its own axis: (i) temperature measured in °C deviations from mid-twentieth century levels; (ii) methane gas (CH_4) levels in parts per billion

Figure 54.1: Vostok ice core data from Antartica over 420kyr for temperature (deviations from mid twentieth century levels), CO_2, CH_4 and dust

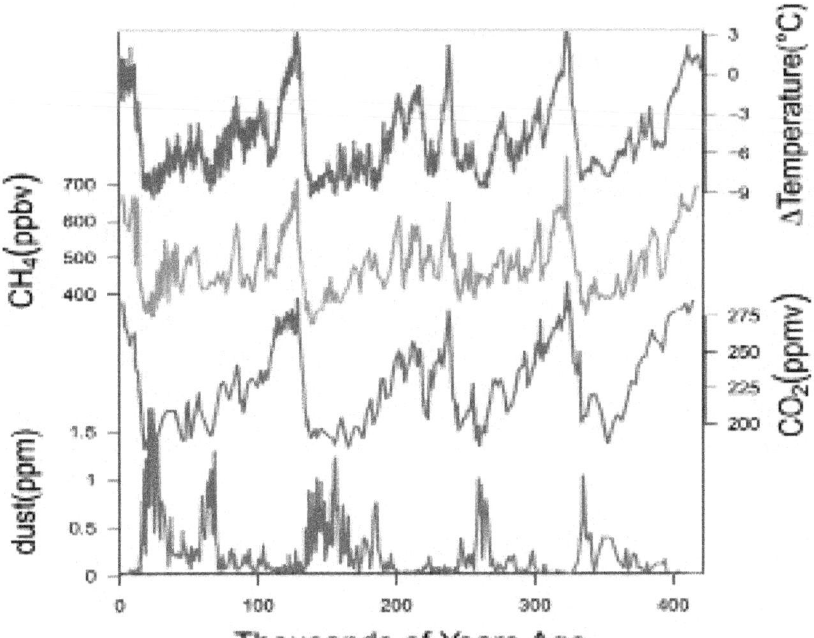

volume (ppbv); (iii) CO_2 levels in parts per million volume (ppmv); and (iv) dust levels in ppm. The temperature graph reveals many well-known features: (i) the (relative) stability of temperatures over the holocene (the last 12kyrs), considered to be decisive in the neolithic revolution and the emergence of human civilization; (ii) the long but variable cycle (with periods between 80–120kyrs) between major glacial epochs; (iii) the relatively short inter-glacial periods; (iv) some less dominant subcycles, also of variable period; and (v) evidence of random wandering behavior between episodes of deglaciation.

Spectral analysis of these series reported in Petit et al. (1999) shows spectral peaks around 100kyr, 41kyr, and 19–23kyr periods. These peaks are thought to be partly associated with certain orbital forcing mechanisms (orbital eccentricities, obliquities and precession), although the links are by no means unequivocal and there is considerable variation in the empirical periods compared with the orbital mechanisms. An alternative astronomical theory involving three dimensional orbital inclination to the invariable plane (the plane of the solar system) leading to 100kyr cycles arising from dust accretion within that plane has been advanced by Muller and MacDonald (1997). Unit root tests that I have conducted confirm evidence of random wandering behaviour in the series between these various glacial epochs, so there is strong evidence of stochastic trends in the data.

No present climatological (or planetary) simulation models are capable of generating time paths of this type over long geologic periods. Frequency domain methods, while informative about dominant periodicities, struggle to deal with the many separate components in these trajectories, particularly the unit root nonstationarity, the irregularity in cyclical behaviour, the abrupt terminations, and the prolonged holocene period which is a singular event in the record. Causal analysis among the series is complicated by the intermittent, irregular and non-concurrent sampling of the different series. Co-movement analysis does not fit within the usual cointegrating model framework of econometrics, yet co-movement is clearly apparent and of great importance, not only in terms of ongoing discussions on anthropogenic driving forces of climate change[5] – measured by recent increases in greenhouse gas emissions (carbon dioxide, methane, and

5 The Intergovernmental Panel on Climate Change (IPCC) Fourth Report released in 2007 confirmed that atmospheric CO_2 concentrations rose from 280ppm in 1750 to 379 ppm in 2005 (see http://www.ipcc.ch/). As is apparent from Figure 54.1, the level 379 ppm exceeds by around 100 ppm all previously recorded levels of atmospheric CO_2 over the last 400,000 years.

nitrous oxide) – but also in terms of the possibly causative relationship between atmospheric dust particulates and temperature.[6]

Another option for modelling these series might be the use of breaking trend functions, such as those that have been popular in econometrics over the last two decades. Structural break models offer flexibility to capture differences as well as commonalities across epochs and could be used to fit trigger point thresholds for the initiation and termination of glacial periods. However, these models have typically been developed in a univariate context and would need to be extended to multiple, sequenced, alternating breaks with common thresholds and feedbacks among the series and to allow for random wandering behaviour and cyclical features associated with orbital forcing in order to achieve congruence with these data. All of these requirements, combined with break point and threshold determination and the singularity of the holocene era, push the envelope of present econometric capability and reveal the fragility and arbitrariness of structural break modelling when it is carried to excess.

Finally, direct nonparametric fitting and data smoothing offer alternate modelling methods. Neither approach deals well with abrupt terminations, threshold triggering or random wandering behaviour within epochs. Neither do these methods allow for the use of astronomical forcing variables or other causal effects known to be important from climate theory, such as greenhouse gas amplification or ocean current influences. Nor do they allow easily for multivariate treatment that permits interaction between the series.

In short, none of the models or econometric methods for studying trends seem to measure up to the task of modelling these series. To take the problem to the next level, these series can be viewed in the context of even longer climate trajectories. Paleoclimate records from various sources are now available over very long time frames extending to hundreds of millions of years. The data are partially based on deep sea sediment cores extracted at a large number of oceanic sites, as described in Muller and MacDonald (1997) and Lisiecki and Raymo (2005a, b).

6 Some alternate planetary evidence of climatic causative forces arising from dust storms is available from astronomical observation. Ten planetary dust storms have been observed on the planet Mars since 1877. Over the last decade two major planetary dust storms (2001 and 2007) have been closely monitored by the Hubble telescope and Mars rovers. It was observed that the 2001 dust storm led to a temperature rise of some 30°C, affirming a strong planetary link between dust and temperature.

These extremely long series raise the difficulties of trend modeling to an entirely different level. Sediment core data reveal a steady downward drift in temperature over the last 5myr period, leading to a growing incidence of glaciation accompanied by an increase in the amplitude of the glacial/deglacial fluctuations (appearing like nonstationary volatility on this time scale). The 41 kyr cycle is a dominant characteristic 3 to 1 million years ago, whereas the ~100kyr cycle appears dominant over the last million years.[7]

The picture is further complicated over the far longer 65myr period following the Cretaceous-Tertiary (or so-called KT) boundary event to the present. While the drift in temperature over this period has generally been in a downward direction, it is by no means linear or monotonic and there have been substantial periods of warming, associated with an Antarctic thawing 25myr ago, prior to reglaciation some 12myr ago. Finally, the estimated climate record over the last half billion years has a pronounced cyclical pattern embodying much of the variation that over shorter geologic periods is reasonably perceived as upward or downward trend.

These long span paleoclimate data highlight that trend is a complex phenomenon with features that are random and endogenous to the sample size. As we lengthen the time span of observation, what first appears as a pattern of drift later becomes absorbed into a cycle with a longer period or even manifests as volatility. The pattern continues to repeat itself over different time scales.

Is trend itself then a phenomenon that is relative to time scale? If so, when we model trend how do we take account of the wider picture presented by a longer time frame when that data is not available to us? And what form of asymptotic theory is appropriate in a finite sample where the trend form is random and endogenous to the sample size? These are hard questions that push the limits of present understanding and methodology. In the absence of data, the answers must lie in good theory, better econometric technique, and fast algorithms for adapting models that are inevitably misspecified.

7 The orbital inclination theory of Muller and MacDonald (1997) offers an explanation of this major change in climate trend. Changes in orbital inclination take the Earth periodically (around 100kyr) into a dust belt. Dust accretion is affected by random astronomical events such as asteroid collisions which periodically replenish dust in this belt around the sun, thereby disturbing the glacial cycle.

To capture the random forces of change that drive a trending process, we need sound theory, appropriate methods, and relevant data. In practice, we have to manage under shortcomings in all of them. It is at least some comfort for the econometrician to know that these manifold difficulties of modelling trend are not confined to economics.

Detecting financial bubbles

In his book *The Adventure of English* the famous author and broadcaster Melvyn Bragg (2003) wrote that "hindsight is the easy way to mop up the mess we call history." While directed towards the study of history, this profoundly perceptive remark exposes some of the limitations in ex post econometric research. It is always easy, and can be misleading, to characterize past data – mop up the sample variation – by adding lags, covariates or using structural breaks to dummy out individually awkward observations. Far more challenging is to develop a truly anticipative ex ante econometric methodology that might be used as a warning alert system of changes in behaviour or system responses.

Some economists believe that the creation of such methodology may be altogether too challenging, especially with regard to financial markets and asset price bubbles – witness the statement of this commonly held position in *The Economist* newspaper (15 June 2005) that "bubbles can be identified only in hindsight after a market correction". Only when the full cycle of exuberance and collapse is complete, it is suggested, can a financial bubble be identified.[8]

Displayed in Figure 54.2 is the dot com bubble in the 1990s which is said to have created and destroyed about 8 trillion dollars of shareholder wealth over a period of 6 or 7 years. The data are given in real terms, including fundamentals – dividends – which behave very differently from prices. From this descriptive characterisation, the market fell first to 36 percent of its peak value and then to 24 percent of its peak value.

The warning cited earlier that Alan Greenspan made in his dinner speech about financial markets in the 1990s was cast as a question – how do we know when

8 Even then, as we have discussed in footnote 4, academic disputes continue over whether a bubble has actually occurred.

Figure 54.2: Monthly real Nasdaq prices and dividends 1973:2 – 2005:6. Both series are normalized to 100 at the beginning of the sample. (Adapted from Phillips, Wu and Yu 2011).

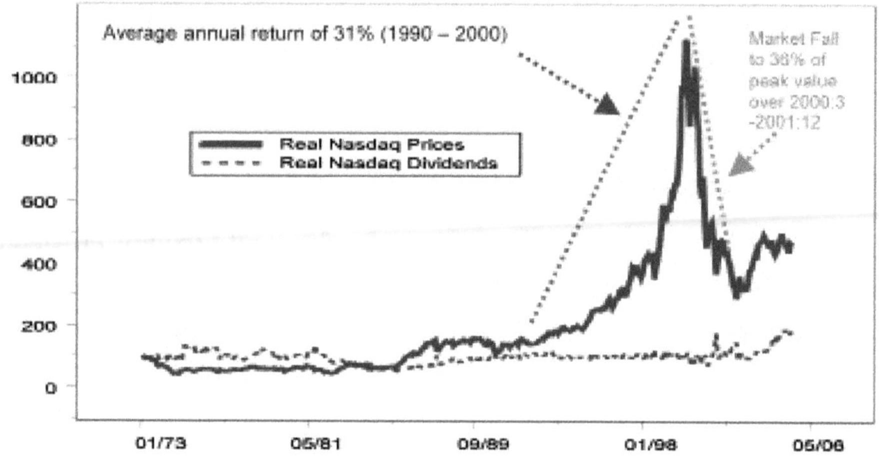

irrational exuberance is escalating asset values? How too might we distinguish between a long-term upward drift in stock prices and such exuberance? Such slow drifts are expected – they represent the long run return from investing in stocks as a risky asset – but they are usually imperceptible and undetectable over short periods of time because their magnitude is swamped by noisy volatility. Figure 54.2 shows that with the Nasdaq data something much more dramatic than a small drift was going on over a short time frame in the 1990s. Greenspan's speech was given in December 1996, by which time the graphic shows that there had been some escalation in prices. The first econometric question is how to define irrational exuberance. The second is how to detect it when it is occurring and the third is whether it can be anticipated. In effect, in December 1996 was Greenspan speaking on the basis of empirical evidence? Did the data at that point in time support his concerns over market exuberance?

It is unclear from Greenspan's speech whether the Fed had conducted any empirical research analysing the data and assessing evidence for exuberance. Given its substantial team of researchers, massive data archives, and expertise in empirics, it seems likely that some empirical analysis had been attempted. However, at that time (1996) there were no ex ante econometric tests for financial bubbles. In recent work Phillips, Wu and Yu (2011) show that by using recursive calculations of right sided unit root tests it is possible to distinguish submartingale (exuberant or mildly explosive) behaviour from martingale behaviour soon after the change in behaviour occurs. These right sided unit root tests are econometric tests for the emergence of a bubble in the data. With this approach it is possible to date stamp the emergence of exuberance and the termination or collapse of the bubble. No methods are currently available to determine the peak of a bubble.

Figure 54.3 shows the results of one of these recursive tests applied to the Nasdaq asset prices and dividends graphed in Figure 54.2. The test used here is a simple ADF unit root test with a 5 percent size. The direction of the test is not against stationarity on the left tail, as the ADF test is commonly used, but on the right tail against explosive (submartingale) alternatives. The test is conducted recursively, so that the calculated statistic provides an observation by observation measure of exuberance in the financial market. When the trajectory of the statistic hits the critical level (obtained from the limit theory of the test statistic under the null hypothesis of unit root or martingale behaviour), the crossing time determines the origination of the financial bubble. As seen in Figure 54.3, empirical application of this test dates the emergence of financial exuberance or mildly explosive market behaviour in Nasdaq prices to June 1995, some 18 months prior to Greenspan's statement about irrational exuberance. Thus, empirical evidence supports the view that Greenspan's remark had evidential basis

Figure 54.3: Time Series of the ADF t-statistic for the log real Nasdaq prices and log real Nasdaq dividends from April 1976 to June 2005. (Adapted from Phillips, Wu and Yu 2011)

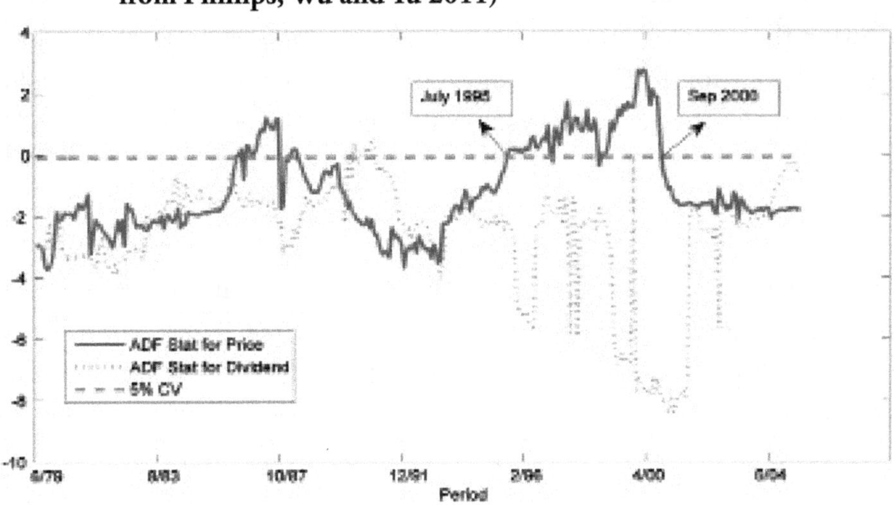

even though this type of anticipative test was unavailable at that time. Similarly, when the time series of recursive calculations falls below the critical value, the crossing time determines the termination of the bubble. Figure 54.3 shows the termination of the Nasdaq price bubble as September 2000, at which point there is a return to normal martingale-like behaviour. Throughout the period of the bubble in the 1990s there is, by contrast, no evidence of ballooning in dividend fundamentals, confirming that Nasdaq asset prices diverged from fundamentals over 1995–2000.

The econometric methodology in this empirical exercise involves the simple reduced form autoregressive model

$$X_t = X_{t-1} 1\{t < \tau_e\} + \delta_n X_{t-1} 1\{\tau_e \leq t \leq \tau_f\} + \left(\Sigma_{k=1+\tau_f}^{t} \varepsilon_k + X_{\tau_f}^{*}\right) 1\{t > \tau_f\} + \varepsilon_t 1\{t \leq \tau_f\}$$

where allowance is made for structural change in the autoregressive coefficient. The time series X_t follows a unit root autoregression with innovation ε_t over period $t < \tau_e$, which transforms into a mildly explosive[9] time series over the period $\tau_e \leq t \leq \tau_f$ (with autoregressive coefficient $\delta_n = 1 + c/k_n > 1$ where k_n tends to infinity slower than the sample size n), and then reverts to a unit root autoregression for $t > \tau_f$ from some re-initialization X^* that may be related to the level of X_t prior to the origination of the bubble. This simple model has two structural breaks that capture the transition to and from a mildly explosive process which characterise the emergence of a bubble and its subsequent collapse. This model is readily extended to accommodate further transitions that might occur during the sample period if multiple bubble episodes were present in the data. Methodology for detecting multiple bubbles is now available using a rolling window version of the recursive tests just described (see Phillips, Shi and Yu 2012).

A central advantage of the autoregressive structure in comparison with more complex time series models is that all of the energy in distinguishing the martingale and submartingale behaviour is concentrated in the autoregressive coefficient which produces a powerful statistical test. Unlike left sided unit root tests against stationary alternatives which are well known to lack power, right

9 The concept of a mildly explosive time series and the associated asymptotics for this type of process were developed in Phillips and Magdalinos (2007a, b).

Figure 54.4: Time series plot of the US monthly real house price index over January 1990 to January 2009 adjusted by the rental price. The estimated bubble origination and collapse dates are shown, together with the August 2007 commencement date of the subprime crisis (Adapted from Phillips and Yu 2011)

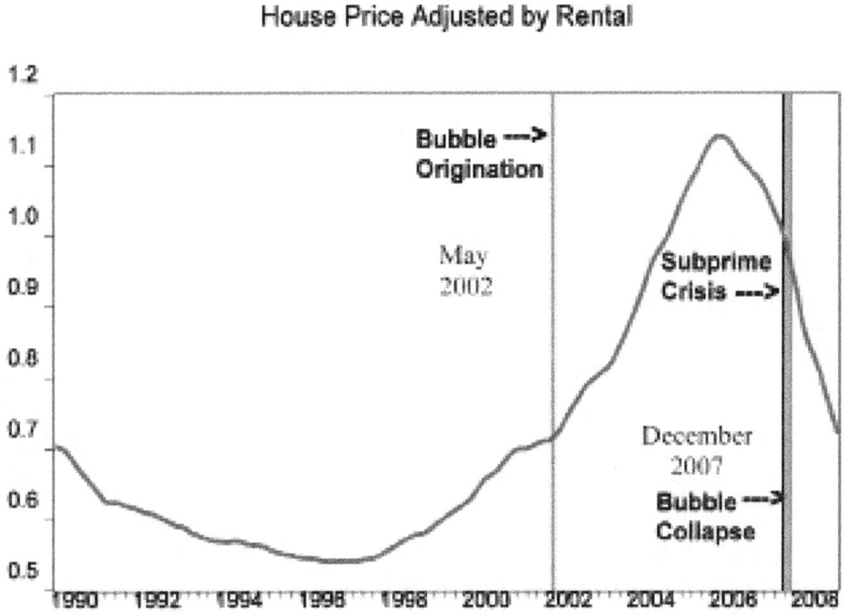

sided tests are very sensitive to explosive departures from the null and this remains so for models with weakly dependent innovations.

In order to ensure a consistent dating algorithm, we arrange for the size of the test to go to zero as the sample size tends to infinity. The critical value of the test then passes to infinity, ensuring that there are no false positives asymptotically and leading to consistent determination of the bubble origination and termination dates. Various modifications of this test procedure are possible to enhance its performance in detection and avoid unnecessary warning alerts when the statistic crosses the threshold for a very short period of time in relation to sample size.[10]

Figure 54.4 shows the results of a further application of this detection procedure by Phillips and Yu (2011) to US rental-adjusted real house prices

10 Technically, this adjustment can be achieved by factoring into the critical value a slowly varying function of the sample size.

based on the Case – Shiller composite 10 index (sourced from Shiller's website) standardized by the CPI. As shown in Figure 54.4, a significant bubble is found by the recursive test during the early part of the 2000s. The estimate of the bubble origination date is May 2002, which strongly supports the position taken by Baker (2002) who claimed that there was a housing bubble at that time, well before other commentators. The dating mechanism shows that the bubble collapsed in December 2007, soon after the subprime crisis erupted. The bubble is analysed by these methods in Phillips and Yu (2011) in the context of the broader timeline of the global financial crisis of 2007–2008 and its aftermath. This study also developed tests of the transmission of exuberance across markets that included housing, commodities (oil) and asset backed commercial paper, finding that there were contagion effects across these financial markets.

Conclusion

One of the recent contributions of econometrics has been the development of tools for studying trends and bubbles. Both phenomena take us away from the regular world of stationary processes into the broad, complex universe of nonstationary time series. Important to the progress that has been made, this work acknowledges salient features of economic and financial reality – that trends have stochastic elements and that bubbles do occur. Accordingly research has fostered new techniques to evaluate trending mechanisms and distinguish among random wandering behaviour, trend stationarity, breaking trend behaviour, and the mildly explosive processes that underlie bubble phenomena. We now have the capability to evaluate nonstationarity in terms of the memory characteristics displayed by the time series and explore potential relationships between variables that embody long range dependence. Many of these elements are relevant in empirical work with trending data such as the climate data discussed in this lecture. In that context, it quickly becomes apparent that trends are poorly understood in relation to both underlying theory and econometric methodology. Without improvements in both theory and methodology, empirical work is simply little more than a glorified version of running a line though a set of points.

Complex models are sometimes needed to provide sufficient detail for empirical research to be useful. But simple econometric models, like simple economic theories, have powerful advantages of focusing attention on key features of interest. In studying bubble phenomena, this principle is well illustrated by a mildly explosive autoregression which captures the key distinguishing characteristic of exuberance and thereby enables powerful new methods of bubble detection. That technology provides a date stamping methodology for use in empirical research and gives policy makers an early warning diagnostic to alert them to changes in financial markets. While further research on theory models and econometric methodology is needed, the methods we have developed are now being used by central bank surveillance teams in many countries. One positive externality of the global financial crisis is that there is now intensive professional interest in this area and much ongoing research that covers theory, econometrics, and empirics of financial bubbles.

References

Anderson, T. (1971), *The Statistical Analysis of Time Series*, New York: Wiley.

Baker, D. (2002), "The Run-up in Home Prices: Is It Real or Is It Another Bubble?" Briefing Paper, Centre for Economic and Policy Research, Washington DC. <http://www.cepr.net/index.php/publications/reports/the-run-up-in-home-prices-is-it-real-or-is-it-another-bubble>

Bragg, M. (2003), *The Adventure of English: the Biography of a Language*, London: Hodder and Stroughton.

Cooper, G. (2008), *The Origin of Financial Crises: Central Banks, Credit Bubbles and the Efficient Market Fallacy*, New York: Vintage Books.

Grenander, U. and M. Rosenblatt (1957), *Statistical Analysis of Stationary Time Series*, New York: Wiley.

Lisiecki, L. E. and M. E. Raymo (2005a), "A Pliocene-Pleistocene stack of 57 globally distributed benthic d18O records", *Paleoceanography* 20: PA1003, doi:10.1029 2004PA001071.

Lisiecki, L. E. and M. E. Raymo (2005b), "Correction to: A Pliocene-Pleistocene stack of 57 globally distributed benthic d18O records", *Paleoceanography*: PA2007, doi:10.1029/2005PA001164.

Muller, R. A. and G. J. MacDonald (1997), "Glacial Cycles and Astronomical Forcing", *Science* 277: 215–18.

Pástor, L. and P. Veronesi (2006), "Was There a Nasdaq Bubble in the late 1990s?" *Journal of Financial Economics* 81: 61–100.

Petit, J. R., J. Jouzel, D. Raynaud, N. I. Barkov, J. M. Barnola, I. Basile, M. Bender, J. Chappellaz, J. Davis, G. Delaygue, M. Delmotte, V. M. Kotlyakov, M. Legrand, V. Lipenkov, C. Lorius, L. Pépin, C. Ritz, E. Saltzman and M. Stievenard (1999), "Climate and Atmospheric History of the Past 420,000 years from the Vostok Ice Core, Antarctica", *Nature* 399: 429–36.

Phillips, P. C. B. (2003), "Laws and Limits of Econometrics", *The Economic Journal* 113: C26–C52.

Phillips, P. C. B. (2010), "The Mysteries of Trend", *Macroeconomic Review* 9(2): 82–89.

Phillips, P. C. B. and T. Magdalinos (2007a), "Limit Theory for Moderate Deviations from a Unit Root", *Journal of Econometrics* 136: 115–30.

Phillips, P. C. B. and T. Magdalinos (2007b), "Limit Theory for Moderate Deviations from Unity Under Weak Dependence", pp. 123–62 in *The Refinement of Econometric Estimation and Test Procedures: Finite Sample and Asymptotic Analysis*, edited by G. D. A. Phillips and E. Tzavalis, Cambridge: Cambridge University Press.

Phillips, P. C. B., S. Shi and J. Yu (2011), "Testing for Multiple Bubbles", Working paper, Yale University, New Haven CT.

Phillips, P. C. B., Y. Wu and J. Yu (2011), "Explosive Behavior in the 1990s Nasdaq: When Did Exuberance Escalate Asset Values?" *International Economic Review* 52: 201–26.

55

Can Asia grow fast on its own? The economics of the dynamic middle

Peter A. Petri[1]

Wall of worry

According to most recent projections (Table 55.1), by 2030 Asia's emerging economies[2] will become larger than those of the United States and the European Union.[3] By then, the world economy should be twice as large as it is today and middle-income countries will dominate demand and production (Appendix Table 55.A). These trends imply extensive (and hopefully peaceful) rearrangements of economic and strategic influence, and could lead to unprecedented innovation and prosperity as well as severe stresses on the environment. In other words, they need to be taken seriously. But are these projections reasonable or even feasible?

Many observers don't think so. The prospects for the "Asian century" (see for example ADB 2011) contrast sharply with recent (August 2012) negative global trends, including in Asia, and much negative commentary. The global recovery has been far slower than expected – even given warnings about the grueling history of financial crises – due to the depth of the initial U.S. financial shock and the extent of its eventual spread to sovereign debt markets in Europe

1 This paper is a revised version of the Joseph Fisher Lecture presented at the University of Adelaide, 13 July 2011.

2 The data used in this paper relate to China, India and Southeast Asia and are based on Petri and Zhai (2012), a background paper for an ongoing study of ASEAN, China and India (a grouping also referred to below as ACI). The diversity of this group cannot be addressed adequately in this short analysis, so the qualitative arguments are dominated by China, which accounts for about two-thirds of the group's GDP.

3 We use projections by CEPII (Fouré et al., 2010) which broadly represent recent studies. Appendix Table 55.1 shows that the region's per capita income would roughly triple and its share of the world output more than double, from 13 percent in 2010 to nearly 30 percent in 2030.

Table 55.1: Projections of real output growth rates to 2030, and actual 1990-2010 (percent per year)

	Actual 1990-2010	IMF (2011)	Fouré et al. (2010)	Lee & Hong (2010)	World Bank (2011)	Goldman Sachs (2007)	USDA (2010)	Mean	Standard deviation	Projection Range: M-SD	M+SD
ACI economies											
ASEAN	5.0	5.7						4.9	1.3	3.6	6.2
Brunei	1.9	2.9	4.5				1.7	3.0	1.4	1.6	4.5
Cambodia	7.4	6.6					6.1	6.3	0.4	6.0	6.7
Indonesia	4.6	6.7	5.4	4.4		4.7	5.0	5.1	0.9	4.3	6.0
Lao	6.6	7.6					6.6	7.1	0.7	6.4	7.8
Malaysia	5.8	5.1	4.5	5.2			4.1	4.7	0.5	4.2	5.3
Myanmar	8.7	5.6					4.5	5.0	0.8	4.2	5.9
Philippines	3.9	5.0	4.4	5.7		5.2	4.4	4.9	0.5	4.4	5.5
Singapore	6.4	4.4	2.3	4.3			4.0	3.7	1.0	2.8	4.7
Thailand	4.4	4.6	4.9	3.8			4.4	4.4	0.5	4.0	4.9
Vietnam	7.4	7.1		4.3		6.8	6.5	6.2	1.3	4.9	7.4
China, PR	10.4	9.5	7.7	5.5	7.0	5.4	7.2	7.0	1.4	5.5	8.4
India	6.5	8.1	6.9	4.5	5.8	6.1	7.5	6.5	1.2	5.3	7.7
Other emerging economies											
Latin America			3.4	3.6			4.2	3.7	0.4	3.3	4.2
Other			3.8	3.9		3.0		3.2	0.9	2.2	4.1
High-income economics											
Japan	0.9	1.5	1.3		1.5	1.2	0.8	1.2	0.3	0.9	1.5
Korea, Taiwan	5.2	4.4	2.2				3.3	3.3	1.1	2.2	4.4
Australia, New Z.	3.0	3.2	2.2				2.8	2.7	0.5	2.3	3.2
Canada	2.4	2.3	2.4				2.3	2.3	0.0	2.3	2.4
United States	2.5	2.7	2.2		1.9	2.5	2.6	2.4	0.3	2.1	2.7
Europe			1.6		2.8		1.9	2.1	0.6	1.5	2.7
World		3.8	3.1		3.3		3.3	3.4	0.3	3.1	3.7

and elsewhere. While Asian economies held up well in the initial stages of the crisis, four years later they are also succumbing to its effects.

Predictions of doom

The structure and durability of Asian growth are now widely questioned. The argument is that rapid Asian growth cannot continue because it has been driven by unsustainable factors. Eventually, some cyclical or unexpected trigger will generate a crash, and growth will then stabilize at much lower levels. These views originate, in part, in a financial community eager to avoid missing still another bubble. James Chanos, a hedge fund manager who earned his reputation by reportedly shorting Enron, has long predicted that the crash of China's real estate markets "is going to be a doozy"[4] (Oprita 2010). Martin Wolf (2011) of the *Financial Times* has compared China to Japan in the 1980s, where "the attempt to sustain

4 Whether intended or not, the term "doozy," which means "something extraordinary" in American slang, is unusually appropriate. This word entered popular use as "Duesy", the nickname of the Duesenberg J-model automobile, which was designed to be the best and most prestigious in the world. The car was launched with much fanfare on 1 December 1928, but soon the Great Depression hit and its markets evaporated. Less than 500 units were ever sold, mainly to movie stars and gangsters. The company collapsed in 1937.

growth in investment-led domestic demand led to a ruinous credit expansion." And two of *The Economist*'s (2011) "most influential economists of the decade," Professors Nouriel Roubini and Tyler Cowen, lead the army of doom: Professor Cowen rhetorically asked: "How about a bone-crunching, bubble-bursting, no soft landing, Chinese auto crash-style depression within the next seven years?"[5] These projections do not merely anticipate a cyclical downturn, or a gradual deceleration as countries approach the global productivity frontier (both of which are inevitable), but the end of growth based on transient causes.

Policy studies have reinforced these worries. While generally hopeful about Asian growth, ADB's *Asia* 2050 report (ADB 2011) is thoroughly hedged and goes to some length to emphasize that growth is not foreordained and could slow dramatically.[6] A prominent Chinese publication noted that "if there's a sustained slowdown, China will find itself in serious trouble without a proper plan. It would be at risk of a financial crisis and social conflict, and unable to pull itself back onto a path of steady growth. Hence, the government cannot afford to ignore these 'prophets of doom.'"[7] Avoiding deceleration – the middle income trap – also became a central theme of the recent World Bank-Development Research Center of the State Council *China 2030* study (World Bank-DRC 2012).

The middle income trap

These concerns have some basis in economic research. For example, by Garrett (2004) and Gill and Kharas (2007) argue that countries tend to get stuck in a "middle income trap" because their wages become too high to compete with low wage economies and they don't have enough technology to compete with advanced economies. The evidence is mostly anecdotal, with Latin American economies often used to illustrate growth deceleration at middle income levels. On the other hand, Japan, Korea, Taiwan and Singapore have clearly sailed past these dangers. In an important empirical contribution, Eichengreen, Park and Shin (2011)

5 That prediction was made about seven years ago (Cowen 2006), and it came true shortly after it was made, but in the United States and Europe and not in China. The Chinese economy has still not experienced a crash, although it is now decelerating. There is an extensive inventory of expired predictions of doom. The most interesting in retrospect is Gordon G. Chang's (2001), *The Coming Collapse of China*, which even identified the precise cause that would precipitate the crash in a chapter entitled: "WTO Accession Will Trigger Collapse."

6 There are some rebuttals to these views – see for example Roach (2011).

7 Caixin editorial, 29 June 2011. <http://english.caing.com/>

Figure 55.1: Growth rate acceleration by country income quartile.

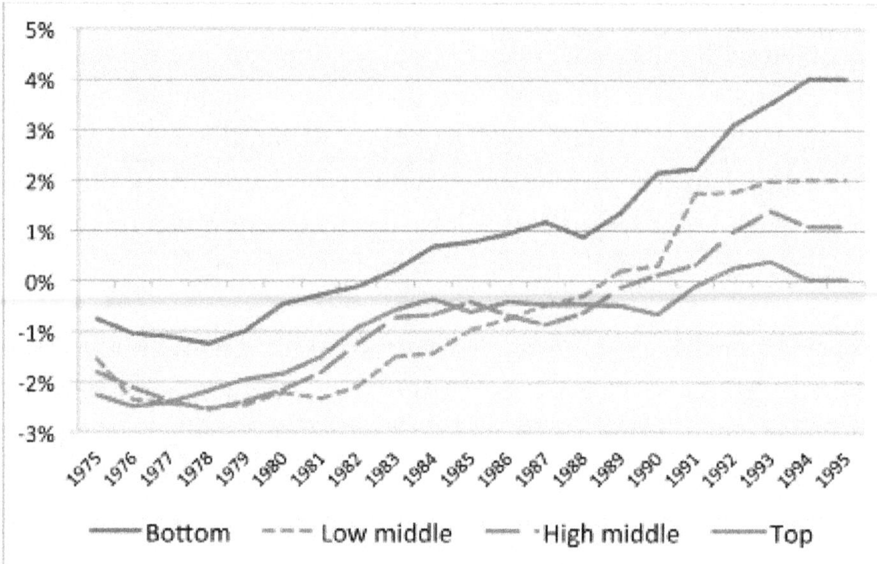

Notes: forward less backward growth rates, each calculated over a 15-year period from the year indicated. Lines are averages for quartiles of countries, ranked according to per capita PPP GDP in the year indicated.

Source: author's calculations based on the Penn World Table, <http://pwt.econ.upenn.edu/>, accessed 10 March 2012.

estimate that the probability of encountering a substantial deceleration in growth rates rises at around $17,000 per capita – a level that the World Bank classifies as high income, and one that China and other Asian economies will approach in the next two decades.

But the empirical case for growth deceleration at middle income levels is far from robust. Figure 55.1 shows retrospective differences between "past" and "future" growth rates (each based on a 15-year interval) for countries in different quartiles of the world's per capita income distribution, centered on years between 1975 and 1995. The bottom and top quartiles are represented with solid lines and middle-income countries with dotted lines. The diagram is dominated by a powerful global trend: general growth deceleration in the early 1980s has gradually turned to acceleration in the 1990s.

From the 1970s to the mid-1980s, both middle income groups lagged the bottom and top quartiles of countries – everyone was decelerating then, but the middle-income groups decelerated more sharply than others. This appears to confirm the hypothesis of the middle income trap. In the late 1980s, however, the middle-income countries began to catch up, and by the end of the data in 1995 the four groups were lined up in order, with the least developed countries accelerating the most and the most developed ones the least. Some obvious implications of Figure 55.1 are that global trends dominate results by country groups, and that differences among the latter don't follow a consistent pattern over time.

Far more detailed analysis is needed to understand changes in long term growth rates, and there may not be enough data to distinguish conclusively among alternative explanations. For example, it is possible that the middle income decelerations in the early years of Figure 55.1 reflected the special circumstances of the 1980s and 1990s, namely the foreign exchange rate crises that roiled middle-income economies during that period. For obvious reasons, middle-income countries then had much larger net, non-official foreign exchange exposures than either poorer or richer economies, and were therefore disproportionately exposed to these shocks. Because of those experiences, most middle-income countries today (along with their creditors) avoid such "currency mismatches" and some have accumulated substantial foreign exchange reserves.

The theoretical underpinnings of the middle income trap are also tenuous. The analogous "low income trap" has a familiar analytical basis: when incomes are low, people are unable to save and therefore cannot accumulate enough capital to raise incomes. No similarly compelling model has been offered to explain why countries should be able to move to middle income levels but not beyond them. Azariadis (1996) provides a survey of theoretical explanations for traps at levels above the low income threshold, but most hinge on peculiarities of demographic and saving functions – such as the possibility of drastic declines in human capital investment – that do not appear to be relevant to Asia's current circumstances.

We offer one possible explanation for the middle income trap in a recent Asian Development Bank study (ADB 2013, Ch. 1). The question that study asks is: why might middle-income countries be unable to switch to new drivers of growth when their wages rise? In other words, what would prevent them following the path traveled by advanced economies by raising skill levels, improving legal and financial systems, and developing better tools to manage demand? There is an important common denominator to the factors required to move beyond middle income stages: they take a long time to develop. If a country grows fast enough – and faces a wall of worry about its future – there will be great uncertainty about when these factors will be needed, and the investments may not be made early enough to assure a smooth transition. This leads to a classic coordination problem, as identified for example by Rodrik (1996).

The "lead time" explanation will be especially relevant to economies that (a) need to switch to more complex production structures that require long-lead-time investments, and (b) approach that stage at a high speed or growth rate. In other words, it is a theory of why fast-growing, middle-income countries decelerate. The hypothesis also contains solutions. It calls for identifying future infrastructure requirements, both institutional and physical, perhaps based on the experience of more advanced economies, as recommended by Lin (2010). It also suggests that planning – not developing sectoral directives, but creating an active dialogue about expected economic conditions – could reduce the chances of poor outcomes by resolving uncertainty about the economic environment. And it may suggest intervention, for example in education and infrastructure, to offset the riskiness of distant future returns.

Scope of this study

We take as given that Asia's growth drivers are changing and that these changes could, in the worst case, lead to a prolonged period of adjustment and slow growth. But the conventional narrative is essentially backward-looking – it argues that historical trends cannot be sustained, but does not pose the question whether "new" growth engines might supplant the "old" ones. That is the subject of this paper.

The thesis of the paper is that new sources of demand, including some already on the horizon, could drive growth at rates similar to those experienced in the past, subject, of course, to gradual deceleration as the gap between Asian and frontier technologies narrows. Moreover, this demand does not require as large a shift in production structures or as much technological upgrading as is commonly assumed. Put simply, China does not have to compete with Boeing and Airbus to grow fast (although it is trying to do that too); it merely has to become good at selling clothes, furniture, apartments, electronics and cars to the Chinese middle class.

To make this case, we assemble evidence that Asia's burgeoning middle spenders – households, firms and governments with relatively low but rapidly growing incomes – will become the most important source of global demand in the intermediate future. Moreover, this demand will be focused on products and services that are similar to those now exported to advanced countries, and may be even better adapted to the production advantages of Asian economies. Asia's potentially massive middle demand could generate exceptional scale economies and play a role similar to that played by exports to advanced countries in the past. Since this demand appears to match the region's comparative advantage, it could continue to drive factors from less to more productive activities, autonomously sustaining high rates of productivity growth and investment.

Even in the best case the transition will not be simple, rapid or smooth. It will take time to shift incomes to households and to government services spending, to design products appropriate for middle income markets, and to develop distribution systems that serve them efficiently. In some cases, challenging policy measures and new institutions will be also required. Some of these factors are examined in ADB (2013) report and will be noted in this paper.

To tackle these issues, we limit the analysis in several ways. First, we focus on *economics* and abstract from the other forces that will affect growth, such as those associated with resource and environmental issues, and the political and social transformations that many emerging economies face alongside economic development. These "other" transformations also pose great risks. To be sure, the pragmatic politics of contemporary East Asia have allowed several countries – Japan, Korea, Indonesia and Taiwan – to complete major political transitions with, if anything, positive effects on growth.

Second, we examine *structural mechanisms* and abstract from cyclical factors that may be more important in a shorter time frame. Even in their periods of miracle growth, Korea and Japan experienced major cyclical setbacks. A significant slowdown appears inevitable across much of Asia at this writing. Asian economies are subject to the usual shocks, from overheating and financial bubbles to global business cycles and raw material price increases. Indeed, economies undergoing rapid change appear to be especially vulnerable to financial crises; Asia has not escaped them in the past, nor will it in the future. From a long-term perspective, however, crises can have positive results: as the region demonstrated in 1997–98, they can trigger reforms that bring economic institutions in line with the current requirements of growth.

Third, we emphasize *autonomous growth*, in the sense of regionally-driven growth, and abstract from the role that trade with advanced economies and other regions will play in Asia's future. This is not to deny the importance of such broader economic integration. Trade is likely to remain central to Asia's growth strategy, especially since the region's reliance on imported raw materials is expected to rise. But it is nevertheless useful to single out regional drivers of growth: if Asia is to develop much faster than the rest of the world, it cannot depend on export deepening as its growth engine.

This, then, is a limited survey of the feasibility of sustained, fast growth. It is not offering a prediction, but rather a demonstration of one of possibly many multiple equilibria.

The dynamic middle as an engine of growth

We use a Shumpeterian analytical framework and emphasize the role of growth engines in driving high rates of investment and productivity growth. We start by defining this concept and then turn to possible growth engines in Asia's future. We conclude with anecdotes on some engines that could be emerging drivers of Asian growth.

The term "growth engine" is not well defined. It is often assumed to be something that we "know when we see," as U.S. Supreme Court Justice Potter Stewart famously said about pornography. The concept of a growth engine was particularly effectively presented in Schumpeter's (1942) explanation of the dynamism of a capitalist economy, although earlier examples can be identified (Kondratiev 1925). Schumpeter argued that the "evolutionary character of the capitalist process is not ... due to a quasi-automatic increase in population and capital. ...The fundamental impulse that sets and keeps the capitalist engine in motion comes from new consumers, goods, the new methods of production and transportation, the new markets, the new forms of industrial organization that capitalist enterprise creates" (p. 82). In other words, dynamic growth is not an automatic product of exogenous changes in factors and productivity. Rather, it results from novel events that provide an impetus for investment and further innovation.

What are growth engines?

Applications of the "fundamental impulse" concept multiplied as economists focused on the problem of development after World War II. Kaldor (1957), for example, emphasized investment in industry which led to productivity gains through scale and innovation. Hirschman (1959) and Nurske (1953) highlighted economies of scale, and Kravis (1970) saw trade as the "handmaiden of growth" because it expanded markets to exploit production advantages and improved productivity. Contemporary endogenous growth theory (Romer 1986) has returned to the concept of the growth engine by emphasizing the self-fueling accumulation of knowledge.

The place of a growth engine in the growth process is schematically illustrated in Figure 55.2. The upper layer of the diagram corresponds to the usual growth accounting equation linking output to labor, capital and total factor productivity, while the lower layer suggests that it is also necessary to study mechanisms that ultimately drive these proximate determinants of growth.

How does a growth engine stimulate investment and TFP growth? Modern growth theory offers several possibilities, including endogenous productivity growth due to accumulating knowledge. In this paper we focus mainly on another candidate, the transfer of resources from relatively low- to relatively high-productivity sectors. To see this, we represent an economy's overall productivity as:

Figure 55.2: Growth engines

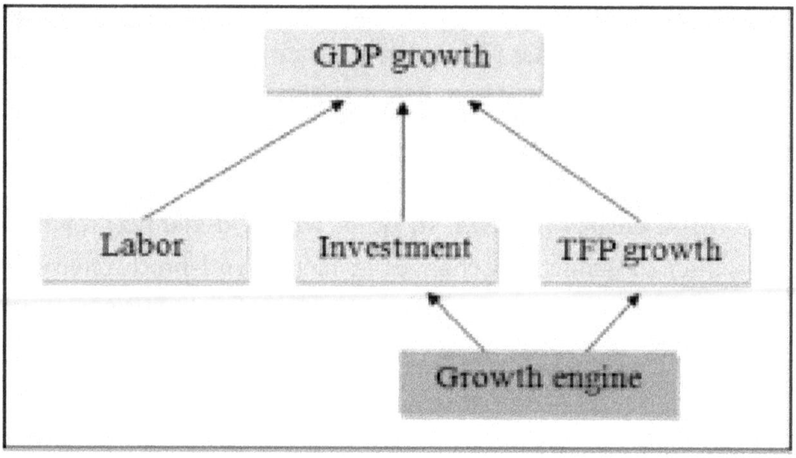

(1) $Q = \sum_i q_i s_i$

where Q = overall productivity
q_i = productivity in i^{th} sector
s_i = share of resources engaged in i^{th} sector

Then the change in productivity is:

(2) $dQ = \sum_i dq_i s_i + \sum_i q_i ds_i$

The variable Q can change either because of productivity growth in the several sectors (the first term) or because of resource shifts among them (the second term). We assume that q_i differ, at least temporarily, hence the second term matters. Productivity differentials between the traditional and modern sectors played an important role in early development theory, which focused on Lewis-style[8] wage setting in agriculture. There is now again interest in such differentials due to firm-level theories that explain international trade in terms of productivity heterogeneity.

Productivity differentials among firms and sectors are presumably due to market imperfections that impede the flow of resources from low- to high-productivity activities. These differences are hard to identify empirically, as it is generally difficult to get accurate measures of absolute productivity *levels*. But

8 See Lewis (1954) and Fei and Ranis (1964).

there is considerable evidence that productivity *growth rates* differ across sectors and among countries for substantial stretches of time, thus creating potential intersectoral and international gaps. For example, Eichengreen, Perkins and Shin (2010) report that Korea's thirty-year productivity growth rates ranged from negative 4 percent in education, health and social work to positive 14 percent in electrical machinery. They also report that almost half of Korea's productivity growth in the 1970s and 1980s was due to resource shifts in the sense of equation 2. Deng and Jefferson (2011) report large labor productivity differentials among sectors and regions within China – on the order of 2:1 two decades ago, and still as high as 1.6:1 recently – despite similar factor market conditions.

If sectoral productivity differentials are large, then the shift effects of engines that move resources into the right industries can be substantial. For example, if productivity is twice as high in a "modern" sector than in a "traditional" sector, then a growth process that shifts one percent of an economy's resources into the modern sector will add one percentage point to the overall productivity growth rate. Korea again offers a useful benchmark: in 15 years between 1975 and 1990, about 30 percent of the economy's labor force moved from agriculture to manufacturing and services.

Against this background, we define a growth engine as a *profit opportunity that induces significant investment* and hence shifts of resources into relatively high-profit activities. Often such an opportunity will arise due to a productivity increase in the target sector itself. This definition does not require, as some do, that a growth engine generate further profit opportunities in the process of its operations.[9] Thus the growth engines we discuss may "run out of steam" as the adjustment to its effects is completed. But we do restrict attention to processes that are significant enough to yield macroeconomic results. Thus, we are interested in potentially large, productive, and fast-growing sectors that can have a macroeconomic impact.

9 A more demanding definition would regard growth engines as processes that not only respond to an exogenous profit opportunity, but also endogenously generate additional opportunities through their operations. For example, Kaldor saw industrial investment as an especially strong engine because he believed that industrial activity led to income distribution effects that expanded opportunities for growth. While scale and agglomeration effects are likely to be associated with many of the engines analyzed in this paper, endogenously generated opportunities are not used as a definitional requirement.

By "profit opportunity" we mean a chance to earn excess return on capital. This will make an activity expand rapidly; it provides a magnet for entrepreneurship, ideas and resources. Such opportunities may emerge spontaneously: the diffusion of the internet in the 1990s led to the US dot-com boom (and eventual bust). In other cases, governments facilitate the exploitation of new opportunities or create them, say, through the adoption of a trade agreement or building new infrastructure such as a highway or train system.

Asian growth engines in practice

An (over)simplified view of the traditional pattern of East Asian development is that exports helped to drive the shift toward more productive industries. Based on technologies borrowed or purchased from abroad, exports offered attractive returns[10] and provided large-scale opportunities for investment and for transferring low productivity agricultural workers into high productivity industrial jobs. (Of course, other enabling factors had to be in place, otherwise the East Asian growth model would have been replicated much more widely.) Over time, as wages increased, export industries were forced to improve productivity and shift to more sophisticated products. It is difficult to imagine how such wide ranging, productivity-raising shifts in output could have been based on domestic or regional demand in the early stages of Asian industrialization.

If Asia's domestic markets are to drive rapid productivity growth today, three conditions will have to be met. First, income growth will have to generate *rapidly expanding demand* for modern products and services, similar to those that were exported advanced countries in recent decades. It appears that investment demand and consumer expenditures by the middle class do in fact generate such shifts, as described below. Extensive needs lie behind this demand: in much of Asia infrastructure and housing are underdeveloped and the natural and built environments are neglected. Firms that address these needs can grow much faster than the economy. If their productivity levels are high, overall productivity growth will follow.

10 In some countries devaluations, subsidies and various types of administrative support helped to highlight export opportunities in the early stages of export development. The large literature on these issues is surveyed in ADB (2008).

Second, the structure of Asian demand will have to *match comparative advantage*. This is likely to be true because middle income growth generates demand for consumer durables. Moreover, the basic, labor-intensive varieties of products favored by lower middle income consumers – so-called frugal innovations, in the terminology of business strategist Prahalad (2010) – correlate well with the strengths of Asian producers. They have the further advantage of proximity to their own markets. In fact, foreign firms serving these markets may also have to invest in Asia for access to market knowledge and production cost advantages. Thus, entrepreneurship, innovation, capital and technology should converge in the relevant industries. Asian firms may themselves master the tools to concentrate these resources, ranging from raising capital and creating international brands to operating fragmented production chains.

Third, there must be scope for *improving productivity* in expanding industries. This condition is also likely to be met: Asia's emerging economies are still well behind the productivity frontier in non-traditional industries and, given their relatively low per capita income levels, will remain so for some decades. (Of course, this generalization inevitably hides important country and sector differences.) The vast economies of scale implied by Asian growth will stimulate and facilitate catch-up. To be sure, to sustain the catch-up process, Asian economies will need to continue improving institutions, including finance and governance.

Examples of sectors that meet these conditions are what are regarded as engines of the "dynamic middle." In these sectors, strong demand is fortuitously matched to productivity-raising opportunities on a relatively large scale. These reinforcing advantages do not necessarily benefit every middle income economy, but they do appear to be working in concert in many Asian countries. Indeed, the fact that the industrial agglomerations typical of Asian economies are lacking in other middle income economies – say in Latin America and the Middle East – may explain why they failed to progress as rapidly at similar stages of development. (Of course, in many cases they also failed to invest heavily, or invested in the wrong industries, or borrowed too much – pitfalls that are less likely to impede Asian growth.)

As with growth based on exports, growth based on the dynamic middle will be amplified by scale effects (including scale, scope, variety and agglomeration effects) and by urbanization. Vigorous investment is both a cause and result of these processes. In fact, there may be even broader pro-growth effects associated with reaching middle income ranks. For example, a rising middle class could also generate greater social cohesion and more effective governance (Easterly 2001).

Potential Asian growth engines: A typology

Growth engines can be categorized by the source of excess profits. *Demand-based* engines reflect new demand for products or services; they generate excess profits while markets adjust. *Productivity-based* engines reflect favorable changes in technology or input prices; they allow firms to realize high margins while the competition catches up. Policy-based engines reflect profit opportunities created by government through direct expenditures, or indirect measures involving regulation, deregulation, taxes and subsidies. Potential Asian growth engines exist in each of these categories.

Demand-based engines

Over the next two decades, the growth in world demand is likely to be dominated by low- and middle-income countries, and especially those in Asia. These trends are illustrated in Figures 55.3a and 55.3b, based on global projections by Fouré et al. 2010). The figures show that the share of low- and middle-income economies in world consumption will reach 53 percent by 2030, while their share in the growth of world consumption, that is, in the new markets that are being established then, will be close to 80 percent. The growth rate differentials between advanced and emerging economies are so large in most projections that the basic message would be the same even if projections at the most conservative end were used.

Figures 55.3c and 55.3d repeat the exercise for investment expenditures. They indicate even larger shares for low- and middle-income countries – which have significantly higher savings rates than advanced economies – amounting to 65 percent of world investment and 90 percent of the growth in world investment. Asia's emerging economies account for roughly two-thirds of these magnitudes.

Figures 55.3a and 55.3b: Global consumption shares

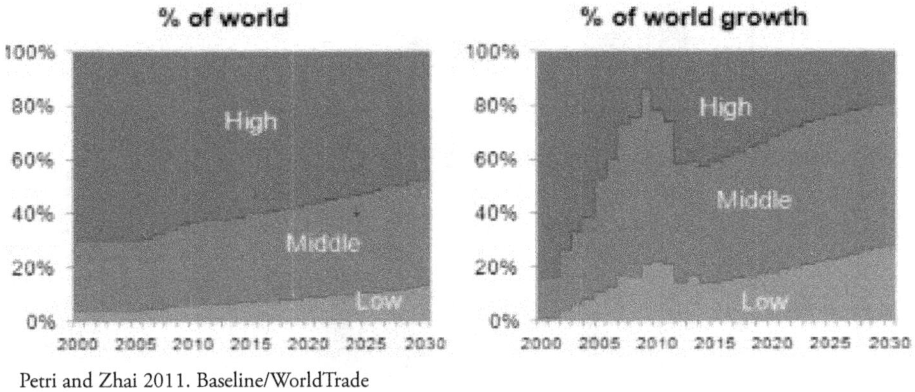

Source: author's calculations based on Fouré et al. (2010)

Figures 55.3c and 55.3d: Global investment shares

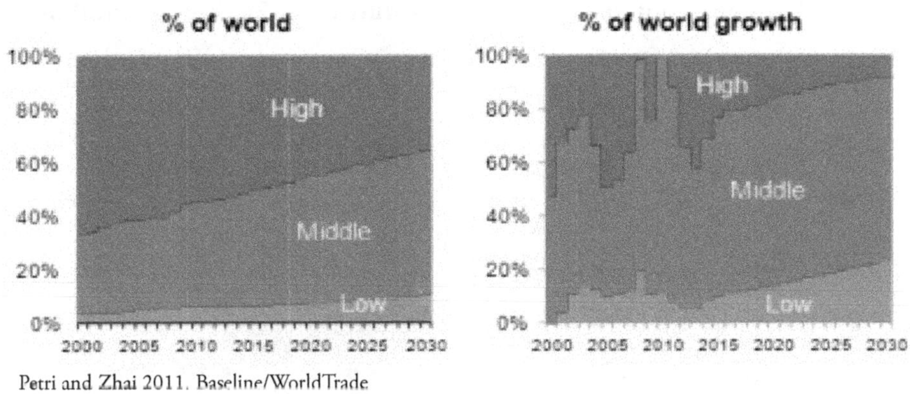

Source: author's calculations based on Fouré et al. (2010)

These changes in international growth patterns will dramatically increase the size of the global middle class (defined as people spending between $10 and $100 per day). In 2010, only one-third of the world's population was in this expenditure category; by 2030 that share is likely to rise to nearly two-thirds (Petri and Zhai 2012). Middle and upper expenditure classes should, by then, account for more than 75 percent of the total population of ASEAN, China and India (see Figure 55.4).

Figure 55.4: Shares of populations by expenditure class

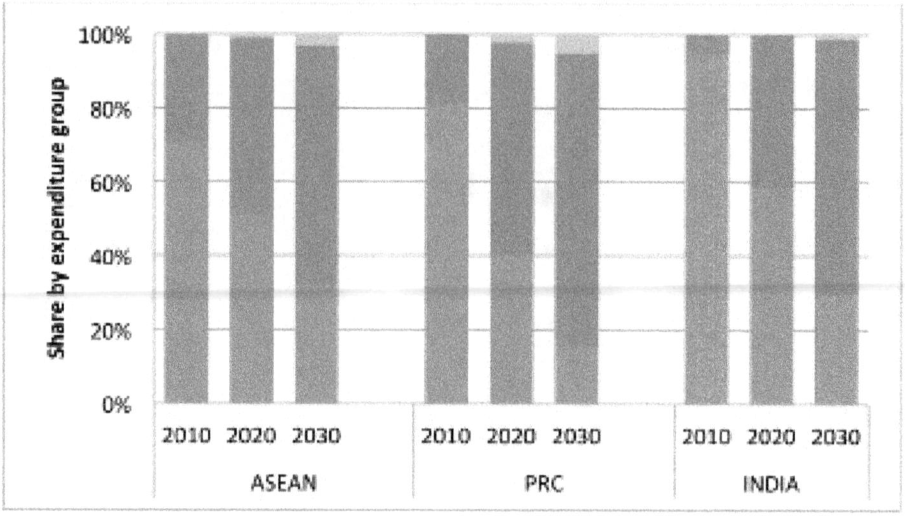

Source: Petri and Zhai (2012)

Figure 55.5: Change in populations by expenditure class, 2010-2030 (millions)

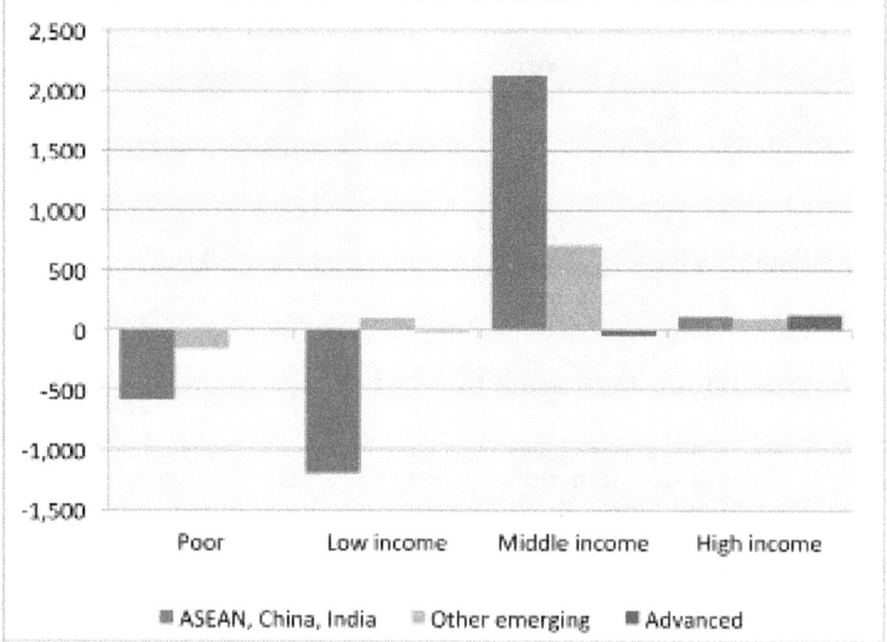

Source: authors' calculations based on Petri and Zhai (2012)

Amplified by large Asian populations, these changes in expenditure composition have major implications for both Asian and global demand. The projected contributions of various groups of economies to global expenditure categories in the next 20 years are summarized in Figure 55.5. The middle class dominates the figure, with Asian economies accounting for most of the expansion in this and other expenditure groups. Two billion Asians – nearly one-third of the world's population – will move from low income categories into the middle class by 2030. By then, extreme poverty will largely end in Asia, and as many Asians will be added also to the *highest* expenditure brackets as in all advanced economies combined (Petri and Zhai 2012).

If other emerging market contributions are added to Asian contributions, virtually all of the growth of the middle class will occur in emerging economies. Emerging economies will also account for about two-thirds of the increase in the world's high expenditure class. Thus, by 2030 more than 80 percent of middle-class and more than 50 percent of upper-class consumers will live in emerging economies. The obvious implication is that Asian producers will have "front row" seats on the major market developments of the next two decades.

Not surprisingly, McKinsey & Company, a prominent consultant to multinational companies, has been eagerly assessing these momentous changes. Much of their work has focused on the BRICs, attempting to identify the product implications of these new markets. They found, for example, that television sets and refrigerators achieve nearly complete penetration as household reach the lower limit of the middle class, but air-conditioners, motorcycles and automobiles begin to take off only as they move higher into the middle expenditure range (Figure 55.6). Most of these durables then reach full penetration at the upper end of the middle expenditure bracket. To facilitate these purchases, in turn, distribution systems tend to become much more sophisticated; supermarket penetration, for example, rises from roughly one-third at average income levels, corresponding to the bottom of the middle expenditure class, to around 90 percent at the upper end (Figure 55.7).

McKinsey has also focused attention on the implications of urbanization, which typically accompanies middle income development. The growth of industry and services promotes agglomeration. China is now in the steepest segment of the

Figure 55.6: Consumer durable penetration by daily income

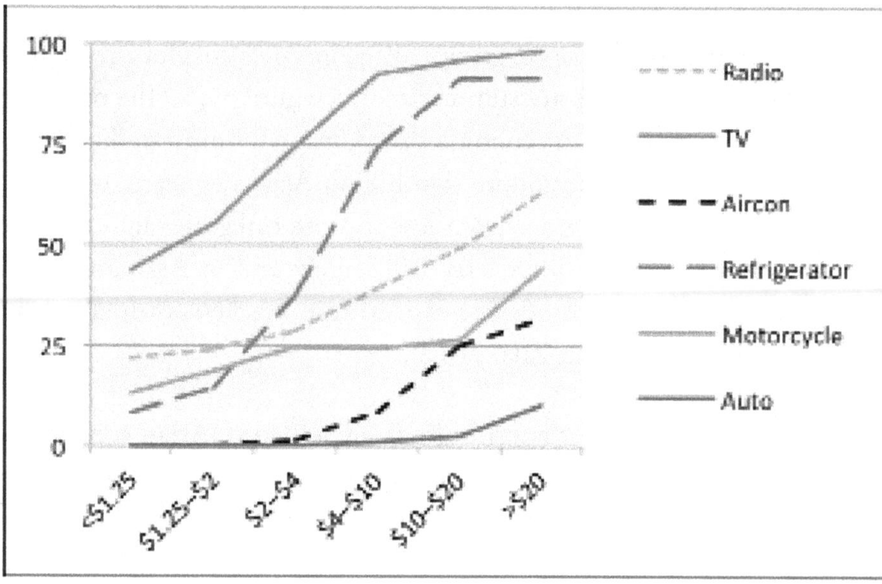

Source: McKinsey Global Institute (2010)

Figure 55.7: Supermarket penetration by income

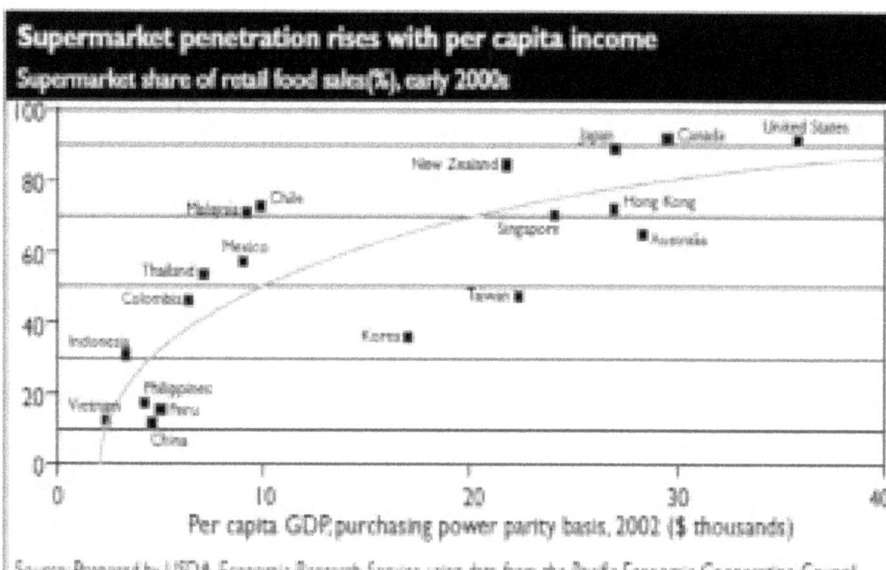

Source: <http://webarchives.cdlib.org/sw1vh5dg3r/http://www.ers.usda.gov/AmberWaves/June06/Features/Revolution.htm>

Figure 55.8: RCA index vs. expenditure shares

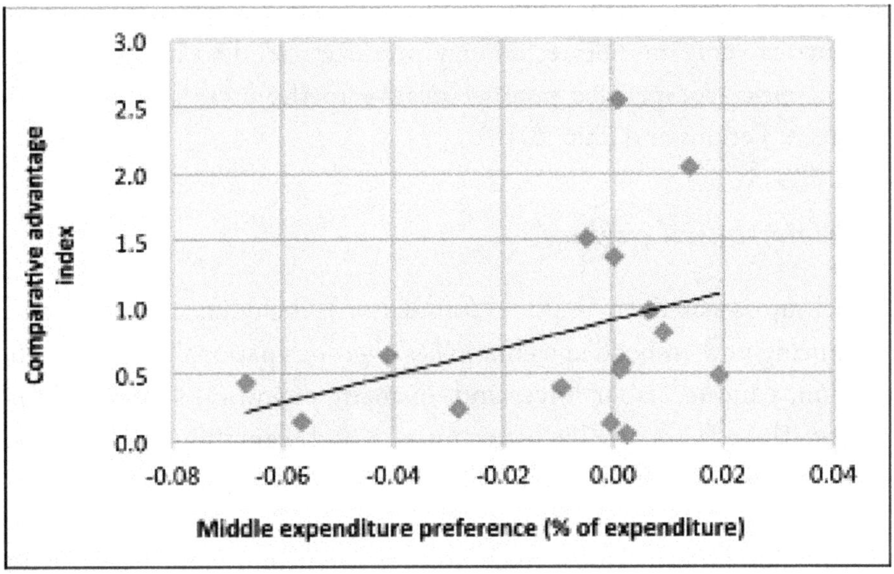

Source: authors' calculations

urbanization process; India is about to enter it. The implications include both demand and production effects; cities require large investments in infrastructure and real estate, and urban densities offer higher rates of productivity and economies of scale. McKinsey projects that there will be 221 cities of 1 million or more in China by 2025, seven times as many as there are in Europe (McKinsey 2009). In rough terms, this growth will require 40 billion square meters of new residential and commercial space, representing an investment of $12–16 trillion, or around $1 trillion annually. In another study, McKinsey (2010) estimates that residential investment in China and India alone would reach $2 trillion in 2030, not counting related infrastructure investments. Examples of these opportunities are provided below.

Importantly, these directions of market growth play into Asia's production strengths. The commonly used method to measure comparative advantage is Balassa's Revealed Comparative Advantage measure, which in Figure 55.8 is plotted against differences in expenditure structure between middle and low income consumers. It shows that Asian RCAs are correlated with middle class expenditure differentials, that is, with the fastest growing markets of the future.

This analysis is conducted on a fairly aggregated level in this paper, but more detailed analysis would likely point to even stronger relationships, since within any product category middle technology producers tend to have an advantage in low-end, price-competitive product relative to the more advanced varieties (Eichengreen, Perkins and Shin 2010).

Productivity-based engines

Asia's catch-up is based on multiple foundations, including ample investment for introducing new embedded technologies, vigorous national and international competition, educated labor forces and, in many countries, substantial foreign investment. These factors are likely to continue, and if anything will be amplified by maturing technological capabilities.

Technological catch-up is likely to remain an important factor in future Asian growth and the substantial opportunities remain for sustained progress. Gaps between productivity levels in emerging Asia and advanced countries are large. At the same time, the environment for technological diffusion and implementation is improving thanks to increased regional competition and integration, high rates of investment, rapid demand growth, and the pressure of rising wages. Meanwhile, advanced-country firms with technology assets have few alternative opportunities to match those offered by Asian markets, and are generally, though reluctantly, willing to trade technology for market access.

Asia's capabilities for absorbing and generating technology are also improving rapidly, although the results are uneven and some countries still have a long way to go (Jimenez, Nguyen and Patrinos 2012). The ratio of R&D investment is rising rapidly and a rapidly increasing proportion of students is enrolled in higher education. The OECD reports, for example, that China increased its R&D expenditures at rates exceeding 20 percent per year throughout the global crisis, roughly doubling its share of world R&D between 2004 and 2009 (OECD 2012). The unusual density of economic activity and industrial and research agglomerations in Asia encourage the flow of ideas and people among firms. These flows are reinforced by research outsourcing and by global technological developments – especially the internet – that were not available to developing economies in the past.

Intra-Asian trade growth will provide additional support for the growth of Asian productivity. Gravity equations suggest a disproportional increase in the bilateral trade of rapidly growing economies – in other words, they will become unusually important partners to each other. Asia is likely to remain the world's industrial belt, although specialization patterns within the region are likely to shift. This will be facilitated by new transport corridors that will link north-south and east-west trade routes. By 2030, the result could be a reasonably integrated industrial belt with 3.2 billion people and $40 trillion of output (ADB 2009).

Trade promotes productivity through multiple channels. It enables production chains to be fragmented across countries with different factor prices and production conditions. While labor costs will rise throughout Asia, differences remain wide and will sustain a range of production techniques for some time to come. Should Chinese wages rise steeply, for example, there would be ample opportunities to relocate labor intensive processes to Vietnam or India. Trade also raises productivity by permitting greater economies of scale in each product variety, and thus generates benefits from access to more diverse final goods and from more productive inputs. Finally, much recent research confirms the new theoretical view that an important consequence of trade is to shift resources to productive firms within sectors (Melitz 2003).

These beneficial effects of trade growth are likely to be amplified by declining trade barriers. Asian economies are now among the most active in negotiating bilateral and regional FTAs. Agreements have been concluded between ASEAN and the so-called "plus 6" (China, India, Japan, Korea, Australia and New Zealand) and other countries in Latin America and elsewhere. Discussions are underway on a Trans-Pacific Partnership agreement among 11 countries including the United States, and on an agreement to connect the large economies of China, Japan and Korea. All of these could eventually lead to a massive Asia-Pacific free trade zone (Petri, Plummer and Zhai 2013). Asia has a particular incentive to pursue global liberalization since its resource-poor economies will increasingly depend on other regions to meet rising food, energy and raw materials requirements.

Policy-based engines

Policy can promote growth by correcting market failures and by removing impediments to economic activity. Recent development theory also emphasizes the need for institutions to support market development. The "new structuralist" approach (Lin 2010) argues that governments need to lay the foundations for economic growth by investing in the soft and hard infrastructure necessary to enter new industrial activities consistent with an economy's comparative advantages.

Soft infrastructure – the institutional, legal and financial framework of economic activity – will be critical for future growth. The World Bank's "Doing Business" indicators rank Singapore, Hong Kong and Korea among the best in the world, but China, Indonesia and India are at or below the global median (91st, 129th, and 132nd, respectively). This is good and bad news. On the positive side, the scope for progress is very substantial and many countries are now aggressively targeting the quality of the business environment. On the negative side, the climate testifies to the strength of traditional impediments to progress, including widespread corruption. Asia's small scale enterprises sometimes also impede progress. For example, many countries greatly restrict large-scale, competitive business models in the service sector. That Asian economies can perform well in services is demonstrated by the success of business process outsourcing in India, the Philippines and other countries; the challenge is to replicate these models in large, domestic markets.

Government expenditures on hard infrastructure should have an even more salient impact, affecting both demand and productivity. ADB (2009) estimates that around $8 trillion will have to be invested in Asian infrastructure over the next decade (Table 55.2). In orders of magnitude, this estimate is consistent with McKinsey Global Institute's projection that China and India alone will spend $1.33 trillion on infrastructure annually by 2030 (McKinsey 2010). Energy, communications, transport and other infrastructure indicators are central to "Doing Business" surveys and hence increasingly the target of "national brands".

Transport is critical in dense, trade-dependent Asia and the region is embarked on many ambitious investments. Seven of the world's ten best airports

Table 55.2: Infrastructure investment requirements, 2010-2020

Sector/Subsector	New Capacity	Replacement	Total
Energy (Electricity)	**3,176,437**	**912,202**	**4,088,639**
Telecommunications	**325,353**	**730,304**	**1,055,657**
Mobile phones	181,763	509,151	690,914
Landlines	143,590	221,153	364,743
Transport	**1,761,666**	**704,457**	**2,466,123**
Airports	6,533	4,728	11,260
Ports	50,275	25,416	75,691
Railways	2,692	35,947	38,639
Roads	1,702,166	638,366	2,340,532
Water and Sanitation	**155,493**	**225,797**	**381,290**
Sanitation	107,925	119,573	227,498
Water	47,568	106,224	153,792
Total	**5,418,940**	**2,573,760**	**7,991,708**

$ = United States dollar

Source: ADB (2009)

(as ranked by London-based Skytrax) and seven of the world's ten largest seaports are in Asia. Much of this capacity is state-of-the-art; the Shanghai port, for example, doubled throughput between 2004 and 2007.[11] In remarkably little time, China built a road system similar in scale to that of the United States and its rail systems now covers 74,000 km (and is scheduled to expand to 120,000 by 2015). Its urban transit systems are highlighted below with the example of the Shanghai metro, now the world's largest. McKinsey Global Institute (2011) estimates that in the next 20 years India will build one subway system equivalent to Shanghai's every year, while China will build two to four. These massive projects have their share of hiccups, ranging from major accidents to financial disasters and extensive corruption – perhaps inevitably, given that these industries are new to the region. Yet many projects are moving forward in an otherwise weak investment environment and are accumulating experience that will improve efficiency over time. Despite inefficiencies, these projects may look like a bargain in retrospect, as wage increases, stiffer regulations, greater political constraints and higher industrial and residential land prices make infrastructure development more difficult and expensive.

11 The infrastructurist.com, 25 June 2011.

Energy output has matched the blistering pace of industrial growth. Increasingly, Asia is also embracing the renewable sector. China and India are now the largest investors in wind energy, and installed 56 percent of the world's new capacity in 2010. China has led infrastructure investment because of its powerful central control: the state has encouraged, funded and facilitated a wide range of investments. A significant share of infrastructure investments (estimates range from $1.6 to over $2 trillion) has been funded by essentially local government debt through financial platforms backed by project revenues. Some of this debt is in trouble and will eventually need to be taken over by the central government. Better models for financing infrastructure will need to be developed in the future, but the progress made has been substantial – and arguably at a cost that cannot be replicated at more advanced stages of development.

New industries may also emerge from social and environmental goals, although their contributions to growth will depend in part on yardstick used. Asia is now the world's leading emitter of greenhouse gases and faces a wide range of environmental problems. Many Asian countries also lag behind in public services, including health, education and public safety (ADB 2013). These concerns will become more prominent as expectations rise and the region's citizens gain influence in political decisions. The resulting expenditures and investments will contribute to welfare growth, but may not increase productivity as conventionally measured. For example, policies that substitute costlier low-carbon fuels for coal would likely increase welfare while reducing conventional productivity.

Some Trillion Dollar Examples

Asia's economic history is punctuated by anecdotes of remarkable innovation. For example, in the mid-1950s when the United States scaled back its expenditures after the Korean War, Korea became desperately short of hard currency earnings and had virtually no raw materials, capital, technology or market connections for building an export industry. Within months, however, it "discovered" the market for wigs made from human hair and quickly became the world's leading exporter. Japan's electronics, Taiwan's computers, Thailand's auto cluster offer other, more advanced examples. What will be the anecdotes of Asia's future? One

Figure 55.9: Tata Nano (l) and Maruti-Suzuki Alto (r)

Source: Nano - , Tata Nano <http://www.mestrecarros.com>, Maruti-Suzuki Alto <http://www.cars4indians.com>

cannot predict or even imagine the industries that will be generated by the forces discussed in previous sections. Nevertheless, some emerging examples illustrate the possibilities.

Tata Nano

By 2030, Asia's emerging economies may purchase 100 million new automobiles a year (up from around 25 million units now), representing annual sales of around $1 trillion. The new kinds of products required by this remarkable market – and more generally by the new middle classes – are illustrated by India's entry-level automobile, the Tato Nano. When introduced in 2008, it attracted worldwide attention and was heralded as the new "Model T."

To be sure, the Nano met with huge skepticism. Some called it two motor scooters with a tent in between. It had five seats, was smaller than the 2-seat Daimler Smart, and had a maximum speed of 60 miles per hour. Its instrument panel was a speedometer (Figure 55.9). But its $2,300 price was less than half that of competitors and sales jumped off to a fast start. In the event, the Nano had problems, including safety issues, and sales fell way behind those of competitors. Today India's low-end market is handily dominated by the locally-produced Maruti-Suzuki Alto, which sells for twice as much as the Nano. It will take more experiments to find the right products for India's middle income market – the

Nano example shows that the price-quality tradeoff will be hard to get right – but the point is that this experimentation is taking place in Asia and to a large extent by Asian firms, and the industries that capture the market are bound to be built in Asia.

Hallstatt, Guangdong?

Housing Asia's urban populations will take extraordinary investments. If 600 million people move into cities in the next two decades, some 150 million apartments will have to be built, requiring investments of at least $20 trillion, or $1 trillion per year. These investments have begun in a spectacular fashion, encouraged by easy credit policies followed during the global financial crisis in China and Southeast Asia. Indeed, many argue that a massive real estate bubble has already formed in China. Real estate prices soared in many cities, and large numbers of new units – maybe as much as one-quarter according to unofficial estimates based on unused electric meters in China – came to be unoccupied. Led by government efforts, prices have since settled back, but they remain high relative to income and there is no evidence of a general market collapse so far. (In contrast to European and US real estate markets, Chinese residential real estate is financed with conservative mortgages and considerable equity.)

The property market will certainly remain volatile, as should be expected given the speed of the region's development and the inherent uncertainties associated with such long-lived investments. But all of this is fully consistent with huge long-term demand. In response to rising social concern about access to affordable housing, the Chinese government is now aggressively building subsidized units – some 36 million units are planned for 2011–2015. Thus, while the market is softening, housing investment remains reasonably strong. Land is still controlled by the state and is easily developed; there are few regulations to protect agricultural land or to require high construction standards, or insist that former occupants be fairly compensated. However one might judge the welfare implications of these factors, they facilitate fast and extensive urban development.

An example of the jubilant competition in the real estate sector is provided by a project to replicate Hallstatt, a prototypical Austrian village and UNESCO World Heritage Site (Figure 55.10), in Huizhou, a city of four million people

Figure 55.10: Hallstatt, Guangdong?

Source: free web image, <http://www.uploadimages4free.com/browse_images/hallstatt_in_winter_austria-221.html>

just north of Shenzhen. The site is complete with lake and a steep mountain backdrop, which is currently being dug from a larger mountain. When the citizens of Hallstatt learned of the project, they were shocked – no one had asked for permission! The owner of Hallstatt's inn was pleased, however, hoping that millions of Chinese would now want to visit the original.[12]

Shanghai Metro

The Shanghai Metro is a remarkable example of large-scale infrastructure investment. Until recently, underground subway systems were mostly built by wealthy cities. In the last 15 years, however, Shanghai developed the world's largest underground system with 427 kilometers of track (Figure 55.11). The cost is not known, but may have been on order of $30 billion ($1,500 per resident). This is a large investment compared to per capita income, but it's difficult to

12 Tony Paterson, "Alpine villagers bewildered as China clones their home", *The Independent*, 20 June 2011.

Figure 55.11: Track length of the Shanghai Metro (km)

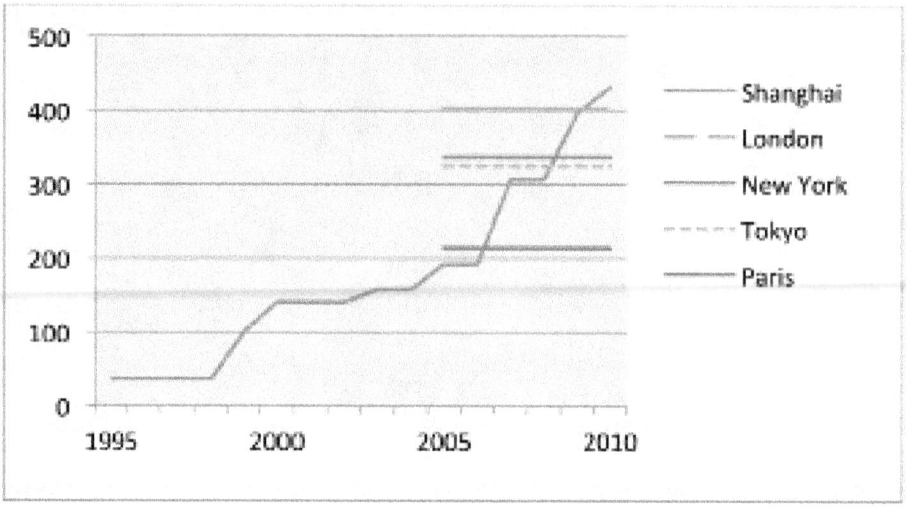

Source: author's calculations based on Wikipedia, accessed 12 July 2011

think of any other investment, in transportation at least, that could have provided similar value. Due in part to improvements in the city's infrastructure, Shanghai's property prices have risen dramatically and are now similar to those in the world's most expensive cities.

The cost of building a subway system in China appears to be at most one-fifth as high as the cost of doing so in an advanced economy, due to low labor costs and few political impediments.[13] Assuming that these differences diminish with development, given usual discount rates – and especially very low current rates – it might even make sense to build a system that is not fully utilized for many years. It also makes sense to factor such expectations of systemic change directly into development policy. For example, the current U.S. interstate highway system (launched in the 1950s) or Japan's Shinkansen rail system (launched in the 1960s) would have been far more difficult and costly to build only a few decades later.

The Shanghai Metro and 14 others already built or in progress in China are also generating technological expertise that will make China a leader in public transport infrastructure. Both Beijing and Shanghai have plans to double their

13 Keith Bradsher, "Clash of Subways and Car Culture in Chinese Cities", *New York Times*, 27 March 2009.

current subway systems over the next decade. Twenty other cities are planning to begin building subway lines. McKinsey (2011) estimates that China and India alone will build 1150–1900 km of subway tracks (three to five times the size of the Shanghai system) every year for the next 20 years. Subway projects can be also become convenient stimulus programs when economic activity slips. For example, the National Development and Reform Commission approved 25 new projects in response to deteriorating economic numbers in 2012.[14]

To be sure, important mistakes have been made in this expansion process. For example, Shanghai's special Maglev line to connect the airport to the city ends in a terminal well outside the center, as it became impossible to continue the line into the city center due to cost and public objections. The high-speed train collision in Wenzhou that killed 40 people is another prominent example. But the Chinese government is not deterred; in 2012 the State Council announced that it will triple the high-speed rail network, from 13,000 to 40,000 kilometers by 2015, connecting virtually every city with more than half million residents. China has also begun to export high-speed rail components to Siemens, the German company that helped to develop some of the Chinese system.[15] The impact of such projects is large compared to the risks, both in generating demand during construction and in raising productivity in the long run.

Conclusions

Asia's future growth will require sustained productivity growth at a rate and over a period of time never before experienced in countries so large. The foundations of Asia's success remain in place, including high savings, entrepreneurial, market-oriented economies and, for the time being, favorable demographics. At the same time, Asia is outgrowing its external drivers of growth and will need to replace them with new, autonomous engines.

There is a now much pessimism about the likelihood that Asian can make these transitions. Powerful global headwinds are slowing Asian growth and there is widespread condemnation of the stimulus programs, particularly China's

14 See "China Make High-Speed Rail Sale to Siemens", *Wall Street Journal*, 9 August 2012.
15 See "Asia: Subways Add to Chinese Stimulus", *Wall Street Journal*, 17 September 2012.

infrastructure investments, that helped Asia ride out the worst of the global financial crisis. There also are worries about the longer-term effects of the middle income trap.

All of these are serious concerns, but this paper argues that Asia's new growth engines are likely to be up to the challenge. Some promise massive new markets in the $1 trillion range. The fuel for these engines is the "dynamic middle", referring to rapidly rising middle class consumption, urbanization and infrastructure investment and the vigorous growth of middle technology industries that are associated with these demands. Moreover, Asia's patterns of comparative advantage should enable the region to capture much of its own new demand, generating economies of scale and new clusters of entrepreneurship, investment and innovation. Asian integration will also permit deeper exploitation of fragmented production based on the region's diversity. Asia's rising multinationals are increasingly spearheading these efforts.

Indeed, the economics of the middle may have wider applications than are discussed in this paper. For example, projections suggest that urban economic growth in coming decades will take place largely in "middleweight" cities, in contrast to megacities, which now face diseconomies (McKinsey Global Institute 2011). A more general formulation may be that all kinds of catch-up processes are accelerating – probably due to improved information flows – allowing middle activities (or countries or cities) to close in on these in the lead, while leaders experience the slower progress characteristic of the frontier.

If this hypothesis is correct, Asia's progress need not be scaled to the growth of the rest of the world or to the size of high-income economies; it can evolve at its own, faster pace. Of course, effective institutions will be essential for steering development through these transitions and managing the inevitable shocks. Asian economies still have far to go in developing the financial systems, business laws and regulations, and mechanisms of public and corporate governance that will be needed to cope with greater prosperity. But most have managed such institutional transformations pragmatically and successfully in the past.

Despite the prospects for autonomous growth, Asia will remain deeply interdependent with the rest of the world. Its rising requirements for energy, food and raw materials will make global trade and trade rules increasingly important. Thus, Asia will need the support of global economy to drive growth with its dynamic middle; it cannot become protectionist or afford protectionism in advanced countries. Increased tensions with advanced or other emerging economies are likely, but so are powerful incentives to manage these strains. Asia's development can serve as an engine of global growth and all countries have a large stake in supporting its rise.

None of this implies that Asia will grow fast. This paper sidesteps questions of political stability and the feasibility of growth in the face of global resource and environmental constraints. Nor does it claim that the "high equilibrium" represented by the region's autonomous growth is the only such alternative. But it does argue that sustained, rapid Asian growth is plausible, even without the growth engines of the past. Among the world's major regions, Asia is best positioned to keep global economic development on track, the headwinds and pundits notwithstanding.

References

ADB (2008), *Emerging Asian Regionalism: A Partnership for Shared Prosperity*, Manila: Asian Development Bank.

ADB (2009), *Seamless Asia*, Manila: Asian Development Bank.

ADB (2011), *Asia 2050: Realizing the Asian Century*, Manila: Asian Development Bank.

ADB (2013), *ASEAN, the People's Republic of China and India: the Great Transformation*, Manila: Asian Development Bank (forthcoming).

Azariadis, C. (1996), 'The Economics of Poverty Traps, Part I: Complete Markets', *Journal of Economic Growth* 1: 449–86, December.

Chang, G. G. (2001), *The Coming Collapse of China*, New York: Random House.

Cowen, T. (2006), "China Skeptics", http://marginalrevolution.com/marginalrevolution/2006/02/china_skepticis.html

Deng, P. and G. Jefferson (2011), 'Explaining Spatial Convergence of China's Industrial Productivity', mimeo, Brandeis University, Waltham MA.

The Economist (2011), 'Economics' most influential people', 1 February. www.economist.com/blogs/freeexchange/2011/02/economics&fsrc=nwl

Eichengreen, B., D. Perkins and K. Shin (2010), *From Miracle to Maturity: The Growth of the Korean Economy*, Cambridge MA: Harvard East Asia Center.

Eichengreen, B., D. Park and K. Shin (2011), 'When Fast Growing Economies Slow Down: International Evidence and Implications for China', NBER Working Paper 16919, Cambridge MA: National Bureau of Economic Research.

Easterly, W. (2001), 'The Middle Class Consensus and Economic Development', *Journal of Economic Growth* 6(4): 317–35.

Fei, J. C. H. and G. Ranis (1964), *Development of the Labor Surplus Economy: Theory and Policy*, Homewood IL: Richard A. Irwin.

Fouré, J., A. Bénassy-Quéré and L. Fontagné (2010), 'The World Economy in 2050: a Tentative Picture', CEPII Working Paper No. 2010–27, Paris, December.

Garrett, G. (2004), "Globalization's Missing Middle", *Foreign Affairs* 83(6): 84–96, Nov/Dec.

Gill, I. and H. Kharas (2007), *East Asian Renaissance*, Washington DC: World Bank.

Goldman Sachs (2003), 'Dreaming with BRICs: the Path to 2050', Global Economics Paper No. 99. New York: Goldman Sachs.

Goldman Sachs (2007), *BRICs and Beyond*, New York: Goldman Sachs.

Hirschman, A. O. (1959), *The Strategy of Economic Development*, New Haven CT: Yale University Press.

IMF (2011), *World Economic Outlook 2011*, Manila, April, and accessible at: www.imf.org/external/pubs/ft/weo/2011/01/weodata/index.aspx

Jimenez, E., V. Nguyen and H. A. Patrinos (2012), 'Stuck in the Middle: How Human Capital Development Can Help Southeast Asian Countries Achieve High-Income Status", Washington DC: World Bank, May.

Kaldor, N. (1957), 'A Model of Economic Growth', *Economic Journal* 67(268): 591–624, December.

Kondratiev, N. (1925), *The Major Economic Cycles* (in Russian), translated in 1984 as *The Long Wave Cycle*,

New York: Richardson & Snyder.

Kravis, I. B. (1970), 'Trade as a Handmaiden of Growth: Similarities Between the Nineteenth and Twentieth Centuries', *Economic Journal* 80(320): 850–72, December.

Lee, J. W., and K. Hong (2010), 'Economic Growth in Asia: Determinants and Prospects', ADB Economics Working Paper No. 220, Asian Development Bank, Manila.

Lewis, W. A. (1954), 'Economic Development with Unlimited Supplies of Labour', *Manchester School*, 22: 139–91.

Lin, J. Y. (2010), 'New Structural Economics: A Framework for Rethinking Development', Policy Research Working Paper 5197, Washington DC: World Bank.

McKinsey Global Institute (2009), *Preparing for China's Urban Billion*, New York: McKinsey Corporation.

McKinsey Global Institute (2010), *Farewell to Cheap Capital: The Implications of Long-Term Shifts in Global Investment and Saving*, New York: McKinsey Corporation.

McKinsey Global Institute (2011), *Urban World: Mapping the Economic Power of Cities*, New York: McKinsey Corporation.

Melitz, M. J. (2003), 'The Impact of Trade on Intra-Industry Reallocations and Aggregate Industry Productivity', *Econometrica* 716: 1695–725.

Nurske, R. (1953), *Problems of Capital Formation in Underdeveloped Areas*, New York: Oxford University Press.

OECD (2012), *Science, Technology and Industry Outlook 2012*. Paris: Organization for Economic Cooperation and Development.

Oprita, A. (2010), 'Jim Chanos: China's Real Estate Bubble is Unprecedented,' http://www.cnbc.com/id/35056774 25 January.

Petri, P. A. M. Plummer and F. Zhai (2013), *The Trans-Pacific Partnership and Asia-Pacific Economic Integration: A Quantitative Assessment*, Washington: Peterson Institute for International Economics (forthcoming).

Petri, P. A. and F. Zhai (2012)', 'Navigating a Changing World Economy: ASEAN, China and India,' Background paper to ACI study, Tokyo: ADB Institute.

Prahalad, C. K. (2010), *The Fortune at the Bottom of the Pyramid: Eradicating Poverty Through Profits*, Upper Saddle River NJ: Prentice Hall.

Roach, S. (2011), 'Ten Reasons Why China is Different', www.project-syndicate.org, accessed 27 May.

Rodrik, D. (1996), 'Coordination Failures and Government Policy: A Model With Applications to East Asia and Eastern Europe,' *Journal of International Economics* 40: 1–22.

Romer, Paul, 1986. "Increasing Returns and Long-Run Growth." *Journal of Political Economy*, 94(5), pp. 1002–37. October.

Schumpeter, J.A. (1942), *Capitalism, Socialism and Democracy*, New York: Harper (1975 edition).

USDA (2011), accessed www.ers.usda.gov/data/macroeconomics/ on 12 November.

Wolf, M. (2011), 'How China Could Yet Fail Like Japan', *The Financial Times*, 15 June.

World Bank (2011), *Global Development Horizons 2011: Multipolarity, The New Global Economy*, Washington DC: World Bank.

World Bank (2012), *China 2030: Building a Modern, Harmonious, and Creative High-Income Society*, Washington DC: World Bank and Beijing: Development Research Center of the State Council.

Appendix

Appendix Table 55.A: GDP at market prices and at purchasing power parity, 2010-2030 (US$2005 billion)

	GDP at market prices			GDP at purchasing power parity		
Region	2010	2020	2030	2010	2020	2030
ASEAN	995	1,597	2,474	2,316	3,752	5,868
China	3,847	8,779	17,091	8,900	20,589	40,246
India	1,180	2,330	4,460	3,522	7,015	13,360
Japan	4,540	5,320	5,860	3,864	4,538	4,965
NIEs	979	1,310	1,500	1,271	1,705	1,950
Australia/NZ	887	1,138	1,376	892	1,144	1,387
USA	12,900	16,400	19,900	12,875	16,398	19,901
Canada	1,200	1,590	1,920	1,193	1,587	1,919
Europe	14,014	17,060	19,303	13,542	16,527	18,697
Latin America	2,570	3,709	5,023	4,484	6,503	8,822
ROW	4,808	7,039	10,177	8,922	13,534	20,511
World	47,920	66,272	89,084	61,778	93,291	137,626

Source: Fouré et al. (2010) and website <http://www.cepii.fr/anglaisgraph/bdd/baseline.htm>

56

Multinational corporations and development: Changing perceptions

Jagdish Bhagwati[1]

It is an honour to be giving the Joseph Fisher Lecture this year. I must say also that I am doubly pleased. The Lecture has been given by international economists whom I much admire. Max Corden, who is Australia's "national treasure" and one of my oldest friends, has given it twice. James Meade who (with Harry Johnson) was the undisputed doyen of international economists has given it also. So has Paul Krugman who was my student and my "discovery" at MIT and from whom I have learnt more than I have taught him. Following in their footsteps is presumptuous but pleasurable.

I also noticed that Mr. Fisher was a man much to admire. He was for long a successful newspaper man. Today, the power that the media exercise is evident even more than in Mr. Fisher's time. All of us who work in public policy are aware of the need to cultivate the media so that our ideas get attraction and therefore traction. My daughter who once worked as an Intern at the *Financial Times* in the Weekend Section being edited then by Robert Thomson (then Editor of the *London Times* and now of the *Wall Street Journal*), told me how even Luciano Pavarotti wanted to take the phone when she said that she was calling for this influential newspaper. She added: "Now I understand why you would dash out of the shower to take the phone if I said that Peter Passell of the *New York Times* was calling!"

Mr. Fisher was also an accomplished businessman who made his money in the apparent belief that economic well-being is hard to sustain unless wealth accumulates. But, like the Dutch burghers of my colleague Simon Schama's *Embarrassment of Riches*, and the Jains and Vaishnavs of my native state of Gujarat

1 Fifty-sixth Joseph Fisher Lecture, 13 July 2012.

(from whose tradition Mahatma Gandhi derived his moral sensibility), he believed that wealth must be deployed, not for self-indulgence, but to do charitable works (of which his endowment of this Lecture is only a small example). I have described such altruism as Personal Social Responsibility.

It is also apparent from all I have read about Mr. Fisher that he brought a sense of moral rectitude in his business dealings. That he was heavily involved in the Bank of Adelaide and never compromised himself strongly suggests that the current preoccupation of the critics of the financial sector, that it undermines morality, reverses cause and effect. We acquire moral values in all sorts of ways: from our parents, from our schools, and from reading great literature that poses moral questions (as in Fyodor Dostoevsky whose *Crime and Punishment* has Sofia turning to prostitution to feed her family, posing a moral conflict instead of suggesting absolutes). We bring these values to where we work. The notion instead that where we work determines our values is for the most part wrong: it is a quasi-Marxist fallacy that argues that where we work, like the means of production, determines our morality. I would suggest also that the fact that the financial sector offers the highest returns to crooked behavior implies that those who are crooked to begin with will be attracted to this sector. The Bernie Madoffs are more likely attracted to finance rather than made by finance.

Since the evolving ideas about Multinationals have led to the notion that they ought to practice Corporate Social Responsibility, I can think of no better subject to address in honour of Mr. Joseph than the evolving role of multinationals in development.

The arguments of both the critics and the proponents have gone through significant changes as structural changes in the world economy have occurred, together with changes in society and governance such as a growing civil society and the spread of democracy worldwide. Equally, it is now clear that, if multinationals are to play a welcoming and beneficial role in the developmental process, they need to re-conceptualize the way they operate in the host countries. If they do so, they will become true friends of the developmental process, and the opponents who charge that they are foes will lose political salience.

Alternative views of the impact of globalization

The earliest arguments as the leaders of the newly independent developing countries began to plan for accelerated growth and resulting poverty reduction.[2] It involved answering a basic economic-philosophical question: how would integration into the world economy on dimensions such as trade, equity investment (i.e., multinationals), migration, and technology (e.g., intellectual property protection) work? Would, as the opponents argued, integration into the world economy on these different dimensions lead to disintegration of the national economy; or would it help instead?

At the time, I distinguished among four different schools of thought (Bhagwati 1977, Ch. 1). First, there was the *benign impact* model: this fitted into economists' thinking, because they are used to "mutual gain" outcomes. Thus, multinationals would earn profits but they would also bring such things as funds and technology to the host countries, and freer trade would or could benefit all. Then, there was also the more-pleasing template of *benign intent*. Multinationals saw themselves as agents of benign change. This was a form of aid given to reflect the white man's burden: it was altruistic. Then there was the *malign impact* view. President Cardoso, who was earlier an eminent sociologist in Brazil, and Raul Prebisch of Argentina and first Secretary General of UNCTAD, were among those who propounded this bleak view. The former is known for the "dependencia" thesis that the developing countries would wind up in a state of dependency with increased international integration: multinationals were seen as sources of a malign impact. Finally, there were many, some in the developed countries as well, who thought in terms of *malign intent*: aid, for instance, was being given to hold the decolonized countries in a neocolonial embrace.

Let me now treat the evolution of thinking about multinationals and their role in development, using this fourfold division of views that characterized different scholars and policymakers in the postwar years.

2 I have called this the progressive and activist "pull up" strategy for reducing poverty, in contrast to the conservative characterization of it as a passive "trickle down" strategy that suggests the Earl of Nottingham and his vassals are eating lamb and venison at a high table, with crumbs falling to the dogs and serfs below.

Benign impact arguments for multinational corporations

At the outset, the benign impact arguments in favour of investing in developing countries came, as one would guess, principally from mainstream economists. Let me recap just a few of the important ones that led many to argue that there was a "presumption" that multinationals (MNCs) brought good to the developing countries.

Several economists focused on the inflow of funds that MNCs would bring to the host countries. If MNCs earned a return equaling the value of their contribution to the host country (i.e., there were no uncompensated externalities or other market failures or policy-imposed distortions), one may deduce that there was neither benefit nor loss to the host country: what the MNCs contributed to the host country was what they earned, leaving no "surplus" that would benefit the host country.[3] But if MNCs are taxed by the host country, as they are, that implies that the MNCs earn less than their contribution to the host country.

Yet another pro-MNC presumption followed from the fact that, if real wages were bounded from below and there was surplus labour available as in the Marx-Lewis model of the reserve army of labour available at a given wage, the social return from funds brought in by the MNC investment would not just be the private return on the investment but also the wages earned by the surplus labour that was hired thanks to the investment influx. Since countries like India and China had abundance of surplus labour at a given wage, the MNC investment would have a social return that exceeded its private return. That reinforced greatly the tax-defined presumption in favour of MNCs.

However, MNCs do not bring in just funds (sometimes they do not even do that, raising all their funds in the host country). They also bring in external (marketing) networks and internal diffusion of knowhow. Again, economists had long hypothesized that MNCs are the source of new management techniques and of new technologies which diffuse at low cost through the host country. There are now numerous empirical studies of the channels through which such diffusion occurs.

3 This argument applies to "small" inflows. If the flows are large and there are diminishing returns, then the inflow of capital will depress the return to capital and generate a "surplus" or gain to the host country.

MNCs now source their inputs from many sources and they virtually guarantee external sales of the components they manufacture. For example, retailers like Wal-Mart are conduits for purchase in the host country and sales in foreign countries.

It is not surprising therefore that worldwide the benign impact view of MNCs has come to prevail. Countries such as India (where the pre-reforms policy based on a malign view of MNCs had reduced equity investment by MNCs to around $100 million) have come around to increasingly opening their doors to welcoming MNCs. The early view of MNCs in many of these countries – that MNCs were foes of development – has changed to the benign view that they are friends instead.

One could even say that there is now a virtual competition among many developing countries for MNCs, much the way states in the United States compete to attract manufacturing firms to locate in them, granting all kinds of rewards such as tax holidays, subsidized land and other benefits, raising the legitimate question whether, once these giveaways are factored in, the MNCs remain beneficial to the host countries/states. A legitimate fear is that we may be getting a race to the bottom, and the presumption that the taxes on MNCs leave the host country better off may be getting reversed by such giveaways. Astonishingly, but not surprisingly (given the self-serving lobbying by MNCs, a subject I turn to later in this Lecture), the MNCs have wanted the OECD countries to reduce taxes, arguing that they distort allocation of investments among host countries of course they have not symmetrically argued that subsidies would do that too!

The malign impact arguments

The specific malign-impact arguments that had provided support for the anti-MNC policies in earlier times have now lost salience. The principal ones related to adverse impacts on local entrepreneurship and to political intrusions. The former has been discredited; the latter is no longer compelling.

Albert Hirschman was the most articulate proponent of the view that MNCs would stifle local entrepreneurship. This fueled attempts at imposing the requirement that only joint ventures with local partners would be acceptable. But it became clear that MNCs could be conduits for increasing the competitiveness of local firms: as noted above, diffusion of technology and "best practices" often follows MNC entry, which can spill over to the competitiveness of domestic rivals. This happens, for the most part, by example; but it also happens because the host country workers employed by the MNCs often acquire the skills and knowhow which lead to their setting up their own new firms.[4] Where local knowhow matters (typically in the shape of contacts and networking which enable the MNC to function more efficiently in the host country), joint ventures often follow. Thus, forcing MNCs into marriage with some local firm/investor is more likely to imply profit-sharing with the lucky firm chosen to meet the host-country requirement, creating rentiers rather than true entrepreneurs.

The question of political intrusion has been one of the greatest concern. Just think of how Pepsi and AT&T got involved with Kissinger and the CIA in facilitating the destabilization of the Allende regime in Chile in 1973 and the military takeover by Pinochet;[5] or of the Katanga intervention in the DRC and assassination in 1961 of Patrice Lumumba by Union Meuniere. Today, with massively increased transparency and the growth of civil society groups that monitor and agitate against such practices by MNCs, it is far less feasible for the MNCs to behave in these reprehensible ways.

Recently, however, new malign-impact arguments have come from the civil society and from labour unions in the developed countries. They are also misplaced, however.

The most astonishing argument has come from groups that argue that MNCs "exploit" local workers by paying them "low wages". Of course poor countries have low incomes and low wages, but instead of comparing the wages paid by MNCs with local wages in non-MNC firms the comparison is made with wages back home. In fact the MNCs win hands down because, for the most part, there is an observed premium for those employed in an MNC – something many scholars have tried to explain in terms of the efficiency-wage and other models. If

4 As an example, Uday Kotak, who represented Goldman Sachs in India, has now set up his own Kotak bank and become the most important financial entrepreneur in India.

5 Ironically, no one remembers the Pepsi story and the beverage firm smells like roses to many who know no history.

one asks workers if they should be paid higher wages, it is not surprising that they say "yes", since income has a positive marginal utility in most settings.[6]

Specious assertions in support of the exploitation argument are also made by saying that MNCs earn high profits and can "afford" to pay higher wages. This supposes that MNCs are earning abnormal profits. But in industries like apparel, which are often the object of agitation by our unions and NGOs that are asserting exploitation, the competition is fierce and I have never seen evidence of abnormal profits.

I have been in debates where a union leader would flamboyantly wave a sweatshirt and say that it costs $10 in New York but the wage paid in Guatemala is only 50 cents. Quite respectable economists at the pro-labor Economic Policy Institute have argued this way also. Typically, for instance, a $100 jacket in an Ann Klein store would be contrasted with a wage of $2 per hour in Nicaragua in the Export Processing Zone. But this is not sensible. For one thing, out of ten coats designed, nine will probably bomb out, leaving the effective sale in New York at $10 instead of $100. Also, transport costs and tariffs (which are high on apparel) push up the retail price but not profits in New York. So we are probably down to $5, which looks far less melodramatic. Likewise, the gross value of the retail sale of diamonds in New York is no index of the value added in Zambia to which the wage paid in Zambia might be related: Zambia may be adding only $100 worth of value to unpolished diamonds that sell, after being polished, for $10,000 in New York.[7]

While many NGOs are simply confused about all this, more importantly labour unions in the developed countries are agitated about competition from the developing countries. Hiding behind the façade of altruistic concern with exploitation of workers abroad, they seek to prevent the outflow of direct foreign investment (DFI) to developing countries abroad and the resulting addition to competition for themselves.

6 I am not sure about the British, who seem sometimes to put conditions on proposed increases in their wages like: "provided" others get wage increases also.

7 See the extended discussion of this specific form of anti-MNC argument in Bhagwati (2004, Ch. 12).

The claim that MNCs exploit and hence harm foreign workers by paying them "low" wages is in fact the opposite of what MNCs manage to achieve for these workers. By increasing the demand for workers, MNCs generally will increase employment and/or improve wages: that is the only successful way to help workers in a sustainable fashion. Take China, for example. The rapid growth in Guangdong province, aided immensely by MNCs spearheading an unprecedented export boom, greatly increased the demand for Chinese workers. As long as workers were in elastic supply (the "reserve army of labour"), the added demand for labour led to increased employment. But then the supply of labour began to increase at a much slower rate as the delayed effect of the one-child policy kicked in, and as the inflow of additional labour from the hinterland (as distinct from the availability of surplus labour within Guangdong province) became difficult because of urban infrastructure problems. The result was that wages began to rise. This also meant that working conditions improved in a market where labour began to be scarce rather than abundant.

The foregoing arguments suggest that MNCs and economic development are generally speaking friends, not foes. But one caveat must be entered. If the host country is not smart about the policy framework within which the MNCs come in, it can turn MNCs into foes of development. As Ian Little of Oxford has wisely remarked, DFI into a country is as good or bad as its own policies. This is best illustrated by the classic contrast between the "Import substituting" (IS) and "Export Promoting" (EP) varieties of DFI, the argument being that the former is likely to be bad for the host country's economy whereas the latter is beneficial because it makes better use of domestic resources.

That an IS strategy has been generally counterproductive, except for an early phase of development, is now conceded by development-and-trade scholars except for a handful of prominent economists, chief among the latter being Dani Rodrik of Kennedy School at Harvard and Joseph Stiglitz at Columbia University. There is far too much empirical evidence now from many economists, including Arvind Panagariya of Columbia, which simply cannot be ignored. There is also compelling evidence that once outward orientation was embraced and growth enhanced, the resulting growth did pull over 200 million above the poverty line. In short, the growth has been "inclusive", contrary to popular assertions. The revenues generated by the enhanced growth are also enabling direct expenditures finally to be undertaken, not just promised, that will (if properly managed) lead to improvements in such things as healthcare and education for the poor.

What Ian Little says is that if the IS strategy is a bad framework to get a lot out of your own resources, it will be bad for the use of foreign resources as well. This sounds like commonsense, and it has also been demonstrated theoretically by many economists including myself, Koichi Hamada, Richard Brecher and Carlos Diaz Alejandro. While India had discouraged DFI prior to the reforms, so we can test for Little's proposition, China certainly was into IS strategy and allowed for more IS-variety DFI inflow, while its DFI in Guangdong Province was based on outward orientation. The earlier IS variety is sometimes described as "tariff-jumping" DFI policy, whereby DFI is attracted by closing the market to imports as against domestic assembly. In China such DFI was often a failure. Mann (1987) has documented beautifully why and how the Beijing Jeep DFI by Chrysler failed, for example. By contrast, the EP variety in China was a huge success.

By way of an aside, now that the Chinese market has become uniquely gigantic, the Chinese are reverting to the old-style IS variety of DFI policy again – but now to great advantage. China is now saying again to foreign firms, as at the time of the Beijing Jeep, if they will not produce in China, enabling the Chinese then to pick up their technology on the cheap, China will simply turn to their rivals. Faced with the choice of losing a huge market to its rivals (e.g., GE versus Siemens) by resisting the Chinese tactic and surrendering to it by investing instead and having the Chinese pick up its technology on the cheap, the foreign firm can do little but choose the latter option. I see no way, short of infeasible collusion among the foreign firms, that this Chinese tactic can be countered. The Chinese, thanks to this tactic of technology-extraction which has become possible now because of the enormous growth of its market, have thus provided a new and favourable twist to the IS type of investment from the viewpoint of the host government. However, it applies only when the host country's market is immense, and – as Baldwin (2012) stresses – only for products whose value chain cannot be fragmented into many stages.

MNCs and rule setting: A problem area

So far, I have been dealing with the question of MNCs and development in terms of the outcomes within a policy framework that they themselves did not manage to define. But once we drop this assumption, as we must, then the benign view of MNCs which now prevails begins to change and the need for international governance to minimize possible malign effects from rules reflecting lobbying interests becomes more evident.

The track record of MNCs in defining rules is not exactly exemplary. Well-known examples include the lobbying by American MNCs against the International Code of Marketing of Breast-Milk Substitutes which had been approved by nearly all nations, with the lobbying going so far as to get the USTR to threaten smaller countries into not enforcing the Code. Similarly, cigarette firms in the US insisted on their being granted the ability to advertise their cigarette brands in Thailand even though it was clear that such a concession would increase sharply the total amount of cigarette consumption, not just increase their share.

American firms have lobbied fiercely to prevent the automatic extension of FDA bans in the US on hazardous drugs to sales abroad on the argument that it is up to these governments to prevent such sales if they care to do so, ignoring the fact that these governments may be ignorant or, more likely, captured/bribed into not enacting such bans by these very firms.

Recent examples include the damage that US multinationals have done to the cause of multilateral free trade. They have been pushing for Free Trade Agreements, which are Preferential Trade Agreements (PTAs) because the trade is free only for members of the FTA. As such, they undermine the principle of non-discrimination and, as I have pointed out in my 2009 book, lead to a veritable flood of FTAs. That flood has now become a "systemic" issue, creating a maze of criss-crossing discriminatory tariffs depending on source and to arbitrary rules of origin that I have called a "spaghetti bowl" phenomenon and affliction. The FTAs also have led to a variety of trade-unrelated and self-serving requirements to be imposed on weaker countries in one-on-one negotiations by the lobbies (including MNC lobbies) of the hegemonic powers such as the US and the EU, turning the trade game into a shell game. At the same time the US MNCs have put their weight behind undermining the Doha Round of multilateral trade negotiations, greedily asking for ever more concessions from other countries when the crying need after ten years of negotiations is to settle with what we have and then to go on to another Round for "unfinished business".

Corporate social responsibility

Having occasionally behaved less than responsibly in defining the rules and institutions that relate to international governance, MNCs now face demands from civil society to step up to what has come to be known as Corporate Social Responsibility (CSR).

Economists such as Milton Friedman have opposed this by arguing that altruism should be left to the shareholders. The shareholders can spend moneys earned by way of dividends and capital gains from their ownership of stocks in the Corporation on doing good in ways they like: there should be no role for the Corporation to do altruism. To put it differently, management should stay out of doing CSR except insofar as CSR is being undertaken with a view to protecting the corporation from unscrupulous attacks on them by NGOs advancing their own agendas.[8]

This is an issue that did not exist when there were family firms since ownership and management were flip sides of the family. Now that management and shareholding are divorced in the case of most corporations, the question of CSR by management on behalf of the corporation as such becomes pertinent.

My own view is that corporations are legal persons. Besides, society today sees them as having an identity that extends beyond ownership. So there is a widespread perception that Corporations should act on altruism as if they were legal persons with an identity of their own. Once this is conceded, it is inevitable that management will take a central role in defining CSR. Legitimacy will then require that CSR be not the sole prerogative of the CEO or the Board of Directors

8 Unscrupulous NGOs in fact will zero in on even good firms which have a big visibility simply because that makes the campaign more "effective"! Naomi Klein once suggested this to me, when I was deploring the campaign against Nike, implying that ends justified the means. For an interesting discussion of this tactic, see the brilliant book by Kleiner (1996, pp. 108–09).

but should require that voices of the workers and lower-level management be heard before any decisions are taken on what the content of the Corporation's CSR program should be.

One of the "efficiency" effects of CSR by management, which makes CSR a matter of "enlightened self interest", is in attracting employees that feel more enthused about the firm. There is much evidence that many lower-level executives want to work for firms that are ethical and seen to be altruistic.

Such CSR by MNCs must reflect some commitment to expenditures on programs in the host, not just the home, countries. This corporate altruism by MNCs should not be seen as atonement for the alleged harm that they do to development. As argued above, I believe that MNCs, by and large, do a lot of good. I see CSR by MNCs as essentially adding to the good they do.

Of course CSR need not be uniform, following the dictates of some zealous activists. Rather, altruism must allow for diversity: let a hundred flowers bloom, not so that Maoists can cut them down but so that they fill spring with their splendor.

References

Baldwin, R. E. (2012), 'Global Supply Chains: Why they Emerged, Why they Matter, and Where they are Going', mimeo, Graduate Institute of International Studies, Geneva, July.

Bhagwati, J. N. (ed.) (1977), *The New International Economic Order*, Cambridge MA: MIT Press.

Bhagwati, J. N. (2004), *In Defense of Globalization*, New York: Oxford University Press.

Bhagwati, J. N. (2009), *Termites in the Trading System: How Preferential Agreements Undermine Free Trade*, New York: Oxford University Press.

Dostoevsky, F. (1866), *Crime and Punishment*, New York: Bantam Books (Classic Edition 1981).

Kleiner, A. (1996), *The Age of Heretics*, New York: Doubleday.

Mann, J. (1987), *Beijing Jeep: A Case Study of Western Business in China*, New York: Simon & Schuster.

Schama, S. (1987), *Embarrassment of Riches: An Interpretation of Dutch Culture in the Golden Age*, New York: Vintage Books.

www.ingramcontent.com/pod-product-compliance
Lightning Source LLC
Chambersburg PA
CBHW081123180926
51611CB00004B/36
* 9 7 8 1 9 2 2 0 6 4 4 2 4 *